THE
COLUMBIA BOOK
OF
MUSICAL
MASTERWORKS

THE

Columbia Book

OF

MUSICAL
MASTERWORKS

Edited by Goddard Lieberson

INTRODUCTION BY EDWARD WALLERSTEIN

NEW YORK
ALLEN, TOWNE & HEATH, *INC.*

1947

FIRST PRINTING

PRINTED IN THE UNITED STATES OF AMERICA
BY THE COLONIAL PRESS INC.
BOUND BY F. M. CHARLTON CO., N. Y.

Editor's Preface

I REMEMBER speaking once with the late Robert Benchley (that wonderful portrayer of the harassed man in modern civilization) about the problems facing record lovers who desire to read the program notes booklet which—at that time—accompanied the albums. It seemed to me a problem that fit very well into his concept of an everyday life made miserable by the so-called "conveniences" which mark the advancement of civilization. To outline the problem, I told him of the happy purchaser of a Beethoven symphony, who hurries home to play his records and finds, upon unwrapping the album, that the descriptive booklet is missing. After a half-hour search he finds it nestling comfortably in the last pocket of the album. Then, just as he is ready to put the records on the machine, the phone rings and he is called out of the room. Meanwhile, his schnauzer dog, "Fidelio," has jumped up on the chair where the booklet was left and makes off with it. Two years later, the booklet shows up in a stack of old *National Geographic* magazines which are about to be given to the local boy scout troop.

That's a brief synopsis. There are a hundred possible variants of a much more dramatic nature.

A few years after this conversation, some of us who work in the record industry felt that the solution to the problem lay in abolishing the elusive booklet in favor of the inside flyleaf of the album cover. There, firmly pasted inside the album itself, and absolutely unlosable (unless you are the kind of person who misplaces pianos or washing machines) one would be sure to find the program notes. Now, under this plan, it is only necessary for the record lover to have two arms each six or seven feet long, or four regular length arms, so that it would be possible at the same time to play the records and read the notes on the album cover, which measures 14½ inches by 12¼ inches closed and 29 inches by 12¼ inches when open. Since it is obviously impossible to read the notes while the album is closed, you are stuck with the larger of the two figures. Furthermore, if you are the kind of a person who likes to smoke a pipe or eat chocolate (and these are not exactly aberrations) while listening to records, it might be advisable to hire a midget to hold the album for you while you read the program notes.

Because of this, and for many other reasons, the Columbia Book of Mu-

[v]

sical Masterworks will, I hope, make life much happier for millions of music lovers! For within these pages are collected practically all of the program notes which have been used in the hundreds of Columbia Masterworks Albums which have so far been issued. To augment these, we have added notes for important works which are so far unrecorded. In those instances, you may feel sure that the unrecorded masterpieces will not stay long in that category, and subsequent editions of this book will include the record numbers assigned to them.

But by its nature, this book is selective rather than inclusive. For instance, under Boccherini, Luigi, you will not find program notes for his twenty symphonies, his one-hundred-and-two string quartets, forty-eight trios, and one-hundred-and-twelve quintets; you won't even find Boccherini; and I do not expect any indignant letters on that account. At the same time, you will find program notes for certain esoteric works which would seem to indicate an inclusive point of view. If this contradiction annoys you, put it down to the perversity and eccentricity of the editor.

Not all of the notes on these pages remain in their original form; for the sake of condensation, unity and readability, it has been necessary to sometimes merge two or three articles into one, or, in some instances, we have divided one article into several.

I believe the reader will find in this book a refreshing variety. We have limited standardization only to format and style; the view points, because of their many sources, are heterogeneous, to say the least, and I for one do not look upon this as a disadvantage. Each set of notes is written from an individual concept: one considers an event in the composer's life as responsible for the creation of a certain work; another reveals the influence of the times on the work which is analyzed; still another proves that a specific work was inspired by a theme of another composer, and so on. If "variety" has the spice with which it is always accredited, I am sure the reader will not find these pages unsalted.

Up to a few years ago, the Columbia program notes were unsigned, and it is therefore impossible in all cases to trace their origin. The best I can do is to express my deepest thanks to the following names, though merely listing them in this cold manner by no means indicates a lesser degree of warmth of appreciation:

JOHN BALL, JR.	ANDRÉ KOSTELANETZ	LEOPOLD STOKOWSKI
JAMES H. FASSETT	LOTTE LEHMANN	HUNTINGTON WATTS
HOLGER HAGEN	PHILIP L. MILLER	BRUNO WALTER
DAVID HALL	NICOLAS SLONIMSKY	FRANZ WERFEL
MORRIS HASTINGS	MOSES SMITH	RONALD WISE

I owe special thanks to my co-workers at Columbia, Paul Southard, Tyle Turner, Alex Steinweiss, Paul Affelder, and numerous others who have assisted with enthusiasm and generosity; also, to Ava Yeargain, who did a heroic job of collecting and collating; to Ann Lingg, for her valuable research assistance; and, finally, to my publisher, David Ewen, who has kept a professional and (because of the sleep of which we have robbed him) an occasionally bloodshot eye on the doings relative to the publication of this book.

G. L.

Table of Contents

[x]

[xi]

Introduction

VIEWED superficially the question might easily be raised as to why the symphony, or better, good music in general should be tied so closely together with records.

This question is completely answered when it is known more fully to what degree modern science has influenced and made possible the growth of interest in good music all over the world and especially in America.

The phonograph was invented in 1878. The impelling force behind the invention was the desire to duplicate the spoken word. The first phonograph was really a dictating machine.

Later, when the device very quickly became an obvious means of home entertainment, the entertainment first took the form of late 19th-century comedy. Both recording and reproduction were of course crude compared to modern standards; and what was offered had to be governed by the limitations of the equipment.

Vocal music soon became possible because the voice was adaptable to these limitations. The early success of the industry was built around operatic arias by the great singers of the early part of this century.

This of course had definite limits, but a new impetus in the form of dance music as we know it today came along and sustained a considerable position in the entertainment field for records in spite of the encroachment of movies, the automobile, and later radio.

In the mid twenties electrical recording was introduced and while the early electrical recordings still had a somewhat limited frequency range, in spite of the extravagant claims, it was a tremendous advance and with it, hand in hand, went the advance of radio and the consequent introduction into the American home of a broad, free musical education.

By the late twenties recording had advanced by a marked degree. With this technical improvement came the first recordings of complete orchestral works.

The first symphonies were recorded by English Columbia and were an immediate success not only in Europe but also by importation in this country, and recording of large works was quickly begun here.

Then strangely enough, just when the new day of recorded home entertainment should have begun, the business nearly died completely.

The causes were comparatively simple: the great depression, and a complete lack of faith on the part of the industry itself.

The faith, however, was soon revived. Beginning in the mid thirties there began a revival which has made available to the public a broader range of musical literature than was ever dreamed of. The field is rapidly expanding to cover modern works made available very soon after they have had a fair hearing. And there will shortly be a great revival of operatic recording in complete form and amazingly improved because of latest techniques.

There has been sporadic criticism of the record industry on the grounds of duplication. This objection has come mainly from the reviewers of records, who ask why, for example, should there be a new recording of Beethoven's 5th Symphony if there is a completely adequate one by Bruno Walter and The New York Philharmonic-Symphony or Toscanini and the NBC Orchestra or Ormandy and The Philadelphia Orchestra.

The question, of course, has answered itself. Who is to say which is adequate to any particular individual? Further, who is to say that all are not both adequate and desirable?

Now, as to the book itself:

Modern science began to bring to Americans only some twenty years ago the opportunity to hear and love great music at will. The speed with which America has grasped this opportunity is one of the great tributes to its people.

This book is the catalyzing agency between the music lover and the music itself; between the record buyer and the recordings of the great musical masterworks. It will, I am sure, bring a clearer understanding of this greatest of all arts to the average American.

EDWARD WALLERSTEIN

Johann Sebastian Bach

1685–1750

THE year 1685 is portentous in the annals of music. During its first quarter were born, in the same country and within a month of each other, two of the greatest musicians the world has ever known: Johann Sebastian Bach and George Frederick Handel.

To Bach, in the words of Schumann, music owes almost as great a debt as Christianity owes to its founder. Under his dominating touch, music took on for the first time the outlines of a science. Musical forms, which through the middle ages had been nebulous and incoherent, were brought into proper relationships and assumed a solidity unknown until his time. And though he was not an innovator, his industry was limitless, his absorptive capacity for study unexampled, his achievements prodigious.

The Bachs were a family of musicians who for a century before Johann Sebastian's birth had exercised their calling in the Thuringian province of Germany. Bach's individual life was one of simplicity, domestic content, and unremitting musical labor. With the generation succeeding him, the musical solidarity of the Bach family was dispersed, the name figuring no more after the passing of Johann Sebastian's son, Carl Philip Emanuel.

Little is known about Bach's earliest years, except that his father, imbued with the musical tradition of the Bach family, gave him violin lessons when he was very young. When Johann Sebastian was ten, his father died, leaving him to the care of his older brother, Johann Christoph, an experienced organist.

Sebastian's mind unfolded rapidly, and it was not long before the brother, who had a churlish disposition, realized with misgiving the astonishing talent of the boy. He set himself to curb these manifestations. In the brother's modest collection of books was one containing manuscript copies of many notable compositions, and to master its contents became Sebastian's ambition. Denied access to it by Christoph, he crept to it each night after the elder brother slept, drew the book through the latticework of the bookcase and, with the moon as his only light, copied it page for page. Six months of this and the work, though far advanced, was not completed; his activities were finally discovered by Christoph, the copy was confiscated, and Sebastian never saw it again. All that remained to Sebastian from this heroic labor was permanently impaired eyesight.

At fifteen, Sebastian was thrown on his own resources. These, however, were to prove amply sufficient for him all his life. His principal asset at that time was a beautiful soprano voice, and making his way on foot to Lüneburg, he obtained a position in the choir of St. Michael's Church, adding a little to his income by playing a violin in the local orchestra.

After three years of Lüneburg, Bach became a member of the orchestra of the Grand Duke Johann Ernst of Weimar, but he left this position almost immediately to take the post of organist at Arnstadt. It was at this time that he began to evidence the extraordinary mastery of the organ which ultimately made him its greatest exponent of his day.

For a time all went well, but in 1705 there began to be murmurings from the more devout members of the congregation. The young organist was playing things which to the ears of these excellent people sounded anything but pious. The great organist from Sweden, Buxtehude, was at that time appearing in Lübeck, and a truce was declared while Bach secured a month's leave of absence to visit him. He overstayed the leave by three months, which further inflamed the townspeople, and they decided to displace him.

But a man such as Bach, even at twenty, is not easily displaced. By one device or another he continued so to bemuse and bewilder the burghers that they were either too timid or too disunited to dislodge him forcibly. Bach himself finally tired of the situation, and as his fame had now spread through many parts of Germany, he had no difficulty in finding a post seemingly to his liking in his native Thuringia, at St. Blasius's Church in Mühlhausen.

In Mühlhausen he married his second cousin, Barbara Bach. Thus commenced Bach's domestic life, which was saddened in 1720 by his wife's death. Not quite two years later he married Anna Magdalena Wülken, of Weissenfels, who survived him. He had in all twenty children, of whom Barbara Bach was the mother of seven.

Bach's tenure of the Mühlhausen appointment was short, for in 1708 he received a call from Weimar to become court organist for Duke Wilhelm Ernst. Here he remained for nine years, his renown constantly increasing. During his Weimar stay he made periodical tours, playing in Leipzig, Halle, Dresden, and other big German towns.

Bach's departure from Weimar was brought about through his resentment at being rejected for the post of Kapellmeister in 1717 in favor of an inferior applicant whose personal influence was more potent. Ignoring the protestations of Duke Wilhelm, he accepted an appointment as Kapellmeister for Prince Leopold at Cöthen and undertook a journey to Carlsbad with the Prince. However, Bach appears never to have been very well satisfied with the Cöthen post, and in 1723 he began to look about for a more lucrative position.

Refusing to be mulcted to the tune of 4,000 marks by those who had in hand the disposal of the great organ position in the Jacobi Kirche of Hamburg, Bach obtained the post of cantor in the Thomasschule in Leipzig. This proved to be his home for the remainder of his life.

Indifferent as was the attention bestowed upon Bach's compositions during his lifetime, there can be little doubt that in his Leipzig days he was regarded as Germany's greatest musician. It is natural to suppose that he would have been officially accorded the consideration that was his due. As a matter of fact, he was greatly respected by the townspeople but continually hampered in his position by the quarrels and jealousies of the rector and other officials of the Thomasschule. These worthies appear to have impeded him in every imaginable way and made his life a burden by their impositions. Affairs reached such a state in 1730 that Bach seriously considered severing his Leipzig connections. But bad as conditions were at times, they never quite inspired a breaking-off point. And when Bach was invested with the more or less empty title of Court Composer of Saxony in 1737, he immediately became, by virtue of this royal condescension, a great man in the eyes of his neighbors. Difficulties were smoothed out for him, and the remainder of his life was comparatively peaceful.

A cherished wish of his whole career—to meet and exchange views with his contemporary, Handel—was never granted. The nearest they came to meeting was in 1719 when Handel, then a resident of England, returned for a short visit to his birthplace, Halle, in Lower Saxony. Bach is said to have made several trips to Halle to effect an acquaintance, but one circumstance or another prevented this on each occasion.

The crowning glory of Bach's life (in his own eyes, at least) was his meeting with Frederick the Great in Berlin, where he went at the behest of this singular and many-sided monarch. Frederick's penchant for music is a matter of history, as is also his amateur standing as a composer. He propounded for Bach an original theme on which the great composer improvised so gloriously that the King was enchanted. He personally conducted Bach through his palace, exhibited his collection of musical instruments, and otherwise conferred unusual marks of favor.

This proved to be Bach's last excursion into the great world. In the following year his eyesight failed almost completely. Other causes, including incompetent medical treatment, combined to wreck his general health, and he died suddenly of an attack of apoplexy on July 28, 1750. While treated not quite so indifferently in burial as was Mozart, his remains, interred in one of the Leipzig churchyards, were long unmarked and forgotten. It was not until 1894 that the location of his grave was ascertained beyond doubt and changed to a crypt underneath the altar of St. John's Church.

Bach's universal genius, overspreading every field of music, laid the foundation for all modern musical art; in majesty and grandeur of musical thought no one has exceeded him.

BRANDENBURG CONCERTOS, FOR ORCHESTRA

THE SIX *Brandenburg* Concertos were milestones in Bach's artistic development. These were his first serious secular compositions, and this was his first use of the orchestra in large-scale works. He wrote each concerto for a different group of instruments.

The Markgraf of Brandenburg, to whom these works were dedicated, was in his day a very notable prince, and a persistent collector of musical works. Soon after the Markgraf met Bach, he was asked to write the concertos, which he completed in 1721. The importance that he attached to the commission may be inferred from the manuscript, in which the notes are written with special care and neatness, the bar lines being drawn with the aid of a ruler.

The manuscript bears an inscription in French, in which Bach asks his patron "very humbly" not to regard the imperfections of the concertos too severely, but rather to find in them "by his very kind consideration the profound respect and humble allegiance which they seek to convey." The concertos went into the Markgraf's library, though they were not numbered among the treasures of his musical collection. When that collection was dispersed in 1734, following the Markgraf's death, Bach's manuscripts were sold in a lot for about ten cents each.

The concerto grosso, so popular with composers of the late seventeenth and early eighteenth centuries, is clearly distinguishable from the solo concerto that we know today. It is a form called forth by the aristocratic patronage of music, by the existence in many noble houses of resident bands of musicians. The concerto grosso is a work not for solo instrument, but for a group of solo instruments opposed to the main body of the orchestra (usually consisting of strings and a clavier).

No doubt the choice of the instruments forming the concertino, or solo group, was often determined by the skill of certain players, but the writing for the solo instruments in classic concerti grossi is not excessively difficult. This type of concerto did not display the virtuosity of a solo performer but merely supplied what might be described as a dialogue between two instrumental groups. In fact, the concerto grosso is more nearly related to the eighteenth-century orchestral overture and suite than to the modern solo concerto.

Bach's *Brandenburg* Concertos exhibit great variety in the composition of the concertino. In the more conventional concerti grossi of his predecessors and contemporaries, this usually comprised two or more stringed instruments. In the *Brandenburg* Concertos we find woodwind and brass instruments sharing the prominence of the solo strings, and in the fifth Concerto, in D, the clavier is elevated from its humble role of filler-in to that of a principal in the solo group. There is variety also in the formal scheme of the concertos, for while the three-movement division adhered to by Bach in his solo concertos predominates, the first Concerto is in four movements, and the third is in two.

The six *Brandenburg* Concertos were written for the following combinations of instruments:

No. 1, in F major, for solo violin, three oboes, bassoon, two horns, and strings.

No. 2, in F major, for solo flute, oboe, trumpet, violin, and strings.

No. 3, in G major, for three violins, violas, and 'cellos, one double bass and cembalo.

No. 4, in G major, for two solo flutes, violin, and string orchestra.

No. 5, in D major, for solo harpsichord, flute, violin, and string orchestra.

No. 6, in B-flat major, for string orchestra, without violins.

M-MM-249, M-MM-250, Busch Chamber Players, Adolf Busch, Director.

CHACONNE, FOR SOLO VIOLIN
See PARTITA NO. 2 IN D MINOR

CHROMATIC FANTASY AND FUGUE IN D MINOR, FOR CLAVIER (OR PIANO)

THIS IS one of many compositions which Bach wrote during periods of comparative relaxation and which cannot be dated with certainty. Forkel, however, believes that it belongs in the second part of Bach's stay in Cöthen, some time between 1720 and 1723.

[8]

It appears that Bach had approached this work in an experimental mood. Its form is free and rhapsodic, and filled with daring bravura passages, instrumental recitatives, rich and novel arpeggios no less challenging to the pianist than the output of the brilliant composer-virtuosos of the nineteenth century. It was essentially in works of this kind that Bach was writing "music of the future." He preceded Classicism in the use of modulation for purposes of expression, and the Romantic movement by placing musical thought above formal symmetry.

CHRISTMAS ORATORIO

THE PERFORMANCE of appropriate music on feast or fast days, as practiced by the Roman Catholic Church, was continued by the Lutherans. Popularized through the introduction of folk-like chorales in the vernacular, it became an important part of Protestant worship. Bach's activities in Leipzig included the composition of such works, and to this fact posterity owes not only his Passions, but his lesser known oratorios for Easter, Ascension Day, and Christmas as well.

The *Christmas* Oratorio is the longest of the three. It consists of six separate cantatas, to be performed on six separate days. The story is based on the Gospels of St. Matthew and St. Luke but differs from the usual oratorio (and Passion) in the absence of dramatic development. Each portion is complete in itself, and each has its own musical character. The continuity of the story alone gives dramatic coherence, and musical unity is achieved through the use of the popular chorale, *O Sacred Head Now Wounded*, in both the first and the last sections.

Each day's music begins with a typical opening number, followed by a recitative relating the incident of the day in a very simple fashion. All the movements, except the second, open with a chorus, and all but the third end with a hymn. The second portion, dealing with the announcement to the shepherds of Christ's birth, starts with a lovely instrumental prelude of pastoral character which reappears between the lines of the closing chorale.

The original score gives the year of composition as 1734. Many musical numbers, however, including three of the five opening choruses, were traced to secular cantatas which Bach had composed during the previous year. This gave rise to much speculation. For a time it was even believed that the *Christmas* Oratorio was no original work at all, but had been compiled by Carl Philip Emanuel Bach after his father's death.

It was not unusual for Bach to borrow from his own works, however. The three earlier cantatas were typical perfunctory compositions, written in honor of the King, Queen, and Crown Prince of Saxony respectively, and performed before an exclusive circle at the Dresden Court. Bach assumed that they would be shelved after having served their purpose and hardly reach Leipzig in their original form. For this reason, he felt justified in using them as sketches for a work of entirely different scope and purpose.

The Oratorio was first performed in Leipzig during the Christmas season of 1734.

CONCERTO IN D MINOR, FOR PIANO (OR VIOLIN) AND ORCHESTRA
Allegro · Adagio · Allegro

THIS concerto is more familiar to the average listener in the version employing the solo clavier or harpsichord than in that using the solo violin. Since Bach had not learned the lesson of musical prudery of later generations of composers, he had not the slightest hesitation in rearranging his works or the works of others for different combinations of instruments from the original scoring. And the study of this feature of his efforts has constituted an extensive subject of research for Bach scholars.

The seven keyboard concertos particularly have given the musical historians much opportunity for illuminating (or obscuring) the mental operations of a musical genius. It has been assumed, from the research of scholars, that most of these concertos, including the one in D minor, were originally written for violin solo and orchestra.

That Bach was not a mere arranger in these matters, but almost always a creative artist at work, is evident not alone in the fact that the clavier version of the D minor Concerto contains features which were not in the original. It is even more apparent in a startling service to which he put portions of the concerto in one of his cantatas, where a brilliant rearrangement of the slow movement is employed as an accompaniment for an independent four-part chorus.

We may settle ourselves at ease, then, to listen to the D minor Concerto as to an original masterpiece. We find in each of the three movements a characteristic device of Bach: the employment of a theme or a fragment of a theme which is frequently reiterated, in one key or another, but with unmistakable identification with the original statement, so that the contrasting elements of the movement are reconciled and the movement itself is given unity.

In the first movement this connecting link is the opening subject, stated immediately by all the instruments. In the slow movement it is not so much a theme as the outline of a sequence of chords. This figure, serving as a sort of ground bass, is heard through most of the movement, while the solo instrument weaves elaborate mosaics around it. The last movement, which is more brilliant than either of the other two, has for its motto parts of the opening theme. Like the first movement, the last has many striking, cadenza-like passages for the solo instrument, which bear out the supposition as to their being originally for the violin.

M-MM-418, Joseph Szigeti, Violin, and Members of the Orchestra of the New Friends of Music Conducted by Fritz Stiedry.
M-MM-624, Eugene Istomin, Piano, with the Busch Chamber Players, Adolf Busch, Director.

CONCERTO IN D MINOR, FOR TWO VIOLINS AND ORCHESTRA

Vivace · Largo, ma non tanto · Allegro

THIS work was written during Bach's Cöthen period when the nature of his appointment forced him to concentrate on instrumental music. It takes a unique position among the many compositions which he wrote for the Court band of some eighteen pieces, for the possibilities of contrasting two solo instruments removed this work substantially from the customary concerto type. This is particularly true of the slow middle movement, in which the discourse of the two violins reduced the orchestra to a very subordinate position.

Bach took full advantage of the aptitude of the violin for melodic beauty. He set the two instruments against each other in a veritable dialogue, with the orchestra providing harmonic and rhythmic background. As in many of Bach's concertos, the slow movement is the point of gravity of the entire composition, flanked by two fast and more or less conventional sections.

The Concerto was later transcribed by Bach himself into a concerto for two claviers, in C minor.

X-MX-253, Adolf Busch, Frances Magnes, Violins, and the Busch Chamber Players.

CONCERTO IN E, FOR VIOLIN
AND ORCHESTRA

Allegro · Adagio · Allegro assai

BACH composed a number of concertos for violin. Three survive in their original form—the solo concertos in A minor and E major, and the Double Concerto in D minor. There are also transcriptions for clavier and orchestra of other concertos known to have been written originally for the violin.

The presumption is that the lost concertos were among the manuscripts that passed at Bach's death to his talented but undisciplined son, Wilhelm Friedemann.

It seems likely that Bach composed his violin concertos during his term of employment with Prince Leopold of Anhalt-Cöthen (1717–1723). It was the usual thing for princelings in Bach's time to maintain bands of court musicians, and Prince Leopold patronized the art out of a genuine liking for it. He sang, he played several instruments, and Bach reported that "he loved music, he was well acquainted with it, he understood it." Not improbably, the violin concertos were written to exercise the virtuosity of the composer's aristocratic patron. If so, Prince Leopold's skill must have been indeed extraordinary, for the concertos are difficult and taxing works.

M-MM-530, Adolf Busch, Violin, and the Busch Chamber Players.

FANTASIA AND FUGUE IN G MINOR, FOR ORGAN

ALTHOUGH no record exists, authorities agree that the Fantasia and Fugue in G minor was probably played by Bach at Hamburg in 1720 where with seven other candidates he auditioned for the post of organist at the Church of St. Catherine. The incumbent whom he sought to succeed was the famed Johann Reinken, still active at the age of ninety-seven. During his two-hour trial, Bach played compositions of his own which he hoped would please the aged master. These consisted mainly of improvisations in the favorite style of the organists of North Germany, among whom Reinken and Buxtehude were prominent. Reinken is said to have been much pleased with Bach's playing and to have been effusive in his praise. Despite this approbation on the part of Reinken, Bach was not awarded the position; one Johann Joachim Heitmann was elected instead. Spitta, who finds in the Fantasia "the imaginative style of the northern masters," believes that the work was composed especially for the occasion.

The Fantasia, which is in the style of a free but highly developed improvisation, is a dramatic example of a form which, like the prelude, evolved from the preliminary flourishes employed (even today) by keyboard soloists as a signal that they are about to begin. The subject of the lively, powerful fugue is one of Bach's finest melodies and is probably hummed or whistled as frequently as any other tune by this master. In order to distinguish it from a shorter and almost equally popular fugue in the same key, the present fugue is known as the "great G minor." Although the Fantasia and Fugue do not appear together in any of Bach's manuscripts, the subject of the fugue was found on the back of a copy of the Fantasia, with an indication to the effect that it should follow the work.

X-MX-244, orchestral transcription, Minneapolis Symphony Orchestra, Dimitri Mitropoulos Conducting.
M-MM-270, Albert Schweitzer, Organ.

ITALIAN CONCERTO, FOR CLAVIER
(OR PIANO)

Allegro · Andante · Presto

THE ORIGINAL title of the work was *Concerto nach Italiaenischem Gusto,* or "Concerto according to the Italian taste." It appeared in 1735 in the second installment of the *Clavierübung,* Bach's collection of piano pieces. Its companion piece was the B minor Partita, which indicates that Bach wanted to devote this volume to the adaptation for solo instrument of a typically Italian, and a typically French, form of orchestral music.

Bach had already transcribed violin concertos by Vivaldi for the clavier, but the *Italian* Concerto remained his only original work of the kind. It was written for harpsichord with two rows of keys, and the idea of composing for this instrument actually may have moved Bach to try the experiment. For the double keyboard offered a splendid opportunity to let two different tone qualities alternate throughout the work, similar to the change of soli and tutti passages in its orchestral model. This intention becomes strongly evident in the first and third movements composed in the typical lively concerto style. Neither has much in common with the melodious Andante, which seems to have been patterned after the slow movement of Italian violin music. The rhapsodic, emotional character of this movement reveals once more Bach's kinship with the Romantic composers of the nineteenth century.

MASS IN B MINOR

WHEN Bach went to Dresden in July 1733 to see his oldest son installed as organist in one of the capital's major churches, he asked King Frederick August for the title of Court Composer as a protection against the continuous frictions with the Leipzig authorities. Along with his humbly penned application went the orchestral and vocal parts of a Kyrie and Gloria, the first two sections of the Roman Mass which had found entrance into the Lutheran ritual. They were, therefore, particularly appropriate to support a petition of a Protestant church official to his Catholic sovereign.

It took Bach five more years to finish the most impressive choral work ever written in Germany. It is uncertain what particular purpose he had in mind as he assembled its sections, but it is almost certain that he did not expect this Mass to be used at church. It takes three hours to perform and is extremely difficult, which makes it unsuitable for other than concert presentation. Its layout is colossal, its musical texture saturated with detail. For all that, it sounds simple and graceful. This combination of sumptuousness and clarity belongs among the major miracles in music.

Bach's accomplishment is even more remarkable when it is noted that the various portions of the Mass were not composed in logical succession. He took much musical material from his own church cantatas, one of them dating back to 1729. The Osanna is an adaptation of a congratulatory evening serenade, while the Credo contains Gregorian Chant in direct quotation. The grandeur of the double choirs is interrupted by graceful airs—mostly duos distributed between two solo voices or a solo voice and solo instrument.

The most contrasting elements are blended with superior mastery into one of the most humane religious compositions in existence. In fact, the convention-pattern of this Mass (Kyrie, Gloria, Credo, Sanctus, Benedictus, Agnus Dei) remained a lone reminder of the ecclesiastic tradition. We come closer to the true significance of the work when we do not consider it a Mass in the clerical sense, but an oratorio composed to words from the Roman liturgy. Its meaning is universal. It shows Bach at his greatest—his seriousness of purpose, his fearless quest for truth. It is the superlative example of a religious composition reaching beyond all boundaries of any one particular faith.

PARTITA NO. 2 IN D MINOR, FOR SOLO VIOLIN

BACH could not have been over thirty-five when he wrote this masterpiece of polyphonic skill and imagination. The manuscript, discovered at St. Petersburg in 1814 by Georg Pölchen, librarian of the Singakademie at Berlin, is not in the handwriting of Bach, but in that of his wife, the incomparable Anna Magdalena, whose penmanship was deceptively like that of her husband.

The Chaconne, known to every frequenter of violin recitals, concludes the second partita and has always been regarded as the classical piece for solo violin—and justly so, since both the theme and its development are consummately adapted to the capacities of the instrument. Out of a single theme Bach conjures up a whole world of musical invention.

A chaconne appears to have been an old Spanish dance form, a slow dance with three beats to the measure. Its musical form is a series of variations on a ground bass. Bach's Chaconne comprises thirty-three variations on a theme of stately majesty which is pronounced by the violin in the very opening measures. The variations that follow are amazing for their variety of mood, color, and feeling.

Spitta describes the Chaconne in these words: "Consider that all this was written for a single violin! And what scenes this small instrument opens to our view! . . . The spirit of the master urges the instrument to incredible utterance; at the end of the major section it sounds like an organ, and sometimes a whole band of violins might seem to be playing."

Although Bach actually wrote three partitas and three sonatas for solo violin, it is usual to speak of these as six sonatas. The second partita belongs to the period during which Bach lived in Cöthen (1717–1723). The oldest known manuscript of the violin partitas and sonatas dates from about 1720, which narrows down the probable date of the composition of the second partita to the three-year period of 1717–1720.

M-MM-276, Nathan Milstein, Violin.

PASSACAGLIA AND FUGUE IN C MINOR, FOR ORGAN

In its earliest form, the passacaglia is said to have been a Spanish street dance (*pasar,* to walk, and *calle,* a street) consisting essentially of free improvisation of one musician over an unvarying bass set by his companion.

Bach was neither the first nor the last great composer to write in the passacaglia form (which even academicians are unable to distinguish satisfactorily from the chaconne). It was the style among the great masters of French opera—Lully, Rameau, and Gluck—to write their operatic finales in this form.

One of the crowning achievements along this line is the celebrated Dido's Lament from Henry Purcell's *Dido and Aeneas*. In each case, the passacaglia consists basically of a set of increasingly elaborate variations on a ground bass. Other magnificent instrumental passacaglias besides Bach's were written by Frescobaldi, Couperin, and Handel; while the most famous later examples are the Thirty-Two Variations by Beethoven and the great finale of Brahms's Fourth Symphony.

Although the exact date of the composition of Bach's Passacaglia and Fugue in C minor for organ is not known, it is thought to have been set down in its final form in or about 1715, during the latter part of the composer's Weimar period (1708–1717). In its original form Bach wrote his Passacaglia for a two-manual clavicembalo with pedals. The first half of his theme he borrowed from a *Trio en Passacaille* by André Raison, a seventeenth-century French organ composer.

On the basis of his eight-bar pedal theme, Bach rears an imposingly monolithic yet many-faceted musical structure of twenty variations, the whole culminating in a gigantic double fugue derived from the first half of the passacaglia theme.

X-MX-216, orchestral transcription, Leopold Stokowski Conducting the All-American Orchestra.

THE ST. MATTHEW PASSION

IT WAS surely one of the great moments in musical history when the 'teen-aged Felix Mendelssohn, browsing among dusty manuscripts by a forgotten provincial church musician, came upon the *St. Matthew* Passion. Overcoming obstacles that then seemed insurmountable, he launched the famous first concert performance of this masterpiece, seventy-eight years after Bach's death, and one hundred years

[17]

after the first performance of this work at St. Thomas's in Leipzig. This monumental concert at the Berlin Singakademie in 1829 set into motion a Bach revival that soon engulfed the entire world of music and that succeeded finally in restoring the master to the limelight he deserved.

Today musicians are generally agreed that this Passion represents not only the climax of German Passion music, but is the crown of Bach's achievements as well.

Bach did not act as his own librettist. The story was arranged by Christian Friedrich Henrici, a postal official at Leipzig who wrote verses under the name of Picander. Bach also secured the cooperation of the able Lutheran preacher, Salomon Deyling, who supervised the writing of the text.

The general layout of the *St. Matthew* Passion is in sharp contrast to that of the *St. John* Passion, since its particular purpose called for the grandest possible effects. In the *St. Matthew,* Bach's purpose was to outdo, or at least to counterbalance, the Latin Passions of the Catholic court chapel at Dresden, which at the time were interpreted by Italian opera singers under the direction of the famous court composer, Johann Adolf Hasse.

The Passion is divided into two parts, the first of which closes with the chorale, *O Mensch, bewein dein Sünden gross,* which Bach had originally intended for the *St. John* Passion. For more than three hours, two choruses, each supported by a separate orchestra and organ, and the customary set of soloists sing the story of the last days of Christ. In its massive design and Gargantuan proportions, the *St. Matthew* is second only to Bach's B minor Mass; but it surpasses the latter work in religious reality.

It might be of interest to contrast the *St. Matthew* Passion with the *St. John.* Where the former gives an exciting account of the historical events (with only stage props lacking to make it actually a mystery play), the latter depicts (so to speak) the reaction of the Christian world of the 1720's to these events. Where the *St. John* is vivid and dramatic, the *St. Matthew* is reflective and more soundly musical. The greatest progress of the *St. Matthew* over the earlier Passion lies, however, in Bach's new representation of Jesus. In the *St. John,* his recitatives are supported by organ and basso continuo; in the *St. Matthew,* Bach adds a string quartet to the conventional accompaniment, thus distinguishing Jesus from the other characters, giving him a more individual and sacrosanct background.

At its first performance, on Good Friday in 1729, a sermon was preached between the two sections of the Passion, as was habitual with many churches in Rome at the time. It is an undeniable fact that the Passion did not please that first audience in Leipzig. It may have been that the performance was inadequate, or that Bach's unorthodox way of presenting religious history proved annoying to the more devout. Some condemned the work as being "operatic," and therefore the very antithesis of the religious.

SUITE NO. 2 IN B MINOR, FOR ORCHESTRA

THE CLASSICAL suite is a collection of dances, with a prelude or an overture to open the series. The number of dances and their nature vary. Usually the first dance is in common time, and in quick movement. The second dance is slow and stately. The third may be a spirited Allegro. Then comes a group known under the comprehensive name of "gallant dances." These may include a minuet or a gavotte, or any of the French dances current in the 16th or 17th centuries. The concluding movement is usually a gigue. In Bach's time not much significance was attached to titles. A suite might be called an overture, a partita, or even a sinfonia. It is only later in history that the titles have assumed the significance of a definite form.

Bach composed four orchestral suites, but of these only the second and third are frequently heard. The second suite is perhaps the gayest of the group. It differs from the other suites in that the concluding movement is not a gigue but a badinerie.

SUITE NO. 3 IN D MAJOR, FOR ORCHESTRA

THE THIRD of Bach's suites is in common time, 4-4, which is the usual time signature for the opening movement. There are three themes in the overture, and the one in dotted rhythm serves as background for

[19]

the entire overture. The counterpoint is not complex as it is in Bach's fugues, and even the Bachian device of inversion is free, so that only the direction of the melody is reversed. The overture consists of two contrasting sections. The first is of a symphonic nature; the second section is based on the imitation of a characteristic rhythmic figure.

The second movement is an air, best known to the general public as the *Air on the G string*. The G-string arrangement, made by the famous violinist, August Wilhelmj, has been called by Tovey a "devastating derangement." Derangement or not, it is an effective piece of music. The third movement consists of twin gavottes, each made up of two sections. The final movement is a gigue; it is in 6-8 time and like all dances of the suite is in two sections.

M-MM-428, Orchestre de la Société des Concerts du Conservatoire, Felix Weingartner Conducting.

TOCCATA AND FUGUE IN D MINOR, FOR ORGAN

BACH's duties at the Weimar court were those of organist and chamber musician and they were reflected in the music that he composed at this time. Virtually all the great organ works—the preludes and fugues, the toccatas, the Passacaglia, the *Orgelbüchlein*, the Vivaldi transcriptions—were products of the Weimar years.

The exploitation of the resources of the instrument and of the skill of the performer was the purpose of the several toccatas composed by Bach. The form of the toccata in Bach's time was vague, but its purpose was well defined: it was a display piece and as such Bach employed it. But everything that Bach wrote had content as well as style; he was incapable of producing even a simple exercise without injecting into it thought and feeling. The massive chord, the long shakes, the tumultuous running passages of the D minor Toccata make up a musical drama of immense power. An impression of intellectual and emotional tension, and of feelings deeply stirred, is inseparable from the mighty fugue that follows.

X-MX-219, orchestral transcription, Leopold Stokowski Conducting the All-American Orchestra.
M-MM-270, Albert Schweitzer, Organ.

THE WELL-TEMPERED CLAVIER

THAT one of the acknowledged masterpieces of music should bear the title, *The Well-Tempered Clavier,* is puzzling. Naturally, we want to understand the meaning of the name. Its quaint title, given in the first of its two books, may be translated thus:

"The well-tuned keyboard, or Preludes and Fugues in all the tones and semitones, alike with the major third, or *Ut Re Mi,* and with the minor third, or *Re Mi Fa.* For the use of young musicians who are eager to learn, and also as a pastime for those who are already skilled in this study, set out and made by Johann Sebastian Bach, Kapellmeister to the Grand Duke of Anhalt-Cöthen and director of his chamber music. Anno 1722."

The system of tuning referred to in the title, and now in universal use under the name "Equal Temperament," needed much support in the days of Bach. If we take a series of perfect fifths and tune them exactly true (C to G, G to D, and so on), it is clear that when the circle of keys is completed, we shall arrive at C again. But this "C" differs from the "C" with which we started by a small interval called a "comma," a mysterious gap which must forever baffle all efforts to keep all keys in perfect tune. It was the old custom to make the simpler keys in perfect tune, and to banish the comma to the keys for which many sharps or flats were needed. The beauty of the pure fifths was as exquisite as those of the stringed instruments, but the remote keys, if attempted, produced an intolerable effect of jarring discord. It was found that this most curious natural error could be distributed equally among the series of fifths, so that each would be slightly—but not objectionably—out of tune. Bach, in this work, gave the strongest possible support to the new system, which made all the keys equally available for use.

Clavier is a term applied not only to the keyboard of the harpsichord, but also to the clavichord, the organ, and the pianoforte. Thus the original destination of this immortal work is a little uncertain, though the internal evidence points to the clavichord as the medium intended for its interpretation.

The fugue is conceived as a composition for several independent voices or parts, interwoven according to certain regulations. A subject is stated by one voice or part and followed, after an interval, by another, giving the same notes at a different pitch. This latter is called the answer, and the first voice, while imitated by the second, has something different to say, this new material being called the counter-subject. When all the voices have entered, they complete what is called the exposition, and soon a new series of entries is contrived, usually in a different order, and called the counter-exposition. Various devices are employed by which the interest of the structure is maintained, and so definite a plan may sometimes result in a mechanical product without any musical value. It is such products that have created a prejudice against the very name of fugue, and hidden from many superficial hearers the extraordinary emotional power and beauty of Bach's greatest works in this, his favorite, form.

The preludes have no such rigid plan as the fugues; they are usually built on a single musical figure, and some were first intended as technical exercises. They were included in a book called *Clavier-büchlein*, compiled for the training of Bach's sons, where they appear in a comparatively simple form.

M-MM-120, Harriet Cohen, Piano.

Béla Bartók

1881–1945

BÉLA BARTÓK was the Janus of modern music. By birth and predilection he was attached to the folklore of his native Transylvania. At the same time he was an extremely sensitive modernist, one of the boldest of our time.

The two natures of his creative mind were reconciled in his music, through his treatment of native melodies and rhythms in an incisive, modern manner. Furthermore, Bartók was not an innovator for novelty's sake; his style has the organic quality peculiar to the materials he used. The exposition of his ideals is always clear and economic: no more, no less than is necessary.

His music has a percussive quality, for percussion is the essence of rhythm; but instead of applying actual percussion instruments, Bartók used special effects—the high treble, or the lowest bass register of the piano keyboard; pizzicato of the violin, asymmetric syncopation. Against this background, his melodies appear unhindered by accompaniment, thus securing the optimum of expressive power.

He was born in Nagyszentmiklós, Hungary, in 1881, and his studies took place first in Pressburg, then at the Royal Academy of Budapest, to whose faculty he was appointed in 1907. During his early years as professor, he undertook numerous trips throughout his country in search of authentic folk music. As a result of his painstaking research, thousands of songs indigenous to Hungary were unearthed from obscurity. After World War I, Bartók traveled extensively throughout Europe and America in performances of his own works, achieving an international reputation. After the outbreak of World War II, Bartók settled in New York City, where he died in 1945.

CONCERTO NO. 3, FOR PIANO AND ORCHESTRA

Allegretto · Adagio religioso · Allegro vivace

THE THIRD Piano Concerto is Bartók's last composition. He was working on it in New York at the time of his death. In fact, he had completed all but the last seventeen measures, and these had already been sketched out, with the bar-lines drawn on the score. The concerto was completed after Bartók's death by his friend, the violist and composer, Tibor Serly. It received its first performance at a concert of the Philadelphia Orchestra, Eugene Ormandy conducting, on February 8, 1946, with Bartók's friend and former pupil, Gyorgy Sandor, as piano soloist. For this première Mr. Serly provided the annotator for the Philadelphia Orchestra with the following notes on the concerto:

"The Concerto, following the traditional classic form, is in the regulation three movements and is of ideal length—twenty-two minutes. It has the brilliance of the typical virtuoso concerto. Dissonances are resolved to a degree of refinement which seems consonant, a tendency strongly characteristic of all Bartók's last works."

The first movement is in the conventional sonata form, and contains brilliant writing for the solo instrument, with strong themes that are delicately embroidered. The second movement is, as is marked, religious in character. "This music," Mr. Serly writes, "is of the out-of-doors at night, the life of birds and insects. It is the life which so fascinated Bartók in his wanderings after folk material." The third movement is a highly spirited Rondo.

M-MM-674, Gyorgy Sandor, Piano, with the Philadelphia Orchestra, Eugene Ormandy Conducting.

CONTRASTS, FOR VIOLIN, CLARINET AND PIANO

VERBUNKOS (RECRUITING DANCE)   PIHENÖ (RELAXATION)
SEBES (FAST DANCE)

Contrasts, three pieces for violin, clarinet, and piano, was written especially for Joseph Szigeti and Benny Goodman. The manuscript bears the date: Budapest, September 24, 1938. These are, as the name implies, studies in contrast. The first movement is in the Hungarian counterpart of the American "blues." The second movement is a short and slow chorale in the two solo instruments. The third piece is a fast dance, opening with the fifths of a mistuned violin, with the E string lowered a semitone, and the G string raised to G sharp. However, there is another violin in reserve, which the player is instructed to pick up when normal tuning is required, much as the clarinet changes from an instrument in A to the one in B-flat.

X-MX-178, Béla Bartók, Piano, Joseph Szigeti, Violin, and Benny Goodman, Clarinet.

QUARTET IN A MINOR, OP. 17

Moderato · Allegro molto capriccioso · Lento

BARTÓK's later quartets are among his severest works and require an intellectual rather than an emotional or aesthetic approach. But his Opus 17 Quartet—his second—while bearing many of the identifiable Bartók traits is easily assimilable and consequently has been more often performed than the other Bartók quartets. The work is modern in its harmonic and melodic structure; but at the same time it makes for pleasurable listening. Only in the opening movement is there a suggestion of that austerity which is so prevalent in later Bartók chamber works. The second movement projects an intriguing attitude of whimsy, while the closing movement achieves a high and eloquent degree of expressiveness.

Ludwig van Beethoven

1770–1827

BEETHOVEN, so often referred to as the great German composer, was actually of Flemish descent. His father's family came from Louvain and Antwerp where his grandfather, an excellent musician, was Kapellmeister in 1737. Beethoven's father, Johann van Beethoven, though of meager talent, was a singer who served at the court of Max Friedrich, Elector of Bonn, and on his small stipend he married Maria Magdalena, daughter of the Elector's cook. Ludwig van Beethoven, the second of their seven children, was born in the attic of a humble dwelling in Bonn in December 1770.

Young Ludwig's father, never a good provider and addicted to the pleasures of the bottle, began exploiting his son's musical talents when Ludwig was only eight years old. Thus it was that Beethoven's general education was put aside as he took his place in the local theatre orchestra. His musical training was stressed, and under good teachers the boy continued his remarkable progress. Before he was twelve, a set of his variations was published, and three of his early sonatas followed. At fourteen, the poverty of his home, due to his father's unreliability, necessitated his applying for the position of Assistant Court Organist. He received the appointment and was able to undertake the support of his family.

Beethoven first visited Vienna when he was sixteen. It was then that Mozart heard him improvise and said, "Watch this Beethoven. Some day he will make the world talk about him." But it was not until 1792 that he permanently settled in Vienna, and in this city the young musician, who had undergone such childhood hardships, rapidly made his way to financial and social success.

Beethoven studied with Haydn for a while, but pupil and teacher were not well mated, and the easy-going Haydn was rather glad to be relieved of the embarrassment of such an ardently inquiring mind.

Beethoven had so thoroughly mastered the rules of composition that he felt justified in shattering them when freedom of expression was at stake. But he never broke down tradition without building something stronger in its place. He worked out his creations gradually from the musical notations he jotted down in his famous "sketch-books," one of which he always carried with him.

Fiercely independent of social conventions and artificialities, Beethoven was unruly—and sometimes even rude. He was clumsy in his motions and spoke with a provincial accent, though what he said and wrote revealed his culture. To compensate for his early lack of schooling, he read and studied constantly. Horace, Homer, Aristotle, and Shakespeare were among his favorite authors. He knew something of Latin and learned to write many of his thoughts in French, Italian, and English.

Because of his obvious genius, he was offered in 1809 an annual pension of 4,000 florins to remain in Austria. But the income, financed by three noblemen—Archduke Rudolph, Prince Lobkowitz, and Prince Kinsky—fluctuated, and soon ceased entirely. By 1818 Beethoven was without funds. He wrote: "I am almost reduced to beggary, and I am obliged to pretend that I do not lack necessities." At this period he owed so much to his publishers that his compositions brought him no profit. The deplorable conduct of his adopted nephew, Karl, and his increasing deafness led to more misery.

The identity of the "Immortal Beloved" of Beethoven's notes has taxed a century of research by skilled biographers. Beethoven, it seems, forever yearned for the beloved one who was too distant to attain. In the meantime his harmless romances were episodic, intense, and seldom flagged. But he never deviated from the high purposes he had set for himself.

The performance of his Ninth Symphony in 1824 was the crown of Beethoven's life. Gleams of happiness again appear, despite new illnesses and total deafness. His one opera, *Fidelio,* unsuccessful in earlier years, was now taking Europe by storm.

In December 1826, a violent cold developed into pneumonia, and dropsy followed. In three months' time, Beethoven died. On his deathbed he is said to have cried, "The comedy is ended." But nature appareled herself for his passing; and the mightiest of geniuses left this world amid the ragings of a thunderstorm on March 26, 1827.

[27]

CONCERTO NO. 1 IN C MAJOR, OP. 15, NO. 1, FOR PIANO AND ORCHESTRA

Allegro con brio · Largo · Rondo: allegro scherzando

THE C MAJOR Piano Concerto was styled by Beethoven the "Grand Concerto" and was dedicated to Princess Odescalchi. Though referred to as the First, it was actually of a later composition than the so-called Second Concerto. Conventional in subject and less significant in technique than later works, it is nevertheless interesting as indicating the early course of the composer's development. It is strictly classical in form, with 18th-century grace; the Titanic force of the later Beethoven is here rigidly held in check by classical formalism.

During Beethoven's early career it was usual for the orchestra to pause—generally on a six-four chord—while the soloist demonstrated his skill and technique in an improvisatory passage founded on a theme from the body of the movement. In the original score Beethoven left the customary pause, but later he wrote three cadenzas for this section.

At the first rehearsal of the C major Concerto, Beethoven is said to have transposed the work to C-sharp as he played, after finding that the piano was tuned too low for the wind instruments of the orchestra.

American music lovers might be interested to know that this work was introduced to New York audiences by Josef Hofmann in the season of 1887-88, when he was a piano prodigy of ten. The Concerto is still in his repertoire.

M-MM-308, Walter Gieseking, Piano, and the Berlin State Opera Orchestra Conducted by Rosbaud.

CONCERTO NO. 4 IN G MAJOR, OP. 58, FOR PIANO AND ORCHESTRA

Allegro moderato · Andante con moto · Rondo

BEETHOVEN began his Piano Concerto No. 4 in 1805, but apparently the composition proceeded slowly. He was in the habit of writing

[28]

several works concurrently and intermittently, without a definite chronology, in which respect he was very unlike Mozart, Haydn, or Schubert, who turned out symphonies in a matter of days or weeks. Thus, while at work on the Concerto, Beethoven was engaged in the composition of the Fourth and Fifth symphonies; and it is probable that the similarity between the rhythmical figure of the first phrase of the Concerto and the famous fate-knocks of the Fifth is not just a coincidence.

Though Beethoven had performed in nearly every great house in Vienna and had won great acclaim for his remarkable improvisations, he disliked playing his own compositions in public. When the Fourth Concerto was completed he asked his pupil and friend Ries to play it. There were only five days left for Ries to learn it before the performance, and Ries begged Beethoven to let him play the C minor Concerto instead. But the great man would tolerate no opposition to his plans. He left Ries in a rage and engaged a young pianist for the performance. At the last moment, however, the audacious younger pianist demurred, and substituted in the program the same C minor Concerto which Ries had wanted to play! Beethoven, though raging, had to submit.

The first performance of the Fourth Concerto took place much later at one of Prince Lobkowitz' palace concerts in 1807, and Beethoven played the piano part.

The Concerto was dedicated to the Archduke Rudolph.

The Concerto is unorthodox for the time in several different ways: in the very opening bars, which are played not by the orchestra, as was traditional up to that time, but by the solo pianist; in the cathedral-like grandeur of the development section of the first movement; and in the poetic expressiveness of the second movement, which achieves Olympian heights of eloquence completely unknown in the concerto literature of the period.

M-MM-411, Walter Gieseking, Piano, and the Saxon Orchestra Conducted by Böhm.

CONCERTO NO. 5 IN E-FLAT (EMPEROR), OP. 73, FOR PIANO AND ORCHESTRA

Allegro · Adagio un poco mosso · Rondo: allegro

WHEN Beethoven wrote his fifth and last piano concerto, he was at the height of his powers as a creative artist. It was not titled *Emperor* by the composer himself. It was written in 1809, a year marked by the investment of Vienna by Napoleon's troops; it was during this occupation that Beethoven's young pupil, Czerny, gave the newly completed concerto its first public hearing in that city. The story goes that a French officer in the audience proclaimed it "an Emperor among concertos." And *Emperor* it is called to this very day.

As in the Fourth Concerto, Beethoven brought in the piano at the very beginning of the Concerto; the *Emperor*, however, is extraordinary for the magnificently rhetorical way in which the piano emphasizes the opening chords. Another high point of the work is the second movement, a set of variations on a theme of typically Beethoven character—majestic and noble.

M-MM-500, Rudolf Serkin, Piano, and the Philharmonic-Symphony Orchestra of New York, Bruno Walter Conducting.

CONCERTO IN D MAJOR, OP. 61, FOR VIOLIN AND ORCHESTRA

Allegro ma non troppo · Larghetto · Rondo

ON DECEMBER 23, 1806, the influential concertmaster of the Theater-an-der-Wien, Franz Clement, gave a recital for which occasion Beethoven composed his only violin concerto. If it is true, as has often been written, that Beethoven did not finish the Concerto until after the last rehearsal of that concert, thus compelling Clement to play *prima vista*, this circumstance must have been highly welcome to the soloist. For Clement, once a child prodigy, was given to musical tricks at his concerts, in which he exploited his digital agility and his memory.

It was, of course, a common practice of the time to interpolate works of other composers between movements of concertos and symphonies. Clement not only included the performance of one of his own works between the first and second movements of Beethoven's Concerto, but wrote this entire piece for one string and played the work holding his instrument upside down. Such goings-on must have infuriated the sensitive Beethoven and may account for the historic fact that the Concerto was not dedicated to Clement but to Stephan von Breuning.

The Allegro opens with four drum taps, a thematic idea which, some say, came to the composer from the tapping on a neighbor's door. The opening movement then proceeds along spacious lines—following a symphonic prologue in which the principal themes of the movement are announced. In the Larghetto, the principal melody is carried by the orchestra, while the solo violin provides embellishments. The final Rondo begins brilliantly with a dance-like subject and advances to a second subject more sensitive and sentimental in mood.

M-MM-177, Joseph Szigeti, Violin, and an orchestra Conducted by Bruno Walter.

CORIOLANUS OVERTURE, OP. 62

THIS overture was written in 1807 and published a year later. It was not composed for the Shakespeare drama but for a tragedy by Heinrich Joseph von Collin, Viennese lawyer and playwright, with whom Beethoven was negotiating about collaboration on an opera. Collin's play deviates from that of Shakespeare in that the hero commits suicide; but, as Wagner was the first to point out, Beethoven had no intention of following either play. Instead, he selected the dramatic highlights of the story—the scene between Coriolanus, his mother and his wife in the enemy camps outside the gates of besieged Rome—to interpret in a tone picture filled with sublime musical concepts. In structure, the piece is based on the sonata form, which is particularly suited for the portrayal of contrasting emotions. The heroic Roman patrician is revealed torn by his inner struggle: patriotism and self-respect (the excited first theme in C minor) vainly trying to resist tender female persuasion (melodious second theme in E-flat), even though his yielding may very well bring death (dramatic coda).

11175-D, Minneapolis Symphony Orchestra, Dimitri Mitropoulos Conducting.

EGMONT OVERTURE, OP. 84

BEETHOVEN's incidental music to Goethe's drama, *Egmont*, dealing with the secession of the Netherlands from Spain in the 16th century, was composed during the first two months of 1810. It was first heard at the Vienna Court Theatre on May 24 of the same year during a performance of the Goethe tragedy.

The Overture is often considered a companion piece to the earlier *Coriolanus* Overture; but there is far greater kinship between it and the prelude to the second act of *Fidelio*. This is emphasized by the fact that both pieces are in the key of F minor and begin with broad, somber chords. Besides, the *Egmont* Overture does not depict any one emotional situation but follows closely the development of the play. There is a striking contrast between the weighty beginning and the jubilant coda: it is the contrast between oppression and freedom, and the full plot develops musically between these two extreme points. It is easy to recognize in this Overture Beethoven's intention to mold his musical material after his characters: a grumbling, oppressed people; a foreign tyrant; a national hero whose execution leads to a successful revolt. It is probable that Beethoven, ever sympathetic to such heroes, tried to picture Count Egmont's ultimate victory not as that of any one individual but rather that of all the oppressed people of the world.

69195-D, Vienna Philharmonic Orchestra, Felix Weingartner Conducting.

FIDELIO, OP. 72

BEETHOVEN began to work on his only opera in 1803. After considering at least fifteen subjects, he finally selected a libretto by Bouilly, a French lawyer, which had already been set to music by a French and an Italian composer. Based upon an actual incident during the Reign of Terror, but transferred across the Pyrenees for reasons of discretion, the plot tells the story of a political prisoner, Florestan, saved from certain death by his wife, Leonore, disguised as the jailer's helper under the name of Fidelio.

Fidelio has much in common with the French "rescue" opera in vogue in those days. The influence of Cherubini, who happened to be in Vienna while Beethoven completed his work, is particularly strong.

In structure, the opera is a Singspiel, the German version of light opera which shares with the French opéra comique (and differs from Italian opera buffa in) the alternation of spoken dialogue and set numbers. The distribution of characters—the pair of lovers, a couple of simpletons, the villain, and the *Deus ex machina*—was derived from 18th-century light opera; but a deviation from this pattern consisted in the introduction of a seventh principal character, Rocco, dramaturgically identical with the "noble father" of the legitimate stage, but in opera mostly identified with the *Deus ex machina*.

Beethoven was neither a vocal nor a dramatic composer. He often professed contempt for singers and once stated that he always thought of new melodies in terms of some instrument. It was inevitable that the composition of *Fidelio* should have involved him in countless artistic difficulties. Even after two revisions, the music remains more symphonic than operatic; and it is significant, indeed, that Romantic opera composers, including Wagner, should have been more strongly influenced by the master's symphonies than by his one completed stage work.

Yet the inner drama—which was always Beethoven's particular kind of drama—is unusually strong. By virtue of its human quality, the dungeon scene in the second act—perhaps the climax of the entire work—has lost none of its electrifying effect. In that scene, Beethoven uses the melodrama, a combination of rhapsodic speech with eloquent snatches of orchestral music; and at times he even resorts to programmatic suggestions in his music.

The première on November 20, 1805 was given under the most unfavorable auspices. Napoleon had just taken possession of Vienna. Most of Beethoven's friends had long since left town, and the theatre, kept open by official command, was occupied by French soldiers who understood no German and shrank at the contemplation of a hapless prisoner left to starve in solitary confinement. There was scant applause, and the opera was dropped after three performances.

Prince Lichnowsky summoned the composer, friends, and literary advisers to his home. After a stormy and lengthy debate—with the Princess virtually on her knees before Beethoven—the composer agreed to some revisions in the opera. The original three acts were compressed into two; three numbers were omitted; others were substantially condensed. In this form, *Fidelio* was performed on March 29, 1806. Improvements in the work had little reaction on the box-office. Beethoven's increasing deafness, irritability, and growing suspiciousness drove him to accuse the theatre employees of unfair business dealings, and he perfunctorily withdrew the score. It lay dormant for eight years—during which time Beethoven increased his musical experiences in virtually every direction. In March 1814, Beethoven again revised certain passages, and on May 23 of the same year *Fidelio* was given in its third and definitive version. The most important additions at this time were the second prisoner's chorus (replacing a conventional ensemble finale) and the second part of Florestan's aria; there were also some changes in Leonore's monologue and in the final chorus.

The great overture known as the *Leonore No. 3*, was for the time discarded. This was a revision of the original overture, published and now known as *Leonore No. 2*, for the 1806 performance. Beethoven, however, felt that the vehemence, passion, and stirring drama, as well as the length of the third *Leonore* disqualified it as an appropriate curtain-raiser. Instead, he wrote a light opera overture which is still in use and is known as the *Fidelio* Overture. (There is still a fourth overture, the *Leonore No. 1*. Much controversy has been aroused about the authentic date of its composition. Some believe it was written for a projected performance of the opera in Prague in 1808, while others claim that it was actually the earliest of the four.) *Leonore No. 3* was revived by Gustav Mahler who established the tradition of having it played during the change of scene in the final act.

69545-D, Fidelio Overture, the London Philharmonic Orchestra, Felix Weingartner Conducting.

71410-D, Florestan's Recitative and Aria, René Maison, Tenor, and Orchestra under Erich Leinsdorf.

X-MX-96, Leonore Overture No. 2, London Symphony Orchestra, Felix Weingartner Conducting.

X-MX-173, Leonore Overture No. 3, Minneapolis Symphony Orchestra, Dimitri Mitropoulos Conducting.

MISSA SOLEMNIS, OP. 123

"COMING from the heart, may it reach the heart," is the motto Beethoven appended to his score. At the beginning of the Kyrie, and again at the Sanctus, Beethoven emphasized in parentheses, "*Mit Andacht*" (With Reverence). Evidently Beethoven felt deeply about this work. The composition preoccupied his mind from 1818 to 1823, and during the last four years of his life he would insist that it was his *magnum opus*.

Actually, Beethoven's love for the *Missa* was that of a parent for a problem child. He never felt fully at ease in the vocal medium, nor did he have much inclination for ecclesiastical music.

Originally planned for performance at the installation of Archduke Rudolph as Cardinal (July 20, 1820), the *Missa* was delayed several years beyond that deadline. As Beethoven immersed himself in this work, he forgot his noble pupil and the purpose of the composition. He was writing a masterwork that could not be tailor-made for a certain date.

Brought up a Catholic and devout in his own way (though indifferent to religious conventions), Beethoven held personal communication with his God in the *Missa*. Beethoven claimed that his main purpose was to evoke in singers and audiences religious sentiments. The work is grandiose in architecture, highly effective, but tremendously difficult to perform and to comprehend at first hearing. The high moments of the work include the long Credo, the sublime melody of the Benedictus (with violin obbligato), the chorus, "Donna nobis pacem"—surely among the most moving passages ever composed.

If not an ecclesiastical work, it is surely a devotional one. It has often been compared to Bach's B minor Mass; but where the latter work attempted to "humanize" ecclesiastical music, the *Missa* tried to bring it to a symbolic and spiritual plane. And in view of the fact that Bach's Mass was unknown in Beethoven's time, the *Missa* can be said to have established a precedent for the performance of ecclesiastical music outside the Church.

It is perhaps inconceivable—yet typical of Beethoven—that a work of such spiritual character, and conceived with such reverence, should have been used as the means for some of the composer's more questionable business deals. Beethoven began by dealing with four publishers simultaneously and ended up by working with seven—accepting advances, stalling off deadlines, raising his price. In addition, he offered the work to several European kings and princes, receiving about ten acceptances. This is the reason why the *Missa*, dedicated to an Austrian Prince Cardinal, was given its world première in St. Petersburg (March 26, 1824). The first performance in Vienna (in parts) took place on May 7, 1824 at the Theater-an-der-Wien, during a concert which also introduced the Ninth Symphony.

QUARTET IN F MAJOR, OP. 18, NO. 1

Allegro con brio · Adagio affettuoso ed appassionato · Scherzo · Allegro

THE SIX quartets of Op. 18 are dedicated to Beethoven's friend and financial benefactor, Prince Franz Maximilian Lobkowitz, who was an amateur musician and a patron of the arts. Many of Beethoven's instrumental compositions were performed for the first time at the Lobkowitz home. Such private performances arranged by a rich music lover were very frequent in the Vienna of Beethoven's time, while public performances in concert halls were rather exceptional.

Beethoven's notebook reveals five attempts at the composition of the very first theme of the Quartet in F major, Op. 18, No. 1. Curiously enough, they were all in 4-4 time, while the final product crystallized into 3-4. The Quartet was completed on June 25, 1799, but a year later the composer wrote to his friend Amenda, to whom he had given the manuscript: "Don't play my quartet—I have modified it very much. I am only now learning how to write quartets, as you will observe when you receive the music." And Beethoven was in his thirtieth year at the time!

All six quartets of this Op. 18 were an immediate popular success, unlike many of Beethoven's later masterpieces. Composed on the general pattern of Haydn's quartets, they equaled that master in melodic beauty and rhythmic grace as they excelled him in profundity and originality. In the slow movements, particularly, the voice is emphatically Beethoven's; and though written so early, it speaks in tones as compelling as those in the greatest works of the mature Mozart. But Beethoven wrote laboriously. While Mozart could turn out a string quartet in an afternoon, it took Beethoven months of revision to bring his early ones into shape.

It was Beethoven, however, who humanized counterpoint. In his student days he practiced strict counterpoint diligently, using for a textbook the famous Latin treatise, *Gradus ad Parnassum*, by the celebrated Fux. But strict counterpoint never appealed to him. He used it as he saw fit, without concerning himself with the pedantry of the science. In quartet-writing he individualized separate instruments by lending melodic interest to their parts, and, in common with all contrapuntal practice, he made ample use of the device of imitation. But it was imitation of pattern rather than strict transposition of intervals.

The first movement of the F major Quartet, Allegro con brio, is based on a single motive which is used 102 times in 313 bars, an amazing proportion for a movement that is not a set of variations. This rhythmic theme appears in every instrument in various melodic forms.

The extremely rare one-hundred-and-twenty-eighth notes are used in the second movement, Adagio affettuoso ed appassionato. Amenda tells us that this Adagio was inspired by the tomb scene in *Romeo and Juliet*. And a sketch of this movement, dated 1799, bears the programmatic designation, *Les Derniers soupirs*.

In the third movement, Beethoven replaces the classical minuet with a scherzo. (As in the minuet, the Scherzo has a trio, so named because in the original classical form three instruments used to perform the middle section.) Beethoven invariably used the word "scherzo" in its etymological sense—namely, the German *Scherz*, meaning jest—thus suggesting a humorous composition.

The last movement is a lively Rondo.

M-MM-444, Budapest String Quartet.

QUARTET IN G MAJOR, OP. 18, NO. 2

*Allegro · Adagio cantabile · Scherzo: allegro
Allegro molto quasi presto*

THIS quartet is known as the *Komplimentierungs,* or "Compliment," Quartet because of its elaborate opening which is suggestive of a court reception. The quartet is short, Mozartean in character, classical in form.

M-MM-66, Lener String Quartet.

QUARTET IN D MAJOR, OP. 18, NO. 3

Allegro · Andante con moto · Allegro · Presto

IN ORDER of composition, this quartet was actually the first to have been written by Beethoven. Most of it was composed as early as 1798, one of the happiest years in the composer's life. Indeed, the work sparkles with good humor. As Beethoven's first quartet, it leans heavily for support on the quartets of Haydn and Mozart and betrays only fugitive signs of Beethoven's subsequent development. The lyrical Andante shows some formal irregularity, and the last movement has individuality of style. But the first movement is entirely formal, with the violin part dominating, and the 'cello completely subordinated, proving no more than a harmonic background. The third movement is in strictly conventional scherzo form.

QUARTET IN C MINOR, OP. 18, NO. 4

*Allegro ma non tanto · Scherzo; Andante scherzoso, quasi allegretto
Menuetto: allegretto · Allegro: Prestissimo*

THE ORIGIN of the C minor Quartet is shrouded in mystery. Since no preliminary sketches of this quartet have ever been found, it is generally assumed that, uncharacteristically, Beethoven must have composed it in a single effort. This is the only quartet of the six in this group that is in a minor key, and its seriousness sets it apart from the others.

The quartet has no slow movement—an unusual feature. Robert

Haven Schauffler singled out the first movement as the "gem" of the whole work—"the precursor of the Ajax-defying-the-thunder mood we are to meet with in the first movement of the *Eroica* and the C minor symphonies." The opening theme of the last movement owes an honest debt (and some of its popularity) to Haydn's *Gypsy Rondo*.

M-MM-556, Budapest String Quartet.

QUARTET IN A MAJOR, OP. 18, NO. 5

Allegro · *Menuetto* · *Andante cantabile* · *Allegro con variazioni*

ONLY by comparison with Beethoven's later masterpieces can this entertaining A major Quartet be regarded as a somewhat trifling achievement. Regardless of how far it was outstripped by its own composer, this quartet can be accepted for what it is worth—a charming and beautifully finished work, delightful and refreshing.

Hasty critics are fond of asserting that Beethoven's early music resembles that of Mozart. A dispassionate study of a work like the A major Quartet reveals that this influence has been overestimated. If any indebtedness is to be discovered, it is to Haydn; but the simple truth is that Beethoven took the idiom current in his time as a working basis, an idiom which happened to be not only Haydn's and Mozart's, but also that of countless minor composers as well. To the classical forms of Haydn and Mozart, Beethoven brings, in this work, a strength of character of his own, a spirit of emancipation which provides a robustness and vigor to his music which that of his predecessors rarely achieved.

M-MM-301, Lener String Quartet.

QUARTET IN B-FLAT, OP. 18, NO. 6

*Allegro con brio · Adagio ma non troppo · Scherzo: allegro
Allegretto quasi allegro*

THE INCLUSION of *La Malinconia* thrusts the B-flat Quartet five years
in advance of the others of Op. 18. Short as it is, this passage is the
soul of the work. Without *La Malinconia,* the quartet is a charming
diversion; with it, the composition becomes an anticipatory hint of
the revelation of the great quartets dedicated to Count Rasoumovsky.
This famous *Malinconia* is heard in the slow introduction to the
finale, and reappears twice in dance-like form.

QUARTET IN F MAJOR, OP. 59, NO. 1

*Allegro · Allegretto vivace e sempre scherzando · Adagio molto e
mesto · Thème Russe: allegro*

THE THREE Rasoumovsky Quartets, Op. 59, were written at the request of Count Andreas Rasoumovsky, the Russian Ambassador to
Austria, a man of great wealth and cultural understanding. The
Count's huge household included a permanent quartet of string
players whose equal was not then to be found in Europe. Rasoumovsky himself often displaced the second violinist, proving a creditable
substitute.

In commissioning the quartets, the Count asked Beethoven to use
Russian folk tunes as thematic material. The composer, who had
often utilized the simplest and most trite of melodies for his greatest
works, was willing to include any air that would impart to the quartets a Russian flavor in honor of Rasoumovsky.

The Russian identification, however, is apparent only twice—in
the finale of the first quartet and in the trio of the second.

In the independence of their form and style, the Rasoumovskys
anticipate more modern works. No wonder, then, that in 1806 many
listeners found them strange and unintelligible. Radicati, the Italian
violinist, saw the quartets in manuscript and remarked to Beethoven,
"Surely you do not consider these works to be music." And Beethoven, unmoved, rejoined, "Not for you, but for a later age."

The finale of this work in F major is a *Thème Russe,* built on a Russian folk song. But in Beethoven's hands its Russian character becomes entirely submerged, and in place of its plaintive andante is heard an energetic statement that draws a smile of admiration for the individuality of Beethoven's methods and of sympathy for the poor theme itself.

M-MM-543, Busch Quartet.

QUARTET IN E MINOR, OP. 59, NO. 2
Allegro · Molto adagio · Allegretto · Presto

THIS, the second of the three Rasoumovsky quartets, is abundant with melody and beauty. Among its many striking features is the solemn and stately theme of the second movement, which seems to anticipate the religious quality of passages in Beethoven's last quartets. Some biographers believe that the composer invented the melody one night while glancing at the star-studded sky. In the trio of the dance-like Allegretto (in scherzo form), Beethoven again uses a Russian national theme to please his sponsor, a theme which was later incorporated by Mussorgsky into the coronation scene of *Boris Godunov;* first played by the viola, the melody is then taken over by the other instruments, first in counterpoint, then in canonic imitation. The finale is full of sparkling gaiety.

QUARTET IN C MAJOR, OP. 59, NO. 3
Andante con moto; Allegro vivace · Andante con moto, quasi allegretto
Menuetto: grazioso · Allegro molto

THE QUARTET in C, sometimes called the *Hero,* is unique in this: that Beethoven wrote no other in which anxiety and distress do not reveal themselves. In the Andante there might be expected an expression of melancholy character; instead, this movement is a lyric narrative, suffused with spiritual contentment.

M-MM-510, Budapest String Quartet.

QUARTET IN E-FLAT MAJOR, OP. 74 ("HARP")

Poco adagio; Allegro · *Adagio ma non troppo* · *Presto* · *Allegretto con variazioni*

IN THE summer of 1809, Vienna once again became a besieged—then a conquered—town. Prevented from leaving the city, Beethoven, whose lodgings were virtually at the city wall, was profoundly upset by the cannon shots and was terrified that they might further impair his hearing. With both hands cupped over his ears, he spent long hours in a cellar. His capacity to compose music under these circumstances was extraordinary: during that very summer he wrote a piano concerto (the Fifth) and began the E-flat major Quartet. The latter was completed in the fall at Baden, where he finally went for his vacation.

This quartet was dedicated to Prince Lobkowitz (the sponsor of the Op. 18 set), who played host to its première. It shows no considerable advance in style over the quartets of the Op. 59 group, but there are here the same richness of invention and unity of design, and the same variety of form. A pizzicato passage in the coda of the first movement, resembling the plucking of harp strings, gave this quartet its nickname.

QUARTET IN F MINOR, OP. 95

Allegro con brio · *Allegretto ma non troppo* · *Allegro assai vivace, ma serioso* · *Larghetto espressivo; Allegretto agitato*

THE TITLE *Serioso* prefaced to the Quartet in F minor, Op. 95, is one of the few that Beethoven actually sanctioned. Imaginative publishers and critics have been responsible for most of his works being known by descriptive labels—the *Moonlight* and *Appassionata* sonatas for piano, and the *Spring* Sonata for violin and piano, among others. Curiously, *their* titles have stuck, while in the case of the F minor Quartet, Beethoven's title has fallen into disuse.

The manuscript of this great work bears, in Beethoven's hand, the following inscription: "*Quartetto Serioso*—1810—in the month of October. Dedicated to Herr von Zmeskall and written in the month of December by his friend, L. v. Beethoven." The Zmeskall who was thus immortalized was a secretary to the Vienna Court and one of the composer's greatest admirers. He helped Beethoven in a thousand ways—from procuring good pens for the copying of music to finding servants for him. The relations between the two men were marked by mutual respect and liking, and the little unpleasantnesses that marred some of Beethoven's other friendships—usually attributable to his difficult temperament—were absent here. Zmeskall received and reverently preserved many letters from Beethoven, and their prevailing tone is one of good humor.

The *Serioso* of Beethoven's inscription needs no explanation, for the epithet characterizes the music. Except for the vigorous and joyous finale, the mood of the music is reflective.

The opening Allegro con brio is followed by the highly original Allegretto ma non troppo which takes the place of a slow movement in this Quartet. The third movement, Allegro assai vivace, ma serioso, follows the second without a break. It has the form of a scherzo, but the content is serious. The Allegretto agitato is introduced by a short Larghetto.

The last chords of the F minor Quartet suddenly change to F major. This transitional ending has been called by d'Indy an "error of genius," and a "Rossinian operatic finale."

M-MM-519, Budapest String Quartet.

QUARTET IN E-FLAT, OP. 127

*Allegro · Adagio, ma non troppo e molto cantabile · Scherzando
Finale: allegro*

BEETHOVEN's quartets marked by opus numbers 127, 130, 131, 132, and 135, are usually called the "last quartets" or the "great quartets." They belong to the last three years of the master's life, and in them the greatness of inspiration is reflected in the greater length of the music itself, as though Beethoven needed a larger canvas on which to develop the dramatic expression of his last period.

The deaf Beethoven's almost exclusive interest in quartet writing at the end of his life is not difficult to understand. He turned naturally to the medium that comes nearest to the ideal of pure design in music, just as a painter who had turned color-blind may be imagined to seek expression in black and white, and to reach the summit of his creative career by means of drawing or etching. Effects of tone-color no longer played any part in Beethoven's music. Instrumental display had ceased to claim the least consideration for its own sake. The technical difficulties—and they are often enormous—which confront the performers of the late quartets are always means to a production of music that is sublimated into pure thought and emotion, music where sensuous beauty and formal polish no longer seem of importance. There are harshnesses, even awkwardnesses, in these quartets which might offend the ear if it were not that they are invariably the carriers of ideas so great as to make us forget the manner of their presentation. It is as sustenance for the mind rather than as solace for the ear that we must listen to these indestructible masterpieces.

These last quartets have a somewhat alarming reputation for surpassing greatness allied with an equal degree of obscurity. Reading much that has been written about these works, *l'homme moyen musicale* is unlikely to rush forward to embrace the difficult, frustrating works. The truth is that the last quartets are difficult only as one goes deeply into them in an attempt to formulate in thought, in language, the experiences they communicate. To the intellectual innocent they present no formidable problems of understanding. They speak to the heart and the spirit—perhaps no other Beethoven works speak to them so directly; and the heart and the spirit, unfettered by the mind, will instinctively understand their message.

The E-flat Quartet is "the last of Beethoven's pastoral symphonies," according to Vincent d'Indy. It breathes the composer's love of Nature, and it was written when Beethoven was in the country. In his sketch books, the motto *La Gaieté* is scrawled above a sketch for this quartet, an indication of the remoteness of Beethoven's own conception of the music from that of most commentators.

M-MM-537, Budapest String Quartet.

[44]

QUARTET IN B-FLAT MAJOR, OP. 130

Allegro · *Presto* · *Andante scherzoso* · *Allegro assai* · *Adagio molto espressivo* · *Allegro*

CHARLES NEATE wrote to Beethoven in September 1824, on behalf of the Philharmonic Orchestra of London, offering him three hundred guineas to come to London to conduct the performance of the Ninth Symphony, which was written for the London Philharmonic. Beethoven asked for one hundred guineas more, to buy a coach in which to travel in greater comfort. For this additional money he offered Neate a string quartet. Neate replied: "If you bring the quartet, it is as good as one hundred pounds more, and, you can be quite sure, I see no obstacle to it that you should earn a sufficient sum of money to take back with you, enabling you to pass your whole life pleasantly and free from care."

This Quartet was the one in B-flat major, Op. 130. Beethoven was agitated by the thought of possible prosperity: "If God would only give me health, I shall be able to accept all commissions I receive from every country in Europe and even from North America."

Quartet Op. 130 was sketched in 1825. As so often in Beethoven's creative habits, he was working on all movements at once. The fourth movement, *Danza Tedesca,* was originally sketched in A major for the A minor Quartet. But later it was transposed into G major and entitled Allemande, which is the French word for the Italian *tedesca,* meaning German dance. There is no organic connection between this German dance and the rest of the Quartet. It is an insertion, an interpolation.

The Grand Fugue, Op. 133, was originally intended as the finale of the B-flat major Quartet, but its length (745 measures) and its polyphonic grandeur were regarded by the publisher as deterrents to success, and he persuaded Beethoven to compose another finale. The new finale was probably the last thing Beethoven ever wrote, and he sent it to the publishers four months before he died.

The only truly slow movement of the B-flat major Quartet is the fifth, Adagio molto espressivo. Beethoven's friends reported that this movement, a Cavatina, was written in tears and agony. An indirect confirmation of this may be seen in Beethoven's expression mark

Beklemmt, with which he marked an episodic passage, and which means "agonized."

The finale was written in the last months of Beethoven's life and demonstrates that the division of Beethoven's music into three styles, accepted by most Beethoven scholars, is at best a convenient chronology. For in his third and last period, Beethoven had not relinquished the youthfulness, vigor, and simplicity of the first.

M-MM-474, Busch Quartet.

QUARTET IN C-SHARP MINOR, OP. 131

Adagio ma non troppo e molto espressivo · Allegro molto vivace · Allegro moderato · Adagio; Andante ma non troppo e molto cantabile Presto · Adagio · Allegro

MUSICALLY speaking, the Quartet in C-sharp minor represents the highest development of Beethoven's new style. It contains innovations extraordinary for his time. The selection of the key itself was unusual, if not unprecedented. The Quartet has seven movements, linked so that there is no distinct separation between the component parts, but a liquid transition from one mood to another. There is an element of experimentation in the use of such effects as the violoncello playing on the bridge in the high treble register, or pizzicato in isolated notes, creating the impression of an intrusive drum beat. The form is extremely free, and yet in the Presto Beethoven reverts to his manner and employs a simple harmony and the rhythm of a country dance.

That the Quartet was conceived as an expression of Beethoven's brighter side is borne out by Beethoven's own inscription on the manuscript: *Zusammengestohlen aus verschiedenem diesem und jenem*—translatable to "Picked up [literally, stolen] in various places, from this and that." Beethoven was in the habit of writing several movements at once, and the seeming synthesis may be explained exactly by Beethoven's word—*Zusammengestohlen.*

The first Adagio is a fugue which Wagner described as "revealing the most melancholy sentiment ever expressed in music." He characterized the fourth movement, Andante ma non troppo e molto

cantabile, as "the incarnation of perfect innocence, revealed in countless aspects." The fifth, Presto, he called "a vision embodied in material form." This movement is similar in character to the Scherzo from
the Ninth Symphony. There is a surprising boisterousness here that
belies the picture of Beethoven as an unchangeably gloomy hypo-
chondriac. The final Allegro suggested to Wagner the picture of "the
indomitable fiddler, whirling us on to the abyss."

The Quartet, Op. 131, had an indirect bearing on Beethoven's
nephew. In a letter written two weeks before his death, Beethoven
asked his publishers to inscribe the score to Baron von Stutterheim,
the colonel of the regiment in which Beethoven's nephew was enlisted. The Quartet was completed and sent to the publishers a few
months before Beethoven's death.

M-MM-429, Budapest String Quartet.

QUARTET IN A MINOR, OP. 132

*Assai sostenuto; Allegro · Allegro ma non tanto · Molto adagio;
Andante; Molto adagio · Alla marcia, assai vivace; Piu allegro; Presto
Finale: allegro appassionato*

THE A MINOR Quartet was more than two and a half years in the
making. Its composition was interrupted by a serious abdominal in-
flammation from which Beethoven suffered in the spring of 1825.
He had to go to the watering place of Baden, near Vienna, where he
could not resume the work until the month of May. It has never been
satisfactorily shown how far it had advanced before his illness,
though a great deal of it appears to have been sketched, and the last
movement is certainly of earlier date, for it was originally conceived
in the key of D minor, and would seem to have been intended as an
instrumental finale for the Ninth Symphony, afterwards displaced by
the choral "Hymn to Joy." The Adagio, on the other hand, was undoubtedly written after the composer's recovery. The superscription,
"Fervent thanksgiving to the Godhead of one who had recovered,"
proves this abundantly.

The Op. 132 was finished about August 1825, while Beethoven
was still at Baden. He did not return to Vienna until September 9,

when the Berlin publisher, Schlesinger, brought him back to the capital to be present at—if not, alas! to hear—a private performance given at the Wild Man Inn. Schlesinger afterwards acquired the work for publication for the sum of eighty ducats, and it received its first public performance on November 6.

M-MM-545, Budapest String Quartet.

QUARTET IN F MAJOR, OP. 135

Allegretto · Vivace · Lento assai · Grave; Allegro

THE QUARTET in F major has caused more flow of commentators' ink than all the others combined, mainly because of Beethoven's curious inscription at the head of the last movement: *"Muss es sein? Es muss sein!"* ("Must it be? It must be!"). These words appear over the musical quotation of the two principal themes. The musical quotation bears a special title, also in Beethoven's hand: *Der schwer gefasste Entschluss* ("a difficult resolution").

Schindler, Beethoven's faithful disciple, offers this prosaic explanation of the mysterious quotation: Beethoven's housekeeper had asked him for money. "Must it be?" Beethoven inquired. "It must be!" the housekeeper answered with emphasis. An alternate suggestion from Schindler is that Beethoven had asked his publishers for money and, anticipating a query, answered it in a musical theme.

Another version is offered by Maurice Schlesinger, the son of Beethoven's publisher—namely, that Beethoven did not care to write this Quartet, but needing money and having promised the work to the publisher, was conscience-bound to write it. Schlesinger's version is more difficult to accept—since he stated it thirty-two years after the event and quoted from memory a letter that Beethoven was supposed to have written to the publishers in explanation of the "must it be" quotation, a letter which was lost during the fire at the publisher's premises, and of which no copy was kept.

A simpler explanation suggests itself in the absence of plausible reports: that Beethoven, thinking about the possibilities of the theme already selected by him, fitted the question and answer to them and set them down in the spirit of a ponderous joke, to which he was addicted.

Beethoven intentionally kept down the length of this Quartet, according to Holz. It seems that composer and publisher had agreed on eighty ducats as the price for the work—but the publisher paid 360 florins instead. And Beethoven's answer was that "amputated ducats deserved an amputated quartet."

Although Beethoven noted at the end of the manuscript "the last Quartet," he could not have foreseen it was to be his last work. This Quartet was Beethoven's Intermezzo, which death converted into a Finale.

M-MM-489, Budapest String Quartet.

SONATA IN C-SHARP MINOR (MOONLIGHT), OP. 27, NO. 2

Adagio sostenuto · *Allegretto* · *Presto agitato*

IT WAS the critic Rellstab who gave the Sonata in C-sharp minor the title *Moonlight,* since he said it made him think of moonlight on Lake Lucerne. He must have named it before he penetrated beyond the opening movement, surely, or he would have seen how poorly the program fitted the lighthearted Allegretto scherzo and the dramatic Presto finale.

This Sonata was suggested by the poem, *Die Beterin,* by Seume, according to Krehbiel. The poem describes a maiden kneeling at the high altar praying for the recovery of a sick father. Angels come to her aid and she glows with the transfiguring light of hope. Krehbiel adds that there is little to commend the poem as literary art, and it is not so easy to connect in fancy with the last movement of the Sonata as with the first and second; "but the evidence that Beethoven paid it the tribute of his music seems conclusive."

Both sonatas of Op. 27 bear for the first time the marking "quasi una fantasia." The Sonata in C-sharp minor was an abrupt departure from the conventionalities of eighteenth-century musical form. Customarily a three-movement sonata opened with the most important movement, written in sonata form. This would be followed by a slow second movement and a rapid finale, possibly in rondo style. But Beethoven, the bold innovator, changed the order and started with the slow movement, a section decidedly in the romantic vein. This is followed by a gay scherzo, with the big section of the work left for the finale and marked Presto agitato—a fiery movement full of drama.

X-MX-237, Rudolf Serkin, Piano.
X-MX-273, Oscar Levant, Piano.

SONATA IN D MINOR (TEMPEST), OP. 31, NO. 2

Largo; Allegro · *Adagio* · *Allegretto*

THIS second sonata of a set of three was probably composed in 1802, and is generally considered the opening work of Beethoven's second period. It was undoubtedly one of the most dramatic works he had written up to this time. Shortly before undertaking this set, Beethoven wrote to Czerny that he was dissatisfied with his earlier work and was about to "strike out in a new direction." And new directions were invariably first struck by Beethoven in his piano music.

The D minor Sonata was his first attempt to free the sonata form from its structural conventions and to make it a vehicle for emotional self-expression. Thus it is the companion piece for the *Eroica* Symphony which Beethoven began composing at this time too. It also represents the key to virtually all of Beethoven's later sonata output; and its kinship with the *Appassionata* was acknowledged by the composer himself.

The Sonata was composed when Beethoven had reached the very peak of his despair in the weeks preceding the Heiligenstadt Testament. The first movement is ghostly and stormy by turns. For two brief passages, Beethoven makes the piano "talk" in an eloquent instrumental recitative. The quiet Adagio is followed by a breezy night-piece almost entirely in triplets and sextuplets, foreshadowing similar pieces by Chopin and Mendelssohn.

X-MX-39, Walter Gieseking, Piano.

SONATA IN C MAJOR (WALDSTEIN), OP. 53

Allegro con brio · Adagio molto · Rondo: allegretto moderato

It was Count Waldstein who first appreciated Beethoven's genius, and through his letters opened the doors of most of the great houses of Vienna to the composer. In the *Waldstein* Sonata, dedicated to the Count, Beethoven leaves behind the comparatively orthodox methods of his earlier sonatas and exhibits a vigor and boldness of idea and treatment which reveal a new outlook. The composer at this time was dejected because of the inroad which deafness had made upon his peace of mind; yet this work divulges nothing of his personal grief, but only the liveliest vitality.

It is interesting that the first movement, Allegro con brio, flowered out of some piano exercises. It does not attempt to deal with any deep or serious issues.

The second movement is in three parts—Adagio molto, Allegretto moderato, and Prestissimo. Beethoven originally intended to use the piece now known as *Andante Favori* as the slow movement of this work, but it was rejected either because of its unusual length or because it was not in keeping with the first movement.

M-MM-358, Walter Gieseking, Piano.

SONATA IN F MINOR (APPASSIONATA), OP. 57

Allegro assai · Andante con moto · Allegro ma non troppo

Beethoven's piano sonatas have been called "mere operas in disguise." Probably the most significant and consistently popular concert hall favorites are three that are known by their bestowed titles —*Appassionata, Waldstein,* and *Moonlight.* But the Sonata in F minor was named *Appassionata* by the publisher Cranz—not by the composer.

Few composers have influenced piano playing as Beethoven did. He had come to regard virtuosity merely as the necessary medium of a new type of musical expression. As he attained freedom in this expression, he enhanced it by technical perfection to set off its beauties and brilliance. He never wrote for superficial effect alone, Bekker tells us, but neither had he an ascetic scorn for arresting devices. And the *Appassionata* is so dramatically effective that it might be called a concerto without orchestral accompaniment.

"There are no minor characters in the *Appassionata*," said Romain Rolland. And he sums up the Sonata in these words: "The *Appassionata* is worthy to take its place between a fresco of the Sistine and a tragedy by Corneille: it is of the same family."

M-MM-365, Walter Gieseking, Piano.

SONATA IN C MINOR, OP. 111

Maestoso; Allegro con brio ed appassionata · Arietta: adagio molto semplice e cantabile

BEETHOVEN's Sonata, Op. 111, has caused much speculation. It consists of two movements only, the first in conventional a-b-a form and the second a theme with variations. These movements are sometimes referred to as "Resistance" and "Resignation." To ears that had long been used to three or four movements in a sonata, two did not represent completeness. In reply to a query, Beethoven said he "had no time to write a third." Even his publisher was insistent about having another, and livelier, movement for the finale—on the grounds that sonatas did not end Adagio. It is known that an Allegro finale was outlined by the composer, but not finished, and it is thought that Beethoven was satisfied with the original ending.

The year that Beethoven composed Op. 111, he said to a friend, "It is long since I have been able to bring myself to write easily. I sit and think and think. The ideas are there, but they will not go down on paper." This Sonata was much revised.

The C minor is Beethoven's farewell sonata for the piano. Bekker remarks that "it is hard to estimate the possibility of his return to the pianoforte after the completion of the great string quartets and the projected Tenth Symphony, even if longer life had been granted him."

In Op. 111, Beethoven wastes little time over preliminary phrases,

[52]

but launches at once into his subject. The opening chord is the most agonized dissonance in this composer's vocabulary.

M-MM-263, Egon Petri, Piano.

SONATA IN F MAJOR, OP. 24 (SPRING), FOR VIOLIN AND PIANO

Allegro · Adagio molto espressivo · Scherzo · Rondo: allegro ma non troppo

BEETHOVEN's sonatas for violin and piano are, as a whole, inferior in quality and interest to those written by him for piano alone. Harvey Grace suggests that the reason may lie in the problem of catering to two virtuosos, and at the same time of producing a good ensemble and a balance of interest throughout. This difficulty is not always solved. Moreover, according to Grace, the needs of the sonata form involve the delivery of a good deal of the material by both soloists. It is inevitable that many themes that suit the keyboard are less satisfactory on the stringed instrument, and vice versa. This is overcome only when the musical worth of the material is so high that an occasional lack of suitability to the medium is scarcely observed. This is not often the case in Beethoven's duo sonatas, because most of those for violin were written rather hastily for the use of eminent players. Thus the element of display had to be considered even at some cost to musical value.

The two violin sonatas in A minor and F major, respectively Op. 23 and 24, were originally meant to form one opus number, No. 23, as they were announced as such in the *Wiener Zeitung* of October 28, 1801. Also an autograph copy of the F major is inscribed as No. 2. The F major sonata is dedicated to Monsieur le Comte Maurice de Fries, at whose house Beethoven's Op. 11, the Trio in B-flat, was first performed. Count Fries, a wealthy merchant and patron of the arts, was instrumental in collecting a sum of money for the last survivor of Bach's children, Regina Susanna Bach.

The *Spring* Sonata belongs to the composer's middle period, and was composed in 1801. The title of "Spring" was not given to this work by Beethoven but by someone whose identity is unknown. It is certainly light-hearted in spirit, and there is nothing incongruous in the idea even if connection of the music with spring and its associations be not especially apparent.

SONATA IN G MAJOR, OP. 30, NO. 3, FOR VIOLIN AND PIANO

Allegro assai · *Tempo di minuetto* · *Allegro vivace*

THE SONATAS of the Op. 30 set are dedicated to Czar Alexander I of Russia and are usually called the *Alexander* Sonatas. Beethoven received 150 ducats for this Sonata No. 3.

The source motive of the Allegro assai is a typical violin finger exercise; Carl Engel thought this might be a souvenir of Beethoven's early violin playing days.

SONATA IN A MAJOR (KREUTZER), OP. 47, FOR VIOLIN AND PIANO

Adagio sostenuto; Presto · *Andante con variazioni* · *Presto*

INTERESTING circumstances surrounded the composition of the *Kreutzer* Sonata. And Leo Tolstoy added to its fascination by writing a celebrated novel about this masterpiece of Beethoven's.

Beethoven composed the music for George Augustus Polgreen Bridgetower, a mulatto violinist who was in Vienna at the time. As usual, Beethoven did not have the music in final shape when the date for Bridgetower's concert drew near. So he took the finale from his Violin Sonata in A major, Op. 30, No. 1, and used it for the *Kreutzer*, writing a new movement for the earlier work at a later time. During the first performance the frantic violinist had to read the variations at sight from Beethoven's hopelessly illegible manuscript. Beethoven's piano part, which he played at the première, was a virtual blank except for the most necessary indications. Despite these facts, the performance was well received, and the audience demanded an encore of the slow movement variations.

After the initial presentation, Beethoven subjected the music to polishing and revision. During this period he quarreled violently with Bridgetower, allegedly over a girl, and transferred the dedication of the new sonata to the French violinist and composer, Rodolphe Kreutzer, who at that time was a professor at the Paris Conservatoire. In a letter to his publisher, Beethoven described Kreutzer as "a good, amiable man, who during his stay here gave me much pleasure. His unaffectedness and natural manner are more to my taste than that of most virtuosi. As the sonata is written for a first-class player, the dedication is all the more fitting." However, Kreutzer himself never appreciated or played the work.

Beethoven's inscription on the title page of the *Kreutzer* Sonata is *Per il pianoforte ed un violin obbligato in un stilo molto concertante* ("For piano and violin obbligato in concerted style"). Exploiting the resources of both violin and piano, it is almost a concerto for solo instruments.

M-MM-496, Adolf Busch, Violin, and Rudolf Serkin, Piano.

SONATA IN A MAJOR, OP. 69, FOR 'CELLO AND PIANO

Allegro ma non tanto · *Scherzo: allegro molto* · *Adagio cantabile; Allegro vivace*

THE SONATA in A major is dedicated "to my friend, Baron von Gleichenstein." Its resoluteness is reflective of Beethoven's renewed determination to make the best of his growing deafness through an increased faith in his art.

Mark Brunswick has characterized the A major Sonata in these words: "This Sonata could be used in any anthology to represent as completely as any one work could the whole style of what has been called Beethoven's middle period. A comparison with the First Sonata shows how Beethoven is here able at last to satisfy his need for broad and definite lines spread over the largest possible canvas. The A major Sonata is what Beethoven wanted to do in his First Sonata, this time fulfilled without recourse to any compromise with his higher

[55]

musical standards. There is virtuosity both in the style of the composition and in the writing for the two instruments, but it is an Olympian virtuosity conferred from above rather than striven for superficially from below."

The A major Sonata is in three movements. The first, an Allegro ma non tanto, is written along broadly melodic lines and opens in an unusual fashion with the unaccompanied 'cello stating the opening theme. The second movement, a scherzo, marked Allegro molto, is dominated by a theme in syncopated form. The only attempt at a slow movement is the Adagio cantabile which serves as the introduction to the final, carefree Allegro vivace.

M-MM-312, Emanuel Feuermann, 'Cello, and Myra Hess, Piano.

SYMPHONY NO. 1 IN C MAJOR, OP. 21

Adagio molto; Allegro con brio · Andante cantabile con moto
Menuetto · Adagio; Allegro molto e vivace

GREAT historical interest is attached to Beethoven's First Symphony, because it is the first work in symphonic form by one who raised that form to so high a point of development. The First Symphony is the work of a man who had carefully studied the symphonies of Haydn and Mozart but whose own individuality was too strong to be subverted by any outside influence. The uncompromising attitude of the composer toward mere conventions even at this early period is admirably expressed by the very opening chord. It is the chord of the seventh, a dissonance, and, to shock the pedants further, a dissonance that does not even belong to the key of the movement! Today it sounds appropriately effective; then, it was rank heresy.

Beethoven had been in Vienna eight years before he ventured to give a concert for his own benefit. This first benefit concert took place at the Burg Theater on April 2, 1800. The program included a Mozart symphony, an aria and a duet from Haydn's *Creation*, and the following compositions by Beethoven: a piano concerto, the Septet, Op. 20, for strings and wind instruments, and the Symphony No. 1. Beethoven also obliged with an improvisation on Haydn's *Emperor's Hymn*—improvisation was then the most admired of his talents.

The concert was far from an artistic success, for the orchestra, disliking the conductor Wranitzky, played atrociously. But Beethoven was not disappointed financially; and badly though it was played, his Symphony earned words of praise. Viennese critics found it "abundant in ideas, and originally conceived," though it was criticized for having too much emphasis in the orchestration and on wind instruments: "The music is more for a band than for an orchestra." Some years later Paris critics reacted quite differently. The not-so-bold dissonance with which the first movement opens horrified them. Beethoven's music, they said, "was a peril to art."

This was not only Beethoven's first symphony, but also his first orchestral work of importance, and it is interesting to find so many of the features that distinguish his mature orchestration already handled with certainty and ease.

M-MM-535, The Cleveland Orchestra, Artur Rodzinski Conducting.

SYMPHONY NO. 2 IN D MAJOR, OP. 36

Adagio molto; Allegro con brio · *Larghetto* · *Scherzo: allegro*
Allegro molto

BEETHOVEN wrote his gay Symphony No. 2 at a time when his growing deafness might more naturally have influenced him to produce a melancholy work. The composer himself admitted that the Symphony was a giant mask.

Today the Second Symphony may seem almost naïve in its simplicity, but its first audience found it too strange to be immediately acceptable. Evidently the work was considerably revised, for several pages of suggestions relating to it are in Beethoven's notebook, and it is said that three scores were written before the existing version was established. Curiously enough, even the critics thought it labored. One contemporary reviewer declared that Beethoven's "anxiety to achieve something novel and surprising was much too evident." Others condemned it as too long, too wild, too bizarre.

The opinion of Berlioz is the opposite, as one would expect: "Everything in it is noble, energetic, and proud." To others it revealed fresh ideas, depth of experience, and individuality.

[57]

Though the Second Symphony is traditional in many respects, the introduction and coda have gained importance. There is greater richness of instrumentation, and the Scherzo has been substituted for the Minuet. Lenz stated that in the history of human achievement recorded in musical symbols, this Symphony "marks the moment when independent, self-conscious genius burst through the fetters of convention."

The Larghetto of this work inspired a famous hymn. It appears in the hymnals under the title *Alsace*, though it is admitted that Beethoven was the composer. Isaac Watts wrote the words, beginning "Kings and thrones to God belong." The beauty of the opening bars so impressed Sir John Goss, the eminent musician, that he also used it. His setting was for Keble's *Sun of My Soul, Thou Savior Dear*, a hymn tune known as *Bonn*—in honor of Beethoven's birthplace.

M-MM-597, Pittsburgh Symphony Orchestra, Fritz Reiner Conducting.

SYMPHONY NO. 3 (EROICA) IN E-FLAT, OP. 55

Allegro con brio · Funeral March: adagio assai · Scherzo: allegro vivace · Finale: allegro molto

WHEN Beethoven dedicated his *Eroica* Symphony to Napoleon Bonaparte, it was Napoleon the republican leader and upholder of freedom whom he wished to honor—not Napoleon the soldier and conqueror. His friend, Ferdinand Ries, saw the work lying on Beethoven's table with but two names on the title page—Bonaparte and Beethoven. Then came the proclamation of Napoleon as emperor, and his series of military conquests. The composer, in a fit of disappointment at the fall of his idol from the lofty ideals with which he had credited him, tore the flyleaf into fragments, exclaiming, "Then he is only an ordinary man after all! Now he will turn tyrant!"

The new title which Beethoven gave the symphony was expressive of his feelings. Napoleon was progressing from one military triumph to another with irresistible force, but Beethoven re-inscribed the work: *Sinfonia Eroica, composta per festeggiare il souvenire d'un grand'uomo* ("Heroic Symphony, composed to celebrate the memory of a great man"). When Napoleon died in 1821, Beethoven remarked, referring to the Funeral March from this Symphony, "I have already written the proper music for that tragedy."

The *Eroica,* so named by Beethoven himself, is the greatest work he had completed up to that time—1804. Many authorities adjudge it the most glorious of his nine symphonies, and even the composer confessed that it was his favorite. "The *Eroica* is a miracle even among Beethoven's works," is Romain Rolland's way of describing it.

The *Eroica* presents two striking innovations: a funeral march, which at that time was unheard of in a symphony; and a Finale comprising a set of variations. A principal theme of the Finale was used earlier by Beethoven in one of his contredanses (No. 7).

M-MM-449, Philharmonic-Symphony Orchestra of New York, Bruno Walter Conducting.

SYMPHONY NO. 4 IN B-FLAT, OP. 60

Adagio: allegro vivace · Adagio · Menuetto: allegro vivace
Allegro ma non troppo

THE POPULARITY of Beethoven's symphonies has always been concentrated on those with the odd numbers—the First, Third, Fifth, Seventh, and Ninth. These works are the more dramatic or profound. The even-numbered symphonies are of a lighter, more straightforward character. This does not diminish their importance or greatness, however, though they receive less attention than their odd-numbered brothers. Perhaps the most obvious exception is the Fourth Symphony, composed in 1806.

When Beethoven visited the castle of Count Franz Oppersdorf, near Oberglogau, in the fall of 1806, Oppersdorf commissioned the composer to write another symphony and paid him 350 florins in advance. The Count was an amateur musician and maintained an excellent orchestra which had performed Beethoven's Second Symphony in the presence of its composer. It was intended that a new symphony should be composed and dedicated to the Count. But in 1808, Beethoven sent the Count, not the symphony, but an apologetic letter, explaining that he had had to sell the symphony—now known as the Fifth—and promising that the work intended for him would

[59]

soon be forthcoming. What he dedicated and actually sent to Oppersdorf was the Fourth Symphony, which had already received its first performance. This greatly irked the Count, especially since the Symphony had not been popular with its first hearers. This episode ended all relations between Beethoven and Oppersdorf.

The Fourth Symphony was written in a single stretch of inspiration with no preliminary notes, an unusual procedure for Beethoven. Schumann compared it to "a slender Greek maiden between two Norse gods"—the latter, of course, being the *Eroica* and Fifth symphonies.

M-MM-197, London Philharmonic Orchestra, Felix Weingartner Conducting.

SYMPHONY NO. 5 IN C MINOR, OP. 67

Allegro con brio · Andante con moto · Scherzo: allegro vivace
Finale: allegro

NEVER in music history was so much written about so few notes as about the opening four notes of Beethoven's Fifth Symphony. The impetus was given by Beethoven himself, if indeed he ever uttered the words ascribed to him: "This is Fate knocking at the door." Rachmaninoff wrote a song based on these four notes to a poem exorcizing the power of Fate. For quite a different purpose Charles Ives used the same four notes in the last movement of his orchestral suite *Three Places in New England.* Orchestra musicians use the motive habitually to whistle greetings or call attention on the streets.

There is another theory of the origin of the motive: namely, that Beethoven used the notes of a birdcall—specifically of a goldfinch. Beethoven did use birdcalls in the *Pastoral* Symphony, which was written at the same period as the Fifth; and the hypothesis is not improbable. Both symphonies were performed for the first time at the same concert in Vienna on December 22, 1808.

The most natural supposition is that the four notes are of a purely musical, non-programmatic origin. The catalogue of all of Beethoven's themes, published by the Beethoven House in Bonn in 1932, lists nineteen examples of the rhythmical figure of the Fifth Symphony, under the heading of "triple repetition in the up beat, followed by a skip." It must be assumed, therefore, that this rhythm was part of Beethoven's natural vocabulary. However, there is no instance of the use of this rhythm in Beethoven's works with the downward skip of a major third, in a minor key, from the dominant to the mediant, except in the Fifth Symphony.

Beethoven was thirty-eight years old when the Fifth Symphony was presented to the public, but sketches of the Symphony refer to a much earlier period. The original four notes are present in the earliest jottings in Beethoven's notebooks, but other thematic material is amazingly different from the final shape.

The Fifth Symphony occupies the midway point in Beethoven's creative life. In it the link with the 18th century is not entirely severed. The traditional form of a classical symphony is still observed. Yet there are in it constantly erupting flames of the Beethoven of the last, his greatest, period; the Beethoven who used the medium of music to express the drama of turbulent emotion, the essence of human struggle, rather than the formulas and usages of the classical art. There are coloristic effects, such as the kettledrum episode in the protracted deceptive cadence of the Scherzo, before the clarifying explosion of the C major fanfare of the Finale, when, for the first time, the trombones enter the scene.

Long after Beethoven's death, young Mendelssohn visited the aged Goethe and played for him the first movement of Beethoven's Fifth Symphony. "This is very great," Goethe remarked, "and quite mad. One fears that the house would come down if all instruments were to play it together."

Schumann wrote of the Symphony: "So often heard, it still exercises its power over all ages, just as those great phenomena of nature, which, no matter how often they recur, fill us with awe and wonder. This Symphony will go on centuries hence, as long as the world and world's music endure."

And Berlioz, the great Romantic and great individualist, saw in the Fifth Symphony the revelation of Beethoven's soul: "He develops in it his own intimate thought. His secret sorrows, his concentrated rage, his reveries charged with a dejection, oh, so sad, his visions at night, his bursts of enthusiasm—these furnished him the subject; and the forms of melody, harmony, rhythm, and orchestration are as essentially individual and new as they are powerful and noble."

M-MM-451, Leopold Stokowski Conducting the All-American Orchestra.
M-MM-498, Philharmonic-Symphony Orchestra of New York, Bruno Walter Conducting.

SYMPHONY NO. 6 IN F MAJOR (PASTORAL), OP. 68

Allegro ma non troppo (The awakening of joyful feelings upon arrival in the country) · *Andante molto moto* (The Brook) · *Allegro* (Village Festival) · *Allegro* (The Storm) · *Allegretto* (Shepherd's Song)

BEETHOVEN loved Nature, and in it he found some of the solace he vainly sought in human companionship. "No man can love the country so much as I. I love a tree more than a man," he wrote.

The *Pastoral* Symphony first bore the heading: "Characteristic Symphony. The recollections of life in the country." This title is in Beethoven's sketchbook attached to the draft of the first movement, and he appended these significant words: "The hearer is left to find out the situations for himself." The precise titles which the movements now bear were added later, perhaps as an afterthought—or possibly by some publisher. Beethoven said the work was "an expression of feelings rather than painting."

The composer pointed out the exact scene that inspired him to write this hymn to Nature. It was in the suburb of Heiligenstadt, and Schindler describes it as "a limpid stream descended from a neighboring height, shaded on both banks by leafy elms."

The opening theme of the Symphony No. 6 is thought to be based on an old Slavonic folk tune. The second movement, in triplets, is easily interpreted as the murmuring of the brook. The third movement is a country dance and is a kindly caricature of a naïvely bad band of peasant musicians. Bekker says of this band, "The fiddles come first, the oboe tries in vain to overtake them, while the bassoon hobbles far behind, heavy and phlegmatic." The Allegretto closes the work in a peaceful mood of thankfulness following the storm.

This Symphony is popular because of the charm of the subject and

[62]

the ease with which it can be understood. Only a genius would have dared to write so representative a work, with the calls of cuckoo, nightingale, and quail reproduced.

Beethoven's close companion, Charles Neate, said that Nature was "almost meat and drink to Beethoven; he seemed positively to exist upon it." And Schindler admitted that the composer taught him even more about Nature than he did about music.

M-MM-631, Philadelphia Orchestra, Bruno Walter Conducting.

SYMPHONY NO. 7 IN A MAJOR, OP. 92

Poco sostenuto: vivace · *Allegretto* · *Presto: assai meno presto*
Allegro con brio

BEETHOVEN had attempted to have his Seventh Symphony performed on several occasions, and it finally received its première at a concert in the great hall of the University of Vienna. This was a performance given for the benefit of Austrian and Bavarian soldiers wounded in the battle against Napoleon at Hanau. The event was organized by Johann Nepomuk Mälzel, a musician and mechanic who is best remembered as the inventor of the metronome. Mälzel also claimed to have invented an automatic chess player, a mechanical trumpeter that played military airs, and a panharmonicon, another mechanical instrument that reproduced the tones of the wind instruments and played symphonies by Mozart and Haydn.

Mälzel had asked Beethoven to write a *Battle* Symphony for the panharmonicon, to celebrate Wellington's victory over Napoleon at Vittoria, so that he might popularize the instrument in London. When the benefit concert was being planned, he suggested that Beethoven arrange the work for full orchestra, augmenting it with special backstage effects, including percussion instruments and cannon.

The concert was such an unqualified success that it had to be repeated four days later. The program opened with the Seventh Symphony, followed by a March by Dussek and one by Pleyel—played by Mälzel's mechanical trumpeter accompanied by the orchestra. The program concluded with *Wellington's Victory, or The Battle of*

[63]

Vittoria. To add glamor to the event, Mälzel persuaded leading musicians and composers to donate their services as members of the orchestra.

Schuppanzigh, first violinist of the ensemble that gave the early performances of Beethoven's quartets, was the concertmaster. Spohr and Mayseder played in the violin section. Dragonetti was among the double basses. Moscheles and Meyerbeer were relegated to the percussion section because of their limited ability as orchestral players. Moscheles played the cymbals, and Meyerbeer beat the bass drum vociferously and—according to Beethoven—"always behind the beat." Hummel and Salieri, Beethoven's composition teachers, gave the cues to the men who released the cannonade backstage.

Beethoven conducted the entire program. Since he was now quite deaf, it was possible for him to hear only the louder passages in the music. Spohr has left us an interesting account of the master's manner of conducting:

"At this concert," he relates, "I first saw Beethoven conduct. As often as I had heard about it, it still surprised me very much. He was accustomed to convey the marks of expression to the orchestra by the most peculiar motions of his body. Thus at a sforzando he tore his arms, which until then had been crossed on his breast, violently apart. He crouched down at a piano, bending lower as the tone decreased. At a crescendo, he raised himself by degrees until at the forte he leapt to his full height; and often, without being conscious of it, would shout aloud at the same time."

Though the *Battle* Symphony, a rather inferior piece, was the hit of the evening, the Seventh Symphony was very well received, and the famed Allegretto had to be repeated.

Many people have tried to read a program into the Seventh Symphony. Wagner and Liszt both called it "the apotheosis of rhythm." Vincent d'Indy pictured the work as a second *Pastoral* Symphony. A contemporary of Beethoven, Dr. Karl Iken, who wrote "programmatic expositions of the symphonies for perusal before the concerts," infuriated the composer by interpreting the Symphony as a musical picturization of a social revolution. Others have linked it with a rustic wedding, a royal hunt, a knightly festival, a dream of love, and a battle of giants.

The Seventh Symphony was completed in 1812. Beethoven indicated the exact date on his manuscript, but a careless binder trimmed off the month.

The score was dedicated to Count Maurice von Fries, and the arrangement for piano was inscribed to the Empress of Russia.

M-MM-557, The Philadelphia Orchestra, Eugene Ormandy Conducting.

SYMPHONY NO. 8 IN F MAJOR, OP. 93

Allegro vivace e con brio · *Allegretto scherzando* · *Menuetto*
Finale: allegro vivace

THE YEAR of 1812 was one of Beethoven's busiest years, for it saw the completion of two symphonies, the Seventh and the Eighth. In the early part of the year the composer's health was not good and the doctor advised him to try the baths of Bohemia. This advice was taken, and the trip had some influence on the character of the Eighth Symphony, for the journey was made easily and under pleasant conditions.

Among Beethoven's friends at that time was the mechanic Mälzel, an ingenious musician credited with the invention of the metronome and its ancestor, the chronometer. At a dinner given to Mälzel, Beethoven improvised a comical canon and sang it to the words: "Ta-ta-ta, ta-ta-ta, lieber Mälzel." Afterwards this canon was used for the ticking accompaniment of the first theme of the Allegretto scherzando of the Eighth Symphony, where the music is noticeably metronomic.

The first performance of the work took place in Vienna on February 27, 1814, at a concert in which the two symphonies composed in 1812 were given. The Seventh, first heard three months before, was a great success, while the Eighth was a failure. The truth is that the program was exceptionally long, and the Eighth was heard at the end of it late in the evening. The audience, surfeited with masterpieces, received it coolly. But Beethoven, with his customary bluntness, said it was not appreciated "just because it is the better of the two." It was not long before the verdict of the Vienna audience was reversed, however, and today the Eighth is one of the most popular of the "immortal nine"—whether or not we agree with the composer that it is better than its predecessor.

[65]

In a letter Beethoven referred to this work as the *"Kleine Sinfonie in F"*—not because it was little, but to distinguish it from the *Grosse Sinfonie in A,* which so closely preceded it.

M-MM-525, Philharmonic-Symphony Orchestra of New York, Bruno Walter Conducting.

SYMPHONY NO. 9 (CHORAL) IN D MINOR, OP. 125

Allegro ma non troppo, un poco maestoso · *Scherzo: molto vivace*
Adagio molto e cantabile · *Presto; Allegro assai*

FOR SEVERAL years Beethoven worked at intervals on his last and greatest symphony, the immortal Ninth. His plans for it changed often during this time, but the basic conception of its scope was fixed in his mind from the beginning. What might be called the distinguishing physical feature of the score—the choral finale—was no part of the early design. His sketches were for a purely instrumental finale; the choral Allegro may thus have been a last-minute inspiration.

Beethoven approached the London Philharmonic Society in April 1822, through his pupil, Ferdinand Ries, to find out how much that organization would offer him for the new symphony. The Society responded seven months later with an offer of fifty pounds for the work, the stipulations being that it was to be delivered the following March and that the Society was to have exclusive performance rights for a year and a half. Beethoven agreed to the arrangement and received the money, but for some unexplained reason he did not keep his part of the bargain. As a result, the Symphony was first performed in Vienna, nearly a year before it was heard in London.

The details of the Vienna première are interesting. Beethoven was rather upset at the acclaim the music of Rossini was receiving in Vienna, and had resolved to give the first performance of his Ninth Symphony elsewhere. But a large group of professional and amateur musicians sent the master a petition, begging him to allow his own city of Vienna to be the first to hear his great new creation. Touched by this show of affection from his colleagues, Beethoven assented, and the following announcement was issued by those of his friends who arranged the concert:

[66]

"Grand musical seance given by Herr Ludwig van Beethoven. The compositions which will be executed are the latest products of the pen of Herr Ludwig van Beethoven.

"Firstly: Grand overture (Op. 124).

"Secondly: Three grand hymns for solos and chorus.

"Thirdly: Grand symphony with a finale, into which enter solos and choruses on the text of the *Ode to Joy,* by Schiller.

"The solos will be sung by Mmes. Sontag and Unger, Messrs. Haitzinger and Seipelt. The direction of the orchestra is confided to Herr Schuppanzigh; the whole will be directed by Kapellmeister Umlauf, and the Musikverein has kindly consented to reinforce the instrumental and vocal bodies.

"Herr Ludwig van Beethoven will personally take part in the direction of the concert."

Herr Beethoven most certainly did take part in the direction of the concert. He was on hand for the rehearsals, and when one of the soloists, complaining about the extreme difficulty of her part, asked him to make a few changes, he flatly refused. To this very day, singers have trouble with many passages in the score.

The concert took place on May 7, 1824, at the Kärnthnerthor Theater. The overture alluded to in the announcement was the *Consecration of the House.* The "three grand hymns" proved to be the Kyrie, Credo, and Agnus Dei of the *Missa Solemnis.* They were so billed on the program because the Archbishop of Vienna forbade the printing of sacred words on a playbill.

During the performance of the Ninth Symphony, Beethoven conducted the orchestra, following the score and indicating the tempo to the leader, Michael Umlauf, at the beginning of each movement. The concert was a tremendous success. When the kettledrums beat out the rhythmic theme-pattern at the beginning of the second movement, the applause all but obliterated the music. At the close of the movement, Beethoven, totally deaf and thus unaware of the demonstration of approval from the audience behind him, was turned around on the conductor's stand by one of the soloists in order that he might witness the gestures of applause which he was never more to hear.

M-MM-591, Stella Roman, Enid Szantho, Frederick Jagel Nicola Moscona, the Westminster Choir, and the Philadelphia Orchestra, Eugene Ormandy Conducting.

TRIO IN B-FLAT MAJOR, OP. 97 (ARCHDUKE)

Allegro moderato · Scherzo: allegro · Andante cantabile ma però con moto · Allegro moderato

COMPLETED in March 1811 and published in 1816, this trio was dedicated to Beethoven's pupil, the Archduke Rudolph of Austria, then twenty-three years old.

It was the last trio for piano, violin and 'cello of Beethoven published during the composer's lifetime. Typical of his music of the second period, it seems designed for a virtuoso, an orchestra, and a large concert hall; its broad themes, generous design, and, above all, the fullness of the piano part reveal a certain kinship with the last two piano concertos.

The middle movements do not follow the customary sonata-form order. The Scherzo becomes the second movement, and the Andante is linked with the finale. The Scherzo shows superior trio-writing technique: a question and answer game passes between violin and 'cello and develops into a dance tune. The slow movement—the finest of the four—is a set of variations on a hymn-like theme, while the closing movement progresses to a brilliant finale.

Vincenzo Bellini
1801–1835

WHOEVER ignores Bellini," wrote one critic, "ignores true melody." Few composers were so richly endowed with Italian song as he. Melody came to him easily and naturally; and just as easily did it come from him, pouring out opulently in his operas as if coming from a seemingly inexhaustible reservoir. Some critics have been impressed by the dramatic quality of Bellini's music; others by his supple use of the recitative. But in the last analysis, Bellini stands for Italian lyricism at its purest, and it is for his lyricism that his greatest operas have survived.

His was a short life—he died at the age of thirty-three—but long enough to produce a few indestructible masterpieces. He was born in Catania, Sicily, in 1801, and studied at the Naples Conservatory where he wrote his first opera. In his twentieth year, Bellini composed the first of his masterpieces, *La Sonnambula*. Introduced at La Scala it was an extraordinary success. One year later came *Norma*, probably Bellini's *magnum opus*. In 1834, Rossini suggested to him that he go to Paris and write an opera expressly for the Théâtre Italien. This opera, *I Puritani*, was the last of Bellini's great operas. Bellini did not live to hear his masterwork. He died in Paris in 1835, and on the eve of his funeral the première of *I Puritani* took place.

NORMA

It is strange that what is probably Bellini's greatest opera should also have been one of his greatest failures at its first performance, which took place on December 26, 1831 at La Scala in Milan. Bellini himself referred to that performance as a "Fiasco! Fiasco! Serious fiasco!" This, in spite of the fact that the opera has such remarkable dramatic verity, has an outpouring of unforgettable melody (including one of the best loved arias in all opera, "Casta Diva") and a nobility and grandeur of style that should have been apparent even upon a first hearing.

Norma, however, did not have to wait long for recognition. Revived, it ran for forty-three performances—the beginning of its long and active career in the permanent opera repertory. As early as 1836, Richard Wagner proclaimed it a masterpiece, an opinion that has since that time been echoed and re-echoed frequently.

The book by Giuseppe Felice Romani centers around the high priestess of the Druids, Norma, who is driven by her great love for Pollio, the Roman proconsul, to break the Druid vow of chastity by secretly marrying him. Pollio's love later turns to the priestess Adalgisa. Ignorant of Pollio's marital state, she confides her passion to Norma and begs for an absolution from her vows. The discovery of Pollio's infidelity enrages both women. When Pollio attempts to snatch his loved one from the altar, Norma orders the Druids to capture him. Given the alternative of renouncing Adalgisa or accepting death, Pollio chooses the latter. This so moves Norma, that she tears the wreath from her head and confesses her own guilt. In atonement, Norma joins her husband at the funeral pyre.

9105-M, "Casta Diva," Claudia Muzio, Soprano, with an Orchestra Conducted by Molajoli.

Hector Berlioz

1803–1869

HECTOR BERLIOZ was one of the first of the great Romantics in music. His works are marked by fiery independence, fearless experimentation, a ceaseless search after new colors, qualities, dimensions. All the later tendencies of the Romantic movement are found suggested, sometimes completely realized, in his works.

He was born in Côte Saint-André, in France, in 1803, and was a pupil at the Paris Conservatory. In 1825, his first work to be performed, a Mass, was heard. Five years later, soon after he had completed the writing of his first famous work, the *Symphonie fantastique,* he won the Prix de Rome. Meanwhile, he had fallen in love with the Shakespearean actress, Henrietta Smithson. This was a turbulent courtship of several years' duration, and in 1833 culminated in marriage. It was an unhappy union and eventually resulted in separation. Despite his anguish over his broken marriage, his pressing financial problems, and his terrible loneliness, Berlioz succeeded in writing several masterpieces, including *Harold in Italy, Romeo and Juliet,* the Requiem, and *Benvenuto Cellini.* A certain amount of recognition came to him in the form of several important cash honorariums enabling him, in 1843, to undertake an extensive tour of Germany as conductor. During the last twenty years of his life, Berlioz's creative powers were at an ebb. The recognition of this fact, combined with his increasing illness and loneliness made him an unhappy man. He died in Paris in 1869.

SELECTIONS FROM THE DAMNATION
OF FAUST, OP. 24

Hungarian March · *Dance of the Sylphs* · *Minuet of the
Will-o'-the-Wisps*

It was during his travels in Austria, Hungary, Bohemia, and Silesia, in 1845 and 1846, that Berlioz began work on his *Damnation of Faust,* which he styled an "Opéra de concert"; afterwards he changed the title page of the manuscript to read simply: *Légende.* It was dedicated to his friend, Franz Liszt. It must not be forgotten that as early as 1828 he conceived his *Eight Scenes from Faust,* which was accorded a cold reception. When Berlioz sent a copy of this earlier work to Goethe, the famed poet was insulted. The character of Faust does not appear in this piece.

The world première of *The Damnation of Faust* in oratorio form at the Paris Opéra-Comique on December 6, 1846 was a dismal failure, in spite of Théophile Gautier's widely circulated pronouncement—while the work was still in rehearsal—that Berlioz, with Hugo and Delacroix, now constituted "the trinity of Romantic art."

Berlioz incorrectly stated that the author of the *Hungarian March* (the renowned *Rákóczy*), from which he derived his own composition, was unknown. But the research of Akos László proves that it was written by one Michael Barna, court musician to Prince Franz Rákóczy the Second (1676–1735). It was later revised by a gypsy violinist named Ruzsitka. In his *Autobiography,* Berlioz, who was criticized for employing this March on the ground that it was alien to the locale of *Faust,* wrote: "The extraordinary effect it produced at Pesth [Budapest] made me resolve to introduce it into *Faust,* by taking the liberty of placing my hero in Hungary at the opening of the act, and making him present at the march of a Hungarian army across the plain. . . . I should not have hesitated in the least to bring him in any other direction if it would have benefited the piece."

The *Dance of the Sylphs* occurs after Faust has been lulled to sleep on the banks of the Elbe. "The spirits of the air," according to the score's directions, "hover around Faust in his slumber, then disappear one by one."

In the *Minuet of the Will-o'-the-Wisps,* the Devil invokes a serenade under Marguerite's window.

X-MX-94, London Philharmonic Orchestra, Sir Thomas Beecham Conducting.

ROMAN CARNIVAL OVERTURE, OP. 9

BERLIOZ composed the *Roman Carnival* Overture as an introduction to the second act of his opera *Benvenuto Cellini.* The opera, first performed in Paris in 1838, was such a failure that it was nicknamed "Malvenuto Cellini." On the other hand, the *Roman Carnival* Overture, written in 1843 and first performed under the composer's direction in 1844, was received with such enthusiasm that it had to be repeated.

This was a great personal triumph for Berlioz. During rehearsals for the première of the opera some six years earlier, he had seriously disagreed with the incompetent and unsympathetic conductor, François-Antoine Habeneck, who was unable to take the *saltarello* in the second act at the proper tempo. (The *saltarello* is a lively Italian leaping dance, which reached the height of its popularity around Rome in the fifteenth and sixteenth centuries. In *Benvenuto Cellini* it is danced during the scene of the Roman Carnival in the Piazza Colonna.) Habeneck attended the concert at which the *Roman Carnival* Overture was first played, expecting—even hoping—for another Berlioz fiasco. When the Overture, which is chiefly concerned with this same *saltarello,* was so well received, Habeneck was disappointed. As Berlioz passed him in the foyer after the concert, he taunted Habeneck with the remark: "Now you can see how it ought to go!"

The Overture opens with a brief quotation from the *saltarello.* Then is heard a beautiful slow section, based on an aria sung by Cellini in the first act. It is played first by the English horn, later by strings and woodwinds, in the form of a canon. The remainder of the piece is taken up with the wildly whirling *saltarello,* with occasional snatches of Cellini's aria.

M-MM-552, London Philharmonic Orchestra, Sir Thomas Beecham Conducting.

[73]

SYMPHONIE FANTASTIQUE, OP. 14

Largo; Allegro agitato e appassionato assai (Dreams, Passions) · *Waltz: allegro non troppo* (A Ball) · *Adagio* (Scene in the Meadows) · *Allegretto non troppo* (March to the Scaffold) · *Larghetto; Allegro* (Dream of a Witches' Sabbath)

WHEN Berlioz completed the score of the *Symphonie fantastique* in 1830, he was twenty-six years old. Beethoven had been dead only two years, and that master's *Leonore Overture No. 3* and *Pastoral* Symphony were the supreme heights to which program music had then attained. Liszt and Wagner were yet to be heard from as significant composers.

Yet this unknown young man burst on the Parisian musical public with a bombshell of a symphony . . . a symphony with a bizarre autobiographical program, calling for orchestral forces of a size and manner unknown up to that time. Besides the usual strings with reinforced woodwinds and brass, Berlioz asked for an English horn, E-flat clarinet, two tubas, two harps, plus a percussion section consisting of four kettledrums, snare drum, bass drum, cymbals, and bells. It is in the more truly fantastic portions of the Symphony that Berlioz' orchestration reveals itself to greatest advantage. Unforgettable even in this day and age of orchestral virtuosity are the gibbering bassoons in the *March to the Scaffold* and the startling effects of E-flat clarinet, brass, and pizzicato strings in the bizarre and wild *Dream of a Witches' Sabbath.*

The composer's own description of this masterpiece runs something like this:

A young and oversensitive musician has poisoned himself with opium in a paroxysm of lovesick despair. The narcotic dose was too weak to cause death, but it has thrown him into a long sleep and most extraordinary visions. The beloved one becomes a melody in his mind, like a fixed idea ever returning.

I. *Dreams, Passions:* At first he thinks of the uneasy condition of his mind, of somber longings, of depression and elation without reason, which he experienced before the beloved one has appeared to him; then the ardent love she roused in him; he thinks of his anxiety, his raging jealousy, his reawakening love, and his religious consolation.

II. *A Ball:* In a crowded ballroom, during a brilliant festival, he finds the beloved one again.

III. *Scene in the Meadows:* On a summer evening in the country he is musing, when he hears two shepherds who play, in alternation, the *Ranz-des-vaches,* a Swiss tune used by the shepherds to call their flocks. This duet, the quiet scene, the sound of the trees stirred by the breeze, some prospects of hope recently coming to him, all impart peace to his heart and a smile to his imagination. Then she appears again. His heart stops beating, forebodings are felt. "Should she prove false!" Only one of the shepherds resumes the air—the other no longer answers him. . . . Sunset. . . . The sound of distant thunder. . . . Loneliness. . . . Silence. . . .

IV. *March to the Scaffold:* He dreams of murdering his beloved; he is condemned to death and is led to execution. A march alternately somber and wild accompanies the procession. . . . The tumultuous outbursts are followed by measured steps. The fixed idea returns—a last thought of love is revived—and is cut short by the death blow.

V. *Dream of a Witches' Sabbath:* He dreams of a witches' revel where he is surrounded by horrible spirits in fearful forms, who have come together for his funeral. Groans, shrill laughter, distant yells, which other cries seem to answer. The beloved melody is heard again, but no longer timid and noble; it is now a vulgar, trivial, grotesque dance tune. This is she who attends the witches' meeting. Riotous shouts greet her arrival. . . . She joins the infernal orgy . . . bells toll for the dead . . . a burlesque parody of *Dies Irae* . . . the witches' round dance . . . The dance and the *Dies Irae* are heard together.

M-MM-488, The Cleveland Orchestra, Artur Rodzinski Conducting.

Georges Bizet

1838–1875

Few composers in history are so completely identified with one single masterpiece as Georges Bizet; the masterpiece, of course, is the opera *Carmen*. Bizet was born in Paris in 1838, and in 1857 he won the Prix de Rome, following his studies at the Conservatory. In Rome he composed several works, including an opéra comique. When he was twenty-five, he saw his first important work, the opera, *Pearl Fishers*, performed by the Théâtre Lyrique in Paris. *Pearl Fishers* was not a success, nor were the other operas which followed it. In 1869, Bizet married the daughter of his teacher at the Conservatory, Genevieve Halévy. Three years later, he was commissioned by the Paris Opéra Comique to compose a score to a libretto which Meilhac and Halévy had prepared from a story by Prosper Merimée. This opera, *Carmen*, was introduced in 1875, and while it was not an overwhelming success, it was no failure either. Bizet died in Paris in June of 1875. In 1883, his opera, *Carmen*, was revived in Paris, and from this time on its acceptance as a masterpiece was world-wide.

CARMEN

THE FIRST performance of Georges Bizet's opera, *Carmen,* at the Opéra Comique, on March 3, 1875, has been said to have been a complete failure and is even believed to have hastened the death of its composer. However, historic truth does not substantiate these often-repeated beliefs. It is quite true that the opera did not at first enjoy the great success it deserved, and that there were some in the audience who reacted to it with hostility. But some of the leading Parisian critics spoke well of it, and the opera enjoyed forty-seven performances—a respectable figure—before it was allowed to lapse into temporary obscurity.

Staging *Carmen* had been an endless series of great disappointments. When the text was finally submitted to the directors of the Opéra Comique by Meilhac and Halévy, one director resigned rather than accept partial responsibility for this work. Putting so questionable a character as Prosper Merimée's cigarette girl on the stage was considered by many as a highly immoral procedure. In order to offset the possible unsavory impression created by Carmen, the librettists created the part of Micaëla as a contrast.

At its first performance there were some critics who condemned the work because of its supposed subservience to Wagner. Some in the audience were shocked at the presence of girls, smoking cigarettes on the stage. In later years, the authenticity of Bizet's Spanish idiom was subjected to much heated discussion. However, *Carmen* has survived all these criticisms and has become one of the best loved operas in the repertory. After its revival in Paris in 1883—a sensational performance—the opera began its march of triumph around the world. Tchaikovsky prophesied that *Carmen* would within a decade become one of the most popular operas in the world. By 1904 it had reached its one thousandth performance on the stage.

The tragedy of the cigarette girl, Carmen, and her lover, the Spanish officer, Don José, is one of the most familiar tales in opera. Arrested for stabbing a friend in a Seville cigarette factory, Carmen works her seductive charms on the officer, Don José, who helps her to escape at the price of his own freedom. After completing his prison sentence, Don José follows Carmen, with whom he is now passionately in love, escaping with her to a lair of smugglers in the mountains. It is not long before Carmen tires of her lover and makes flirtatious overtures to Escamillo, the famous toreador. Micaëla, sweetheart of Don José, comes to the mountains to beg her lover to return home to visit his dying mother. José, however, can think of nothing and no one but the seductive Carmen. He begs for her love and receiving only apathetic disdain, he kills her.

In this opera, Bizet had no intention of writing authentic Spanish music; consequently the criticisms leveled against the opera on this point, by Turina and other similar critics, are not justified. It is true that certain Spanish forms were interpolated by Bizet—that of the Habanera, for example, in Carmen's famous aria, and that of the Seguidille. But this was only to give the work some authentic local color. What Bizet tried to do—and what he did with consummate success—was to give in his music suggestions of Spanish backgrounds; but his style of music remained essentially French.

Bizet himself arranged two orchestral suites comprised of excerpts from *Carmen*.

OP-MOP-1, Artists of the Paris Opéra Comique, Cohen and Gaubert Conducting.
M-MM-607, Excerpts, Risë Stevens, Nadine Conner, Raoul Jobin, Robert Weede, the Metropolitan Opera Chorus and Orchestra, George Sebastian Conducting.
X-MX-144, Suite, London Philharmonic Orchestra, Sir Thomas Beecham Conducting.

Ernest Bloch

1880–

ERNEST BLOCH was born in Geneva, Switzerland, in 1880, the son of a merchant. His study of music was intensive, taking place in Switzerland (Dalcroze and Rey), Brussels (Ysaÿe and Rasse), and Munich (Knorr and Thuille). In 1902 he composed his first symphony which failed to get a performance; this so discouraged Bloch that he decided to enter business. For several years he combined work in his father's shop with composition in his spare hours. Thus he composed the opera, *Macbeth*, which was introduced at the Paris Opéra Comique in 1910. This opera attracted the attention of Romain Rolland who henceforth became one of Bloch's most staunch supporters and who was instrumental in convincing the composer to abandon business for creative work.

In 1916, Bloch came to the United States as conductor of the Maud Allen troupe. The bankruptcy of this organization left Bloch stranded without funds. A few influential musicians, however, worked on his behalf; their efforts resulted in several major performances of Bloch's music in this country, performances which first helped to establish Bloch's reputation in America. His reputation was further enhanced in 1919 when he was awarded the Elizabeth Sprague Coolidge prize of $1,000 for his *Suite for Viola and Orchestra*.

In 1920, Bloch became director of the Cleveland Institute of Music, holding this post for five years. In 1927, his symphony, *America*, won the $3,000 *Musical America* award, the unanimous choice of the judges, and was given a simultaneous first performance by several of America's foremost orchestras. For several years, Bloch was enabled to live in Switzerland by virtue of an endowment. He returned to the United States in 1934 to conduct the première of his *Sacred Service*. He has since then lived in this country devoting himself to composition and teaching.

[79]

BAAL SHEM SUITE, FOR VIOLIN AND PIANO

Vidui (Contrition) · *Nigun* (Improvisation) · *Simchas Torah*
(Rejoicing)

Baal Shem is a suite for violin and piano picturing three aspects of Hassidic life.

Baal Shem was the founder of a new sect, Hassidism, which flourished in Poland beginning with the mid-18th century. His followers regarded him as a prophet and a saint. Hassidism was built around the belief in joy, pleasure, love; that an element of the divine exists in everything that lives; that no one is beyond redemption. Baal Shem's followers celebrated their holidays with elaborate feasts, dances, and throbbing music—music that had that same quality of ecstasy that was found in the Hassid's worship of God.

The first picture, *Vidui*, portrays the mood of contrition, with a characteristic falling fifth of the Jewish ritual song. The second, *Nigun*, is an improvisation. Here the mood is aspiration, reflected in the motto of a rising fourth. This movement is also the most popular of the three. The third section of the suite, *Simchas Torah*, pictures a joyful, festive mood—for *Simchas Torah* was the holiday in which Jews commemorated the handing down to them of the Torah.

In all three pieces the rhythm is as free as the Jewish chant that inspires Bloch's music. The intervallic structure is peculiar to the Hebrew modes—in western music the nearest equivalent of Bloch's scale is the Mixolydian mode with the lowered sixth.

X-MX-188, Joseph Szigeti, Violin, Andor Farkas, Piano.

CONCERTO FOR VIOLIN AND ORCHESTRA

*Allegro; Moderato · Andante; Piú calmo · Deciso; Moderato;
Allegro moderato; Animato*

THE VIOLIN Concerto was, so far as its composer can trace its derivation, the work of several years—1930 to 1937. Bloch cannot recall precisely how the many sketches for the work originated and still less how they happened to be gathered together to form a whole. "They arose," he says, "mostly on the inspiration of the moment and

[80]

with no preconceived idea of a violin concerto, though most of them were orchestrally or 'violinistically' conceived."

He continues: "However, music being for me a kind of language, it is easy to discover in the chosen material that went to make this Concerto, parentage or affinities, either in the expressive or the purely musical-thematic frame of the motives. They combine with each other in a rather intricate way throughout the score, appearing and disappearing like characters in a drama. But it would be impossible for me to delineate any plan or 'programme' in this work—I can only say there is in it no 'Jewish' inspiration or intention, as was the case in my *Israel* Symphony, *Schelomo* Rhapsody or the *Three Jewish Poems*, for instance.

"The idea of the Concerto itself may date from 1935 when part of the introduction was written in Paris. Its progress was several times interrupted—for the completion of two works which I had already partly written and for the composition of the orchestral suite, *Evocations*."

The style of the Concerto is rhapsodical; it is, in the most innocuous sense of the word, atonal in that the music does not move in settled tonalities. It makes great play with the interval of the "fourth," a cluster of which enters in the second and fourth bars. This interval is of great importance throughout the work, creating its own peculiar timbre.

The writing, although favoring no particular key in a general sense, makes occasional sojourns in this or that tonality. As a whole, however, the music is in no sense "modernist"; beauty of sound inspired by emotion and imagination is the keynote, for Bloch himself, in the words of a student of his music, "disdains and abhors the preciousness and intellectuality of the cerebral sterilized moderns, whenever it obstructs true feeling and emotion."

The Concerto was finished at Châtel, Haute Savoie, in January 1938. The first performance was in Cleveland by Szigeti with the Cleveland Orchestra, conducted by Dimitri Mitropoulos, on December 15, 1938.

M-MM-380, Joseph Szigeti, Violin, with the Paris Conservatoire Orchestra Conducted by Charles Münch.

QUARTET, NO. 1

Andante moderato · *Allegro frenetico; Molto moderato; Allegro
frenetico* · *Andante molto moderato* · *Finale: vivace*

"DURING the summer of 1915," wrote Ernest Bloch, "a friend of mine,
Alfred Pochon of the Flonzaley Quartet, visited me in the country
near Geneva. I showed him, among other works, rough sketches of
a string quartet. . . . Pochon . . . then advised me strongly to go
on with the string quartet. In a few months the first three movements
were completed. It was then necessary for me to leave for America.
. . . I was dazed by American life, after the atmosphere of Europe.
I could hardly find myself . . . it seemed another world, almost another planet. However, I worked in a fever, and the last movement
—the first music I wrote on this continent—was achieved in about
a week.

"Thus this string quartet was composed at a period of double
crisis: the crisis of the world, at the outside, and the crisis of my own
life, the expatriation from my native country, Switzerland. It certainly shows the traces of both. Without being an autobiography
. . . it embodies in a certain sense my *Weltanschauung* at the age
of thirty-six—a kind of synthesis of my vision of the world at that
period. No work of mine, since that time, can be compared to it in
this respect.

"The whole quartet falls into the regular classical form. It may
appear very free at times, melodically, modally, rhythmically, but
it certainly is neither 'rhapsodical' nor freer, for instance, than the
first movement of the *Eroica*."

M-MM-392, Stuyvesant String Quartet.

Alexander Borodin

1833–1887

ALEXANDER BORODIN was an integral member of that school of composers known as the "Russian Five," whose artistic mission it was to create a nationalistic music. The spirit of Russia pervades Borodin's music which combines Western culture with the savage emotion and spirit of the Orient.

Borodin was born in St. Petersburg in 1833. An intensive academic education was combined with his musical studies, for Borodin showed an equal aptitude for both science and music. Ultimately he became professor of chemistry at the Academy of Medical and Physical Sciences. In 1862, Borodin met Balakirev, a decisive moment in Borodin's life, for from then on music assumed with science a major role for him. Soon after his first meetings with Balakirev, Borodin began composing his first symphony.

Borodin was not destined to write many works, for he was a fastidious worker. No more than a half dozen major compositions represent the fruits of his maturest creative powers. But he was an influential force in the development of a nationalist school, and his compositions represent some of the most successful realization of that school's ideals. Borodin died in St. Petersburg in 1887.

One of Borodin's first ardent protagonists was Franz Liszt, who set a fashion in the appreciation of Borodin that soon spread throughout western Europe. Borodin had a reputation in Germany, France and England before Rimsky-Korsakov, Mussorgsky, or even Tchaikovsky did.

BORODIN has left us the following program for this famous tone poem, which he composed in 1880 and which was introduced in St. Petersburg during the festivities honoring the twenty-fifth anniversary of the reign of Alexander II:

"Through the silence of the steppes of Central Asia is heard the strain of a peaceful Russian song. Sounds of horses and camels come from the distance, approaching ever nearer, and with them the strains of a haunting eastern melody. A caravan is crossing the desert escorted by Russian soldiers. It progresses on its long journey confident in the protection afforded it by the soldiers. The caravan disappears into the distant horizon. The song of the Russians blend with that of the Orientals in a common harmony, until both fade away from the plains."

PRINCE IGOR

THE TWO works by which Borodin is best known, the works on which, indeed, the whole of his reputation rests, are the opera, *Prince Igor,* and the Second Symphony. Borodin never finished *Igor*. Begun in 1867, it was still incomplete when Borodin died twenty years later. He had anticipated the possibility:

"We old sinners," he wrote, "are, as always, in the whirlwind of life—professional duty, science, art. We hurry on and do not reach the goal. Time flies like an express train. The beard grows grey, wrinkles make deeper hollows. We begin a hundred different things. Shall we ever finish any of them? I am always a poet in my soul and I nourish the hope of leading my opera to the last measure. Yet I often mock at myself, and there are great gaps in my work."

Igor was completed after Borodin's death by Rimsky-Korsakov and Glazounov. The opera, as we know it, is partially their work. Rimsky's hand can be detected in the brilliant instrumentation of the score, so much more elaborate than Borodin's own orchestral writing.

Shortly after the opera was begun, friends discouraged Borodin from continuing with it. The day had passed, they argued, for operas on historical subjects. He was almost persuaded that they were right, and sought some other use for the musical material he had assembled for the opera.

Borodin was ever the conscientious workman. Before undertaking *Igor*, he made exhaustive researches into the history—social, cultural and political—of medieval Russia. What he read, what he studied, affected him profoundly, and exerted great influence on his musical imagination. Hence the epic character of the score, its bardic ring, its high, barbaric color.

This opera—which concerns the capture of Prince Igor and his son by a Tartar race known as the Polovtzi, in the 12th century—is rarely heard today. But the celebrated Polovtzian Dances—a great favorite on concert programs—keep the name of the opera alive.

X-MX-54, Polovtzian Dances, Leeds Festival Chorus, and the London Philharmonic Orchestra, Sir Thomas Beecham Conducting.

SYMPHONY NO. 2 IN B MINOR

Allegro · Scherzo · Andante · Finale

BORODIN began writing this symphony in 1871, but did not complete it until six years later. Its première took place in St. Petersburg on March 10, 1877, Nápravník conducting. The symphony was not immediately successful. The Russian public, more especially the critics, were indifferent to the aims and ideals of the nationalist school and were critical of Borodin's orchestration. However the critic Ivanov said that the work reminded him of "ancient Russian knights in all their awkwardness and also in all their greatness'"—an opinion that must have pleased Borodin, for he had sought to make that very effect in this work.

At the time he wrote this symphony, Borodin was deeply steeped in the creation of *Prince Igor*. It is, therefore, not surprising that so much of *Prince Igor* is in this music, not only in the atmosphere and spirit of the work but even in the actual duplication of musical sketches. Like *Igor*, the symphony is most notable for its passionate and savage utterances, for its Tartar wildness and strength.

M-MM-528, Minneapolis Symphony Orchestra, Dimitri Mitropoulos Conducting.

Johannes Brahms

1833–1897

IT HAS been said, more or less aptly, that a history of Johannes Brahms is a history of his works. There are indeed few lives as rich in accomplishment which present so little on the surface that is colorful and arresting. Though never a man of affluence, material problems seem to have bothered him little; except for his long devotion to Clara Schumann, who as wife and widow of the great Robert did much to promote Brahms's success and whom he regarded with almost filial affection, women apparently figured in his life scarcely at all; the radius of his traveling was limited mainly to the German-speaking communities; his dislike of all social lion- izing was marked and his desire to pursue a quiet existence in the intimacy of a few tried and true friends was one of his notable char- acteristics. In all matters of life and social contact he was an apostle of true simplicity; under a rough and burly exterior he concealed a warmth and kindliness of disposition that frequently surprised those who in a long acquaintance had seen only his more obvious traits; and he could on occasion exercise the most felicitous tact, as when, asked for his autograph by Mme. Johann Strauss, wife of the cele- brated "Waltz King," he wrote on a card the introductory bars of the *Blue Danube* Waltz, adding underneath "Unfortunately not by me—J. Brahms."

Primarily, therefore, it is not as a personality of rich and varied experience but as one of the greatest and most profound of the creators of music that Brahms is to be considered, and the facts of his life may be set down briefly.

Brahms was born in Hamburg in 1833. His father, a double-bass player in the Hamburg City Theatre, is said to have run away from home in his early days in order to gratify his desire to study music professionally; it is natural to find, therefore, that he viewed with much sympathy the inclination for music which Johannes showed at a very early age. He procured for him the tuition of Otto Cossel, a pupil of the eminent master Eduard Marxsen, of Altona. With Cossel young Brahms pursued his studies for some years until the teacher, finding that the boy could learn no more from him, turned him over to Marxsen, with whom he practically completed his technical education. During much of this time he composed, at first secretly, though his principal aim was to perfect himself at the piano.

His first public engagement of note was as accompanist to the famous Hungarian violinist, Reményi, with whom, at the age of twenty, he made a tour of some length. It was during this tour that there occurred an incident which was to have a not inconsiderable effect upon Brahms's whole career. On reaching the town of Goettingen for a concert it was discovered that the piano sent to the concert hall was a half tone under concert pitch. It was impossible to delay further the beginning of the concert. Without a moment's hesitation and without a mistake Brahms transposed from memory the entire piano part of the *Kreutzer* Sonata thus enabling Reményi to contribute his part of the evening. In the audience at this concert was another and still greater violinist, namely, Joseph Joachim. Struck with admiration at the feat performed by Brahms, Joachim asked to be introduced to the young musician, from which introduction proceeded a lifelong friendship. In the course of a visit to Joachim later that year, Brahms was given introductory letters to Liszt, in Weimar, and Schumann, at that time living in Düsseldorf. The introduction to the latter was to lead to the real establishment of Brahms's fame, for Schumann, impressed to the point of intense enthusiasm by Brahms's compositions up to that time and his deep knowledge of musical subjects, published in the *Neue Zeitschrift für Musik*, a journal of criticism which he had founded, an article so laudatory of Brahms that musical circles throughout the length and breadth of Europe were set agog.

Untroubled by the stir thus created, Brahms pursued the even tenor of his way, though he well knew that for the rest of his career each new composition by him would provoke almost endless controversy, which in truth proved to be the case. The friendship of Robert and Clara Schumann, thus established, became one of the bulwarks of Brahms's existence, and following Robert Schumann's tragic end in 1856, Brahms's relationship to Mme. Schumann was practically that of a devoted son for the remainder of her life.

Later in 1853, Brahms made a permanent arrangement with the great music publishing firm of Breitkopf & Härtel of Leipzig for the publication of his compositions, and in the following year, being offered two important appointments, he chose that of Director of Court music for the Prince of Lippe-Detmold. This post he retained for four years, but finally resigned it and returned to Hamburg, making a few public appearances during the next two years in that city and in Cologne, Leipzig and Zürich.

In 1862 Brahms went to Vienna, and while regarding the Austrian capital as his home for the rest of his career, he led for some years a restless and wandering existence. In 1863 he was appointed director of the Vienna Singakademie but abandoned the post after a few months. Concert tours with Joachim and Stockhausen figure in his public appearances for some years following. From 1871 to 1874 he conducted the concerts of the Gesellschaft der Musikfreunde in Vienna and from the latter year until 1878 lived near Heidelberg. From his return in 1878 to the end of his life his permanent home was in Vienna. By this time a creative musician of world fame, his life flowed quietly along in the even channel of the firm friendships which he had consolidated in the small intimate social circle of which he had become the center. Occasional visits to Italy and Switzerland formed his main recreation. From Cambridge University he received the degree of Doctor of Music; Breslau conferred upon him a Ph.D. in 1881; and in 1886 he was awarded the most distinguished of Prussian orders, *Pour le Mérite*. In 1889 he was given the freedom of the City of Hamburg.

In 1897 at the funeral of Clara Schumann he contracted a chill which, aggravating a malignant condition of some standing, led to his death on April 3 of that year.

ACADEMIC FESTIVAL OVERTURE, OP. 80

BRAHMS spoke of the *Academic* Overture as a "potpourri on students' songs à la Suppé"; but he was notoriously irreverent toward his own music. Max Kalbeck, Brahms's Boswell, whose four-volume biography of the master sets all records for detail, finds in the *Academic* Overture more than a token of appreciation for an honor. He believes the Overture is an ode to the spirit of freedom, comradeship, and joy of living at the old German Universities. He finds in the opening theme a double reminiscence of the *Rákóczy* March (the Hungarian *Marseillaise* of 1848) and the *Paris Entrance* March of 1813, symbolizing the emergence of the spirit of liberation from the armies of military conquest and from the oppressive reaction in post-Napoleonic Europe. The concluding song, *Gaudeamus igitur*, was indeed a symbol of students' rebellion against the police surveillance in German Universities.

Four students' songs are used in the *Academic* Overture, apart from original thematic material. The first song *Wir hatten gebauet ein stattliches Haus* ("We Had Built a Stately House") makes its appearance softly in the brass after a long drum roll. The second song is *Der Landesvater* and may be construed as a second movement, an Andante.

The third movement in all of Brahms's four symphonies is a Viennese scherzo. In the *Academic* Overture, the scherzo effect is provided by the *Fuchslied*, introduced, appropriately enough, by the laughing bassoons. This song is a hazing song for a freshman, who is asked impertinent questions about his family, and then is given a pipe too strong for a freshman's lungs.

The concluding song is *Gaudeamus igitur*, the finale.

Brahms went to Breslau to conduct the Overture himself, and the first performance took place at the Breslau University on January 4, 1881. Other performances followed immediately, and very soon the *Academic Festival* Overture became an orchestral favorite the world over.

X-MX-200, Philharmonic-Symphony Orchestra of New York, John Barbirolli Conducting.

BALLADES, FOR PIANO

AMONG Brahms's many collections of piano pieces there was only one which he explicitly entitled Ballades. This was Op. 10, composed during the summer of 1854. Like his piano sonatas, these Ballades are built on a large pattern. And they are intense and expressive. Emotional expression was still more important to Brahms than the solution of the problems of form. However, these Ballades are also filled with a Northern predilection for the fantastic, nightmarish, melancholy; for veiled colors and sharp contrasts. It is frequently cruel, cold, frightening music.

In technical treatment, in the development of the melodic line and the application of harmonic color, these Ballades suggest the mastery to be found in his later piano works. Here Brahms's piano style had improved greatly over that of the E-flat minor Scherzo composed three years earlier. Brahms no longer aimed at a maximum of polyphonic (orchestral) effect, a tendency that makes so many of his early piano works unpianistic. He gradually came to learn the subtler qualities of the instrument. His friendship with Robert Schumann, whom he had met a year earlier, was largely responsible for this development.

The Ballades were Brahms's last works of his so-called first period. The very first Ballade is still the most widely performed. It was inspired by the Scottish ballad, *Edward*, a pianistic tone-poem with tragedy sounding with dramatic impact through the three pages. (Twenty-three years later, Brahms once again set the *Edward* ballad to music; this time as a duet for alto and tenor, included in a collection of vocal duets, Op. 75.)

Another of Brahms's Ballades—that in G minor—is found in a volume of five piano pieces published as Op. 118, and composed during a vacation in Ischl in 1893. Brahms was at that time preoccupied with his edition of German folk songs. In general, his piano pieces of this period are marked by simplicity, brevity and naturalness. The G minor Ballade is the only boisterous piece of the entire volume.

69280-D, D minor Ballade, "Edward," Anatole Kitain, Piano.

CAPRICCIOS, FOR PIANO

Most of Brahms's Capriccios are included in his collections of piano pieces entitled *Klavierstücke* and *Fantasien,* Opp. 76 and 116. Brahms began writing his Op. 76 in 1871, and completed it seven years later during a vacation in Pörtschach in Carinthia. This eight-piece collection appeared in two volumes, each of which contains two Capriccios (Nos. 1 and 2, 5 and 8).

Compared with Brahms's earlier piano pieces, these are much simpler, more genuinely pianistic, more intimate. The second Capriccio, in B minor, betrays the composer's interest in Hungarian music.

Brahms composed his Op. 116 in Ischl during the summer months of 1892 and 1893. Brahms no longer wrote great orchestral music, but concentrated on the more intimate forms of chamber music, piano pieces, and songs. Simple modulations and harmonies, three-part song forms, and uncomplicated rhythms are typical of Brahms's tendency toward economy during his last years. The texture of these pieces is delicate; they are so thoroughly pianistic that to transcribe them for any other instrument is unthinkable.

All three Capriccios are in the minor mode. Hanslick appropriately referred to them as "monologues."

CONCERTO NO. 1 IN D MINOR, OP. 15, FOR PIANO AND ORCHESTRA
Maestoso · Adagio · Allegro non troppo

In 1853, Johannes Brahms brought some of his piano pieces and chamber music works to Robert Schumann. Schumann was much impressed with the young man's output and predicted big things for him. He even wrote a special article on Brahms in his musical paper, *Neue Zeitschrift für Musik,* in which he said: "If he would only point his magic wand to where the might of mass, in chorus and orchestra, offers him its power, yet more wondrous glimpses into the mysteries of the spirit world await us."

With the almost fantastic praise of Schumann ringing in his ears, Brahms felt a great responsibility toward the world of music. He moved very cautiously, lest he make a musical misstep, and he certainly did not rush right home and write a symphony (it was to be another twenty-three years before the world would hear his first symphony).

The following January, however, Schumann received a letter from Brahms which stated: "I have been trying my hand at a symphony during the past summer; have even orchestrated the first movement, and have composed the second and third." But Brahms was not at all satisfied with his new creation. He had been receiving counsel in matters of orchestral writing from Julius Otto Grimm, but felt that he was not yet ready to attempt the symphonic form. Consequently, he reduced the embryo symphony to a sonata for two pianos. Clara Schumann recorded in her diary that "I tried over with Brahms at Klems three movements of his sonata for two pianos. They appeared to me to be quite powerful, quite original, noble and clearer than anything before. We played them twice, and on Sunday I shall play them with Dietrich, so that he may hear them from a distance and be able to obtain an idea of the sound of the instruments."

When Brahms heard the work from a distance he was still dissatisfied. Grimm then tried the sonata with Mme. Schumann, and came up with the suggestion that Brahms combine his symphonic and pianistic ideas in a concerto for piano and orchestra. Thus the D minor Piano Concerto was born. Brahms utilized only the first two movements of the sonata, composing a new third movement for the concerto. He saved the original third movement, however, and it finally made its appearance as the chorus, "Behold All Flesh," in the *German* Requiem.

It was not until the spring of 1858 that the Concerto was sufficiently refined and polished to satisfy its fastidious composer. It was tried out at a rehearsal of the orchestra at Hanover, of which Brahms's friend, the noted violinist, Joseph Joachim, was the conductor, on March 30 of that year. The composer was at the piano for this first reading which created a favorable impression on the players. The same artists were involved in the first public performance of the Concerto, which took place at the Royal Theatre, Hanover, on January 22, 1859. It was not particularly well received by the general public, though it earned the respect of the musically informed.

When Brahms performed the Concerto five days later at the Gewandhaus in Leipzig, Julius Rietz conducted the orchestra.

It is hardly surprising that early audiences found the Concerto difficult and strange. In sharp contrast to the smooth-flowing, melodic works in this form by Mozart—and even Beethoven—Brahms's First Concerto must have fallen upon their ears with arresting starkness. For the first time, too, the soloist did not stand out above the orchestra, but was united with it, almost as if he were another member of the ensemble. The Concerto offers little opportunity for virtuoso display, but much opportunity for purely musical expression.

The first movement is a dramatic and powerful Maestoso, which begins with a long orchestral introduction. The first theme is somber in character; the second, announced by the piano alone, is considerably brighter. The second movement, Adagio, is placid and songful. The manuscript score for this movement bears above it the inscription, "*Benedictus qui venit in nomine Domini.*" Brahms's biographer, Max Kalbeck, took this to be a tribute to Schumann, whom Brahms sometimes addressed as "Mynheer Domini," but others believe that the composer had Clara Schumann in mind, for, in a letter to her about the Concerto, he wrote: "I am also painting a lovely picture of you; it is to be the Adagio." The final Allegro non troppo is a vigorous rondo, which includes a fugato for the orchestra and a short cadenza —the only one in the concerto—for the solo piano.

M-MM-652, Rudolf Serkin, Piano, and the Pittsburgh Symphony Orchestra, Fritz Reiner Conducting.

CONCERTO NO. 2 IN B-FLAT MAJOR, OP. 83, FOR PIANO AND ORCHESTRA

Allegro non troppo · *Scherzo: allegro appassionato* · *Andante*
Allegretto grazioso

AFTER a trip through Italy, Brahms returned to Pörtschach in the Austrian Alps on the eve of his forty-fifth birthday in 1878. Immediately he made some sketches for his second piano concerto. Three years elapsed before he attempted anything more on the work. Then he made another journey to Italy, in March 1881, and the spring sunshine inspired him to finish his Concerto. He returned to Vienna on his forty-eighth birthday, May 7, and on May 22 retired to a villa at Pressbaum, west of Vienna, where he set to work seriously, and completed the composition on July 7.

Brahms was extremely self-conscious about any of his new musical creations and made sarcastic, deprecatory remarks about them to his friends. Thus, on the very day the Concerto was finished, he wrote to his old friend, Elisabeth von Herzogenberg, whose musical opinion he valued most highly: "I don't mind telling you that I have written a tiny, tiny pianoforte concerto with a tiny, tiny wisp of a Scherzo. It is in B-flat, and I have reason to fear that I have worked this udder, which has yielded good milk before, too often and too vigorously."

Four days later, he sent the manuscript of the concerto to Dr. Billroth, the renowned surgeon and amateur musician, with the remark that he was sending him "some little piano pieces." Brahms was frequently in the habit of seeking Billroth's advice on his new works, and his friend once wrote: "It is always a delight to me when Brahms, after paying me a short visit, during which we have talked of indifferent things, takes a roll out of his greatcoat pocket and says casually, 'Look at that and write me what you think of it.'"

The Concerto had its first hearing at a rehearsal of the Meiningen Orchestra, conducted by Hans von Bülow, with Brahms at the piano, on October 17, 1881. Its first public presentation took place at the Redouten Saal in Budapest on November 9. Alexander Erkel conducted the orchestra of the National Theatre, and the composer was again the soloist.

The Concerto was not too enthusiastically received at its first performances in Germany and Austria. One of the reasons for this may have been that Brahms was a pianist who cared far more about interpretation than technical perfection, and was not above changing certain passages in his own music so that he would be better able to play them. Yet he would not entrust the first performances to others. As time went on, and better pianists played the Concerto, it gained in popularity, until today it is considered one of the finest compositions for piano and orchestra ever created.

Despite Brahms's reference to it as "a tiny, tiny pianoforte concerto," it is one of the most extensive, most difficult works in the entire concerto literature. Even the composer once remarked to a young lady who was to play it in Vienna: "It is decidely not for little girls." It has been described as a symphony with piano obbligato, since it is definitely not a display piece for the piano. However, it might better be characterized as a symphony for piano and orchestra.

Brahms departed from custom when he divided the B-flat major Concerto into four, instead of the usual three, movements. He explained this procedure by saying that he had placed the Scherzo (which is the extra movement) between the opening Allegro non troppo and the Andante, as he wished to avoid having what he called the "Adagio mood" dominate the whole composition. He believed that the "simple" first movement and the "simple" third movement should be separated by a more vigorous and passionate section.

M-MM-584, Rudolf Serkin, Piano, and the Philadelphia Orchestra, Eugene Ormandy Conducting.

CONCERTO IN D MAJOR, OP. 77, FOR VIOLIN AND ORCHESTRA

Allegro non troppo · Adagio · Finale: allegro giocoso

BRAHMS remarked to Clara Schumann in 1895 that "one composes only until one's fiftieth year; then, the creative power begins to diminish." He was within five years of that precipice when he wrote his Concerto in D major for violin and orchestra, having composed it in 1878. Still, it would be rash to say that in this work there are premonitions of impaired creative power. As a matter of fact, there is the powerful Symphony No. 4 in E minor to refute Brahms's statement: it belongs to his fifty-second and fifty-third years. Though this Violin Concerto is now considerably more than half a century old, it is still fresh and companionable—of notable imagery.

The name of Joseph Joachim, the great violin virtuoso, is closely linked with this work. Not only is it dedicated to him, but he was the soloist when the Concerto was given its première under Brahms's direction at a Gewandhaus concert in Leipzig on New Year's Day, 1879. It is significant that Brahms consulted Joachim on the merits of the violin passages. Joachim even furnished a cadenza, and the fingering and bowing indications are his, not Brahms's. Before its publication in October 1879, Joachim made further alterations, to which the composer yielded. Eduard Hanslick was not exaggerating when he termed this Concerto "the ripe fruit of the friendship between Joachim and Brahms." Brahms was ultimately so satisfied with the work that he wrote his publisher, Simrock: "It is well to be doubted whether I could write a better concerto."

Evidently a Scherzo was included in Brahms's original draft. This was removed "for reasons of style," according to Richard Specht, and the composer lamented: "The middle movements have gone, and of course they were the best." Max Kalbeck affirms that the Scherzo was later incorporated in the Piano Concerto No. 2 in B-flat major.

The Leipzig critic, Dörffel, wrote of the première as follows: "Joachim played with a love and devotion which brought home to us in every bar the direct or indirect share he has had in the work. As to the reception, the first movement was too new to be distinctly appreciated by the audience, the second made considerable way, the last aroused great enthusiasm."

Constructed mainly along classical lines followed by Mozart and Beethoven in their concertos, the Brahms Violin Concerto is also closely linked to those of Mendelssohn and Bruch in romantic feeling. It is typical of Brahms in its supreme blend of reflective breadth and warm humanity of mood and melody.

M-MM-603, Joseph Szigeti, Violin, and the Philadelphia Orchestra, Eugene Ormandy Conducting.

HUNGARIAN DANCES, FOR FOUR HANDS

THE *Hungarian Dances,* for four hands, were published in two installments, two volumes each, in 1869 and 1880. They have no opus numbers, and with good reason: Brahms wished to emphasize the fact that they were not new and original compositions, but arrangements of traditional melodies. The word "arranged" appears prominently on the title page and played an important part in Brahms's defense when Hungarian composers (among them Brahms's former friend, Reményi) charged him with plagiarism.

Reményi had been responsible for Brahms's predilection for Hungarian music. Ever since his early tours with the Hungarian violinist, Brahms had been collecting Hungarian folk songs, to which Reményi

[96]

had originally introduced him. Often, in his serious works, when striving for rhythmic animation and variety, Brahms would inject the Hungarian manner. And a Magyar flavor filtered through even some of his Waltzes, try though he did to keep them Viennese.

Patient studies of old music and folk material had made Brahms a discriminating connoisseur. It remains amazing that he should have been able to understand so intimately and personally the national music of a foreign people. He actually succeeded in translating these genuine, uninhibited and often exotic melodies into his personal idiom without violating their individuality. The *Hungarian Dances* are not only genuine Brahms, but genuine gypsy music as well.

This is particularly true of the first two volumes, published in 1869. The later set occasionally sounds like Brahms compositions based on Hungarian themes. It is consequently not surprising that the later volumes were not quite so successful as the first. The first two books, as a matter of fact, enjoyed the greatest success that Brahms was ever to achieve, and were the first of his works to bring him an international fame.

Numerous different arrangements exist of these *Hungarian Dances*. Brahms himself transcribed three of them for orchestra (Nos. 1, 3, and 10).

17352-D, Dance No. 2 arranged for violin by Joachim, Nathan Milstein, Violin.
1211-D, Dance No. 5 arranged for orchestra, Philadelphia "Pops" Orchestra, Eugene Ormandy Conducting.
17340-D, Dance No. 5 arranged for violin, Joseph Szigeti, Violin.

INTERMEZZI, FOR PIANO

BRAHMS did not follow any particular order in bracketing assorted piano pieces under one opus number. Thus, Intermezzi are interleaved with Capriccios or Rhapsodies in various groups.

Intermezzo Op. 118, No. 6, is in E-flat minor. In this Intermezzo Brahms delights in long appoggiaturas, projected upon the harmony notes at close range, so that a sensation of acute discord is created. Brahms applied this method consciously. Writing to Clara Schumann about another piece similarly constructed, he confesses: "It teems with discord. These may be all right and quite explicable, but you

[97]

may not perhaps like them." He adds with a touch of Brahmsian humor, "And if so, I might wish that they were less right and more pleasing to you." Apart from the conscious use of discord, the Intermezzo in E-flat minor is extremely pure in its form, which is ternary.

Edwin Evans, in his handbooks to Brahms's complete works, has this to say about this Intermezzo: "This is a movement portraying the utmost grief and passion. . . . There is no bending of the form to his will; nothing (except maybe a highly refined pianism) to point particularly to Brahms." The pianism is indeed quite extraordinary, almost acrobatic, in that Brahms makes the left hand cross the right in light arpeggios, at times in the identical register, to the point of collision and coincidence.

Intermezzo No. 3 of Op. 76 is one of the shortest pieces Brahms ever wrote. It is in A-flat major and comprises only thirty bars. Huneker describes this Intermezzo in his impressionistic language as a "tender wreath of moonbeams and love." Edwin Evans comments upon the form: "Notwithstanding its shortness, it is divided into two portions, which are practically a repeat of one another. But the repetition only seems to respond to the listener's longing to hear the lovely strain again, and in doing so to make it even more charming than before."

Intermezzo No. 4 of Op. 76 is remarkable for the use Brahms makes of tonality. The key signature is in two flats, and the opening bar is the dominant seventh of B-flat major. But having implied the principal key by aural harmony and visual time signature, Brahms shuns the tonic in a most deliberate manner. He veers momentarily toward G minor in a deceptive cadence, and then proceeds enharmonically to remote keys, farther and farther away from the tonic. It is only in the second section that the tonic makes its appearance in the pedal, and even then as the bass of the minor subdominant. Clear and unadulterated B-flat major appears for the first time only in the last two bars. This Intermezzo is thus the extreme instance of Brahms's tonofugal idiosyncrasy, for here the tonic triad is not reached until the very last bars.

Intermezzo Op. 116, No. 4 is an Adagio in the clearly expressed key of E major. The piece is a study in acceleration and retardation, secured not by the actual increase and decrease of tempo, but by the quicker rate of motion in a given metrical unit. Harmonically and melodically, the important effect is that of the upward resolution of the augmented triad in the opening phrase.

Intermezzo Op. 119, No. 2 is another instance of Brahms's tono-fugal harmony. Ostensibly, the piece is in E minor, with a middle section in E major. But the E minor triad never appears at all, and when the final cadence seems to lead to the tonic, it is the major tonic of the middle section that provides the resolution. The movement is toccata-like, with both hands alternating in quick groups of two notes. The second section is, rather unexpectedly, a Viennese waltz, as charming as any of Brahms's. The concluding section is almost an exact repetition of the first.

X-201, Walter Gieseking, Piano.

QUARTET NO. 1 IN G MINOR, OP. 25, FOR PIANO AND STRINGS

Allegro · Intermezzo: allegro ma non troppo · Andante con moto Rondo alla Zingarere: presto

THIS Quartet, in which Brahms introduced the Hungarian element into his chamber music, was begun in 1857, completed in 1861, and published in 1863. It is one of his richest chamber-music works, for it combines extraordinary fertility of melodic invention with plasticity of form. If at first hearing it appears over-elaborate, it is only because of Brahms's amplified piano writing.

The second and fourth movements introduce elements which were to become characteristic of Brahms. The second movement, originally a scherzo (later renamed Intermezzo), is a night-piece in a veiled, mysterious mood, far removed from our accepted idea of the scherzo. Brahms was to write many such pieces, and in precisely the same way. Then the Rondo alla Zingarese shows for the first time Brahms's preoccupation with the Hungarian folk idiom; this is one of the most genuinely Hungarian pieces he ever wrote.

The Quartet was first performed (from manuscript) at the concert of the Hellmesberger Quartet soon after Brahms's arrival in Vienna, with Brahms himself officiating at the piano. This was his first appearance before a Viennese audience, and his success was so great that he received immediate offers from publishers, and was encouraged to undertake a concert of his own only two weeks later.

QUARTET NO. 2 IN A MAJOR, OP. 26, FOR PIANO AND STRINGS

Allegro non troppo · Poco adagio · Scherzo · Finale: allegro

THIS is the companion work to the G minor Quartet, and was introduced by Brahms and the Hellmesberger Quartet in Vienna on November 29, 1862. Like the first quartet, it dates from Brahms's last days in Hamburg. It was dedicated to Mrs. Elisabeth Rösing, his widowed landlady, and the aunt of two attractive members of his ladies' vocal quartet.

When Brahms wrote works in pairs—which he did on occasion—the first is usually more effective and more fertile in melodic invention, while the second is invariably superior in architectonic construction and in refinement of details. It is almost as if he intentionally gave full rein to his creative urges before settling down to careful and fastidious workmanship.

The first two movements of this Quartet are better balanced than those of the G minor, even though Brahms experiments with the use of variations in the development section of the first movement. The Scherzo suffers from Brahms's intensive studies of counterpoint during the two years prior to the composition of the Quartet: the trio, a full-fledged canon, appeared "rough and dull" even to the sympathetic Clara Schumann. The third movement is again a nocturne in mood and tone color; the fourth, a Hungarian piece, though with a more restrained palette than that employed in the G minor.

QUARTET NO. 3 IN C MINOR, OP. 60, FOR PIANO AND STRINGS

Allegro ma non troppo · Scherzo: allegro · Andante · Finale: allegro commodo

"PICTURE to yourself a man who is about to shoot himself, because that is all that remains for him to do." These are the words Brahms used to explain the meaning of the first movement of the C minor Quartet as late as 1868—almost fourteen years after he had first drafted the music! And in the 1870's he still identified its youthful composer with Goethe's Werther, a character symbolic of the young man dying of unrequited love for a married woman.

Actually this very difficult piano quartet was Brahms's first composition in this form. Its proximity to the First Symphony, in the same key, is unmistakable, not merely for chronological reasons but also for the emotional upheavals that precipitated its composition.

The first version was completed in 1854 or 1855. It was Brahms's own Werther period—that of his friendship with the Schumanns, his concern over Robert's illness, and his growing attachment to Clara. He discussed the Quartet with Joachim, whom he still considered his superior as a composer; both were dissatisfied with it, and it was shelved. Brahms, however, remained sentimentally attached to the work. Through the ensuing years he continued to correct and revise parts of it until he gave it its final shape and form during the happy summer of 1875.

In spite of drastic revisions, Brahms was not altogether successful in assimilating the styles of the uncontrolled Romantic he had been in the 1850's, with that of the well-balanced admirer of classical form he became later on. "The Quartet," he confessed to his publisher, "is half old and half new, and not worth much."

The first version was in three movements, without a scherzo, and in the key of C-sharp minor. In the new one, the first two movements remained unchanged; a scherzo was written and introduced between these two movements, and the old Finale was discarded to make way for an altogether different movement.

Again, as in the A major quartet, Brahms utilizes variations in the sonata form: the beautiful second subject of the first movement appears in four variations. The mood of this movement is tragic despair, fraught with dramatic struggle, touched with gloom. Actually, the entire work would appear to have been drenched in somber colors were it not for the romantic and beautiful Andante. The new movements (the Scherzo and the Finale) are models of brevity and restraint: the trio of the Scherzo is reduced to a brief episode, and the Finale was so concisely written that Brahms later inserted thirty-three additional bars. The changing styles of the various movements, however, are rendered less striking by the unity of the atmospheric mood of the entire work.

QUARTET IN C MINOR, OP. 51, NO. 1

Allegro · Romanze: poco adagio e commodo · Allegretto molto moderato · Allegro

THE FIRST two of Brahms's three string quartets were completed in the summer of 1873. They were, however, not his first experiments in that form. For many years he had tried to acquire fluency in quartet-writing, and later admitted that he had sketched at least twenty string quartets before permitting one to be published.

He had written no chamber music in the eight years preceding the writing of these two quartets. Meanwhile his style had developed into full maturity. He had acquired conciseness and architectural balance; he had lost most of his Romantic exuberance. He had learned that which he considered the composer's most difficult problem: to "leave out unnecessary notes."

The first quartet is in the same key as his two other important "firsts"—the symphony and the Piano Quartet. It finds Brahms at a climax of his "C minor mood"—gloomy, angry, desperate, resigned. It is perhaps the least attractive among Brahms's chamber-music works, appealing exclusively to the intellect and leaving unanswered the listener's yearning for sonorous beauty. It is Brahms at his moodiest, presented in all his North-German harshness—not the Brahms who wrote the waltzes and gypsy melodies. This atmosphere is maintained throughout.

A brief motive at the beginning of the first movement reappears in the Romanze and becomes the main subject of the concluding Allegro. This attempt at cyclic writing greatly increases the feeling of unity between the movements.

QUARTET IN A MINOR, OP. 51, NO. 2

*Allegro ma non troppo · Andante moderato · Quasi minuetto
moderato · Finale: allegro non assai*

THE SECOND quartet is somewhat more cheerful than the first. Although it begins in a melancholy deliberation over the Brahms-Joachim motto "FAE" (*Frei aber einsam*—free but lonely) which becomes the basis of the entire movement, it soon progresses into happy exuberance in the full-fledged gypsy manner. The Hungarian-flavored motive of the concluding rondo appears in all of the three preceding movements (another attempt on the part of Brahms at cyclic writing).

The solemnity of the Andante is interrupted by a lovely discourse between first violin and 'cello. The Minuet consists of a vivid alternation of lyrical and febrile passages. The Finale is a rondo on two themes, with the principal subject, a Czardas, reappearing in six masterful variations.

QUINTET IN F MINOR, OP. 34,
FOR PIANO AND STRINGS

*Allegro non troppo · Andante un poco adagio · Scherzo: allegro
Finale: poco sostenuto*

BRAHMS'S last months in Hamburg, prior to his removal to Vienna, were congenial, stimulating, and prolific. However, he still struggled with the technical problems of his craft, complaining once to Clara Schumann that everything still went hard with him. Among the works dating from this period (1862), was a quintet for strings which developed into something of a problem child. Unable to make it "sound right," Brahms decided never to publish it, and later actually destroyed the manuscript. However, during the winter months of 1863–64, he arranged the material into a sonata for two pianos (subsequently publishing it as Op. 34b); the peculiarly symphonic quality of this music appeared to him to be well suited for the richness of the piano tone. A few months later, Clara Schumann objected to the absence of string sonorities. Then and there, in the congenial atmosphere of Clara's summer home near Baden-Baden, Brahms recast the music into its third, and definitive form—a piano quintet.

The public was slow in appreciating this beautiful work. It is a work of transition, carrying Brahms's emotional self-expression to the limit and at the same time suggesting his growing tendency toward more universal thought. Here, for the first time perhaps, is Brahms the Romantic classicist, whose musical affinities were soon to turn sharply away from Schumann and toward Haydn and the early Beethoven; whose classical clarity was not likely to find appreciative ears in an age of Romantic diffuseness.

The work is comparatively complicated, elaborate in its development, and crowded with thematic material. The first movement contains not two but five contrasting themes; their development, though elaborate, is packed into an incredibly narrow space. The third movement is built around three themes, and keeps changing in rhythm and mode. The very long Finale is an excellent example of Romantic lack of organization; the sonata form is vaguely suggested, yet the exposition is preceded by the entire unorthodox introduction which establishes the basic mood of the entire movement.

The slow movement, with its folk-song simplicity, offers the only page of uncomplicated music in the entire work.

QUINTET IN B MINOR, OP. 115,
FOR CLARINET AND STRINGS

Allegro · Adagio · Andantino · Con moto

BRAHMS discovered the clarinet at a time when he was on the verge of abandoning composition altogether. In the spring of 1891, on a visit to the ducal court of Meiningen, he heard Richard Mühlfeld, whom he considered one of the greatest woodwind players he had ever heard. Promptly, Brahms started work on a trio and a quintet for Mühlfeld. He completed both works during the summer, and before the end of the year they were introduced at Meiningen and Berlin by the Joachim Quartet and Richard Mühlfeld.

In this Quintet, Brahms seems to have summed up his life and work; the prevailing mood is that of resignation without bitterness. The mellow timbre of the clarinet, with its different registers and tone colors, lends itself particularly well to this kind of meditation. Both the melancholy pages and the fragmentary moments of bliss seem to be veiled by an autumnal mist.

The Quintet is one of Brahms's most accomplished compositions. It is a model of everything for which he stood artistically: intensity of feeling, classical simplicity, economy and transparency of writing, sheer beauty of sonority. The fusion of classicism and Romanticism was fully achieved without any suggestion of contradiction.

Here, Brahms seems to have been working *toward* his main theme rather than away *from* it; not until the final movement does it appear in its fully developed form. Generally speaking, the melodic material of the various movements is cut from the same cloth, but variety is achieved through the interpolation of rhapsodic passages. Some of the passages echo Hungarian themes; the solo clarinet, over mysterious string tremolos, in the second movement seems to speak of the melancholy expanses of the Hungarian plains.

RHAPSODIES, FOR PIANO

ON A CONCERT tour, Brahms stopped at Leipzig one day in 1879, and called on his dear friends, the Herzogenbergs, to play for them his two newly composed piano pieces. Herzogenberg was a plodding composer and his wife was an excellent and intelligent pianist. The original titles of the two pieces, Op. 79, were *Capriccio, presto agitato,* and *Capriccio, molto passionato.* Later Brahms decided to rename them, and wrote to Frau von Herzogenberg, asking what she thought of Rhapsody for a title. He playfully added that he could not improve on the dedication, which was made to her. She replied that the simpler title, *Clavierstücke,* would suit the pieces better, since the music did not conform to the general idea of rhapsodies, but admitted that Rhapsody was the best of the descriptive titles.

James Huneker liked the second Rhapsody as much as he disliked the first. "This B minor Rhapsody," he wrote in the preface to the selected edition of Brahms's piano works, "sounds as if its composer were trying to make a harsh pragmatic statement; in it there is more intellectual acrimoniousness than rhapsody. . . . Acrid as the patina on antique metal, this first Rhapsody is for the head rather than for the heart."

This judgment is puzzling: the musical analysis would tend to show that the first Rhapsody is much more human than the second. It is in perfect three-part form; the main section, which is repeated in full in the third part of the piece, is tonally clear, and the modulations take place only after the fundamental key is established. There is a touch of humor in the lyric D minor phrase, which is a quotation from Grieg's theme in "Åse's Death," from *Peer Gynt*. Brahms no doubt intended it as an amortization of the melody-loan Grieg had made for his Piano Concerto from Brahms's E-flat minor Scherzo.

Huneker is enthusiastic over the second Rhapsody: "A wonderful, glorious, bracing tone picture, in which Brahms, the philosopher, burns the boats of his old age and becomes for the time a youthful Faust in search of a sensation. A hurricane of emotion that is barely stilled at the end, this Rhapsody reminds me of the bardic recital of some old border ballad. . . . It is an epic in miniature."

The last Rhapsody is the fourth piece of the four *Clavierstücke*, Op. 119, and is the last original piano piece that Brahms composed.

X-MX-183, Egon Petri, Piano.

SONATA IN D MINOR, OP. 108, FOR VIOLIN AND PIANO

Allegro · Adagio · Un poco presto e con sentimento · Presto agitato

THE SONATA in D minor, the last of the three sonatas for violin and piano, is the least known, possibly because of its reputed austerity. The biographer Specht suggests that when Brahms dedicated the Sonata in D minor to Hans von Bülow, he had the dedicatee so firmly in mind that the work is like a portrait of the pianist with its restless excitement, feverish visions, and scarcely relieved tension, to which lyric portions make a provisional contrast, and threaten to change from fantastic humor to the deepest solemnity, from agitation to serious contemplation. The listener can shape the work to this program as he thinks fit.

Another view is interesting. Frau von Herzogenberg stated that the finale reminded her of a picture by Guido Rene, of Aurora sprinkling flowers before the Sun God's chariot, a copy of which hung in Brahms's studio in Vienna.

M-MM-324, Joseph Szigeti, Violin, and Egon Petri, Piano.

SONG OF DESTINY (SCHICKSALSLIED), OP. 54

IN THE summer of 1868, while vacationing in the north of Germany, Brahms read, and was much impressed with, *Hyperion's Song of Destiny* by the German Romantic poet, Friedrich Hölderlin. The poem contrasts the calm, untroubled life of the celestials with the unrelieved misery and futile striving of mankind here on earth. The composer made the first musical sketches for the poem on the beach at Wilhelmshaven on the same day that he first read the lines, but it was not until three years later that the work was completed.

The work opens with the orchestral prelude, a twenty-eight-bar passage of luminous beauty and simplicity that has been acclaimed by critics one of the finest creations of this master. The spirit of the prelude carries over into the first choral section, which deals with the life of the gods. A sudden change in mood is ushered in with a brief but menacing orchestral interlude, following which the chorus hurls forth in passionate—sometimes violent—tones its dissatisfaction at the sorry lot of earthly mortals. The work ends, as Geiringer remarks, "on a note of sorrowful resignation."

The *Song of Destiny* was first performed from manuscript on October 18, 1871, by the Karlsruhe Philharmonic Society, the composer conducting. It was published two months later.

X-MX-223, Philharmonic-Symphony Orchestra of New York and the Westminster Choir, Bruno Walter Conducting.

SONGS

BRAHMS wrote approximately 200 songs for solo voice and piano accompaniment. It was the only major branch of music which he practiced uninterruptedly throughout the forty-four years of his creative life. His first group of songs, six in number, was begun in 1852 (Op. 3); the *Vier Ernste Gesänge*, completed in 1896, was the last opus (121) he lived to see published.

We look vainly for a persistent development in Brahms's writing, or for much variety of feeling. Love songs predominate, and most of these are sad. In songs like the famous *Mainacht* and *Feldeinsamkeit* the melancholy mood of an individual is reflected in the atmosphere or landscape background; other love songs are more passionate (*Meine Liebe ist grün; Von ewiger Liebe*), or tender (*Immer leiser wird mein Schlummer*), or slightly humorous (*Vergebliches Ständchen, Tambourliedchen; Der Schmied*).

Though there are between four to nine songs to each opus number, Brahms wrote only one song-cycle of larger proportions: 15 Romances from Ludwig Tieck's *Magelone* (Op. 33). Ballad-like dramatic narrations appear only in solitary instances, such as in *Verrath*. Brahms himself insisted that he preferred his little songs to his big ones, "little" meaning the simple strophic form which predominates in his beloved folk music. Between this form and the (numerically less) "through-composed," are songs with different accompaniments for each stanza, such as the celebrated *Wie bist du, meine Königin*.

During the closing years of Brahms's life, Dr. Gustav Ophüls, of Krefeld collated the poems which Brahms had set to music into a carefully annotated volume. A critical survey of these poems betrays surprising findings—surprising when Brahms's remarkable literary background is taken into account. Although Goethe and a few of the great Romantic poets appear in considerable proportion, there is a surprising representation of obscure poets whose names would surely have been forgotten but for Brahms's music. It seems apparent that Brahms looked for a poem frequently after he had planned the music in detail, and he was more often guided by the atmosphere of a poem than by its literary quality. Although Brahms tried to do justice to the lyrics, to treat pauses according to the structure of the verse, to keep the rhythm of words and music uniform, he was ever ready to sacrifice such considerations if his musical expression required him to do so.

In his songs, Brahms proved again that good music could still be written in a conservative manner. An avowed and enthusiastic disciple of Schubert (more than of Schumann!), he reduced coloristic effects to a minimum. Melody ruled supreme. Far removed from the German disposition to exploit harmony for musical expression, Brahms's songs—with their full abandonment to the human voice—might very well have been written under the cerulean skies of Italy. Italian, too, is the high importance he assigned to the bass. "The bass," Brahms used to say, "must be a mirror of the melody"; and he covered the harmonic middle voices to put the last touches on the contrapuntal treatment of melody and bass. Sometimes he considered it sufficient to sketch his songs according to the ancient method of basso continuo.

Brahms's melodies are very expressive, sometimes so simple in design that they might be mistaken for folk songs. Actually a great number of his songs were purposely written in the folk-song manner, or based on folk material. Some song groups include numbers plainly entitled *Volkslied*, which indicates that the composer was resetting the lyrics of a traditional song. North-German folk material predominates, of course; but some titles betray other musical influences, such as *Magyarisch* (in Op. 46) or *Aus der Moldau* (Op. 32). Apart from an occasional Spanish or Oriental tinge, Austrian and Hungarian sources provided most of the non-Germanic material. Among Brahms's last publications were numerous German folk songs which Brahms had edited and arranged with loving care. The last volume adds a mixed chorus to the supporting piano accompaniment—an old North-German practice.

For many years Brahms's songs were considered harsh and unsingable. Yet eventually they found their way into every great singer's repertory. They do not place exaggerated demands on the voice, but they do require a maximum of stylistic refinement and good taste.

M-MM-453, A Brahms Recital, Lotte Lehmann, Soprano.

SYMPHONY NO. 1, IN C MINOR, OP. 68

Un poco sostenuto; Allegro · Andante sostenuto · Un poco allegretto e grazioso · Adagio, più andante; Allegro non troppo ma con brio

MANY of music's greatest composers began to experiment with the symphonic form almost as soon as they had mastered the elements of composition and orchestration. Mozart had completed his twentieth symphony by the time he reached his sixteenth year. Not so Johannes Brahms. It is characteristic of this great master that he did not essay the symphonic form until he had attained artistic maturity. He was forty-two years old and had behind him such achievements as the *German Requiem*, the D minor Piano Concerto, as well as many lesser works. There is hardly a parallel case of a composer so well qualified who waited so long to test his symphonic powers. As would be fully expected under the circumstances, when Brahms did elect to turn his talents to writing symphonies, he revealed a mastery at once complete and full-grown. Of the four symphonies which Brahms wrote, all are acknowledged masterpieces, and each reveals a different facet of the composer's technical mastery and the nature of his personal outlook on life.

Brahms could be both profound and informal, serious and gentle. These contrasts are especially evident in the flowing lyricism of the Allegretto e grazioso (third movement) and in the impressive chorale which occurs in the last movement. To many, this chorale is the crux of the entire work, much as the fugal finale of Mozart's *Jupiter* Symphony is a climax to which preceding movements are but a prologue.

It also demonstrates a peculiar Brahmsian talent to be heavy without being wearisome. The near-violence of some of his movements have a certain infectious enthusiasm of which the listener becomes a willing partner.

This work reveals a richness of feeling which is without precedent or successor. It has the honesty and rebelliousness of Beethoven, and a magnificence of its own which might have been foreshadowed with much less intensity in the symphonies of Schumann.

M-MM-621, Philharmonic-Symphony Orchestra of New York, Artur Rodzinski Conducting.

SYMPHONY NO. 2 IN D MAJOR, OP. 73

Allegro non troppo · Adagio non troppo · Allegretto grazioso
Allegro con spirito

BRAHMS was convinced that his music brought little cheer into the world. Even regarding his Second Symphony, conceived in the summer of 1877 in the pleasant surroundings of rural Pörtschach and permeated with pastoral charm and lightness, the composer wrote to his publisher: "I have never written anything quite so sad. The score should be printed with black edges." It is possible that in making this singularly misleading estimate of the Second Symphony, he was thinking chiefly of the Adagio, which indeed is profoundly meditative, if not hopelessly sad.

In any event, his dearest friends did not all agree with him. Clara Schumann's diary contains the following entry, made after Brahms had played portions of the Symphony to her: "Johannes came this evening and played the first movement of his Second Symphony in D major, and it delighted me. . . . Also, he played some of the last movement, which gave me great joy. This Symphony will bring him more success than the first, and its genius and marvelous workmanship will impress the musicians, too."

The Symphony No. 2 was completed in only a few months, which was remarkable, considering that it took Brahms fifteen years to compose his First Symphony. The composer was naturally eager to hear the new work performed as soon as possible. But there were obstacles. Finally these were overcome and a performance was announced in Vienna. But the copyist entrusted with the task of preparing the parts for the orchestra had not finished his work when the time for rehearsals arrived and the première was postponed for three weeks. Eventually it took place on December 30, 1877, at a concert of the Vienna Philharmonic, Hans Richter conducting.

The Symphony had an immediate success with the Viennese public, which found its tender, lyric moods more to its taste than the austerities of the C minor Symphony. Brahms himself conducted the first Leipzig performance some little time later, and here the music had a mixed reception: there were "Brahmins" who evidently felt it beneath the dignity of their idol to deal in charm. There is evidence that Brahms was influenced by their opinions. For, three days after the Leipzig performance, he wrote to his publisher and asked him whether the first movement should not be rewritten. Characteristically, he inquired whether the new first movement should not be in a minor key. However, his doubts were soon suppressed, all thought and talk of revising the work came to an end, and the published edition conformed in all essential details to the manuscript score from which the Symphony received its first performances.

M-MM-493, London Philharmonic Orchestra, Felix Weingartner Conducting.

SYMPHONY NO. 3 IN F MAJOR, OP. 90

Allegro con brio · Andante · Poco allegretto · Finale

BRAHMS completed the Symphony No. 3 in the summer of 1883, shortly after the death of Wagner, his great rival in musical aesthetics. To Brahms and to the "Brahmins" this symphony was a reassertion of the classical faith. The Symphony was performed for the first time at a Philharmonic concert in Vienna on December 2, 1883, under the direction of Hans Richter. Hanslick, the powerful Vienna critic, declared that the Third Symphony was superior to the first two, "the most compact in form, the clearest in the details, and the most plastic in the leading themes."

There were several attempts by Brahms's friends to affix a durable subtitle to this Symphony. Both Hanslick and Richter suggested *Eroica,* but admitted that the parallel with Beethoven's Third was not complete: the heroic element lacked defiance and tragedy. Clara Schumann thought that the best name for the Symphony would be *Forest Idyl,* and even wrote a tentative program to fit the description. Finally, Max Kalbeck, the author of the most worshipfully detailed biography of Brahms, declared that the Symphony was inspired by the sight of the statue of Germania at Rüdesheim. While it is true that Brahms believed in the great destiny of the German race, particularly its North-German branch, it can be questioned whether he needed a statue of stone for musical inspiration.

The first performance of the Third Symphony was given at Karlsruhe on November 4, 1876, with Dessoff conducting. Unfortunately, at that time the senseless feud between the proponents of Wagner and Brahms was in full blossom. Instead of recognizing or attempting to understand the music of both of these men, the partisans were divided into two hostile camps, with each striving to ridicule the work of the opposite composer. At this performance the Wagnerites were out in force to destroy as far as possible the success of the occasion. They failed. The reception of the new work by the rest of the audience resulted in such a gratifying ovation that the hisses of the Wagnerites did nothing but add to the general din of approval.

The first movement, Allegro con brio, opens, as might be expected, with three chords which state the F—Ab—F motif. Then the interplay of themes begins with a breadth and strength that caused Niemann to describe this section as "a North-German epic." After a characteristic climax in the Coda, the movement subsides and ends on a calm note. The Andante is song-like in character; a resemblance has been noted to the Prayer in Hérold's opera, *Zampa*. Beginning almost like a chorale, the music resolves itself into a magnificent hymn-like tune which then fades away at the end of the movement. The third movement, Poco allegretto, has been described as the dance of a melancholy dryad. The phrase is apt. Dance-like themes and melodies are constantly present; there is even a fragment of a waltz which appears and then vanishes. In this movement Brahms was peculiarly and particularly at home. The final movement, Allegro, begins in a weird, mysterious minor, a new device in symphonic construction. The suspense builds gradually until the whole orchestra breaks out into a wild burst of sound which ceases just as abruptly. The suspense motif then enters into a complex development, leaping about the orchestra and building in intensity until the whole ensemble has been awakened into furious sound. No sooner has this been accomplished than a pastoral calm begins to assert itself, and before long the storm has given way to a twilight calm with crepuscular shafts of sound coming from the oboe. Then, when the calm is complete, the opening motto of the whole symphony appears once more, resigned and placid. In reversed form it descends on the strings of the first violins and the symphony dies away.

M-MM-642, Philadelphia Orchestra, Eugene Ormandy Conducting.

SYMPHONY NO. 4 IN E MINOR, OP. 98

*Allegro non troppo · Andante moderato · Allegro giocoso
Allegro energico e passionato*

BRAHMS wrote his Fourth Symphony in 1884–85, under the fresh impression of his fourth trip to Italy, where he was an observant student of Roman antiquities. It is also known that he was reading the Greek classics in a translation at the time. The Fourth Symphony may not have been directly conditioned by Brahms's interest in classical art, but a certain congeniality of inspiration, a certain austerity of expression, may have been the result of these classical leanings.

This Symphony in E minor was composed when Brahms was in his early fifties. After an ardent youth and formative middle age, he had now reached the philosophical period of his life. He was serene, secure in the knowledge of his own powers, working systematically and evenly. He had recently grown a flowing beard. When his friend Widmann, the distinguished poet, saw him bearded for the first time, he found in Brahms's appearance "a symbol of perfect maturity of his powers."

The Fourth Symphony is indeed a symbol of perfect maturity of Brahms's genius. Hans von Bülow, interpreter of Brahms's orchestral music, referred to it reverently as the Thirteenth Symphony, taking Beethoven's nine Symphonies into the count, and continuing with Brahms's four. "Number 4 is colossal," wrote Bülow. "It breathes inexhaustible energy from A to Z."

Brahms himself had no reverence for his music. He jocularly called the Fourth Symphony the "Waltz and Polka affair," the waltz being the last movement, and the polka the third. But he liked it better than any other of his works. He also liked to conduct the Fourth, although he was no match for Bülow in the art of orchestral conducting. For the first performance, which took place at Meiningen on October 25, 1884, Bülow prepared the Symphony at painstaking rehearsals, but let Brahms conduct the concert. Richard Strauss, who was assistant conductor at Meiningen at the time, tells that Brahms, as conductor, made no great impression, but "one did hear the music." Brahms subsequently went on tour with the orchestra as guest conductor in his Symphony, and precipitated a minor

quarrel with Bülow when he insisted upon conducting a second performance of the Symphony at Frankfort, a performance which had
been promised to Bülow.

Unlike Wagner, Brahms was never the target of criticism as an
innovator. But he was often accused of being over-scientific. It was
said that Brahms's themes, at least in symphonic and chamber music,
were derived from the development, which was first formed in the
composer's mind.

The triumph of Brahms as a scientist of music comes in the last
movement of the Fourth. It is a Passacaglia, a continuous set of
variations never departing from the key of the symphony, E minor.
The theme is derived from the bass of the *ciaconna* from Bach's
Cantata No. 150. Elisabeth von Herzogenberg, a musical friend of
Brahms, was dismayed by the technical complexity of the last movement when she played it in a piano arrangement. "It is more for the
lens of a microscope," she wrote to Brahms, "for the erudite and the
scientific than for an average music lover." But when she heard it in
the orchestra she forgot her misgivings: "The movement might as
well be three times as long, and the audience would have enjoyed it,
even without knowledge and understanding of Passacaglia and such
things as that."

M-MM-452, Leopold Stokowski Conducting the All-American Orchestra.
M-MM-567, Philadelphia Orchestra, Eugene Ormandy Conducting.

TRAGIC OVERTURE, OP. 81

OF THE two overtures which Brahms composed at Ischl during the
summer of 1880 he wrote, "One weeps; the other laughs." The *Tragic*
Overture, despite its later opus number, was composed first. Then
came the ever-popular and lusty *Academic Festival* Overture. While
the *Academic Festival* has long been a perennial concert hall favorite, the *Tragic* Overture, among all Brahms's major orchestral
works, has yet to achieve enthusiastic response comparable to the
four symphonies.

Actually the *Tragic* Overture is a perfect orchestral masterpiece—

music of sternly controlled power, unerring in its orchestration, utterly devoid of rhythmic and figurative padding.

Program annotators, particularly those of Europe, have cudgeled their brains in fruitless speculation about the particular tragedy Brahms had in mind when he composed the Overture. Hanslick, *factotum in excelsis* of the Vienna Brahmins, would have us believe it was *Hamlet*. Other critics make much of the fact that Brahms had at one time considered writing incidental music for Goethe's *Faust* as produced by Franz von Dingelstedt at Vienna's Burgtheater.

X-MX-214, Chicago Symphony Orchestra, Frederick Stock Conducting.

TRIO IN C MINOR, OP. 101, FOR PIANO AND STRINGS

Allegro energico · *Andante grazioso* · *Presto non assai* · *Allegro molto*

COMPOSED during a summer vacation at Thun, Switzerland, in 1886, this Trio is characteristic of all Brahms's works in C minor. They all reflect a dramatic, somber, passionate struggle; they all suggest defiance and pessimism at turns. This C minor Trio is the most important Brahms work for three instruments and is something of a counterpart to the C minor Piano Quartet. But while the latter work reflects the emotional disturbances of early manhood, the Trio is the product of a mature man who has learned restraint, resignation, and suppressed feelings.

The opening movement is built entirely from a four-note motive, characteristic of Brahms's vigor and terseness. (It is remarkable, indeed, that Brahms's method of composition seemed to grow increasingly involved as he grew older, while the musical substance became simpler.) The second and third movements provide relaxation; they are written in a light and charming vein, employing thematic material that has folk-song simplicity. An unusual combination of double and triple time in the third movement compensates for lack of melodic variety. The finale has a scherzo character and develops into a powerful Coda.

VARIATIONS ON A THEME BY HAYDN,
OP. 56a

BRAHMS was fond of variations, in which he could demonstrate his contrapuntal skill. While he always embellished any theme, it was still recognizable underneath a garland of appoggiaturas and scale passages. Also, the tonic key in Brahmsian variations remains a tonic, major or minor, in the variations. In short, the composer believed that variations should be transfigurations of the theme, rather than aberrations from it.

Brahms composed the *Variations on a Theme by Haydn* in 1872–73. Some years earlier Haydn's biographer, C. F. Pohl, had shown him a number of unpublished compositions by the eighteenth-century master. From one of these, a Divertimento in B-flat for wind instruments, Brahms copied the theme used in the Variations. This theme, labeled *Chorale Antoni* in the manuscript of the Divertimento, may not have been original with Haydn.

Brahms's Variations exist in two forms—for orchestra, and for two pianos. There is disagreement as to which preceded which. The two-piano version was the first performed (by Brahms and Clara Schumann, before an audience of friends in the late summer of 1873) and the first published. But there is some evidence that the orchestral version was written first.

Kalbeck, Brahms's biographer, who suggested that the Variations were intended as musical illustrations of the temptations of St. Anthony, saw in the seventh variation visions of Leda and the Swan. But the sentiment of the music is untinged by voluptuousness.

X-MX-225, for orchestra, Dimitri Mitropoulos Conducting the Minneapolis Symphony Orchestra.
X-MX-181, for two pianos, Bartlett and Robertson, Duo-Pianists.

WALTZES, OP. 39, FOR PIANO

"BRAHMS and waltzes! The two words stare at each other in amazement!" cried the Viennese critic, Hanslick. And he greeted Brahms's Op. 39, which was dedicated to him, "as a sort of conversion on the part of Brahms to the creed of Haydn, Mozart, and Schubert."

The volume of 16 four-hand Waltzes, composed in January 1865, was Brahms's first tangible reaction to his new surroundings in Vienna. There the Johann Strauss madness was at its peak. The appearance of each new waltz was celebrated as a major artistic event. Brahms did not intend to keep aloof from this general passion for waltzes. (Actually, the later mutual admiration of, and friendship between, the morose North German and the Waltz King belong among the curiosities in musical history.)

Brahms did not dance; and his Waltzes are not ballroom music. Brahms brought waltz melodies and rhythms into artistic form, and intended that his pieces be played by two persons in intimate performances. These pieces catch Brahms in his most social mood. They reveal the intimate side of his nature—his pleasure at little things. The Waltzes are short and simple. Some resemble a Schubert *Ländler;* others, a gypsy dance; some are tender or dreamy; others, playful, excited, corybantic. In the last of the Waltzes the stern North-German musician asserts himself: it is a graceful piece in double counterpoint.

The Waltzes were at once made available in numerous arrangements. One of the best known of these arrangements today is that of the graceful A-flat major Waltz, by David Hochstein for the violin.

Two more volumes of Waltzes appeared in 1869 and 1877 respectively. These were the *Liebeslieder* Waltzes, Op. 52a, and the *Neue Liebeslieder* Waltzes, Op. 65a, piano arrangements of his vocal quartets with piano accompaniment (Opp. 52 and 65).

M-MM-342, Anatole Kitain, Pianist.

Max Bruch

1838–1920

M AX BRUCH, German Romantic, was not a first-line composer. His reputation rests almost entirely on a half dozen concert pieces for solo violin or solo 'cello and orchestra. Clearly his was a lesser talent, yet it sufficed for the uses to which he put it. His best works, in which ends and means are perfectly balanced, are admirable, and deservedly popular with performers and general public alike.

He was born in Cologne in 1838, and took to music early. A symphony, composed and performed when he was only fourteen, brought him a scholarship with Ferdinand Hiller. In 1863, Bruch composed his first successful work, the opera *Die Loreley*. In 1865, Bruch became conductor of orchestral concerts in Coblenz. After holding various other musical posts, he settled permanently in Berlin to become one of its dominant musical figures for many decades. From 1892 to 1904 he was head of the master school of composition of the Royal High School of Music. He died in Berlin in 1920.

CONCERTO IN G MINOR, OP. 26, FOR VIOLIN AND ORCHESTRA

Allegro moderato · Adagio · Allegro energico

CHIEF among Bruch's works is the beautiful First Concerto in G minor for violin and orchestra which Bruch began when he was nineteen, but which he completed nine years later. Bruch, himself a pianist, understood perfectly the nature and capacity of the violin, and the solo part of the concerto is a masterly exercise in idiomatic writing for that instrument. This is one reason for its continuing popularity with performers. Its appeal for listeners is due to Bruch's melodic fluency and charm, his unabashed frankness of sentiment. The slow movement is a melody of surpassing sweetness and beauty which belongs with the best lyric writing of the Romantic period.

The Concerto was first introduced in April 1866, but later Bruch subjected it to very extensive revision on the advice of Joseph Joachim.

M-MM-517, Nathan Milstein, Violin, with the Philharmonic-Symphony Orchestra of New York, John Barbirolli Conducting.

KOL NIDREI, OP. 47, FOR 'CELLO AND ORCHESTRA

ON THE eve of their Day of Atonement, Jews sing a prayer called the *Kol Nidrei*, the melody of which is one of the most celebrated and one of the most moving in all Hebrew liturgy. It is this melody that Bruch uses as the basis for his famous work for 'cello and orchestra, introducing it simply with the solo instrument at the opening of the work, subjecting it to a series of ingenious variations, and then contributing to it a counter-melody of his own creation, no less poignant.

Bruch's *Kol Nidrei* was first introduced in Leipzig on October 20, 1881, with A. Fischer playing the solo 'cello. It has since then become a standard work in the 'cellist's repertory.

[120]

Anton Bruckner

1824–1896

ANTON BRUCKNER considered himself Beethoven's successor in
the realm of the symphony, and there are those who feel that
he was justified. These protagonists of Bruckner's music point
out his expansion of the symphonic form, his intensification of a
poetic idea, and the grandeur and nobility of his musical speech.
But there are others—and they are equally articulate—who feel that
Bruckner's grandeur is only bombast, that his poetry only overwritten
prose, his expansive style and form only so much pomposity. And so,
the battle over Bruckner has been waged for many years—and for
that matter is still being waged—making him one of the most provocative figures in the music of the past six or seven decades.

Born in the small Austrian town of Ansfelden, Bruckner spent most
of his life in his native country. For a while he taught music at the
St. Florian secular music school where he had formerly attended as
a pupil; it was in this post that, in 1849, he wrote his first talented
work, a Requiem. In 1853, he settled in Vienna, with whose musical
life he was henceforth to be intimately associated. For a while he
served as a choral director; then, in 1868, he was appointed Professor
at the Vienna Conservatory, filling this position with great honor for
many years. Meanwhile, he heard Wagner's *Tannhäuser*, an experience that overwhelmed him and henceforth made him a passionate
disciple of the master. Wagnerian influences are frequently in evidence in his music, while his Third Symphony is openly dedicated
to Wagner.

The controversy over Bruckner's music began early—indeed, with
the very first performances of his first symphonies. One of the officials
at the Conservatory, studying his early manuscripts, advised him to
throw his symphonies in a trash basket. The first performance of the
Third Symphony was an outright fiasco. The critics were savage in

their denunciation; and famous musicians, among them Brahms, were undisguisedly hostile to him.

Toward the close of his life, Bruckner found a certain measure of recognition and appreciation. Performances of his later symphonies by Nikisch, Hans Richter, Mottl, Hermann Levi, and Karl Muck were comparatively successful. In 1891 Bruckner received an Honorary Doctorate from the University of Vienna, and a few years later the the Emperor presented him with a stipend and a decoration. His seventieth birthday was the occasion for a nationwide celebration. However—despite this increasing favor—Bruckner still had his hostile critics. And, after his death in 1896, his symphonies still continued to arouse controversy outside of Austria.

SYMPHONY NO. 4 IN E FLAT (ROMANTIC)

Ruhig; Bewegt · *Andante* · *Scherzo: bewegt* · *Finale: Mässig bewegt*

BRUCKNER's first symphony to achieve success at its première was his fourth; and to this day it has remained the one most frequently performed. Hans Richter conducted its first performances in Vienna in 1881 (seven years after Bruckner finished writing it) and achieved such a resounding success with it that, after the performance, Bruckner came to him weeping with gratitude. As a matter of fact, Bruckner—whose excessive naïveté caused as much merriment in Vienna as his music—came to Richter after the final rehearsal and, in compensation for that magnificent performance, tried to force a gulden into Richter's hand.

Except for its slow movement—a funeral march—the *Romantic* Symphony has a contagious buoyancy throughout. Of all Bruckner symphonies, it makes the most pleasurable listening. The first movement is of broad outline and is highly charged throughout with electrifying thematic material which, at the close, is built into a monumental coda. The Scherzo skillfully uses a hunting subject in music that suggests the Viennese countryside and peasant humors. In the closing movement, the composer utilizes the thematic material of the three preceding sections in a sort of summation which seems to foreshadow the cyclical method of César Franck.

Emmanuel Chabrier

1841–1894

EMMANUEL CHABRIER was born over a hundred years ago, on January 18, 1841. His fame today rests chiefly on his brilliant orchestral piece *España*. Apart from this work, Chabrier's best music was written for the piano. He himself was an excellent pianist and understood the technique of the instrument. In some ways he was an innovator. Parallel formations of languid ninth chords, characteristic of French impressionism, are found in Chabrier's piano music at an early date. Chabrier boldly used unresolved dissonances, particularly seconds. These excursions into the future are notable, but otherwise Chabrier's piano music is in Schumann's tradition, romantic and picturesque.

He was born in Ambert, Auvergne, France. He was, at first, intended for the legal profession. After completing his studies he was given a post in the office of the Ministry of the Interior. During this period he continued his music studies, which had begun in childhood. It is said that a performance of *Tristan und Isolde* in Munich decided him to turn completely to music. He took this step in 1882, became an assistant conductor of the Lamoureux Orchestra, and plunged into composition. One year later he wrote the composition which established his reputation at the time and which, more than any other single work, has left his name alive—*España*. Subsequent compositions included several operas, strongly influenced by Wagner, the most notable of which was *Gwendoline*. During the last two years of his life, Chabrier was a victim of paralysis. He died in Paris in 1894.

ESPAÑA

Historically *España* is significant as one of the early examples of Spanish music by French composers. Debussy and Ravel elevated the French cult of musical Spain to a position of great art, but Chabrier was a worthy precursor.

Chabrier composed this work after a brief visit to Spain. It vividly records the impression made upon him by the folk music and dances of that land. Chabrier incorporated actual Spanish folk materials in his work, including two Spanish dances, the Jota and the Malaguena. In main, the composition may be regarded as a free fantasy on Spanish melodies and rhythms.

España was introduced by the Lamoureux Orchestra on November 4, 1883.

71250-D, London Philharmonic, Sir Thomas Beecham Conducting.

TROIS VALSES ROMANTIQUES, FOR TWO PIANOS

Written for the Société Nationale de Musique in Paris, the *Trois Valses Romantiques* was performed at one of the concerts of that society by the composer and André Messager, well-known writer of light music, on December 15, 1883. There also exists an orchestral version, by Felix Mottl.

The touch of irony in the title is intentional. These waltzes are true to the Romantic tradition. They are brilliant, sentimental, and at the same time they poke fun at the romantic style they represent. This type of musical irony is elaborate to the point of absolute perfection in Schumann's *Carnaval* and, in another century, in Ravel's *Valses nobles et sentimentales*. Chabrier's waltzes, placed in time between Schumann and Ravel, constitute a link between the two eras and two types of musical humor, and symbolize Chabrier's own position in music history, as a Romantic who prepared the rise of impressionism.

X-MX-209, Robert and Gaby Casadesus, Duo-Pianists.

Gustave Charpentier

1860–

GUSTAVE CHARPENTIER was born in Dieuze, Lorraine, in 1860. At the Paris Conservatory, he was a pupil of Massenet, winning the Prix de Rome, in 1885. While in Italy, he wrote his first successful work, the orchestral suite, *Impressions of Italy*. Returning to France, he settled in Montmarte, intimately associating himself with the working classes; his experiences and his backgrounds were to provide him with the materials for his greatest work, the opera *Louise*. An ardent Socialist, Charpentier founded in 1902 the Cercle Mimi Pinson and the Conservatoire Populaire for the purpose of providing music for working girls. In 1913, Charpentier's second opera, *Julien,* was introduced in Paris, and though it attracted a great deal of attention, it was a failure. Meanwhile, in 1912, he succeeded Jules Massenet as a member of the Institute. Since 1913, Charpentier has done virtually no composing to speak of, and up to the present time his reputation rests exclusively on his opera *Louise*.

LOUISE

REALISM entered opera with Gustave Charpentier's *Louise*—realism in the story, setting, costuming and even in the use of actual Parisian street cries in the musical texture. When Charpentier first submitted the manuscript of his "musical romance" (as he described it) to the Paris Opéra, the directors were aghast at this attempt to break down the long-established tradition of a make-believe world for opera. Ten years after this, it was accepted and performed by the Paris Opéra Comique (February 2, 1900) and proved so successful that there was a demonstration for the composer. Since then, of course, *Louise* has become one of the best-loved operas in the contemporary repertory, and has known more than a thousand performances on virtually all the great opera stages of the world.

"The universe is contained within the district where I live," wrote Charpentier. And the world of *Louise* is, indeed, the world that Charpentier knew so well: Montmarte. Charpentier's book, which he wrote himself, was based on a true-to-life incident. Julien, a painter, and the dressmaker Louise, are in love, but frustrated in their efforts to marry by Louise's father, who is suspicious of all artists. The lovers elope and settle in the picturesque environment of Montmarte. Word that her father is dying brings Louise to his bedside. However, Louise remains deaf to her father's demands that she abandon Julien and the Bohemian life.

Louise is most noteworthy as a picture of Bohemian Paris which Charpentier drew with amazing fidelity in both book and music. The use of recitative, on which Charpentier relied greatly and which he employed with great skill and variety, does not deny the composer the opportunities to write fulsome lyrical pages ("*Depuis le jour,*" for example), exquisite atmospheric music (Prelude to Act II, and parts of Act IV), and music that draws richly from the folk tunes of Paris's city streets. The opera is genuinely dramatic, vibrantly original in conception and projection, and continually varied in mood and emotion.

OP-MOP-12, Vallin, Thill, Pernet, with Chorus and Orchestra Conducted by Bigot.

Ernest Chausson

1855–1899

Two dominating influences can be discovered in Chausson's best work. The more important is that of César Franck, whose pupil Chausson became in 1880. The other, and lesser, is that of Richard Wagner. Yet Chausson was not an imitative composer by any means; though he was influenced by others, he was able to achieve a charm, beauty, and power of his own.

Chausson was born in Paris in 1855, of wealthy parents. Powerfully gifted in music, he was allowed by his parents to study it seriously. Though he entered the Conservatory in 1880, he did not remain there long, because he soon met César Franck and was determined to study privately with the master. This he did over a period of several years, becoming one of Franck's most ardent disciples and assimilating some of Franck's creative traits in his own composition. In 1888, Chausson became secretary of the Société Nationale de Musique, which Franck and d'Indy had founded to bring performances to younger and lesser-known composers. In 1899, Chausson was killed in a bicycle accident. He had not produced many works, but those that he had were of such distinction and growing importance and independence that it is reasonably certain that this unfortunate accident robbed the music world of a major creator.

POÈME, OP. 25, FOR VIOLIN AND ORCHESTRA

IT IS the influence of Franck rather than that of Wagner that is to be found in this work: Franck's mysticism, poetic divinations, spiritual calm. Written in 1896, and dedicated to Eugène Ysaÿe, it was introduced by that violinist and the Colonne Orchestra in Paris one year later.

The *Poème* is a one-movement rhapsody that opens in a mood of mystery and closes with a full-throated reiteration of the opening theme by the entire orchestra. In between, the melodic writing for the solo violin is full and soaring, with frequent overtones of tenderness and melancholy.

SYMPHONY IN B-FLAT, OP. 20

Lent · Très lent · Animé

THE ECHOES of Wagner heard in Chausson's Symphony are found in the rich orchestration, the sensuous moods, the striking dramatic climaxes and the chromatic harmonies. This Symphony was the first work of Chausson to be performed successfully—heard at the concerts of the Société Nationale de Musique in Paris in 1891 and repeated a year later in Germany under the baton of Nikisch. The most striking part of the symphony—and the one in which Chausson's individuality is most strongly assertive—is the middle one, a beautiful lyric theme first heard in the English horn and 'cellos, and later carried by the whole orchestra. The first and third movements have a rhapsodic character.

Frédéric Chopin

1810–1849

THE name of Chopin inevitably connotes the piano, for with the exception of a few songs and chamber music pieces he wrote nothing except for this instrument, and for it contributed the most voluminous and most poetical literature the world has inherited from any composer. To the poetry of music he stands in the same relation as do Keats and Shelley to the poetry of words. His works, mainly the product of ecstatic, evanescent moods, are compact of fleeting loveliness; they express in accents of unexampled eloquence the love of beauty, the sadness and the brilliance of the deeply wronged people from whom Chopin derived and amongst whom he was cradled.

Though his headstone in the cemetery of Père Lachaise proclaims that he was born in 1810, there have been much discussion and uncertainty on this point, some claiming that the actual date was March 1, 1809, his birthplace Zelazowa Wola, near the Polish capital, Warsaw. (The 1810 date, it might be said, seems now to be accepted by standard authorities.) Frédéric's father, Nicholas Chopin, though himself apparently of Polish extraction, hailed from Nancy, in Lorraine, and had settled in Poland only after maturity. Following an unsuccessful start in business and a brief military career, he became a professor of French, married a Polish woman of gentle birth, and established a boarding-school which, as it was attended by the children of the local landed gentry, became in time reasonably prosperous, and young Chopin spent his early years in a *milieu* which though far from that of affluence was decidedly one of culture and refinement.

There is no evidence that Chopin was in any sense an infant phenomenon, musically speaking. On the contrary there are indications that as a baby the sound of music caused him actual distress,

Whether or not this was so, it seems certain that at about the age of seven he had developed a lively interest in musical study, taking piano lessons of Adalbert Zywny, of Warsaw. That Zywny was a competent teacher is shown by the fact that although Chopin attained world-wide fame as a pianist in addition to immortalizing himself as a composer, Zywny was his only piano teacher, and this only up to Chopin's thirteenth year. To dispose at once of his formal study of music it should be said that in 1824, after discontinuing his lessons with Zywny, Chopin took up composition with Joseph Elsner, of the Warsaw Conservatory, a learned and masterful instructor, to whose diligence and strict surveillance Chopin undoubtedly owed much of his success as a composer. In this same year also he entered the Warsaw Lyceum for completion of his general education, graduating from this in 1827.

Chopin's boyhood presents not a great deal of special interest to the biographer. Almost from the first he evidenced a certain delicacy of constitution, amply borne out by his general aspect of form and features, which, while by no means effeminate, were of the type which seemingly attract adulatory feminine attention to a boy-child. Chopin apparently was favored with more than a little of this. Almost at the commencement of his piano lessons with Zywny he began composing little pieces—miniature mazurkas, waltzes and so on—and under Elsner he really began to develop as a serious composer, though apparently he started with no definite plan for a musical career. His temperament in childhood and early youth was lively and affectionate; he was fond of practical jokes and private theatricals and made many friends among his Lyceum associates. There is record of a play which he wrote, at the age of fourteen, in collaboration with his youngest sister. Incessant attention to studies, musical and general, necessitated in 1826 a summer devoted completely to rest and recreation at one of the Silesian spas. In 1825 the publication of his first work took place, the Rondo in C minor; in 1827 he was graduated from the Lyceum, from which time he devoted all his energies to music, and in the following year had his initial glimpse of the European world of fashion in a journey taken to Berlin with one of his father's old friends, Dr. Jarocki, a professor at the University of Warsaw. A congress of scientists was in session, and Chopin had the opportunity to meet numerous famous men, but his shyness was such that apparently he took little advantage of the circumstance. He spent his time mainly attending the operas popular in that day, and returning to Poland continued his musical studies for another year. A journey to Vienna in 1829, whither he went in company with three friends of his Warsaw school days, signalized Chopin's entry into the musical life of Europe. He had appeared in public twice before, once at the age of eight and again in 1825; his variations on the Mozart air, *"Là ci darem la mano"* (*Don Giovanni*) Op. 2, had attracted wide attention (it was this which called forth Schumann's famous panegyric: "Hats off, gentlemen—a genius!"); the Sonata Op. 4 and several other compositions had been published. In Vienna Chopin was introduced to a wider audience, though he had to overcome a besetting diffidence at appearing in the city where Mozart, Beethoven, and Haydn had flourished. His concert in the Kärntnerthor Theatre was however a great success, and he was encouraged to appear again before turning his steps homeward. Back in Warsaw he applied himself once more to study and composition. Stirrings of romance also appear in an attachment to a fair pupil at the Warsaw Conservatory; this however went the way of most immature and unencouraged affairs of its kind. In 1830, Chopin left his native land, never to see it again.

For the better part of a year he toured through central Europe, spending, however, much of the time in Vienna, where several of his compositions were published by Haslinger. He was saddened beyond measure by reports of the Russian invasion of Poland, the capture of Warsaw and the final dismemberment of his oppressed country. Toward the end of September, 1831, he set out from Vienna for Paris, which was to be his home from that time to the end of his life.

For all the trepidation experienced by Chopin in hazarding his fortunes in Paris, his success there was almost immediate. In musical and literary ways this was one of the most brilliant epochs in the history of the French capital. Liszt, Berlioz, Bellini, Meyerbeer, Halévy, Cherubini, Auber, and Rossini, in music, and Balzac, Dumas, Hugo, de Musset, Lamartine, Gautier, and Mérimée, in letters, were almost at the height of their fame. Chopin was fortunate in his introductions and soon found himself accepted as a member of this extraordinary galaxy. His success as a teacher to the fashionable world was likewise pronounced. As he grew older Chopin's public appearances became less frequent, and practically ceased after 1835.

This period of substantial development was clouded by only one circumstance, namely, Chopin's constantly increasing tendency to delicate health, this pointing always to pulmonary weakness.

Early in 1837, Chopin was introduced by Liszt to George Sand. Aurore Dudevant, *née* Dupin, a high-spirited girl of good family, finding herself married to a boorish, jealous husband, had summarily left him and established herself in Paris, bent upon a literary career. She took the pen name of George Sand, which in time was practically adopted as her own. With a flair for writing which eventually attained high development, making her one of the literary sensations of her time, she combined a nature energetic, eager and passionate. With astonishing rapidity she made her way into the most exclusive art circles of Paris. After *affaires* with several notabilities of the day, of each of whom she successively tired, she had drifted into a rather more enduring liaison with the famous poet, Alfred de Musset. The cause of their rupture in 1837 is uncertain and immaterial. The salient fact seems to be that in the rebound of her shattered affections, being introduced by Franz Liszt to our young composer, she cast her eyes upon poor Chopin and marked him for her own.

There is no reason to suppose that Chopin, for his part, was in any sense a reluctant swain. On the contrary, though he probably did not fall immediately in love, he became in time entirely devoted to her; it is more than likely that her watchful care during his attacks of illness prolonged his life for several years, and it is certain that he never recovered from the final breaking of their friendship in 1847.

The winter of 1837–38 was approaching and Chopin's physician made plain to him the fact that Paris would be no place for him at this season. Aurore with characteristic energy settled the matter by literally carrying him off to Majorca, in the Mediterranean. Here they inhabited a dismantled monastery a short distance from Palma, principal settlement on the island; with much difficulty a piano was brought from Paris and the two settled down to a winter of work in their respective fields.

It would be pleasant to record an idyllic existence for the pair in these romantic surroundings, and doubtless for a while it was, but eventually they appear to have got on each other's nerves a good deal. The food was bad, the natives of the island rude and insensitive; Chopin gave way to febrile complainings, and Aurore's patience, never very great, became severely taxed. With the commencement of regular sailings between the island and Barcelona in the early spring of 1838 they returned to the continent and, Aurore's divorced husband having accommodatingly given up his house in Nohant to her, they went there for the summer, proceeding to Paris on the approach of cold weather. Here Chopin recommenced his teaching and renewed contact with his many illustrious friends.

The remainder of his career is summed up largely in summers spent at Nohant with Aurore and a select company of their intimates; winter in Paris; feverish creative activity in which at times he despaired of ever setting down his elusive and exquisite musical ideas in a manner satisfactory to him.

Early in 1847 came the final break with Aurore, the result of many small irritations which in the large made their continued association impossible. It proved, however, the final blow for Chopin. He lingered on for two years, a man plainly marked for death, which came to him on October 17, 1849, in his fortieth year.

BALLADES, FOR PIANO

UNDER the title of ballades, Chopin has left us four of his most characteristic compositions. They are the G minor, Op. 23 (1836), F major, Op. 38 (1838); A-flat, Op. 47 (1841), and F minor, Op. 52 (1842).

Inspired by poems by Mickiewicz, the ballades might aptly be described as "arias without words." The form is rhapsodic, not subject to any particular rules. Artistic detail is determined by the "story" and the good taste of the composer. (This was a typical Romantic device of musical expression, and particularly congenial to Chopin.) Each ballade follows a definite story or emotional program.

The four ballades are all in triple time, but each is different in mood. Chopin's contemporaries were bewildered at the novelty of these "poetic stories," and expressed amazement at the eloquence of the piano. Historians consider the ballades Chopin's most valuable contributions to music because here his poetic inclinations were not stifled by technical requirements of any kind.

The most popular ballades are the first and the third. The first was Schumann's favorite, just as it was Chopin's. It is long, dramatic, frenetic; yet in spite of its impassioned speech, careful of details. The second ballade, written in Majorca and dedicated to Schumann, is less artistic and sophisticated than the first. Its first theme is suggestive of a country atmosphere; Rubinstein interpreted it as a struggle between a wild flower and the wind. The third ballade is different from the others. Characterized by a syncopated rhythm, it is lighthearted and slightly ironic, one of the few works of Chopin's mature years suggesting happy overtones. The fourth—whose technical difficulties infuriated Chopin's contemporaries—is perhaps the most poetic, the most deeply felt, and the saddest of the four. It has chromatic coloring, and is a typical Romantic mood picture.

CONCERTO NO. 1 IN E MINOR, OP. 11, FOR PIANO AND ORCHESTRA

Allegro maestoso · Romanze · Rondo

CHOPIN composed two concertos for the piano. The second, in E minor, was the first to be published and is known as No. 1. Both date rom the years 1829 and 1830, and little time elapsed between the completion of one and the commencement of the other. There are many references to both works in an interesting series of letters from Chopin to his friend, Titus Wojciechowski.

In a letter of March 27, 1830, Chopin indicated that the Second Concerto in E minor was already under way. In May, there was more news of the work: "The rondo of my new concerto is not finished, but I am in no rush about it, for once the first movement is off my mind, the rest ceases to trouble me. . . . The slow movement is in E major and of a romantic, calm, somewhat melancholy character. It is intended to convey the impression one receives when gazing on a beautiful landscape that evokes in the soul beautiful memories—for example, on a fine moonlit spring night. For this reason I have muted the string accompaniment."

In August, Chopin announced that the concerto was finished and rehearsals about to begin. The first performance took place on October 11, and the following day Chopin sent Wojciechowski a full account of it.

"I hasten to let you know that yesterday's concert was a huge success. I was not in the least degree nervous, but played as I do when I am by myself. Everything went well. Goerner's symphony came first, followed by the first movement of my E minor Concerto, which I shook from my sleeve. The applause was thunderous. Soliwa was very pleased. He conducted because the program included his aria with chorus, sung by Wolkow. Following the aria came the slow movement and rondo of the Concerto, then an intermission. . . ."

The second half of the program included Rossini's *William Tell* Overture, an aria from the same composer's *Lady of the Lake,* sung by Constantia Gladowska, with whom the twenty-year-old Chopin imagined himself in love, and Chopin's Fantasia on Polish Themes, for piano and orchestra. "Now," Chopin wrote to Wojciechowski, "I was in the vein and so was the orchestra and the audience understood. . . . I had four recalls. . . . Things might have gone differently yesterday had Soliwa not taken my music home for study, afterwards conducting so that it was impossible for me to rush ahead at a breakneck rate. He held us all together admirably, and I can assure you that I have never played so comfortably with an orchestra."

Shortly after this concert Chopin left Warsaw for Vienna. On the eve of his departure he was serenaded by a group of friends, including his teacher Elsner, and given a silver goblet filled with the soil of Poland, on which he was never again to set foot. While he was in Vienna, war broke out between Poland and Russia; Warsaw was taken and burned, and Chopin turned west to Paris and a life of exile.

Chopin's concertos have been thought inferior to his best work, and perhaps they are. Yet the E minor Concerto unquestionably has many great qualities. The noble opening Allegro maestoso is scarcely matched in dignity and affirmative eloquence elsewhere in Chopin's work, and the Romanze is loveliness incarnate. The accompaniment has been revised by more than one editor, but Chopin's writing for orchestra is less inept than this would suggest. The Concerto is now commonly heard in its original form, and it is doubtful if one listener in a thousand senses any inadequacy in the scoring.

M-MM-515, Edward Kilenyi, Piano, with the Minneapolis Symphony Orchestra, Dimitri Mitropoulos Conducting.

CONCERTO NO. 2 IN F MINOR, OP. 21, FOR PIANO AND ORCHESTRA

Maestoso · Larghetto · Allegro vivace

THE F MINOR Concerto, known as No. 2, was actually the first to have been written by Chopin. It was composed during the winter of 1829–30, but was published three years after the E minor Concerto. Chopin himself introduced the F minor in Warsaw on March 17, 1830.

The Second Concerto consists of exquisite pianistic interludes which could stand independently as an etude, prelude, nocturne, or mazurka. The first movement includes brilliant passage-work suggestive of Chopin's later etudes; the last movement has a melody with echoes of a mazurka. But the high point of the entire work is the Larghetto, possibly one of the greatest pages written by Chopin. Inspired by Constantia Gladowska, a young voice pupil with whom Chopin was madly in love, it is sensuous and romantic, in the vein of Chopin's greatest nocturnes.

M-143, Marguerite Long, Piano, and the Paris Conservatory Orchestra, Philippe Gaubert Conducting.

"I HAVE composed a study in my own manner," wrote Chopin in October 1829, when he was nineteen. In his "own manner" meant that for the first time he had written an emotional and spontaneous piece of music under a general classification which offered no clue to its musical content.

Two groups of twelve etudes each were composed by Chopin between 1829 and 1834. Op. 10 was dedicated to his "friend," Franz Liszt; Op. 25, to Countess Marie d'Agoult, that fabulous personality who wrote novels under the name of Daniel Stern, who was Liszt's lover, and whose daughter, Cosima, later married Richard Wagner. A group of three later studies is believed to have been written to order for a piano method by Moscheles and Fétis (1840); intended exclusively for pedagogical use, they are of little musical significance.

The first twenty-four etudes have educational utility; but they have aesthetic value as well. This raises them from above the level of the classroom, and even in Chopin's day they were considered not merely important experiments in piano technique but important works of art as well. Composed early in Chopin's career, many of them are in the grand manner, and often very brilliant, displaying the uncommonly wide range of Chopin's piano technique.

The first etude in Op. 10 (C major) is devoted to the practice of arpeggios; the second (A minor) to exercises in the chromatic scale; the third (E major) and sixth (E-flat minor) are studies in expression, the former in the manner of Mendelssohn, the latter in the subtle style of one of Chopin's nocturnes. No. 5 (G-flat major) is the famous "Black Key" study, a bravura piece of the first order but little appreciated for its sound musical values even by Chopin himself. Nos. 7 (C major) and 9 (F minor) are highly emotional, but not quite so much as the No. 12 (C minor), the so-called "Revolutionary" Etude which Chopin composed in September 1831 under the immediate impression that Warsaw had been conquered by the Russians; this etude is extremely difficult and a striking bravura exercise for the left hand.

Chopin was often criticized for his alleged neglect of the left hand. The "Revolutionary" Etude is an exception to this rule; and so is the seventh etude of Op. 25 (C-sharp minor) entitled "Duo," in which the bass carries the melody and the right hand fills in the harmonic background. Op. 25 also includes the studies known as the "Shepherd Boy" (A-flat major), one of the rare instances in which Chopin himself supplied the clue for its program, the "Butterfly" (G-flat major) and the "Winter Wind" (A minor). The fourth etude (A minor) is a study in syncopation; the sixth (G-sharp minor) in thirds; the eighth (D-flat major) in sixths; the tenth (B minor) in octaves; and the twelfth (C minor) in arpeggios. In all of them, Chopin manages to make a technical problem appear artistically important and interesting in a unique way.

Numerous editions of the Chopin etudes are in existence. Those by Klindworth, Kullak, and von Bülow are most widely used.

M-MM-368, Op. 10, Edward Kilenyi, Piano.
M-MM-473, Op. 25, Edward Kilenyi, Piano.

MAZURKAS, FOR PIANO

THE MAZURKA is a Polish national dance, and can be traced back in history as far as the sixteenth century. In one respect it remains distinct from the other more formal national dances—the comparative freedom of form and treatment allowed. Repeats can be made and the dancers may improvise steps of their own.

In rhythm the mazurka has always retained the fundamental principle of a marked "three" time accent. In this it is somewhat similar to the waltz. But whereas the waltz makes for an accent upon the first beat, in the mazurka the accent comes upon the third.

Chopin took the mazurka as a form for pianoforte compositions and put new life into something which had not until his time been treated as a vehicle for serious music. The grace of this particular dance, its rhythmic stress, its freedom, were only some of the boundless possibilities of which he made such rich use. Again and again he turned to the mazurka and wrote three or four pieces in this form and published them under one group. In this way the store of Chopin Mazurkas increased rapidly, so that no less than fifty-one of these compositions now exist to enrich the repertoire of the pianoforte.

M-MM-159, Ignaz Friedman, Piano.

NOCTURNES, FOR PIANO

CHOPIN's first three nocturnes, Op. 9, were published in 1833, when the composer was twenty-three. The same year saw the publication of the first twelve etudes; the young Chopin had thus already worked out for himself a completely new piano idiom and a new technique. John Field, the creator of the nocturne, passed the winter of 1832–33 in Paris, and his playing of his own works may have had some influence on Chopin. The latter, however, at a bound carried the nocturne beyond the best of his predecessors.

The second set of three, Op. 15, was published in 1834. The early one in E minor was found among his papers and published after his death as Op. 72, No. 1; another youthful nocturne, in C-sharp minor, was not issued until 1895. This last is little known, and is not of great musical value. The fastidious Chopin would hardly have approved of its publication.

While the "nocturne," as a form of music, was created not by Chopin but by Field, there can be little doubt that it was Chopin who realized its fullest possibilities as a medium for expressing some of his most sensitive and poetic thoughts. To Field's form, Chopin brought breadth, expanse, and nobility, while he filled this form with moods, nuances, and atmospheres—gentle and comforting as the moonlight—not to be found in Field's pieces. "They have," wrote Huneker of the Chopin nocturnes, "the exotic savor of the heated conservatory, not the fresh scent of the flowers grown in the open by the less poetic John Field. . . . Chopin loved the night and its starry mysteries; his nocturnes are truly night pieces, some wearing an agitated, remorseful contenance; others seen in profile only; while many are like whisperings at dusk—Verlaine moods."

Some of these nocturnes are among Chopin's best known pieces. That in A-flat major (Op. 32, No. 2) is familiar to all lovers of ballet because of its prominence in *Les Sylphides*. The Nocturne in E-flat (Op. 9, No. 2) is almost as well known in its violin transcription as it is in its original form. Others no less famous are the ones in F-sharp major (Op. 15, No. 2), C-sharp minor (Op. 27, No. 1), C minor (Op. 45, No. 1), and C-sharp minor, (Op. post.).

M-MM-112, Leopold Godowsky, Piano.

THE POLONAISE is the most characteristic of Polish dances. It is believed to have originated in 1574 when Henry of Anjou, ascending the throne of Poland, held a reception in Cracow. As noblemen and their ladies passed before the throne, they were accompanied by a stately and measured music adapted for the occasion from an old processional country dance. This ceremonial was repeated whenever a foreigner ascended the Polish throne. Gradually, the music became the opening dance at all court festivities. It developed into a pageant, and sometimes was converted into a song with a political text. It became a symbol of Polish chivalry in war and in love.

It was during the 17th century that it assumed its later form and adopted its strongly national character. In the early 18th century, it became internationally popular. Shortly after the rise of the King of Saxony to the throne of Poland (1733) we find it described in a German theoretical work by Mattheson. Bach twice included polonaise movements in his larger works; and so did Handel on one occasion. The heyday of the polonaise was virtually over when Chopin was born; yet this Polish patriot, living abroad during revolutionary wars at home, found this form to be the most adequate medium through which to express his loyalty to his motherland.

The polonaise is in simple two or three part form and always in triple time. Accentuation on the half beat and frequent syncopations are characteristic.

Chopin began to compose his polonaises early. The first, in G-sharp minor (published posthumously without opus number) is unofficially dated 1822; some biographers believe that its style was too developed and integrated for the work of a twelve-year-old boy.

The first polonaise which can be dated with certainty is the one in E-flat minor, published posthumously without opus number—1826.

Twelve more were to follow within the next twenty years. They reflect in a curious manner Chopin's development both as an artist and as a man. Three polonaises, published as Op. 71 are sad in mood, written under the immediate influence of Poland's vain struggle for independence. The dance and bravura character is still present; yet another trait is in evidence—a trait characteristic of all the polonaises —that of virility, defiance. It is as if the hapless condition of his

country inspired in Chopin not weakness but strength, not submis-
sion but revolt. Occasionally a note of melancholy is sounded; but
the general atmosphere is heroic.

Op. 40 impressed Rubinstein as musical pictures of Poland's greatness and downfall. The first (A major) has been described as one of
the most brilliant pieces of music Chopin wrote, and it is one of the
most popular of all the polonaises. Liszt used to play it frequently.
It contains a strongly martial passage, an imitation of the rolling of
drums.

Another polonaise with distinct political associations is the E-flat
minor, Op. 26, No. 2, subtitled the "Siberian" or "Revolt." Contemporaries saw in it a picture of Polish citizens in chains being dragged
to their exile in Siberia.

All of the polonaises, except two, are for piano solo. The exceptions
include the E-flat, Op. 22 (Grande Polonaise Brilliante) for piano
and orchestra, and the C major, Op. 3, for 'cello and piano.

17377-D, A-flat major, Op. 53, Egon Petri, Piano.
71812-D, B-flat major, Op. 71 No. 2, Maryla Jonas, Piano.

PRELUDES, OP. 28, FOR PIANO

As THE name implies, a prelude is an introductory section leading to
the main portion of a composition, sometimes only a few bars long,
sometimes an elaborate composition in free rhapsodic style.

The contemporary music lover associates the term with an orchestral passage serving as a prologue to an act in opera. In pre-classical
days a prelude served as a short introduction to a fugue or suite.

Chopin, creator of new forms under old titles, expropriated the
name and its tendency toward brevity. But while the preludes
written before Chopin were built on a single theme and were usually
very ornamental in style, Chopin's were frequently built around several subjects at a time, and were austere in their directness. Chopin's
preludes do not claim to serve as introductions to anything. Each of
them contains a musical thought, fully developed. Their form—or
should we say lack of form?—was particularly congenial to Chopin.
Some of these little pieces seem to come out of his sketchbooks in

one piece. Close examination, however, reveals their superior finish, the roundness of their form, their fine workmanship. They are little masterpieces which Rubinstein considered the "pearls of Chopin's work."

The French edition of the preludes is dedicated to Pleyel; the German, to J. G. Kessler, a composer of studies. It was Pleyel who actually commissioned the preludes; his advance of two thousand francs enabled Chopin to take his coveted vacation with George Sand in Majorca. He composed most of these pieces before he left, but organized and completed the series during his unhappy sojourn on the island.

Published in 1839 as Op. 28, the preludes consist of twenty-four little pieces in all the major and minor keys. They cover a wide range of emotions. Yet it is noteworthy that a "positive" mood (grace, even gaiety) prevails over a "negative" one of conflict and grief.

Among the most famous of this group are the following: No. 7 (A major), a mazurka in miniature; No. 13 (F-sharp minor), considered by many the most beautiful of the group, possessing a strong religious feeling; No. 15 (D-flat major), subtitled the "Raindrop" Prelude because a brief note in the accompaniment is repeated almost without interruption suggestive of descending raindrops; No. 17 (A-flat major), a lovely melody superimposed on a simple harmonic background—a piece said to have overcome Moscheles's antagonism to Chopin.

The fourth and sixth preludes were played at Chopin's funeral services at the Madeleine church.

M-MM-523, Egon Petri, Piano.

WALTZES, FOR PIANO

During his visit to Vienna, Chopin wrote: "I have acquired nothing particularly Viennese; and I still cannot play waltzes."

Perhaps he could not play waltzes in the traditional Viennese ballroom manner, but he certainly could compose dance poems in that form. His fifteen waltzes were inspired by Johann Strauss I (the father), whose popularity was at a peak when Chopin came to Vienna. Some of Chopin's waltzes are stylized dances and could well be utilized in the ballroom; others, however, are lyric poems in waltz-time, which some biographers have described as "dances of the soul." All of them are characterized by aristocratic elegance.

The first of the waltzes is the one in E-flat, Op. 18. It is the most rhythmic of them all, and is subtitled "Grande."

Op. 34, published in 1838, consists of three waltzes. The third of these (F major) is sometimes called the "Cat" Waltz. According to a story by no means authentic, Chopin's cat ran up and down the keyboard as he was in the act of composing, and gave him the idea for the appoggiatura passage in the fourth section.

The waltz in A-flat, Op. 42, was published in 1840. It is the most interesting of these pieces from the point of view of its adaptability to the dance, containing as it does an intricate combination of double and triple time.

Three waltzes are found in Op. 64, published in 1847. The first (D-flat) has acquired the sobriquet of "Dog" Waltz because, according to legend, it was inspired by the sight of George Sand's dog chasing its own tail.

The seven posthumous waltzes include two early ones (1829) published without opus numbers in 1868 and 1872 (E minor and E major respectively).

In 1855, five waltzes were published as Opp. 69 and 70. The former contains two dating from 1835 and 1829 the latter, three waltzes composed in 1835, 1843, and 1829. Two of these were composed while Chopin was violently in love, the one in F minor (Op. 69 No. 1) inspired by and dedicated to "Mlle. Marie," whom Chopin had met during a holiday trip, and the one in D-flat (Op. 70, No. 3) written for Constantia Gladowska, Chopin's sweetheart at the Warsaw Conservatory.

M-MM-626, 4 waltzes, Maryla Jonas, Piano.

Aaron Copland

1900–

FEW will deny Aaron Copland a position of first importance among the American composers of our time. Through the written and spoken word, and through his association with important organizations, he has been a passionate advocate of the modern American composer; but it is perhaps in his own music, which forms a basic part of the concert repertory of our times, that he has most successfully furthered the cause of contemporary musical expression in this country. He was born in Brooklyn, New York, in 1900. After preliminary studies with Victor Wittgenstein, Clarence Adler and Rubin Goldmark, he went to Paris (in 1921) to become the first enrolled pupil of the newly founded Fontainebleau School of Music. There he came into contact with Nadia Boulanger, who became his teacher and exerted a profound influence on his development.

Copland first achieved success as a composer with music written in a jazz style, notably the *Music for the Theatre* and the Concerto for Piano and Orchestra. Since then, his style has undergone subtle changes, has arrived at greater directness of speech and simplification, and has absorbed within itself American folk traits.

In 1930, Copland won a $5,000 award of the RCA Victor Company for his *Dance Symphony,* and five years after that he received the Pulitzer Prize. Besides his great success as a composer for the concert stage, Copland has also won high praise for his musical contributions to radio and the screen.

EL SALÓN MÉXICO

Mr. Copland has provided the following information about this work:

"During my first visit to Mexico, in the fall of 1932, I conceived the idea of writing a piece based on Mexican themes. I suppose there is nothing strange in such an idea. Any composer who goes outside his native land wants to return bearing musical souvenirs. In this case my musical souvenirs must have been very memorable, since it wasn't until 1933 that I began to assemble them into the form of an orchestral work. From the very beginning, the idea . . . was connected in my mind with a popular dance hall in Mexico City called *Salón México*. . . . I realized that it would be foolish for me to attempt to translate into sounds the more profound side of Mexico: the Mexico of the ancient civilizations or the revolutionary Mexico of today. In order to do that one must really know a country. All that I could hope to do was to reflect the Mexico of the tourists, and that is why I thought of the *Salón México*. Because one felt, in that 'hot spot,' in a very natural and unaffected way, a close contact with the Mexican people. It wasn't the music I heard, but the spirit that I felt there, which attracted me. Something of that spirit is what I hope to have put into my music.

I followed no general rule in the use of the themes that I treated. Almost all of them come from the *Cancionero Mexicano* by Frances Toor, or from the erudite work of Ruben M. Campos, *El Folk-lore y la Musica Mexicana*. To both authors I owe thanks. Probably the most direct quotation of a complete melody is that of *El Mosco* (No. 84 in the book by Campos), which is presented twice, immediately after the introductory measures (in which may be found fragments of *El Palo Verde* and of *La Jesusita.*)"

A LINCOLN PORTRAIT

The composer has this to say of the *Lincoln Portrait:*

"It was in January, 1942, that André Kostelanetz suggested the idea of my writing a musical portrait of a great American. He put teeth into the proposal by offering to commission such a piece and play it extensively. My first thought was to do a portrait of Walt Whitman, the patron poet of all American composers. But when Mr. Kostelanetz explained that a series of portraits he was planning already included a literary figure, I was persuaded to change to a statesman. From that moment on the choice of Lincoln as my subject seemed inevitable.

"On discussing my choice with Virgil Thomson, he amiably pointed out that no composer could possibly hope to match in musical terms the stature of so eminent a figure as that of Lincoln. Of course he was quite right. But secretly I was hoping to avoid the difficulty by doing a portrait in which the sitter himself might speak. With the voice of Lincoln to help me I was ready to risk the impossible.

"The letters and speeches of Lincoln supplied the text. It was a comparatively simple matter to choose a few excerpts that seemed particularly apposite to our own situation today. I avoided the temptation to use only well-known passages, permitting myself the luxury of quoting only once from a world-famous speech. The order and arrangement of the selections are my own.

"The first sketches were made in February and the portrait finished on April 16. The orchestration was completed a few weeks later. I worked with musical materials of my own, with the exception of songs of the period: the famous *Camptown Races* and a ballad that was first published in 1840 under the title of *The Pesky Sarpent,* but is better known today as *Springfield Mountain.* In neither case is the treatment a literal one. The tunes are used freely, in the manner of my use of cowboy songs in *Billy the Kid.*

"The composition is roughly divided into three main sections. In the opening section I wanted to suggest something of the mysterious sense of fatality that surrounds Lincoln's personality. Also, near the end of that section, something of his gentleness and simplicity of spirit. The quick middle section briefly sketches in the background of the times he lived in. This merges into the concluding section, where my sole purpose was to draw a simple but impressive frame about the words of Lincoln himself."

X-MX-266, Kenneth Spencer, Narrator, and the Philharmonic-Symphony Orchestra of New York, Artur Rodzinski Conducting.

Arcangelo Corelli

1653–1713

IT IS rare that the inventor of a new technique in music leaves his musical footprints in the history of interpretative or creative music. Arcangelo Corelli was such an exceptional figure. He is justly renowned as the father of the new school of the violin, in which the instrument is treated in a virtuoso fashion rather than as a member of the accompanying body of players, subordinated to the vocal line and the text. In the form of the concerto grosso, which he cultivated, he lifted the string instruments to a position of absolute eminence. He pursued the same task even with more emphasis in his six books of sonatas. It must be recalled that the name "sonata" in Corelli's time did not imply the classical form, with two contrasting subjects, but meant merely a sound piece, to be played and not sung.

Arcangelo Corelli, whose time span was sixty years between 1653 and 1713, was one of the greatest violin players of the time. With the allusion to his Christian name, he was described as the "archangel of the violin." He was no less celebrated for his instrumental works. His fame spread far beyond the borders of his native land.

He was born in Fusigano, and after study with Bassani, he toured extensively, achieving considerable fame as a virtuoso of the violin; indeed, in the history of interpretative music, he appears as the first professional concert violinist.

LA FOLIA, FOR VIOLIN AND PIANO

La Folia is the last of the twelve sonatas of the fifth book (each book contained twelve sonatas). There is nothing to justify the title, unless *La Folia* was to mean passion, vogue, or fashion, rather than madness. The origin of the dance itself seems to be Portuguese. At least, Francisco Salinas, the learned blind organist of the sixteenth century, when speaking of Folia in his treatise on music, published in 1577, refers to it as originating in Lusitania—that is, Portugal. But in France the Folias were known as Folies d'Espagne, which is not surprising seeing that the dance must have come to France through Spain, for geographical reasons.

In its meter and rhythm, Folia closely resembles the stately Sarabande. There is the characteristic 3-4 time, with an emphasis on the second beat. Very often the bass figure serves as a constant drone for a set of variations. Corelli, in his *La Folia*, has twenty-three variations. Rachmaninoff wrote a set of piano variations on *La Folia* in 1932.

X-MX-202, Joseph Szigeti, Violin, Andor Farkas, Piano.

Claude Debussy

1862–1918

THE curious feline fellow with the beard who walked about Paris with a cape over his shoulders, and who was sometimes called "Claude de France," was born in simple surroundings in Saint-Germain-en-Laye within sight of Paris on August 22, 1862. On his birth, he was called Achille-Claude Debussy; but this son of a typical French family of farm laborers, city artisans and small merchants later dropped the Achille, and for a while in his teens, spelled his last name De Bussy.

Much of Debussy's life was either run or influenced by women. First, it was his mother who hearkened to his sensitivity and probably protected him, at least emotionally, from a father who had planned the life of a sailor for his sons. His aunt, Mme. Roustan influenced his education, which, at the most, was meager. His studies with Mme. Mouté de Fleurville, a pupil of Chopin, led to his entering the Paris Conservatoire in 1873. (There, his recalcitrance in questions of musical theory made him somewhat of a problem for his masters.) In 1880, a meeting with Mme. von Meck, Tchaikowsky's patroness, led to trips to Switzerland, Italy, Austria and eventually, two trips to Russia. On these travels, Debussy acted as pianist in the group of household musicians maintained by Mme. von Meck. When he was nineteen, he became enamoured of Mme. Vasnier, the wife of an elderly architect. He spent much time at the Vasnier home, and later dedicated the first of his *Fêtes galantes* to her.

Debussy won the coveted Prix de Rome in 1885, and while in Rome, a city he disliked intensely, he worked in a desultory manner; but he was already noted for his restless modulations and his early scores show clearly what could be expected in the way of harmonic innovations. In 1887, Debussy met Mallarmé and began attending the famous "Tuesdays" where he was to meet many of the Symbolist poets. This is an important fact, for it has often been contended that

Debussy was more the product of the literary Symbolist movement than of the parallel Impressionism of the painters of his time.

Debussy's most notable success was, of course, *L'Après-midi d'un faune*; in the orchestral field, he went to further triumphs with works like *Nuages* and *Fêtes* and the larger score of *La Mer*. But his genius as a composer also served to revolutionize the whole art of pianism. Debussy was himself primarily a pianist, and the master of no other instrument. It is only natural, therefore, that he should have given so much attention to the piano, and when his genius is admitted, only natural that he should have contributed so much to that instrument. In short, Debussy gave the piano the full expression of an orchestra: no idea was too big or too small for adequate expression on the keyboard. Such a belief led him to find undreamed-of paths.

Of the actual music of Debussy, much has been written and said. Attempts to classify it as symbolistic, impressionistic, medieval or Russian, have given ammunition to writers, but have failed to change the essential qualities of beauty inherent to the music. Dissonance is only a relative term, and by this time the dissonances of Debussy which were once dubbed "harsh" or "biting" have come to seem "melting" or "iridescent." Though Debussy did use the whole-tone scale, he used it much less often than is generally supposed. And although there are echoes of medieval organum throughout his works, it is pointless to characterize all of his music as medieval.

In commenting on his own work, and in commenting, as a professional critic, on the works of other musicians, Debussy sought to give the impression that the artist was a free agent. "The artist," he wrote, "should be independent of rules; rules are established by, not for, works of art. The artist must seek discipline in freedom." Analytic criticism, he said, is "murder as a fine art," quoting De Quincey.

Debussy avoided the subject of technique, or treated it with studied vagueness. His spoken and written comments on music were deliberately "impressionistic." Yet the evidence of his work shows that he composed carefully, even scientifically. There was nothing spontaneous about the origin of his revolutionary technique; we can study its development, stage by stage, in his works. Nor did he compose rapidly, in a trance of inspiration. The perfection of each of his larger works was achieved laboriously: *Pelléas et Mélisande* was a decade in the making; he occupied himself with *La Mer* for two years.

L'APRÈS-MIDI D'UN FAUNE

THE FOLLOWING is a summation of the theme of Stéphane Mallarmé's poem which inspired Debussy's tone-poem:

"A faun is lying on the borderland of waking and sleeping in a grove. The atmosphere is palpitating with the golden midday heat of an Eastern day. He has seen some slender-limbed, light-footed nymphs flit by; he would perpetuate the lovely vision. But he asks himself, Am I in love with a dream? Fully awake, he begins to reflect and analyze. He dissects the sensations and emotions he has experienced; questions the truth of the dream; recalls it again and again. . . . His thoughts become exaggerated, distorted; his senses predominate. . . . The current of his ideas becomes more and more realistic; at last he imagines himself under the shadow of Etna with Venus in his arms. And while he is anticipating punishment for such desecration sleep visits his eyelids once more; he bids adieu to waking facts and reality and in the shades of oblivion he will go to rightful quest of the shadowy, vanished dream."

L'Après-midi d'un faune was written in 1892 and was introduced on December 23, 1894 by the orchestra of the Société Nationale de Musique, Gustave Doret conducting.

69600-D, London Philharmonic Orchestra, Sir Thomas Beecham Conducting.

CHILDREN'S CORNER SUITE, FOR PIANO

The Children's Corner Suite (titled in English by Debussy himself) appeared in 1908, bearing the dedication "To my dear little Chouchou, with her father's apologies for what follows." The charming way in which the composer has captured the viewpoint of childhood firmly establishes the Suite among the handful of musical masterpieces written for children. Like most of the other great works of this kind, however, this is by no means music for the child to play, but a work to be enjoyed by all and, indeed, appreciated to the full only by those of us who are no longer very young.

What memories of piano practice are called up by the first piece, "Dr. Gradus ad Parnassum"! And with what naïve tenderness we hear the child rocking her toy elephant to sleep in "Jimbo's Lullaby"! The

"Serenade for the Doll" is whimsical and colorful, and "The Snow is Dancing" is a picture of simple charm. "The Little Shepherd" is full of the tender unreality of the toy world, and the "Golliwog's Cake-walk" (containing, we are told, a tune Debussy heard played by the Grenadier Guards in London) takes an unusual interest as one of the forerunners of the modern so-called "classical jazz." The cake-walk, a popular Negro dance of the time, had just become popular in France when this Suite was written.

M-MM-314, Walter Gieseking, Piano.

IBÉRIA

Par les rues et par les chemins · Les Parfums de la nuit · Le Matin d'un jour de fête

I<small>T IS</small> difficult to explain how Debussy produced such masterpieces in the true Spanish spirit as *Ibéria*, and the works for piano, *La Soirée dans Grenade* and *La Puerta del Vino*. For during his lifetime Claude Debussy visited Spain only once, and that was primarily to attend a bull fight at the border town of San Sebastian. However, he had also had the opportunity of hearing authentic Andalusian *flamenco* singers and guitarists at the famous Exposition Universelle of 1889–90 in Paris.

His success may have been due to the fact that the folk music of Spain possessed so many elements in line with his own creative instincts—irregularly accented melodies, shifting and conflicting rhythms, the frequent use of consecutive fourths and fifths. Indeed, Spain's most eminent composer, Manuel de Falla, asserted that without knowing Spain, Debussy had written better and more authentic Spanish music than many a native Spanish composer.

Ibéria, the second of a set of three *Images* for orchestra, was begun in 1906; but it was no easy task to bring into shape. Originally the composer planned it as a work for two pianos, but when, on Christmas Day of 1908, the rough draft of *Ibéria* was completed, the end-result was an orchestral masterpiece in the Hispanic idiom surpassed today only by the finest works of Falla. The first performance took place at a Colonne Concert, Paris, on February 20, 1910. Gabriel Pierné conducted.

Despite a formidable array of instruments, Debussy uses his full orchestra sparingly. Rather, with the daring and subtlety of a master supremely sure of his craft, he conjures up a whole host of miraculous orchestral effects, all backed by unerring feeling for the essence of the Andalusian dance, and a sense of construction and balance.

That Manuel de Falla fully appreciated Debussy's genius for capturing the unique tonal effects of Spanish folk music in his instrumental works may be seen in an article he wrote for the January, 1921 issue of *The Chesterian:* "The Andalusians obtain these sounds from their guitars; needless to say, in a rudimentary form and quite unconsciously; and curiously enough, Spanish composers have neglected and even despised these effects, which they looked upon as something barbaric, or they might have at most sought to reduce them to old musical forms, until the day on which Claude Debussy showed them how they could be used."

The music of *Ibéria* divides itself into three contrasting sections played without pause: (1) *"Par les rues et par les chemins"* ("In the Streets and Byways"), (2) *"Les Parfums de la nuit"* ("Perfumes of the Night"), (3) *"Le Matin d'un jour de fête"* ("Morning of a Festival Day").

M-MM-491, Pittsburgh Symphony Orchestra, Fritz Reiner Conducting.

LA MER

De l'aube à midi sur la mer · Jeux des vagues · Dialogue du vent et de la mer

La Mer was begun in Burgundy in 1903. A letter to André Messager is assumed to contain a reference to the work: "You may not know that I was destined for a sailor's life and that it is only quite by chance that fate has led me in another direction. But I have always retained a passionate love for the sea. . . . My sea-scapes might be studio landscapes had I not an endless store of memories, worth more than reality, in my mind."

A year later the score was still unfinished. It was not completed until shortly before its première in Paris at a Lamoureux Concert on October 5, 1905. The reviews were mixed, and the strain of hostility that ran through some of them was directed in all probability more at the man than at his work. In 1905, Debussy's music had ceased to shock sophisticated auditors; he was admitted to have talent, even genius. But a short time before the première of *La Mer* he had precipitated a scandal by deserting his wife and eloping with Mme. Bardac, whom he later married. Mme. Debussy unsuccessfully attempted suicide. The incident earned a bad review or two for *La Mer.*

Debussy supplied no program for these sea pieces beyond that suggested in the titles of the separate movements—"From Dawn 'till Noon on the Sea"; "Play of the Waves"; "Dialogue of the Wind and the Sea." And the average listener remains indifferent to the virtuosity that the score reveals; to him its wonder consists in its evocation of the multifarious sea.

M-MM-531, Cleveland Orchestra, Artur Rodzinski Conducting.

PELLÉAS ET MÉLISANDE

IN *Pelléas et Mélisande,* Debussy made a conscious effort to free opera of some of the stilted conventions which still clung to it even after Wagner. The most important of his revolutions was the complete replacement of declamation for the aria. As Debussy explained: "The characters of the drama endeavor to sing like real persons, and not in an arbitrary language on antiquated traditions." Besides, the employment of the whole-tone scale in opera, the emphasis not on dramatic action or climaxes but on moods and atmospheres, and the use of a shimmering and exquisite orchestral background to the proceedings on the stage, all heightened the exotic quality of the opera.

To the audience that first heard the opera—at the Opéra Comique on April 30, 1902—what was happening on the stage, and what was emerging from voices and musical instruments proved mystifying, indeed. The première was a fiasco—there were hisses and noisy demonstrations when the opera was over. The critics, too, had a field day.

"The music," wrote H. Imbert, "is . . . indefinite, strange, escaping, full of harmonic hardness." "Rhythm, melody, tonality—these are three things that are unknown to M. Debussy," said Pougin. "His music is vague, without color or nuance, without motion, without life. It is not even declamation, but a continual melopoeia, without vitality or vigor, deliberately shunning all semblance of precision."

But an unappreciative audience and annihilating press were not Debussy's only troubles. There was also the scandal created by Debussy's collaborator, Maurice Maeterlinck, in which the poet completely disassociated himself from the project. It seems that Maeterlinck had intended his common-law wife, Georgette Leblanc, for the principal role; and the directors of the Paris Opéra Comique, together with the composer, went over Maeterlinck's head and chose Mary Garden, then a little-known American singer. Maeterlinck announced publicly that Pelléas was now "an enemy alien" as far as he was concerned and that he wished for it a "resounding and prompt" failure; and he did everything in his power to bring upon the new opera added ridicule and abuse.

Despite this highly inauspicious birth, Pelléas et Mélisande was one of the momentous historic events in the evolution of the opera. The entire development of contemporary opera was affected by it. More than that, it is a masterpiece, the beauty of which has held operagoers fascinated for several decades; it has opened new vistas of musical expression for opera, to the spell of which music lovers everywhere have succumbed.

Maeterlinck's dramatic poem draws upon a subject familiar in literature and legend. It concerns Golaud who falls in love with Mélisande and brings her back with him to the castle of his father, King Arkel. Pelléas, brother of Golaud, is so taken with Mélisande's beauty that he succumbs to it; Pelléas and Mélisande become lovers. When Golaud discovers this, he kills them both.

OP-MOP-13, Nespoulous, Maguenat, Croiza, and Dufranne, and Orchestra Conducted by Truc.

IN 1910, while Debussy's orchestral works were the subject of impassioned debate, the much-discussed composer again submitted a large number of chamber music works for the consideration of an undecided public. These included the first volume of the Preludes for piano. Debussy himself played some of his Preludes at the Société Musicale Indépendante in May, 1910.

The Preludes comprise twenty-four pieces in all, divided into two books of twelve each. They were composed between 1910 and 1913, and are improvisations. Owing to their picturesque titles which Debussy—for purely musical reasons—inserted only at the end of each piece, the twenty-four Preludes aroused the interest of commentators, many of whom displayed great ignorance. Debussy does not adopt any strict form in these pieces, but gives them the character of improvisations or fantasias—extremely free types of composition.

The romantic conception of the prelude as Chopin imagined it, would suit Debussy only if it were transposed according to the exigencies of a more objective art and of a less impulsive sensibility. This is not to say that Debussy ignores the penetrating accents of music, nor is he neglectful of the tumultuous and agonizing power of a sonorous paroxysm. But he does not abandon for them the exact control of his emotion. When he intends to provoke ours, it is not by the feverish means of a passionate inspiration. "He insists, on the contrary, in his last works, on that apparent reserve of feeling, which determines not only the personal character of his piano music, but also the special pleasure it gives us" (Cortot).

Of the twenty-four Preludes, there are a few which the composer probably published merely to complete his two dozen. Debussy did not like the complete series to be played as a whole, according to modern practice. "They are not all good," he himself admitted. And pianists do not always choose the best.

It is probable that in some cases Debussy utilized old sketches, as an examination of the harmonies would suggest. Again, many of the Preludes have the intimate quality of genuine chamber music, and lose a great deal of their effect in large concert halls. People are also apt to forget the meaning of the word "prelude," which the composer did not choose heedlessly. Debussy regarded these little pieces less as works intended to be played themselves than as real preludes: short introductions to more important pieces in the same keys. Indeed, this so-called revolutionary showed many conservative traits.

The two sets of Preludes contain perhaps the most comprehensive exposition of Debussy's dramatic miniatures. In some, one feels that he almost exceeds the legitimate province of musical impressionism, but in general they are original and expressive of their titles.

M-MM-352, M-MM-382, Walter Gieseking, Piano.
M-MM-644, Book II, Robert Casadesus, Piano.

QUARTET IN G MINOR

Très modéré · Assez vif et bien rhythmé · Andantino doucement expressif · Très modéré

DEBUSSY did not write much chamber music, only three sonatas and the Quartet. Referred to as the First Quartet it is, nevertheless, the only work of its kind left us by Debussy who planned a second but never wrote it. And it is one of his masterpieces.

The form of the Quartet is more classic than that usually employed by Debussy. The first movement is in a recognizably sonata form; the second is a scherzo in ternary form; the third—and the most effective of the four movements—an extended A-B-A song form; and the fourth a rather conventional finale.

But there is no mistaking the identity of the composer. Here, as elsewhere in Debussy, there is the beauty of writing, the exquisite detail work, the highly sensitized harmonic structure to delight the senses.

The Quartet was composed in 1893, and on December 29 of the same year was introduced by the Ysaÿe Quartet, to whom it was dedicated. When the Quartet was published, Dukas praised it highly and referred to its composer (then comparatively unknown) as "one of the most gifted and original artists of the younger generation of musicians." However, the general music public and the critics did not take to it at first, and it was virtually a decade before the Quartet took its deserved place among the great chamber-music works of its time.

M-MM-467, Budapest String Quartet.

TWO NOCTURNES

Nuages · Fêtes

ON SEPTEMBER 22, 1894, exactly three months before the première of *L'Après-midi d'un faune*, Debussy wrote to his friend, the renowned Belgian violinist, Eugène Ysaÿe, that he was composing three nocturnes for him, for solo violin and orchestra. The first was to be for strings, the second for three flutes, four horns, three trumpets, and two harps, and the third was to combine the two previous groups. "It is a fact," wrote Debussy, "an experiment in the different combinations that can be achieved with one color—what a study in gray would be in painting." Though these projected nocturnes for violin and orchestra never reached completion in that form, they must have served as the foundation for the three *Nocturnes* for orchestra as we have them today.

The first two, *"Nuages"* (Clouds) and *"Fêtes"* (Festivals), were first performed by the Lamoureux Orchestra of Paris, Camille Chevillard conducting, on December 9, 1900. The three *Nocturnes*, including *"Sirènes"* (Sirens) which is scored for orchestra with women's voices, singing without words, were first heard in their entirety in 1901.

Though Debussy was openly averse to written explanations of his music, he did write this description of the *Nocturnes:* "The title *Nocturnes* is to be interpreted here in a general and, more particularly, in a decorative sense. Therefore, it is not meant to designate the usual form of the nocturne, but rather all the various impressions and the special effects of light that the word suggests.

"*'Nuages'* renders the immutable aspect of the sky and the slow, solemn motion of the clouds, fading into the poignant gray softly touched with white. *'Fêtes'* gives us the vibrating, dancing rhythm of the atmosphere with sudden flashes of light. There is also the episode of the procession (a dazzling fantastic vision) which passes through the festive scene and becomes merged in it. But the background remains persistently the same: the festival with its blending of music and luminous dust participating in the cosmic rhythm. *'Sirènes'* depicts the sea and its countless rhythms and presently, amongst waves silvered by the moonlight, is heard the mysterious song of the Sirens as they laugh and pass on."

X-MX-247, Philadelphia Orchestra, Eugene Ormandy Conducting.

Frederick Delius

1862–1934

FREDERICK DELIUS was one of the strangest figures in modern music. Born in England, he was of German blood, and indeed made his first successes as a composer in Germany. Then he moved to France, and lived there until the end of his days. He died an innocent victim of an hereditary disease that reduced him to a human shell. He was blind and crippled, but his hearing and his speech were unimpaired. Then a young British composer, Eric Fenby, an admirer of Delius, volunteered to serve as his musical amanuensis. In his memoirs, Fenby describes this unique process of musical dictation, note by note, bar by bar, instrument by instrument. True, the pieces thus composed were not of great complexity, nor of great significance in Delius's creative catalogue, but the episode is extraordinary.

The pathetic contrast between Delius in his manhood and Delius in his state of physical disintegration is brought out by two personal accounts, the first by John F. Runciman in the *Musical Courier* of March 25, 1903, and the second in the *Memories of My Brother* by Clare Delius, published after Delius's death. "He is about forty years of age, taller than one at first thinks, lean, wiry, strenuous in every movement, a fine face with piercing eyes. Every movement he makes is rapid, decisive; he is a prodigious walker, bicyclist, and swimmer." This is Runciman's description of Delius in his French retreat. Clare Delius portrays her brother as he was taken to London to attend a festival of his works in October, 1929. "He was carried in his invalid chair, propped up with cushions, down the gangway to a waiting ambulance. All that the pressmen, who had come down to witness his return, could see, was a figure with silvered hair, wearing a gray felt hat, a heavy overcoat, with his sightless eyes shielded by tortoiseshell glasses, and a pale, wrinkled, ascetic face."

Thirty years before, Delius appeared for the first time in London, at a concert of his works on May 30, 1899. He announced his name then as Fritz Delius. The writer has secured a copy of Delius's birth certificate testifying that his full name was Fritz Theodore Delius, that he was born at Bradford, England, on January 29, 1862, the son of Julius Delius, a stuff and yarn merchant, and Eliza Paulina Delius, formerly Kronig. The dictionaries usually give the date of Delius's birth as January 29, 1863, and, indeed, Delius himself believed that he was a year younger.

As a composer, Delius combines traits characteristic of neo-romanticism and German impressionism. His music comes closest to that of Sibelius; there is the same rhapsodic tension, fluidity of form, and an eclectic musical vocabulary. Delius's technique, as that of Sibelius, is purely harmonic, and the solo voices are brought out against the background of subdued colors. Both Sibelius and Delius use simple melodies of folk-song flavor, but are reluctant to develop these melodies in established classical forms. Both are chiefly composers of instrumental music, with abundant coloristic effects in unconventional but effective orchestration.

BRIGG FAIR

Brigg Fair is a famous English folk song which was rediscovered by Percy Grainger and which forms the basis for Delius's rhapsody, composed in 1907, and introduced in Liverpool one year later. The folk song is first heard in the oboe, and is then subjected to elaborate growth. The pastoral mood of the folk song dominates the atmosphere of the entire rhapsody which, from beginning to end, is of a calm beauty.

X-MX-30, London Philharmonic Orchestra, Sir Thomas Beecham Conducting.

[160]

IN A SUMMER GARDEN

In a Summer Garden was written in 1908 at Grez-sur-Loing in France, where Delius was living since 1899. The score is prefaced with the lines from D. G. Rossetti:

> "All are my blooms; and all sweet blooms of love
> To thee I gave while Spring and Summer sang."

It is typically rhapsodic work, with themes arrayed in a simple succession, without any attempt at formal connection. The pastoral mood prevails. The harmonic idiom is homophonic, and parallel chord formations in simple triads abound. The omission of certain scale notes in thematic figures produces an effect of pentatonic construction.

M-MM-290, London Philharmonic Orchestra, Sir Thomas Beecham Conducting.

ON HEARING THE FIRST CUCKOO IN SPRING

THIS exquisite musical-pastoral scene is said to have been inspired by the Norwegian countryside; and, as if to substantiate this contention, Delius injected into his score a Norwegian folk song (second subject). The singing of the cuckoo can be heard in the first theme.

This tone poem was composed in 1912 and was first performed by the London Philharmonic under Mengelberg in 1914.

67475-D, London Philharmonic Orchestra, Sir Thomas Beecham Conducting.

OVER THE HILLS AND FAR AWAY

Over the Hills and Far Away is a simple piece in a folk-song style, inspired by the Yorkshire moors. A comparatively early work, it retains a greater symmetry of structure than found in most of Delius's music, and there is some formal treatment in variations. It also presents a rare example of a Delius ending in *fortissimo,* for most of Delius's music fades away in the softest colors.

M-MM-290, London Philharmonic Orchestra, Sir Thomas Beecham Conducting.

Sea Drift is one of Delius's tributes to America, where he lived first in Florida, and later as an organist in New York. The poem is the first in Walt Whitman's collection under that name, and in it Whitman recalls his childhood on Long Island, or, as he calls it by its Indian name, Paumanok.

Walt Whitman's lines are divided between the chorus and the baritone solo. The chorus takes up the epic geographic description of rugged nature, and the soloist relates the piteous tale of "two feather'd guests from Alabama." The orchestration is light, with many solo passages in various instruments.

The work was composed in 1903, and produced for the first time at the festival of the *Allgemeiner Deutsche Musikverein* at Essen on May 24, 1906.

M-M-290, John Brownlee, Baritone, London Select Choir, London Philharmonic Orchestra, Sir Thomas Beecham Conducting.

Gaetano Donizetti

1797–1848

D ONIZETTI, the son of a weaver, was born in Bergamo in 1797.
Music study took place at the Naples Conservatory, and later
with Padre Mattei in Bologna. His father chose a teaching
career for the boy, a choice so distasteful to young Donizetti that he
joined the army instead. While quartered in Venice he composed his
first opera, *Enrico di Borgogna* (1818), a work imitative of Rossini.
Four years later came success: *Zoraïde,* introduced in Rome, was
such a sensation that it brought its composer release from military
duty as well as fame. Now able to devote himself exclusively to composition, Donizetti became highly prolific. Between 1831 and 1834,
for example, he wrote eight operas, among them the charming opera-
buffa *L'Elisir d'Amore,* and *Lucrezia Borgia.* In 1835, *Lucia di Lammermoor* brought Donizetti to the very peak of his fame.

In 1839, Donizetti visited Paris to assist in the production of several of his operas. Later, in Vienna, he was given the honorary titles
of Hofcompositeur and Kapellmeister.

But the closing years of Donizetti's life were somber. From de-
pressions and hallucinations he progressed to insanity, and for a
period had to be confined to an asylum. Released from this confinement in 1847, he developed paralysis. In 1848, he died in the city of
his birth.

A facile composer, Donizetti always wrote with consummate ease;
ideas came readily to him, and he had the gift of spontaneity to a
marked degree. His operas have the charm of easy writing, and frequently the superficiality as well. However, in his greatest operas—
and in their best pages—he was able to attain extraordinary inventiveness. In both tragic and comic styles, he had a sense for the
theater, a talent for ensemble writing, and abundant melodic resources which rarely deserted him.

DON PASQUALE

DONIZETTI's *Don Pasquale*—which he wrote in the amazing period of eleven days—is one of the happiest examples of opera-buffa writing. It was first performed at the Théâtre des Italiens in Paris on January 4, 1843, and today is a fitting companion to such classics of opera-buffa as Rossini's *Barber of Seville*. It has a witty and light-hearted libretto that on occasion is not afraid to yield to burlesque and nonsense; and its score is ebullient throughout, as bold-faced in its absurdity as the book. Few pages in all comic opera are so broadly farcical as the effervescent quartet that closes Act II. Yet there is no sacrifice of wonderful melody, of which the soprano aria of Act I (*"So anch' io la virtu magica"*) and the tenor serenata from Act III are notable examples.

Don Pasquale is a wealthy, fussy bachelor who refuses to give his nephew permission to marry the widow, Norina. An elaborate plot is concocted in which Don Pasquale is introduced to a charming, seductive woman (Norina in disguise). He falls victim to her wiles, and then "marries" her—a false notary performing the ceremony. After marriage, the charming woman turns out to be an extravagant, unfaithful termagant. Don Pasquale is so relieved to learn that his "marriage" was only a fraud that he willingly gives his consent to his nephew to marry his loved one.

LUCIA DI LAMMERMOOR

Lucia is a characteristic example of grand opera—grand opera at its best and worst. At its best, it contains magnificent music—one of the truly great pieces of concerted vocal music (the Sextet), a brilliant page of coloratura writing (the Mad Scene), and a highly effective piece of atmospheric writing (the Tomb Scene). But it is also grand opera in its more objectionable form—particularly in the incredibility of the book, in its stock-theater dramatics, and false-toned tragedy.

It is based on a novel of Sir Walter Scott, *The Bride of Lammermoor*. Lucia, who is in love with Edgar Ravenswood, is driven by her brother to marry Lord Arthur Bucklaw in order to rehabilitate the family fortunes. To influence Lucia further, her brother forges letters from the absent Ravenswood to prove his infidelity of Lucia. The marriage contract is drawn up and signed when Ravenswood returns suddenly. Discovering that his beloved is about to wed someone else, he curses the house of Lammermoor. Lucia goes mad on the evening of her wedding, kills her husband, and commits suicide; and Ravenswood, who learns that his beloved had been faithful to him after all, kills himself in the tombs of his ancestors.

Characteristic of Donzietti's facility is the fact that this, his most important grand opera, was written within the space of six weeks. It was introduced at the San Carlo Theatre in Naples with outstanding success on September 26, 1835.

OP-MOP-20, Soloists and Chorus of La Scala, Molajoli Conducting.
17313-D, Cavatina, Lily Pons, Soprano.
9145-M, Sextet, Molinari, Mannarini, Caspir, Lomanto, Baccaloni and Venturini, and Chorus and Orchestra of La Scala.
71642-D, Mad Scene, Lily Pons, Soprano.

Paul Dukas

1865–1935

O F PARISIAN birth—in the year 1865—Paul Dukas was trained in the Paris Conservatory where he won the Second Prix de Rome. He was thirty-two years old when *The Sorcerer's Apprentice* brought him fame as a composer. Paul Dukas was essentially a minor poet of French music, a musician of the stage and the ballet. He left little music other than stage works and symphonic poems, and before his death—which took place in Paris in 1935—he destroyed several manuscripts on which he had laboriously worked. To most music lovers, Dukas remains the composer of a single piece, and that piece is *The Sorcerer's Apprentice.*

THE FULL title of the work is *The Sorcerer's Apprentice, Scherzo, after Goethe's Ballad*. A translation of Goethe's poem is printed in the score, and the music follows it with illustrative fidelity. It is as perfect an example of program music as ever was written. The music tells the story so clearly that there is never any doubt as to the correspondence between a particular section of the score and the action intended.

The score of *The Sorcerer's Apprentice* begins softly in the strings and flutes; the harmonies are based on the whole-tone scale, characteristics of French impressionism. After a progression of languorous chords in the strings and some suggestion of the principal theme in the woodwinds, there is an outburst of gaiety: "At last, the old master is gone, and I can now command the spirits. I have caught the magic word, and I remember the formula. With the aid of spirit force, I, too, can work miracles." The excitement in the orchestra grows, and suddenly everything stops. The drum strikes, and the next bar of the score is marked with the word "silence."

Then the scherzo proper begins. It is a beginning unique in orchestral literature. There is a drop of a chord in the low register of the wind instruments, followed by five bars of rest. Three bars of rest are found in classical music, but five bars are a record. The time signature is 3-8, and the musical unit is designated by the composer as comprising three bars. Another low chord falls, and another silence of five bars.

Then the bars begin to be filled with dash-and-dot rhythms. The Apprentice calls on the broom: "Up on your legs, head high! Make haste, and fetch some water." The bassoons, accompanied by the strings pizzicato, give the motive of the broom in full. The ironic B-natural, off the principal key of F minor, suggests that things might come to a bad end. Languorous chords in whole-tone harmonies reappear in a quick tempo. Then the horns proclaim the motive of the broom in a whole-tone progression, emphasizing the sinister significance of the events. A chromatic avalanche is precipitated in the violins.

Now the trumpet plays the broom theme, and is answered by the theme of distress: "Stop! Stop! There is enough water . . . I have forgotten the word that would make this broom what it was before. . . . More and more water. . . . This flood engulfs me. . . ."

But the magic broom now proclaims its triumph in the horns and trumpets, and water flows in running arpeggios in the whole orchestra, and the whole-tone harmonies are here again. No sooner has the first flood reached its high point than the second wave appears, growing from small beginnings in the strings and woodwinds to menacing proportions in the brass. The motive of distress is louder and louder, and there is a break. A third wave of the flood follows the second; the broom motive is distorted and harried, but it mounts higher and higher.

Finally, an ominous augmented triad is sounded in the bass against the metallic roll of the cymbals. The lamenting violin chords are heard again. The unhappy Apprentice addresses the broom: "Be quiet, you, piece of lumber, or else I shall split you in two with an ax. . . . Here you come again. Wait till I get you. A moment, and you will be down. The ax has fallen. A fine blow! The broom is split in two."

The music stops. There is nothing except drops of low F's in the double bassoon and double basses. But the double bassoon shows signs of life. It plays alone, gathering force to reach B-flat, and soon the unholy Scherzo is set in motion once more. But it is doubled by a fugato: "Woe begone! The two pieces of the broom begin to move and stand up like servants awaiting orders." The motive of distress is now contrapuntally projected against the broom theme, but is drowned out. The split of wood is now triumphant in the bass instruments. The agonizing trills of the woodwinds and high strings are a prelude to a new explosion of triumph.

The orgy continues until the solemn sound of augmented triads announces the return of the Master. "Oh, Master, the peril is great! I cannot tame the spirits I have evoked." This last sentence from Goethe is famous among literary quotations.

"Back in the corner, you broom! . . . The old Master brings you to life only when it serves his purpose." The chords of the introduction reappear. The bassoon plays a fragment of the broom theme. There is a quick epilogue: C, D, E, and F, and the adventure is over.

X-MX-212, Minneapolis Symphony Orchestra, Dimitri Mitropoulos Conducting.

Antonin Dvořák

1841–1904

ANTONIN DVOŘÁK has brought the soul of the Slavic people into his music. He was not an experimenter, not the adventurer seeking new worlds. The expression of beauty—and its expression with directness and simplicity—was his guiding mission. He felt he could do this by writing honestly what he felt and in forms and idioms that he had learned from his predecessors. He was best when he spoke about his native land, Bohemia, of its people and dances and folk strains; and even when he chose to write works in tribute to America (a land he admired and in which he lived and worked for several years) the flavor of his native Bohemia lends a rich and spicy tang.

His birthplace was a small town near Prague, in 1841. His father, an innkeeper and butcher, saw to it that Antonin be well educated, academically as well as musically. In 1857, Antonin prevailed upon his father to send him to Prague for a more intensive musical education. Three years of great hardship and deprivation followed, years of study at the Organ School—hardship and deprivation that were only slightly alleviated when, through the intercession of Smetana, Dvořák was given a job at the National Theatre. Greater financial stability did not come until 1873 when Dvořák became organist at the St. Adelbert's Church. Greater recognition, too—for in that very same year the performance of a cantata brought Dvořák to the attention of the Bohemian music world. A commission now came to him from the National Theatre in Prague to write an opera. At first a failure, this opera—*The King and the Collier*—was revised by Dvořák several times, and in its final form was a great success.

It was Johannes Brahms who first recognized Dvořák's exceptional, though still latent, creative gifts, and who used his own influence to bring the younger man some recognition. Brahms induced the pub-

lisher Simrock to commission a work from the Bohemian. That work
—a set of Slavonic Dances based on actual Bohemian dances—
made Dvořák famous.

Within a few years, Dvořák's reputation as a composer spread not
only throughout Europe but across the Atlantic as well, bringing him
an invitation to become director of the National Conservatory of
Music in New York. Dvořák accepted, arriving in October 1892, and
remaining in America for three years. He occupied an apartment on
East 17th Street, close to the Conservatory, and during the summer
months he took his wife and six children to the little town of Spill-
ville, Iowa, which was settled predominantly by Bohemians.

While in America, Dvořák was introduced by the critic Krehbiel
to Negro folk music, which so impressed the Bohemian composer
that he incorporated the Negro idiom into several major works, including the symphony *From the New World*, the *American* Quartet,
and the Quintet.

Though Dvořák enjoyed the greatest successes of his career in
America, he felt continual pangs of homesickness. In 1895, he turned
down the offer of another handsome contract with the Conservatory
and sailed for home. After returning to Prague, Dvořák became director of the Prague Conservatory, remaining in this post up to the
time of his death from apoplexy, which took place in 1904.

CONCERTO IN B MINOR, OP. 104,
FOR 'CELLO AND ORCHESTRA

Allegro · Adagio ma non troppo · Allegro moderato

Dvořák's Concerto for 'Cello and Orchestra, like the *New World*
Symphony, was written while the composer was in America. Unlike
the *New World* Symphony, it contains no American-inspired thematic material; its flavor is Bohemian throughout.

Sir Donald Tovey states that when Brahms saw the score of the
Dvořák Concerto he exclaimed: "Why on earth didn't I know that
one could write a violoncello concerto like this? If I had only known,
I would have written one long ago!"

The Concerto is in three movements. The first movement in an even-flowing Allegro, with a sturdy first subject and a rich, melodic second theme. There is a feeling of quiet reserve about the second movement, Adagio ma non troppo, which includes a brief cadenza for the solo instrument. The finale, Allegro moderato, is almost marchlike in character. Its rather unusual ending has already been described, in the composer's own words.

The accompanying orchestra employed by Dvořák includes two flutes, two oboes, two clarinets, two bassoons, four horns, two trumpets, three trombones, tuba, kettledrums, triangle and the usual strings.

M-MM-658, Gregor Piatigorsky, 'Cello, and the Philadelphia Orchestra, Eugene Ormandy Conducting.

QUARTET NO. 6 (AMERICAN) IN F MAJOR, OP. 96

Allegro ma non troppo · Lento · Scherzo: molto vivace · Vivace ma non troppo

THIS melodious and effective Quartet represents, with the symphony *From the New World* and the Quintet in E-flat, Dvořák's contribution to the idea of an American school of music which he believed could be made to germinate from the melodies of the Southern plantations. That the idea has so far proved abortive in no way lessens our debt to the composer for these beautiful and stimulating works.

In the *American* Quartet we may recognize many simple tunes, artfully developed—paraphrases of figures of melody that have been familiar to millions of Americans from childhood. With this there is a curious mingling of old-world ideas that lends an added charm to the composition as a whole. The resemblance of this work to the *New World* Symphony is marked.

Sometimes called the "little sister of the *New World* Symphony," this is one of the most melodious and successful string quartets ever written.

M-MM-328, Roth String Quartet.

THESE pieces were originally intended as counterparts for the famous *Hungarian Dances* of Brahms. This, at any rate, was the intention of the publisher Simrock when he ordered a set of national dances from Dvořák. Where Brahms had used actual gypsy melodies, however, Dvořák merely borrowed native rhythms, while inventing his own melodic ideas.

The first set of dances appeared in 1878 (Op. 46), a second set in 1886 (Op. 72). They were originally written for four hands, but as soon as their success became assured Dvořák himself adapted them for orchestra.

Before this, Dvořák had frequently used the rhythms of the Polka and Furiant in his music. Here, for the first time, he concentrated on many different national Czech dance forms, notably the Dumka, the Sousedska, the Skoena, as well as the Polka and Furiant.

These dances made Dvořák internationally famous. Overnight they became best sellers. Dvořák's unprecedented mastery in the treatment of folk material, combined with the rising tide of nationalism which seized eagerly upon all native musical expressions, made these dances beloved throughout Europe.

11667-D, No. 1, G minor, Philharmonic-Symphony Orchestra of New York, Bruno Walter Conducting.
17338-D, No. 2, E minor, Joseph Szigeti, Violin.
11645-D, Nos. 1 and 3, Minneapolis Symphony Orchestra, Dimitri Mitropoulos Conducting.
12210-D, No. 10, E minor, Philadelphia Orchestra "Pops," Eugene Ormandy Conducting.

SLAVONIC RHAPSODIES, OP. 45, NO. 3

The third of Dvořák's three rhapsodies, in the key of A-flat, is believed to describe the court life of many years ago—the royal hunts, tourneys, and the "service of fair ladies." The principal theme is first played by solo harp, then remerges as a dance (now subjected to a series of variations) and finally brings the Rhapsody to a close with majestic pomp.

It was completed in 1878, and was introduced the same year in

Berlin. All three of Dvořák's *Slavonic Rhapsodies* are filled with folk colors and rhythms.

X-MX-55, London Philharmonic Orchestra, Sir Thomas Beecham Conducting.

SYMPHONY NO. 5 IN E MINOR (FROM THE NEW WORLD), OP. 95

Adagio; Allegro molto · *Largo* · *Scherzo* · *Finale: allegro con fuoco*

ANTONIN DVOŘÁK's Symphony in E minor, popularly known as the *Symphony From the New World,* is the best known of his works in this form. Although this work is catalogued as No. 5, it is actually the last of the nine symphonies. Being dissatisfied with his first four symphonies, the composer disregarded them in the numbering, and counted his fifth symphony as No. 1, and so on.

There has been considerable discussion as to whether Dvořák used Indian, Bohemian, or Negro themes in his *New World* Symphony. Opinion was divided roughly into two schools. One group, supported by the German musician Kretzschmar, accepted the work as a species of rhapsody on American Negro and Indian motives. The other side attacked the theory, emphasizing the strong Czech flavor of its pages, and barely admitting random echoes of American folk music. Of course, it was true that the Negro baritone and arranger, H. T. Burleigh, showed Dvořák many Negro folk tunes, often singing them at the composer's home.

Dvořák settled the issue later when he flatly denied incorporating folk songs verbatim into his Symphony. "Omit the nonsense about my having made use of 'Indian' and 'American' motives," he wrote to the Berlin conductor, Oscar Nedbal, enclosing Kretzschmar's analysis. "That is a lie. I tried to write only in the spirit of those national American melodies."

Dvořák came to America in 1892, as director of the National Conservatory, for which he received a salary of $15,000 a year. But by 1895 he had grown homesick for his native land, and he refused the offer of a renewed contract, sailing home in the spring of that year. He orchestrated large parts of this Symphony in Spillville, Iowa, where he spent his summers in a Bohemian colony. There he joked and chatted with compatriots, and was freed from the constant necessity of conversing in English, a tongue he never mastered.

Anton Seidl conducted the première, which took place with the New York Philharmonic Orchestra on December 15, 1893.

The symphony is in the usual four movements. In the first movement, Adagio; Allegro molto, there is a substantial introduction mostly for the creation of atmosphere, which may be taken as suggestive of the great wide spaces of the West. Later comes a theme not unlike the familiar Negro spiritual, *Swing Low, Sweet Chariot*.

The famous Largo is the slow movement, to which William Arms Fisher wrote the words *Goin' Home*. That Dvořák had in mind the story of Hiawatha in Longfellow's poem can hardly be doubted.

The Scherzo has been called "eager, impetuous, aggressive . . . sportive in the Trio."

The first theme of the Finale, Allegro con fuoco, is in the minor key, but demonstrates that peculiar thrusting, nervous energy so typical of this composer. Here, Dvořák shows very clearly that the minor need not necessarily express a sad or doleful sentiment.

M-MM-416, Leopold Stokowski Conducting the All-American Orchestra.
M-MM-570, Philadelphia Orchestra, Eugene Ormandy Conducting.

Sir Edward Elgar

1857–1934

Sir Edward Elgar was born in Worcester, England, June 2, 1857. His father, W. H. Elgar, was for a long period organist of the Roman Catholic Church of St. George, in Worcester, and was also proprietor of a thriving sheet-music business. The famous Three Choirs Festivals being such a feature of musical and social life in Worcester, it is natural to find that young Elgar became early associated with this annual event, and his interest in music in early youth was such that his adoption of it as a profession was a foregone conclusion. He also took active part as a boy in glee-club and chamber-music events in his native city. At his school, near Worcester, where his father was also organist, he was permitted frequently to assist at the organ.

At twenty, Elgar went to London, after a plan for his entrance to the Leipzig Conservatory had proved abortive. (He visited Leipzig briefly, however, in 1882.) In London he studied violin a while with Pollitzer, but his formal musical education seems to have been very desultory, as the violin lessons are said to have been the last in actual musical instruction that he ever had. He made it his business, however, to gain first hand experience in all branches of orchestral playing and orchestration. For a while he conducted the band in one of the Worcester County institutions, making his own arrangements for the heterogeneous group of players he was called upon to direct; he also played for a season in Stockley's Orchestra in Birmingham, where for the first time one of his compositions—an intermezzo—was played in public. From 1882 to 1885 he found time also to conduct the concerts of the Worcester Amateur Instrumental Society. In the latter year he succeeded his father as organist of St. George's Church.

In 1889, Elgar married and removed to London, but the change of residence was not auspicious; he received little encouragement either from publishers or concert managers and after two years of struggle went to live in Malvern, where a teaching opportunity had opened and where in a small way he could continue his conducting. Here he remained for some years.

His first real recognition came in 1896 when his *Scenes from the Saga of King Olaf* was given at the North Staffordshire Festival with outstanding success. In the same year his short oratorio, *The Light of Life,* was performed at the Worcester Festival and his *Scenes from Bavarian Highlands* was introduced by the Worcester Choral Society. With this beginning, the appearance of two of his greatest and most characteristic compositions, the *Enigma* Variations and the cycle *Sea Pictures,* in 1899, soon brought his name to the attention of the music world. Their success was such that the Birmingham Festival Committee at once asked the composer for a work to be produced the following year. The result of this commission was what is regarded by many authorities as Elgar's greatest work, the oratorio, *The Dream of Gerontius,* the music set to the poem by Cardinal Newman. Received at first with moderate enthusiasm, it was later declared a work of genius, especially after Richard Strauss, following its performance at the Niederrheinische Fest in 1920, spoke of it with unqualified praise. In 1904, it was performed in London in the course of a three-day Elgar Festival. Elgar received the honor of knighthood in the same year. For the coronation exercises of Edward VII in 1901 Elgar composed what are perhaps his most popular compositions, the two *Pomp and Circumstance* marches.

After *Gerontius,* Elgar composed many works of value, including symphonies, oratorios, a violin concerto, and smaller works. The death of his wife in 1920 was a shattering blow to Elgar who refused to compose a note of music for almost a decade thereafter. In or about 1930, Elgar began composing a third symphony which he was never fated to complete. He died in 1934, three years after receiving a baronetcy from the Crown.

Elgar's music is the emotional expression of a romanticist who is not interested in discovering new idioms or directions but strives to achieve poetic discourses in the traditional forms. He had a splendid melodic gift, a mastery of orchestration, and a feeling for dramatic climax.

VARIATIONS ON AN ORIGINAL THEME (ENIGMA), OP. 36

THIS exceptional work, on which a great deal of Elgar's reputation rests, at least outside the British Isles, was composed in 1899, in the composer's forty-third year. It was Hans Richter, early champion of Wagner, who first made the composition known in England and other parts of Europe, playing it first at one of his London concerts in June 1899. It was heard in revised form at the Worcester Festival in September of that year, the composer conducting, and before long had been played in all of the great European capitals and in America, where Theodore Thomas conducted it first in Chicago in 1902.

The term "Enigma" as applied to the work did not emanate from Sir Edward himself, but was given to it at an early date by those intrigued by the mystery inherent in its conception and execution. Just what this is can best be stated by quoting a remark made by the composer in answer to questioning on the subject:

"I have sketched, for their amusement and mine, the idiosyncrasies of fourteen of my friends, not necessarily musicians; but this is a personal matter, and need not have been mentioned publicly. The Variations should stand simply as a piece of music. The Enigma I shall not explain—its 'dark saying' must be left unguessed, and I warn you that the apparent connection between the Variations and the Theme is often of the slightest texture. Further, through and over the whole set, another and large theme 'goes' but is not played. . . . So the principal theme never appears, even as in some . . . dramas . . . the chief character is never on the stage."

Since each of the variations is preceded by a fanciful cognomen, a set of initials or a group of asterisks, various conjectures, which may or may not be pertinent, have been made as to the identities of the composer's friends: G. R. S. is assumed to be Dr. George Robertson Sinclair, organist of Hereford Cathedral; "Nimrod," August Johannes Jaeger, adviser to the house of Novello, and former editor of the London *Musical Times;* C. A. E. may be identified as the initials of Lady Elgar—and so on. The composer steadily declined to offer further enlightenment on the subject or to elucidate the melody which goes over all but is never heard.

Georges Enesco

1881–

RUMANIA is the meeting ground of many cultural influences, Latin, Slavic, Magyar, Gypsy. But Enesco is a Rumanian Rumanian. His blood and his heritage are free from admixture. His father was a farmer in the village of Cordaremi. When Enesco was a moppet of three, he asked his father for a fiddle. When he was given one with only three strings, he objected: "I want a fiddle, not a plaything." At least this is the way the family legend has it.

A wandering musician taught Enesco to read music. When Enesco was seven he was taken to the Vienna Conservatory. Hellmesberger, the violin professor, said, "The Conservatory is not the cradle," but accepted the child in his class. Enesco took the Conservatory prize for violinists at the age of eleven. In the meantime he began to compose. He then went to Paris where he studied further with Massenet and Fauré. His source of inspiration was Rumanian folklore, seasoned with Gypsy orientalism. This Gypsy inflection in Enesco's music, as in the music of Liszt, is so completely fused with the pure national element, that the product ceases to be synthetic. Generally speaking, the Rumanian element is reflected in the wide intervals in the major mode, while the Gypsy element is revealed by narrow semitones and "crooked" augmented seconds.

Enesco's first orchestral composition, *Poème Roumain*, which he wrote at sixteen, is imbued with the spirit of national folk song. He has remained faithful to this spirit throughout his career as a composer.

To American music audiences, Enesco is not only recognized as a composer, but as a violinist and conductor as well.

RUMANIAN RHAPSODY NO. 1

The fine Rumanian Rhapsodies are outstanding examples of national music in Enesco's catalogue. As it often happens, the earliest work in a series of similar works is the most popular. So it is not surprising to find that Enesco's first Rumanian Rhapsody in A major is the most frequently played.

The early criticisms of the first Rumanian Rhapsody were without exception favorable. The only complaint was that Enesco stuck to the principal tonality, and allowed little variety in his thematic material. But it is by no means certain that in a rhapsody, which is essentially a set of variations, obdurate adherence to tonality is not a virtue. And has not Ravel shown in his *Bolero* that amazing variety can be achieved without departing from the fundamental key?

When the first Rumanian Rhapsody was performed at the Promenade Concerts in London in August 1911, it was so successful that it had to be repeated by request two weeks later. The London *Times* wrote in the issue of September 14, 1911: "Its repetition is not unnatural, for it is just the kind of work which makes an immediate appeal to a Promenade audience. The fresh melodious themes, the clearly cut rhythms, the bright orchestration, the absence of anything in the nature of formal development, and the preservation of the simplicity of the folk tunes in the manner associated with Smetana and Dvořák, all help to make it an attractive work for a miscellaneous programme on a warm evening."

Many years later, when Enesco conducted the Boston Symphony Orchestra on another American tour, Moses Smith gave on the pages of the Boston *Evening Transcript,* of March 19, 1938, his impressions of Enesco as an interpreter of his own music: "The playing of Enesco's first Rumanian Rhapsody had wildness without roughness. Gypsy abandon without cheapness, fire, so to say, without smoke. As a result, the composition, over-familiar from ubiquitous performances, emerged as something of a masterpiece of its type, rather than merely another instrument for generating specious excitement."

X-MX-203, Chicago Symphony Orchestra, Frederick Stock Conducting.

Manuel de Falla

1876--1946

MANUEL DE FALLA's birthplace was Cádiz, the beautiful white
city guarding the mouth of the Guadalquivir. His first
teacher was his mother, who combined uncommon pianistic
ability with a high degree of musical taste and feeling. Among his
earliest teachers were also Odero and Eloisa Galuzzo of Cadiz, and
the famous bandmaster Broca. His talents developed rapidly and at
an early age he was sent to the Royal Conservatory in Madrid, where
he made phenomenal progress in composition under Pedrell. In piano
study he accomplished much under José Tragó, winning the special
conservatory prize for piano playing.

His first signal honor was in the crowning of his short opera *La
Vida Breve* by the Royal Academy of Fine Arts in 1905. Yet even
this brought him very little in the way of necessary financial support,
for, ignoring the stipulations of the contest, the directors of the
academy failed to produce the work in public at that time.

Now nearing his thirtieth birthday, Falla felt it necessary to
make a decisive change. In 1907, he removed to Paris where he was
welcomed with generous acclaim by the most eminent musicians of
France, among whom Debussy, Dukas and Ravel extended sincere
and helpful friendship.

In 1914, with the outbreak of World War I, Falla returned to
Spain, establishing himself in the city of Granada, where within
sight of the incomparable palace of the Alhambra he found a physical
and intellectual environment conducive to the highest development
of his genius. Here many of his most significant works have been
composed.

In 1939, dissatisfied with the new regime in his native land, Falla
abandoned Spain and settled in Argentina, to spend there the remaining years of his life. He died in 1946.

EL AMOR BRUJO

El Amor Brujo is a Choreographic Fantasy, or ballet, based directly on Gypsy material, as its subtitle, "Gitaneria," indicates. (The word is almost impossible of accurate translation. *Gypsyishness* has been suggested as the closest English approximation.) Falla composed the work at the request of the eminent Spanish dancer, Pastora Impervio, who wished a work in which she could both sing and dance. It was written, according to Gilbert Chase, at white heat, each section being put into rehearsal as it came fresh from the pen of the composer. The libretto is by Gregorio Martinez Sierra who in turn derived his material directly from an authentic Andalusian Gypsy tale. It was Impervio's mother, herself a Gypsy, who related to the librettist the story on which the ballet is based. The first performance was given at the Teatro de Lara in Madrid on April 15, 1915, with Impervio creating the role of Candelas. At that time, the following statement was issued: "The composer, whose feeling for and command of his country's folk-music are well-known, saw that it would be possible to write true gypsy music by restricting himself to instrumental dances alone, and without resorting to the gypsies' most characteristic feature, their songs. But he has by no means used actual folk-melodies. Every song is his own invention, and it is his particular glory that he has succeeded in making it almost impossible to believe that they are not actual popular material."

The story, as given in a preface to the score, is as follows: "Candelas is a young, very beautiful and passionate woman who has loved a wicked, jealous, dissolute, but fascinating and cajoling gypsy. Although her life with him had been a very unhappy one, she has loved him intensely, and mourned his loss. She is unable to forget him; her memory of him is like some hypnotic dream, a morbid, gruesome, and maddening spell. She is terrified by the thought that the dead may not be entirely gone, that he may return, that he continues to love her in his fierce, shadowy, faithless, caressing way. She lets herself become a prey to her thoughts of the past, as if under the influence of a spectre. Yet she is young, strong and vivacious.

"Spring returns and with it love in the shape of Carmelo. Carmelo, a handsome youth, enamoured and gallant, makes love to her. She, not unwilling to be won, almost unconsciously returns his love, but the obsession of her past weighs against her present inclination. When Carmelo approaches her and endeavours to make her share in his passion, the Spectre returns, and terrifies Candelas, separating her from her lover. They cannot exchange the kiss of perfect love.

"Carmelo being gone, Candelas languishes and droops; she feels as if bewitched, and her past loves seem to flutter heavily round her like marvelous and foreboding bats. Carmelo is determined to break this evil spell, and he believes he has found a remedy. He was once the comrade of the dead lover, whom he knew as a typically faithless and jealous Andalusian gallant. Since he appears to retain, even after death, his fancy for beautiful women, he must be taken on his weak side and diverted by means of a decoy, Lucia, a young and enchantingly pretty girl.

"Lucia, out of love for Candelas and from feminine curiosity, would flirt even with a ghost, and anyway the dead was so mirthful in life! And so eventually the Spectre appears and makes love to Lucia, whose coquetry almost brings him to despair. In the meantime, Carmelo succeeds in convincing Candelas of his love and good faith, and life triumphs over death and over the past. The lovers at last exchange the kiss that defeats the evil influence of the Spectre, who perishes, definitely conquered by love."

Perhaps the high point of the score comes midway when, following the episode of the Magic Circle, the clock strikes twelve and Candelas prepares herself to dance the dance that will banish all evil spirits. This is the celebrated *Ritual Dance of Fire*, perhaps the most famous excerpt from any of the composer's works.

M-MM-633, Carol Brice, Contralto, and the Pittsburgh Symphony Orchestra, Fritz Reiner Conducting.

NIGHTS IN THE GARDENS OF SPAIN

IN THE GARDENS OF THE GENERALIFE   A DISTANT DANCE TUNE
IN THE GARDENS OF CORDOVA

Nights in the Gardens of Spain was completed in the year 1916 and first performed in London during 1921, with the composer at the piano. Falla published his compositions only after tireless revision and attention to detail. His sensitive perception of beauty in color, rhythm, and design won for him an unchallengeable position as a composer of outstanding merit.

Unlike many of his works, *Nights in the Gardens of Spain* has no definite program. Although the movements have definite titles, the course of the music proceeds on a free plan and has no connection with definite pictorial images. The work is scored for orchestra with an important part for the piano.

En el Generalife (In the Gardens of the Generalife) refers to the gardens of the castle at Granada. This is night music in the impressionist sense, as Mozart's *Eine Kleine Nachtmusik* is also night music in the classical sense.

Danza Lejana (Distant Dance Tune) comes as a more rhythmic—but still graceful—interlude between the first and third movements.

In the Finale—*En las Sierras de Córdoba* (In the Gardens on the Slopes of Cordova)—the feeling is more vigorous, and this movement follows the second without pause.

M-156, Manuel Navarro, Piano, and the Orquesta Bética de Cámara, Ernesto Halffter Conducting.

Gabriel Fauré

1845–1924

IN FRANCE the name of Gabriel Urbain Fauré stands high as a composer. No less a luminary than Roger-Ducasse has paid him this tribute: "More profound and mysterious than Saint-Saëns, more varied than Lalo, more spontaneous than d'Indy, more classical than Debussy—and, I add in spite of my old enthusiasm for the composer of *Le Roi malgré lui,* more warm-hearted than Chabrier—Gabriel Fauré is the master par excellence of French music, the finished specimen of our art, the perfect mirror of our musical genius."

This distinguished composer, conductor, and teacher was born at Pamiers, near Foix, on May 12, 1845. He studied at the Ecole de Musique Religieuse in Paris from 1854 to 1866 under Niedermeyer, Dietsch, and Saint-Saëns. In 1866, he became organist of the church at Rennes, returning to Paris in 1870 to become organist at St. Sulpice. Subsequently he held the same post at St. Honoré. In 1877, he was appointed choir master at the Madeleine and succeeded to the position of organist in 1896, remaining there until 1905.

Fauré was professor of composition at the Conservatoire from 1896. In 1905 he succeeded Dubois as director and held that post until his resignation in 1920. During his career as teacher, Fauré had many pupils who later became internationally famous, among whom are Aubert, Nadia Boulanger, Georges Enesco, Ravel, and Roger-Ducasse.

Unlike many other composers, Fauré was honored in his own country as well as abroad. He succeeded Guiraud as Inspecteur des Beaux Arts in 1892, was elected to the Académie in 1909, was promoted to the rank of Commandeur in the Légion d'Honneur in 1910, and was elected honorary member of the Academy of St. Cecilia at Rome in 1916 together with Sibelius, Ravel and Stravinsky. In 1922 he was given an homage of national devotion.

As in the cases of César Franck, Dubois, Widor, Pierné, Niedermeyer, Saint-Saëns and others of the same tradition, Fauré's background was largely that of the organ loft and of French religious music. But while the others are known equally well for their organ compositions and for their secular music, Fauré's religious works are fewer than his other compositions. One exception, however, is his celebrated Requiem.

Fauré's compositions seem to have attracted attention for the first time in 1873, establishing his earliest and lasting reputation as a composer of songs.

Fauré died in 1924 at the age of eighty. The popularity of his works has grown steadily since that time, and there will be few to deny today that he is one of the great creative figures of the past half century.

QUARTET IN C MINOR, OP. 15, FOR PIANO AND STRINGS

Allegro molto moderato · *Scherzo* · *Adagio* · *Finale: allegro molto*

ALTHOUGH the reputation of Fauré seems to rest chiefly upon his song literature, which together with Debussy's has long been ranked among the best of French achievements in that form, his principal development has been in the sphere of chamber music, which has been critically appraised with the best that was produced during the latter part of the nineteenth century.

Through Fauré's Piano Quartet in C minor, Op. 15, it has been said that chamber music in France won its right to endure. Although over fifty years have passed since its creation, its charm has not lessened. Fauré's first chamber music came after he had written piano music and songs, and the expression of his melodic gifts had undeniably freely established themselves.

Fauré had a rare gift for melody—which he never permitted at any time to descend to the banal. There is an irresistible bloom and a fluidity to his lyricism. The slow movement of this Quartet has been called perhaps the most perfect and most deeply expressive one in all French chamber music.

M-MM-255, Robert Casadesus, Piano, Joseph Calvet, Violin, Léon Pascal, Viola, Paul Mas, 'Cello.

REQUIEM, OP. 48

THE REQUIEM occupies a position unique among modern choral works, and certainly ranks with the finest religious music ever composed in France. Though it dates from 1887 the freshness of its conception is striking even today, and it is one of the few works of its time and type that is not overshadowed by the spirit of Gounod.

Inspired by the passing of the composer's father, the Requiem is an expression of a deeply sincere and moving grief, yet the grief of a man who can accept death and its terrors in a wise and confident tranquillity. This is not a dramatic work as is the Requiem of Verdi.

Dynamically the music is scaled rather low throughout its duration; there is nothing to startle or to come between us and the message of the timelessly beautiful text. Of all the myriad and varied settings of this ritual, surely none is more convincingly right than this—the listener may easily imagine that he has conceived it himself, or, on first hearing, wonder how it is possible that he has not known it all before. This, of course, is the result no less of the matchless craftsmanship of Gabriel Fauré than of his unfailing inspiration.

M-MM-354, M. Didier, Baritone, S. Dupont, Soprano, Les Chanteurs de Lyon and Le Trigintour Instrumental Lyonnais, E. Bourmauck Conducting.

SONGS

FOR THE delicate and soft-spoken Fauré, songs were a most appropriate form of musical expression. He was the prototype of the aristocratic musician who instinctively shunned mass effects. He preferred small forms, expressive detail, intimacy of effect. He made a fetish of good taste, elegance, noble restraint. His credo was art for art's sake, the creation of pure music whose basis was melody.

Characteristically enough, his songs are not classified as *chansons*, which would be their proper designation in French, but as *mélodies*. He wrote about a hundred of them, beginning in 1865 (Opp. 1-8). His last songs appeared two years before his death—*L'Horizon chimérique*, Op. 118. It may be said that his complete evolution as a musical poet is reflected in the development of his song writing.

Fauré selected his lyrics with fastidious taste. His poets were in the very front ranks, and even as he grew old he preferred to select them among the younger generation. His favorites included Leconte de Lisle, Victor Hugo, Théophile Gautier, Sully Prudhomme, Charles Baudelaire, and, above all, Paul Verlaine. He set his first Verlaine poem in 1887 (*Claire de lune*), and four years later wrote music for nine love songs out of the twenty-one poem cycle, *La bonne chanson* (Op. 61), which is the most important work of Fauré's middle period.

Fauré's first song, *Le Papillon et la fleur* is still influenced by Saint-Saëns; but a few songs contained in that first volume, and written in the same year, already show Fauré's growing independence—*Sérénade Tuscane, Après un rêve, Sylvie,* and *Lydia.* The second volume of songs, beginning with Op. 18 (1880) reveals Fauré to have grown to full individuality. The most famous songs are *Nell, Rencontre* and *Chanson d'amour;* the delicate *Le Secret;* the exotic *Les Roses d'Ispahan. Au cimetière, Prison, Soir,* in the third volume, are characteristic of Fauré's most melancholy style.

These songs alone would justify Fauré's claim to immortality. They raised the French song on a level with the German, perhaps less dramatic and emotional, but certainly more subtle and poetic. Most of Fauré's later songs are contained in four cycles: *La Chanson d'Eve,* Op. 95 (1907–10); *Le Jardin clos,* Op. 106 (1915–18); *Mirages,* Op. 113 (1919); *L'Horizon chimérique,* Op. 118 (1922).

The distinguishing characteristics of Fauré's songs are: variety of mood; refinement and imagination; expressive modulations; a tendency toward mediant harmonies; the frequent use of ninths, elevenths, and thirteenths of the whole-tone scale; augmented triads; Gregorian modes.

César Franck

1822–1890

IN CÉSAR FRANCK we have a musician of the highest significance of whom it may be said, as in the case of Brahms, that his work was his life. In the midst of turmoil and revolution his existence was simple and serene, his mind subjective and introspective; his music was the efflorescence of a great soul finding expression in terms of loftiest and purest musical thought.

The chronicle of his days is soon told. Franck was born in Liège on December 10, 1882. His father's family had for many generations been located in a north-eastern corner of Belgium bordered by a portion of the German Rhineland and the Hollandish province of Limberg. His mother, a German, was a native of Aix-la-Chapelle.

It is probable that young Franck commenced the study of the piano in his tenth or eleventh year, as his parents removed to Paris in 1835, and he had been attending the Liège Conservatory for some time before that. It was his father's idea that he should become a virtuoso pianist, and now, in Paris, private lessons were arranged for him with Reicha, one of the famous masters of the time. Reicha's death the following year put an end to this, and Franck thereafter gained admission to the Paris Conservatory. Here, between his fifteenth and twentieth years he made a notable record, achieving, successively, the Grand Prize of Honor for pianoforte, first prize for fugue and second prize for organ. Probably it was at this time that the organ began to take precedence in his mind as a medium of expression, for there is found little further allusion to the piano in any of his memoirs whereas the former was to become his inseparable companion for the remainder of his life and he one of its most finished and revered exponents. It is true of course that in the teaching which afforded so much of his livelihood he came in contact with piano work but this was purely as a part of his pedagogic activities.

For some reason never adequately explained, Franck's father deprecated so authoritatively his contesting for the great honor of the Prix de Rome, in the young man's twentieth year, that César left the Conservatoire (1842) and returned to Belgium, where he remained for two years. There exists very scant record of his activities during this time, but no one can doubt that with the sincerity of nature that was his from the beginning he spent the time in earnest preparation for the arduous and at times humdrum existence which awaited him. Returning to Paris in 1844 he entered upon a laborious course of teaching, reserving a part of each day for composition. In the latter he revealed almost from the start a mystical trend, his works strongly tinged with a definite if unconventional religious feeling. The subtle and delicate harmonic effects which he achieved were destined in fact to prepare the way for the cult of the modernist so ably carried forward by Debussy, Ravel and certain others.

Franck's uneventful life at this time offers little for the commentator. The devoted band of disciples headed by Vincent d'Indy, whose appreciation was to be the reward and solace of his later life, was still far in the future. The present was plainly a necessary round of hard work for the support of himself and his parents. The revolution of 1848 found him, though still struggling, in somewhat better financial circumstances, and in the midst of this troubled time he married. It cannot be said that this proceeding excited any enthusiasm on the part of his parents—quite the contrary in fact, but the young man asserted and maintained his right to lead his individual existence and to have a home of his own. The young girl Franck married was the daughter of Mme. Desmousseaux, famous actress of the Comédie Française. Through this famous and brilliant woman, whose salons Franck and his wife frequented, the young composer became *en rapport* with the elite of artistic circles of Paris. He became organist of Notre Dame de Lorette, while still keeping up his teaching and reserving always a definite part of his time for composition, in which he was gradually beginning to find himself, though doomed to serious disappointments before he finally achieved the medium of expression which he was to make his own. His first considerable work, the oratorio *Ruth,* was given an initial performance in 1846, and certain of his instrumental writings began to attract attention, but in 1850, with the partial completion of an opera which baffled all attempts to bring to a conclusion satisfying to his ideals of art, he appears to have become discouraged with his progress, and for ten years thereafter practically nothing appeared from his pen. The years 1860 to 1870 also constituted a most unfruitful decade in creative activity. With his growing fame as an organist it seemed for a long time in fact that this was to be the absorbing activity of his later life. As an improvisator on the organ he is said to have been without peer amongst all the great exponents of this instrument. Holding in succession several important posts of this nature in Paris he finally took charge of the organ and choir of the aristocratic church of St. Clotilde, a position which he retained to the end of his life.

In reality during all this time, however, Franck was simply gathering his energies for the succession of masterpieces produced during the last twenty years of his career. Of these it is pertinent to mention two, namely, the oratorio, *The Beatitudes* and the Symphony in D minor. The former, a work of profoundly religious feeling, gorgeous in its polyphonic orchestral coloring and strongly tinged with the mysticism characteristic of Franck, is regarded as uniquely significant and beautiful among works of its kind.

Franck commenced his *Beatitudes* in 1869, and in 1870 the Franco-Prussian war, throwing Europe into a turmoil and turning France into a vast armed camp, cast its blight upon composition as upon everything else. Franck, though not a naturalized Frenchman (he became such in 1873) naturally followed the French fortunes with fervid anxiety. During the famine conditions of the siege of Paris he suffered with the fortitude characteristic of those terrible days, and on conclusion of peace took up once more his interrupted work.

In 1872, he returned to the Paris Conservatory, taking charge of the organ class at this famous institution. For almost ten years much of his time aside from his Conservatory and private classes was devoted to the progress and completion of *The Beatitudes,* to which he wrote the last note in 1879. The final ten years of his life were most fruitful in masterpieces of the first rank.

In the spring of 1890, Franck suffered apparently slight injuries in a carriage accident. The effect of these lingered on however and when in the autumn of the same year he was attacked by pleurisy his system was unable to rally.

LES EOLIDES

Les Eolides, a symphonic poem composed in 1876, was Franck's first orchestral venture. It is said that the composer's inspiration for this work came from the first lines of a poem by Leconte de Lisle, although the score is not so designated.

According to Greek mythology, which holds the source of the title, the seven islands between Italy and Sicily were called Aeoliae and were ruled by King Aeolus. Poets called Aeolus the "God of the Winds" because he could predict how the winds would blow. Aeolus (a word meaning rapidly turning or moving) was also a skillful astrologer, and was the father of six sons and six daughters.

The première of *Les Eolides* took place in Paris at a concert of the Société Nationale on May 13, 1877.

X-MX-145, Columbia Broadcasting Symphony, Howard Barlow Conducting.

PRELUDE, CHORALE AND FUGUE, FOR PIANO

CÉSAR FRANCK wrote his most significant works at an advanced age; the *Prelude, Chorale and Fugue* was the fruit of vigorous old age, and wisdom. In it, Franck intended to write in the spirit of Bach; but this spirit is here refracted through a Gallic temperament.

The Prelude is based on the rhythmic figure of arpeggio passages, with the melodic line projected over it. There is a contrasting second theme of emotional, even passionate, nature. The form is classical, in two sections, the second being a transposition of the first a fifth upwards. The Chorale is also composed of two themes, a meditative initial phrase, and a bell-like progression of falling fourths and rising seconds against the diatonically descending bass. The chromatic subject of the Fugue is foreshadowed in the Chorale, but the Fugue proper does not enter until another section of the Chorale is completed.

Finally, after a short cadential transition, the subject of the Fugue is announced in descending chromatics. The subject is imitated in the dominant, according to the established rules of the classical fugue, and again in the tonic. When four voices have completed their entries, marking the end of the exposition, the subject is played freely in various keys, with intervening episodes. The subject is then taken up in octaves in the treble. The bass then imitates the subject upside down (inverted), so that the tones of the subject rise chromatically instead of descending. A new rhythm is introduced by figures in triplets, and the subject enters against this background. There is a protracted cadenza. For the concluding section, the composer unites the elements of all three movements, Prelude, Chorale, and Fugue. Of the Prelude, there is the characteristic figure in arpeggios; the Chorale is represented by the bell-like theme of falling fourths, and rising seconds; and the Fugue subject is combined contrapuntally with these elements, thus establishing the unity of the entire composition.

X-MX-176, Egon Petri, Piano.

QUARTET IN D MAJOR

Poco Lento; Allegro · Scherzo · Larghetto · Finale: allegro molto

THIS Quartet, perhaps one of the most beautiful of all in the whole realm of chamber music, was the composer's only work in this form. He had long thought of writing it before finally, when well over sixty years of age, he took up the idea in earnest. Living a life of hard work, devoting all his spare time to composition when his duties allowed him, the story of the reception of Franck's music as it came out is almost one long list of disappointment to him, for no composer has been more misunderstood through the lack of knowledge and sympathy on the part of his hearers. Encouraged by a small band of followers, Franck went on until this Quartet was performed—in his sixty-ninth year—at a concert given in Paris by the Société Nationale de Musique in 1890—when its performance was greeted by tremendous applause. "There, you see," he said, when discussing the concert, "the public is beginning to understand me at last." This remark, from a man close on seventy years of age, is typical of Franck, who was not to enjoy the sunshine of recognition for long, but this quartet won for him, during his lifetime, a taste of those fruits of popularity which he so richly deserved.

The Quartet contains some of the most spiritual passages ever written by César Franck, and to appreciate his very individual musical "idiom"—or language—a sympathetic understanding of the composer is essential. Simple and kind, working hard as a teacher and an organist, the picture of him sitting alone in his organ-loft has often been drawn, but it was when there that he seems to have received so much inspiration. Having an intense, mystical nature, much of his music seems to express a personal "groping" for happiness, and all of a sudden, as if lit by an unearthly light, his music glows with a spirit that lifts both it and the hearer far above this world, so that one seems to be approaching—with Franck—the realms of that peace and happiness which is always just "out of reach" for so many, and which it is granted to few to hand on the torch to lead us there.

M-MM-128, London String Quartet.

QUINTET IN F MINOR, FOR PIANO AND STRINGS

Molto moderato quasi lento; Allegro · Lento con molto sentimento Allegro non troppo ma con fuoco

IN HIS youthful days Franck composed four trios for piano and strings, three being written in 1840 and the fourth in 1842. In these four early works we find little or nothing to foreshadow the glory of the composer's later and only piano quintet. The Quintet in F minor was first played at a concert of the Société Nationale de Musique by the Marsick Quartet with Saint-Saëns at the piano.

The Quintet by Franck is a forerunner of a large class of the more recent ensemble works of this nature. It was composed on what was then considered broad modern lines, the string sounds being more a single mass, treated as one voice rather than as four. Much of the writing for the strings is in unison, and the piano part is always extremely interesting and melodious. In the slow movement Franck reveals many new beauties of ensemble writing full of delicacy and with a profound depth of sentiment.

M-MM-334, E. Robert Schmitz, Piano, and the Roth String Quartet.

[193]

SONATA IN A MAJOR, FOR VIOLIN AND PIANO

Allegretto ben moderato · Allegro · Ben moderato: recitativo-fantasia Allegretto poco mosso

THIS work was the composer's only venture into chamber music for two instruments. It was composed in 1886, and was introduced by Eugène Ysaÿe, to whom it was dedicated.

According to Franck's pupil, Vincent d'Indy, the entire work develops from a simple basic idea—a rising and falling inflection—which adds to the feeling of unity already obtained through the use of the cyclic form. Though the four movements contrast emotionally, the basic mood of the entire sonata remains the same, that of mysticism; toward the end of the work a strong religious note is sounded.

The second movement is in strict sonata form, while the first deviates from the classic pattern. The emotional plan of the first movement demanded that the development section be eliminated (the exposition leads directly into the recapitulation) and that the movement be played in a "fairly moderate" pace, which is slightly slower than the customary Allegro. The second movement is more varied and agitated than the first and makes elaborate use of chromaticism. The third is partly in recitativo, partly in an impressive rhapsodic style, very long, serious and in the "grand manner." The finale begins with a classical example of canonic writing.

SYMPHONIC VARIATIONS, FOR PIANO AND ORCHESTRA

FRANCK composed his *Symphonic Variations* in 1885, and it was introduced at a concert of the Société Nationale on January 30, 1887. The work had been poorly rehearsed, and the audience appeared completely cool to the new work. Yet, despite this inauspicious birth, this work grew up to be one of the most frequently heard of Franck's compositions.

It was not Franck's intention in this work to state a theme and then to follow it with a series of variations. He had in mind a large and integrated work of symphonic scope, in which ideas are presented and enlarged and in which variations are bridged together by amplified transitions. Indeed, the theme does not introduce the work. The opening consists of a meditative recitative for strings which is followed by piano unaccompanied. A hint of the theme appears, pizzicato in the strings, and it is only after the Allegro develops that the theme appears in its fully developed form. The symphonic variations now follow, though frequently interrupted by extended passages of varying moods. The middle of the work consists of a poignant slow section, divided into two parts—music of introspection and mysticism. The piano makes a transition to the finale which consists of a highly gay Allegro non troppo.

X-MX-10, Walter Gieseking, Piano, and the London Philharmonic Orchestra, Sir Henry J. Wood Conducting.

SYMPHONY IN D MINOR
Allegro · Allegretto · Finale

CÉSAR FRANCK completed the composition of his only symphony on August 22, 1888, when he was nearly sixty-six years old. He was a professor of organ at the Paris Conservatoire, and a respected figure in the musical world. What, then, is the explanation of the fact that the majestic and solemn creation of so venerable a *vieillard* should have been attacked in the press? Franck's Symphony was not a work by a bold modernist; its form, its construction, its orchestration had elements of novelty, but all entirely within the compass for a generation that heard Berlioz and Wagner.

After its initial performance on February 17, 1889, Arthur Pougin, the Hanslick of the Paris press, allergic not only to all that was new, but to all that was unusual in the old, wrote a vicious account in *Ménestrel*, the influential Paris weekly, finding "a lack of fire of genius, lack of inspiration, lack of freshness." Hanslick found the orchestration "without verve and color," the harmonic progressions "drab and enwrapped in fog." He granted that the work was "estimable," but said it did not excite the listener.

On the other hand, Gustave Derepas, Franck's early biographer, tells us that Franck's Symphony has been compared to an algebraic equation, scientifically contrived and solved. He is willing to grant science of structure, but proposes another formula, geometric rather than algebraic, determining the dimensions and proportions of component parts. He sees in the Symphony a Cologne cathedral, whose dimensions are ideally proportioned.

Taking stock of the half century of Franck's Symphony, we find that it ranks among the most popular symphonies in the orchestral repertoire the world over. The criticism of its orchestration seems puzzling. Franck's orchestra is, if anything, too luscious for modern ears. The Conservatory professor, who, according to the report of Vincent d'Indy, was shocked by the employment of the English horn in the second movement (for it was "unsymphonic"), would now find unexpected allies among modernists. But even by a statistical measure of orchestral variety, Franck's Symphony is far ahead of his Romantic contemporaries.

From the harmonic standpoint, the moderns will demur to Franck's chromaticism and his fluid use of tonality. The inspiration of Franck's Symphony may seem too lofty, with too narrow a margin between loftiness and pompousness. Be that as it may, César Franck's Symphony is a distinctive form, affiliated with Schumann and Wagner, but with differences of treatment so unmistakable that there can be no confusing Franck's style with that of any other musician. And this secures his musical immortality.

M-MM-608, Philadelphia Orchestra, Eugene Ormandy Conducting.

George Gershwin

1898–1937

S INCE his death, Gershwin has lost little of that phenomenal popularity that was his during his lifetime. His best songs are still heard frequently; his serious works still attract capacity audiences. Indeed, all-Gershwin concerts have become something of a ritual; and the life of Gershwin has been commemorated in a successful motion-picture.

His music—that wonderful melodic vitality, that remarkable variety of rhythm, that charm and sophistication—seem to defy the passing of time and remains as fresh today as when first composed. Today we are less concerned with the fact (important though it is) that he was a historic force—that it was he, more than any other composer, who brought our popular idiom into serious musical forms. What is more important is that his music remains vibrantly alive, is still an eloquent expression of things American. What Eva Gauthier said of him when he died remains true: "George Gershwin will live as long as music lives. . . . He will never be forgotten, and his place will never be filled."

He was born in Brooklyn, New York, in 1898, but spent his boyhood days in the city streets of Manhattan's East Side. Except for the fact that he revealed a love for music, he gave little indication that he was talented. He began studying the piano with local teachers, the most important of whom was an operetta composer named Charles Hambitzer who was the first to recognize his latent gifts. Ever strongly attracted to popular music, Gershwin became a songplugger in Tin Pan Alley. At the same time, he continued his music study, sometimes by himself, sometimes with teachers (one of whom was Rubin Goldmark).

Inevitably, he began writing popular songs. Success came to him early. By the time he was nineteen, he had written a smash hit,

Swanee, and the scores of several musical comedies. There followed a series of brilliant scores for the Broadway stage, including several for George White's annual *Scandals.* By 1924, he was considered among the most brilliant and successful composers in Tin Pan Alley.

It was at this time that Paul Whiteman commissioned him to write a large work in the jazz idiom for a concert of popular music at Aeolian Hall. That work—*Rhapsody in Blue*—made Gershwin internationally famous. It brought him out of the ranks of popular-song composers and placed him with the important serious writers of the time.

After that, Gershwin's career was divided between the writing of popular music for the Broadway stage and subsequently for the Hollywood screen, and the creation of serious works for symphony orchestras and for the opera house. In both fields he proved to be uniquely successful. *Of Thee I Sing!* became the first musical comedy to win the Pulitzer Prize.

Gershwin died in Hollywood in 1937 following an unsuccessful operation on the brain.

AN AMERICAN IN PARIS

In the spring of 1928, Gershwin took a trip to Europe. For some years his had been a magic name in America. He was Broadway's favorite composer, earning as much as a quarter of a million dollars a year from his musical comedy scores. Furthermore, he had achieved quite a name for himself in the field of serious music with the *Rhapsody in Blue* and Concerto in F. But he was not satisfied. His crowded everyday schedule of composing and rehearsing new shows left him no time for the concentrated study of music. He felt that his training along formal musical lines was not sufficient, and he hoped that in Europe he might find the seclusion which he needed for study, and the composers from whom he could learn the finer points of orchestration.

But when he arrived on the other side of the Atlantic, he found that his music was almost as popular as it was in America, with the result that most of the great composers politely refused to accept him as their pupil. Maurice Ravel asked, "Why do you want to become a second-rate Ravel when you are already a first-rate Gershwin?" And when Igor Stravinsky learned that Gershwin made from one to two hundred thousand dollars a year from his compositions, he said: "In that case, perhaps it is *I* who ought to study under *you!*"

The only composition to come out of this European journey was *An American in Paris*. Gershwin had the idea for this work before he even landed on the Continent, and once he arrived in the French capital, and visited its museums, its many historic sights, its cafés, and rode down its boulevards in noisy taxicabs, his musical ideas took definite form. Through an interviewer for the magazine *Musical America*, he made the following remarks about this work:

"This new piece, really a rhapsodic ballet, is written very freely and is the most modern music I've yet attempted. The opening part will be developed in typical French style, in the manner of Debussy and the 'Six,' though the themes are all original. My purpose here is to portray the impressions of an American visitor in Paris as he strolls about the city, listens to the various street noises, and absorbs the French atmosphere.

"As in my other orchestral compositions, I've not endeavored to present any definite scenes in this music. The rhapsody is programmatic only in a general impressionistic way, so that the individual listener can read into the music such episodes as his imagination pictures for him.

"The opening gay section is followed by a rich 'blues' with a strong rhythmic undercurrent. Our American friend, perhaps after strolling into a café and having a few drinks, has suddenly succumbed to a spasm of homesickness. The harmony here is both more intense and simple than in the preceding pages. The 'blues' rises to a climax followed by a coda in which the spirit of the music returns to the vivacity and bubbling exuberance of the opening part with its impressions of Paris. Apparently the homesick American, having left the café and reached the open air, has downed his spell of the blues and once again is an alert spectator of Parisian life. At the conclusion, the street noises and French atmosphere are triumphant."

It is not difficult to realize that the "homesick American" was the composer himself.

Gershwin worked further on his new composition during his subsequent visit to Vienna, and completed the orchestration when he returned to Paris. By the end of the summer, when he again set foot on his native soil, the work was ready for performance.

The Philharmonic-Symphony Orchestra of New York gave *An American in Paris* its first performance at a concert conducted by Walter Damrosch in Carnegie Hall on December 13, 1928. The audience went wild with enthusiasm; the critics, as usual a bit skeptical about the musical value of Gershwin's serious compositions, were divided in their opinions.

It was with this piece and this orchestra, too, that Gershwin made his debut as a conductor. When the first all-Gershwin concert was given by the Philharmonic at New York's Lewisohn Stadium in the summer of 1927, it was such a success that it has been repeated every season.

The composer appeared as piano soloist in the *Rhapsody in Blue* and the Concerto in F at the first two of these concerts. At the third annual concert on August 26, 1929, he took a baton in his hand for the first time, and directed a most competent performance of *An American in Paris*.

X-MX-246, Philharmonic-Symphony Orchestra of New York, Artur Rodzinski Conducting.

CONCERTO IN F, FOR PIANO
AND ORCHESTRA

Allegro · Andante · Allegro agitato

GERSHWIN composed his Concerto in F on a commission from the Symphony Society of New York. The commission was the one important result of Paul Whiteman's celebrated "experiment in modern music"—the Aeolian Hall concert of February 12, 1924, at which the *Rhapsody in Blue* had its first performance. All of the credit for the Rhapsody went to Gershwin. As a matter of fact, not quite all of it was earned by him, for the Rhapsody had been packaged by other hands. The orchestration was Ferde Grofé's, and a few of the effects which became inseparable from the texture of the music were, it is said, improvised by Whiteman's players in rehearsal. But to score this point against the Rhapsody is to score another in favor of the Concerto. The Concerto, written the following year, owes nothing to any hand but Gershwin's. A much more ambitious musical undertaking, he accomplished it unaided from beginning to end.

The first performance took place at a concert of the New York Symphony Society. Walter Damrosch conducted, and Gershwin himself played the solo part. The audience applauded for several minutes, but reviewers were temperate in their praise of the work. They spoke of defects of form and of inexpert treatment of the orchestra. But little attention was paid to them. What they said might be true though it was not important. What was important was the gaiety, the charm, the originality, the infinite resourcefulness of the music.

Never at a loss for a good tune, Gershwin had poured dozens of his best into the Concerto. And the tunes were treated with unfailing skill. In the face of this display, reviewers' strictures were accepted for what they very often are—cautious quibbling. It is worth noting that the Concerto was heard more and more frequently in the years that followed, and that estimates of its quality rose with every hearing. Today it is over twenty years old, but its freshness and its fascination seem to have increased with time. Of what other American work, contemporaneous with the Concerto, can we say as much?

M-MM-512, Oscar Levant, Piano, and the Philharmonic-Symphony Orchestra of New York, André Kostelanetz Conducting.

[201]

PORGY AND BESS: A SYMPHONIC PICTURE

(Arranged by Robert Russell Bennett)

Porgy and Bess was Gershwin's last major composition. He had long cherished the idea of writing a truly American opera, one that would utilize an American theme, but he could not find a suitable story.

Then he came across the play *Porgy*, about Negro life in Catfish Row in Charleston, South Carolina, written by DuBose and Dorothy Heyward, and produced with great success by the New York Theatre Guild in 1927. This was the play for which he had been searching. He became absorbed in the idea of making an opera out of *Porgy*, and in his effort to put an authentic flavor into the music, he took DuBose Heyward down to a little island near Charleston, where the two spent several months making a first-hand study of the music of the Southern Negro. This observation at close range enabled Gershwin to inject into the music for *Porgy and Bess* a note of folklike authenticity.

Returning from Charleston, Gershwin worked for nearly two years on his folk opera. It received its initial performance in a production by the Theatre Guild on September 30, 1935, in Boston, and it met with immediate success. After its Boston tryout, *Porgy and Bess,* with its all-Negro cast, opened in New York on October 10. It ran for 124 performances, and was heard by more people than had ever heard an American opera before. Since then the work has had a number of revivals, each of which has played to capacity houses.

In 1942, Fritz Reiner, conductor of the Pittsburgh Symphony Orchestra, asked Gershwin's friend, the well-known American composer, conductor, and arranger, Robert Russell Bennett, to make a symphonic arrangement of the principal music from *Porgy and Bess.* Mr. Bennett tells us that "Dr. Reiner selected the portions of the opera that he wanted to play and also set the sequence of the excerpts. He expressed his ideas as to instrumentation, wishing to make generous use of saxophones and banjo, and to dispense with Gershwin's pet instrument, the piano.

"I proceeded not only to follow Dr. Reiner's ideas faithfully," he continues, "but also to remain completely loyal to George's harmonic and orchestral intentions. In other words, although carrying out Dr. Reiner's approach, I have been careful to do what I knew—after many years of association with Gershwin—Gershwin would like as a symphonic version of his music."

The "Symphonic Picture" had its première by Reiner and the Pittsburgh Symphony on February 5, 1943. It consists of the following excerpts from the opera, not just thrown together as a medley, but carefully woven into a compact orchestral composition: Scene in Catfish Row (with peddlers' calls), Opening of Act III, Opening of Act I, *Summertime, I Got Plenty o' Nuttin'*—Storm Music—*Bess, You Is My Woman Now*, The Picnic Party, *There's a Boat That's Leavin' Soon for New York, It Ain't Necessarily So, Finale (Oh, Lawd, I'm On My Way)*.

M-MM-572, Pittsburgh Symphony Orchestra, Fritz Reiner Conducting.

RHAPSODY IN BLUE

LIKE all great successes, that of Gershwin's *Rhapsody in Blue* was unpredictable. The Rhapsody was one of the many pieces on the program of Paul Whiteman's concert in New York on the afternoon of February 12, 1924. The concert was announced as "an experiment in modern music." Paul Whiteman asked the twenty-five-year-old Gershwin to write a piece for this concert, but Gershwin was busy with his current revue *Sweet Little Devil*, and hesitated to accept, until he read in the New York *Herald Tribune* that he, Gershwin, was at work on a symphony. This garbled report made Gershwin think of writing for Whiteman something more ambitious than just a short jazz piece. Gershwin told the story of the Rhapsody to his friend and biographer Isaac Goldberg:

"Suddenly an idea occurred to me. There had been so much chatter about the limitations of jazz. . . . Jazz, they said, had to be in strict time. It had to cling to dance rhythms. I resolved, if possible, to kill that misconception with one sturdy blow. Inspired by this aim, I set to work composing with unwonted rapidity. No set plan was in my mind—no structure to which my music would conform. The *Rhapsody*, as you see, began as a purpose, not a plan.

"At this stage of the piece, I was summoned to Boston for the première of *Sweet Little Devil*. I had already done some work on the

Rhapsody. It was on the train, with its steely rhythms, its rattle-ty-bang that is often so stimulating to a composer. . . . I frequently hear music in the very heart of noise. And there I suddenly heard—and even saw on paper—the complete construction of the Rhapsody, from beginning to end . . . as a sort of musical kaleidoscope of America."

The date of completion of the score is marked on the manuscript: January 7, 1924. Gershwin wrote the piano score in about three weeks, but a few figurations were still left out. Gershwin was so pressed for time that he had to improvise these little details at the first concert, for he was the soloist with Paul Whiteman's orchestra.

Gershwin left the orchestration to Ferde Grofé, and the latter completed the job in ten days. In this orchestration, Grofé opened a new chapter in the art, and set an example for countless jazz arrangers after him. Many textbook rules of orchestration went into discard, but the effect was electrifying. Incidentally, the famous *glissando* at the end of the "ascending whoop" in the opening clarinet passage is not indicated in the score, and was, according to authentic accounts, the inspiration of the clarinet player of the occasion, Ross Gorman, who had to experiment for five days before he found a reed that could turn the trick.

All newspaper critics acknowledged Gershwin's inventive talents, but also found defects of structure in the piece. Deems Taylor said that the Rhapsody had "all the faults one might expect from an experimental work," but remarked that "it hinted at something new, something that has not hitherto been said in music," and expressed the belief that Gershwin "may yet bring jazz out of the kitchen." W. J. Henderson called the Rhapsody "a highly ingenious work, treating the piano in a manner calling for much technical skill," and commented further that Gershwin should "keep to the field in which he is a free and independent creator, and not permit himself to be led away into the academic groves and buried in the shadows of the ancient trees." Olin Downes wrote that "the audience was stirred, and many a hardened concertgoer excited with the sensation of a new talent finding its voice, and likely to say something personally and racially important to the world."

X-MX-196, Alec Templeton, Piano, and André Kostelanetz and his Orchestra.
X-MX-251, Oscar Levant, Piano, and the Philadelphia Orchestra, Eugene Ormandy Conducting.

Christoph Willibald Gluck

1714–1787

THE music drama, as distinguished from grand opera, was born with Gluck. It was he who struck an altogether new path for opera by replacing the florid and often artificial writing of the Italians with forthright simplicity and naturalness and direct emotions; by using texts that had dramatic truth; by consciously trying to create an artistic unity out of play and musical score. That path—and its source was *Orfeo ed Euridice*—was to become a mighty highway on which Weber, Wagner, Debussy and Richard Strauss were later to travel.

Gluck was born in Weidenwang in 1714 on the lands of Prince Lobkowitz, by whom Gluck's father was employed as forester. Gluck's youth was marked by wanderings through Bohemia, taking whatever jobs were at hand, mostly musical ones. In 1736, he came to Vienna, there to be employed by Prince Lobkowitz. Another prince, Melzi, impressed by his musical gifts became his patron, taking Gluck to Italy and enabling him to study for several years with Sammartini. Before long Gluck composed his first opera, *Artaserse*, then several others, eventually becoming known throughout Europe as a composer of successful Italian operas.

After a devious route that took him to England and Germany, Gluck returned to Vienna in 1748. One year later, the Burgtheater was reopened with one of Gluck's operas. The popularity of this work, and that of several others which followed it, made Gluck a favorite in court (where for ten years he was employed as Kapellmeister) and fashionable in the palaces of the nobility.

The year of 1760 was the turning point of Gluck's career. With the collaboration of Calzabigi, Gluck slowly evolved theories about opera which were sharply in conflict with those held by Italian composers then so greatly in vogue in Vienna as elsewhere. *Orfeo ed Euridice* was the first opera of Gluck's to translate these theories into practice, and to this very day this opera remains Gluck's most famous and one of the treasures in the operatic repertory. *Orfeo,* at first, was not successful; nor were its immediate successors—*Alceste* and *Paride ed Elena.*

In 1773, Gluck—disheartened by his failures in Vienna—left for Paris where his latest opera, *Iphigénie en Aulide* was successfully introduced. In Paris Gluck became the center of a historic controversy—the fight between French opera (or music drama) and Italian opera. The spearhead for the opposition was a composer named Piccinni. During the climax of the struggle—which split musical Paris into two warring camps—the Paris Opéra commissioned both Gluck and Piccinni to write an opera on the same text, *Iphigénie en Tauride.* The triumph of Gluck's opera brought an end to the conflict with a decisive victory for Gluck and his followers.

Gluck spent the closing years of his life in Vienna—now a composer of international fame, and of substantial means. Most important of all, he lived to see full vindication for his theories of the music drama. He died of an apoplectic stroke in 1787.

ORFEO ED EURIDICE

THE TALE of Orpheus and Euridice had appealed to composers of opera long before the time of Gluck. Jacopo Peri, a member of that historic "camerata" that actually brought opera into existence, composed *Euridice* in 1600; so did still another "camerata" member, and in the very same year—Giulo Caccini. And only six years after that came Monteverdi's *Orfeo*.

The story is famous, and it appears in all these operas—and in that by Gluck—with little variation: Orpheus, who bewails the death of his beloved Euridice, is permitted to rescue her from the underworld, but only on the condition that he does not look at her face until they emerge. He finds Euridice in the Elysian Fields, only to succumb to her entreaties that he look at her. He loses his loved one again. But the Goddess of Love pities Orpheus and reunites the lovers in her Temple.

It is this simple and affecting tale, memorable in legend and opera, that Gluck turned to in his first experiment in the creation of his new kind of musical drama.

The setting used by Gluck was prepared by Calzabigi; and the opera was introduced at the Burgtheater in Vienna on October 5, 1762 to an audience that included the Empress and Vienna's leading nobility.

The audience did not like *Orfeo*—it was too much of a revolution from what these people were accustomed to witness in the opera house. The threadbare simplicity of Gluck's opera—and that simplicity was evident in both the libretto and the musical score—appeared stark; many of Gluck's realistic effects, particularly his use of dissonance, sounded brutal. Eighteenth-century ears liked florid airs, meretricious vocal runs, humdrum orchestral accompaniments; they got none of these in *Orfeo*. What they could not recognize then—and what the world of music has learned to recognize long since—was that Gluck's unornamented melodies spoke a heart-stabbing poignancy (as in the celebrated soprano air, *Che faro senza Euridice*); that Gluck's rich-textured orchestral setting carried with it the impact of the drama, as in the corybantic description of Hades and the dance of the Furies.

OP-MOP-15, Soloists. Vlasoff Chorus and Orchestra, Tomasi Conducting.

[207]

Karl Goldmark

1830–1915

O F THOSE composers who write from the sheer necessity of expressing their emotions in music, no better example could be
found than Karl Goldmark. Born in the small Hungarian
town of Keszthely, on May 18, 1830, Goldmark had early contacts
with music. His father was the cantor in the Jewish synagogue in
Keszthely, too poor to pay for regular music lessons. Thus it was that
the young Karl's early training was at the hands of the village school-
master who taught him the simplest rudiments of music. But with a
marked aptitude, particularly for the violin, Goldmark won enough
attention to warrant a trip to Vienna in 1843 where he studied with
Leopold Jansa for two years and then entered the Conservatory. During the political disturbance of 1848, the institution was closed; Goldmark, faced with the problem of supporting himself, managed to do
so by playing in a theatre-band at Raab. With the capitulation of that
town to the government forces, Goldmark was arrested with others
suspected of being "rebels" and was actually led out to face a firing
squad. Fortunately, intercession and explanation by a friend halted
the orders, and Goldmark's life was spared.

Goldmark returned to Vienna in 1850, where, save for short periods, he spent the rest of his life. Until 1857, he worked intensively,
becoming familiar with all the orchestral instruments and making
various attempts at original composition. Serious works—a quartet
for piano and strings, an overture and songs—by Goldmark began to
appear on programs. These were received with encouraging success,
and it was but a short time until such works as *The Rustic Wedding*
Symphony and the overture *Sakuntala* carried his name to every musical center of the world. Along with his work as a composer, Goldmark found time to serve as a music critic for the *Konstitutionelle
Zeitung*, for which he wrote several articles in support of Wagner,

[208]

whose works he had carefully studied so far as they were at that time available. Curiously enough, he also maintained a friendly relationship with Brahms, whom he also admired.

Goldmark's early struggle and privations were well repaid by the success of his most famous work, the opera *The Queen of Sheba*, to whose composition and revision he devoted nearly ten years. This work won immediate favor, and Goldmark's reputation as a composer of standing was assured. He died in Vienna on January 2, 1915.

RUSTIC WEDDING SYMPHONY, OP. 26

WEDDING MARCH   SERENADE
BRIDAL SONG   DANCE

IN THE *Rustic Wedding* Symphony, Goldmark succeeded in catching the mixed gaiety, sentimentality, lugubriousness, and quaint naïveté of rural Central Europe. Strictly speaking, the work is not a symphony, for it is not in the sonata form, though the composer divided it into the conventional movements. It is rather a suite or a series of musical tableaux, illustrative of the program inferred by the title. Noticeable in this work is the composer's complete mastery over every kind of musical effect.

Goldmark's Symphony is marked by his instinctive feeling for folk music combined with a remarkable sense of color. both in his harmonies and in his orchestration. In his day the accusation was made of subservience to Wagner, but study of his scores today tends to prove that this accusation was the result of a prevailing prejudice, for Goldmark speaks with an exceptionally individual musical language. In achieving this language, he performed no extraordinary feat of invention; he merely spoke of those things he knew well, and clothed his musical sentences with an Oriental opulence, though this is more apparent in *The Queen of Sheba* than in the *Rustic Wedding* Symphony.

M-MM-385, Columbia Broadcasting Symphony, Howard Barlow Conducting.

Charles Gounod

1818–1893

CHARLES FRANÇOIS GOUNOD was born in Paris in 1818. In 1836 he entered the Paris Conservatory where he was a pupil of Halévy. Three years later, he won the Prix de Rome. In Italy he was strongly influenced by the church music of the early polyphonic composers, notably Palestrina, and inspired by it he wrote several Masses one of which was performed in Italy and Vienna. After returning to Paris, Gounod served as organist at Les Missions Etrangères. During this period, he began writing operas, one of which, *Sapho,* was presented at the Paris Opéra in 1851.

Gounod composed several operas—as well as two symphonies and a very successful Mass—before writing the masterpiece which was to make him immortal, the opera *Faust.* With *Faust* Gounod reached full maturity as a composer. Two other gifted operas came from his pen, *Mireille* and *Roméo et Juliette;* but while the latter one is still fresh in the operatic repertoire, neither of these two works is a *Faust.*

During the Franco-Prussian War, Gounod visited England where he was fêted and performed. In 1875, he returned to Paris, now giving himself up equally to religion and music. Indeed, his last works were religious in nature, including several important sacred Masses. Gounod died in Paris in 1893 of a stroke, while deep at work on a Requiem.

His musical style was exquisitely French in its sweetness, eloquence, refinement, and charm. Saint-Saëns was of the belief that the greater Gounod is to be found not in the operas but in the religious works; but Time has still to substantiate this opinion. To the music world at large, Gounod remains known as the composer of *Faust* and *Roméo et Juliette*—and a beautiful melody called *Ave Maria* built to the accompaniment of a Bach piano prelude.

FAUST

OF THE many musical settings of Faust which are in existence—by Berlioz, Liszt, Boïto—the most popular is the opera by Charles Gounod. A veritable gold-mine of glittering melodies (the "Soldier's Chorus," the "Flower Song," "Mephisto's Serenade," the "Jewel Song," the Waltz, etc.), it has maintained its great popularity with opera audiences for more than half a century. Yet when it was first performed—at the Théâtre Lyrique in Paris in 1859—Faust was not successful. Strange to say, the audience found it unpalatable to the ear, the critics thought it too experimental, the publishers said it was uncommercial. Only after several years did Faust achieve popularity. Published by Choudens it brought in through its publication more than three million francs' profit, much to the surprise of the publisher himself. And a revival of the opera on March 3, 1869 was so well received that it now had to stay permanently in the repertoire.

For all its weak pages—and there are many stretches of pedestrian writing—Faust is in the best traditions of French opera. In its construction and in the fidelity of the music to the text it is a sharp departure from operas then being written by the Italians. If a work is to be measured by its best pages rather than by its weakest, Faust is a masterpiece which maintains an extraordinarily high level of beauty, and not only beauty in its abundant melodies, but also in its use of harmony and orchestration.

The story of Faust is drawn from those parts of Goethe's poem dealing with Faust and Marguerite. Faust consigns his soul to Mephistopheles in return for recaptured youth. He sees Marguerite again, tempts her with jewels, seduces and abandons her. Marguerite's brother, Valentin, vows revenge. Challenging Faust to a duel, he is killed. Meanwhile, Marguerite kills her child and is incarcerated. Faust visits her cell and begs her to escape with him; but Marguerite prefers death to Faust.

9019-M, Death of Valentin and Prison Scene, Artists of the Paris Opéra, Chorus and Orchestra conducted by Gaubert.

71770, Jewel Song, Bidu Sayao, Soprano, and the Metropolitan Opera House Orchestra, Fausto Cleva Conducting.

69031-D, Waltz, transcribed for piano by Liszt, Egon Petri, Piano.

Edvard Grieg

1843–1907

BECAUSE he was a sensitive tone poet, Grieg is sometimes described as the "Chopin of the North." Like Chopin's, Grieg's music was tender, imaginative, fastidiously wrought in every detail; but unlike Chopin, Grieg was no mere miniaturist, but able to write spaciously and with breadth in the larger forms. His best vein was a national one. He modeled his melodic material after that of Norwegian folk music and succeeded to a marked degree in transferring the gray colors and gentle moods of that folk music into his own works.

He was born in Bergen in 1843. Ole Bull, the famous violinist was the first to recognize his talent. Seeing some of Grieg's youthful pieces, Ole Bull urged the boy to go to Leipzig for the full development of his gifts. This Grieg did in 1858, studying for two years with Richter, Reinecke, Rietz, and Moscheles. After completing his studies —and with honors—Grieg went to Copenhagen. There he was thrown in with a group of young, idealistic musicians who influenced him greatly. Grieg's latent nationalistic ardor—first awakened when he took a tour through Norway with his father—was further aroused by Nordraak. The death of Nordraak in 1865 inspired Grieg to carry on alone a mission the two young men had discussed long and passionately—the stimulation of Norwegian music and the encouragement of Norwegian composers. In Christiana, Grieg founded and directed the Musical Union, with which organization he performed many new Norwegian works. At the same time, in his own compositions, he adopted traits and mannerisms of Norwegian folk music, besides making fetching new arrangements of native Norwegian songs and dances.

In 1867, Grieg married Nina Hagerup, for whom he had composed what is probably his most famous song, *I Love You.* Some measure of recognition now came to him in the form of a government grant of 1,600 kronen. This sum enabled Grieg to indulge in travel—to visit Liszt in Rome (where the master warmly praised the young man's talent), and to help found the Danish Opera Company in Denmark.

Meanwhile, Grieg's national—even international—significance as a composer became recognized. This clearly became evident in 1874 when Henrik Ibsen called upon him to write incidental music for his play *Peer Gynt*. When performed in 1876, the *Peer Gynt* music further extended Grieg's reputation.

From now on, he was generally accepted as Norway's leading composer, and as such he was the recipient of numerous honors. The government gave him a substantial annual pension, thereby relieving him of all economic worry for the rest of his life. The Swedish Academy made him a member, as did the Musical Academy of Leyden. Tributes also came to him from the French Academy and the University of Cambridge.

Grieg died in 1907 in the city of his birth. His body lay in state in the Museum of Art in Bergen where thousands filed passed his body to pay last homage to Norway's greatest composer.

CONCERTO IN A MINOR, OP. 16, FOR PIANO AND ORCHESTRA

Allegro molto moderato · Adagio · Allegro moderato molto e marcato—Andante maestoso

LISTENING to the tonal effects in this Concerto, it is hard to realize that it was Grieg's first piano work in which the orchestra was used. His previous output consisted almost entirely of piano music with a few songs, and the Sonata for Violin and Piano, yet here is a work that, apart from its wonderfully effective writing for the solo instrument, contains beautiful and original orchestration.

The Concerto was written during a holiday at Sölleröd in Denmark in 1868. It is full of the Norwegian atmosphere so characteristic of Grieg's music, and is a peculiarly happy work. In 1870, the composer went to Rome, and there met Liszt who was much impressed by the Concerto. He played it through and when he reached the passage nearly at the end of the finale where the piano repeats, with a subtle alteration, the theme previously thundered out by the full orchestra, Liszt stopped and cried, "G, G! not G-sharp! Splendid! That is the real Swedish Banko!"

It was the performance of this Concerto by the composer at a Gewandhaus Concert at Leipzig in 1879 that laid the foundations of the great popularity of his music.

There are many moments of high inspiration in the Concerto. There is, first of all, the effervescent opening which is followed by a contrasting second subject tender and wistful; there is the song of the second movement—surely one of the most lyrical pages in all the piano-concerto repertoire; and, finally, there is the brilliance and color of Norwegian folk festival in the closing section.

M-MM-313, Walter Gieseking, Piano, Berlin State Opera House Orchestra, Hans Rosbaud Conducting.

PEER GYNT SUITE NO. 1, OP. 46

MORNING SCENE   ANITRA'S DANCE
ÄSE'S DEATH   IN THE HALL OF THE MOUNTAIN KING

PEER GYNT was not actually invented by Ibsen, but was part of the Scandinavian legend. In his play *Peer Gynt*, Ibsen made him a philosophical character in a semirealistic, semifantastic world. Peer Gynt starts his career by kidnaping a village bride at her wedding, and taking her to his mountain cabin for a night. He is declared an outlaw, but another girl, Solvejg, is willing to consort with him despite the peril and disgrace. He leaves her, too, and goes away for forty years, during which he pursues a varied life as a slave trader in America, a pretended prophet in Arabia, and a man of the world elsewhere.

Solvejg waits for him to the end, when, finally, he comes to her to die. Death confronts him in the person of a Button Moulder, whose business is to use worthless scrap for something useful—buttons. Peer Gynt's devoted mother Äse, and all the girls in his life, whom he treated so unjustly, keep faith with him and help him to redeem his soul.

Ibsen asked Grieg to write incidental music to certain parts of the play, and Grieg composed, in all, twenty-three numbers. From this music he drew two orchestral Suites. The first performance of *Peer Gynt* with Grieg's music took place in Oslo, then named Christiania, in 1876. Grieg was not particularly happy about the conditions of performance, and wrote bitterly in a letter that the Swedish management of the theatre gave him specifications as to the duration of each number and its order, without allowing him any margin. "I was thus compelled to do patchwork. . . . In no case had I an opportunity to write as I wanted. . . . Hence the brevity of the pieces."

The music, however, was an instantaneous success. The two orchestral Suites very soon became great favorites in the orchestral repertoire. Grieg's *Peer Gynt*, for better or for worse, lacked the philosophical gloom of Ibsen's character, and possessed, in happy recompense, an easy melody and stimulating grotesqueness.

The first Suite includes the *Morning Scene*, which is conceived in the barcarolle style. The second number of the Suite, *Äse's Death*, for strings alone, is one of the best examples of musical threnody. The third number is *Anitra's Dance,* in a stylized Oriental manner. The fourth movement, *In the Hall of the Mountain King,* is a grotesque march of the gnomes.

X-MX-180, The London Philharmonic Orchestra, Sir Thomas Beecham Conducting.

SONATA IN C MINOR, OP. 45, FOR VIOLIN AND PIANO

Allegro molto ed appassionata; Presto · Allegretto espressivo alla romanza; Allegro molto · Finale: allegro animato; Cantabile; Prestissimo

GRIEG composed three sonatas for violin and piano, each of which is marked by chamber-music writing of great refinement and a sensitive adjustment of the two instruments to each other. It is generally conceded that the third of his sonatas, the one in C minor, is the greatest. Less ebullient, less irrepressible in its good spirits than the one in G, Op. 13, the C minor is—on the other hand—wiser, deeper in thought, more mellow in concept, more genuinely national in spirit. At times there is a healthy peasant vigor to it, as in the last movement, which betrays its ancestry to be the Norwegian folk dance. But in its best pages—and these are found in the middle movement—there is a gray and tranquil beauty which finds Grieg in one of his happiest poetic moods.

George Frederick Handel

1685–1759

THE year 1685 is marked as one of the most notable in the history of music, for it gave to the world Bach, and Handel, who was his senior by less than a month. Both were voices to be heard round the world, and to echo through the subsequent centuries with an ever increasing popularity.

This popularity, the genius which they shared, a mutual facility and profusion of output, and a common tradition and homeland, were, however, the limit of their resemblances. Bach became the prophet of fervent, subjective piety, of lofty masses of impressive tonal architecture, of that awesome feeling attendant upon one's presence before a power greater than oneself. His work came from the confines of a comparatively narrow environment, and suffered so casual a reception as to shock us who know his present position.

From every point of view, Handel's was a different story. He was a man of the world, a boulevardier. Throughout his life, Handel lived, wrote, played in the grand manner. He was a giant who could blast or whisper with equal grace, was never uneasy in the presence of the great, and not above throwing an obdurate soprano out of the window. Hardships there were, but his music and his memory are unshadowed. During his life, his music met with enthusiastic reception. He deserved and received the patronage of influential contemporaries, and managed to say the right thing at the right time.

Handel was the first of the three great German composers whose second country was England (the other two being Haydn and Mendelssohn). Of the three, Handel was the only one who became a naturalized English citizen. The quibble as to whether Handel's name should have an *Umlaut* on the "A" is settled by Handel himself who, during his life in England, signed his name without one. He also changed the German form of his name Georg Friedrich to the half-English, half-Gallic form George Frederick. But he spoke with a heavy German accent to the end of his days.

De Quincey gives a vivid picture of Handel in England. "A Polyphemus as to enormity of appetite," Handel used to order a dinner for seven. "He rang furiously for dinner to be served upon which the waiter would timidly suggest that perhaps his honor might choose to wait for the six *commensales* who had not yet arrived. "De who, de what?" would Handel exclaim. "The company, sir," was the waiter's reply. "De gombany!" ejaculated Handel. "I am de gombany!"

Handel died in England and was buried in the Westminster Abbey at the foot of the coffin of the Duke of Argyle. One hundred and eleven years later, Charles Dickens was to become Handel's "silent neighbor."

CONCERTI GROSSI, FOR ORCHESTRA

"Twelve Grand Concertos" for strings (some with oboe parts) were composed by Handel within the space of a month and a day, in Handel's fifty-fifth year.

The London *Daily Post* of October 29, 1739, said: "This day are published proposals for printing by subscription, with His Majesty's royal license and protection, Twelve Grand Concertos, in Seven Parts, for four violins, a tenor, a violoncello, with thorough-bass for the harpsichord. Composed by Mr. Handel. Price to subscribers, two guineas. Ready to be delivered by April next. Subscriptions are taken by the author, at his house in Brook Street, Hanover Square, and by Walsh." The concertos were published for the composer, by Walsh, on April 21, 1740.

The characteristic of each of these eighteenth-century concerti grossi, so different from what we call a concerto today, is the contrasting of a small group of solo instruments (*concertino*) against a full body of instruments (*ripieno*) augmented by an accompanying cembalo. Less elaborately worked out than those of Bach, Handel's concertos usually contain more movements and more thematic variety than the *Brandenburg* Concertos.

The Fifth Concerto Grosso, one of the longer works of the twelve, is one of the best and represents the composer's finest instrumental style. The *Grave* is a stately short introduction, sort of a "curtain-raiser" which leads to a fugal Allegro. The Presto, in 3-8 time, is in a rather fresh vein. This is followed by the Largo, a short movement, which shows how to sustain a line of thought upon one figure. There is a second, well developed Allegro, followed by a final movement, Menuet, which combines dance motion with warm melodic line.

M-MM-685, complete, Busch Chamber Players, Adolf Busch Director.
X-MX-142, No. 5, London Philharmonic Orchestra, Felix Weingartner Conducting.

(ROYAL) FIREWORKS MUSIC

| OVERTURE | BOURRÉE |
| ALLA SICILIANA | MENUETTO |

IT WAS in October 1748, that England signed the Peace of Aix-la-Chapelle (in German, Aachen) which brought to a close the War of the Austrian Succession. Although England's part in the war itself had been marked by brilliant achievements, her role in the peace was less successful. As George II knew that the House of Hanover was to retain the succession in its German states as well as in Great Britain, he decided the time was ripe for celebration.

Accordingly, George Frederick Handel was summoned by the Court, and commissioned to prepare music for a mighty public entertainment to take place on April 27, 1749, in the Green Park, London. For this occasion—which was to include a gigantic display of fireworks such as England had never seen—Handel was instructed to write *al fresco* music.

The celebrated Italian architect and showman, Jean-Jérôme Servandoni, was commanded to design a "machine" as a backdrop. His architecture took the form of a huge Doric temple of wood: a center structure 100 feet high, with wings which measured more than 400 feet. A gigantic figure of Peace, attended by Neptune and Mars, and a likeness of equal size of King George delivering peace to Britannia adorned the pavilion. An enormous sun completed the picture, and for musicians there was a special gallery large enough to accommodate a hundred men.

After the public rehearsal in Vauxhall Gardens, attended by 12,000 people, the *General Advertiser* described the band as "the brightest and most numerous assembly ever known." Handel, Composer to the Royal Chapel, had completed the score a week in advance. Reported the *Gentlemen's Magazine:* "So great a resort occasioned such a stoppage on London Bridge that no carriage could pass for three hours. The footmen were so numerous as to obstruct the passage, so that a scuffle ensued in which some gentlemen were wounded."

Apparently this confusion was to be a precursor of the unfortunate happenings at the event itself. On the day of the celebration a week later, the enthusiasm of the people surpassed all bounds. Great crowds jammed their way into Green Park. Even the King could not contain his excitement.

But the celebration was a dismal failure—not to say disaster. Wrote Horace Walpole: "The fireworks by no means answered the expense, the length of preparation, and the expectation that had been raised. . . . The rockets, and whatever was thrown up into the air, succeeded mighty well; but the wheels, and all that was to compose the principal part, were pitiful and ill-conducted, with no changes of colored fires and shapes: the illumination was mean, and lighted so slowly that scarce anybody had patience to wait the finishing, and then, what contributed to the awkwardness of the whole, was the right pavilion catching fire and being burnt down in the middle of the show. . . . Men climbed like monkeys with torches and lit things, and lit them again. Hours passed with fitful display, followed by intervals of irritating failure. After the Temple of Peace caught fire, the whole wooden structure burst into a bright flame. Panic seized the crowd, and even hysteria was felt by the distinguished architect Chevalier Servandoni, for, when he beheld his masterpiece lighting the sky, he lost his head, and drew his sword upon the Duke of Montagu, Controller of the Ordnance, and was promptly arrested, but was released the following day."

Fortunately, Handel's music escaped the calamity. The original score for the *Royal Fireworks Music* is merely entitled *Concerto A* and *Concerto B*, two orchestral concertos that are to be found in Vol. XLVII of the *Deutsche Handel Gesellschaft*. It was not until the work was published, in 1786, that it was given its present name.

With an extravagance in keeping with the event, Handel lavished himself upon this music. "After a grand Overture of wind instruments, composed by Mr. Handel," reported the *Gentlemen's Magazine*, "a signal was given for the commencement of the Fireworks, which opened by a Royal Salute of 101 brass ordnance, viz., 71 six-pounders, 20 twelve-pounders, 10 twenty-four pounders, etc." Romain Rolland has likened the Overture to Beethoven's *Ritterballet*—"a march in D Major, full of pomp and, like it, joyous, noble and sonorous."

This Suite was conceived in two parts. After the Overture and the Royal Salute come five lesser movements intended to portray and accompany one or the other of the allegorical set pieces. The directions in Handel's score are an amusing mélange of Italian, French, and English.

In arranging his Suite, Sir Hamilton Harty has included all the movements of the original score, save one. He has omitted the Allegro (*La Rejouissance*); the Overture he follows with the music *La Paix*, calling it merely Alla Siciliana; then comes the Bourrée, and finally the Menuetto. In the latter, Sir Hamilton has combined the two minuets of Handel's score, using the first as the Trio of the second dance.

Already firmly established in royal and public favor, Handel became the man of the hour in music after his composition of this Suite.

X-MX-51, London Philharmonic Orchestra, Sir Hamilton Harty Conducting.

THE HARMONIOUS BLACKSMITH

IN THE fifth harpsichord suite there appears a movement which consists of a jaunty theme followed by a set of routined and rather academic variations. The Suite is rarely heard; but this movement has become famous under the name of *The Harmonious Blacksmith*. This name is believed to have been given the work in or about 1820 because a blacksmith in Bath was associated with the tune, having whistled it consistently; when, therefore, a Bath publisher decided to issue the piece, he decided to utilize what he considered a rather droll and salable title. It is not true, however, that the music was suggested to Handel by the rhythmic beating of the blacksmith's hammer on the anvil—a story that was believed for so long a time that actually a monument was erected to the smithy.

MESSIAH

THE *Messiah* is unquestionably one of the greatest works of its kind ever conceived by the mind of man. In its pages will be found music of both the simplest and most complex nature, but all of it is on the highest plane of inspirational beauty. This massive Oratorio requires approximately two and a half hours for its complete performance, yet it was composed in the incredibly short span of twenty-four days between August 22nd and September 14th, 1741.

Handel used as his text certain passages selected from the Bible and arranged by a clergyman named Pooley. Credit for the text, however, was claimed by Handel's friend, Charles Jennens, Jr., a wealthy but literally unscrupulous man, whom Pooley served as secretary.

Shortly after the completion of the *Messiah*, Handel received an invitation from William Cavendish, Duke of Devonshire and Lord Lieutenant of Ireland, to visit Dublin and there present some concerts of his music. Since, at that time, his compositions were being received with indifference—and even outright opposition—by the London public, he accepted the invitation eagerly, hoping to find a more cordial audience for his works in the Irish capital. Consequently, he left London early in November 1741, spent a few days in Chester, awaiting favorable weather to make the voyage across the Irish Sea, and finally arrived in Dublin on November 18th. The following month he began a series of highly successful subscription concerts, devoted entirely to his own compositions.

A public rehearsal of the *Messiah* was held on April 8th before a large audience, and the next day *Faulkner's Journal* stated that "it was allowed by the greatest Judges to be the finest Composition of Musick that ever was heard, and the sacred Words as properly adapted for the occasion." This preliminary review then went on to say that the actual first performance of the Oratorio was to be postponed one day, until April 13th. It also carried a request that, in order to accommodate a larger audience, ladies should please come without hoops and gentlemen without swords.

The first concert performance must have been as successful as the rehearsal, for three Dublin papers used almost the same words to describe it as had *Faulkner's Journal* in reviewing the rehearsal. Handel presided at the organ, his friend, Matthew Dubourg, led the orchestra, and two famous singers of the day, Signora Avolio and Susanna Maria Arne Cibber, sang the soprano and contralto solos respectively. Authorities disagree as to the identity of male soloists.

Handel's old patron, King George II, attended the London première, and legend has it that he was so moved by the Hallelujah Chorus that he rose and remained standing until its conclusion. Naturally, when the King stood up, everyone was obliged to rise. Since that time it has been the custom for the audience to stand during the singing of this inspiring chorus. It was this portion of the Oratorio to which Handel referred when he said that, while composing it, "I did think I did see all Heaven before me, and the great God Himself."

Handel divided the *Messiah* into three sections. Part I contains the prophecy and the narrative of the Nativity; Part II tells the story of the Passion and Resurrection, reaching a climax in the mighty Hallelujah Chorus; Part III deals with man's hope of his own resurrection.

M-MM-666, Isobel Baillie, Soprano, Gladys Ripley, Contralto, James Johnston, Tenor, Norman Walker, Basso, the Huddersfield Choral Society and the Liverpool Philharmonic Orchestra, Malcolm Sargent Conducting.

WATER MUSIC

Allegro · Air · Bourrée · Hornpipe · Andante · Allegro deciso

THERE is a pretty tale told about the origin of this work which, though often retold, is unfortunately a legend. This story tells that Handel wrote this music to placate the anger of his employer, the Elector George of Hanover, who resented the composer's prolonged absence. The music—the story tells further—was performed during a royal water party on the Thames held to celebrate the ascension of the Elector to the throne of England as George I. The King was not apprised of the identity of the composer, but he was so delighted with the music that when he learned it was by Handel he forgave him, reinstated him in his good graces, and even gave him a handsome pension besides.

The *Water Music*, however, was composed not in 1714—the date of the royal fête—but three years after that. It is, however—even without a charming origin—one of Handel's most delightful suites.

X-MX-279, Philadelphia Orchestra, Eugene Ormandy Conducting.

Howard Hanson

1896–

AMONG present-day American composers, Howard Hanson is the romanticist who, in his music, searches restlessly for the expression of beauty in forms and idioms that are essentially conservative. He was born in Wahoo, Nebraska, in 1896. His education took place at Luther College, Nebraska, at the Northwestern University in Illinois and at the Institute of Musical Art in New York. In his twentieth year he was appointed professor of theory at the Conservatory of the College of the Pacific in California, soon rising to the position of Dean. For three years, from 1921–1924, he lived in Europe as a Fellow of the American Academy of Rome. Upon returning to this country, he was appointed director of the Eastman School of Music in Rochester, New York, a position he has held since that time with considerable honor. He has been a vital force in American music, not only as the director of a great musical institution, but also as a conductor, and as a founder and director of the annual festival of American music in Rochester, New York. He has also been a highly fertile composer, his orchestral works having been performed extensively by most of the major American orchestras, and his opera, *Merry Mount*, having been produced successfully at the Metropolitan Opera House in 1934.

SYMPHONY NO. 2, OP. 30 (ROMANTIC)

Adagio; Allegro moderato · Andante con tenerezza · Allegro con brio

DR. HOWARD HANSON has provided the following information about his symphony:

"My Second Symphony, to which I have given the subtitle 'Romantic,' represents my escape from the rather bitter type of modern musical realism which occupies so large a place in contemporary thought. Much contemporary music seems to me to be showing a tendency to become entirely too cerebral. I do not believe that music is primarily a matter of the intellect, but rather a manifestation of the emotions. I have therefore aimed in this symphony to create a work that was young in spirit, lyrical and romantic in temperament, and simple and direct in expression. The work is in three movements. The first, Adagio—Allegro moderato, begins with an atmospheric introduction in the woodwinds joined first by the horns, then the strings and finally the brass choir, and then subsiding. The principal theme is announced, Allegro moderato, by four horns with an accompaniment of strings and woodwinds, and is imitated in turn by the trumpets, woodwinds, and strings. An episodic theme appears quietly in the oboe and then in the solo horn. A transition leads into the subordinate theme, Lento, with the theme itself in the strings and a counter-subject in the solo horn.

"The development section now follows, with the principal theme announced in a changed mood by the English horn and developed through the orchestra. The episodic theme, influenced by the principal theme, takes an important part in this section.

"The climax of the development section leads directly to the return of the principal theme in the original key by the trumpets. This is followed in turn by the episodic theme, now in the clarinets and then in the first horn, with canonic imitation in the oboe. The subordinate theme then follows, and the movement concludes quietly in a short coda.

"The second movement, Andante con tenerezza, begins with its principal theme announced by the woodwinds with a sustained string accompaniment. An interlude in the brass, taken from the introduction of the first movement and interrupted by florid passages in the woodwinds, develops into the subordinate theme, which is taken from the horn solo in the first movement. A transition, again interrupted by a florid woodwind passage, leads into a re-statement of the principal theme of the movement.

"The third movement, Allegro con brio, begins with a vigorous accompaniment figure in strings and woodwinds, the principal theme of the movement—reminiscent of the first movement—entering in the four horns and later repeated in the basses. The subordinate theme, Molto meno mosso, is announced first by the 'cellos and then taken up by the English horn, the development of which leads into the middle section, Più mosso.

"This section begins with a pizzicato accompaniment in the violas, 'cellos and basses, over which is announced a horn call. This call is taken up by the trombones, and leads into a fanfare first in the trumpets, then in the horns and woodwinds, and then again in the trumpets and woodwinds. The climax of this fanfare comes with the announcement of the principal theme of the first movement by the trumpets, against the fanfare rhythm in woodwinds. The development of this theme leads into a final statement of the subordinate theme of the first movement, fortissimo.

"A brief coda of this material leads to a final fanfare and the end of the Symphony."

The Symphony, commissioned by the Boston Symphony Orchestra, was performed by that organization on November 28, 1930 in commemoration of its fiftieth anniversary.

Roy Harris

1898–

Roy Harris is a rare musical phenomenon, a composer who uses a scientifically worked-out system of composition—yet succeeds in writing music with a mass appeal. This happy combination of qualities is due to the fact that Roy Harris is a melodic composer, to whom the singing line comes first. His melody suggests the spaciousness of the western plains, and, if, indeed, musical inspiration can be brought into connection with the geography of a composer's birthplace, then Harris's music furnishes excellent material in favor of this contention. For Roy Harris was born in a log cabin in Lincoln County, Oklahoma, on Lincoln's birthday in 1898. His parents, of Scotch-Irish extraction, were pioneers who settled in Oklahoma. Roy Harris continued the tradition of pioneering. He was in turn a farmer and a truck driver for a butter and egg company; and he served in the heavy artillery in a training camp toward the end of World War I.

Meanwhile he was studying the clarinet and pipe organ, comparative philosophy and social sciences. Then he discovered that "tone was the only *a priori* value that humanity possesses, all other values being transitory and relative." This led him to the study of creative composition. He mastered the technique of composition with extraordinary rapidity, and exhibited a strong predilection for polyphonic style from the very first. With the aid of a Guggenheim Fellowship he went to Paris where he studied with Nadia Boulanger. On his thirtieth birthday the League of Composers presented in New York his Concerto for Piano, Clarinet, and String Quartet, his first important work in which the essentials of his compositorial style are already well established.

For several years, Harris was head of composition at the Westminster Choir School, later becoming Composer-in-Residence at Cornell University and at Colorado College.

FOLK SONG SYMPHONY

IN COMMENTING on his *Folk Song* Symphony, Roy Harris wrote: "If . . . folksongs stimulate him [the composer] to his best creative ingenuities, he may put the folk tune into a new form, serviceable to his people. He may find the material an aesthetic chart which leads him to new riches. He may even enhance the beauty and scope of natural folk tunes, and in so doing learn to sense the inherent values of musical materials, follow the natural flow of creative form, to gather his creative thoughts into a homogeneous stream of musical continuity."

In his Symphony, Harris has proved his argument admirably: The work is enriched in its employment of indigenous American folk tunes, and in turn it enriches the tunes themselves. The work abounds with quotations of famous melodies: *When Johnny Comes Marching Home* (Part I); *Oh Bury Me Not on the Lone Prairie* (Part II); fiddle tunes (Part III); *Jump My Lady* (Part V) and many others. But these folk strains become inextricable parts of the fabric of Harris's symphony, bringing to Harris's own thematic materials additional color and musical interest, at the same time acquiring new dimensions.

Composed for orchestra and chorus to be performed by schools throughout the country, the *Folk Song* Symphony was introduced (in parts) by Howard Hanson in Rochester in 1940, and in its entirety by the Cleveland Orchestra under Ringwall. The Symphony received the $500 award of the National Committee for Music Appreciation as the best new work of the season.

QUARTET NO. 3

THE STRING Quartet No. 3 was written in 1939, and is a suite of four movements, each containing a prelude and a fugue. Each prelude is written in a definite mode, while the fugues are bi-modal, using the mode of the prelude and another mode obtained by the change of one tone in the original mode. This bi-modality results in a characteristic fluctuation of one of the tones of the chosen mode, creating a coloristic, chromatic effect.

Roy Harris has elaborated an interesting color scheme of modes, in which a mode is "dark" when its tones lie nearer to the tonic, and "bright" when they lie farther. Thus, the Lydian mode is brightest because its intervals from the tonic are largest (major second, major third, augmented fourth, perfect fifth, major sixth, major seventh), while the Locrian mode is darkest because its intervals from the tonic are smallest (minor second, minor third, perfect fourth, diminished fifth, minor sixth, minor seventh).

The complete Spectrum of Modes, from the darkest to the brightest part, is then as follows: Locrian, Phrygian, Aeolian, Dorian, Mixolydian, Ionian, and Lydian, each mode differing by one tone from its neighbor. Modes equidistant from the middle mode are inversions of one another. The Dorian mode, being in the middle, is the inversion of itself. This scale of comparative brightness is paralleled in Harris's scheme by a scale of psychological states, from the most subjective (darkest) to the most objective (brightest). The most subjective mode is then Locrian; the most objective, Lydian. The Dorian mode, which is the only invertible mode, is neutral, neither subjective nor objective.

The Prelude of the first movement is in the Dorian mode, and the Fugue, being bi-modal, adds the Aeolian mode, which is the neighbor of the Dorian mode in the Spectrum of Modes. The second subject of this Fugue is the Mixolydian mode, which is here used not as a new mode, but as the inversion of the Aeolian mode.

The second movement is in the brightest and most objective mode, the Lydian. According to Harris's own description, the Prelude of this movement is canonic in its structure, and carries a sustained bass figure (*ostinato*). The Fugue adds the Phrygian mode to the original Locrian.

The fourth movement is in the Ionian mode (major scale), suggesting, in Harris's words, "color, vitality, animal spirits." The Fugue is bi-modal, adding the neighboring Mixolydian mode to the Ionian.

M-MM-450, Roth String Quartet.

Joseph Haydn

1732–1809

IN THE great chain of master composers linking the earliest musical forms to those of the contemporary era, Haydn, chronologically speaking, follows Bach and Handel; and though he outlived Mozart, was twenty-four years his senior and in essential respects his musical predecessor. Under him the string quartet had its real beginning and the symphony evolved approximately to the construction which endured for much over a century, though further developed by Mozart and Beethoven. Haydn was one of the greatest melodists the world has known.

Franz Joseph Haydn was born March 31, 1732, in the village of Rohrau, near the Austro-Hungarian border. His talent for music was noticeable at an early age. In his ninth year he was admitted to the choir of St. Stephen's Cathedral, Vienna, where he remained until he was rendered unfit for service by his changing voice. Porpora was reputed to be the best teacher and composer in Vienna and it was the desire of Haydn to study with him. Porpora was now ill, disgusted with life, and bitter at what he termed the ingratitude of his former pupils. When it was suggested that Haydn study with him, he fell into a rage. Undaunted by the rebuff, Haydn entered Porpora's household as a valet, and through his good humor and intelligence won the master's friendship, with the result that the coveted lessons followed. Through Porpora, Haydn made many acquaintances in the great Viennese world of society and art, including the illustrious Gluck. At length he attracted the attention of Prince Nicolaus Esterházy, one of the noblest patrons music has ever known. Haydn was made chapelmaster and established a lifelong friendship with the Prince. Living at the regal estate near Suttor, named Esterház, the composer was given complete authority over orchestra, soloists and chorus engaged by the Prince for both chapel services and the very frequent concerts given for the guests and townspeople. Haydn very quickly became, in fact, indispensable to the Esterházy family.

For twenty-eight years, from 1762 to 1790, Haydn remained with the Esterházys. By 1776 he had written over fifty symphonies, numerous operas, masses, and cantatas, and almost innumerable lesser works ranging from concertos down through the various branches of chamber music to simple songs. While much of this music remains, much of it also has fallen into oblivion. The fact that even authorities' estimates of the number of symphonies written by Hadyn vary from 118 to 180 is significant proof of this.

During the 1780's, perhaps the outstanding features of Haydn's life were his very profitable relations with the publisher Artaria and his friendship with Mozart, which commenced about 1781. Despite the very considerable disparity of their ages and the fact that Haydn's long absences from Vienna rendered any continuous contact impracticable, the affectionate regard of the two continued to the end of Mozart's life.

It was in 1790, in the composer's fifty-ninth year, that the next great change in his life took place. Prince Nicolaus Esterházy died, and Haydn, deeply affected—for he had had for the Prince a very real affection—said farewell to the chapel at Esterház and his life in those quiet precincts.

Established in Vienna, Haydn was soon thereafter approached by the composer-impressario Salomon, who had long wished to arrange for Haydn a series of appearances in England. Now, without ties, Haydn consented, arriving in London on New Year's day, 1791.

No ordinary space would permit a detailed story of Haydn's sojourn in England. It was a continuous triumph, royalty and society doing him unstinted honor at every turn. It was during this and a following visit that the composer wrote twelve famous symphonies (including the *Surprise,* the *Military,* and the *Clock*) which mainly perpetuate his fame in orchestral music.

The crown of Haydn's artistic career was signalized by the first production in 1799 of his majestic oratorio *The Creation.* He was to live to see his proud country humbled by Napoleon in 1805, and the breaking up of the Holy Roman Empire in the following year. He died, full of years and honors, in 1809.

CONCERTO IN D MAJOR, OP. 101, FOR 'CELLO AND ORCHESTRA

Allegro moderato · Adagio · Allegro

NOT ONLY did Haydn write six concertos for the 'cello—and perhaps the solo part of a seventh—but he was so much interested in the instrument that he provided two of his symphonies with obbligato 'cello parts. The Concerto in D major, Op. 101, is the third of the 'cello concertos and is the only one played extensively today. It was written for Anton Kraft, whose father was a brewer and a music lover. Born in Pilsen in 1752, Kraft went to Vienna and became a member of Prince Esterházy's orchestra, for which Haydn engaged him as 'cello soloist. Kraft remained with the orchestra for twelve years when Haydn, after twenty-nine years of service, retired on a pension.

Later Kraft joined the orchestras of Prince Graffalkowitsch and Prince Lobkowitz. His popularity had increased. The 'cello part in Beethoven's Triple Concerto was written for him, and Haydn taught him composition. When Haydn observed that Kraft's 'cello playing was being sacrificed to his interest in composition, he stopped the lessons, assuring Kraft that "he had acquired all the knowledge he needed for his purposes."

This Concerto in D is likely to hold its place in the 'cellist's repertoire after others have faded. It still retains its original fragrance, but demands an unusually high level of performance. The work appears to have been composed between 1781 and 1784. It has not only maintained the recognition that it won, but has increased in popularity throughout the world. The work as we now know it was first published under the editorship of François Auguste Gevaert, who was the director of the Conservatory of Music in Brussels. Gevaert dedicated the work "to the memory of the highly gifted virtuoso, Joseph Servais."

The Concerto is in three movements. Originally a small classical orchestra was used, comprising two oboes, two horns, and strings. When Gevaert re-scored the Concerto, he added two flutes, two clarinets, and two bassoons, elaborated the solo part, and also wrote two cadenzas. It remains a small-scale work and, like Haydn's other concertos of the period—to quote Pitts Sanborn—"resembles a vocal *scena* with the 'cello as a prima donna of the virtuoso type."

M-MM-262, Emanuel Feuermann, 'Cello, with Orchestra Conducted by Malcolm Sargent.

QUARTET IN F MINOR, OP. 20, NO. 5

Allegro moderato · Menuetto · Adagio · Finale: fuga a due soggeti

JOSEPH HAYDN has long been associated with the sobriquet "father of the string quartet." He originated and developed that wonderfully independent form of the string quartet which became the fundamental pattern as adopted later by Mozart and Beethoven, and which has come down to the present day. "It is seldom that an artist has been so successful in discovering the fittest outcome for his individual productiveness," observes Otto Jahn, Mozart's biographer. "The quartet was Haydn's natural expression of his musical nature. The freshness and life, the cheerful joviality which are the main characteristics of his compositions, gained ready and universal acceptance for them."

Strange to say, Haydn seems to have come by the quartet form inadvertently. In his day it was the custom to write for whatever instruments were available; the clear distinctions now so popular and descriptive were quite unknown at that time. So loose was the nomenclature of the period that Haydn's First Symphony, Op. 1, No. 5, came to be included, not among his symphonies, but among his quartets. By the middle of the 18th century, Haydn's early period, the distinction between orchestral and chamber music had not yet been definitely fixed. Nobody knew or observed the exact difference between an overture and a serenade, a cassation and a divertimento, and what was called a sinfonia might resemble any of these and have elements of the concerto, with its use of solo instruments as well. Haydn's earliest quartets and first symphonies were not sharply defined in form and no definite distinction between them is apparent. The early quartets represent works in several movements scored for

[234]

strings in four parts. They could be played either by four solo instruments or by a string orchestra with double bass.

With the arrival of the set of six quartets of Op. 20 (1772) known as *Die Grossen* and *Die Sonnen* (the "Sun") Quartets, an advance was to be observed in Haydn's style and technique. In this series of quartets Haydn discloses a better appreciation and keener technique of writing for his lower voices, the 'cello especially profiting from a more individual treatment. The viola, too, is given greater freedom and individuality, although Haydn never completely realized the innate qualities of this instrument. Particularly significant is the fugue form of the finale, an important innovation, since it assigned equally difficult parts to all players, and for the first time in chamber music writing.

The Quartet in F minor, No. 5 of this opus, is among the most remarkable of Haydn's early essays in the form. In it are some of the warm, romantic qualities anticipating Schubert and Schumann; one noted critic finds it "the most nearly tragic work Haydn ever wrote."

M-MM-228, Roth String Quartet.

QUARTET IN E-FLAT MAJOR, OP. 33, NO. 2

Allegro moderato; Cantabile · Scherzo: allegro · Largo sostenuto
Finale: presto

THE SIX quartets which Haydn composed in 1781—and which had such a profound influence on Mozart's quartet-writing—are known as the "Russian" group. The second in this group is particularly famous for its closing movement, one of those musical pranks that Haydn so delighted in perpetrating in his music. Insisting that ladies always talked during the performance of music, Haydn composed this quartet—or so the legend goes—to prove his point. Within the last movement he inserted unexpected rests which were intended to catch the ladies at their gossiping. Consequently, the E-flat major Quartet has acquired the nickname of "The Joke." The good humor of the last movement is the characteristic mood of the entire work.

QUARTET IN D MAJOR, OP. 50, NO. 6

Allegro · Poco adagio · Menuetto · Finale: allegro con spirito

This Quartet is sometimes known as the "Frog" because the principal theme in the last movement is played across open strings, giving (to some at least) the suggestion of a frog. But this last movement is distinguished quite apart from this rather remote association with animal life. In it Haydn uses brilliantly a technical effect in which the same note is sounded alternately on two adjacent strings—an effect found in the old Italian masters. Beyond this last movement, the Quartet is outstanding for a charming theme and variations (Poco adagio), and for a delightful use of Hungarian folk rhythms in the Minuet.

QUARTET NO. 30 IN G MINOR (HORSEMAN), OP. 74, NO. 3

Allegro · Largo assai · Allegretto · Allegro con brio

The Quartet in G minor Opus 74, No. 3, is one of the works which falls in the composer's final period. It was in all probability written in London circa 1794 and reveals on every page of the score the consummate mastery of the technique of composition which was now Haydn's. The figure which opens the last movement has suggested a man on horseback to some listeners; for this reason, the Quartet is usually referred to as either the "Horseman" or the "Rider." The whole Quartet is infused with the optimism and gaiety which is characteristic of practically all of Haydn's music, as well as of the man himself. The last movement is much more intense than the rest of the composition, so much so in fact that it evokes at times the vision of the Beethoven yet to come. The work is not allowed to end on this note, however, for just when the mood appears to be firmly established, the irrepressible Haydn sunshine bursts into the score and the Quartet comes to its conclusion in a gay burst of buoyant melody.

X-MX-274, Budapest String Quartet.

QUARTET IN D MINOR, OP. 76 NO. 2

Allegro · Andante e più tosto allegretto · Menuetto: allegro ma non troppo · Vivace assai

BESIDES being one of Haydn's greatest quartets, it is also one of his most integrated ones. All four movements were written in the same key; beyond this they have a unanimity of spirit which makes one movement a fitting—perhaps inevitable—partner of the other. This work is frequently referred to as the "Quinten"—or "Fifths"—quartet; this is because the opening theme of the first movement consists of descending fifths. The slow movement is one of Haydn's most soulful songs; surely it would be difficult to find music more serene and exquisite than this is. The sobriquet of the Minuet—"Hexen" or "witch"—describes the character of the third movement, which is feverish and savage; and this same mood is sustained in the closing movement.

QUARTET IN C MAJOR (EMPEROR), OP. 76, NO. 3

Allegro · Adagio: cantabile · Menuetto: allegro · Finale: presto

THE SIX quartets in Op. 76 were written when Haydn was matured and capable of sustaining the very highest level of artistic creation. At this point the extraordinary inter-reaction of Mozart on Haydn (after Haydn had influenced Mozart) is most strongly in evidence. Haydn may now be discerned reaping the benefit of Mozart's inspired writing, tapping new veins of profundity and eloquence never before found in Haydn's chamber music writing.

The third number in this series is familiarly known as the *Emperor* Quartet, since it incorporates variations on Haydn's famous Austrian National Hymn as its slow movement. Count Saurau has told the story of his Hymn and its inception; how he perceived the necessity of some musical vehicle for the adequate conveyance of loyal sentiments in an age of revolt, and so had the words written by Haschka and the music by Haydn. The Emperor was so pleased with the tribute when it was first sung at the National Theatre in Vienna on his birthday in 1797, that he sent Haydn a gold box inscribed with his portrait. "You have expressed what is in every loyal Austrian heart," the Emperor told Haydn, "and through your melody Austria will always be honored."

It is said that when the French were bombarding Vienna in 1809, some five days before he died, Haydn asked to be led to the piano where he played the Hymn three times with sacred respect and intense expression.

The affinity of this tune with a certain Croatian folk tune has been pointed out. Haydn often based his themes on fragments of Croatian songs, but, except for a vague family resemblance, their primitive impulsiveness bears little likeness to the comparatively sophisticated and highly polished themes of the symphonies and quartets.

M-MM-246, Lener String Quartet.

QUARTET IN D MAJOR, OP. 76, NO. 5

Allegretto; Allegro · *Largo: cantabile e mesto* · *Menuetto* · *Presto*

THE QUARTET in D major, the fifth of the six in Op. 76, is characteristic of Haydn's later style, which had passed from the facile to the mellow. There are gaiety and good humor here: the light heart of the last movement is in Haydn's best vein. But a deeper note is sounded as well. The Largo movement is one of the most poignant melodies that Haydn ever put to paper, and one of the most moving pages of music found in all chamber-music literature. Indeed, so famous is this movement that the entire quartet is frequently called the "Largo."

M-MM-400, Roth String Quartet.

SYMPHONY NO. 45 (FAREWELL)
IN F-SHARP MINOR

Allegro assai · *Adagio* · *Menuetto* · *Presto; Adagio*

HAYDN is termed the "father of the symphony," but a truer title might be that of "stepfather," for his is not all the credit. He was preceded by several older contemporaries who produced symphonies before him. Also, on his own declaration, Haydn was greatly indebted to Philip Emanuel Bach in this respect. It has been declared that Johann Stamitz was the inventor of the form, and that what Haydn achieved was not actually the invention of the symphony but the development of its structure. He deepened its significance, exalting it into a form of music which made a perfect vehicle for the highest thoughts and emotions of the composer. In a word, he changed it from diversion to drama.

Haydn's life was chiefly passed in the service of the house of Esterházy, which he entered in 1761. Prince Anton died in 1762, being succeeded by his brother Nicolaus who was called the "Magnificent" because of his love of munificent display. He was the ideal patron of music, and Haydn remained in a subservient but distinguished relationship with him until the Prince's death in 1790. In this position as Kapellmeister, Haydn wrote some of his best-loved symphonies and quartets.

The Prince sometimes thoughtlessly retained his musicians at his estate too long without a holiday. On one of these occasions the disgruntled musicians enlisted their conductor's aid, and Haydn agreed to place this matter before their master. This he did by writing a special symphony as the last number for a concert which the Prince attended, a symphony in which Haydn's humor and naïve character are illustrated.

At the performance, the work followed the usual symphonic lines until the last movement. Candles were used to illuminate the music desks, and Haydn so arranged the score that one by one the musicians were to blow out their candles, pick up their music, and depart. At the end of the symphony only two violins were left in the orchestra, quietly playing a few soft chords. The Prince took the hint, and granted a holiday the next day.

In 1939, the Boston Symphony Orchestra under Serge Koussevitzky (all dressed in 18th century costumes) reproduced this very pantomime in a performance of the *Farewell* Symphony in Boston.

Apart from the interest in its origin, this symphony is also noteworthy as an excellent example of Haydn's method of organizing the symphony into a great art form. The first three movements illustrate the working plan while the last movement displays a remarkable facility of innovation. Only a musician wonderfully sure of himself would have dared to depart so radically from the accepted form.

M-MM-205, London Symphony Orchestra, Sir Henry J. Wood Conducting.

SYMPHONY NO. 92 (OXFORD) IN G MAJOR
Allegro spiritoso · Adagio · Menuetto: allegretto · Presto

ONE OF the most notable figures in London musical circles during the last two decades of the 18th century was one Johann Peter Salomon, a German violinist of considerable ability who had been concertmaster of the orchestra of Prince Henry of Prussia. When the Prince disbanded his orchestra in 1780, Salomon moved to London, where he became popular as a performer of chamber music. But in 1786 he began to give concerts of his own, and soon developed into a leading impresario.

In order to heighten the prestige of his concerts by bringing to London a musical celebrity of the times, Salomon sent a personal ambassador to Haydn, in the person of the London music publisher Bland, to try to induce the Austrian composer to come to London for a series of concerts. Haydn, however, was in the employ of Prince Esterházy and had no desire to leave Austria. In 1790, Prince Nicolaus died, and his successor, Prince Anton, who was no music lover, dismissed the orchestra and kept only a brass band. But he increased by 400 gulden the annual pension of 1,000 gulden bequeathed to Haydn by Prince Nicolaus. When Salomon, who was visiting in Bonn at the time, heard of this change in Haydn's status, he hurried to Vienna where he was finally successful in persuading the master to make the trip to London.

Haydn composed six symphonies for his first London visit in 1791. These he conducted from his place at the harpsichord. The London public received him with much enthusiasm, and his triumph was so great that Salomon immediately arranged for a second series of six concerts. These, however, did not materialize until 1794.

During his first visit in London, in 1791, Haydn was conferred an honorary degree of Doctor of Music by Oxford. For these ceremonies,

Haydn composed a new symphony. This new work proved so difficult that he substituted an earlier symphony. This earlier symphony, though composed some years before Haydn's visit to London, now is included in the Salomon group and has acquired the subtitle of "Oxford." Light, graceful, pleasing from the first bar to the last, this symphony is characteristic Haydn music.

SYMPHONY NO. 94 (SURPRISE) IN G MAJOR

Adagio cantabile: vivace assai · Andante · Menuetto · Finale: allegro di molto

IN THE *Surprise* Symphony, as in so many other compositions of this most genial of masters, there is the simplicity that conceals great art. Nowhere is this more subtly achieved than in the Andante which, with the other three movements of this completely captivating work, fulfills to perfection Haydn's plain purpose to provide a piece that would entertain—and perhaps surprise—through a series of joyous melodies and a deft working-in of harmonic changes. Though by no means the only one of his symphonies to survive in the general repertoire, it is by general consent the most popular of the composer's great number of works in this form.

Composed in 1791, this Symphony in G major was performed for the first time on March 23, 1792, at the sixth Salomon concert in London. The success of the work was immediate and great. Since then it has become generally known as the *Surprise*. It is the third ("Salomon No. 3") of the twelve symphonies as arranged in the order of their appearance in the catalogue of the Philharmonic Society in London.

M-MM-363, Columbia Broadcasting Symphony, Howard Barlow Conducting.

SYMPHONY NO. 101 (THE CLOCK) IN D MAJOR

Presto · Andante · Minuet · Finale

THE NICKNAMES that were imaginatively applied to the Haydn symphonies, such as *The Bear, The Philosopher, The Hen, The Surprise,* and *The Clock*, were, of course, not of Haydn's invention. These names usually reflected some similarity between a phrase in the symphony and an animal cry or some other sound. The *Clock* Symphony received its sobriquet from the tick-tacking bassoons in the opening of the Andante. It is amusing to note that the English word *Clock* was mistranslated by some German publishers as *Glocken*, which, of course, means chimes.

In the late eighteenth century, the clock was not exclusively a timepiece, but served as an ornament and a musical instrument as well, so that the naming of a symphony after the clock brought familiar associations. Haydn himself wrote thirty pieces for musical clocks, and three of these clocks are still preserved. They were constructed by Haydn's friend, the monk Primitivus Niemecz. Haydn never wrote out these pieces on paper, but, fortunately, the mechanism on which the music was recorded has remained in perfect condition, so that the music could be taken down and published. It is just as if a phonograph record of Haydn's times has come down to us over the span of a century.

Indeed, these mechanical clocks performed a function of present-day juke boxes. They recorded familiar pieces, and even complete overtures. Viennese restaurants used them for the entertainment of guests. Beethoven liked to dine to the sound of a recorded Cherubini overture, and he, too, composed music for these instruments.

The first performance of the *Clock* Symphony was given in London at Haydn's benefit concert on May 4, 1795, and the Symphony was labeled simply *The New Overture*. It is well to remember that in the eighteenth century, Overture was often synonymous with Symphony.

The second movement of the *Clock* symphony, Andante, is the one that gave the work its nickname. The tick-tacks are heard in the bassoons as accompaniment to the violin theme in G major. The orchestration is light at first, then grows simultaneously with the increased rhythmic tension. The middle portion of the movement is in sonorous G minor and its relative major. The clock movement returns, with the flute and the bassoon ticking at the distance of two octaves and a third. The violins play the subject against the gurgling woodwinds. Then the theme is given to the strings with the flute trills over it. The tick-tacks are magnified, and the rhythms are

[242]

quickened. After a dynamic ascent toward fortissimo, the sonority
fades to the vanishing point toward the end.

M-MM-459, Columbia Broadcasting Symphony, Howard Barlow Conducting.

SYMPHONY NO. 103 (DRUM ROLL) IN E-FLAT MAJOR

Allegro con spirito · Andante · Menuetto · Allegro con spirito

IT WAS for the second series of Salomon concerts in London that
Haydn composed the Symphony in E-flat major, sometimes called
the *Drum Roll* Symphony. But his love for the drum and his first
use of it go back to his early childhood.

On a certain occasion a drummer was needed for a street procession. Haydn, then a small boy, was allowed to fill the vacancy after
he learned to make the drum stroke. He was so little that the drum
had to be adjusted to his height by being carried ahead of him on
the back of another short person—a hunchback. This was the beginning of Haydn's "drum rolls." He never lost interest in the instrument,
and prided himself upon his skill in playing it, even taking his turn
at the drums in Salomon's orchestra when he was in London.

The *Drum Roll* Symphony opens with a slow introduction marked
Adagio, the first bar of which consists of a roll on the tympani, or
kettledrums. It is from this roll that the work derives its name.
Known in Germany as the *Symphonie mit dem Paukenwirbel* ("Sym-
phony with the Kettledrum Roll"), it is not to be confused with the
Symphony No. 94 in G major—*mit dem Paukenschlag* ("with the
Kettledrum Stroke") which is more familiar to us as the *Surprise*
Symphony.

Some authorities believe that many of the themes in the *Drum Roll*
Symphony were taken from Croatian folk songs popular in the district where the composer was born. The Symphony was composed in
1795, most probably in London, and received its initial hearing in
that city the same year.

M-MM-547, Hallé Orchestra, Leslie Heward Conducting.

SYMPHONY NO. 104 (LONDON) IN D MAJOR

Adagio: Allegro · *Andante* · *Menuetto* · *Allegro spiritoso*

IT IS usually by the number in the Salomon series that the so-called *London* Symphony is identified. Otherwise, it is no easy matter to designate a Haydn symphony. Mandyczewski, the editor of the early volumes of Haydn's collected works, begun in 1907, has listed 104 Haydn symphonies, which he considered authentic. He also disposed of thirty-six spurious symphonies, written by Haydn's contemporaries and credited to Haydn by unscrupulous publishers. In Mandyczewski's list the *London* Symphony is the last, presented as No. 104.

For reference to other catalogues, Mandyczewski identifies each symphony by a row of symbols: "London Symph. No. 7. H. 118. P. 109. F. W. 144. Z. 75." "No. 7" refers to the order of occurrence in the catalogue of the Philharmonic Society of London. "H. 118" is the number according to Haydn's own list dictated to his copyist in 1805 ("Catalogue of those Compositions, which I recall having composed from my 18th to my 73rd year"). The number with the letter "P." applies to the list made by Haydn's biographer Pohl. The letters "F," "W," and "Z" refer to the lists made by Fuchs, Wotquenne, and Zulehner.

The date of the performance would never have been established had Haydn not identified the new Symphony, performed in London on May 4, 1795, as *die 12., und letzte der englischen.* The program of the concert listed a *New Overture,* and, in parenthesis, *Sinfonia.*

The *London* Symphony was given for Haydn's last benefit concert. Haydn wrote in his diary in his realistic manner: "The hall was filled with a picked audience. The whole company was delighted, and so was I. I took in this evening 4000 gulden. One can make as much as this only in England." At that time, 4000 gulden was equivalent to about $2,000.

M-MM-409, London Philharmonic Orchestra, Sir Thomas Beecham Conducting.

[244]

Paul Hindemith

1895–

ONE of Hindemith's recent works is a monumental contrapuntal opus called *Ludus Tonalis* which some critics have compared to Bach's *Well-Tempered Clavier.* This work is perhaps a key to the composer's complex style, which combines the polyphony of Bach with the most modern harmonic and rhythmic devices. It was this curious blend of the past and the present that made one German critic describe some of Hindemith's music as "Brandenburg concertos upside down."

Hindemith was born in Hanau in 1895. After a period of study at the Hoch Conservatory in Frankfort, he became concertmaster of the Frankfort Opera House Orchestra, and founder and director of the Amar String Quartet which specialized in the performance of modern chamber music. He also did a great deal of composing—his works beginning to attract attention through performances at the Donaueschingen Festivals of 1891, 1922, and 1923. By 1925, with a series of works he called *Kammermusik,* his style became crystallized, and he produced compositions of striking originality in which the resources of modern counterpoint were fully exploited. He also achieved considerable fame with two operas (*Cardillac* and *Neues vom Tage*) and a series of functional works for radio, the theater, the screen, etc.

For a long while he taught composition in Berlin. After the rise of the Nazis, and the controversy over *Matthis der Maler* which made him unacceptable to the new regime, Hindemith left Germany permanently. He went to Turkey, on an invitation from that government, to reorganize its musical life. In 1937, he visited the United States for the first time. Since then, Hindemith has settled in this country permanently, serving on the music faculty of Yale University, and composing numerous works of extraordinary distinction.

MATTHIS DER MALER, SYMPHONY

THE ANGELIC CONCERT   ENTOMBMENT
THE TEMPTATION OF ST. ANTHONY

AT THE time that Hindemith composed his opera *Matthis der Maler*, in 1934, he also wrote a Symphony collating three passages of the opera into a symphonic opus. The overture of the opera became the first movement of the Symphony; music from the sixth scene was developed into a second movement; and for the final section, Hindemith chose the intermezzo which is heard in the closing scene. The titles of the various movements were derived from the names of three paintings found on the famous Isenheim Altar of the painter Matthias Grünewald.

Hindemith prepared his own libretto for his opera, using the painter Grünewald as his central figure, but building his plot around the Peasant War of 1524 in Southern Germany.

It will be recalled that this opera became something of a *cause célèbre* in Nazi Germany. Wilhelm Furtwängler, the conductor who had introduced the Symphony on October 4, 1934, scheduled the opera for Berlin in 1935. But the Nazis were afraid of a theme that treated rebellion against autocracy; and they were hostile to Hindemith's music anyway. They refused to permit the performance to take place. Furtwängler insisted on the production, and fought so stubbornly for Hindemith that he was finally punished by banishment from Germany's musical life for about a year. And Hindemith's music was pronounced by the *Kulturkammer* to be unacceptable in the new Germany.

The opera was finally performed in 1938 in Zurich; and it scored a tremendous success.

Hindemith's Symphony is one of his most palatable scores. It combines poetry with mysticism; it culls forth the medieval period with amazing authenticity (largely through the use of authentic church melodies and old modes) without ever becoming esoteric. Indeed, it is one of Hindemith's most popular works. For here Hindemith's complex art has been greatly simplified.

Engelbert Humperdinck

1854–1921

GERMAN musical histories assign to Humperdinck a special niche as the creator of the operatic fairy tale, or a Wagnerian music drama for children. That Humperdinck was a pocket-size Wagnerian is quite true, and he worked with Wagner in Bayreuth.

In his harmonic idiom Humperdinck follows early Wagner, and the significance of certain chords is the same in Humperdinck's musical dictionary as in Wagner's. Thus, the foreboding apprehension of children lost in the woods is conveyed by the augmented triad. This chord has retained its sinister import in programmatic music of the post-Wagnerian composers.

Humperdinck was born in Siegburg, Germany, in 1854. His musical studies took place at the Cologne Conservatory (with Hiller, Gernsheim and Jensen) and at the Munich Royal School (with Rheinberger). In 1879, he toured Italy as a result of winning the Mendelssohn Prize. There he met Richard Wagner who was so impressed by his talent that he invited the young man to come to Bayreuth and become stage manager. This marked the beginning of Humperdinck's lifelong devotion to Wagner and the Wagnerian music-drama. In 1885, Humperdinck was appointed professor at the Barcelona Conservatory. Five years later he filled a similar post at the Hoch Conservatory in Frankfort. Meanwhile, in 1893, his opera *Hänsel und Gretel* was performed in Weimar and made him famous. Humperdinck's last important pedagogical post was that of director of the Akademische Meisterschule in Berlin, which he assumed in 1900. Humperdinck died in Berlin in 1921.

HÄNSEL UND GRETEL

THE SUBJECT of Humperdinck's operatic fairy tale is the truculent story by the brothers Grimm. In it the children are driven by a heartless mother to pick berries in a forest known to harbor a "crunch" witch, whose specialty is to entice children and bake them for gingerbread. However, she is no match for the sly Hänsel and the resolute Gretel, and, after some astute maneuvering around the fateful stove, the little heros of childhood manage to push the old woman into the oven, where she herself is baked into a *Lebkuchen*. This outcome calls for general merrymaking, in which the fearful and repentant parents take part.

From this story, Humperdinck's sister, a professional librettist, extracted a workable book in three acts. Humperdinck's music is based on German folk song. The composer does not use actual folk melodies, but writes original tunes in the folk manner. According to his biographers, these innocent little melodies are the product of hard work and much revision.

The opera was completed during the year 1893 when Humperdinck was thirty-nine, and was produced in Weimar on December 23 of that year. Richard Strauss, who was the regular conductor of the Weimar Opera, led the performance. It was an instantaneous success. Performances followed in Munich, Karlsruhe, Frankfort, Breslau, Darmstadt, Mannheim, Hamburg, and Berlin.

Richard Strauss wrote to Humperdinck admiringly: "Dear friend, I want to tell you to what extent I am enchanted with your opera. What refreshing humor, what preciously naïve melodies, what art and subtlety in orchestral treatment, what perfection in the shaping of the whole work, what flowering invention, what marvelous polyphony, all so original and new, and yet so genuinely German!"

Even Brahms, though generally little sympathetic with the pictorial type of post-Wagnerian music, remarked to Humperdinck at their meeting: "Our roads are divergent, and yet we meet here," and he put his hands on the score of Wagner's *Meistersinger*.

The texture of Humperdinck's music in this opera is lighter than Wagner's or Richard Strauss's. Humperdinck is a Wagner in miniature, and as such, he is eminently successful.

M-MM-424, Suite, Columbia Broadcasting Symphony. Howard Barlow Conducting.

Vincent d'Indy

1851–1931

VINCENT D'INDY came under the influence of César Franck early in his life, but never allowed his individual talent to be submerged by devotion to his master—indeed that was the last thing Franck strove for in his pupil. D'Indy developed into the most eminent French composer, conductor, teacher, and musical writer of his time. As Lawrence Gilman wrote: "He was honored wherever the sense of a noble and plastic tradition of musical excellence was influential. An aristocrat in his art, a creator whose purity of style and loftiness of aim caused the hasty to think of him unjustly as 'austere,' he nevertheless was an audacious experimentalist, an innovator who did not hesitate to expand the traditional moulds."

Vincent d'Indy, who was born in Paris in 1851, began his professional career as an orchestra violinist. In 1872 he became a pupil of César Franck. A strong bond developed between master and pupil which was to have a far-reaching influence on the development of the younger man. A symphony, *Jean Hunyade*, already revealed the effect of Franck's influence on d'Indy. But from Franck d'Indy also acquired that high integrity, that idealism, that severe artistic conscience which marked the entire career of the pupil.

Together with Franck, d'Indy founded the Société Nationale de Musique, an organization which dedicated itself to the performances of music by the younger composers of France. When Franck died, d'Indy became the president of this important society.

Vincent d'Indy was one of France's great music teachers. For many years he was professor at the Paris Conservatory where he helped to give direction to an entire generation of rising composers. He also helped to bring about a reorganization of the Conservatory. Vincent d'Indy died in Paris in 1931.

[249]

SYMPHONY ON A FRENCH MOUNTAIN AIR, OP. 25, FOR ORCHESTRA AND PIANO

Assez lent · Assez modéré · Animé

VINCENT D'INDY's symphony, written in 1886, shows traces of influences that can be definitely labeled as German romanticism, or as Franckian, or Wagnerian. The main influence of Franck is in the form—that evolved by the master and known as "cyclical" (a treatment by which the principal themes are taken from one common melodic source); that of Wagner is less obvious and lies only in certain instrumental phrases.

The title of the work suggests that the piano is integrated with the orchestra and not used in concerto fashion as the principal instrumental protagonist. The Symphony, which is sometimes known as the *Symphonie Cévenole*, is one of d'Indy's two works with a folksong basis. In its three movements this genuine native theme is ingeniously transformed to fit varying moods.

The mountain air used in the Symphony was inspired by a melody d'Indy heard during one of his visits to the French Alps. It forms the greater portion of the thematic material and is introduced by the English horn in the second measure of the first movement. The flutes repeat the melody and fragments are heard elsewhere in the orchestra. The air returns at the close of the movement, and throughout the remainder of the Symphony we get persistent reminders of this theme.

M-MM-211, Marguerite Long, Piano, and the Colonne Symphony Orchestra of Paris, Paul Paray Conducting.

Edouard Lalo

1823–1892

VICTOR ANTOINE EDOUARD LALO was born at Lille, France, on
January 27, 1823. He was descended from an old Spanish family that had lived in France for generations. He studied violin
and 'cello at the local conservatory, but parental objection to his pursuit of a musical career caused him to leave home at the age of sixteen
to further his musical studies in Paris. Enrolling at the Conservatoire,
he continued his violin studies with Habeneck and took private lessons in composition. His first compositions appeared in 1845, and
three years later he attracted some small attention when a group of
his songs was published. In 1867 he entered a contest sponsored by
the Théâtre Lyrique, submitting an opera, *Fiesque*. It won only third
prize, but the ballet music from the opera, performed under the title
of *Divertissement*, brought the composer his first real recognition
when it was performed by the Colonne Orchestra at a Concert Populaire in 1872.

Lalo's fame increased when, in 1874, the great Spanish violinist,
Pablo de Sarasate, introduced his Violin Concerto in F major, Op. 20,
at a Concert National. That same year, Lalo composed and dedicated
to Sarasate the *Symphonie espagnole*, Op. 21, and the violinist performed it for the first time at a Concert Populaire in the Châtelet on
February 7, 1875. It was with this work that Lalo achieved his greatest fame and by which he is best known today. Subsequent successes
included his opera, *Le Roi d'Ys* (the overture to which is second only
in popularity to the *Symphonie espagnole*), a ballet, *Namouna,* the
Cello Concerto in D minor, *Rapsodie norvégienne* and *Concerto
russe.* In 1880, his talent was officially recognized and he received
the decoration of the Légion d'Honneur.

His death (April 22, 1892) during the commotion excited by dyna-miters at Paris awakened little attention, and there were no funeral eulogies in the journals; but nearly all the French musicians of re-nown were present at his burial, and thus paid tribute to a composer of the highest character and talent.

SYMPHONIE ESPAGNOLE, OP. 21, FOR VIOLIN AND ORCHESTRA

Allegro non troppo · *Scherzando* · *Allegro molto* · *Andante*
Rondo

LALO's *Symphonie espagnole* captured Tchaikovsky's interest in 1878. On March 15 of that year, he wrote to his patron Mme. von Meck: "Do you know the *Symphonie espagnole* by the French composer Lalo? The piece has been recently brought out by the very modern violinist, Sarasate. It is for solo violin and orchestra, and consists of five independent movements. It is so fresh and light, and contains piquant rhythms and melodies which are beautifully harmonized. It resembles many other works of the modern French school with which I am acquainted. Like Léo Delibes and Bizet, Lalo is careful to avoid all that is *routinier,* seeks new forms without trying to be profound, and is more concerned with musical beauty than with tradition, as are the Germans. The young generation of French composers is really very promising."

Pablo Sarasate, to whom the work is dedicated, played the *Symphonie espagnole* for the first time at a Concert Populaire in Paris in February 1875. Lalo was then over fifty; yet it was only a year earlier that the production of his Violin Concerto, Op. 20—also dedicated to and first played by Sarasate—had made him famous. Indeed, Lalo's early neglect by the public caused him such depression of spirit that, a decade before, he had abandoned composition and turned for precarious solace to matrimony with a contralto.

The *Symphonie espagnole* added to his renown; indeed it is now the most popular of Lalo's concert works. But he had to wait more than a dozen years before the production in 1888 of his opera *Le Roi d'Ys* placed him securely among the foremost composers of his day. In 1880, he had received the decoration of the Légion d'Honneur. At its first performance, the *Symphonie espagnole* had a magnificent reception, and since that day it has been a favorite with all violinists.

Although originally in five movements, the *Symphonie espagnole* is rarely performed in its entirety today, the Scherzando or the Intermezzo often being omitted.

M-MM-564, Nathan Milstein, Violin, and the Philadelphia Orchestra, Eugene Ormandy Conducting.

Ruggiero Leoncavallo

1858–1919

LEONCAVALLO belongs with that group of opera composers who have achieved a permanent place in operatic history with a single work, that work being *Pagliacci*. He was born in Naples in 1858, and was educated at the Naples Conservatory and the University of Bologna. For several years he traveled restlessly throughout Europe, sometimes working as a hack pianist and composing popular tunes for the Parisian music halls, while dreaming of a Gargantuan artistic venture in which he would re-create the Italian Renaissance in a trilogy of operas in the manner of Wagner. Upon his return to Milan, Leoncavallo was subsidized by the publisher Ricordi to begin work on this monumental venture, and he produced the first opera of that trilogy, *I Medici*. Meanwhile, the great success of Mascagni's *Cavalleria Rusticana* inspired him to write an opera in a more popular vein. He played that opera, *Pagliacci*, for Sonzogno the publisher who was sufficiently impressed with it to arrange for its performance.

The overwhelming success of *Pagliacci* made Leoncavallo famous and brought performances to his earlier opera, *I Medici*. It was a failure. Discouraged, Leoncavallo abandoned his Renaissance project, and turned to the writing of other operas more popular in vein. None of these duplicated the great success of *Pagliacci*, though one of them—*Zaza*—is occasionally performed by major opera houses. Leoncavallo died in Montecatini in 1919. The fact that, despite his fertility, he was to remain a one-opera composer to the end of his life was one of his great personal tragedies.

PAGLIACCI

THE HISTORY of opera is rich with tales of famous operas failing dismally at their première performances. *Pagliacci* is a notable exception. When it was introduced at the Teatro dal Varme in Milan, on May 21, 1892, under the direction of Arturo Toscanini, Leoncavallo was a struggling and unknown composer. The morning after the première he was famous. Rarely did an opera meet with such a riotous approval as *Pagliacci* did on its first night. At the end of the performance pandemonium broke out. *Pagliacci* had arrived; Leoncavallo became the talk of Milan; and arias like the baritone Prologue and the "*Ridi Pagliaccio!*" were on everyone's lips.

Leoncavallo wrote his own libretto. The Prologue introduces the clown Tonio who explains that the play about to take place is not fiction but fact, and the players are not actors but actual human beings. The first act tells of the triangle love affair existing in a company of theatrical players, among Canio, its director, his wife Nedda, and a young man from the village, Silvio. The clown Tonio—who is repulsed by Nedda when he pathetically tries to make advances—leads Canio to a rendezvous between Silvio and Nedda. Canio tries to kill Silvio, but fails; and he brings the act to a close with his heart-breaking apostrophe, "*Ridi Pagliaccio!*" The second act comprises an actual performance by this theatrical troupe of a play which closely resembles the incidents in Canio's personal life. During the course of this performance, Canio kills his wife; and when Silvio jumps up to the stage from the audience, he, too, is killed by the enraged husband.

OP-MOP-22, Pampanini, Merli, Galeffi, Vanelli, Nessi, Chorus and Orchestra of La Scala, Molajoli Conducting.

Franz Liszt

1811–1886

IT HAS been astutely observed that Liszt made the best of two
worlds. An Abbé, honorary canon of Albano, a sincere mystic,
and at the same time one of history's most publicized lovers, incredible showman, hypnotic virtuoso, an astonishing amalgam of
magician, zealot and philanthropist, Liszt is easily the most colorful
personality in the history of music.

He was a grateful subject for biographers, factual and fictional. He
possessed every feature of a romantic personage, as we of the twentieth century are apt to portray the men of the nineteenth. He had a
brilliant beginning as a child prodigy; he was kissed on his brow by
Beethoven; as a youth he was the prince of pianists and the leading
artistic figure in European capitals at the time when European capitals were, according to our dearest beliefs, gay and preoccupied with
glamor rather than work or war; he wore flowing hair; he loved
women, and women loved him; and in his middle age he became an
Abbé, as sinners do in romantic novels. He wrote music with expressive and meaningful titles, often with a poem for an epigraph; and
he was with Wagner the co-author of the "music of the future," so
designated by the despairing contemporaries for its quality of huge-
ness of design and grandiloquence of idiom.

His name would have become famous had it identified only his
creative talents. Abundant exhibitionism and an astounding virtuosity as a pianist hastened this fame, with the result that Liszt never
faced the unhappy lot of poverty, disappointment and despair which
are the commoner rewards of genius. From his entry into the musical
circles of Vienna, at the age of eleven, to his ultimate emergence as
foremost piano virtuoso of his time, Liszt enjoyed the constant plau-
dits of the musical world.

Critics have felt some disappointment at this state of affairs, believing that a less comfortable life might have stimulated more meaningful composition. But one might, with equal justice, blame an impresario for not being a physician. Liszt was what he was by virtue of innate endowments, and the fruit of his work has its singular, if not supreme, place in musical literature.

In his mature years Liszt became a great progressive force in music. It may be true that now much of his golden garment seems tinfoil, and his grandiloquence appears an expansion of fundamentally unimportant thoughts. But his contribution to instrumental and orchestral technique and color, and his liberating influence in musical form cannot be questioned.

Franz Liszt, who was born in Raiding, Hungary, in 1811, was a phenomenal child prodigy of the piano. He outgrew his prodigy status to become one of the truly great virtuosos of his generation. He also became famous as a conductor, holding the post of Kapellmeister at Weimar from 1848 until 1861. It was at Weimar that Liszt first met Richard Wagner, with whose career his own was so intimately linked. After 1861, Liszt drew closer to the Church, assuming the honorary title of Abbé in 1865, and submitting to the tonsure and taking vows of four minor orders in 1879. He died in Bayreuth in 1886.

CONCERTO NO. 1 IN E-FLAT MAJOR, FOR PIANO AND ORCHESTRA

Allegro maestoso · *Quasi adagio; Allegro vivace; Allegro animato*
Allegro marziale animato

THE CONCERTO No. 1 in E-flat major was composed in 1848 and first performed on February 17, 1851, by the composer himself, with Berlioz conducting. The work is dedicated to Henri Litolff, a composer of Alsatian descent who is still known for his overtures *Robespierre* and the *Girondists,* and for the delightful Scherzo from the *Concerto symphonique.*

If we must divide Liszt's compositions into categories, it will be most convenient to call one kind the brilliant-spectacular, and the other the poetic-spiritual. The E-flat Concerto belongs to the brilliant-spectacular and is therefore the type of work which is scoffed at

[257]

and condemned by Liszt traducers, of whom Hanslick was a good specimen when he called it the "Triangle Concerto"—merely because that inoffensive member of the orchestral family for once had a chance to shine.

But the triangle was not long to be so honored. For the story goes that at the first public performance of the Concerto the triangle player was so nervous over the prospect of solitary prominence in his solo passage that he failed to come in at all. And in later editions of the score these measures were given to oboes and flutes.

Nevertheless, this Concerto, which might reasonably be called a rhapsody, contains much fine music which can stand on its own legs as music. In general feeling and technical cleverness the work rightly maintains its place as a leading figure in the repertoire of piano concertos. Every virtuoso who has the necessary technical equipment plays the work, and the brilliant success of such performances has proved its genuine merits. As he played the Concerto, Liszt used to sing the very first theme to these words: *"Das versteht ihr alle nicht!"* ("None of you know how to do this!")

Liszt made an innovation in this Concerto by altering the idea of separate movements, unconnected musically except by contrast, to one in which the movements are loosely strung together and the themes employed as leitmotifs throughout the sections or movements. The result therefore amounts to more or less a work in one movement, such as his B minor Sonata and A-flat Concerto. The themes are varied by metamorphosis, and thereby is obtained a unity to which orthodox sonata form is alien because in it everything must develop according to rule.

X-MX-17, Walter Gieseking, Piano, and the London Philharmonic Orchestra, Sir Henry Wood Conducting.
M-MM-371, Emil Sauer, Piano, and the Paris Conservatoire Orchestra, Felix Weingartner Conducting.

HUNGARIAN FANTASIA, FOR PIANO
AND ORCHESTRA

THE Hungarian Fantasia actually exists in three forms: the original version, known as the Hungarian Rhapsody No. 14, which was written at Weimar in 1852 for Hans von Bülow; the Fantasia on Hungarian Melodies for piano and orchestra, arranged from the foregoing; and the original version scored for orchestra by Liszt and Albert Franz Doppler.

It must be remembered that in 1842, Liszt was appointed Kapellmeister "in extraordinary" at Weimar, and from 1848 until 1861 he lived there, actively engaged as director of the court musical enterprises. It was during this period that the Hungarian Fantasia was written. Until 1847, the composer had continued his career as a piano virtuoso, but at Weimar he abandoned concertizing in favor of composing, conducting, and teaching. In the twenty-four years that had elapsed since his arrival in Paris, Liszt had become Europe's greatest pianist—even being called by one critic "the Paganini of the pianoforte."

The first performance of the Hungarian Fantasia was given by Hans von Bülow at the Hungarian National Theatre in Budapest on June 1, 1853, after the second act of Nagy Ignacz' play *Parisi Napló*. Franz Ertel was the conductor. Bülow performed it again three months later in Dresden, and in January of the following year in Hanover. He did not always play the work under the same title, however. At the première the program announced it as *Magyar rapsodia*. Later Bülow played it as Hungarian Fantasia, and again as Hungarian Rhapsody for Piano and Orchestra.

X-MX-120, Edward Kilenyi, Piano, and the Grand Orchestre Philharmonique de Paris, Selmar Meyrowitz Conducting.

HUNGARIAN RHAPSODIES, FOR PIANO

THERE is no doubt that the twenty famous Hungarian Rhapsodies did as much to enhance Liszt's popularity as the Hungarian Dances did for Brahms, though the two composers are quite dissimilar in every respect. These Rhapsodies are very brilliant and demonstrate the pianist's technique to such advantage that their genuine musical worth has often been underestimated. They are full of vitality and passion, and their rhythm is irresistible. Among the composer's works they occupy a special place, and their history is curious. At first they were merely short transcriptions of Hungarian tunes. These were elaborated, republished, and canceled—then rewritten and published again. They reflect faithfully all the characteristics of the *tzigan* (gypsy)—his sadness as well as his buoyancy of spirit.

In his volume entitled *Des Bohémiens et leur Musique en Hongrie,* Liszt has explained his ideas at length, the term Rhapsody being chosen by him to designate the "fantastically epic element" present in pieces intended to evoke "the expression of certain states of the soul in which are resumed the ideals of a nation." Thus, they are in reality a species of glorified Hungarian Gypsy music. In general, they consist of two connected movements: the first, of a mournful or contemplative character, labeled *Lassan;* and the second, *Friska,* instinct with wild exuberance of spirit.

The wide keyboard range that Liszt used in his piano works is explained in this superb tribute he made to the piano as an instrument: "To me my pianoforte is what to the seaman is his boat, to the Arab his horse; nay, more, it has been till now my eye, my speech, my life. Its strings have vibrated under my passions and its yielding keys have obeyed my every caprice. It may be that the secret tie which binds me to it so closely is a delusion, but I hold the pianoforte very high. In my view, it takes the first place in the hierarchy of instruments. It is the most often used and the widest spread. In the circumference of its seven octaves it embraces the whole range of an orchestra, and a man's ten fingers are enough to render the harmonies which in an orchestra are brought out only by the combination of a hundred musicians.

"The pianoforte has on the one side the capacity of assimilation, the capacity of taking unto itself the life of all instruments; on the other hand, it has its own life, its own growth, its own individual development. My highest ambition is to leave to the piano players to come after me, some useful instructions, the footprints of advanced attainment, something which may some day provide a worthy witness of the labor and study of my youth."

Not all the rhapsodies are equally celebrated. The second is, of course, the most famous of all, and probably the most famous and widely performed composition by Liszt. The ninth, subtitled "Carnaval de Pesth," the twelfth and the fourteenth rhapsodies are also frequently heard.

69004-D, No. 2, for Piano, Louis Kentner, Piano.
11646-D, No. 2, for Orchestra, Leopold Stokowski Conducting the All-American Orchestra.
7243-M, No. 12, for Orchestra, the Hallé Orchestra, Sir Hamilton Harty Conducting.
71718-D, No. 15, for Piano, Gyorgy Sandor, Piano.

LES PRÉLUDES

LISZT created the symphonic poem, a freely constructed orchestral composition with a definite literary program. This new form proved so useful that even composers who were not in sympathy with Liszt's musical philosophy—Tchaikovsky, for instance—adopted the form of the symphonic poem as a rich medium of free musical expression.

The greatest and most perfectly constructed of Liszt's symphonic poems is *"Les Préludes."* The quotation marks appear on the title page, for the title is itself a quotation from the writing of the French poet-philosopher-statesman, Alphonse de Lamartine. The passage which served Liszt as the program for the *Préludes* pictures life as a series of preludes to the unknown song of death. The dawn of life is love; the tempest dispels love's illusions, and creates a desire to thrust the memories away in some peaceful retreat in the country. But the trumpet sounds, and the rested soul returns to combat.

Such is the romantically vague outline of Liszt's *Préludes.* The music illustrates the changing moods. It opens with an Andante in C major, leading to Andante maestoso, in which the brass sounds full-blooded major harmonies against the accompaniment of running string passages. The major mode prevails even with the advent of a lyric theme, with the key shift from C to E major.

A new theme, emotional and pleading in character, is heard in the strings, and the major mode soon gives way to ambiguous diminished seventh chords, moving in chromatic parallels. This chord is a nineteenth-century cliché for stormy moods or sinister premonitions. The storm follows in the section marked Allegro tempestuoso. The chromatics rage; an avalanche of chromatically falling six-four chords against the bass progression along the chord notes of the diminished

[261]

seventh chord marks the climax. A rhythmic figure in the brass indicates a clearing in the atmosphere, although the diminished seventh chord harmonies are still heard. The major mode reasserts itself.

There is a pastoral interlude in the section marked Allegretto pastorale, and bits of song are echoed in the woodwinds. The pleading theme is heard again, and repeated in several keys. The brass intones the principal theme in martial accents, while the trombones punctuate it with mighty steps. Andante maestoso returns to complete the cycle.

Liszt himself was a professional conductor, and conducted the first performance of "Les Préludes" in Weimar on February 23, 1854.

X-MX-198, London Symphony Orchestra, Felix Weingartner Conducting.

MEPHISTO WALTZ

"Heavenly maid" though she is, music has often related adventures of the Prince of Darkness. Not the least of these Satanic episodes is the *Mephisto* Waltz, which was completed in 1860 and was described by Frederick Niecks as "the *ne plus ultra* of weirdness and unbridled sensuality in the whole domain of music, and one of the most remarkable *tours de force* of imagination, combination, and instrumentation." The work, which carries the subtitle *The Dance in the Village Inn,* is an orchestral setting of a portion of the Faust legend, as recounted by the German poet, Nicholas Lenau. An English paraphrase of Lenau's lines which are reprinted on the score of the *Mephisto* Waltz runs as follows:

"There is a wedding feast in progress in the village inn, with music, dancing, carousing. Mephistopheles and Faust pass by, and Mephistopheles induces Faust to enter and take part in the festivities. Mephistopheles snatches the instrument from the hands of the lethargic fiddler, and draws from it indescribably seductive and intoxicating strains. The amorous Faust whirls about with a full-blooded village beauty in a wild dance; they waltz in mad abandonment, out of the room, into the open, away to the wood. The sounds of the fiddle grow softer and softer, and the nightingale warbles his love-laden song."

X-MX-281, Philharmonic-Symphony Orchestra of New York, Artur Rodzinski Conducting.

Charles Martin Loeffler

1861–1935

CHARLES MARTIN LOEFFLER has been aptly called a musical enigma, since his art although evincing the development of his time, nevertheless, seems to have sprung from an older world—a world of medieval classicism. He was one of the most reticent, retiring artists of his time. Few people knew him intimately, and those few seem to regard their close affinity so highly that they preserve a curious silence regarding his unpublished music, his manner of composition, and any confidences that may have been a part of their friendship. For this reason, whether they actually know how he courted the muse of music or not may well be questioned. Loeffler always kept his music making largely to himself. Like a recluse or a medieval monk, he lived and worked apart from the eyes and the ears of mankind, and only permitted the world to hear his music after much revision, contemplation and reconsideration. It is whispered that there are almost as many works in the larger forms still in manuscript as have been published. Thus, it will be noted Loeffler was given to great self-criticism.

Loeffler preferred suburban to city life. In this way, he was able to evade much of the restlessness and the tension of modern living. His artistry, although evincing the development—as we have noted—of the period in which he lived, nevertheless belonged to another era. Carl Engel has stated, although "born into the crude light of our day," Loeffler however seemed to belong to the "dim and shadowy middle ages." His music, it has been aptly observed, creates the past anew, as though it emanated from a realm of shadows—a dream world—another life.

Charles Martin Loeffler was born on January 30, 1861 at Mulhouse in Alsace. His father was a consulting scientist, whose chief hobby was music and his mother was an ardent devotee of poetry. Thus we can trace Loeffler's fondness for finding inspiration for many of his most outstanding works in literary subjects.

While still a boy under ten, Loeffler was taken to Russia, where under the guidance of a German musician connected with the Imperial Orchestra in St. Petersburg, he had his first violin lessons. Later his family moved to Hungary. These early environments are said to have had an incisive influence upon his musical tastes and tendencies.

At the age of fourteen, after two years spent in Switzerland, Loeffler decided to become a professional violinist. Going to Berlin, he became a violin pupil first of Rappoldi and then of Joachim, and a student of harmony under Kiel. Later he continued his studies on the violin in Paris under Massart, whom he found more agreeable to his temperament, and in composition with Guiraud.

In 1881, Loeffler came to America, where he first played in the orchestras of Leopold Damrosch and Theodore Thomas. In 1882, he became a member of the Boston Symphony Orchestra, where from 1885 to 1903, he shared the first violin desk with Kneisel. In 1903, he resigned his position to devote himself exclusively to composition.

For the remainder of his life, Loeffler lived in semi-retirement in his home in Massachusetts, composing only a handful of works of considerable beauty, such as the *Evocation,* written to dedicate Severance Hall in Cleveland. He died in Medfield, Massachusetts, in 1935.

A PAGAN POEM, OP. 14

HERE we have Loeffler's impressionism at its purest and best, the completest realization of the composer's ideals of tonal beauty. In its original form, composed in 1901, *A Pagan Poem* was scored for a chamber-music ensemble. This evidently dissatisfied the composer, for two years later he arranged the music for two pianos and three trumpets. Finally, he rewrote it for piano and full symphony orchestra. In this form it was introduced by the Boston Symphony Orchestra under Karl Muck in 1907; and in this form the work has become famous.

This exquisite tone poem was inspired by Virgil's eighth Eclogue, but is by no means a literal musical interpretation of the magic powers of the Thessalian maiden to bring back her estranged lover. The music rather attempts to re-create the mood of the poem, its ethereal atmosphere, its delicate feelings, its sensual qualities. Loeffler here succeeded in producing a delicate and sensitive masterpiece in which the writing is sustained from beginning to end on a high plane of beauty.

PARTITA, FOR VIOLIN AND PIANO

Intrada; A Merry Fugue · Sarabande · Divertissement · Finale des tendre adieux

AMONG Loeffler's works, his Partita ranks as one of his finest chamber compositions. It is dedicated to Mrs. Elizabeth Sprague Coolidge, the sponsor of so many chamber compositions, and is founded upon a motive derived from the initials of her name. The note E-flat in German being known as Es, her initials transcribed into music become E, E-flat, C. This musical motto appears in the very beginning and at the end of the composition.

The Partita, which was first performed at a festival of chamber music in Chicago in the autumn of 1930 is, as its name implies, conceived in the manner of a classic suite. It is in four movements. The Intrada is in a fugal form, beginning with a broad and expressive introduction, and passing on into a "merry fugue." The Sarabande consists of a stately theme and variations. In the third movement, elements of jazz are introduced, bringing a striking note of modernity to this classic form. The last movement is in modified rondo form and is Gallic in flavor.

M-MM-275, Jacques Gordon, Violin, and Lee Pattison, Piano.

Edward MacDowell

1861–1908

Edward MacDowell, dean of nineteenth century American composers, was born in New York City on December 18, 1861. His first teachers were various Latin-Americans, among them the celebrated pianist, Teresa Carreño; but like so many of his compatriots, he looked to Europe for the completion of his musical education and became a pupil at the Paris Conservatoire in 1876. There he remained for three years before moving to Germany to add yet another influence to his completely international training, a training that is rather strange for a man whose name was to become associated with the best music to be composed in America.

In 1888, MacDowell returned to America and settled in Boston where he prospered as a pianist and composer, playing his own music and the music of others with the Boston Symphony Orchestra, the Kneisel Quartet and at private solo concerts. Twelve years later he was called to New York to accept the first chair of music at Columbia University. MacDowell was never very happy with the Columbia post, although it relieved him of the economic apprehension that troubles artists in general. He finally resigned in 1904 after much disagreement with the administration over the importance of music and the fine arts in the curriculum. Resignation from the Columbia faculty virtually marked the end of MacDowell's career, for although he was free from the strain of harrowing arguments, the impact of bickering affected his nerves and in the spring of 1905 he broke down completely. He died three years later at New York on January 24, 1908.

As a composer MacDowell advocated a just measure for the American musician. He wanted to have American composers judged without condescension by the same standards as were European composers. Musically, he was a romanticist. He expressed himself according to programmes, but he strove to achieve moods and emotions evoked by moods, rather than musical pictures of the subject matter. He was a great lover of nature and received the inspiration for many of his loveliest works from the woods.

SUITE NO. 2 (INDIAN), OP. 48

LEGEND	IN WAR-TIME
LOVE SONG	DIRGE

THE *Indian* Suite was first performed at a concert of the Boston Symphony Orchestra on January 23, 1896, Emil Pauer conducting. A note in the score states that the thematic material was suggested by the music of the Indians of North America. MacDowell had made an intensive study of native Indian music and was powerfully attracted to it; in his Suite he tapped this folklore vein for his melodic material. Frequently, the melodies were subjected to subtle rhythmic changes; but their Indian identity is always recognizable.

In the "Legend" movement, MacDowell uses an Iroquois theme, reserved by these Indians for sacred ceremonies; a Kiowas love song is interpolated in the "Love Song"; in the "In War-Time," the principal subject is one believed by the Indians of the Atlantic Coast to have supernatural origin; a Kiowa tune is heard in the "Dirge," while a dance and war song indigenous with the Iroquois Indians appear in the "Village Festival."

Though composed in this country by a native American, the *Indian* Suite was first published in Germany, by Breitkopf & Härtel in 1897. It is dedicated to Emil Pauer and the Boston Symphony Orchestra.

M-MM-373, Columbia Broadcasting Symphony, Howard Barlow Conducting.

Gustav Mahler

1860–1911

Gustav Mahler was born in a little town in Bohemia. Melodic are the very whisperings of Bohemia's groves and meadows, the murmuring of its fertile fields and streams, and song accompanies the women at their work. This song remained ever the primal song in Mahler's heart and lives in his symphonies in the ever recurring voices of Bohemia—even the horn and trumpet signals of the soldiers in the barracks to which he so often listened as a child.

As a boy Gustav Mahler was sent to Vienna to study music at the Imperial Conservatory. Now he became acquainted with a landscape which, though new, had familiar features. All the world knows the greatness, the uniqueness, the bitter-sweetness of the melody of Vienna and the Austrian land from the works of Haydn, Mozart, and Schubert. Young Mahler drank in this Austrian melody and in his soul it blended with the Bohemian in a sublime unison.

Gustav Mahler's life is an explanation and verification of his music. He rose out of the most confining circumstances. When eighteen he was already conductor at a small theatre. Then for years he worked in the provinces until finally through his talent and energy he rose at thirty-seven to the all-powerful post of Director of the Imperial Opera at Vienna, in the face of the most embittered opposition. His activity there meant a reformation of the entire musical life. Ten years later he came to New York as one of the greatest and most celebrated conductors of his time. He died at the age of fifty. His activity as conductor and operatic director might well have filled another's life to the brim. While others rested he created his great work, the nine mighty symphonies and many Lieder cycles, works which today speak ever more forcibly to us. Thus, in the short pauses which his duties allowed him, he became the last of that line of great men, which begins with Haydn and culminates in Beethoven.

DAS LIED VON DER ERDE (THE SONG OF THE EARTH)

THE LIFE and music of Gustav Mahler can be fully understood only in the setting of his time and place, the pre-war Vienna, Janus-like in its dual aspect of the gay capital of the Waltz, and the seat of heavy intellectualism and searching philosophy. This was the city of Freud; of the pleasure-loving royalty, and of the tragic Mahler. It must be understood that at that time the Wagnerian wave was still rolling strong; composers did not merely write music: they created philosophies, founded religions. Although Mahler invariably denied that his symphonies had a program or a story behind them, each work was a chapter in his struggle with himself or, as he believed, a struggle with some mystical evil force.

Bruno Walter, Mahler's friend and interpreter, tells us a strange story which seems to have come from out of Edgar Allan Poe: "While at work in his cottage in Toblach, he was suddenly frightened by an indefinable noise. All at once something terribly dark came rushing in by the window, and, when he jumped up in horror, he saw that he was in the presence of an eagle which filled the little room with its violence. The fearsome meeting was quickly over, and the eagle disappeared as stormily as it had come. When Mahler sat down, exhausted by his fright, a crow came fluttering from under the sofa and flew out."

Bruno Walter thinks that this episode happened at the time Mahler was composing *Das Lied von der Erde,* and that Mahler referred to the work as a symphony in songs: "It was to have been his Ninth. Subsequently, however, he changed his mind. He thought of Beethoven and Bruckner, whose Ninth had marked the ultimate of their creation and life, and did not care to challenge fate. He turned to the *Abschied* (last movement) and said: 'What do you think of it? Will not people do away with themselves, when they hear it?'" But Mahler *did* write a Ninth Symphony, and even started on a Tenth.

As to *Das Lied von der Erde,* it is not numbered among Mahler's symphonies at all. It must therefore be considered, as Mahler said to Bruno Walter, a symphony of songs, separate from his purely symphonic works.

The selection of texts to these songs is also characteristic of the spirit of pre-war Europe. It was a set of Chinese poems translated into German. Chinese poetry and Japanese art were extremely popular among European intellectuals before the cataclysm. The Orient was believed by them to possess an immediacy of feeling, a spirit of communion with the eternal that no white man could approach. The selection of poetry cannot, therefore, be accidental, and must be regarded as part of the design.

All the songs of *Das Lied von der Erde* are united by a leading motive, a descending progression of three tones—A, G, E. These three tones may, of course, be regarded as a part of the Chinese pentatonic scale, but there is no evidence to support this assumption. The motive was not used explicitly; rather it was Mahler's private magic formula which he employed in various forms, in augmentation, or diminution, played twice as fast. All three tones appear together in the concluding chord of the entire work, signifying unity. The symbolic quality of *Das Lied von der Erde* is thus plainly indicated.

There are altogether six songs. The first is a "Drinking Song of the Misery of the Earth." The pessimistic refrain of the song "Dark is life, and so is death," is heard in a lugubrious phrase in G minor.

The second movement, or the second song, is entitled "The Lonely One in Autumn." The characteristic indication in lieu of the tempo mark is: "Somewhat dragging. Tired out." Against the background of muted violins, the oboe intones sadly the three notes of the leading motive. The contralto sings the song of loneliness and soul fatigue.

The third song, "Of Youth," is the scherzo of this symphony of songs. The Chinese pentatonic scale is used in this movement explicitly, imparting to the piece a definite local color.

The fourth movement is entitled "Of Beauty." The text of the song describes young maidens at play, and once more the pentatonic scale is explicitly employed. There are rhythmic figures that suggest a light dance.

The fifth movement is called "Drunkard in Spring." But the drinking is not gay; it is an escape from life's troubles. The theme is gay but wry, with melodic intervals distorted to express bitterness in artificial gaiety.

The sixth movement is "The Farewell." This is the movement that

Mahler thought would inspire suicidal thoughts. The song describes the death of the day, when the sun sets, and the world falls asleep.

M-MM-300, Kerstin Thorborg, Contralto, Charles Kullman, Tenor, and the Vienna Philharmonic Orchestra, Bruno Walter Conducting.

SONGS OF A WAYFARER

The *Lieder eines fahrenden Gesellen*—variously translated *Songs of a Wayfarer*, *Songs of a Traveling Apprentice*, *Songs of a Wandering Youth*—were composed in 1883, when Mahler was only twenty-three, but were not published until fourteen years later. At the time of their composition, Mahler, who was serving as assistant conductor of the Opera at Cassel, Germany, was in the midst of a youthful love affair with Johanna Richter, one of the singers. The shock of being rejected in his suit caused the young composer to express his feelings in six songs, for which he wrote both the words and music.

Mahler himself wrote of the Songs as follows: "I have written a song-cycle, at present six songs, all of which are dedicated to her. She does not know them. But they can tell her only what she already knows. Their burden is a man who has found only sadness in love and who goes forth into the world as a wanderer."

These songs also served as a prelude to Mahler's Symphony No. 1 in D major, the thematic material from the second and fourth of them figuring prominently in the symphony.

The songs were first heard at an orchestral concert under Mahler's direction in Berlin in March 1896, with the Dutch singer, Anton Sistermans, as soloist.

X-MX-267, Carol Brice, Contralto, and the Pittsburgh Symphony Orchestra, Fritz Reiner Conducting.

SYMPHONY NO. 1 IN D MAJOR
Langsam · Kräftig bewegt · Feierlich und gemessen Stürmisch bewegt

MOST of Mahler's youthful works, including chamber and symphonic music as well as opera, he destroyed. But in the years 1883 and 1884 he composed the *Lieder eines fahrenden Gesellen* ("Songs of a Way-farer"), while the initial version of *Das klagende Lied* ("Song of Lament") goes back at least to 1880. By 1888, Mahler had completed the First Symphony, which employed for two of its principal themes, melodies from *Lieder eines fahrenden Gesellen*. The Symphony received its first performance, under the direction of the composer, in Budapest during the following year.

At first the symphony, dubbed "The Titan," was a failure. The young conductor scarcely found an audience prepared for his sensationally complex and sharply individual music. Even the printed program referred to the new work as a symphonic poem in two parts.

The composer himself at one period believed that his music would not make its way without explanation. Although the first performance in Budapest was unaccompanied by any "program," subsequent performances in Weimar and Hamburg quoted the following remarkable description by the composer:

"Part I. The Days of Youth. Youth, flowers and thorns. (1) Spring without end. The introduction represents the awakening of nature at early dawn. (2) A Chapter of Flowers (Andante). (3) Full Sail! (Scherzo). Part II. Commedia umana (Human comedy). (4) Stranded. A funeral march à la Callot.

"The following remarks may serve as an explanation *if necessary*. The author received the external stimulus to this piece from a pictorial parody well known to all children in South Germany, 'The Hunter's Funeral Procession.' The forest animals accompany the dead forester's coffin to the grave. The hares carry flags; in front is a band of Gypsy musicians and music-making cats, frogs, crows, etc.; and deer, stags, foxes, and other four-footed and feathered denizens of the forest accompany the procession in comic postures. In the present piece the imagined expression is partly ironically gay, partly gloomily brooding, and is immediately followed by (5) *Dall' Inferno al Paradiso* (Allegro furioso), the sudden outbreak of a wounded heart."

M-MM-469, Minneapolis Symphony Orchestra, Dimitri Mitropoulos Conducting.

SYMPHONY NO. 4 IN G MAJOR

*Bedächtig, nicht eilen · In gemächlicher Bewegung, ohne Hast
Ruhevoll · Sehr behaglich*

No COMPOSER is more completely absorbed in Nature than Gustav
Mahler. In all his nine symphonies he reveals its mysterious force,
from the bud to the flower, from wastrel profusion to decay; and
again and again, Death. The very symphonic form, the origin and the
development of the themes seem to repeat the fate of organic matter.
Mahler's music has no program, but it is poetic music, full of imagery,
metaphors, crises. Its eternal fundament is wondrous and pitiless
nature. And in the middle stands Man.

The first movement of the Symphony No. 4 depicts the lovely
landscape of the environs of Vienna in a conscious revival of the
warmly staid style of Haydn. At the same time the main theme reveals the most genuine Mahler inspiration.

In the second movement the composer was under the spell of the
self-portrait by Arnold Böcklin, in which Death fiddles into the
painter's ear while the latter listens entranced.

The third movement transports us to the realm of heavenly bliss,
which is presented to us plastically by the text of the fourth movement.

About this fourth movement Mahler spoke frequently and in
detail. A poem, *The Heavenly Life,* in Arnim and Brentano's collection, *Des Knaben Wunderhorn,* had bewitched him. Medieval
mysticism was akin to his nature. He wanted to write something
archaistic. He wanted to paint a *quattrocento* picture on gold base.
He wanted to set to music the stiff figures with the transfigured faces:
the hurrying angels . . . St. Peter calmly observant . . . St. John's
escaped lamb innocently led to death by Herod . . . the ox, sacrificed without hesitation . . . fish and deer, leaping joyfully to death.
Over it all the abundance of bread and wine! And St. Cecilia's music
transports them all into eternal bliss.

To the composer all this seemed to be his own personal experience.
He wanted a voice of silver purity for the soprano solo, and regretted
that a child could never sing it.

At its conclusion the Symphony fades into a mere breath.

M-MM-589, Dési Halban, Soprano, and the Philharmonic-Symphony Orchestra of
New York, Bruno Walter Conducting.

[273]

Pietro Mascagni
1863–1945

PIETRO MASCAGNI was born in Leghorn in 1863. His father wanted him to become a lawyer and frowned upon his wishes to study music seriously. For a while, Mascagni studied music secretly; then, after being adopted by an uncle, turned to it openly and completely. Mascagni's early works for chorus showed so much promise that their composer was subsidized to study at the Milan Conservatory. He did not remain there long. He joined up with a touring opera company as conductor, then settled at Cerignola as a music teacher.

A one-act opera suddenly swept him to fame—*Cavalleria Rusticana,* which won first prize in a contest sponsored by the publisher Sonzogno and then was produced in Rome in 1890. *Cavalleria* made its composer a musical figure of international importance. He composed other operas after that, mild successes like *Iris* and *L'Amico Fritz.* But to the end of his life he remained known primarily for *Cavalleria.* Mascagni, who toured America several times, was the recipient of many honors, and in the closing years of his life was considered the *grand homme* of Italian music. He died in Rome in 1945.

CAVALLERIA RUSTICANA

THE NAME of *Cavalleria Rusticana* recalls one of the most instantaneous, complete and astonishing successes ever achieved in the presentation of a new opera. Pietro Mascagni, a young musician hailing from Leghorn, had long struggled, against parental opposition and very uncertain fortune, to make his mark in the musical world of Italy. After a wandering existence covering a period of several years, conducting for one small opera troupe after another, he had settled in the town of Cerignola as teacher in the local music school. The announcement came of a competition for a new opera, instituted by the famous music publishing house of Sonzogno, and pushing to completion the score of a one-act opera on which he had been working, Mascagni submitted it for the contest. It bore away the prize and on May 18, 1890, *Cavalleria Rusticana* was produced in Rome. The performance ended in such a scene of enthusiasm as had probably never before attended an operatic première. Mascagni became a world figure overnight. He returned to his native Leghorn to be invested with the order of the Crown of Italy by the King and to find that a medal had been struck in his honor.

The plot of the story is direct, forceful and dramatic, leading with lurid intensity to its tragic finale. Lola, youthful sweetheart of Turiddu, during the latter's prolonged absence on military duty, has married Alfio, the village teamster. Turiddu, returning, addresses his attentions to Santuzza, whom he wrongs. Tiring of her, he enters into an intrigue with Lola, whose husband is frequently absent from the village. The scene opens in the little Calabrian town on Easter morning. Alfio returns after an absence of some days and meets Santuzza who, in a jealous fury, after a passionate and futile argument with Turiddu, informs the teamster of his wife's unfaithfulness. Alfio encounters Turriddu and after the ancient Calabrian fashion of biting the ear challenges him to fight. Turiddu, too late repenting his actions, accepts the challenge and is killed by Alfio.

The opera is full of memorable melodies. The best known of these —a staple in the repertory of salon music—is the Intermezzo, which is performed during the Mass scene. The Siciliana air, sung backstage in the Prelude, is one of the most lyrical tenor arias in Italian opera.

OP-MOP-7, Lombardi, Castagna, Mannarini, Melandri, Lulli, Chorus of La Scala, and the Milan Symphony Orchestra, Lorenzo Molajoli Conducting.

Jules Massenet

1842–1912

JULES MASSENET composed over a score of stage works, and excelled in mobile and easily assimilable melodies. He wrote his music rapidly, thereby inviting superficiality and discouraging profundity and scholarship. But he never failed, at least in his best operas, to cast a spell of enchantment over his audiences. His sweet and sympathetic nature induced a languorous sentimentality which developed music that is frequently tender and feminine. And he was a master in evoking sensitive moods that are irresistible.

He was born in Montaud, St. Etienne, in 1842. After removing to Paris in 1851, he entered the Paris Conservatory. While there he found it difficult to provide for himself with the necessities of life His parents were too poor to remit a regular allowance, and he was forced to obtain a position playing the triangle in an orchestra, following this with an engagement at the Théâtre des Italiens where he played the drums three times a week. His perseverance and his application to his studies at the Conservatory eventually gained him the much coveted Grand Prix de Rome in 1863.

He wrote his first opera soon after his return to Paris from Rome— *La Grand 'tante,* performed at the Opéra Comique in 1867. But he achieved his first marked success not with an opera but an oratorio This was *Les Erynnies,* one number of which is the world famou "Elégie." Indicative of his now expanding fame was his election to the Académie des Beaux Arts, and his appointment as professor o composition to the Paris Conservatory.

His most productive period were the two decades between 188(and 1900 when he wrote those operas by which he is today best re membered: *Manon* (1884), *Le Cid* (1885), *Werther* (1892), an *Thaïs* (1894). He died in Paris in 1912.

MANON

IT IS generally conceded that *Manon* is Massenet's greatest opera.
Here we have pure Massenet melody at its very best, and much more
besides. Massenet also displays a mastery of orchestration by which
he succeeds in resuscitating the time, spirit, and scenes of the early
part of the 18th century. And in his dances, he imitates the style of
Lully and Rameau "with extraordinary cleverness."

The influence of Wagner runs through this opera. Massenet stated
that it was based on a set of motives, one for each character, with
two for Manon exemplifying the duality of her nature—sadness and
gaiety. Each scene has its own special local atmosphere, while the
differentiation of Manon and Des Grieux suggests that the composer
anticipated the theory of the "Life-force" that Bernard Shaw dis-
cuses in *Man and Superman*. In the two lovers Massenet forges
a link that shows the inseparability of life and passion.

The opera is based on Abbé Prevost's *Histoire de Manon Lescaut
et du Chevalier des Grieux*. Meilhac was one day discussing the
novel with Massenet and suggested that the subject would make an
excellent opera. "Yes," replied Massenet, "we'll call it *Manon*." It was
produced on January 19, 1884, at the Opéra Comique in Paris.

The opera is centered around the tragic love of Manon Lescaut
for Chevalier des Grieux. They flee to Paris where Des Grieux is
abducted by his father who objects to this affair. Manon, now a mistress of Des Grieux' cousin, learns that her beloved is about to take
holy orders. She prevails on him to run away with her. Des Grieux
becomes a gambler and a cheat, and Manon his accomplice. They become entangled in the law, from which Des Grieux successfully ex-
tricates himself through the influence of his father; but Manon is
sentenced for deportation to America. Des Grieux comes to Le Havre
to try to effect Manon's escape; but Manon is mortally ill, and she
dies in his arms.

OP-MOP-10, Artists, Chorus and Orchestra of the Opéra Comique, Élie Cohen Conducting.

Felix Mendelssohn

1809–1847

MENDELSSOHN is properly classed among romantic composers. He was born a year before Schumann and Chopin; but the path of his life was far too smooth for a romantic biography. He was one of the few celebrated composers who did not have to struggle for a living. His grandfather was a philosopher, but his father was a banker; and it was the banker who made Mendelssohn's life easy. The piercing intellectual eyes, familiar in Mendelssohn's portraits, he inherited from the philosopher, and from the banker he acquired the quiet and assured manner of life.

Mendelssohn was a common Jewish name in Germany, a compound of two words, Mendels Sohn (hence two s's), that is, Mendel's son. The name Bartholdy was added when the family adopted the Protestant faith. Bartholdy was the name of the former owner of the garden bought by Mendelssohn's uncle. And it was that uncle who persuaded the banker Mendelssohn to embrace the religion that was prevalent in the country.

He was born in 1809 at Hamburg, Germany, and died on November 4, 1847, at Leipzig. One scarcely realizes that his life span was only three years longer than that of Mozart. When the Nazi regime in Germany came into power, Mendelssohn's music was banned there, because of his Jewish origin. A statue that stood as a memorial to him in Leipzig was completely demolished.

As a youth, this composer had every educational advantage that a city like Berlin could offer. His instruction in music was superlative: he mastered the piano sufficiently to appear in public at the age of nine; he was an accomplished violinist; his early compositions furnished a large part of the program at the musical evenings at the Mendelssohn home. These Sunday evening concerts became one of the central attractions of Berlin musical life. They were not only of inestimable value to the youthful composer as opportunities to hear performances of his own works, but they attracted musicians from all over Europe who constantly visited Berlin.

There is a certain parallel between his life and Mozart's, for before Mendelssohn reached the age of sixteen, he had a wide acquaintance among the intellectual and artistic leaders of Europe. He knew Spontini in Berlin. Cherubini—whom he had met in Paris—wanted him as a pupil. He had been a guest at Goethe's home in Weimar. Weber he knew and greatly admired. Ignaz Moscheles, an admirer, friend and pupil of Beethoven, and one of the leading pianists of the time, was a welcome visitor in the Mendelssohn home. At the age of seventeen, young Felix had composed the Overture to *A Midsummer Night's Dream* (1826), than which no prelude to Shakespeare's eerie comedy could be more appropriate. In this work he demonstrated that he had not only attained a complete mastery over his materials, but was already a mature and original composer.

Between 1827 and 1835, Mendelssohn's activity took him from city to city on the Continent and in England. His popularity increased to a point where he was deluged with invitations to the finest homes. Some have said that this acclaim was unwarranted; but his works today speak for themselves and bear the stamp of genius. In 1829 he conducted the first performance, after Bach's death, of the great *St. Matthew* Passion. During the same year he spent some time in England, where the performance of his C minor Symphony and the *Midsummer Night's Dream* Overture laid the foundation for his international fame as a composer. Known as pianist, conductor and composer, he was in constant demand throughout Europe. This period saw the production of many important works, among which were the first volume of the *Songs Without Words*, the *Hebrides* Overture, the *Italian* and *Reformation* symphonies, and the G minor Piano Concerto.

In 1835, Mendelssohn became the conductor of the Gewandhaus Orchestra in Leipzig, and eight years after that he helped to found the Leipzig Conservatory.

Mendelssohn displayed certain qualities which, if not inimical to creative musicianship, are certainly not general hallmarks of genius. It was his misfortune to suffer none of the dramatic adversities which

[279]

make composers attractive to the public. He was without guile, well-bred, free from complaint, and gentle-natured.

It has been suggested that the world would have been musically richer had Mendelssohn endured the privation so frequently the lot of his spectacular predecessors. One critic notes that he wrote "as he looks in his picture, smiling, and with a stickpin in his ruffled shirt," and continues to ask wistfully, "What might he not have accomplished if he had been poor and less respectable!" Mendelssohn did smile—constantly—he smiled sincerely, graciously, and also, with some depth of feeling. But most later critics have passed upon him a verdict of "charming, but not profound."

Mendelssohn eloquently refuted this notion, though it is also true that his work is not uniform, and in spots, mediocre. Something more than a superficial gaiety accounts for the modern popularity of his symphonies. Perhaps it is his unfailing courtesy, his broad tolerance, his neatness and order. These were all qualities in which he excelled. But they are qualities which set forth something more than themselves. They are not empty form. Mendelssohn did express more than an empty etiquette. He entered wholeheartedly, if somewhat discreetly, into the spirit of his experiences, and in his larger works has preserved the inner substance of those experiences, refined and distilled in his music. If he does not attempt the objectives of a Beethoven or Brahms, it cannot be said that he is any less successful in what he did attempt, or even, in view of the result, that his music is to be compared unfavorably with that of others.

Mendelssohn was a most popular composer in his day, and perhaps because of that fact the reaction against his music was stronger after his death. His sentimentality and moderation became and remained the butt of critics well into the present century. Fortunately the tide has turned in his favor, and with it a more just and profitable estimate is now prevalent.

CONCERTO IN E MINOR, OP. 64, FOR VIOLIN AND ORCHESTRA

Allegro molto appassionato · *Andante* · *Allegro molto vivace*

MENDELSSOHN'S Violin Concerto was the result of a long friendship between the composer and the prominent violinist Ferdinand David. Mendelssohn did not meet him until he was sixteen, though the two were born in the same house in Hamburg. When Mendelssohn took over the conductorship of the Leipzig Gewandhaus Orchestra in 1835, he made David his concertmaster, a post David retained for thirty-seven years.

Though Mendelssohn's principal instrument was the piano, he had studied both the violin and viola as a youth, and enjoyed playing the viola when he participated in informal performances of chamber music.

This Violin Concerto was first mentioned in a letter that the composer wrote to David in 1838, in which he said: "I should like to write a violin concerto for you next winter. One in E minor runs through my head, the beginning of which gives me no peace." Evidently the work did not haunt him too much, for he did not compose it the following winter. David must have kept after him, however, as evidenced by another letter from Mendelssohn a year later: "It is nice of you to press me for a violin concerto! I have the liveliest desire to write one for you, and if I have a few propitious days here, I'll bring you something. But the task is not an easy one. You demand that it should be brilliant, and how is such a one as I to manage that? The whole of the first solo is to be for the E string."

It was another five years before the Concerto was completed, with many consultations between the composer and the violinist over details of the solo and orchestral parts. Mendelssohn put the final note on the score on September 16, 1844, and it was sent to the publisher in December. But even then, there were further revisions which were not completed until February. David offered suggestions regarding the solo parts, and it is believed that the cadenza, in its present form, is substantially his.

David was the soloist when the E minor Concerto was first performed at a Gewandhaus concert on March 13, 1845. Unfortunately, Mendelssohn was unable to be present, as he was taking an enforced

[281]

rest at Frankfort. His duties as conductor were taken over by the Danish composer, Niels W. Gade. Two weeks after the première, David wrote to Mendelssohn: "I should have written you before of the success that I made with your violin concerto. Forgive me if I do so only now. The work pleased extraordinarily well, and it was unanimously declared to be one of the most beautiful compositions of its kind." This opinion has been echoed during the more than a hundred years of the Concerto's existence, and today it is considered the favorite of all compositions for violin and orchestra.

The Concerto is written in three movements, which should be played without pause. Perhaps no other Mendelssohn work sustains such a high plane of melodic beauty throughout, beginning with the exquisite melody of the solo violin in the very beginning of the Concerto, through the eloquent measures of the ethereal slow movement, and up to the closing pages with their sunny humor and sparkle.

M-MM-577, Nathan Milstein, Violin, and the Philharmonic-Symphony Orchestra of New York, Bruno Walter Conducting.

ELIJAH, OP. 70

FROM the time he achieved his spectacular success with his oratorio *St. Paul* at the Birmingham Festival of 1837, Mendelssohn was fired with the ambition of writing an even more elaborate work around the prophet Elijah. He sketched parts of it from time to time, spoke about it to various people, concentrated on it for a while in 1843. Yet the impetus for its actual completion did not come until 1845 when Birmingham asked him to prepare a new oratorio for its festival the following year.

Elijah was one of the most powerful of the Hebrew prophets. Mendelssohn wanted his story to be told in a dramatic, almost operatic, manner, with a good deal of dialogue. The Oratorio, in two parts, opens with the prophet's announcement of the coming drought; it pictures the miracles performed by the Prophet and the hostility he had to endure; it concludes with his ascent to Heaven, carried by flames. Aided by Julius Schubring, pastor at Dessau, Mendelssohn prepared his libretto; the translation into English (by Bartholomew) was sent to him as he composed his music, and he himself made last-minute alterations in the text to avoid discrepancies between words and music.

His friendship with Jenny Lind inspired much of the beautiful music of *Elijah*. It was with her voice in mind that Mendelssohn wrote many of the soprano arias. Lind did not sing in the première performance, but she did participate in many subsequent presentations. Shortly after Mendelssohn's death she organized and supervised a performance of *Elijah* to raise funds for a Mendelssohn music school (the first scholarship going to Arthur Sullivan).

The première of the new oratorio, on August 26, 1846, went exceedingly well. Four choruses and four arias had to be repeated. Mendelssohn himself regarded it as one of the greatest successes of his life. To the present day, *Elijah* enjoys in England a popularity second only to that of the *Messiah*.

The oratorio is rich with dramatic music, effective recitatives, moving choruses, and beautifully melodious arias. It is a simple and direct expression of sincere religious feelings. The direct use of the Psalms, with simple music merely underlining the meaning of the text, is highly effective. And some of the greatest arias are so wonderfully lyrical that they have acquired a permanent place on concert programs ("*It Is Enough,*" "*O Rest in the Lord,*" and "*If with All Your Hearts*").

After the première, Mendelssohn subjected his oratorio to extensive revision, adding a few numbers, including the trio "*Lift Thine Eyes,*" and the final chorus. He worked on the score for many months before he permitted Simrock to publish it (in June 1847). In the spring of 1847—on his tenth (and last) visit to England—he conducted the new version, giving six performances, four of them in London. Queen Victoria and Prince Albert were in the audience at the concert of April 26, and were so pleased that the Prince wrote a spontaneous and highly laudatory tribute to the composer on the back of his program.

THE HEBRIDES (FINGAL'S CAVE) OVERTURE, OP. 26

In 1829 Mendelssohn, accompanied by his friend Klingemann, visited the Island of Staffa, a tiny member of the Hebrides group, on which is situated the famed Fingal's Cave. Klingemann described the visit as follows: "We were put out in boats, and lifted by the hissing sea up the pillar stumps to the celebrated Fingal's Cave. A greener roar of waves surely never rushed into a stranger cavern—its many pillars making it look like the inside of an immense organ, black and resounding, and absolutely without purpose, and quite alone, the wide gray sea within and without."

But Mendelssohn did not set down his impressions in words. Instead, on the very same day that he visited the cave, he wrote to his sister Fanny: "That you may understand how extraordinarily the Hebrides affected me, the following came into my mind." And he noted down the twenty-one measures of music that were to form the opening of the Overture.

The composer worked for some time on this piece of picture music, and in December 1830, while he was in Rome, the score was completed. Even then Mendelssohn was not satisfied with it. In January 1832, he wrote from Paris: "The middle portion is too stupid, and the whole working out smacks more of counterpoint than of train oil, sea gulls and salt fish, and must be altered." That he was finally successful in painting a wonderfully vivid musical picture of the seascape is evidenced by the immense popularity that the work has enjoyed. It was first performed on May 14, 1832, at a Philharmonic concert in London, and was most enthusiastically received.

The double title of this Overture results from the fact that the original score was marked *Fingal's Cave*, while the orchestral parts bore the title *The Hebrides*.

M-MM-552, London Philharmonic Orchestra, Sir Thomas Beecham Conducting.

A MIDSUMMER NIGHT'S DREAM, SUITE, OPP. 21, 61a

OVERTURE

SCHERZO

NOCTURNE

INTERMEZZO

WEDDING MARCH

MENDELSSOHN was seventeen when he composed the Overture to *A Midsummer Night's Dream;* he was thirty-four when he completed his incidental music to Shakespeare's comedy with the addition of the Scherzo, Nocturne, Wedding March and several other orchestral and vocal numbers. It is thought remarkable that Wagner was able to achieve continuity of style and mood in the *Ring,* on which composition was suspended for a twelve-year period. But Wagner was a man of forty-four when the interruption occurred, the plan of the *Ring* was formulated in detail in his mind and on paper, the text was written, and the source material for music of the last act of *Siegfried* and the whole of the *Götterdämmerung* existed in the completed portions of the score. The circumstances in Mendelssohn's case were very different. The *Midsummer Night's Dream* Overture was the work of an inspired boy. Its perfection of form, the sure handling throughout of the materials of musical composition, testify to fully developed technical powers. But the spirit of the music is the spirit of youth—fanciful, extravagant, naïvely romantic. Yet Mendelssohn at thirty-four could recapture it perfectly.

The completion of the *Midsummer Night's Dream* music was undertaken at the request of the King of Prussia. In the printed score the Overture is succeeded by twelve separate numbers and a finale. No. 1 is the Scherzo, intended as an interlude between the first and second acts of the play. No. 2, written to accompany stage action, employs thematic material from the Scherzo. No. 3 is the song "You spotted snakes," for solo voice and chorus. No. 4 is background music, No. 5 an Intermezzo intended to follow Act 2. Printed above it in the score is the following descriptive note: "Hermia seeks Lysander and loses herself in the wood." No. 6 is music to accompany the scene of Titania's infatuation with Bottom. No. 7 is the celebrated Nocturne. No. 8 again is background music. No. 9 is a miniature March, No. 10 an even briefer Funeral March. No. 11 is dance music accompanying stage action. No. 12 is the Wedding March.

Aside from the Overture, Scherzo, Nocturne and Wedding March, only a single number of the score is suitable for concert hall performance: the brief descriptive piece (No. 5) composed as a musical epilogue to Act 2. It is included in this Rodzinski-Cleveland Orchestra Masterworks recording.

The *Midsummer Night's Dream* music was completed in the summer of 1843. It was first used in conjunction with a performance of Shakespeare's comedy given in the Neue Palais at Potsdam on October 18, of that year. Public performances at the King's Theater, Berlin, followed immediately. Mendelssohn had enemies in the Prussian court and in Berlin musical circles. But his music had irresistible charm and it was received with the greatest favor.

M-MM-504, Cleveland Orchestra, Artur Rodzinski Conducting.

SYMPHONY NO. 3 IN A MINOR (SCOTCH), OP. 56

*Andante con moto; Allegro un poco agitato · Vivace non troppo
Adagio · Allegro vivacissimo*

THE NUMBERING of the Mendelssohn symphonies, like that of the Schumann symphonies, is misleading. The *Reformation* Symphony, No. 5, is really No. 2; the *Italian* Symphony, No. 4, is really No. 3, and the *Scotch* Symphony, No. 3, is really No. 5 in order of composition, the latest and most mature of Mendelssohn's works in the form, completed in 1842 and first played on March 3 of that year, at a Gewandhaus concert in Leipzig, the composer conducting.

Mendelssohn was the most peripatetic of composers, always on the move, driven from Germany to England, from England to Switzerland, from Switzerland to Italy, from Italy to France, not by circumstances beyond his control, as in the case of other musical wanderers (Chopin, Liszt, Wagner), but simply by love of travel and an amiable willingness to indulge friends and impresarios who desired his presence now in Berlin, now in London, now in Rome, now in Paris. He had a special fondness for England, which he visited no fewer than ten times between 1829 and 1847, the year of his death.

His travels supplied the inspiration for a number of his works. The deep impression made on him in 1829 by the natural and historical

[286]

monuments of Scotland resulted in the composition of the *Hebrides* Overture and the A minor Symphony. The designation *Scotch* was originally no part of the official title of the latter work, but it stems nevertheless from Mendelssohn, who made use of it in his correspondence from 1832 on. To the same source—the composer's letters —must be ascribed the tradition which associates the Symphony with the story of the murder of David Rizzio, at Holyrood Castle.

Mendelssohn visited Holyrood in July, 1829, and wrote this account of the experience: "We went, in the deep twilight, to the castle where Queen Mary lived and loved. There is a little room to be seen there, with a winding staircase leading up to it. This the murderers ascended, and finding Rizzio, drew him out. Three chambers away is a small chamber where they killed him . . . I believe I found today the beginning of my Scotch Symphony." Then or later he jotted down that beginning—a ten measure phrase—but thirteen years were to pass before the Symphony was completed.

Though it is not easy to associate the melodrama of Mary and Rizzio and Bothwell with Mendelssohn's music, that music does somehow manage to suggest typically Scottish scenes—somber, treeless hills, interspersed with lakes whose unruffled surfaces reflect the whiteness of an overcast sky. To impose no more detailed a program than this on the music accords with Mendelssohn's own inclinations, for he combatted vigorously the efforts of his contemporaries to read meanings into his compositions, rebuking Schumann almost harshly when the latter professed to discover "red coral, sea monsters, magic castles and ocean caves" in the *Beautiful Melusine* Overture. Mendelssohn's point was not that his music had no meaning, in the programmatic sense, but that on the contrary, "notes have as definite a meaning as words, perhaps an even more definite one." And having expressed himself thus definitely in notes, he considered it an impertinence that anyone should reframe his thoughts in words.

The *Scotch* Symphony is in traditional form. The four movements, in accordance with the composer's wishes, are played without intervening pauses.

M-MM-540, Minneapolis Symphony Orchestra, Dimitri Mitropoulos Conducting.

SYMPHONY NO. 4 IN A MAJOR (ITALIAN), OP. 90

Allegro vivace · Andante con moto · Con moto moderato · Presto

MENDELSSOHN's *Italian* Symphony was inspired by a visit to Italy, just as his *Scotch* Symphony had its source in his travels in Scotland. From Rome he wrote to his sister Fanny: "I am making great progress with the *Italian* Symphony. It will be the most mature thing I have ever done, especially the last movement, Presto agitato." According to his letter, he planned to finish the work in Naples.

But the Symphony was not finished while the composer was in Italy, nor for some time afterwards. Possibly the invitation from the London Philharmonic Society in November 1832, to compose "a symphony, an overture, and a vocal piece," stimulated Mendelssohn to complete the *Italian* Symphony in Berlin on March 13, 1833. It was first performed by this same Philharmonic under the composer's direction exactly two months later. The Symphony made a great impression on the audience, as did Mendelssohn's performance of the solo part in the Mozart Piano Concerto in D minor.

But Mendelssohn was not satisfied with the Symphony. The following year he began to make revisions in the score, and even contemplated rewriting the first movement. This dissatisfaction prevented the publication of the work during his lifetime. Therefore, the *Scotch* Symphony, which was composed nine years after the *Italian,* was given the opus number 56, and is known as the Third, while the *Italian,* published in 1851, was assigned the opus number 90, and is known as the Fourth.

The second movement, Andante con moto, has often been referred to as the "Pilgrims' March."

For those who doubt the source of Mendelssohn's ideas for this Symphony, there is the characteristically Italian finale in the form of a saltarello. The saltarello is one of the most ancient of Italian dances, dating from the sixteenth century or before. It is in rapid time, and the name is derived from the Latin *saltare*—to jump. Mendelssohn has used the form most effectively, combining with two saltarello themes a whirling tarantella figure even wilder in its rhythm.

M-MM-538, Philharmonic-Symphony Orchestra of New York, Sir Thomas Beecham Conducting.

SYMPHONY NO. 5 IN D MAJOR
(REFORMATION), OP. 107

Andante; Allegro con fuoco · Allegro vivace · Andante
Allegro maestoso

THE *Reformation* Symphony opens with a slow introduction, marked Andante, which contains music of a dark and foreboding character. There is a hint of the chorale which comes in a later movement, then the familiar motif associated by most hearers with Wagner's *Parsifal*, which, however, was borrowed by both Wagner and Mendelssohn from the Saxon Liturgy. It is usually known as the "Dresden Amen." The principal section, Allegro con fuoco, opens with an agitated, restless passage, and continues with upward surges of tone, punctuated by staccato chords and accented passages in the brass. This restlessness continues with recurrence of the ascending sixths (the *Parsifal* motif), alternating with occasional waves of tone in the strings. The movement closes in a passage of deep melancholy.

In the second movement, the composer is heard in a more characteristic mood, as if, done with the formalities of introduction, he relaxed to his usual good nature. Woodwinds and horns set the atmosphere for the entire movement in a passage suggestive of the composer's *Italian* Symphony. Strings echo the theme and soon the full orchestra joins in, relapsing into a smooth-flowing, less intense melody in strings against a mosaic of woodwinds. The movement comes to a tranquil close.

The third movement opens with a wistful passage, growing more somber as it proceeds. After a crescendo and quiet major modulation the chorale, "*Ein' feste Burg*," is given out by flutes, to which are added the brasses, increasing in power and motion, as the third movement passes without pause into the fourth, an Allegro maestoso.

Marked ascending chords make a joyful beginning to this movement, while incisive passages for the strings lead to a contrapuntal development of considerable proportions, the chorale furnishing a sturdy background. The development of the chorale theme continues in widening contrapuntal patterns. The brass restates the chorale at intervals, giving way to one last tender statement by woodwinds, after which the full orchestra reunites in a powerful conclusion.

M-MM-391, Columbia Broadcasting Symphony, Howard Barlow Conducting.

Giacomo Meyerbeer

1791–1864

MEYERBEER was born in Berlin in 1791, the son of a wealthy banker. His real name was Jakob Liebmann Beer, but he later Italianized Jakob into Giacomo, and prefixed to his own name that of a relative, Meyer. His musical precocity was unusual. Studying under Lauska and Clementi, he made his pianistic debut with Mozart's Concerto in D minor at the age of seven. Subsequently, he was accepted by Abbé Vogler as a musical apprentice, Vogler's household at the time including another outstanding pupil, Carl Maria von Weber. An oratorio and two operas were written by Meyerbeer at this time, one of which—the opera *Alimelek*—was highly successful, and was accepted for performance in Vienna.

Upon Salieri's advice, Meyerbeer went to Venice, where his musical style underwent the first of its remarkable transformations. Rossini was at the time at the height of his fame. Copying the style of the master, Meyerbeer managed to change his manner of writing from German to Italian.

However, it was not in Italian opera that Meyerbeer achieved his greatest successes, but with the French style. A resident of Paris after 1826, Meyerbeer studied French opera assiduously. The first result of these studies was his opera *Robert le Diable*, produced on November 21, 1831 with spectacular success. Later operas in the same vein included *Le Prophète* and *L'Africaine*.

In his operas, Meyerbeer achieved a singular combination of musico-dramatic elements, new orchestral colors, and grandiose effects. In his passion for theatrical effect, he found a uniquely sympathetic collaborator in the librettist, Eugène Scribe, who favored historical subjects.

Meyerbeer did not live to see the first performance of his last opera, *L'Africaine*, which took place in 1865, one year after the composer's death in Paris.

L'AFRICAINE

L'Africaine is the story of the famous Portuguese explorer, Vasco da Gama, and the self-sacrificing love of Selika, an Indian queen whom he brings home as a slave girl. A third principal character is Inez, daughter of Don Diego, who is deeply in love with the explorer. Don Pedro, selected by Don Diego for his daughter, seeks out the new lands about which Vasco speaks as having discovered, and takes with him both Selika and her servant Nelusko (as guides), as well as Inez. Vasco da Gama uncovers a plot of Nelusko to destroy Don Pedro's ship, and rushes to him with a warning which is not heeded. Nelusko's men capture the ship and either kill or take as captive everyone on board. Selika effects Vasco's escape to her own land. There Vasco learns that Inez is still alive. When he tries to seek her out, Selika commits suicide.

In this opera, Meyerbeer reveals all his passion for spectacle and drama. His opera employs all the resources of dramatic theatre, including shipwreck, battle, suicide. It is, for the most part, dramatic hokum. But the score does contain some of Meyerbeer's finest music, including the tenor aria *"O Paradiso,"* Selika's poignant *"Adieu, mon doux rivage,"* and Nelusko's ecstatic *"Adamastor, roi des vagues."*

Meyerbeer considered this his crowning masterpiece, and lavished upon it more care and attention than he did on other operas. He completed the score in 1860, but up to his dying day, he continued to make revisions—the last of them being entered on the day before his death.

The première took place on April 28, 1865, one year after Meyerbeer's death, and was highly successful.

71343-D, O Paradiso, Nino Martini, Tenor, with the Columbia Concert Orchestra, Howard Barlow Conducting.

Darius Milhaud

1892–

Darius Milhaud was born at Aix-en-Provence, France, in 1892. Almost from the time he emerged from the cradle, he showed an intense interest in music. When he was two, his mother found him laboriously picking out street songs on the piano. When he began the serious study of music four years later, however, it was the violin, not the piano, that engaged his attention. At ten, he gave his first public concert, and at eighteen, he was enrolled as a student at the Paris Conservatoire. There he studied not only the violin but conducting and composition.

It was not long before his abilities as a composer came to light. In 1912, when he was twenty, a sonata for violin and piano was performed in public in Paris, and three years later he won a prize in composition.

Matters diplomatic occupied Milhaud's attention from 1917 to 1919, when he was attached to the French Legation in Brazil. While in South America, however, he gathered musical material for such famous works as *Saudades do Brazil, Scaramouche* and *Le Boeuf sur le toit*. On his return to France—via the West Indies and the United States—he joined five of his fellow composers to form the group known as *"Les Six."* The other members of this group, which led the way in a reaction against the influence of the post-Debussy impressionists, were Louis Durey, Arthur Honegger, Germaine Tailleferre, Georges Auric and Francis Poulenc. The poet, Jean Cocteau, and the composer, Erik Satie, gave counsel to *"Les Six,"* which many have compared to the great Russian "Five."

The remainder of Milhaud's career has been devoted to composing, playing (he is an accomplished pianist) and lecturing all over Europe and America. He has received numerous awards, and is a Chevalier de la Légion d'Honneur.

The occupation of his native land by the Nazis in 1940—just six days after the première in Paris of his opera, *Medée*—caused Milhaud to flee to the United States. Since his arrival here, and up to the time of his return to France in 1945, he lectured at Mills College in Oakland, California, and made many concert appearances throughout the country.

Milhaud is an extremely prolific composer. To date, he has written fifteen ballets (including his most famous work, the jazz ballet, *La Création du monde*), fourteen operas, ten cantatas, thirty-three pieces of theatre music, eighteen scores for motion pictures, thirteen string quartets, fifteen sonatas, twelve concerti, four orchestral suites, two symphonies, six chamber symphonies and a host of vocal and piano works.

THE *Suite française* was originally written for band, and in that form, received its world première at a concert of the Goldman Band, Edwin Franko Goldman conducting, on the Mall in Central Park in New York City on June 13, 1945.

An outdoor concert in New York was also the scene of the first performance of the *Suite française* in orchestral form. It was first heard on July 29, 1945, at a Lewisohn Stadium concert by the Philharmonic-Symphony Orchestra of New York, conducted by Maurice Abravanel. At that time Milhaud provided this additional information about the music:

"The five parts of the Suite are named after French Provinces, the very ones in which the American and Allied armies fought together with the French underground for the liberation of my country: Normandy, Brittany, Ile-de-France (of which Paris is the center), Alsace-Lorraine, and Provence.

"I used some folk tunes of these Provinces. I wanted the young Americans to hear the popular melodies of those parts of France where their fathers and brothers fought to defend the country from the German invaders, who in less than seventy years have brought war, destruction, cruelty, torture and murder three times to the peaceful and democratic people of France."

In a letter Milhaud expressed himself further regarding the use of folk material. "I think that there are only two ways of facing the problem," he wrote. "1. By collecting folk music as exactly as possible, and leaving it as it is for archives in libraries. The danger here is that it will gather the dust of forgetfulness. 2. By using a folk melody with all possible freedom in a composition as if it were the composer's own theme, interpreting it in any kind of character, and mixing it with original themes that seem like folk music but are not."

It is this second course that Milhaud has taken in his *Suite française,* and in many other compositions as well, and the excellent results he has obtained have proved his wisdom.

X-MX-268, Philharmonic-Symphony Orchestra of New York, Darius Milhaud Conducting.

Wolfgang Amadeus Mozart

1756–1791

A LITTLE boy of three, earnest and serious of face, sits watching his sister Marianne, five years his senior, taking a music lesson. The lesson over and the girl returned to her play, the boy clambers upon the harpsichord bench and amuses himself by picking out chords, simple but always harmonically correct, with his baby hands. The child is Wolfgang Amadeus Mozart, the time 1759, the place, the ancient Austrian cathedral city of Salzburg.

The little boy's father, Leopold Mozart, an accomplished musician, whose understanding and affectionate care of his marvelously gifted son was to continue from this period of childish helplessness on until he had reached maturity, soon perceived that in Wolfgang there dwelt the germ of a genius for musical creation such as the world had never before known. Lessons in simple composition, which commenced as play for the little boy of three, became for the budding genius of five a work of serious endeavor. The extraordinary incongruity of his years with these proceedings seems never to have occurred to him. At four he was dictating minuets of his own to his father and in his sixth year he was trying to compose a concerto.

Leopold Mozart, while a most affectionate father, was also a shrewd man-of-affairs where his children were concerned. Realizing, as would be said nowadays, their box-office value, he early contemplated a tour that would take advantage of the local fame of the children and further extend it. An opportunity to bring Wolfgang before the world as a musical prodigy of the first order before long presented itself. To Munich, thence to Vienna, the children were taken, creating a furore in both places, especially the Austrian capital. The story of Wolfgang climbing into the Empress's lap and giving her a resounding kiss is amongst the classics of musical anecdotes. Emperor and Empress were both delighted with the children and lavished attentions upon them. The auspicious visit was broken by Wolfgang contracting scarlet fever.

Arrived back in Salzburg, more ambitious projects began to stir in Leopold Mozart's brain. With Paris as their immediate goal we find the trio—the father, seven-year-old Wolfgang and twelve-year-old Marianne—soon setting out. Stopping at many places on the way, Wolfgang exhibited his extraordinarily versatile powers to the wonderment of all who saw and heard him. Apparently nothing in musical performance, either creative or interpretative, was more than play to him, whether performing on the harpischord, violin or organ, his own compositions or those of others. Five months of furore and success in Paris, then to London where for over a year the same sensation attended him. Leaving England in July 1765, the family traveled by many stages back to Salzburg, the journey interrupted on three occasions by the serious illness of one or other member of the trio, and it was not until almost a year and a half later that they finally arrived home.

For young Mozart, now ten years old, there followed a period of hard and serious study, interrupted by an unfortunate visit in 1767 to Vienna, where both children fell ill of small-pox. Wolfgang, on his recovery, was gladdened by the production, first of his miniature opera *Bastien und Bastienne* in Vienna and his first serious opera *La Finta semplice* in Salzburg under the auspices of the Archbishop, after his return.

Space unfortunately renders impossible anything more than a summary of Mozart's extraordinary career from this point on to his lamentably early death. During 1770 and 1771, he toured Italy with his father, visiting all the principal cities and making the same deep, lasting impression by his astounding capabilities. Two shorter visits to Italy followed, the last one ending in March 1773. Saving a visit to Bavaria in 1775, the next four years were spent by Mozart mainly at home in quiet study and in employment as an orchestra violinist.

During all this time his prodigious progress in composition continued without break. At eighteen he had numbered two hundred works worthy of preservation in published form.

The time was now at hand, however, when, with the oncoming of manhood, there was to appear for Mozart a radical change in the aspect of all worldly things. No longer a child phenomenon, it must be his lot to stand up to the world foot to foot with other men. In Vienna, the Emperor to whom Mozart the wonder-child had made such a strong appeal was dead; the Empress who had held him on her knees was in mourning. The Archbishop of Salzburg who had made Mozart, at the age of fourteen, Kapellmeister of the cathedral was also dead, and his successor, a man whose harshness and vanity seem to have been his most salient characteristics, was neither of the nature nor the inclination to foster a genius such as Mozart's. It is necessary to note here that in the age of the aristocratic patron the musician was often regarded as no more than a glorified lackey. Not until Beethoven, in the next century, by overwhelming force of his great dominating personality and superb consciousness of his God-given powers, made princes and potentates bid for his favor was there any real indication of a change in this revolting condition.

At twenty-one, Mozart, impatient and chafing at a situation which he could only regard as an ignoble bondage, yet still lacking the courage openly to rebel, applied through his father for leave to take an extended professional tour. The Archbishop, coarse and insensitive as ever, refused, whereupon Mozart driven at length to desperate expedients asked to be discharged from his service, a request which the prelate finally granted, with expressions appropriate to his character.

From this turning-point in his career to the beginning of its next and final phase—the commencement of his permanent residence in Vienna in 1781—Mozart was engaged mainly in travel which, however it may have added to his artistic stature, did little to improve the condition of his exceedingly lean purse. A journey to Munich and Mannheim, undertaken with his mother in 1777, led to his meeting with Aloysia Weber, who profoundly influenced his life, directly in that she caused his first great heartache; indirectly in that through her he met her sister Constanze whom he married in 1782. Leopold Mozart, learning of his son's infatuation for Aloysia, expressed his strongest disapproval and in a letter virtually commanded Wolfgang to go to Paris and keep his mind on his career. Mozart, always an obedient son, with heavy heart obeyed. Returning to Germany the following year he found that Aloysia scarcely remembered him; it was then presumably that he turned to Constanze. Leaving the Weber family in 1779 he returned to Salzburg where for the next

year he accomplished prodigies in composition. In 1781, the Arch
bishop being in Vienna he was ordered to attend him. This service
proved to be a repetition of the ignominious experience in Salzburg
years before, and finally Mozart in desperation again demanded his
discharge, which was ultimately given after a disgraceful scene in
the Archiepiscopal palace.

Settled now in Vienna, Mozart's life for its remaining ten years
was one of magnificent and phenomenal accomplishment in the creation of immortal music and a continuous battle against penury which
at times approached absolute want. In his twenty-seventh year, still
contrary to the wishes of his father, Mozart married Constanze
Weber. The marriage generally speaking was a happy one, as the
devotion of the two never faltered, but Constanze, unfortunately, was
quite as bad a manager as Wolfgang, and the result was only confusion worse confounded as far as practical needs were concerned.
Great as his compositions were, the monetary returns to Mozart from
them were slight, and though he disliked teaching he was obliged to
rely upon it frequently for such slender income as he had.

With his *The Marriage of Figaro* in 1786 commenced that galaxy
of masterpieces by which Mozart is mainly known to the modern
world. The following year *Don Giovanni* had its first performance
in Prague. In 1788 came, in the incredible space of three months,
the three great symphonies, in E-flat, G minor and C major (the
Jupiter); in 1791 *The Magic Flute* and the marvelous Requiem, still
uncompleted at his death.

With all his growing fame it seemed impossible for Mozart to
escape from the net of disheartening financial circumstances which
surrounded him.

In 1791 at the age of thirty-five, while working on the score of *The
Magic Flute*, Mozart's health broke badly. Completing this, however,
he commenced work on his Requiem, the commission for which had
come to him from an unknown hand. Before this could be finished
he was attacked by a kidney disease, which his weakened condition
could not withstand. He died on December 5th, 1791. To the shame
of his contemporaries and his age he was buried, unattended, in the
common burial ground reserved for paupers, the exact place of his
interment unknown.

CONCERTO IN E-FLAT MAJOR (K. 271), FOR PIANO AND ORCHESTRA

Allegro · Andantino · Presto

OVER thirty concertos for piano are listed in Köchel's catalogue of Mozart's works. It may be assumed that he composed still others, which have not survived. When he was only four he was discovered by his father and the court trumpeter Schachtner putting notes to paper. When asked what he was doing, the answer was prompt and unembarrassed: "Why, composing a concerto for piano!" We are told that this fledgling effort was "correctly written but impossibly difficult."

The first piano concerto wholly Mozart's of which we know is the one in D major composed in 1773. But his first masterpiece in this form is the E-flat concerto, K. 271. This Concerto was composed in Salzburg in 1777 when Mozart was twenty-one. It was written for a French pianist, Mlle. Jeunehomme, who was one of the most celebrated pianists of her day.

It is of particular historic importance that this is the first concerto in which the individuality of the virtuoso is pronounced, and in which the sonata form is so clearly defined. Thus the E-flat major Concerto struck a pioneer trail which was soon to lead to the greatest of Mozart's concertos, as well as to the developing concerto form of Beethoven. For Mozart is generally credited with having established the form of the modern concerto, a form which has undergone little change since his time. Before his innovations, the soloist had little importance in the concerto. He was either a member of a small group playing against the full orchestra, as in the concerto grosso, or he was simply an outstanding voice in the orchestra. But Mozart gave the soloist a definite importance, at the same time increasing the significance of the orchestral accompaniment, producing a form that had more musical balance.

M-MM-291, Walter Gieseking, Piano, and the Berlin State Opera Orchestra, Hans Rosbaud Conducting.

CONCERTO IN A MAJOR (K. 414), FOR PIANO AND ORCHESTRA

Allegro · Andante · Rondo

THE CONCERTO in A major is the second of three of his small piano concertos. Writing to his father of these works, in December 1782 Mozart said: "They are a compromise between the too easy and the too difficult, pleasant to the ear and very brilliant without, of course sounding empty. Some passages will appeal only to connoisseurs but others will also be satisfied and enjoy them without, perhaps, knowing why."

Mozart appears to have been very fond of the A major Concerto. He performed it frequently in public and taught it to his favorite pupils. Furthermore, he left two complete sets of cadenzas for it, a practice quite unusual for one who was accustomed to writing only rough, perfunctory sketches for these display sections.

M-MM-544, Louis Kentner, Piano, and the London Philharmonic Orchestra, Sir Thomas Beecham Conducting.

CONCERTO IN D MINOR (K. 466), FOR PIANO AND ORCHESTRA

Allegro · Romanza · Rondo

THE D MINOR Concerto is one of the greatest Mozart composed, and one of the epical works in which the later Beethoven is foreshadowed. The dramatic impact of its very opening bars has a Beethoven quality about it, as has the spacious development of the principal themes of the first movement. The slow movement is, however, pure Mozart—a Romanza which (as so often is the case with Mozart) carries over the Italian aria into concerted music. The melody—announced first by solo piano and then erupting with full orchestra—is sustained throughout the movement. There is a suggestion of restlessness in the finale, but good spirits finally prevail, and the work ends with a feeling of exuberance.

[300]

CONCERTO NO. 23 IN A MAJOR (K. 488), FOR PIANO AND ORCHESTRA

Allegro · Andante · Presto

IT WAS on the eve of the climax of his career that Mozart composed his Piano Concerto in A major. The production of his opera *The Marriage of Figaro* soon followed. This Concerto was his twenty-third work for piano and orchestra. (An earlier A major Concerto—K. 414—dates from 1782.) Mozart wrote his father in December, 1785, that he expected to give three subscription concerts during Lent, and that he had 125 subscribers. For these Lenten concerts he wrote three concertos, including the one in A major.

It is interesting to find that two clarinets are used in the score, to the exclusion of oboes. The score calls for one flute, two clarinets, two bassoons, two horns, and the customary strings.

In the bold modulations and the lack of conventional figures, this Concerto reveals a mature manner. There appears in the Concerto a broader use of counterpoint and a more subtle tonal architecture that distinguish such later works as the *Jupiter* Symphony and the Piano Sonata in F.

The first movement is very simple, almost conventional in its soli-tutti relationship. The omission of trumpets and percussion instruments gives the movement a brightness which, incidentally, was Mozart's characteristic A major mood. The Adagio, in F-sharp minor, is however characterized by passionate despair. With the beginning of the final rondo the somber mood is dissipated and contagious cheerfulness sets in.

M-MM-261, Marguerite Long, Piano, and Orchestra Conducted by Philippe Gaubert.

CONCERTO IN C MINOR (K. 491), FOR PIANO AND ORCHESTRA

Allegro · Larghetto · Allegretto

THIS is one of but two concertos by Mozart written in the minor key (the other being the popular D minor Concerto). In Mozart's C minor Concerto there is none of the gay writing that characterize much of his more lighthearted music. This is a somber and melancholy work, in which the composer plumbs profound emotional depths.

There are several unusual features about this Concerto. For one thing, most of the first movement is built around the principal theme; the second theme does not appear until after the piano has entered and remains in a subordinate position throughout the movement. In direct contrast, the second theme in the second movement assumes more importance than the first theme. Then again, presaging the piano concertos of Beethoven, the second movement of the C minor opens with a solo for the piano. Finally, Mozart reverses his own concerto formula by writing the second movement in rondo form and the third movement, an Allegretto, in the form of a theme with variations.

M-MM-356, Robert Casadesus, Piano, with the Orchestre Symphonique de Paris, Eugène Bigot Conducting.

CONCERTO IN B-FLAT MAJOR (K. 595), FOR PIANO AND ORCHESTRA

Allegro · Larghetto cantabile · Allegro scherzando

THE CONCERTO in B-flat was Mozart's last, composed in the year of his death. Otto Jahn, the musicologist, comments briefly on it: "For his own playing, no doubt, at a concert, he wrote pianoforte in B-flat which like most of the compositions of this period is characterized by its mild and earnest tone and charming euphony." Indeed, this is one of Mozart's most buoyantly lighthearted works, pervaded throughout by an almost magical gaiety. The Larghetto is a song of simplicity and directness which could come only from a spirit free from care, while the last movement is full of irrepressible good humor.

M-MM-490, Robert Casadesus, Piano, with the Philharmonic-Symphony Orchestra of New York, John Barbirolli Conducting.

CONCERTO IN E-FLAT MAJOR (K. 365), FOR TWO PIANOS AND ORCHESTRA

Allegro · Andante · Rondo: allegro

MOZART's Concerto in E-flat major for two pianos and orchestra is by far the best known and most frequently played of the handful of compositions for this combination of instruments. It was composed in 1780, and was first performed the following year in Vienna by Mozart and Josepha Aurnhammer, a young pupil with whom the composer did a considerable amount of two-piano work. It is believed that the Concerto was originally written with the idea that Mozart should play it in concert with his sister, Marianne, but there is no record of its ever having been thus performed.

Mozart, who was given to voluminous letter writing, and whose letters have been collected and translated by Emily Anderson, had this to say about Josepha Aurnhammer: "The young lady is a fright, but plays enchantingly, though in cantabile playing she has not got the real delicate singing style. She clips everything. She has told me (as a great secret) of her plan, which is to work hard for two or three years more and then go to Paris and make music her profession. She said: 'I am no beauty—*au contraire*, I am ugly. I have no desire to marry some chancery official with an income of three or four hundred gulden and I have no chance of getting anyone else. So I prefer to remain as I am and to live by my talent.' And there she is right."

The rumor circulated in Vienna that Mozart and his keyboard partner were to be married. Concerning this, the enraged composer wrote to his father: "She [Josepha] told me that when anything of the kind was said to her she always laughed at it; but I know from a certain person that she confirmed the rumor, adding that we would then travel together. That enraged me. So the other day I gave her my mind pretty plainly and wanted her not to abuse my kindness. Now I no longer go there every day, but only every other day, and I shall gradually drop it altogether. She is nothing but an amorous fool." Evidently, he did not live up to his promise, for he continued to visit the Aurnhammers, and gave several concerts with Josepha.

The gay Concerto bears no trace of the composer's troubles with his keyboard partner. The first movement is a vigorous Allegro, the principal theme of which opens with a downward leap of an octave. The same leap, in the same rhythmic pattern, occurs at the beginning of Mozart's Symphony in C major (K. 338) and starts the overture to his opera, *La Clemenza di Tito*. The second movement is beautifully tranquil, and the work is brought to a joyous conclusion with a lively Rondo, marked Allegro.

M-MM-628, Vita Vronsky and Victor Babin, Duo-Pianists, with the Robin Hood Dell Orchestra of Philadelphia, Dimitri Mitropoulos Conducting.

CONCERTO NO. 4 IN D MAJOR (K. 218), FOR VIOLIN AND ORCHESTRA

Allegro · *Andante cantabile* · *Rondo*

MOZART wrote five violin concertos in Salzburg in 1775, of which the D major is probably the most famous. According to his custom, he went thoroughly into the subject from its very foundation, gaining proficiency by continuous work in the one direction. These concertos indicate a high standard of technical attainment, and beyond that, they show fertility and inventiveness in composition. They are all serious works, skillfully planned and generally greatly in advance of his contemporaries.

The violin concertos are all written in three movements—the first of which "the most elaborate, is more suggestive of the aria," says Jahn, "than is the corresponding movement of the symphonies. The passages grow out of the principal subjects, converting and adorning them. The movement falls generally in three main divisions, the middle one—corresponding to the same division in the symphony—passes into another key and elaborates one or more motifs more freely than in the symphony, and chiefly by changes of modulation and modification of passages whereby the repetition of the first division is affected . . . The second movement is simple and rests essentially on the tuneful and artistic delivery of the *cantilene* . . . embellishments are not excluded, but they are kept in the background . . . The last movement is, as a rule, in the form of the rondo, in which

[304]

the solo part moves more freely, especially in the connecting middle passages . . ."

Mozart displayed his interest and talent for the violin when he was a child, and his father encouraged him to develop this talent. In 1777, Mozart received a letter from his father which read: "You have no idea yourself how well you play the violin. If you only do yourself justice, and play with fire, heartiness, and spirit, you may become the first violinist in Europe." Mozart remembered his father's words, and after he played the violin at Munich and at Augsburg in October of that year, he wrote home that "they all stared—I played as if I were the first violinist in Europe."

The D major concerto opens with a stately introduction for orchestra in which the principal themes of the movement are stated. The solo violin then carries the themes and embellishes upon them. Two beautiful melodies comprise the slow movement, while the rondo has the stately grace of a dance at an imperial court.

M-MM-224, Joseph Szigeti, Violin, and the London Philharmonic Orchestra, Sir Thomas Beecham Conducting.

DIVERTIMENTO IN E-FLAT MAJOR (K. 563), FOR VIOLIN, VIOLA AND 'CELLO

Allegro · Adagio · Menuetto No. 1: allegretto · Andante Menuetto No. 2: allegretto · Allegro

MOZART's only string trio, this Divertimento in E-flat, was composed in September, 1788, soon after the completion of his last three magnificent Symphonies. It was apparently written for his friend and benefactor, Johann Michael Puchberg.

Although the string trio presents more difficulties than the string quartet, Mozart proves in this unique example that he was capable of overcoming every obstacle in technical presentation. The writing is rich and the work is full of the inspiration that had overflowed from the preceding symphonies. There are six movements in the Divertimento, including two minuets divided by an Andante.

M-MM-351, Pasquier Trio.

[305]

DON GIOVANNI

Mozart's opera, *The Marriage of Figaro,* had met with such success in Prague that he was commissioned to write another opera to be performed in that city. Lorenzo da Ponte, the librettist of *Figaro,* was chosen to furnish the text for the new opera. He selected the popular legend of Don Juan and delivered the libretto to Mozart in April 1787. The composer completed the score just in time for the initial performance on October 29.

Many legends have arisen concerning Mozart's composition of *Don.* It is said that he composed part of the opera during his trip to Prague, part of it between shots at bowling games, part during drinking sessions with da Ponte. Perhaps the most famous legend concerns the writing of the overture, during the night preceding the première. His wife is said to have kept him awake with punch and jokes; and the copyist delivered the parts to the members of the orchestra only a few minutes before official curtain time compelling them to play the music at sight.

Don Giovanni has been described as the "ideal" opera. It covers a wide range of human emotions, not only in the play but in the musical score as well. The Don's bristling "Champagne" aria and tender Serenade, Leporello's "Catalogue" aria, the Mask Trio, the conventional but beautiful solo numbers of Donna Anna and Don Ottavio, the instrumentation of the cemetery scene, the ballroom scene with its three orchestras performing simultaneously, the last scene (considered by some critics as the ultimate in theatrical effect for opera) with its quotations from *Figaro,* Solar's *Una cosa rara* and a Sarti opera—all this reveals superior mastery of musical devices and rare subtlety of expression.

Don Giovanni is no opera buffa, although Mozart himself called it that. Da Ponte knew better: the libretto describes it as a *dramma giocoso*—"gay drama." Actually, *Don Giovanni* contains elements from both opera buffa and seria. However, some authorities insisted on considering it exclusively as a serious opera; in support of this, some opera companies in Europe omitted the last sextet, with the traditional gay ensemble finale of the surviving leading characters. With the curtain falling on the Don's descent to Hell, the aspects of the entire work were altered.

[306]

Many people wonder why Mozart wrote his title role for a baritone instead of tenor. Dramaturgically, the Don is not the hero of the opera but the villain. Traditionally, the villain in opera was a basso, frequently a comic basso: basso because he was old; comic because deserved punishment always has about it a flavor of ridicule to the simple mind. Since the Don could not be made to appear either as old or as essentially comic, the authors furnished Mozart with Leporello (god-child of "Lipperl," a Viennese buffoon) as a second caricature. The real heroine, borrowed from grand opera, is Donna Elvira (not Donna Anna!). The remaining five characters include the conventional two pairs of lovers (exalted and simple), and the "noble father" officiating as the *deus ex machina*.

Mozart was severely criticized for *Don Giovanni* outside Prague. The virtuous Germans (Beethoven among them) were shocked at the impossible situations. The German press found the subject dull, the music noisy and artificial. Among the great of Mozart's day who rose to defend the opera were Goethe and Haydn.

The first performance in Vienna took place on May 7, 1788. Mozart, for this occasion, had made further alterations and additions in order to please the supposedly more sophisticated tastes of the Viennese public. Even so, *Don Giovanni* achieved only 15 performances. The Emperor found it superior to *Figaro* but felt that it was too difficult for the Viennese. It was not given in Vienna again until seven years after Mozart's death.

Strange to say, Lorenzo da Ponte was present at the American première of the opera, in 1825. He had left Vienna in 1791, a few weeks before Mozart died. After a period in England, he came to New York where he was, at turns, a grocer, and an instructor of Italian at Columbia University. He was deep at work writing his memoirs when the Garcia operatic troupe came to New York and presented *Don Giovanni* in its repertory.

Three women are involved in Don Giovanni's escapades, in the da Ponte libretto: Donna Anna, whose father (the Commendatore) he kills; Donna Elvira; and the peasant girl, Zerlina. Retribution comes to Don Giovanni when the stone statue of the Commendatore comes alive, visits the Don while he is at his meal, and consigns him to the flames of Hell.

70365-D, Overture, London Philharmonic Orchestra, Sir Thomas Beecham Conducting.

71577-D, Batti, batti, Bidu Sayao, Soprano, with Orchestra Conducted by Erich Leinsdorf.

71048-D, Catalogue Aria, Salvatore Baccaloni, Basso-buffo, with Orchestra Conducted by Erich Leinsdorf.

71577-D, Vedrai, Carino, Bidu Sayao, Soprano, with Orchestra Conducted by Erich Leinsdorf.

EINE KLEINE NACHTMUSIK—SERENADE IN G MAJOR (K. 525)

Allegro · Romanze · Menuetto and Trio · Allegro

Mozart composed *Eine kleine Nachtmusik* in Vienna on August 10, 1787, as a piece of the order we now would call *Gebrauchsmusik*—utility music—to be played by students or amateurs. *Eine kleine Nachtmusik* is classified as a Serenade, which in Mozart's usage was not very different from a little symphony. In fact, the piece is entirely symphonic. It was originally written for two violins, viola, 'cello, and bass, but is usually performed today by a full string orchestra.

Eine kleine Nachtmusik is built in four movements. In the initial Allegro in G major, the development is exceedingly brief, and there is nothing experimental in the use of different keys. The second, slow movement, Romanze, is in C major, in ternary form. The phrases are sharply subdivided into four-bar phrases, or their multiples. The middle section of Romanze is in C minor, with characteristic simple figures imitated by one instrument after another. Then the C major theme returns, and the movement is concluded with the feeling of a perfect ending.

The third movement is a Minuet in G major, with a Trio in the dominant. The last movement is an Allegro, called Rondo by Mozart himself, although the structure is close to sonata form. The initial vivacious theme dominates the movement, appearing in the tonic, then in the dominant, and in the middle section also in other keys. The movement is further consolidated by an extended coda.

X-MX-187, London Symphony Orchestra, Felix Weingartner Conducting.

THE MAGIC FLUTE (DIE ZAUBERFLÖTE)

THE HISTORY of *The Magic Flute* is intimately connected with that of its librettist, the impresario, Emanuel Schikaneder. Mozart first met him in 1780, and at once became interested in those light operas (or *Singspiel*) which Schikaneder was at that time producing in a theatre opposite Mozart's home. In 1789, Schikaneder took over the direction of a shabby theatre in Wieden, a suburb of Vienna. His repertory consisted chiefly of fairy comic operas—heroic, sentimental, romantic farces with music, thriving on a curious mixture of ghosts, fairies, villains, princes, and burlesque.

The story has it that Schikaneder asked Mozart to write the music for one of his plays in an effort to stave off bankruptcy. While Mozart hesitated to write for the suburbs, he had come on evil days, and a commission was not to be refused. Work on this project proceeded so slowly that Schikaneder prevailed on Mozart to move into a little pavilion in the courtyard of his theatre, so that the impresario and his singers might keep an eye on the composer. For a while, composition of *The Magic Flute* was interrupted by a commission from Prague for Mozart to write the opera *La Clemenza di Tito*.

The Magic Flute was intended to be just another popular fairy opera. When most of the first act was written, both Mozart and Schikaneder decided to change the whole course of the libretto. Villains became angels, and vice-versa. A glorification of Freemasonry now became the new underlying theme.

It is habitual to describe the libretto as silly. Its theme is, indeed, confused; its humor is somewhat puerile; the verses are amateurish. Yet Schikaneder did have a sophisticated instinct for stage effect and emotional expression. For all its absurdities, the play makes for entertaining, often dramatic theatre.

Beginning with the first finale, the opera abounds with Freemasonic allusions. This scene, which takes place in front of the Masonic temple and contains Tamino's significant dialogue with the Speaker, is the spiritual highlight of the opera. It became the nucleus of German Romantic opera, used as a model by Weber for his famous Wolf's Glen scene in *Der Freischütz* and by Wagner. Mozart was careful to underline the Masonic meanings of the plot. The Masonic number "three," recurs constantly (three boys and three ladies appear three times; three doors lead into the inner sanctum, etc.); the wind instruments are handled in a fashion characteristic of bands of Viennese lodges; E-flat minor, with which the work begins and ends, was the Masonic key.

In the 19th century, someone tried—with typical Romantic imagination—to interpret a yet deeper symbolism into the opera. According to this commentator, the Queen of the Night was supposed to represent Empress Maria Theresa (who disliked Freemasonry); Tamino—Emperor Joseph (who had supported it); Pamina—the people; and so forth. This, of course, is absurd. Mozart was far too attached to the ruling house, and to the late Empress particularly, to become partner to this kind of political satire.

The highly involved plot can be reduced to its essentials. Sarastro, high priest of Isis, kidnaps Pamina, the daughter of the Queen of the Night, for the purpose of teaching her wisdom. The Queen of the Night prevails upon Tamino to regain her daughter for her. During this mission, Tamino is converted to the faith of Isis, and after undergoing numerous tests to prove his bravery is accepted into the religious sect and is given Pamina as bride.

Mozart's treatment of the musical score is simple, indeed. The most heterogeneous elements are mixed together and then organized into a unity with a sureness of which only Mozart was capable. These elements are French, Italian, or German in origin. Forms range from a Bach chorale and opera seria arias for coloratura soprano, to light opera ditties. Between these extremes are moving love arias, the majestic pronouncements of Sarastro, and ensemble numbers of extraordinary lucidity.

The overture anticipates the Masonic elements of the opera, beginning with three significant chords. The Allegro is a brilliant fugato based on a theme found in a Clementi piano sonata.

At the première of the opera, Mozart thought he had a failure on his hands, and refused to take a bow after the first act. Schikaneder, however, virtually forced the opera on the public by giving it night after night. Gradually, trips to Schikaneder's theatre became a fashion in Vienna. Even Salieri, Mozart's enemy, came and congratulated the composer. The success of *The Magic Flute* was Mozart's last pleasure in life. On his deathbed, he followed the proceedings on Schikaneder's stage in his imagination, a watch in his hand. Had he ived, *The Magic Flute* would probably have made Mozart a rich man, for it did that to Schikaneder.

67660-D, Overture, Symphony Orchestra Conducted by Bruno Walter.
17345-D, Queen of the Night aria, Lily Pons, Soprano, and Symphony Orchestra Conducted by Bruno Walter.

THE MARRIAGE OF FIGARO
(LE NOZZE DI FIGARO)

AFTER a much-publicized three-year war with censorship, the French author, Beaumarchais, staged his controversial play, *Le Mariage de Figaro*, in 1784, before a delighted Parisian audience. It was a sequel to his own *Le Barbier de Seville*, later to be made into a famous opera by Rossini. *Figaro's* satire on the master-servant relationship and on nobility privileges in general was presented so brilliantly that even court circles (not excluding the Queen herself) took a fancy to its author. The King alone recognized its revolutionary implications; and so did the Emperor of Austria, who prohibited the production of the play in Vienna.

Mozart somehow saw the book and at once recognized its operatic potentialities. Lorenzo da Ponte declared himself ready to collaborate with Mozart. He succeeded in transforming the *Figaro* plot into a libretto sufficiently harmless in its political and social theme to be acceptable for aristocratic consumption. The two authors worked in secrecy. When they were half through they presented their product to the Emperor who not only gave his approval but promised all-out support.

After numerous obstacles placed in its way by envious Italian composers, *Figaro* was introduced on May 1, 1786. It was a gala affair. According to Mozart's friend, the Irish tenor, Michael O'Kelly (who sang two minor roles), encores and da capos almost doubled the performance time. But then came summer, with the Court and nobility leaving town; hostile theatre officials shelved *Figaro* after only nine performances. The opera, however, had better luck in Prague where it actually saved the bankrupt opera troupe of Bondini. This success brought Mozart an opera contract from Bondini, a circumstance to which we owe the existence of *Don Giovanni*.

[311]

Figaro was justifiably classified not as opera buffa but as "*commedia per musica.*" It is a comedy of intrigue between Count Almaviva and his wife's maid, Susanna. The Countess, learning of this situation, disguises herself in Susanna's clothes, to make love to the Count in the garden; meanwhile, Susanna is making love to Figaro. The Count, discovering this rival rendezvous, suspects that Figaro's beloved is none other than his own wife. Eventually, however, all turns out well, as the identity of each one is revealed.

Mozart here succeeds in raising opera buffa to high artistic levels. With the most skillful use of musical characterization, buffo types suddenly become human beings. Their arias express a wide gamut of feelings ranging from Cherubino's effeminate tenderness to the Count's tragi-comic wrath. The orchestra excels in its role as commentator. There is an exquisite balance between voices and instruments, between musical numbers and recitatives. Duets and ensemble numbers no longer interrupt the flow of the plot but share, with recitatives, in the development of the action.

Mozart's favorite numbers were Figaro's aria, "*Non più andrai,*" (Act I), and the sextet in the third. But audiences throughout the world have selected their own favorites as well, and these include the celebrated "Letter Duet," Cherubino's two solo numbers (particularly "*Voi che sapete*"), and Susanna's poignant aria in the last act.

71606-D, Overture, London Philharmonic Orchestra, Sir Thomas Beecham Conducting.

17331-D, Non Più Andrai, Nelson Eddy, Baritone, and Orchestra Conducted by Robert Armbruster.

17298-D, Non So Più, Risë Stevens, Soprano, and Columbia Concert Orchestra, Erich Leinsdorf Conducting.

17331-D, Se Vuol Ballare, Nelson Eddy, Baritone, and Orchestra Conducted by Robert Armbruster.

71193-D, La Vendetta, Salvatore Baccaloni, Basso-buffo, with Orchestra Conducted by Erich Leinsdorf.

17345-D, Voi Che Sapete, Lily Pons, Soprano, with Orchestra Conducted by Bruno Walter.

REQUIEM, K. 626

MYSTERIOUS, indeed, were the circumstances surrounding the composition of this masterpiece. In the summer of 1791, a solemn-looking stranger, dressed in gray, and masked, brought Mozart the assign-nent, promising to pay whatever fee the composer considered reaonable, but specifying that under no condition was Mozart to try to uncover the patron's name. From time to time, he returned to inquire about the progress of the work.

Then already aware of his physical disintegration, Mozart was obsessed with the idea that this stranger was actually a messenger from the other world urging him to complete his own requiem.

The composition of the Requiem was interrupted by other assignments; but when Mozart returned to it it was with renewed passion and industry. He felt he was living on borrowed time, and that he had to hurry if he were to finish his own requiem before it was too late. Early in November he suffered a nervous breakdown; his wife, Constanze, managed to hide the score from him. But Mozart was determined to finish it. Even on his deathbed he worked feverishly. When he grew too weak to write, he dictated his intentions to his pupil Süssmayer. When friends came to see Mozart, they all joined with the composer in singing parts of the Requiem. When they came to the Lacrimosa, Mozart suddenly suffered a passionate crying spell. A few hours after this he was dead.

Süssmayer completed those parts of the Requiem which the master had left undone. Only after Mozart's death was it discovered who Mozart's unknown patron was: He was Count Franz von Walsegg who made it a practice to commission composers to write works which he later palmed off as his own.

The Requiem is a monumental church work which mirrored Mozart's faith in the delights of the world and in the transfiguration of eternal life. The Kyrie contains a fugue on two themes—one quiet, the other agitated. The Rex Tremendae is a superb example of canonic writing. The Recordare, in which the solo voices combine into a quartet, is one of the longest and most beautiful passages of the Requiem. After the antiphonal Confutatis comes the Lacrimosa, which rises to a high pitch of emotional expression. It is here that Mozart's work ends as he wrote it. He left indications and the musical materials for the remaining movements; that these are still products of Mozart's genius and not those of any pupil are proved by the unearthly beauty of the Benedictus and Agnus Dei. As Beethoven said: "If Mozart did not write this music, then the man who wrote it was a Mozart."

QUARTET IN D MINOR (K. 421)

Allegro · *Andante* · *Menuetto and Trio* · *Allegro ma non troppo*

WHEN Haydn's *Russian* Quartets appeared in 1781, the many new developments in these works inspired Mozart to compose a series of six quartets which he dedicated to Haydn. These quartets were begun in 1782 and completed in Vienna in 1785. When they were published they bore the following elaborate dedication:

"A father who had once decided to send out his sons into the great world deemed it his duty to entrust them to the protection and guidance of a man of great fame, who, moreover, was also his best friend. In like manner I send my six sons to you, most celebrated and very dear friend. They are, indeed, the fruit of a long and painstaking endeavor; but the hope, corroborated by many friends, that this toil will be in some degree rewarded, flatters me and encourages me in the belief that some day these children may prove a source of consolation to me.

"During your last stay in this capital you, my very dear friend, personally expressed to me your approval of these compositions. Your kind opinion encourages me to present them to you, and lets me hope that you will find them not entirely unworthy of your favor. I pray you, then, receive them kindly, and be a father, guide and friend to them. From now on I surrender my rights over them to you. I beseech you not to be severe to faults that may have eluded a father's partial eye, and to preserve your generous friendship towards one who so highly treasures it."

Though Mozart quite obviously had his tongue in his cheek when he wrote the above dedication, he felt a sincere attachment to these works. They were the one means he had of repaying a debt of gratitude to Haydn, who had "shown him the way" in the matter of quartet writing. These six quartets are among the very few compositions by Mozart which were produced neither on commission nor on command.

The six so-called *Haydn* Quartets represent Mozart at the peak of his creative powers, and show with what beautiful effect he could make four stringed instruments sing as one. Each member of the quartet is given equal importance, and the parts are handled with an ease and freedom seldom, if ever, equaled by any other composer.

[314]

The D minor Quartet is the second of the quartets dedicated to Haydn, and the only one of the six in a minor key. It was written in Vienna when Mozart was twenty-seven years old.

The first movement is an Allegro in recognizable sonata form. The harmonic progressions follow the classical alternation of the tonic and the dominant, but soon the Mozartean plaintive harmonies of the augmented sixth appear, with their inevitable resolutions into the octave. There are bold modulations in the development, transitions to remote keys—at one juncture connecting E-flat minor and A minor by a sudden chromatic move. It is of such enharmonic changes that Robert Browning wrote:

> "And music: what? that burst of pillar'd cloud by day
> And pillar'd fire by night, was product, must we say
> Of modulating just by enharmonic change,
> The augmented sixth resolved. . . ."

M-MM-462, Budapest String Quartet.

QUARTET (HUNTING) IN B-FLAT MAJOR (K. 458)

Allegro vivace assai · Menuetto · Adagio · Allegro assai

MOZART's *Hunting* Quartet is the third of the six dedicated to Haydn. It was written in a single day in November, 1784, in Vienna.

The sobriquet *Hunting* Quartet is suggested by the opening theme of the first movement, which is based on a well-known figure of the so-called "Horn Fifths." In reality, there is only one fifth on the second degree of the scale, preceded by a sixth on the tonic, and followed by thirds on the mediant, subdominant, and dominant, but such are the vagaries of musical terminology. These tones were the natural tones of a hunting horn, and were used for hunting episodes, journeys, or leave-takings. Schubert used them in his song *Die Post,* Beethoven in his *Farewell* Sonata, Mendelssohn in his *Hunting Song.* It is interesting to observe that these hunting-horn intervals are generally used in the key of B-flat major, the key in which natural bugles, trumpets, and postillion horns were actually constructed.

M-MM-438, Roth String Quartet.

QUARTET (DISSONANT) IN C MAJOR
(K. 465)

Adagio: allegro · *Andante cantabile* · *Menuetto* · *Allegro molto*

MOZART's Quartet in C major is the last of the six quartets he wrote
for Haydn. Mozart composed it in Vienna in one day—on January 14
1785.

The C major Quartet is a celebrated one in the annals of Mo
zartology. In the opening Adagio, Mozart uses combinations of chro
matics that create what is known in harmony textbooks as "cros
relations." Natural and altered tones brush each other in closes
proximity, and there is a strange feeling of the absence of key
C major is expressed only by the initial tonic in the cello, while the
viola and the two violins hover perilously on the fringe. All kinds o
subtle explanations have been advanced to account for these chro
matic vagaries, but Haydn, to whom the Quartet was dedicated
merely remarked: "If Mozart wrote it, he must have had a good
reason to do so."

Mozart purposely used dissonances and forbidden progressions ii
a little parody which he called *A Musical Joke,* and which he wrot
for the amusement of friends. In this *Musical Joke* Mozart deliber
ately used consecutive fifths, a whole-tone scale in the violin cadenz:
and finished the piece in five different keys. He could hardly foresee
that the employment of several keys in simultaneous harmony woul
be taken seriously a hundred odd years thence, and that it woul
even receive a scientific-sounding name—polytonality.

Mozart and dissonances! We are so familiar with the picture-boo
presentation of Mozart, a genius unconscious of his own powers, a
eternal child with an angelic face in a frame of artificial curls, tha
it is naturally shocking to discover he could be mischievous in his ar
Yet this Mozart is much more human than the tinseled creature c
conventional biography.

M-MM-439, Kolisch Quartet.

QUARTET NO. 2 IN E-FLAT MAJOR
(K. 493), FOR PIANO AND STRINGS
Allegro · Larghetto · Allegretto

EARLY in 1786, Mozart's friend, Franz Anton Hoffmeister, published
he Quartet No. 1 in G minor for Piano and Strings (K. 478). The
noted Mozart authority, Alfred Einstein, quotes Georg Nissen (who
married Mozart's widow and was one of his earliest biographers) as
aying that this was to have been the first of three such works. "When,
however," says Nissen, "Hoffmeister complained that the public
ound the work too difficult and would not buy it, Mozart voluntarily
eleased him from the contract and gave up the project of continuing
he series." He even states that Hoffmeister allowed Mozart to keep
he advance payment, on the condition that he would not compose the
other two quartets. Mozart kept his promise only halfway, for he did
compose another piano quartet—the one in E-flat. It was published
not by Hoffmeister but by another Viennese publisher, Artaria.

It is understandable why the public did not fully appreciate the
wo piano quartets, for they were the first works of their kind ever to
be written. Previous compositions for piano with three stringed in-
truments were in the form of miniature piano concerti. To this day,
hese two quartets, despite the excellence of their musical content,
re seldom performed.

The E-flat Quartet which was finished on June 3, 1786 is in three
movements. The opening is bright-hued and smooth-flowing; the sec-
nd movement is a songlike dialogue between the piano and the
hree stringed instruments; and the finale brings the quartet to a
lose in a delightful, quasi-playful mood.

M-MM-669, George Szell, Piano, and the Budapest String Quartet.

QUINTET IN C MAJOR (K. 515), FOR STRINGS
Allegro · Allegretto · Andante · Allegro

THE MONTH of May 1787, was a fateful one for Mozart. It marked his
rst meeting with Beethoven, and the young man made a great im-

[317]

pression on him. It also marked the passing of Mozart's father, Leopold, at the age of sixty-eight. He had been very close to his father
despite occasional differences between them, and his death deeply
affected the sensitive Wolfgang.

It was during this period that Mozart's two most important string
quintets were composed. Though the C major (K. 515) Quartet
which was completed in May, is fairly serious, its composer was still
able to rise above his personal troubles to write a bright piece of
chamber music.

All of Mozart's string quintets were written for two violins, two
violas, and 'cello. Boccherini had composed a number of quintets
which used two 'cellos instead of two violas, but Mozart felt that this
gave too much thickness to the bass line. He was particularly attracted to the dark tones of the viola, and the combination of two
violins, two violas, and 'cello was particularly well suited to his thematic and contrapuntal style.

M-MM-586, Milton Katims, Viola, and the Budapest String Quartet.

QUINTET IN A MAJOR (K. 581),
FOR CLARINET AND STRINGS

Allegro · Larghetto · Menuetto · Allegretto

THE QUINTET in A major was composed at the request of Anton Stadler, a clarinetist of no small merit, and a friend of both Mozart
and Haydn. Mozart had just returned from a concert tour in
Germany which, while increasing his reputation as a composer and a
performer, did little to relieve him of his financial worries. But it was
soon after this that a successful revival of his opera *Figaro* led to a
commission from the Emperor for another opera by the same authors. This was to be *Così fan tutte*, which was occupying Mozart's
chief thought and time when this Clarinet Quintet was composed.

The unusual combination of instruments in the Quintet in A major
reveals Mozart as a pioneer composer in this form. By adding a clarinet to the string quartet he adds interest to his coloring. The clarinet
—Mozart's favorite instrument—dominates the entire work; occa-

sionally the Quintet appears like a clarinet concerto with string-quartet accompaniment. This is particularly true of the first movement, written in the customary sonata form, with a lyrical second theme, and of the romantic and sentimental slow movement. Compositions for this group of instruments are rare, and the only other contribution worthy to stand with this one is the Quintet in B minor, Op. 115, by Brahms.

Mozart's Clarinet Quintet was composed in 1789 at the end of nine years of prodigious creative activity, during which time Mozart wrote nearly 200 works of varying character. The preceding year had marked the high point of his creative genius. Now still hard at work and impoverished as ever, he wrote this Quintet. His hitherto indomitable spirit was beginning to fail him, and into his music had crept—almost imperceptibly—a change. The world that was so good to him as a child prodigy, turned a heart of stone to him through the years of his early manhood, and his former moods of reckless gaiety gave place to a more thoughtful frame of mind. It was only two years later (1791), when Mozart was still in the thirties, that his early death robbed the world of one of its greatest geniuses.

The Menuetto has two trios, one in the minor mode for string quartet alone, and the other a typical Ländler in which the clarinet assumes leadership. The variations of the finale are built on a brief and simple theme and are extraordinarily colorful; the work ends in dashing brilliance.

M-MM-293, Simeon Bellison, Clarinet, and the Roth String Quartet.

SYMPHONY (HAFFNER) IN D MAJOR (K. 385)

Allegro con spirito · *Andante* · *Menuetto and Trio* · *Finale: Presto*

WHEN Mozart re-examined the score of his *Haffner* Symphony some time after composing the work, he was "quite surprised" and felt that "it must have had a very good effect." The fact that he wrote it in all possible haste in two weeks' time when he was only twenty-six years old is quite surprising to the listener as well.

"Very good" is something of an understatement. The *Haffner* Symphony may fall short of the last three monumental works composed in a six-weeks' period during 1788, but if it does, the difference in quality is scarcely perceptible.

The *Haffner* Symphony was the first of Mozart's six last symphonies which are usually grouped together as the culmination of his labors. It was composed in 1782, to the order of his father's friend, Haffner, the mayor of Salzburg.

The first movement is high spirited, with its opening theme leaping an octave in a burst of ebullience. But tranquillity returns with the next movement, one of Mozart's heavenly pages of song.

M-MM-399, London Philharmonic Orchestra, Sir Thomas Beecham Conducting.

SYMPHONY (LINZ) IN C MAJOR (K. 425)

Adagio; Allegro spiritoso · *Poco adagio* · *Menuetto and Trio*
Finale: presto

MOZART and his wife visited Linz in 1783, where they were most hospitably received by Count Thun, father-in-law of a distinguished pupil of Mozart's in Vienna. The Count was enthusiastic about Mozart's music and asked him to write a new symphony for a private concert he had organized for November 4.

On the thirty-first of October, Mozart wrote to his father, "When we arrived at the gates of Linz, a servant was standing there to conduct us to the old Count Thun's where we are still living. I really cannot tell you how they overwhelm us with kindness in this house. On Thursday, November 4th, I am going to give a concert in the theatre, and as I have not a single symphony by me, I am writing away over head and ears at a new one, which must be ready by then. I now end because I positively must get on with my work."

The Symphony Mozart thus composed is the one known as the *Linz,* and is the second of his last six works of that type.

The Symphony was finished by the third of November and dedicated to the friendly Count Thun. The earliest edition was issued as Symphony No. 6, as one of a set of twelve of Mozart's most important symphonies, but this numbering now has no significance. Köchel

ranks it as 425, while Wyzewa and Saint-Foix call it No. 414. It bears
the impress of Haydn's influence and, although composed hastily, is
a work of the first order, revealing great vitality, invention, and maturity of style.

M-MM-387, London Philharmonic Orchestra, Sir Thomas Beecham Conducting.

SYMPHONY (PRAGUE) IN D (K. 504)

Adagio; Allegro · *Andante* · *Finale: presto*

THE CITY of Prague was the scene of some of Mozart's most substantial successes during the closing years of his life. It was there that he
conducted the first performance of his new Symphony in D, a symphony now called *Prague*. Even had it been an indifferent work, it
would have been well received, for Mozart was a favorite with
Prague music lovers; but it was a work of quality, and its reception
was tumultuous. At that concert the acclaim was so great that Mozart
had to sit down and improvise at the piano for over half an hour.

Commentators describe this Symphony as a "transitional work," of
the development in the composer of a new attitude toward life, the
product of the frustration and disillusionment consequent on his failure to stabilize his position in Vienna. The absence of the traditional
minuet is supposed to signify a serious mood. But minuets are lacking
in other Mozart symphonies, and it is possible that he had doubts as
to the appropriateness of a dance movement in this symphonic
scheme.

The *Prague* Symphony has its place among Mozart's finest works
in this form. Its character is dramatic. Liberal use of dissonance, of
chromatic harmony, a new freedom in the treatment of the orchestra,
may be observed. Another feature is the extended, slow introduction
to the first movement, a device seldom employed by Mozart. Free
and extensive, this introduction establishes a background of melancholy, and the Allegro that follows (with hints of melodic ideas used
in *Figaro* and *Don Giovanni*) is tense rather than joyful. The Andante is an interlude of exquisite grace. Here neither trumpets nor

[321]

drums are used; the instrumental scheme parallels the simplicity of the music's line and texture. The Symphony concludes with a brilliant but agitated rondo on three themes.

M-MM-509, London Philharmonic Orchestra, Sir Thomas Beecham Conducting.

SYMPHONY NO. 39 IN E-FLAT MAJOR
(K. 543)

Adagio; Allegro · *Andante* · *Menuetto and Trio* · *Allegro*

ONE OF the marvels in the history of musical composition is the creation by Mozart of his three last and greatest symphonies within a period of only six weeks. And the circumstances under which these works were composed would hardly be considered as conducive to the creation of musical masterpieces.

When these three symphonies were written in the summer of 1788, Mozart was living in Vienna. As usual he was beset by debts, worry, and discouragement. A year earlier he had had to give up a number of his pupils in order to prepare and rehearse his opera, *Don Giovanni*, for its première in Prague. But he realized only a small amount of money from its production, and when it was repeated in Vienna in 1788 it was a failure.

Then, too, the composer Gluck had died in 1787, leaving vacant a remunerative post as Court composer of chamber music to Emperor Joseph II. Mozart, as he had every reason to believe, succeeded to this position; but the thrifty Joseph appointed him at the meager salary of 800 gulden. Mozart described this as "too much for what I do, too little for what I could do." For the Emperor did not want symphonies, concertos, or string quartets; all Mozart was to compose for him was dance music for the court balls at the Redoutensaal. Desperately in need of funds, the composer was frequently forced to write to his friend Michael Puchberg to borrow sums of money. It was under these pitiful conditions that the three symphonies were written.

Even without the knowledge that Mozart completed his E-flat Symphony in June, one could guess that this music was written in late spring or early summer, for it is a summer symphony in its leisurely gait. The introductory Adagio is a musical landscape: quiet Nature with man. The principal movement, Allegro, in the regular sonata form, is pastoral in an almost Beethovenian sense, where serenity foreshadows an explosion of latent power.

The second movement, Andante, paints a pastoral mood even more definitely; and the tension here is shown in the development that is carried, in a modulatory digression, from the principal key of A-flat major to its minor antipode in the cycle of fifths, B minor.

The Minuet with a Trio also suggests the June day outdoors rather than the mannered dance of the salon, and the poetic figures of the woodwinds enhance this feeling.

The finale, Allegro, in sonata form, is lively to the point of boisterousness. It ends with the principal theme used as the final cadence— an instance of formal perfection in which Mozart knows no rivals.

M-MM-456, London Philharmonic Orchestra, Sir Thomas Beecham Conducting.

SYMPHONY IN G MINOR (K. 550)

Allegro molto · *Andante* · *Menuetto* · *Allegro assai*

THE SYMPHONY in G minor (K. 550) is one of which Schubert said: "You can hear the angels singing in it." And, indeed, it almost appears an angel *is* singing the ethereal first theme with which the work opens following one measure of accompaniment. It is unusual for a symphony to open on a lyrical note, as this one does, without any formal introduction; it is almost as if Mozart himself felt that a melody of such beauty requires no preliminaries.

The work is of a quieter character, and of more lyric beauty, than is usually found even in Mozart symphonies. It has been well said that "the consoling thoughts that spring out of human suffering" find expression in the first movement. The entire Symphony suggests the waning summer days giving place to autumnal shades. Yet it contains the dignity and power of nature, the dignity that implies the unchanging processes of life, which in proper perspective are noble— however sad.

[323]

As originally written, there were no trumpets, drums, or clarinets in the score, and a very small orchestra was used.

M-MM-316, London Philharmonic Orchestra, Sir Thomas Beecham Conducting.

SYMPHONY NO. 41 (JUPITER) IN C MAJOR (K. 551)

Allegro vivace · *Andante cantabile* · *Menuetto and Trio* · *Finale: allegro molto*

No ONE seems to know who gave the C major Symphony its title of "Jupiter," but most authorities believe it was Johann Baptist Cramer, German-born pianist and composer, and founder of a London publishing house, who was profoundly impressed by the divine perfection of this work. Indeed, as Tovey pointed out, this Symphony has the "youthful majesty of a Greek god." In its spacious form, in its often fiery temperament and—particularly in the closing movement —in the grandeur of its architectonic construction, this, the last of Mozart's symphonies already casts a warning shadow of the Beethovenian symphony to come.

M-MM-565, Philharmonic-Symphony Orchestra of New York, Bruno Walter Conducting.

Modest Mussorgsky

1839–1881

MUSSORGSKY belonged to the group of Russian composers known as "The Five," who were guided by the ideal of creating a nationalist art; and there are few to deny that he was one of the most powerful, original and imaginative composers of this clique. He was born in Karevo, Pskov, in 1839. His father, a prosperous landowner, planned a military career for the boy: after being graduated from the Military School for Ensigns, Modest Mussorgsky became an officer. It was while he was in uniform that Mussorgsky became acquainted with such nationalist composers as Dargomijsky and Balakirev. The latter, particularly, impressed the young man with his own ideals for the creation of a new Russian school of music deriving its inspiration and strength from national sources. And it was under Balakirev's guidance that Mussorgsky composed his first works.

From 1863 to 1879, Mussorgsky—now out of the army—earned his living by working as a government official. But his major preoccupation was composing. In 1867 came *The Rout of Sennacherib*, some songs, and the first draught of *A Night on the Bald Mountain*. After this, he wrote a one-act opera *The Marriage*, based on Gogol's play and began working on his masterpiece, *Boris Godounov*.

In his operatic writing, Mussorgsky was bent on a realistic adaptation of the inflections of human speech to his melodic line. "If I have managed to render the straightforward expression of thoughts and feelings as it takes place in human speech," he once wrote to Rimsky-Korsakov, "and if the rendering is artistic and musicianly then the deed is done."

Boris was followed by two other important operas, *Khovantschina* and *The Fair at Sorotchinsi*. Epilepsy, which in turn brought on paralysis, brought Mussorgsky's artistic career to a premature end, and when it was at its height. He died in 1881.

[325]

A NIGHT ON THE BALD MOUNTAIN

"ON THE eve of St. John's night, June 23, 1867, I finished, with God's help, *St. John's Night on the Bald Mountain,* a tone picture consisting of the following episodes: 1. Assembly of the Witches, Hubbub and Chatter; 2. Satan's Pageant; 3. Ceremonies in Honor of Satan; 4. Witches' Dance. . . . You do not know the Witches' Dance yet. It is compact and glowing. I think the form was the most suitable in which to cast the evocation of the pother. The general character of the thing is warmth; nothing drags, all is firmly connected. Please God, and you will hear and judge."

Thus wrote Mussorgsky to Rimsky-Korsakov.

Begun in 1863 as an opera, this composition was later recast by the composer into an orchestral fantasy. The score was revised and re-orchestrated by Rimsky-Korsakov before it was published and performed.

A brief synopsis of the action around which Mussorgsky built his score is found in the published score. It reads: "A subterranean din of unearthly voices. Appearance of the Spirits of Darkness, followed by that of Tschernobog. Glorification of the Black God. The Black Mass. The Revelry of the Witches' Sabbath, interrupted from afar by the bell of a little church, whereupon the spirits of evil disperse. Dawn breaks."

12470-D, Pittsburgh Symphony Orchestra, Fritz Reiner Conducting.

BORIS GODOUNOV

MODEST PETROVITCH MUSSORGSKY's opera, *Boris Godounov,* has probably precipitated as much discussion among musicians as any work in the entire history of the tonal art. Based on Pushkin's historical drama, the work was composed between the fall of 1868 and the end of 1869. When it was submitted to the committee on acceptance of the Maryinsky Theatre in St. Petersburg, it was promptly rejected, the reason being that it lacked an important female part and also that it treated an episode in Russian history that was highly unpopular with the political authorities.

[326]

Three years later, *Boris*, with an enlarged female role for Marina, was again put before the committee, and was again rejected. This time, however, pressure from various interested groups was brought to bear, and the committee finally agreed to produce the opera. The première, with certain small cuts, took place on February 8, 1874. So enthusiastically was *Boris* received that it had to be repeated nine times during the first season. It was not heard in this country until March 19, 1913, when Toscanini conducted a performance in Italian at the Metropolitan Opera in New York.

Most of the arguments over *Boris Godounov* have raged around the various revisions made in the original score. As has already been stated, Mussorgsky made a number of changes himself. Then, about ten years after the composer's death in 1881, his friend, Rimsky-Korsakov, undertook the extensive task of completely revising the opera. He believed that *Boris* was the work of a genius, but a genius who was unfamiliar with the finer points of harmony and orchestration. Therefore, he set about to polish off the harsh harmonic dissonances and abrupt orchestral scoring. From the middle 1890's until his death in 1908, he worked on this labor of love, and even then did not complete the job. In his first revision he made many cuts in the original score and changed the sequence of several scenes; in the second version he made further changes, but restored certain scenes previously omitted. It is this second revision by Rimsky-Korsakov which is usually used in operatic performances today.

Authorities have differed widely over the relative merits and demerits of the Rimsky-Korsakov alterations, some asserting that he did the work a great service by refining Mussorgsky's rough passages, while others contend that in so doing he utterly destroyed the dramatic power of the opera.

The complete original version of *Boris* was not heard until 1928, when it was made available by the State Music Publishers in Moscow. More recently, the renowned contemporary Soviet composer, Dmitri Shostakovich, has made what is said to be a most successful revision of the score that adheres very closely to Mussorgsky's original creation.

Whatever the discussions there have been concerning Mussorgsky's opera or the changes that time and other men have wrought in it, the fact remains that *Boris Godounov* is one of the greatest of Russian masterpieces for the lyric stage.

Boris Godounov has no closely knit plot sequence; it is more a series of scenes and incidents. The action takes place at the beginning of the seventeenth century. Boris, a privy councilor in the court of the Czar Theodore, has had the Czar's young brother and sole heir to the throne, Dimitri, put to death. When Theodore dies, Boris pretends not to desire the throne, but secretly orders the officers to force the populace of Moscow to come before him and beg him to assume their leadership. In the Prologue, the people, under threats from the officers, kneel before the Novodievitch Convent, where Boris is in seclusion, and plead with him to become their Czar. When Boris pretends to be inflexible, a group of pilgrims enters and joins in the supplication.

In a cell in a nearby monastery Pimen, an old monk, relates to Gregory, a young novice, the story of Dimitri's assassination. When he learns that Dimitri was about his own age, Gregory is determined to spread the rumor that Dimitri is still alive, disguise himself as the young heir and usurp the throne.

In the great square between the Cathedral of the Assumption and the Cathedral of the Archangels is laid the massive Coronation Scene. Amid the pealing of bells and the acclamation of the people, Boris and his procession move across the square and into the Cathedral of the Assumption, where all the czars are crowned. The principal melody in this scene, which is the most familiar strain in the entire opera, is taken from an old Russian folk song. (This same song was also used by Beethoven in the third movement of his Quartet No. 8 in E minor, Op. 59, No. 2, which was dedicated to the Russian Count Rasoumovsky.)

The scene shifts to an inn on the Lithuanian frontier. Gregory, together with two accomplices, has escaped from the monastery. After a brief encounter with some soldiers, who are searching for him, he also manages to escape across the border.

Back in the Czar's apartments in the Kremlin, Boris tries to comfort his daughter, Xenia, who has recently lost her betrothed, and sends her out to seek the companionship of her friends. Left alone, he bemoans his fate in the Monologue of Boris. Though he has achieved the highest power, he can find no peace of mind. There is a disturbance outside, and Prince Shouisky enters to tell Boris that the populace has heard that Dimitri still lives. If he enters the country, Boris's throne will surely fall. As Shouisky leaves the room, the Czar sinks back, half mad with the thought of the murderous deed he has done and fearful lest Dimitri really be alive. In the Hallucination Scene Boris believes he actually sees the body of Dimitri bathed in blood. Falling on his knees, he prays for mercy.

Concealed in a garden outside the Polish Castle of Mnichek, Gregory is waiting for the Polish lady, Marina, with whom he is in love. Marina and her banquet guests come out into the garden and dance the Polonaise. As they dance, the guests toast Marina and swear to vanquish the hateful Boris and his Moscovite followers. There is a love scene between Marina and Gregory, during which the young man is induced to lead the attack against Moscow and seize the throne.

In the Forest of Kromy a crowd of peasants taunts one of Boris' Boyars, whom they have captured. A village fool joins in mocking the nobleman, but is himself ridiculed by a group of urchins. Gregory's two cohorts, Varlaam and Missail, appear, singing the praises of Czar Dimitri. When two Jesuits enter, also hailing Dimitri, however, the crowd does not trust them, and they are led off to be hanged. At this point, the false Dimitri (Gregory) passes through the forest with some troops on his way to Moscow, and the revolutionists follow him, acclaiming him their lawful Czar.

The final scene of the opera is laid in the Palace of the Kremlin. The Duma of Boyars has met to decide what punishment should be meted out to the usurper. Before they consider the issue, however, Prince Shouisky asks Boris to grant an audience to Pimen, who is waiting outside. In Pimen's tale the aged monk relates how one night an old shepherd, who had been blind since childhood, came to him and told him that the Czarevitch Dimitri appeared to him in a dream, telling him to go to the Cathedral at Ouglitch and pray before the boy's tomb. When he awoke, he went to the cathedral and prayed, and miraculously his vision was restored to him. As Boris listens to this narrative, the emotional strain becomes too great; with an anguished cry, he falls in a faint. Shouisky rushes out and returns with the Czarevitch Theodore. Regaining consciousness, Boris dismisses the Boyars and asks to be left alone with his son. In Boris's farewell to his son the Czar counsels the boy to rule wisely, protect his sister and crush the uprising in Lithuania. There is a sound of bells tolling. Outside the people are heard praying for the soul of their ruler. Pointing to Theodore as his successor, Boris falls to the floor in fright and agony, crying to Heaven for mercy. The Boyars enter in time to witness the tragic Death of Boris.

M-MM-563, Excerpts, Ezio Pinza, Basso, and Chorus of the Metropolitan Opera with Orchestra Conducted by Emil Cooper.

M-MM-516, Symphonic Synthesis, All-American Orchestra, Leopold Stokowski Conducting.

PICTURES AT AN EXHIBITION

ALTHOUGH Mussorgsky's *Pictures at an Exhibition* is one of the most popular works in the modern orchestral repertory, it was not written for orchestra. It was composed as a piano suite. Orchestral versions have been made by Ravel, Cailliet, Leonardi, Wood, and Stokowski.

In 1873, the Russian painter and architect, Vladimir Hartmann, died. Mussorgsky, who had known him intimately, was deeply affected. Attending an exhibition of Hartmann's work held in St. Petersburg (now Leningrad) shortly after his death, Mussorgsky conceived the idea of composing a suite of pieces illustrative of Hartmann's designs. *Pictures at an Exhibition* was the result.

The piano Suite consists of ten episodes, each with the title of one of Hartmann's drawings, preceded by a brief prelude, the *Promenade,* the theme of which recurs several times as a connecting link between the pictures. The Suite is in the following order:

1. *Promenade.* The Russian critic Stassov, to whom Mussorgsky dedicated the *Pictures,* thus explained this prelude: "The composer pictures himself walking idly through the gallery, pausing occasionally to observe a picture and think sadly of his friend."

2. *The Gnome.* One of Hartmann's pictures showed a diminutive, misshapen, comical figure. According to Stassov, this was an ornament fashioned for the Christmas tree at the Artist's Club.

3. *Promenade.*

4. *The Old Castle.* An ancient castle, with the figure of a minstrel in the foreground.

[330]

5. *Bydlo* (a Polish ox-cart). A peasant's ox-drawn cart lumbering across the fields.

6. *Promenade.*

7. *Ballet of the Chicks.* This episode was evidently inspired by one of the designs made by Hartmann for a ballet in which the dancers were costumed as chicks emerging from their shells.

8. *Samuel Goldberg and Schmyle.* Two Polish Jews, one rich, the other poor, meet and pass the time of day.

9. *Catacombs.* A musical impression of a drawing which shows the artist Hartmann exploring the Paris catacombs by lantern light.

10. *Baba-Yaga.* Baba-Yaga, the witch, is a familiar figure in Russian folk tales. Hartmann drew a clock to represent Baba-Yaga's house. Mussorgsky was inspired by the drawing to depict a witch's dance.

11. *The Great Gates of Kiev.* A sonorous evocation of Hartmann's design for the great gate of Kiev. Through the gate a pageant of Russian history passes.

M-MM-641, Philharmonic-Symphony Orchestra of New York, Artur Rodzinski Conducting.

Jacques Offenbach
1819–1880

IT TOOK a German Jew to bring French opéra comique to its highest point of development. One might say of Offenbach's music that it is as Parisian as the boulevards—full of the joy of living, of effervescence, of grace and charm.

He was born in Cologne in 1819—his name, originally, being Judah Eberscht. A child prodigy, he made a name for himself in his native city before setting out—in his fourteenth year—for Paris. In Paris, Offenbach studied at the Conservatory, at the same time earning his living by playing in professional orchestras. His professional career, following the completion of his studies, began with the baton, as the conductor of the Comédie Française orchestra.

In 1855, Offenbach leased the Bouffes Parisiens theatre for the purpose of presenting comic operas to the French public. His initial offering was a work of his own, *Les deux aveugles*, which was outstandingly successful. During the next few years, Offenbach presented other comic operas of his own; and the greatest of these were *Orphée aux enfers* and *La Belle Hélène*.

In 1866, Offenbach gave up the Bouffes Parisiens, which had been extraordinarily successful. A second venture at being an impresario, undertaken in 1872, was, however, disastrous. It was to help pay off the onerous debts which he had incurred in this venture that Offenbach undertook a tour of the United States.

Strange to say, Offenbach's last years were tragic ones, even though there was little question of his greatness in the comic vein. He was sick and discouraged, given to melancholia, and even hallucinations. During these last somber years he was hard at work on a grand opera—serious in vein—which he considered his *magnum opus*. It was the *Tales of Hoffmann*. Unfortunately, he did not live to hear the first performance of that opera, which was produced four months after his death.

ORPHEUS IN THE UNDERWORLD

No HAPPIER or apter example of opéra comique exists than this gay and witty satire on the Olympian gods who are endowed with human frailties. Orpheus, unhappily married to Euridice, turns to the shepherdess Chloe; and his wife favors the shepherd Aristeus (actually Pluto in disguise). When Euridice elopes with her lover, Orpheus is delighted. But convention demands that he assume the pose of the suffering husband, which he does before Jupiter. The god decrees that Orpheus may reclaim his wife and save. her—but only on the condition that he does not look at her face until he reaches the Styx. But Jupiter himself is now in love with Euridice. He throws a thunder-bolt which so startles Orpheus that involuntarily he turns around and looks at his wife. Thus Jupiter is enabled to take Euridice for himself (as a Bacchante), and Orpheus is free to follow Chloe.

Performed for the first time at the Bouffes Parisiens in 1858, *Orpheus* would have been an outright failure were it not for the fact that it was violently attacked in the *Journal des Debats* as a "blasphemous" work. A spirited battle followed in the press; and when the smoke was cleared, *Orpheus* was famous.

TALES OF HOFFMANN

THREE fantastic tales of E. T. A. Hoffmann were adapted by Barbier and Carré as the book for Offenbach's last opera. It is a strange libretto, evoking an unreal world of make-believe characters; but it has brought from Offenbach some of his most exquisite music.

The three principal episodes of the opera concern the three tragic love affairs of Hoffmann: for the doll Olympia, which Dr. Spalanazi creates and fools Hoffmann into believing as real; for the beautiful Giulietta, for whom Hoffmann kills a man only to have her escape with another lover; and, finally, for the sick Antonia, who dies from singing too much, only to have Hoffmann accused of the murder. Some writers have interpreted the first episode with Olympia as a bitter satire on the vanity and artificiality of the Second Empire.

68692-D, Barcarolle, London Philharmonic Orchestra, Sir Thomas Beecham Conducting.
71681-D, Dapertutto's Air, Martial Singher, Baritone, with the Metropolitan Orchestra, Paul Breisach Conducting.

Walter Piston

1894–

Walter Piston was born at Rockland, Maine, in 1894, to a family of Italian descent. He first cultivated his artistic talents in drawing and painting, and was graduated from the Massachusetts School of Art in 1916. A strong impulse to work at music, however, induced him to matriculate at Harvard, where he received the Bachelor of Arts degree, *summa cum laude*, in 1924, and was elected to the Phi Beta Kappa. Mr. Piston continued his musical studies in Paris under the direction of Nadia Boulanger. He has held both the John Knowles Paine and the Guggenheim Fellowships.

Now an assistant professor of music at Harvard, Piston composes steadily, his works including compositions for orchestra, chamber music ensembles, ballet, and chorus. His works have been extensively performed, particularly by the Boston Symphony Orchestra, and he is now accepted as one of the major creative figures in American music. No experimentalist, Piston writes in the traditional forms with a superb sense of form, an abundance of ideas, and fine imagination.

THE INCREDIBLE FLUTIST, SUITE FOR ORCHESTRA

In 1938, Walter Piston composed gay and intriguing music for a ballet for Hans Wiener in which the central character is a flutist of a circus who can charm not only snakes but women as well with his enchanted pipings. The orchestral suite comprises major sections from the ballet score. In this form—first introduced by the Pittsburgh Symphony Orchestra under Reiner on November 22, 1940—the work has achieved great popularity.

The suite is divided into the following sections: Introduction; Siesta Hour in the Marketplace and the Entrance of the Vendors; Dance of the Vendors; Entrance of Customers; Tango of Four Daughters; Arrival of the Circus and Circus March; Solo of the Flutist; Minuet—Dance of the Widow and Merchant; Spanish Waltz; Eight o'clock Strikes; Siciliano—Dance of the Flutist and the Merchant's Daughter; Polka and Finale.

STRING QUARTET, NO. 1

Allegro · Adagio moderato un poco mosso · Allegro vivace

THE COMPOSER himself describes his String Quartet, No. 1, as follows:

"The Quartet was composed in 1933. It is dedicated to the Chardon Quartet of Boston, and was first performed in Cambridge, Massachusetts, in March, 1934.

"The first movement opens in the key of C with the first theme, vigorously rhythmic and dissonant. There follows a rhythmic, contrapuntal development, leading to a lyrical second theme in F minor. The theme is introduced by the viola, and there are answering phrases in the first violin. After a somewhat slower statement of this theme, inverted in the 'cello and the low register of the viola, a return to the spirit of the opening of the movement is the signal for the beginning of an extended development of motives from both themes. Variation and canonic treatment are prominent in this section. At the height of the climax the first theme reappears in recapitulation. The second theme, now in C minor, is given to the violin and 'cello. It is followed by a short *coda* that brings the movement to its end in the *staccato* character of the first theme.

"The key center of the second movement is E. The two motives from which the movement is constructed appear in the recitative-like 'cello declamation and the answering figure in the other instruments. These elements appear in alternation and finally in combination. Contrapuntal treatment of the material leads at times to polytonal writing, as in the canonic passage for the violins over a placid accompaniment. The recitative of the 'cello seems about to end the movement when a fugal passage, its subject based on the second element of the movement, enters in the viola. This passage moves to a climax, with the stretto of the fugue subject appearing in the four voices. The opening mood returns to end the movement in calmness and serenity.

"The original tonality of C returns in the third movement, a lively rondo which makes use of whimsical changes of meter and irregular accents. Measures of 5-8 alternate with measures of 2-4 and sometimes 3-8. The form of the rondo might be described as A-B-A-B-A, in the course of which the themes appear often in varied form. The A begins the movement and is characterized by quick, repeated notes in all four instruments. B appears as a tune for the first violin over an off-beat accompaniment. One of the variations of A takes the form of a pizzicato for all instruments. The tempo of the movement is accelerated to increase the brilliance of the ending."

M-MM-388, Dorian String Quartet.

Amilcare Ponchielli

1834–1886

AMILCARE PONCHIELLI was born in Cremona in 1834. For eleven years—from the time he was nine—he studied at the Milan Conservatory. He composed his first opera soon after his graduation from the Conservatory. It was based on Manzoni's *I Promessi sposi,* and was produced in Cremona in 1856. For the next few years, Ponchielli worked as a bandmaster, at the same time composing numerous operas. One of these opened the new opera house in Milan, the Teatro dal Verme; it was a tremendous success. *La Gioconda,* produced in 1876, confirmed Ponchielli's fame. He never succeeded in duplicating the success of *La Gioconda,* however. He died in Milan in 1886 after having served for several years as Kapellmeister in the Cathedral of Bergamo. Of his many operas, only *La Gioconda* has survived him; but that opera has succeeded in keeping his name alive in operatic history.

ARRIGO BOITO adapted the Victor Hugo drama, *Angelo, Tyran de Padoue* for Ponchielli. To each of the four acts he appended a descriptive title: Act I: "The Lion's Mouth"; Act II: "The Rosary"; Act III: "The House of Gold" and Act IV: "The Orfano Canal."

La Gioconda purchases the safety of her lover Enza from the spy Barnaba even though she learns that her lover is interested in Laura Adorno. When La Gioconda discovers that Laura's husband threatens to kill Enza, she offers herself to Barnaba in return for Enza's safety. Subsequently, she commits suicide rather than live up to her bargain.

La Gioconda was introduced at La Scala in Milan on April 8, 1876. After that performance, Ponchielli subjected the opera to extensive revision. The new version was introduced in Genoa in December of the same year, and in its new form it was an unqualified success.

Richly lyrical, with many deservedly famous arias, the opera is nevertheless most famous for its brilliant ballet music. The "Dance of the Hours," which appears in the third act, has become a staple in salon-music repertory and was interpreted in the successful Walt Disney motion picture *Fantasia*.

11621-D, Dance of the Hours, Chicago Symphony Orchestra, Frederick Stock Conducting.

71276-D, Voce di Donna O d'Angelo, Bruna Castagna, Contralto, with Orchestra directed by Antonini.

Serge Prokofiev

1891–

SERGE PROKOFIEV's imperial position in Soviet music has been accepted ever since 1934 when he returned to his native land to make his home there permanently and to identify himself and his art with Soviet ideals. But even before then he belonged with the great composers of our time.

He was born in Ekaterinoslav, South Russia, in 1891. The study of the piano began in his fifth year (with his mother); and before he reached his tenth birthday he was already the proud composer of an opera. Taneiev saw his boyish compositions and recommended the boy to Glière. With Glière to guide him, Prokofiev composed one work after another in an irrepressible burst of industry. It was on Glière's advice that Prokofiev now entered the St. Petersburg Conservatory. For ten years he studied there with Rimsky-Korsakov, Liadov, and Tcherepnine; during these student days he composed numerous works.

On the eve of World War I, Prokofiev was graduated from the Conservatory with three diplomas and the Rubinstein Prize for piano. The war years—even though they were years of deprivation and suffering—was a period of rich achievement for the young composer; for it was now that he wrote his first famous works including the *Classical* Symphony and the First Concerto for Violin and Orchestra.

Soon after the Revolution, Prokofiev toured the United States for the first time, appearing in performances of his own works, and composing an opera for the Chicago Opera Company, *The Love for Three Oranges*. For the next decade and a half, Prokofiev lived in Paris, embarking frequently on concert tours. However, in 1934, he decided to return permanently to the Soviet Union. There he assumed a position of major importance in its musical life. During World War II, he composed several works inspired by the Soviet struggle, as well as an opera of major proportions, *War and Peace*.

In 1938, in connection with a renewed interest in Russian history—
and a certain degree of anti-German feeling in Russia—the Soviet's
leading motion picture director Sergei Eisenstein, in collaboration
with Vasiliev, produced the stirring picture *Alexander Nevsky*. This
eminently successful film portrayed in a masterly fashion the Russians' defense of Novgorod against the invading Knights of the
Teutonic Order in 1242. These knights, who were originally cru-
saders, turned militaristic and, on the pretense of Christianizing East
Prussia and portions of Russia, overran these territories.

To meet the onslaught in the land of Novgorod, the people called
upon their Prince, Alexander Yaroslavitch Nevsky, to lead them
against the foe, as he had against the Swedes two years before.
Nevsky organized a large militia to supplement the regular army.
On April 5, 1242, the people of Novgorod met the Germans on the
ice of Lake Chud, near Pskov, and defeated the enemy in a fierce
battle, during which many Germans were driven through the ice and
drowned. As the result of this heroic defense of his country, Alexander Nevsky became an immortal Russian hero and a fine symbol of
valor to the present-day fighters in the Soviet Union.

The musical score for the film was composed by Serge Prokofiev
who, in addition to his wide reputation as a leading composer of concert music, had won international acclaim for his musical score for
an earlier Soviet film *Lieutenant Kije*. Prokofiev was so impressed
with the story of Alexander Nevsky, however, that he expanded his
cinema music into a cantata for mezzo-soprano, chorus, and orchestra. He wrote the text himself, with the collaboration of V. Lugov-
skoi. The Cantata was completed in Moscow on February 7, 1939,
and had its initial performance, under the composer's direction, by
the Moscow Philharmonic Orchestra and Chorus on the following
May 17.

Alexander Nevsky was first presented in America via the radio.
Leopold Stokowski conducted the NBC Symphony Orchestra in a
performance of the work on March 7, 1943. He was assisted by the
Westminster Choir and Jennie Tourel. Miss Tourel was also the
soloist on May 24, 1944, when the Cantata was broadcast by the
Columbia Broadcasting Symphony and the Collegiate Chorale, con-

ducted by Bernard Herrmann, during the CBS *Invitation to Music* program. The first concert performance in this country took place on March 23, 1945, with Eugene Ormandy conducting the Philadelphia Orchestra and the Westminster Choir, and with Rosalind Nadell as soloist.

The Cantata is composed of seven musical pictures, each of which presents a phase of this famous national epic.

M-MM-580, Jennie Tourel, Mezzo-Soprano, the Westminster Choir, and the Philadelphia Orchestra, Eugene Ormandy Conducting.

CONCERTO NO. 3 IN C MAJOR, OP. 26, FOR PIANO AND ORCHESTRA

Andante; Allegro · Theme and Variations · Allegro ma non troppo

IN HIS biography of Prokofiev, Israel Nestyev traces four predominant characteristics in his music—classicism (or neo-classicism) and frequent use of old classical forms and patterns, fantasy and grotesqueness, lyricism, and humor. Though all of these do not make their appearance in every work by this composer, they are all amply represented in the Third Piano Concerto.

Ideas for this concerto were accumulated over a period of years— one or two are traceable as far back as 1911—but actual work was not begun on it until 1917, while Prokofiev was in Leningrad. Shortly thereafter, however, the composer embarked on a tour which took him to the United States, and the composition of the Concerto was temporarily suspended. It was ultimately completed at St. Brevin, France, in October 1921. The first performance was given by the Chicago Symphony Orchestra, Frederick Stock conducting on December 16th of that year, with Prokofiev himself playing the solo piano part. It was well received by the public and press of Chicago, but when the composer played it with the New York Symphony Orchestra under Albert Coates ten days later, it was condemned.

The first movement is a brilliant Allegro with an introduction (Andante) that reappears in the middle as a lyrical contrast. The second movement is a marchlike theme with five variations, and the third movement is alternately dancelike and broadly lyrical.

M-MM-667, Dimitri Mitropoulos, Piano, and the Robin Hood Dell Orchestra, Dimitri Mitropoulos Conducting.

[341]

CONCERTO IN D, OP. 19, FOR VIOLIN
AND ORCHESTRA

Andantino · Scherzo; Vivacissimo · Moderato; Andante

PROKOFIEV, one of the most talented and original of modern composers, wrote this Concerto in 1913. It is unquestionably the most consequential addition to violin literature since the concerto of Sibelius. It has all the qualities of Prokofiev's music at its best—wit, charm, and distinction.

The vogue of the work dates from the Prague International Festival of Contemporary Music in 1924 when Szigeti's playing of it resulted in invitations from almost every conductor of note in Europe to introduce it in his particular series. Szigeti played it with Furtwängler, Bruno Walter, Malko, Ansermet, Fritz Reiner, and many other conductors in virtually every capital in Europe. Russia first heard it from Szigeti and it created such a stir that the Scherzo had to be encored at all performances. Szigeti also played it in the United States with the New York Philharmonic, the Philadelphia and Boston Symphony orchestras, and introduced it in Tokyo, Shanghai, Sydney, and Melbourne.

While the Concerto has some dazzling pages of characteristic Prokofiev whimsy (as in the Scherzo), it is essentially a work of great lyric beauty, with more than one passage of introspection. It opens and closes with the same subject, a slow theme of gentle loveliness, and the entire closing movement is a broad melody of great feeling.

M-MM-244, Joseph Szigeti, Violin, and the London Philharmonic Orchestra, Sir Thomas Beecham Conducting.

CLASSICAL SYMPHONY IN D MAJOR, OP. 25

Allegro · Larghetto · Gavotte · Finale: molto vivace

HAVING secured an excellent musical education, Prokofiev began almost at once to compose in an idiom so unconventional and barbaric as to cause downright embarrassment to his teachers. While all of the time staying within the proper limitations of musical form, he seemed to take fiendish delight in indulging in unheard of modulations, sudden violent jumps of the melodic line, and other departures from Romantic tradition. Before long he held unquestioned honors as an *enfant terrible* in Russian music.

In 1916, Prokofiev decided to answer his critics and enjoy himself at the same time. He planned a classical symphony. His first work to be published in this form was sketched in precisely the form employed by the classic masters. The same instrumentation was specified. The work became a Mozart symphony as it might have been written had that profound master lived 100 years later than he did. Mozart would recognize the form and instrumentation at once, but hardly so the music itself. That is pure Prokofiev. The composer darts up and down the scale in his characteristic way. Nevertheless, the color combinations are crisp and clear, the indigestible elements of the *Scythian* Suite are absent.

Despite his deviations from the usual path followed in harmony and modulation, Prokofiev is a master of dynamics, and at all times knows what he is about. The *Classical* Symphony fits neatly and precisely into the classical pattern—all that is out of place is the chronology. Unmistakably the work is twentieth century, and equally clear is the fact that its composer is a musician of wit, ingenuity, and remarkable creative ability.

The four movements of the Symphony are short and neatly worked out. The first contains no ear-pounding climaxes. Its two themes weave their way in miniature form through the traditional pattern, punctuated at intervals with loud chords from the whole orchestra. The second movement begins and ends softly, scampering up to a mild climax and right back down again. The third movement is a Gavotte rather than the expected minuet. The dance form is delightfully worked out, complete with the octave jumps so dear to the composer's heart. The Finale, Molto vivace, is perhaps the movement most completely in the spirit of the classic masters. Once again the modern composer shines through, but the music conjures up the silks and powdered wigs of another day.

X-MX-166, Minneapolis Symphony Orchestra, Dimitri Mitropoulos Conducting.

IN *Peter and the Wolf,* Prokofiev has created a masterpiece which possesses an appeal to sophisticated adults as well as to children. The children learn to recognize the instruments of the orchestra, as each character is represented by an instrument: the bird by the flute, the duck by the oboe, the cat by the clarinet in the low register playing staccato, Grandfather by the bassoon, the wolf by the chord of three French horns, Peter by the strings, the shots of the hunters by the kettledrums and the bass drum. Each character is also given a special leading motive.

The story, Prokofiev's own, is told by the narrator to the accompaniment of the music, or between the episodes. The tale has also an implied political significance, for in it the wolf, who during his career as a ruthless aggressor has gobbled up a defenseless duck, and threatened the safety of the cat and the bird, is finally outwitted by the Soviet boy scout Peter, is caged by the hunters who came to Peter's aid, and is placed in the zoo for everyone to behold and marvel.

M-MM-477, Basil Rathbone, Narrator, and the All-American Orchestra, Leopold Stokowski Conducting.

SYMPHONY NO. 5, OP. 100

Andante · Allegro marcato · Adagio · Allegro giocoso

IN JANUARY, 1945, Prokofiev conducted the first performance of his new Fifth Symphony in Moscow, and immediately it joined the ranks of his most popular works. When it received its American première by Serge Koussevitzky and the Boston Symphony Orchestra later the same year it was so enthusiastically acclaimed that it has since been assimilated into the standard repertoire of practically every major orchestra.

Though some fifteen years elapsed between the appearance of the Fourth and Fifth symphonies, the Moscow correspondent of the New York *Times,* Robert Magidoff, quotes the composer as saying that he had been working on the Symphony for several years, collecting themes for it in a special notebook. "I always work that way," stated Prokofiev, "and probably that is why I work so fast. The entire score of the Fifth was written in one month in the summer of 1944. It took another month to orchestrate it, and in between I wrote the score for Eisenstein's film, *Ivan the Terrible*.

"When the war broke out," the composer continued to relate to Magidoff, "I felt that everyone must do his share, and I began composing songs, marches for the front. But soon events assumed such gigantic and far-reaching scope as to demand larger canvases. I wrote the Symphonic Suite *1941*, reflecting my first impressions of the war. Then I wrote *War and Peace*. This opera was conceived before the war, but the war made it compelling for me to complete it. Tolstoy's great novel depicts Russia's war against Napoleon, and then, as now, it was not a war of two armies but of peoples. Following the opera I wrote the *Ballad of an Unknown Boy* for orchestra, choir, soprano and dramatic tenor, to words of the poet Pavel Anatakolsky. Finally I wrote my Fifth Symphony."

Written in the usual four movements, the Fifth Symphony is conceived along decidedly melodic lines. The opening movement is of a rather broad, dramatic nature. The second movement, probably the most easily appreciated of the four, is a scherzo. The principal section contains a jaunty theme, under which is a steady staccato accompaniment. A brief bridge passage for woodwinds leads into the contrasting middle section—somewhat akin to the classical Trio. This same bridge passage leads back into an altered reiteration of the opening section. The third movement described as tragic in character, is quite songlike, and certain passages are reminiscent of Prokofiev's Second Violin Concerto. The lower strings, playing a variation on the opening theme of the first movement, provide a slow introduction to the finale. This mood is quickly dispersed, and is replaced by a very lively theme, Allegro giocoso, that begins the main portion of the last movement. The entire movement smacks of satire, and there are many brutal thrusts that remind one of Shostakovich. A lengthy, turbulent coda brings the Symphony to a close.

Although the Fifth Symphony is intended as pure music, and although Prokofiev insists it is without a program, he himself has called it "a symphony about the spirit of man."

M-MM-661, Philharmonic-Symphony Orchestra of New York, Artur Rodzinski Conducting.

Giacomo Puccini

1858–1924

Puccini was born at Lucca in 1858. Beginning with his great-great-grandfather (born 1712), his ancestors were musicians, mostly in the service of local or nearby churches. Giacomo took elementary lessons in voice from an uncle; later, he studied with one of his father's pupils. To help support his family, Giacomo accepted employment as an organist, and played in dance halls, during this period of study.

He scored a remarkable success as a composer before he was twenty, with a cantata *June*. Thus encouraged, Puccini proceeded to write a motet for the Feast of San Paolino, and a variety of other works including a mass and some chamber music.

A performance of *Aida* at nearby Pisa awakened in him the desire to write for the stage. Sponsored by the Queen of Italy, and supported by a generous relative, he entered the Milan Conservatory in 1880, where one of his teachers was Ponchielli. It was Ponchielli who officially launched Puccini in an operatic career by encouraging him to submit a one-act opera in the competition sponsored by a publishing house. *Le Villi* did not win the prize, but it did enjoy a *succès d'éstime* at its performance at the Teatro dal Verme in Milan on May 31, 1884. A commission from the publishing house of Ricordi followed. That opera—*Edgar*—was a failure at its première at La Scala in 1889.

His next opera was *Manon Lescaut* based on Prevost's novel. Its first performance in Turin in 1893 was a signal success. It was exactly three years after the première of *Manon* that Puccini became world famous. On February 1, 1896 the world première of *La Bohème* took place in Turin under the baton of twenty-nine-year-old Toscanini.

With *La Tosca* and *Madama Butterfly* Puccini definitely established himself as the greatest composer of Italian opera after Verdi. In January 1907, Puccini visited North America for the first time. It was during these days in New York that he decided to collaborate with Belasco on an operatic adaptation of the latter's play, *The Girl of the Golden West*. The première took place at the Metropolitan Opera House on December 10, 1910 with Toscanini conducting. It is not one of Puccini's successful works.

Puccini's last opera (though not fully completed by him) was *Turandot*. Musically, this is one of his most interesting works. There are in it echoes from Wagner, Richard Strauss, Debussy, Stravinsky, and even Schönberg; and yet it remains genuine Puccini. It even contains some elements of Chinese music.

For over twenty years, Puccini had been suffering from a slight case of diabetes. Disturbances gradually took on alarming proportions. In the fall of 1924 he had to leave for Brussels to be operated on for cancer of the throat. The operation was pronounced successful. Puccini's heart, however, could not stand the strain of a post-operation radium treatment. He collapsed on the evening of November 29, 1924. On April 25, 1926, Puccini's last opera *Turandot*—which was completed by Franco Alfano under the supervision of Toscanini —was introduced at La Scala. After Liu's wailing farewell song, Toscanini terminated the performance that night with the words: "And here ends the work of the master."

LA BOHÈME

PUCCINI's *La Bohème* was performed for the first time at Turin in 1896. Toscanini conducted. The opera did not have the immediate success of its predecessor *Manon Lescaut*. The episodic character of the action, the simplicity of the music, the substitution in both of pathos for melodrama and of sentiment for passion, seem to have affected the audience with mingled emotions of surprise and displeasure. But this reaction was temporary. There was enough interest in the rising star of Puccini to bring about repetitions of his newest work, and through these repetitions the qualities of that work asserted themselves. Today *La Bohème* is one of the most popular of all operas, and musicians rate it as high as does the uninstructed public.

The libretto, by Giacoso and Illica, is based on Murger's once-popular novel *La Vie de Bohème,* and may be briefly summarized as follows:

Act I. A garret in the Latin Quarter of Paris. Here the four Bohemians—Rodolfo, a poet; Marcello, a painter; Schaunard, a musician; and Colline, a "philosopher"—live merrily in a state bordering on destitution. It is Christmas Eve, and while Schaunard and Colline are out foraging for provisions, Rodolfo and Marcello sacrifice, the one the manuscript of the tragedy he has just completed, the other the frame of the portrait he is painting, to warm their chilly quarters.

Schaunard and Colline return; the former has had a windfall and brings fuel, food, wine, and money. The friends make merry and decide to adjourn to a café. Rodolfo is left alone to complete an article. There is a knock, and on opening the door Rodolfo discovers a pretty girl holding an unlighted candle. He lights it and she departs, only to return almost at once—a draft has again extinguished the candle. She drops her key, and in the darkness she and Rodolfo grope for it; their hands touch. Hers are icily cold, and Rodolfo feels a surge of pity and tenderness. He asks her name and learns that it is Mimi. They exchange confidences and go out together to join Rodolfo's friends at the café.

Act II. The Café Momus. Rodolfo introduces Mimi to his friends. Musetta, a former sweetheart of Marcello, appears in the company of an old and wealthy admirer whom the friends trick into paying their bill while they make off, taking Musetta with them.

Act III. A city gate on a winter morning. Mimi confides to Marcello that she can no longer live with Rodolfo, who is jealous. When Rodolfo appears, Mimi hides, but her coughing—she is ill of consumption—reveals her presence. She asks Rodolfo to pack her belongings, but to retain a pink bonnet in memory of her. Rodolfo's tenderness reawakens, and the parting of the lovers is postponed.

Act IV. The garret where the action of the play began. Rodolfo and Marcello have again been deserted by their sweethearts and are miserable, though each strives to conceal the fact. Colline and Schaunard arrive in a despondent mood—the friends as usual are short of funds, and this time all that Schaunard has are four rolls and a herring. To offset the depression which all of them feel, the four friends pretend that they are attending a court ball.

At the height of the ensuing hilarity the door opens and Musetta enters. Breathless and in great distress, she tells them that Mimi is desperately ill and has hardly strength to climb the stairs to the garret. Rodolfo and Marcello go to Mimi's assistance, Schaunard and Colline prepare a bed for her. She greets them and thanks them for their kindness. Rodolfo she embraces—may she stay with him? "Forever!" he answers, and implores her not to exhaust herself talking. Musetta removes her earrings and gives them to Marcello—he is to sell them and get a doctor and medicine for Mimi. In the same spirit of sacrifice, Colline removes his overcoat and bids it a fond farewell.

Rodolfo and Mimi are now left alone. Opening her eyes, the dying girl confesses that she shammed sleep in order to bring this about. Together, the lovers recall the happy past. Schaunard is the first of the friends to return, closely followed by Musetta and Marcello, who bring medicine and a muff and word that a doctor is on his way to their patient. Mimi fondles the muff with childish pleasure; her hands are much warmer now, and sleep comes. The friends speak in whispers in order not to disturb her.

Rodolfo is impatient for the doctor's arrival, and Marcello reassures him. Musetta kneels in prayer by the window. Colline returns at this juncture with money, which he gives to Musetta. But the end has come; Schaunard, approaching the bed, sees that Mimi has expired. Rodolfo cannot understand the whisperings of his friends. Then the truth dawns on him, and with a cry of despair, "Mimi! Mimi!" he falls sobbing at Mimi's side.

OP-MOP-5, Soloists and Orchestra of La Scala Opera, Lorenzo Molajoli Conducting.

M-MM-274, Act IV, Perli, Andreva, Nash, Brownlee, Alva and Easton, and the London Philharmonic Orchestra, Sir Thomas Beecham Conducting.

MADAMA BUTTERFLY

ORIGINALLY a magazine story by John Luther Long, and dramatized by the author and David Belasco, *Madama Butterfly* came to the notice of Puccini during his visit to London in 1900. The Italian adaptation was made for Puccini by Giuseppe Giacosa and Luigi Illica, the composer's collaborators on *La Bohème* and *Tosca*.

Puccini took infinite pains to catch in his score both Japanese and American flavors. He imported hundreds of records from Japan in order to learn what he could about Japanese music; he went to Milan to see performances of a visiting Japanese troupe; he traveled to Viareggio to consult with the Ambassadress of Japan. On the other hand, he tried to make Pinkerton "as American as possible," and rather naïvely used the American national anthem as a sort of *leitmotif*.

Puccini was always in love with his heroines, especially when they were pathetic and frail. He was so enthusiastic about Cio-Cio-San and (probably for the first time) so fully satisfied with the libretto that he paid little attention to occasional spells of fever, throat irritations and diabetic disturbances which he was suffering at this time. The composition of the opera was, however, interrupted by an automobile accident which almost took the composer's life and confined him to bed for eight months.

Madama Butterfly always remained Puccini's favorite opera. He who never liked to listen to his own music claimed that *Butterfly* never ceased to interest him. He considered it his most modern opera, probably because of his occasional use of the whole-tone scale for exotic colors.

He was so certain of its triumph that, for the first time, he invited his brothers and sisters to attend the première at La Scala in 1900. At that performance, at any rate, *Butterfly* was a miserable failure. Even after the newsboys screamed out the headline in the street about the "fiasco of Maestro Puccini," the composer kept repeating that this was his most beautiful opera.

No one knows precisely why *Butterfly* failed as conclusively as it did at that première performance. It is likely that the exotic subject held no interest for a Milanese audience; that the division into two very long acts fatigued them; that vague reminiscences of *La Bohème* struck it as repetition; that the novelty of the atmosphere and the harmony proved annoying. It is just as likely that Puccini's enemies—a formidable clan—were well organized to provoke a disturbance.

Puccini withdrew his score and refunded the royalties to the opera house. Three months later, he emerged with a revision of the opera. A performance in Brescia on May 28, 1904 established the opera as a huge success.

The sad tale of the American sailor Pinkerton and his Japanese "port-wife," Cio-Cio-San, is well known. During Pinkerton's absence, Cio-Cio-San gives birth to a child. The next time Pinkerton returned to Japan it was with his legal American wife. When Cio-Cio-San discovers this, she turns over their child to Pinkerton and kills herself.

OP-MOP-4, Pampanini, Granada, Vanelli, Baccaloni, and Chorus and Orchestra of La Scala conducted by Lorenzo Molajoli.

TOSCA

OF THE four Puccini operas antedating *Tosca,* i.e. *Le Villi, Edgar, Manon Lescaut* and *La Bohème,* only the last named, produced in Turin in 1896, had up to that time attracted world-attention (though of late years *Manon Lescaut* has also taken its place as one of this composer's admired works). The dramatic intensity of *Tosca* (as reflected in both libretto and music) quickly made its impression, following the première in Rome in 1900, and from this time Puccini's place was assured as one of the most prominent of modern Italian writers of opera. From Rome the new work traveled by swift stages to other centers in Italy, across the Alps to London, Paris, Vienna, Berlin and some three years later New York. It has come to be regarded as one of the finest examples extant of the type of music drama so successfully developed by Puccini.

As is well known, the basis of the drama is Sardou's celebrated play *La Tosca*. Stripped of certain scenes rather too starkly realistic for lyrical presentation, it offers a swiftly moving series of melodramatic incidents and effects of which Puccini was not slow to take advantage. The close knitting of the plot with the music is a triumph of both stagecraft and composition. The characters, too, offer contrasts and vivid outlines which have called forth the best in the impersonating powers of opera's most eminent exponents. The beauty, charm and wit of the singer Tosca, the romantic character of the painter Cavaradossi, the silken brutality of the Minister of Police, Scarpia, the humorous interjections of the Sacristan and his boys, the sustained excitement of the leading motives in the orchestra, so admirably employed to carry the drama forward to its tragic finale—all these factors have challenged the resources of the world's greatest operatic organizations and resulted in some of the most memorable performances in operatic history. All in all, the modern repertory holds no more incisive and enthralling drama of love and hate, passion and death.

Tosca is perhaps the most theatrical of Puccini's operas. Many critics found the libretto repulsive. But they had to confess that the composer had succeeded beautifully in humanizing outrageous situations—seduction, torture, execution, suicide. Puccini utilized illustrative music when the stage action became too realistic; and he indulged in passionate cantilene at the proper psychological moments. He paid particular attention to plastic declamation and obtained novel effects through the use of whole-tone scales and modern harmonies.

OP-MOP-6, Scacciati, Granada, Molinari, Baccaloni, Baracchi, Venturini, Cortellini, Chorus of La Scala and the Milan Symphony Orchestra conducted by Lorenzo Molajoli.

Serge Rachmaninoff

1873–1943

SERGE RACHMANINOFF occupies a unique position in the world of music. From his student days at the Moscow Conservatory until the time of his death at Beverly Hills, California, on March 28, 1943, he was world famous as a composer, pianist, and conductor. Yet, though he lived during a period that began when the nationalistic music of his native Russia was in ascendancy, and that saw the rise of Richard Strauss, the French impressionists, Stravinsky, Schönberg, the modern Soviet composers and American jazz, Rachmaninoff, as a composer, remained aloof from all trends and all musical experiments. Throughout his entire career, his music was marked by conservatism, though it could never be called reactionary. What gave it universal appeal was the constant presence of a beautiful, original melodic line, supported by richly colored harmonies and, in the case of his symphonic works, a wonderfully woven orchestral fabric.

Rachmaninoff composed four symphonies during his lifetime, though *The Bells*, a symphony for chorus and orchestra based on the poem by Edgar Allan Poe, bears no number. The First Symphony, written in 1895, had a single—and unsuccessful—performance in St. Petersburg, and has never been heard again. It brought rebuke from critics and friends alike, and César Cui, one of the famous Russian "Five," remarked caustically that "if there was a Conservatory in Hell, Rachmaninoff would gain the first prize for his symphony." Even the composer was dissatisfied and discouraged. Though he had already won considerable renown as a pianist, and though no less a musician than Tchaikovsky had praised his early opera *Aleko,* and had arranged for its première a few years earlier, Rachmaninoff resolved to abandon composition entirely. A considerable amount of persuasion by his friend Count Tolstoy, some lessons in self-assertion by a psychologist and his marriage to Natalie Satin—all these factors helped the young man to overcome his inferiority complex; and he returned to his musical life with renewed vigor and confidence.

By 1906, when he was thirty-three, Rachmaninoff's musical and social activities had reached a high pitch. For the past year he had been conductor of the Imperial Grand Opera in Moscow, besides making frequent concert appearances as pianist. Then for the next two years Rachmaninoff, together with his wife and baby daughter, lived in virtual seclusion in Dresden, occupying a little house with a garden. There he composed three important works: *The Isle of the Dead,* the Piano Sonata (Op. 28), and the Second Symphony.

Rachmaninoff visited the United States for the first time in 1909, appearing in numerous concerts which introduced him to America as pianist, conductor, and composer. When he returned to the United States in 1917, it was as an exile from his native land. Thereafter, he lived permanently in Switzerland, but spending a great part of each year in concert tours of the United States. After the outbreak of World War II, Rachmaninoff remained in this country, and here he died in 1943.

CONCERTO NO. 2 IN C MINOR, FOR PIANO AND ORCHESTRA, OP. 18

Moderato · Adagio sostenuto · Allegro scherzando

RACHMANINOFF's Second Piano Concerto has become so popular that it is one of the most widely played works of its kind. Even the writers of popular song hits have snapped up several of its leading melodies and have put words to them; and, in recent years, it has been heard in several motion pitcures, forming an integral part of the plot of one of them.

The circumstances surrounding the composition of the Concerto are among the most unusual in the history of music. In 1895, Rachmaninoff composed his unsuccessful First Symphony. Discouraged, Rachmaninoff felt that his career as a composer was over and that he would have to spend the rest of his life as a piano teacher—for concert engagements were still few and far between. Feeling that his career had already ended, he fell into a state of apathy and despair. A few concerts, including a highly successful appearance in London, failed to bring him out of the doldrums.

Finally, in 1900, his family and some friends, the Satins (with whom he was living and a member of whose family he married in 1902), sent Rachmaninoff to a Dr. Dahl, a specialist in the new science of auto-suggestion. Dr. Dahl kept repeating to the young composer that he was not through, that the work he was even then planning—a piano concerto—would be excellent, that Rachmaninoff would henceforth work with great facility. "Although it may sound incredible," wrote Rachmaninoff many years later, "the cure really helped me. Already at the beginning of the summer I began again to compose. The material grew in bulk, and new musical ideas began to stir within me—far more than I needed for my concerto."

The concerto Rachmaninoff wrote following this cure was to become his most famous and successful work, the Second Piano Concerto. Its first complete performance took place at a Philharmonic Society Concert in Moscow on October 14, 1901, with Rachmaninoff at the piano. It was published the same year, and in 1904 became the first of a series of Rachmaninoff's works to win the Glinka Prize of five hundred rubles. This award was made possible through a bequest by Mitrosan Petrovich Belaieff, who had sponsored the work of many Russian composers and had, in 1885, established a music publishing house for Russian compositions in Leipzig.

The entire Concerto is marked by a warm lyricism; it fairly bulges with hauntingly beautiful melodies. There is a certain sturdiness about the opening movement, though the second theme is of a more relaxed nature. The second movement is placid, while the third movement has a marchlike character. The second theme of this third movement, like that in the first movement, is gorgeously songful, and it is this theme, stated in a triumphal outburst, which brings the Concerto to its conclusion.

M-MM-605, Gyorgy Sandor, Piano, and the Philharmonic-Symphony Orchestra of New York, Artur Rodzinski Conducting.

CONCERTO NO. 3 IN D MINOR, FOR PIANO AND ORCHESTRA, OP. 30

Allegro ma non troppo · Adagio · Alla breve

It was the American music-loving public that Rachmaninoff had particularly in mind when he composed his Third Concerto for Piano and Orchestra in 1909, for he had been invited to come to this country for his first concert tour in the fall of that year, and he planned to give the work its world première here. There was considerable pressure from his native Russia for a first performance there, but Rachmaninoff remained firm in his resolve to play the Concerto for the first time in America. He completed it during the summer, but did not have sufficient time to practice it thoroughly before sailing for New York. Consequently, he took with him what he described as a "dumb piano," a keyboard upon which he could practice while crossing the ocean. It was the first and only time he used this type of instrument.

He gave the first performance of the Concerto with the New York Symphony Society under Walter Damrosch in Carnegie Hall on November 28, 1909. According to all accounts, it was brilliantly played and as brilliantly received by the capacity audience.

The Third Concerto is in the customary three movements. The opening movement begins almost immediately with the flowing principal theme; the second theme is simple and lyrical. The second movement is an intermezzo, and is full of poignant beauty. The sombre mood is relieved by a middle section in the waltz tempo, the theme of which is based upon the principal subject of the first movement. After a return to the Adagio, the finale is ushered in without a pause, fairly overflowing with brilliance and the soaring melodies and harmonies so typical of Rachmaninoff.

M-MM-671, Cyril Smith, Piano, and the City of Birmingham Orchestra, George Weldon Conducting.

THE ISLE OF THE DEAD, OP. 29

In 1906, Rachmaninoff, at the age of thirty-three, occupied an important position in Russian musical circles. For the past year he had been conductor of the Imperial Grand Opera in Moscow, besides making frequent concert appearances as pianist, and he was constantly sought after socially. All this left him little or no time for composing. Consequently, he decided to resign his conductorial position, retire temporarily from public life, and devote himself wholeheartedly to the creation of new works.

Taking his wife and baby daughter with him, he retired to a quiet little house in Dresden, where for two years he lived in virtual seclusion. He did make occasional trips to nearby Leipzig, however, to hear the famous Gewandhaus Orchestra under Artur Nikisch, and it was during one of these visits that he saw Arnold Böcklin's painting, *Die Toteninsel—The Isle of the Dead.*

It was painted for the Countess Marie von Oriola, one of Böcklin's patrons, and when he delivered it to her, he said: "You receive, as you wished, a dream picture. It must produce such an effect of stillness that anyone would be frightened at hearing a knock on the door."

Rachmaninoff has captured this effect in his symphonic poem. There is a somber stillness, interrupted only by the constant lapping of the water against the rocks. The music gradually rises in intensity until, in the middle of the work, it bursts into a song of lamentation for the dead. Toward the end there is a reference to the *Dies Irae* from the Mass for the dead, a passage frequently used in compositions having to do with death. Finally, there is a return of the un-

[357]

dulating rhythm, suggesting the motion of the water, and the music dies away into the peace and calm suggested by the picture.

Written in the spring of 1907, *The Isle of the Dead* was one of three important works composed by Rachmaninoff during his sojourn in Dresden, the others being the Piano Sonata, Op. 28, and the Second Symphony. The composer returned to Russia in 1908, and on May 1, 1909, he conducted the first performance of *The Isle of the Dead* at a concert of the Philharmonic Society in Moscow. He was also on the podium for the American première of the work by Theodore Thomas' Orchestra in Chicago on December 3 of the same year.

Not long before his death at Beverly Hills, California, in 1943, Rachmaninoff said: "Of all my compositions, *The Isle of the Dead* is dearest to my heart."

M-MM-599, Minneapolis Symphony Orchestra, Dimitri Mitropoulos Conducting.

SYMPHONY NO. 2 IN E̸ MINOR, OP. 27

Allegro moderato · *Allegro molto* · *Adagio* · *Allegro vivace*

THE COMPOSER himself conducted the première of this symphony on February 8, 1908 at one of six subscription concerts given by his cousin Siloti at St. Petersburg. The following December the symphony won the Glinka Prize of 1,000 rubles. On February 15, 1909, Rachmaninoff directed the first Moscow performance, and its success was immediate. He gave the first American hearing of the Symphony with the Philadelphia Orchestra on November 26, 1909.

The Symphony opens with a slow, rather somber, introduction, which contains thematic material to be heard later in the work. The principal section however is a fluent Allegro moderato that is highly melodic from start to finish. The second movement is a carefree scherzo; the trio—or middle section—is unusual in that it starts off with a little fugue and utilizes material based on the principal theme of the main section. The Adagio is slow, serene, and often majestic. It contains a particularly lovely solo passage for clarinet. The finale is restless, and vivacious. An extended coda weaves together fragments from the first and fourth movements.

M-MM-569, Philharmonic-Symphony Orchestra of New York, Artur Rodzinski Conducting.

Maurice Ravel

1875–1937

MAURICE RAVEL was born on March 7, 1875, in Ciboure, Pyrenees, France, the lovely mountain section just over the
border from the country of the Basques, that mysterious
race inhabiting the northwestern corner of Spain. Brought early
to Paris, he received most of his education in the capital. At the usual
tender age he was admitted to the Conservatoire, where he was
grounded in piano and composition by the two famous masters De
Beriot and Pessard. The highly individualistic nature of the boy's
talent was from the beginning apparent both to his teachers and to
all who came within the range of his acquaintance. At twenty-two
he was delving deeply into the intricacies of counterpoint with
Gédalge and Gabriel Fauré. For the latter, whose strong champion-
ship of the utmost freedom in the working out of melodic ideas
within the limits of established classical forms excited the lad's deep
admiration, Ravel developed a sympathy the results of which have
been noted from the first in his writing.

In his *Habanera*, composed in 1895, Ravel first gave notice to the
musical fraternity that a new composer whose progressive and individualistic ideas were to be reckoned with had appeared on the
scene. This engaging composition was later incorporated in the *Rapsodie Espagnole* which remains one of the most considerable of his
works.

Continuing his studies and creative activities in Paris, Ravel during
the next few years produced several works of importance, among
them the *Sites auriculaires* and the exquisite *Pavane pour une In-
fante défunte*. In 1901, with his cantata *Myrrha* he captured the
much-coveted Prix de Rome, a scholarship entitling the winner to
residence in Rome at the expense of the French Government.

With the publication of his Quartet in F in 1904, Ravel may be said to have established himself definitely in public favor. This genuinely masterful work proclaimed a new Ravel's fertility of invention and his faculty for expressing the best in modern musical thought. It was followed in the same year by his *Three Melodies for Voice and Orchestra* and *Schéhérazade,* the latter one of the notably impressionistic of his writings.

At a slightly earlier period Ravel had become much attracted by the compositions of Erik Satie, that eccentric futuristic genius whose highly original and extraordinary nomenclature for his various writings (*Cold Pieces, Pear-shaped Pieces, Limp Preludes*—[to a dog], etc.), had so bewildered the public as to discourage a proper estimate of their really interesting qualities. His more robust mentality prompting him to avoid the error of emulation, Ravel nevertheless became convinced of Satie's unique merit. He was, however, unable to stem the tide of popular disfavor and help his friend to real recognition.

In 1905, Ravel entered the lists again for the Prix de Rome but was declared ineligible, owing to his former success, much to the disappointment and resentment of his friends. The composer, however, accepted the decree with equanimity and continued composition in Paris. In 1908 appeared the *Valses nobles et sentimentales, Ma mère l'oye (Mother Goose)*, in 1907 his uniquely clever opera *L'Heure espagnole.*

The outbreak of war in 1914 dealt a severe blow to Ravel's activities. He joined the colors and though shortly afterwards returned home it was some time before he could resume his work. Since then he published his gorgeous ballet *Daphnis and Chloé* (generally regarded as his masterpiece), *Le tombeau de Couperin, La valse, Bolero,* two concertos and several minor works.

Ravel died in 1937. He was then the unquestioned leader of French music and no one thus far has succeeded to his position. He himself was the successor of Saint-Saëns. Less prolific and more critical than his great predecessor, he resembled him in his possession of a clear and logical mind, in his facility as a technician. It was once usual to compare him, to his disadvantage, with Debussy, by whom he was said to have been unduly influenced. As a matter of fact, it was Debussy, in all probability, who was influenced by Ravel, especially in the development of his pianistic style.

ALBORADA DEL GRACIOSO

This is one of Ravel's most felicitous works in the Spanish idiom of which he was so fond. An "alborada" is a song for the morning, in the same way that a "nocturne" is a song for the evening. "Gracioso" —in the apt description of Jean-Aubry—is "something like a jester full of finesse, a wit always aroused and an irony always reading: something like Figaro." Ravel originally composed this as a piano piece (1906), but fourteen years later he orchestrated it.

17137-D, Walter Gieseking, Piano.
11910-D, Cleveland Orchestra, Artur Rodzinski Conducting.

BOLERO

In the summer of 1928, the dancer Ida Rubinstein asked Ravel to make an orchestral arrangement of Albéniz' piano suite *Iberia* for her forthcoming dance recital at the Paris Opéra. Finding that *Iberia* had recently been orchestrated by Arbós, Ravel proposed to Mme. Rubinstein that he write an original Spanish piece for her. The result was the *Bolero.*

The *Bolero* had its première at the Paris Opéra on November 22, 1928, with Ida Rubinstein dancing the principal part and Walter Straram conducting the orchestra. The London *Daily Telegraph* gave this description of the action on the stage: "In *Bolero,* Ravel has once again produced a little masterpiece. There is no story. The scene represents an inn in Spain, and a woman dances on a trestle-table. The men who surround her, calm at first, as the dance progresses are gradually worked up to a frenzy; knives are drawn; the woman is tossed from arm to arm; her partner intervenes; and together they dance until the tumult dies down and peace is restored again."

The piece is constructed on a single theme and counter-theme, repeated over and over again, without any variation in the slow 3-4 beat. The tremendous effect is achieved through the marvelous orchestral scoring. The sensual excitement aroused by the *Bolero* might be compared to that engendered by the insistent beating of African tribal drums; it has the same primitive effect.

Ravel expressed his own attitude toward the *Bolero* to the critic M. D. Calvocoressi. "I am particularly desirous that there should be no misunderstanding about this work," said the composer. "It constitutes an experiment in a very special and limited direction, and should not be suspected of aiming at achieving other or more than what it actually does. Before its first performance, I issued a warning to the effect that what I had written was a piece lasting seventeen minutes, and consisting wholly of 'orchestral tissue without music'— of one long, very gradual crescendo. There are no contrasts, and there is practically no invention save the plan and the manner of execution. The themes are altogether impersonal . . . folk tunes of the usual Spanish-Arabian kind, and the orchestral writing is simple and straightforward throughout, without the slightest attempt at virtuosity. . . . I have carried out exactly what I intended, and it is for the listeners to take it or leave it."

Despite its title, the piece is actually not a true bolero, which is a much livelier dance than the one composed by Ravel, and customarily accompanied by the clacking of castanets. Ravel's work is more a study in orchestration than an example of a Spanish dance.

There have been statements that Ravel never expected his *Bolero* to be a success; that he was amazed at the world-wide popularity it attained. But the eminent pianist Robert Casadesus relates the following incident in his *Memories of Ravel*, published in the magazine *Musical America*:

"One day in Havre, he [Ravel] confided to me that he was at work on a new composition. This was unusual, for he was ordinarily very reticent about his own music, and once it was finished, popular acclaim was a matter of indifference to him. But this time he said: 'This piece I am working on will be so popular even the fruit peddlers will whistle it in the streets.'

"Five years later, I was in Rome giving some recitals. One morning I was awakened at 7 o'clock by the sound of someone whistling shrilly outside my hotel window. The melody was haunting and familiar, but I could not place it. Suddenly I knew; it was Ravel's *Bolero*. I hurried to the window and looked for the whistler. He was a fruit peddler."

X-MX-257, André Kostelanetz Conducting the Robin Hood Dell Orchestra.

DAPHNIS AND CHLOÉ (SECOND SUITE)

DAYBREAK
PANTOMIME
DANSE GÉNÉRALE

MANY of the composers who made their reputations during the first decades of the century made them with the ballets they wrote for the fabulous Serge Diaghilev. Diaghilev was a genius of the theatre unrivaled in his day. He had everything—taste, imagination, extravagance. He was part Maecenas, part Lorenzo di Medici, part P. T. Barnum—and part Mephistopheles.

In 1909, in Paris, he organized the Ballets Russes, commissioning scenery and costumes from Bakst, Benoit, Matisse, Derain, music from Stravinsky, Falla, Debussy, Ravel, Prokofiev, assembling a corps of choreographers and dancers that included Fokine, Nijinski, Bolm, Pavlova, Karsavina. The result was something altogether new—a dazzling synthesis of the arts, a kind of musical-dramatic spectacle Wagnerian in the amplitude of its conception, the magnificence of its execution. Those who saw the productions of the Ballets Russes in their great days will never forget them.

Ravel composed his masterpiece, the ballet *Daphnis et Chloé*, for Diaghilev. When *Daphnis* was commissioned, Ravel already had to his credit his finest songs and piano pieces, his opera *L'Heure espagnole*, his Overture *Schéhérazade*. But the inspiration of the Ballets Russes, organized by Diaghilev, was to draw from him his finest work. He composed to a scenario derived by Fokine from Longus's pastoral romance *Daphnis and Chloé*—a tale of the loves of Greek shepherds. He worked slowly, taking infinite pains with the detail of his score.

Commissioned in 1910, *Daphnis* was not ready for performance until more than a year later. At rehearsals, friction developed between dancers Fokine and Nijinski, maliciously abetted by the feline Diaghilev. Disorder ensued and the première was postponed. Eventually it took place in June of 1912, but in the meantime Ravel's music had been published and performed in a concert version.

As a ballet, *Daphnis and Chloé* was not a success, but in the form of the orchestral suite it is the work by which, with the exception of

[363]

the tricky *Bolero*, Ravel is most frequently represented on orchestral programs today.

X-MX-230, Cleveland Orchestra, Artur Rodzinski Conducting.

INTRODUCTION AND ALLEGRO

RAVEL'S *Introduction and Allegro* is, in essence and form, a concertino, or little concerto, for harp, accompanied by flute, clarinet, and string quartet. Ravel wrote it in 1906, when he was thirty-one years old. A year before, he had failed for the third and last time to obtain the Grand Prix de Rome, and this rejection, brought about by the old guard of the French Academy, put Ravel in the center of a controversy as the bearer of the new spirit in French music.

Jules Renard, the French writer, noted in his diary on November 19, 1906, in reference to Ravel: "a musician of the advance-guard, for whom Debussy is already an old beard." This is, of course, a literal translation: the French *vieille barbe* means a back number, a has-been, and the fact that Debussy wore a beard and Ravel was always close-shaven, has no bearing on the case. Jules Renard's remark is interesting in that many critics accused Ravel of imitating Debussy, who, consequently, could not be just an old beard for him.

In the light of history, Ravel is bracketed with Debussy as representative of French impressionism. The term impressionism itself originated in 1874, when Claude Monet exhibited his picture *Impressions,* and the critic Louis Leroy, in the French publication *Charivari* of April 25, 1874, called Monet and his followers "impressionists" in derision. The name stuck, and was later applied to Debussy and the modern school of French music. The impressionist school has developed a style, characterized by subtly changing moods, languorous melodies, and highly individualized instrumentation; and these traits are in evidence in this *Introduction and Allegro*.

X-MX-167, Laura Newell, Harp, John Wummer, Flute, Ralph McLane, Clarinet, and the Stuyvesant String Quartet.

PAVANE POUR UNE INFANTE DÉFUNTE

A PAVANE is a slow and stately dance, which was sometimes sung as
well as danced. And Ravel's gentle piece is a stately dance of grief in
honor of a dead Spanish princess—not, as it is sometimes carelessly
translated, for a dead child. Ravel originally composed this piece for
piano in 1899, and in this form it was introduced by Ricardo Viñes in
1902. In 1910 Ravel orchestrated it for the following instruments:
two flutes, oboe, two clarinets, two bassoons, two horns, harp, and
strings.

7361-M, André Kostelanetz and his Orchestra.

QUARTET IN F MAJOR

Allegro moderato · *Assai vif* · *Très lent* · *Vif et agité*

WHEN the Kneisel Quartet gave the first American performance of
Ravel's String Quartet in F major in New York on December 11,
1906, the music aroused wonderment among New York music critics.
History repeats itself with monotonous regularity. Going over a stack
of clippings from the time of Berlioz down to the time of Arnold
Schönberg, one finds the same sort of incomprehension, dubious
brand of humor, and polysyllabic invective. These critical outbursts
have a semblance of humanity in them when they are directed
against revolutionary works, such as Stravinsky's *Le Sacre du printemps.* But the innocent music of Ravel's Quartet lacks all revolutionary elements, and it is baffling that the New York music critics of
1906 should have been perturbed by it. Yet the adverse judgment
was unanimous.

Wrote the New York *Tribune:* "M. Ravel is content with one theme
which has emotional potency of one of those tunes which the curious
may hear in a Chinese theatre, shrieked out by an ear-splitting clarinet. This theme serves him for four movements during which there is
about as much emotional nuance as warms a problem in algebra. In
the second movement, which stands for the old-fashioned scherzo,
the four viols essay the noble language of the banjo effectively. This,
we suppose, is the cerebral music, and the psychical music that we

[365]

read about in the dithyrambs sung by the young men of France." The reviewer added, with sesquipedalian humor, that Ravel's music was "a drastic dose of wormwood and asafoetida" which caused a "horripilation of nerves." He complimented the audience on their tolerance: "The audiences of the Kneisel Quartet are a gentle and well-bred folk. Even when music revolts them they do not utter catcalls or throw missiles at the performers. Instead, they give a respectful hand to the musicians, evidently crediting them with good intentions."

The New York *Sun* was no less outspoken. "Ravel is of the school of d'Indy and Debussy. He hates common triads and dotes on chromatic complications. He can make chords out of any notes that happen to be lying around."

The New York critics were not alone in being nonplussed by Ravel's simple music. The London *Times* wrote on December 7, 1907, after the first performance of Ravel's Quartet in England: "There is no recognizable principle of construction, and the only wonder is how the thing is kept going so long without a principle."

Ravel's Quartet was performed for the first time in Paris on March 5, 1904, at a concert of the Société Nationale, under the auspices of the famous Schola Cantorum. The Société Nationale was not devoted exclusively to the cause of modern music. In fact, the organizers of the Société Nationale fought shy of extreme examples of modernity so that eventually the more modern members bolted, and formed a new organization definitely modernistic in its aspirations, under the name Société Indépendante.

Charles Koechlin wrote to Nicolas Slonimsky: "The Société Nationale had been very useful to French art, but since about 1900 it found itself under the influence of Vincent d'Indy. While pieces of mediocre students of the Schola Cantorum were performed at the Society's concerts, works of real value were often rejected. Even Ravel was accepted with suspicion, and at the first performance the whole clan of the Schola was hostile to the point of impoliteness." Still the Quartet was performed, and d'Indy praised the music in a public statement.

M-MM-425, Budapest String Quartet.

RAPSODIE ESPAGNOLE

PRÉLUDE À LA NUIT   HABANERA
MALAGUEÑA   FERIA

THE FOLK and popular music of Spain has appealed powerfully to composers of non-Spanish nationality. Bizet's *Carmen,* Debussy's *Iberia,* Rimsky-Korsakov's *Capriccio espagnol,* Lalo's *Symphonie espagnole,* Chabrier's *España* are but a few of the masterpieces that owe their origin to this fascination. Ravel's music provides several additional examples—the opera *L'Heure espagnole,* the famous *Bolero,* and the *Rapsodie espagnole.* Moreover, these works of Spanish inspiration are among Ravel's finest, though everything that he wrote —everything, at any rate, that his severely self-critical nature allowed him to publish—has distinction.

The *Rapsodie espagnole* dates from Ravel's most productive period. It was composed in 1907, a year which also saw the completion of *L'Heure espagnole,* and was followed shortly by his piano masterpiece *Gaspard de la nuit,* and the ballet *Daphnis et Chloé.* The first performance of the *Rapsodie* took place on March 15, 1908, at a Colonne concert.

Ravel's *Rapsodie* and Debussy's *Iberia* have many points of similarity. But Debussy began work on *Iberia* in 1906 and had completed it before Ravel's *Rapsodie* had its première, and the relationship of the two works is entirely coincidental. The *Rapsodie* is in four movements, the first and second of which are connected. The first movement, *"Prélude à la nuit,"* is similar in mood to the second movement of Debussy's *Ibéria—"Les parfums de la nuit";* it is a night piece— fireflies in an acacia-scented garden, with dance music in the distance. The second movement is a *"Malagueña,"* a characteristic Spanish dance in triple time. The name suggests that the dance originated in Malaga, but tradition names Flanders, at the time of the Spanish occupation, as its home.

The third movement of the *Rapsodie* is a *"Habanera."* The rhythm of the typical habanera is familiar to all—a dotted eighth, followed by a sixteenth and two eighths. The dance did not originate in Spain but in Cuba, where it is said to have been introduced by African Negroes. From Cuba it was imported to Spain, where it took root, undergoing modifications. The *"Habanera"* in Ravel's *Rapsodie* is a languorous dance in 2-4 time, an adaptation of an earlier piece for two pianos.

The fourth and final movement of the *Rapsodie* is entitled *"Feria,"* "the Fair." It is the most elaborate of the four movements, simple in basic design, but complex in detail. Again we are reminded of Debussy and *Iberia,* which closes with a section entitled *"Le Matin d'un jour de fête"*—"The Morning of a Fête Day."

X-MX-234, Cleveland Orchestra, Artur Rodzinski Conducting.

LA VALSE

THE ORIGINAL title of *La Valse* was simply *Wien* (German for Vienna). It is a pity that this title was not allowed to stand. *Wien* evokes in the mind a definite picture of the carefree, amorous atmosphere of the imperial city, which an indefinite title, *La Valse,* fails to convey. When the title was changed, it was necessary to add an explanatory note, in which the locale of the scene was marked with deliberate latitude: "An imperial court *circa* 1855."

The score is subtitled *Choreographic Poem,* which shows that Ravel had in mind a ballet interpretation of the music. He marks the places in the score, when the waltzing crowd appears through the rifts in the clouds, and the *fortissimo* passage where the light of the chandeliers suddenly illuminates the scene.

La Valse was performed for the first time at the Concerts Lamoureux in Paris on December 12, 1920. The elimination of *Wien* from the title misled the critics. In one of those vague reviews in which there are more literary allusions than relevant analysis, the critic of *Le Ménéstrel* gives this description: "To the grace and languor of a Carpeaux is here opposed the anguish of Prud'homme: 'We are dancing on a volcano.' This bacchanale has in its joy something foreboding, like drunkenness betraying a debility, perhaps by the dissonances and shocks of orchestral colors. . . ."

Henry Prunières is much more scholarly and literary. Writing in *La Revue Musicale,* he gives a specific program of *La Valse.* "A Classical Viennese Waltz, or rather a phantom of a waltz in a dream. Crushed with fatigue after the ball, one falls asleep, and the rhythms

[368]

just heard haunt him. Indistinct at first, they gradually take shape. Shreds of phrases emerge, the melody is organized, and the waltz appears, quite simple, a bit caricatured, a waltz of Johann Strauss and Offenbach. It sweeps the couples, it hurries along, pressed, out of breath, hesitating for a moment, but never stopping. . . . The dancers whirl, the heads are dizzy, the walls, the floors vibrate. The gyrating hallucination reaches a paroxism. Suddenly, awakening comes, or perhaps a plunge into unconsciousness, and all disappears.

"Never has Ravel's art been more perfect. This is a tour de force, this waltz that lasts twelve minutes without an episode, without a stop. Inexhaustible verve animates this whole piece, written with a dizzy virtuosity, and visibly to the great enjoyment of the author himself."

Alfredo Casella, who was closely associated with Ravel, describes *La Valse* as "a mask of human life, with its pomp and glory, its luxury of sight and sound, its hours of golden youth, one generation treading upon the receding footsteps of another."

X-MX-207, The Philharmonic-Symphony Orchestra of New York, John Barbirolli Conducting.

Ottorino Respighi

1879–1936

IN THE annals of musical history, Ottorino Respighi will certainly be ranked as one of the leading Italian composers of the twentieth century. Born on July 9, 1879, at Bologna, he showed an early interest in music. He received his first instruction from his father, who was a pianist, but at the age of twelve, he entered the Liceo Musicale in his native city, studying composition with Giuseppe Martucci and violin with Frederico Sarti. For a time, young Respighi played violin in a chamber-music group. Then, when he was twenty-two, he went to Russia, where he played viola in the orchestra of the St. Petersburg Opera and studied orchestration with Rimsky-Korsakov. Shortly thereafter he moved on to Berlin, where he worked with Max Bruch.

Returning to Italy, Respighi devoted himself entirely to composition. By 1913, his reputation was so great that he was engaged as instructor of composition at the Conservatorio Musicale di Santa Cecilia at Rome, and ten years later became the institution's director. In the ensuing years, his symphonic and operatic works brought him world-wide fame. He made three trips to America—in 1925, 1928, and 1932—when he conducted many of these works with several of the nation's leading orchestras. A heart ailment caused his untimely death at Rome on April 18, 1936.

THE PINES OF ROME

THE PINES OF THE VILLA BORGHESE   THE PINES OF THE JANICULUM
THE PINES NEAR A CATACOMB   THE PINES OF THE APPIAN WAY

RESPIGHI will probably be best remembered for his three suites of orchestral arrangements of old Italian dances and airs for the lute and his three symphonic poems about Rome—*The Fountains of Rome, The Pines of Rome,* and *Roman Festivals.* The second of these, *The Pines of Rome,* was composed in 1924, and was first performed in the city that inspired its creation during the following year by the Augusteo Orchestra, under the direction of Bernardino Molinari. It was first heard in this country on January 14, 1926, at a concert of the New York Philharmonic Orchestra under Arturo Toscanini, and the very next day the composer gave the work its Philadelphia première when he performed it with the Philadelphia Orchestra.

The Pines of Rome is in four connected sections, which are described as follows in the preface to the score:

I. *The Pines of the Villa Borghese* (Allegretto vivace). Children are at play in the pine-grove of the Villa Borghese, dancing the Italian equivalent of *Ring Around a-Rosy,* mimicking marching soldiers and battles, twittering and shrieking like swallows at evening, and they disappear. Suddenly the scene changes to—

II. *The Pines Near a Catacomb* (Lento). We see the shadows of the pines which overhang the entrance to a catacomb. From the depths rises a chant which re-echoes solemnly, like a hymn, and is then mysteriously silenced.

III. *The Pines of the Janiculum* (Lento). There is a thrill in the air. The full moon reveals the profile of the pines of Gianicolo's Hill. A nightingale sings (represented by a gramophone record of a nightingale's song, heard from the orchestra).

IV. *The Pines of the Appian Way* (Tempo di marcia). Misty dawn on the Appian Way. The tragic country is guarded by solitary pines. Indistinctly, incessantly, the rhythm of innumerable steps. To the poet's phantasy appears a vision of past glories; trumpets blare, and the army of the consul advances brilliantly in the grandeur of a newly risen sun toward the sacred way, mounting in triumph the Capitoline Hill.

M-MM-616, The Philadelphia Orchestra, Eugene Ormandy Conducting.

Nicolai Rimsky-Korsakov

1844–1908

D URING the period of Rimsky-Korsakov's youth, musical composition was not encouraged as a profession for those of the upper class. When he took it upon himself to compose an overture—at the age of ten—he did so furtively. His education for this essay consisted of piano lessons, which began in his sixth year the examples of folk songs furnished by an eccentric uncle, the singing of monks at a neighboring monastery, and the assistance of three old ladies of the village who augmented his adventures with the piano.

Glinka's *A Life for the Czar* became his favorite. But the young man determined to follow his ancestors in becoming a sailor. At the age of twelve he was placed in the Corps of Naval Cadets at St Petersburg. For two years more he studied piano. His teacher was not the most competent, and Nicolas learned no theory whatever. But his musical interests became stronger. He was able to attend symphony concerts, and was much impressed with the works of Beethoven, Mendelssohn, Meyerbeer and others making up the mid-19th century symphonic repertoire. Still, it was Glinka who enthralled him.

Whatever pocket money could be spared went to purchase Glinka's operas. Rimsky took delight in arranging them for various groups of instruments. He found fascination in the intricacies of instrumental transposition and the Italian nomenclature on the scores.

Another and better teacher soon took him in hand, provided an introduction to the German Romantics, to Bach, and to his contemporary and friend, Balakirev. Though Rimsky was still ignorant of the commonest principles of theory, he was encouarged by these stimulating contacts to attempt his first symphony.

Almost immediately thereafter—when he was eighteen years old—

Rimsky was dispatched aboard a training vessel for a three-year cruise. Composition was, of course, difficult. But he managed to complete his Symphony during this time, and to see *Robert le Diable* and *Faust* when on shore leave.

In December of 1865, after Rimsky had returned to St. Petersburg, the Symphony was presented by Balakirev at the Free School of Music. The first symphony of any importance by a native composer, it received an ovation from the audience which called enthusiastically for the composer. Rimsky appeared, much to their surprise, very young, and in the uniform of a naval cadet.

Thereafter it was his good fortune to remain in St. Petersburg and to resume his association with the nationalist group of Balakirev. He continued to compose. In 1871, he was appointed professor of composition and instrumentation at the Conservatoire.

The eventful year of 1873 marked his resignation from the navy, his marriage, and his appointment as inspector of naval bands. This post afforded an opportunity to study closely the wind instruments and their possibilities. Rimsky acquired thereby an acquaintance with this group, and a facility in its use unexcelled by any other composer. Largely through him and his influence orchestral color became one of the marked characteristics of the Russian school.

With many successes already behind him, Rimsky-Korsakov began to regret his limitations of formal study and immediately set about the study of counterpoint and fugue. This enabled him to do some much-desired revising of his earlier works, and to attempt some part writing for piano and strings. The Third Symphony was also a product of this academic awakening. When the air had cleared and Rimsky's attention was attracted by folk music he ceased theorizing; but the training it had given him was to prove useful in the later periods of his activity.

Rimsky-Korsakov now holds an important place between Glinka—whose heir he was—Liszt and Balakirev, and such differing luminaries as his pupils Stravinsky, Glazunov, Respighi, Liadov, and Ippolitov-Ivanov. A magnificent orchestrator, he epitomized, as a composer, the achievements of the nationalists of the last century.

CAPRICCIO ESPAGNOL, OP. 34

ALBORADA

VARIATIONS

ALBORADA

SCENE AND GYPSY SONG

FANDANGO OF THE ASTURIAS

THE MOST effective Spanish pieces for orchestra have been written by Frenchmen and Russians. Rimsky-Korsakov's Spanish Suite of five pieces, played without pause and entitled *Capriccio espagnol,* is a particularly brilliant example of Russian-Spanish orchestration. In a letter to Yastrebtzev, Rimsky-Korsakov's Boswell and "phonographic and photographic" biographer, as he was known in Rimsky-Korsakov's family, Rimsky-Korsakov writes: "How strange! It seems that I like to orchestrate better than to compose." In his *Chronicle of My Musical Life* Rimsky-Korsakov points out the difference between a "well-orchestrated piece," and a "brilliant composition for orchestra." He puts his *Capriccio espagnol* in the latter category, a piece conceived for orchestra, and inseparable from orchestral timbres. Instrumental cadenzas, the role of percussion, figurations and embellishments, all these, he maintains, are not mere elaborations and exercises in tone color, but integral parts of the whole.

The composition of *Capriccio* was completed on August 4, 1887. A year later *Scheherazade* was written. These orchestral works mark the conclusion of a period in Rimsky-Korsakov's evolutionary style which he defines by two characteristics, the attainment of a virtuoso style in orchestration, without Wagner's influence toward the enlargement of sonorous means, and the lessening of purely contrapuntal writing. In place of elaborate polyphony, Rimsky-Korsakov makes increasing use of melodic ornamentation and its logical outgrowth, the art of variation.

The first performance of *Capriccio espagnol* was given in St. Petersburg at one of the Russian Symphony Concerts on November 12, 1887, conducted by Rimsky-Korsakov himself. (The date of October 31, 1887, given in the dictionaries and orchestral program notes, is the old-style date of the Russian calendar, which in the nineteenth century was twelve days behind the West.)

Capriccio espagnol obtained a great success at its initial performance, and quickly became a repertoire piece. Its hispanism is, of course, external, but the stylization of Spanish melodies and rhythms is remarkably effective. The name of the opening dance, *"Alborada"* (from the Latin and Spanish word *albor*—whiteness, dawn), is often defined as "morning serenade." But since a serenade is itself an evening song, *Alborada* is a morning evening song, which is as complicated a description as Erik Satie's *Crépuscule matinal (de midi)*, "morning twilight at noon." Rimsky-Korsakov's *Alborada* is an explosive orchestral dance with several instrumental solos for contrast. It leads to a movement entitled *"Variations."* The next movement is a return of the *Alborada*.

The fourth movement is a series of instrumental cadenzas, under the general title *"Scene and Gypsy Song."* The gypsyness of the song is indicated by a sort of illegitimate Mixolydian, or Hypo-eolian, mode, derived from a minor scale, with the dominant serving as a tonic. This mode has done excellent service in nineteenth-century music as has ersatz for nontempered Oriental or near-East scales. Cadenza is picturesquely defined by Webster as "a parenthetic flourish or flight of ornament." Certainly there is a parenthetic flourish in the opening fanfare for horns and trumpets, and there is a flight of ornament in the ensuing violin cadenza.

The last number of the suite is an Asturian *"Fandango."* The derivation of the name *Fandango* has been traced by amateur etymologists to the playing on the lute (*fidicinare*), but it seems that the dance and the name were brought to Spain from the West Indies. The rhythm is similar to that of *Bolero,* but it has been said that while *Bolero* intoxicates, *Fandango* inflames.

X-MX-185, Philharmonic-Symphony Orchestra of New York, John Barbirolli Conducting.

RUSSIAN EASTER OVERTURE (LA GRANDE PÂQUE RUSSE), OP. 36

THE RUSSIAN critic, Montagu-Nathan, informs us that in this work the composer portrays "the contrast between the orthodox celebration of festivals and the pagan rites in which they originated." The melodic sources are drawn from Russian liturgical music. The overture was composed in 1888 and was dedicated to the memory of Borodin and Mussorgsky.

[375]

A Russian chant opens the work, followed by a short section depicting graphically the mystery and gloom of the sepulchre. The overture proper begins with the development of the theme in the characteristic modes of the Russian church. A grave and solemn chant appears in the trombone, as though some priest were intoning in the cathedral. The first theme then returns and leads into a final coda which conjures up the image of the cathedral, the dazzling splendor of the altar, and the clanging of the triumphant bells proclaiming the glory of the risen Lord.

X-MX-276, Philadelphia Orchestra, Eugene Ormandy Conducting.

SCHEHERAZADE, OP. 35

I. THE SEA AND SINBAD'S SHIP
II. THE STORY OF THE KALANDER PRINCE
III. THE YOUNG PRINCE AND THE PRINCESS
IV. FESTIVAL AT BAGDAD; THE SEA; THE SHIP GOES TO PIECES ON A ROCK SURMOUNTED BY A BRONZE WARRIOR

THE SYMPHONIC suite *Scheherazade* is based on tales from *The Thousand and One Nights*. The printed score bears in French and Russian an epitome of the literary framework upon which the tales are strung:

"The Sultan Schahriar, convinced of the duplicity and infidelity of all women, vows to slay each of his wives after the first night. The Sultana Scheherazade, however, saved her life by the expedient of recounting to the Sultan a succession of tales over a period of a thousand and one nights. Overcome by curiosity, the monarch postponed from day to day the execution of his wife, and ended by renouncing altogether his bloody resolution.

"Many were the marvels recounted to Schahriar by Scheherazade. For the telling of these she drew from the verses of the poets and the words of folk songs and tales, connecting her stories one with the other."

Rimsky-Korsakov originally provided the following outline for the four movements: (1) *The Sea and Sinbad's Ship;* (2) *The Story of the Kalander Prince;* (3) *The Young Prince and the Princess;* (4) *Festival at Bagdad. The Sea. The Ship Goes to Pieces on a Rock Surmounted by a Bronze Warrior. Conclusion.*

[376]

These titles were published at the time of the first performance under the composer's direction in 1889 and are usually associated with the work today. Later, however, they were withdrawn, as the composer felt that they were too definite in associating the various themes with the characters and incidents suggested. The truth is that in the story these four episodes are almost wholly unrelated, whereas in the music the four episodes are connected by frequent recurrences of certain thematic material. Rimsky-Korsakov tells in his autobiography that he had intended to label the movements Prelude, Ballade, Adagio, Finale, but that in the end he abandoned even this identification. Further in his book he gives an interesting commentary on these various discarded headings:

"In composing *Scheherazade* I meant these hints to direct but slightly the hearer's fancy on the path which my own fancy had traveled, and to leave more minute and particular conceptions to the will and mood of each listener. All I had desired was that the hearer, if he liked my piece as symphonic music, should carry away the impression that it is beyond doubt an Oriental narrative of some numerous and varied fairy-tale wonders, and not merely four pieces played one after the other and composed on the basis of themes common to all the four movements. Why then, if that be the case, does my suite bear the name, precisely, of *Scheherazade?* Because this name and the sub-title ("After The Thousand and One Nights") connotes in everybody's mind the East and fairy-tale wonders; besides, certain details of the musical exposition hint at the fact that all of these are various tales of some one person (which happens to be Scheherazade) entertaining therewith her stern husband."

Two "unifying threads," as the composer calls them, link the movements together. These are the thunderous motif of the stern Sultan, always with full orchestra, which introduces the first and fourth movements, and the delicate, cadenzalike theme for violin solo, appearing at frequent intervals throughout the work, delineating the narrator Scheherazade.

This Suite represents at its greatest Rimsky-Korsakov's amazing faculty for orchestration—in which he has been only rarely eclipsed by even such giants as Wagner, Richard Strauss, Berlioz, and Ravel—and his exceptional native gift of original thematic creation.

M-MM-398, Cleveland Orchestra, Artur Rodzinski, Conducting.

Gioacchino Rossini

1792–1868

Gioacchino Rossini was born at Pesaro, near the Adriatic Sea, in 1792. His father was a talented amateur musician. From him the boy inherited not only his aptitude for music but his good humor, love of life and contagious gaiety.

Father Rossini's republican sympathies caused him to lose his civic jobs as supervisor of a slaughter house and town trumpeter, and sometimes even landed him in jail. The boy, therefore, was brought up mostly by relatives. He began studying music early, sang in churches and played in theatre orchestras when he was only ten, and at fourteen was made a member of the Accademia Filarmonica of Bologna. In 1807—his fifteenth year—he entered the Bologna Conservatory, and one year after that won a prize with a cantata.

He turned to the writing of operas soon after he left the Conservatory, and saw some of them performed in major opera houses, including La Scala. First signs of genius were revealed in two operas written in 1813, *I Tancredi* and *L'Italiana in Algeri*. Both were written for Venice, and both scored tremendous successes.

On February 20, 1816, Rossini saw one of the big fiascos of his career—and with an opera which, with crowning irony, is the one which is generally considered his masterpiece, *The Barber of Seville*. The conservative Rome audience resented young Rossini's "preposterous" choice of subject which their beloved Giovanni Paisiello had used for an opera thirty years earlier. The première inspired hisses and vocal denunciations. But the second performance established the opera firmly in the hearts of operagoers.

In 1823, Rossini bade farewell to the Italian stage with *Semiramide*. He left for Paris where, in 1824, he became director of the Théâtre Italien. It was in Paris that Rossini composed another of his masterpieces, *William Tell*. No one at the time would have guessed that *William Tell*, written by Italy's greatest opera composer at the age of thirty-seven, was actually destined to be his operatic swan song.

Why Rossini, who was to live for another thirty-nine years, was never again to write an opera is one of the inexplicable mysteries in musical history. Was it the fact that Rossini, naturally indolent, could now afford to pamper himself? Was it that he was jealous of the rising popularity of Meyerbeer? Did his own personal problems—his divorce, his growing poor health—so sap his energies that he could no longer find the strength to create for the theatre? Whatever the reason, Rossini spent the remainder of his life in Italy and Paris, in comparative idleness. Only two major works left his pen during these four decades—the *Stabat mater* and the *Petite messe solenelle*.

After a minor operation, Rossini died in Paris in 1868. His remains were transferred to Florence in the spring of 1887, where they were buried to the music of four military bands.

Rossini has been called by Franz Werfel "the only creator of truly comic music." Despite occasional spurts of seriousness, his true ambitions never really transcended the limits of opera buffa. At its best, his music is brilliant and witty; his characterizations masterful. Almost proud of his "passion for laziness," he jotted down his bubbling masterpieces at a breathtaking speed. He wrote for his own enjoyment primarily, and never tried to improve the tastes or standards of his audiences. He never pretended that he had an artistic mission to perform. Often condemned for having delayed the "progress" of operatic composition, he actually was a powerful contributor to those foundations upon which such later composers as Verdi and Wagner were to build in some of their works. His operas mark the end of a glorious period of opera buffa; and in that period he was one of its most lustrous figures.

BEAUMARCHAIS's sensational comedy, *Le Barbier de Seville*, had been used for an opera libretto by one of Rossini's eminent predecessors, Giovanni Paisiello, a version that was extremely popular. With extreme tact, young Rossini approached the dying Paisiello for permission to use the libretto and, in addition, offered to use for his own opera the title of *Almaviva*. These facts notwithstanding, Paisiello's friends were not soothed. When Rossini's opera was introduced in Rome on February 20, 1816, they skillfully organized the opposition to the new opera which, combined with a series of mishaps on the stage, brought Rossini the most formidable fiasco of his entire career. At the second performance, however, the opera began to catch on. Within a year, it was the rage in Italy; in a few years' time, its popularity spread throughout Europe.

The libretto is the time-tested story of the repulsive old bachelor who wants to marry his wealthy ward secretly betrothed to someone else. The lovers are usually brought together by a cunning servant responsible for many of the seemingly hopeless situations, but who finally contrives a happy ending. A popular variant of the servant was the barber whose profession brought him into most of the households of his town or village—news reporter, pharmacist, letter-writer, matchmaker, trouble-shooter all rolled into one. He was, therefore, a highly important member of his community, and a highly useful character for opera buffa.

Figaro the barber (whom the Count gratefully takes into his service) is the central character of Rossini's opera. His *pièce de résistance,* the famous aria *"Largo al factotum"* comes dangerously early in the first act; but the opera is so fascinating throughout that this slight lack of balance passes unnoticed. This aria is a so-called patter song in which the singer tells of his profession, experiences, and achievements. The soprano aria, *"Una voce poco fa"* is a masterpiece of fioritura; that of Basilio, the "Calumny Song," a gem of characterization.

Rossini composed the opera in two weeks' time, which may explain its amazing spontaneity and freshness. It oozes good humor, has a sly air of mischief about it, is rich in imagination and skillful in craftsmanship.

The overture used for the Rome première is not the one we know today. The original one, based on Spanish themes which Rossini had obtained from Manuel García (the Almaviva of that first performance) somehow went astray after the first Roman season. The present overture comes from another Rossini opera, *Elisabetta*.

Some good music originally written for the *Barber* has been lost. Rosina was originally a contralto, until the objections of sopranos compelled Rossini to change the range of his principal female character. Rossini himself transposed the part, but—with his customary indolence—he failed to rewrite the music for the lesson scene in the second act. Since then it has been habitual for prima donnas to interpolate any aria they prefer into this part of the opera.

The merry story concerns the triangular love affair of Count Almaviva, Rosina, and Doctor Bartolo. Doctor Bartolo wants his ward Rosina for himself, but the Count is supported by the barber Figaro. After numerous episodes, Rosina marries the Count, and Bartolo is finally consoled when he learns that the Count waives his right to Rosina's dowery in favor of the doctor.

OP-MOP-8, Stracciari, Caspir, Borgioli, and Chorus and Orchestra of La Scala, Lorenzo Molajoli Conducting.

WILLIAM TELL

ROSSINI wrote this opera under the immediate influence of Beethoven's scores which he was at that time studying. His choice of subject was the result of his contact with Schiller's plays which were then becoming available in French translations.

In his role as manager of the Parisian Théâtre Italien, Rossini had been personal witness of the sorry degeneration of opera in France, and he was inspired with the mission of inaugurating a new era. He almost succeeded, even though *William Tell* was destined to be his last work for the stage. It combines elements of opera seria, French revolutionary opera, and opera buffa, with those of the music drama and grand opera of the future. It had a tremendous influence on Meyerbeer (who underwent his important period of germination just then); since Meyerbeer was an important precursor of both Wagner and Verdi, the significance of Rossini's last stage work cannot be overestimated.

Rossini employs the familiar story of the rebellion of the Swiss against their tyrannical governor, Gessler, and the latter's assassination by the heroic patriot and super-marksman, William Tell. The libretto is rather clumsy and much too long, requiring six hours for performance. With drastic, even fatal, cuts a practical necessity, the opera has never achieved general popularity. From the day of its première, on August 3, 1829 in Paris, it has been much more successful with critics and scholars than with the public at large. For this opera reveals Rossini in disguise, even though it must be confessed he wears that disguise with a great deal of dignity. Rossini is not at his best weighing and deliberating. Except for an aria or two (such as "*Sombre foret*") the opera is chiefly known for its overture and the ballet music from Act III. The overture is an excellent piece of programmatic music, poetic and dramatic at the same time. It suggests a sunrise and a storm in the Swiss Alps, includes a shepherd song and rustic dance, and ends with a highly effective march.

Critics are generally agreed that *William Tell* marks an epoch in the development of so-called "symphonic" opera. Rossini's orchestration was daring and progressive for his day, and had an influence on all major opera composers who followed him.

X-MX-60, Overture, London Philharmonic Orchestra, Sir Thomas Beecham Conducting.

Camille Saint-Saëns

1835–1921

IN A valedictory speech on the occasion of the election of Saint-Saëns to the Institute of Fine Arts, the orator remarked that Saint-Saëns alone had written more chamber music than all of his colleagues put together. This does not speak well for the productivity of the members of the Institute as a body, for at the time he was elected to occupy Cherubini's chair in the Institute on February 19, 1881, Saint-Saëns had not composed a great quantity of music. The same orator said something more significant, if his statement could be proved: "If it were necessary to characterize Saint-Saëns in a few words, one should call him the best musician of France."

Saint-Saëns may not have been the greatest French musician, but he was probably the most roundly gifted and the most conspicuously successful one. He started his career as a child prodigy. When, at the age of nine, he played a piano recital in Paris, *La Revue et Gazette Musicale* of July 7, 1844, commented: "Mr. Saint-Saëns, whose name is pronounced like that of a bank-note representing one-half of a thousand francs, is an artist of eight years of age who began to play piano at the age of thirty months." The reference to five hundred francs is explained by the fact that the French words *cinq cents* is homonymous with the composer's name. As a child, Saint-Saëns received a medallion with the silhouette of Mozart from the famous painter Ingres. Berlioz and Gounod entertained a high opinion of Saint-Saëns, and so did Liszt. The only honor which Saint-Saëns coveted, but failed to achieve, was the Prix de Rome.

When Saint-Saëns was only seventeen years old he obtained the first prize in a competition of an Ode for St. Cecilia Society in Paris. He had many influential patrons who believed in his genius. One of them arranged a performance of his early Symphony, written at the age of eighteen. To inflame the curiosity of the public, this Symphony was produced anonymously. It was not a new idea, for a work of Berlioz' had been similarly presented without his name some years before. The Berlioz work was deliberately misattributed to Pierre Ducre, a seventeenth-century ecclesiastical composer. Many years later, on May 9, 1911, the Société Independante de Musique in Paris presented a whole concert of chamber works without the composer's names, leaving it to the audience to guess the authorship. Among them was a new work by Ravel, *Valse nobles et sentimentales*.

In his operas, in his symphonies, in his concertos, in his chamber music, Saint-Saëns had a peculiar knack of creating successful music. There is in his music emotion and pathos, brilliance and humor, all in the right proportion, and right measure.

As happens with so many composers, the early music of Saint-Saëns is more successful than his later works. In the second half of his long life, he departed from the Gallic simplicity which was his greatest natural endowment, and introduced heavier elements of Germanic romanticism. Yet Saint-Saëns was rabidly anti-Wagnerian and anti-German. Once he refused to receive a musician who had presented some Schumann at his concerts. By his intransigeance he endeared himself in the eyes of many French nationalists; but critics pointed out that Saint-Saëns had kept an autographed picture of the Kaiser in his room up to the very moment of the declaration of War. Saint-Saëns died peacefully in Algiers at the age of eighty-six.

SAINT-SAËNS subtitled this Suite of tonal pictures about animals, a "grand zoological fantasy for orchestra." With a great deal of wit, sentiment, and charm, the composer has here given us some remarkable animal pictures. The composition is in fourteen sections, and their titles are descriptive of the music: (1) Introduction and Royal March of the Lion; (2) Hens and Cocks; (3) Mules; (4) Tortoises; (5) The Elephant; (6) Kangaroos; (7) Aquarium; (8) Personages with Long Ears; (9) Cuckoo in the Woods; (10) Birds; (11) Pianists; (12) Fossils; (13) The Swan; (14) Finale.

The inclusion of "pianists" in this zoo of animals is characteristic of the composer's bent for satire. Characteristic, too, is the skillful and apt interpolation of musical quotations throughout the score. Among the works thus quoted are Saint-Saëns's own *Danse Macabre*, Rossini's *The Barber of Seville*, Offenbach's *Orpheus in the Underworld*, Berlioz' *Ballet of the Sylphs*, and Mendelssohn's Scherzo from *A Midsummer Night's Dream*.

The thirteenth section—"The Swan"—is perhaps the most famous single movement of the entire work, a beautiful melody for solo 'cello. In the finale, the composer reintroduces all his characters.

The Carnival of Animals was written in 1886 and is scored for two pianos and orchestra.

CONCERTO NO. 1 IN A MINOR, OP. 33, FOR 'CELLO AND ORCHESTRA

WHEN Saint-Saëns finished the composition of his first concerto for violoncello, he declared that never again would he undertake another 'cello concerto, so restricted are the technical means of the instrument, and so difficult is it to make it sound effectively against a full orchestra. But Saint-Saëns did not keep his pledge. Thirty years later he wrote another concerto for 'cello and orchestra, and made it so complex that, for clarity of the writing, two staves were used in the 'cello part, in G and F clefs, as in piano music.

The Concerto No. 1 in A minor is by far the more popular of the two. It was first performed at a concert of the Paris Conservatoire on

January 19, 1873, and the soloist was the French cellist Tolbecque, to whom the Concerto was dedicated. It was written in 1873. In 1875, Saint-Saëns wrote his universally popular *Danse macabre,* and in the same year he completed his opera *Samson and Delilah.* The composer is still best known by these early works, although he continued to write music until the year of his death.

The 'Cello Concerto in A minor is sectional rather than articulately symphonic. There is no break between the movements—only short transitions. The treatment of the instrument is novel for the time. The entire range of the 'cello is used, and there is a great deal of technical brilliance, unusual in early 'cello music. The rhythmic design is built not on metric dichotomy, or subdivisions into two, four, eight, and sixteen notes to a measure, but includes graduated grouping in triplets as well. This rhythmic variety permits effects of gradual acceleration and deceleration of movement, and contributes to the kinetic force of the whole.

There are also combined rhythms, as in the animated middle section, where the theme of the muted strings suggesting a minuet is contrasted with the slow waltz time of the 'cello solo. The tonal relationship of principal themes and sections is nonclassical. Thus, the opening section is in A minor, and the following section, the minuet-like Allegro, is in B-flat major, a semitone distant, which is an uncommon key relationship. The Concerto ends in a brilliant A major finale.

X-MX-182, Gregor Piatigorsky, 'Cello, and the Chicago Symphony Orchestra, Frederick Stock Conducting.

CONCERTO NO. 4 IN C MINOR, OP. 44, FOR PIANO AND ORCHESTRA

Allegro moderato; Andante · *Allegro vivace; Andante; Allegro*

SAINT-SAËN's Fourth Piano Concerto was written in 1875. It had its first performance on October 31 of that year at a concert of the Colonne Orchestra in the Châtelet, Paris. The composer played the solo part, as he had in the premières of the three preceding concertos, and as he did twenty-one years later when his fifth and last piano concerto was first heard in a program commemorating the fiftieth anniversary of its creator's concert debut.

Saint-Saëns had always created a sensation as a pianist. Beginning the study of the instrument when he was only three, he was able to play operas from score by the time he was five. In 1860, it is reported, he amazed Wagner by playing from memory long passages from *Tristan und Isolde*. He was always admired for his technical fluency, intense vitality, and mastery of style, and this skill is reflected in the way he wrote for the solo piano in his five concertos.

The Concerto No. 4 in C minor, like the composer's Symphony No. 3 in C minor, and Sonata for Violin and Piano, is unique in its division into two movements, instead of the usual three or four. It was Saint-Saëns's colleague, the editor and musicologist Charles Malherbe, who gave the best analysis of the Fourth Concerto. He pointed out that the work contains the four movements of the classical symphony, only they are condensed and paired off into two sections, resulting in a greater "economy of formulas more in accordance with the musical habits of our time."

"The themes are distinct, peculiar to each movement," he continued, "but they intermingle at times in the developments, and the return establishes a sort of natural bond between the different portions of the work. Thus the Andante in 4-4 of the first section is transformed to triple time in the second, and the first Allegro reappears with a different measure in the Finale."

M-MM-566, Robert Casadesus, Piano, and the Philharmonic-Symphony Orchestra of New York, Artur Rodzinski Conducting.

DANSE MACABRE, OP. 40

Danse macabre—the third of the four tone poems by Saint-Saëns—is based on a poem by Henri Cazalis. At the hour of midnight, Death tunes his violin, the flute strikes up a diabolical dance tune, and a mad dance begins. The xylophone imitates the rattling of skeleton bones. Suddenly, the strains of the *Dies Irae* are sounded. The dancing continues until dawn is ushered in by the crowing of the cock. The dance is dissipated and the dancers vanish.

Saint-Saëns wrote this work in 1874, and on January 24, 1875 it was introduced by the Colonne Orchestra in Paris. It has been arranged for solo piano by Franz Liszt, and for two pianos by the composer himself.

11251-D, Chicago Symphony Orchestra, Frederick Stock Conducting.

SAMSON AND DELILAH

SAINT-SAËNS's opera follows the Biblical story from the Book of Judges closely. Delilah, mistress of Samson whom she hates because she knows he does not love her, lends a willing ear to the plan of the high priest Dagon to uncover the source of Samson's strength. She discovers that the secret lay in Samson's hair, which she manages to cut off. Robbed of his hair—and strength—Samson is now weak and blind, a helpless victim of the Philistines who come to capture him. Tied to the pillar of the Temple, as the Philistines celebrated in a lavish feast below, Samson begs God for a brief renewal of his strength. His prayer answered, Samson brings down the pillars of the Temple on himself and the Philistines.

Samson and Delilah was no overnight success. The first act was performed by the Colonne Orchestra in 1875 and was received frigidly. The first complete operatic performance took place two years later in Weimar under Franz Liszt with less hostility perhaps but hardly greater success. Not until 1892 did it enter the repertoire of the Paris Opéra.

The justly celebrated *"Mon coeur s'ouvre"*—one of the most famous contralto arias in all opera—is found in the second act; the equally famous Bacchanale, with its strong Semitic colors, takes place in the third act at the Feast of the Dagon.

71390-D, Amour, viens aider, Bruna Castagna, Contralto, with Columbia Opera Orchestra, Alfredo Antonini Conducting.
71058-D, Fair Spring Is Returning, Bruna Castagna, Contralto, with Orchestra conducted by Alfredo Antonini.
71058-D, Mon coeur s'ouvre, Bruna Castagna, Contralto, with Orchestra conducted by Alfredo Antonini.

Domenico Scarlatti

1685–1757

DOMENICO SCARLATTI, the son of the celebrated Italian opera composer Alessandro Scarlatti, was born in Naples in 1685. His father was his first teacher. In 1702, Domenico Scarlatti went to Rome and three years after that he began to grow famous as a performer on the harpsichord. Cardinal Ottoboni arranged a competition between Scarlatti and Handel to ascertain who was the greater virtuoso; and there were many who felt that it was Scarlatti who emerged the winner.

In 1709, Queen Marie Casimire of Poland engaged Scarlatti for her musical staff; for the next six years he devoted himself to the writing of operas. An appointment in 1715 as Kapellmeister of St. Peter's in Rome directed him toward the writing of church music. For twenty-five years, Scarlatti lived in Spain as music master to the royal family. It was during this period that he wrote his sonatas—or *Esercizi*, as he called them. In 1754, Scarlatti returned to the city of his birth, where he died three years later.

SONATAS FOR HARPSICHORD

THE MUSICAL depth and ingenuity of Domenico Scarlatti's harpsichord sonatas contradict the preface to one of his works which reads: "Pray do not expect in these compositions a profound programmatic idea, but just accept them as artful 'scherzos' devised to improve your proficiency on the harpsichord."

Scarlatti, the son of Alessandro Scarlatti, was the greatest harpsichord virtuoso of his time. And it is not surprising that his music demonstrated the widest opportunities to display the technical possi-

[389]

bilities of the instrument in its variety of registration, in the over-
lapping of the hands on two manuals and in virtuoso technique.
Scarlatti is to the harpsichord what Chopin is to the piano. Both
combine with profound inspiration the utmost technical possibilities
on their respective keyboard instruments.

In Scarlatti's long and rich life he wrote more than 500 known
sonatas. Almost all sonatas of Scarlatti consist of a single movement,
usually in two parts. Some resemble the traditional dance forms to
be found in suites. They are dominated by one rhythmic idea, and
accordingly follow the style of the slow Sarabande in 3-4 as in the
Longo collection 434 B-flat major Sonata, of the Siciliana in 6-8 in the
Longo 218 C major Sonata, of the Neapolitan Dance in the Longo
205 C major Sonata, of the Gavotte in the Longo 58 D minor Sonata.
Other pieces again are characterized by the perseverance of rhythmic
ideas, as in the Longo 384 F major Sonata, Longo 327 B-flat major
Sonata, and Longo 243 A minor Sonata. In the Longo 205 C major
Sonata this stubbornness in the bass, with almost modern disso-
nances, summons a rural fiesta in an impressionistic manner.

The classical style was finally encompassed within the relatively
short forms of Scarlatti in those pieces where an entirely new theme
is introduced in the second part. The new theme may still be recognizable as a distant relative of the original theme, like the cadence-
like passage in the elaborate Sonata 407, or it may be an entirely
novel thought as in 129, calling for a special register—theorbe stop.

On such occasions Scarlatti utilized the registers of the clavicembalo not only as a means for shading, but as an inherent factor of
his compositions, on equal footing with diversities of rhythm, mode,
and key. Echolike imitation and restatement of the theme in different registers, as in 218 and 434, resemble alternations of string and
woodwind groups as in contemporary orchestral music. Whereas
Bach's work formed the apogee of keyboard music in general in
forms derived from the organ, his contemporary, Scarlatti, individualized and specialized the music of the instrument of which he was
the master, and stands, looking forward, at the threshold of modern
pianism.

M-MM-298, Yella Pessl, Harpsichord.
M-MM-372, Robert Casadesus, Piano.

Arnold Schönberg

1874–

ARNOLD SCHÖNBERG did not invent the twelve-tone system, but it was he who developed that technique so completely and with such infinite resources that it is inextricably associated with his name. Through this formula, Schönberg has arrived at a musical expression that is complicated and cerebral, often ugly to the ear, often completely devoid of all sentiment. But it is music that has extended the resources of the art considerably, and has explored new horizons.

Schönberg did not arrive at his twelve-tone technique overnight. Early in his career, he wrote conventional music which had strong Romantic and Wagnerian overtones. Slowly and inevitably he outgrew his Romanticism and guided by his theories and convictions turned to expressionistic writing of the severest kind in which the new system of music—the twelve-tone system—became the guiding principle. His music has influenced the direction of numerous other composers, notably Alban Berg and Ernst Křenek.

Schönberg was born in Vienna in 1874, and early in life he became a pupil of Arnold Zemlinsky whose influence on the young man was profound. (Later, in 1901, Schönberg was to marry Zemlinsky's sister.) It was under his teacher's influence that Schönberg composed his first works, including a string quartet, performed in Vienna in 1897, and a set of songs. Of these early works—in none of which the future revolutionist of tones asserts himself—the most famous is the *Verklärte Nacht*.

A *Kammersymphonie* was the transition from the old style to the new. Slowly and subtly—between 1909 and 1912—Schönberg developed his new manner of writing music, producing in this idiom works like *Five Pieces for Orchestra, Pierrot Lunaire,* and *Six Pieces for Piano* which scandalized the more conservative world of music.

Battles were fought in Schönberg's name; frequently concerts featuring Schönberg's music developed into riots.

During World War I, Schönberg served in the Austrian army. His fame as a composer—and as a vital force in contemporary musical expression—developed rapidly after this war. And while his works continued to inspire provocative arguments, there were few to deny that he was a force in music to reckon with.

With the rise of Hitler in Germany, Schönberg voluntarily left Europe to settle permanently in this country. For a while he taught at the Malkin School in Boston. But later on, he established his home in Los Angeles, where he taught music, and devoted himself assiduously to composition. His seventieth birthday, in 1944, was the occasion for a nationwide celebration in which numerous articles were written about him and numerous of his works were performed by our most prominent musical organizations.

PIERROT LUNAIRE

Schönberg's *Pierrot Lunaire* is a set of "thrice seven" melodramas, short poems by Albert Giraud, translated into German by Erich Hartleben. The scoring is extremely tenuous, employing the piano, flute (interchangeable with piccolo), clarinet (interchangeable with bass clarinet), violin (interchangeable with viola), and 'cello. The poems are not sung, but spoken along a given melodic line. The music is not necessarily a reflection or illustration of the text. At times it deliberately deflects from the meaning of the words in the poems. Thus, in "Serenade," Pierrot is pictured as playing on the viola, but the setting is for 'cello, and when the word pizzicato occurs in the text, the 'cello continues to play *arco* (with the bow).

The idiom of *Pierrot Lunaire* is expressionistic. The subjective world of the moon-struck Pierrot is here made into a private reality, which a breath of oxygen would instantly destroy. Expressionism in poetry is reflected by integral chromaticism in music, with chromatic tones now crowding narrowly, then dispersing widely through several octaves, creating the feeling of tenseness or spaciousness, according to the design of each piece. This is the language of atonality: there is no determinable key, and the acoustically sharp intervals, major sevenths and minor ninths, prevail over milder dissonances. But this chromatic idiom does not yet constitute the logical system in which the twelve tones of the chromatic scale are arranged in a fundamental series. This twelve-tone technique was not elaborated by Schönberg until twelve years later.

The twenty-one pieces of *Pierrot Lunaire* were written in 1912. It took forty rehearsals to bring the work to performance, which took place in Berlin on October 16, 1912. *Pierrot Lunaire*, like every epoch-making work, met with derision on the part of the music critics. The American correspondent for the *Musical Courier* described the music as "the most ear-splitting combination of tones that ever desecrated the walls of a Berlin music hall," and the critic of the *Boersen-Courier* in Berlin exclaimed in mock horror: "If this is the music of the future, I pray my Creator not to let me live to hear it again."

M-MM-461, Stiedry-Wagner, Kolisch, Auber, Steuermann, Posella, and Bloch, with Arnold Schönberg Conducting.

VERKLÄRTE NACHT (TRANSFIGURED NIGHT)

Verklärte Nacht belongs to that period in Schönberg's career when he was still strongly influenced by Wagner, and before he turned to the writing of expressionistic music in the twelve-tone scale. The year of its composition was 1899—Schönberg's twenty-fifth; at this time it appeared as a sextet. In 1917 Schönberg arranged the work for chamber orchestra, and it is in this form that it is most frequently heard.

The music—which throughout is romantic in mood and atmosphere, and sensuous in colors—describes the moonlight walk of two lovers through a forest. The woman confesses that she is soon to have a child by another man, but that she is still profoundly in love with the one now at her side. He forgives her, saying that the baby soon to be born will be *their* child. The lovers kiss, and then proceed walking through the dark and silent forest.

Franz Schubert

1797–1828

O N JANUARY 31, 1797, in Lichtenthal, a suburb of Vienna, there was born, to school teacher Franz Schubert and his wife Marie Elizabeth, a son who was promptly christened Franz Peter. Fortunately for the world, if not for himself, young Franz escaped the appalling infant mortality rate of the Schubert family of which nine out of their fourteen died. School teacher Schubert was a kindly man and interested himself in his children as much as the struggle of existence would permit, especially in Franz, whose genius even in infancy he seemed dimly to perceive. Franz, Sr. imparted to Franz, Jr. the fair knowledge he had in the general rudiments of music, and at the age of eight the boy was playing the violin with remarkable skill for his years. The boy also studied voice and so developed it that at the age of ten he was given solo parts in the Lichtenthal church.

In 1808, after passing the official admission test, the youth entered an Imperial institution where young singers were trained for the Imperial Chapel Choirs. During the lad's stay at this school he made such friends as Spaun, Holzapfel, Senn and Stadler, and all clung to him till death. Spaun was older and much larger than Schubert and did much to achieve his own immortality by helping and championing Schubert at all times. Franz left the Imperial institution in 1813 (his seventeenth year) still saddened by the death of his mother in 1812. Returning home, he escaped the rigor of service in the army and took a Normal School course which qualified him to teach in the school conducted by his father.

Throughout his life Franz liked nothing so much as to be with companions of his own choosing. Mayrhofer, the poet, Schubert first met in 1814. Vogl, an accomplished baritone singer, who did most of what little was done to spread the gospel of Schubert's marvelous songs, came into his life at about the same time. In 1816 he first met Franz von Schober, a young man of family and wealth, who recently had come to Vienna to study law and who was to exercise an important influence on the young composer. Earlier he had formed an intimate friendship with the Grob family, mother, son and daughter, cultured people much interested in music.

It was in 1815 that Schubert gave the first real evidence of the torrential rush of musical thoughts that fairly overwhelmed him. In the course of these twelve months he produced his second and third symphonies, two masses, five operas, an almost incredible number of piano and chamber music pieces and one hundred and forty-six songs! Among the last named was a composition which was to blaze a new trail for song-writing, i.e., *Der Erlkönig* ("The Erl King").

His friend Vogl, in 1816, sensing the greatness of "The Erl King," sang the song in most of the great salons of Viennese society. Schober offered to undertake Schubert's maintenance until he could become established, and at his house in fact Schubert lived for the greater part of that year; other friends helped him during the difficult and infertile year of 1817, when having thrown over the schoolteaching he was in even worse case than before. In 1818, his position was much improved temporarily by his official appointment as music master to the noted patron of music, Count Johann Esterházy, at whose castle in Zselész, Hungary, he passed the summer.

Year after year continued to bring forth an abundance of compositions by Schubert—as well as life devoid of luxury. Of the *Unfinished* Symphony in B minor little is known except that it dates from 1822 and that upon completion of the first two movements and nine bars of the Scherzo with sketches for the remainder of this movement, it was either consciously abandoned or laid aside and forgotten. It was unearthed years after the composer's death from amongst the great pile of manuscripts found in his room.

Of the remaining days of Schubert's inauspicious earthly career the tale is soon told. The year of 1827 saw the completion of the great song-cycle *Die Winterreise*, and the last illness and death of Beethoven (March 26th). Schubert's last year, 1828, was signalized by the completion of the "great C major" Symphony. Early in November, typhus, sinister product of unsanitary conditions and undernourishment, made its appearance, and the ill-fated young genius died on the nineteenth of that month, and was buried within a few steps of Beethoven.

FANTASIE ("WANDERER"), FOR PIANO

Allegro con fuoco, ma non troppo · Adagio · Presto · Allegro

SCHUBERT's Piano Fantasy, Op. 15, written in 1820, is sometimes labeled *Wanderer-Fantasie*, because the slow movement is a set of variations on a melody from the song *Der Wanderer* written four years before.

The form and material of Schubert's piano works were not essentially different from the average style between Mozart's time and Beethoven's. Schubert lacked Mozart's professional technique, and wrote for the piano in terms of an instrumental ensemble, a procedure which produced the effect of an arrangement rather than a work using the resources of the instrument. The Fantasy in C is no exception.

The second movement is based on a theme from *Der Wanderer*. The final Allegro is fugally constructed, and Schubert himself was never able to play this effectively because of its technical difficulties.

Liszt made a faithful transcription of the Fantasy, following Schubert's music without gratuitous additions. Where the piano plays solo, Schubert's music is left untouched. When the orchestra comes in, it either reinforces the harmony or takes over the melody, the basses or the underlying rhythm leaving the piano freedom of action in elaborate passage work. Schubert's trills are enlarged into Lisztian rumbling chromatics, and the simple arpeggios and chords are magnified so that the piano achieves a maximum of sonority. Where Schubert has a short cadenza, Liszt spreads it over several octaves. The result is a Concert Piece for piano and orchestra, in which the pianist is a collaborator subordinating the importance of his part to the greater significance of the whole.

Schubert's simplicity and Liszt's grandiloquence may not form a perfect union of spirit, but Liszt, superimposing his personality on Schubert, did it reverently, enlarging—not canceling or altering—the essential elements of Schubert's great music.

M-MM-426, Edward Kilenyi, Piano, and Symphony Orchestra Conducted by Selmar Meyrowitz.

IMPROMPTUS

"IMPROMPTU" is a French word meaning "improvisation." In the 19th century it was one of the many names given to small pieces for the piano which met the typically Romantic need for intimate expression in short and simple forms.

Schubert wrote eight impromptus, contained in two volumes (Op. 90 and Op. 142) of four pieces each. The four pieces of Op. 90 are well balanced, though contrasted in mood. Melody, grace, sentiment, often brilliancy, are their outstanding traits. Op. 142 moved Schumann to write one of his most enthusiastic articles, in which he suggested that the first, second and fourth numbers might have been planned by Schubert for a piano sonata in F minor, since the first impromptu has the character of a first movement. The third impromptu in this set is one of Schubert's own favorite melodies, since he used it in *Rosamunde* and in the A minor Quartet.

It was the publisher Haslinger, and not Schubert, who entitled these piano pieces Impromptus.

LÄNDLER, OP. 171, FOR PIANO

SCHUBERT composed his Ländler, Op. 171, in 1823. Known also as the German Dance, the Ländler was popular, especially in Austria, during the eighteenth and the early part of the nineteenth centuries. It served as the connecting link between the Minuet and the Viennese Waltz. Besides Schubert, such immortals as Haydn, Mozart, and Beethoven composed Ländler for dancing.

X-MX-236, Robert Casadesus, Piano.

MOMENTS MUSICAUX, OP. 94, FOR PIANO

LIKE the impromptus, this is a set of smaller pieces for the piano of extempore character which helped to pave the way for the rich pianistic literature of the 19th century.

The six *Moments musicaux* appeared in two volumes as Op. 94

and includes one of the most famous piano pieces of all time, the enchanting F minor *Moment musical*. In the form of the *Moment musical,* Schubert was free from the fetters of the sonata form and the conventions of classical restraint. The length of the pieces could be adapted to the requirements of the musical material. If these pieces are lacking in the dramatic power found in some of the impromptus, they are, on the other hand, more delicate and lucid. Pure melody here reigns supreme.

17079-D, F minor, Walter Gieseking, Piano.

QUARTET NO. 13 IN A MINOR, OP. 29

Allegro ma non troppo · Andante · Menuetto: allegro · Allegro moderato

THIS is the only one of Schubert's string quartets published in his lifetime. It was dedicated to Schuppanizgh who participated in its first performance in the spring of 1824.

As the composer stated in a letter to a friend, he sought, in the writing of this Quartet, to find distraction from personal worries and extreme loneliness. However, Schubert's prevailing mood at this time is clearly reflected in the music. The painter Schwind found the music "smooth and gentle . . . the kind of melody that is usually associated with song." But it has a somber overtone which, at moments, makes it an almost pessimistic pronouncement. The very opening subject of the first movement sets the mood of intense melancholy which pervades the entire work.

Technically, this Quartet is a marked progress over Schubert's earlier works in this form. It is a successful attempt at developing musical material logically and organically, and creating a certain unity among the respective movements. This unity is particularly evident in the first three movements. The finale is relief from the intense tension that has prevailed.

In two different passages, Schubert quotes himself in this Quartet. The slow movement is an adaptation of one of his impromptus, a melody of such surpassing beauty that it provides for H. L. Mencken the incontrovertible proof that God must exist. The Minuet opens with the theme of one of Schubert's songs, *Gods of Greece.*

[398]

QUARTET NO. 14 IN D MINOR

Allegro · Andante con moto · Scherzo: allegro molto · Finale: presto

OF SCHUBERT'S many great songs, few have impressed themselves upon succeeding generations more forcefully than his *Death and the Maiden*. The beautiful Andante of the Quartet in D minor, which is founded on this song, is generally considered Schubert's finest work in chamber music. It was written at the end of 1825 and the early part of 1826, and had its first performance in Vienna on January 29, 1826.

The Quartet was well received, but the composer's friends considered the last movement too long and he accordingly condensed it. This is one of the few instances in which Schubert revised a work after its completion; as a rule his music was dashed down at a furious rate, and, once written, the urge to pour out yet more from his unfailing well of melody prevented anything in the way of revision. In this case the original manuscript has disappeared, so it is not known exactly what was deleted. But an unusually compact movement remains.

The slow movement is not the only place where Schubert quotes himself. In the Presto we hear brief suggestions of still another Schubert song, *Der Erlkönig*, as if to carry out once again the idea suggested in the slow movement—namely, a struggle with Death.

QUINTET IN A MAJOR ("TROUT"), OP. 114, FOR PIANO AND STRINGS

Allegro vivace · Andante · Scherzo: presto · Andantino Finale: allegro gusto

SCHUBERT wrote this Quintet—which is unusual in that it calls for a double-bass—during the summer of 1819 while he was vacationing at Steyr in Upper Austria. It was his second visit to the old picturesque town where he enjoyed that popularity that was denied him in Vienna. His music was constantly being played there at informal chamber-music sessions. It was for just such an occasion that this work was written. It was dedicated to Sylvester Paumgartner who is believed to have suggested to Schubert that he use his own song "The Trout" (*Die Forelle*) as one of the movements.

The major mode which is maintained throughout the work gives the work its fundamental optimistic mood. The work is light-hearted and carefree except for ephemeral moments of melancholy in the Andante, which offers a brilliant contrast to the animation of the first and third movements. The fourth movement is a set of six variations, some of them highly formal, on the "Trout" theme, while the closing movement—with its Hungarian echoes—leads the Quintet to a gay conclusion.

QUINTET IN C MAJOR, OP. 163, FOR STRINGS

Allegro ma non troppo · Adagio · Scherzo · Allegretto

SCHUBERT dated his Quintet in C major 1828, and it was probably composed in September. There are no references to it in Schubert's meager correspondence.

It is a work of deeply personal character; commentators have not hesitated to read autobiographical meanings into its content: confessions of discouragement, even despair, presentiments of death. The instrumental combination for which Schubert composed the Quintet has been thought significant: a second 'cello, rather than the more conventional second viola, is the fifth instrument of the group, imparting a darker color to the music.

The Quintet opens with an Allegro ma non troppo in C major, distinguished by a wonderful melody first assigned to the two 'cellos. An Adagio in E major follows—one of Schubert's loveliest slow movements, in which suggestions of the song *Death and the Maiden* are heard. The somber Trio is the glory of the Scherzo. A lyrical Allegretto then concludes what Cobbett described as the "most romantically conceived work in all chamber music."

M-MM-497, Budapest String Quartet.

SCHUBERT's cycle of the lovely miller maid, set to the poems of Wilhelm Müller, reveals the whole gamut of human emotion, from the buoyant hope and joy of a youth in love to utter disillusionment.

Through the fields wanders the carefree young miller boy filled with joy of living. Before him his road stretches like a bright ribbon edged by wooded hills, and he follows its way with a gay song on his lips. Suddenly he hears the murmuring of a brook as it splashes through the rocks and rushes merrily toward the valley. The miller boy stops and listens to the sound of the water which he knows and loves so well. It is always a brook which makes this lad, who so loves to wander, want to stop and linger. He roams from hill to hill, always finding work until his wanderlust again drives him on, but ever again a brook calls: Halt! Here is a new mill! New work, a new place to rest! But today the brook sings a strangely enticing song. It is as if the voices of fairies called to him, luring and leading him. He follows the brook as though in a dream—half against his will. He would have liked to wander on to another mill, perhaps, of which he has been told, far ahead on a sunny mountainside. But he must follow the brook. Suddenly he knows that the brook has meant it well: between the alders stands a mill, and its shining windows seem to welcome him. The lad thanks the brook for finding him such a friendly place in which to work. And the miller's young daughter—perhaps the brook wanted to lure him on her account? The lad has fallen head-over-heels in love with her; he works with redoubled energy in the hope of winning her. The brook, his best friend, is his confidant. Yet it gives no answer to his yearning plea. "Does she love me?"

For a short time the miller's daughter is attracted by the lad, and he in his exuberance believes that he has found unending happiness in her pledge of love, and pours out his ecstatic delight in the song *Mein!* But his good fortune is short-lived. A dashing hunter has now captured the fancy of the light-hearted miller girl. Because of his green hunting coat, green is now her favorite color. This color, green, gradually becomes an obsession for the poor youth fallen so rudely from his heaven; green pursues him wherever he looks; he hates green because it symbolizes the end of all his happiness; he loves green with a despairing grief because it is his beloved's favorite color. Standing upon the bank of the brook, he asks it to bear him to eternal rest, to put an end to all his misery. But the brook warns him that life will go on with unceasing changes; misery will be followed by new joy. It is in vain: the longing for death is too great. Slowly the boy bends down. The cool waters receive him and close over him.

Now the brook sings an eternal slumber song, and green willows hang over him as he rests; green meadows surround his cool bed and earth and heaven are far away; joy and pain pass from him like the flowing water.

M-MM-615, Lotte Lehmann, Soprano, with Paul Ulanowsky, Piano.

SONATA NO. 9 IN A MAJOR, OP. 120

Allegro moderato · *Andante* · *Allegro*

Schubert's piano music has suffered undeserved neglect chiefly because this music offers little opportunity for external display on the part of the pianist. Since technical showmanship elicits applause and the acclaim of the masses, the virtuoso seeks it in the works of other composers. The beauty of Schubert's piano compositions is found in subtle rhythms and tone shading. And, most important, his music always sings.

The piano sonatas provide a musical diary of Schubert's development as an instrumental composer. Whereas in the symphonies there is the inexplicable leap from the first six, with their frankly Haydnesque and Mozartean characteristics, to the mature, Romantic, and well-orchestrated *Unfinished*, and the monumental C major Symphony, in the piano sonatas there is a continuous line of struggle and experiment.

There has been some little dispute as to when the Sonata No. 9 was composed. In Breitkopf & Härtel the date given is 1825, but three authorities, Scheibler, Költzsch, and Glock, feel that the Sonata has little in common with the other sonatas of that period, and therefore have assigned it to the year 1819. In the works of most composers the opus numbers bear a direct relation to the dates of their compositions, but with Schubert this is not the case. Some of his earliest works have high opus numbers, while some of the later ones have low numbers.

This Sonata in A major is marked by an economy of material skillfully used. An unusual feature of the opening Allegro moderato is the single bar of transitional passage work that separates the two themes used in both the opening and closing sections. In the Andante there is a slight resemblance to the famous Minuet in Mozart's opera *Don Giovanni*. Only in the final Allegro is there any brilliance or opportunity for the display of virtuosity, and even here the rapid passages are directly bound up with the musical scheme and are never employed for the flaunting of mere technical prowess.

At no point does the Sonata leave the listener with a feeling of agitation. It might be characterized as a musical expression of peace and well-being, best described by the untranslatable word from Schubert's homeland—*Gemütlichkeit*.

X-MX-236, Robert Casadesus, Piano.

SONGS

ONE SUMMER evening in 1826, seated at a table of one of the suburban cafés he so loved to frequent, Schubert fingered a volume of Shakespeare which a friend happened to bring with him. Suddenly Schubert said: "Such a wonderful melody came to me. If only I had some music paper!" His friend quickly drew a few staves on the back of the menu. Then and there, in the midst of the café-house hubbub, Schubert sketched his immortal song, "Hark, Hark, the Lark."

This anecdote forcefully describes the working habits of the one who is generally regarded as the creator of the German song—the *Lied*.

Actually there were composers of German song before the time of Schubert. Haydn, Mozart, Beethoven all wrote songs. But it was Schubert who most fully realized all its artistic potentialities and who recognized that in the song form lyric and music were equal partners. Blessed with a reservoir of melody the like of which is not duplicated in musical history, Schubert could provide the lyrics of

[403]

more than a hundred different poets with melodies of inexhaustible beauty and variety of expression. His insufficient schooling (which sometimes handicapped him in his approach to the larger forms) was no impediment, for his musical ideas could pour forth freely and copiously unrestricted by too many technical considerations.

While Schubert most certainly had good taste in poetry (Goethe and Schiller were his favorites), bad verse did not discourage him from writing music to it. When he read melodious lines, some beautiful theme would immediately spring up in his mind. He was as directly inspired by the poetic word as Mozart was by the dramatic situation or pointed dialogue. Some poems were used by Schubert over and over again. He wrote easily, swiftly. "Why," he once explained, "when I have finished one song I start another."

The literary approach to music was a characteristic Romantic phenomenon, and Schubert was its first major exponent. Whether he used good poetry or bad, his music fit the words neatly. Words and music, voice and accompaniment, appear in perfect partnership. The accompaniment sometimes characterizes and illustrates the text, leaving the voice to embellish on the emotional quality of the poem. This threefold unity of words, melody, and accompaniment marks a new era in song literature.

Schubert wrote 603 songs. They vary in length, form, and mood. Schubert completed his first songs in 1811, at the age of fourteen. His early works show a youthful predilection for dramatic topics and, at the same time, astounding maturity of feeling and an almost unbelievable versatility of expression. His big "song years"—1814–16 —coincided with his assignment as a schoolteacher in his father's school. Between, during, and after classes he would turn out one song after another. In 1815 alone he wrote 144 of them, eight on a single day (October 13). From this period date some of his masterpieces including *Der Erlkönig* (Schubert's Opus 1, published in 1821), *Gretchen am Spinnrade, Heidenröslein, Am See, Rastlose Liebe, Die Mainacht, Vergebliche Liebe,* and *Der Fischer.*

As he matured, he sought more and more for personal and intimate communication in his songs. The best known of these (outside of those included in cycles, which are treated separately in this section), are perhaps *Ave Maria* (from Scott's *Lady of the Lake*), *Ständchen* (or Serenade), *Du bist die Ruh', An die Musik.* Two songs of 1817 were later used for variation-movements in important chamber-music works: *Die Forelle* (The Trout) for the A major Quintet, and *Der Tod und das Mädchen* for the D minor Quartet. Schubert himself transcribed *Der Wanderer* into a piano fantasy, which was later arranged for piano and orchestra by Franz Liszt.

M-MM-89, Selected Songs, Sophie Braslau, Contralto, Alexander Kipnis, Bass, Elsa Alsen, Soprano, and Charles Hackett, Tenor.

SYMPHONY NO. 5 IN B-FLAT MAJOR

Allegro · *Andante con moto* · *Menuetto and Trio* · *Allegro vivace*

THE SYMPHONY No. 5 was written in 1816 in a little over three weeks' time when Schubert was only nineteen years old. The first performance of this work was executed by the amateur orchestra which used to meet at Otto Hartwig's house in the Schottenhof, and took place shortly after the completion of the Symphony. This orchestra had grown out of the string quartet in which Schubert himself played the viola and which originally met at his father's house.

The first public presentation was probably that on February 1, 1873 at the Crystal Palace, England. The work was conducted in manuscript by the indefatigable August Manns, who directed the Crystal Palace concerts for no less a period than from 1855 to 1901.

The greater number of Schubert's symphonies were composed before 1818, the year he was twenty-one years old. These works reflect the style of the earlier composers. His technique is immature, and his habit of eking out ideas by sequential repetition instead of by true symphonic development and counterpoint was in evidence, but rich melody and harmony made up for these deficiencies.

The Symphony in B-flat follows the *Tragic* Symphony and is a striking contrast with its full happy feeling. It might well be called the Joyful.

M-MM-366, London Philharmonic Orchestra, Sir Thomas Beecham Conducting.

SYMPHONY NO. 7 IN C MAJOR

Andante; Allegro ma non troppo · *Andante con moto* · *Scherzo*
Finale

Schubert's Symphony in C major was discovered by Schumann along with two other symphonies in the possession of Schubert's brother. Schubert himself never heard a performance of it, and it was with some difficulty that friends finally persuaded the Gesellschaft der Musikfreunde of Munich to present it on December 14, 1828—about two weeks after the composer's death. It was not heard again until its performance at a Gewandhaus concert in Leipzig under the direction of Mendelssohn the following year. Mendelssohn later tried to interest the London Philharmonic Society in the work—without success. And London did not hear the Symphony until 1856.

There is some question as to whether Schubert actually wrote nine or ten symphonies. This is because many of his compositions came to light only after his untimely death. The Symphony in C major is known as the Seventh, and is probably Schubert's greatest symphony. Schumann wrote of it: "This heavenly, long-drawn-out symphony is like some romance of Jean Paul's, which ought never to end." Actually, it is not longer than many symphonic compositions, but it marks the end of the classical period and the beginning of the Romantic.

The Symphony opens with an extended, dignified introduction, Andante, which gradually increases in tempo and excitement until it leads into the main body of the first movement, a buoyant Allegro ma non troppo. At the conclusion of the movement, without a slackening of pace, the theme of the introduction makes a triumphant reappearance. The second movement is a subdued, marchlike Andante con moto that features a plaintive melody sung by the oboe. The vigorous scherzo that follows is marked Allegro vivace; its Trio—or middle section—is more relaxed to provide appropriate contrast. Allegro vivace is also the tempo indication for the boisterous, onrushing finale, which brings the symphony to a wildly joyous conclusion.

M-MM-403, Chicago Symphony Orchestra, Frederick Stock Conducting.
M-MM-679, Philharmonic-Symphony Orchestra of New York, Bruno Walter Conducting.

SYMPHONY NO. 8 (UNFINISHED)
IN B MINOR

Allegro moderato · Andante

WHEN Schubert died at the age of thirty-one, he left so many un-published works that the flow of his new music continued for years after his death. So extraordinary was the quantity and quality of this posthumous output that a London publication, the *Musical World*, in a correspondence from Paris in 1839 expressed doubts whether these unknown works were indeed Schubert's. "A deep shade of suspicion is beginning to be cast over the authenticity of posthumous compositions," wrote the *Musical World*. "All Paris has been in a state of amazement at the posthumous diligence of the song writer F. Schubert, who, while one would think that his ashes repose in peace in Vienna, is still making eternal new songs."

The *Unfinished* Symphony, discovered more than thirty years after Schubert's death, was first performed in Vienna in 1865, and published in 1867. In that year, Grove, the founder of the famous dictionary of music, and Sullivan, the composer, made a musical pilgrimage to Vienna and discovered more Schubert manuscripts. The "posthumous diligence" of the "song writer F. Schubert" was indeed amazing.

By a whim of popular taste, the *Unfinished* Symphony has become the best-known orchestral composition of Schubert. It has been made a subject of novels and motion picture films. In the cinema version, Schubert writes a symphony for his pupil, young Carolyn Esterházy. He is awkward, bespectacled, timid. He declares his love for Carolyn in music. She is sympathetic and understanding, but she cannot love Schubert. When her engagement to another is announced, Schubert folds the manuscript of a Scherzo he had just begun to compose. The Symphony will never be finished, as his love has never been consummated.

There is a modicum of evidence to support the cinema version in the part concerning his tender feelings for the younger of the two Countesses Esterházy, who was seventeen years old in 1822 when Schubert was her music tutor. It is said that Carolyn asked Schubert why he had not dedicated anything to her, and that he replied: "Why should I? All I have written is dedicated to you."

[407]

The established facts are these: Schubert began the composition of the Symphony in Vienna, on October 30, 1822. The Symphony was intended as a gift to the city of Graz, which had elected Schubert an honorary member of the Music Society. Two movements were completed, and nine bars of the following movement, a Scherzo, was sketched. It is still a question why Schubert presented an unfinished manuscript as a gift.

The *Unfinished* Symphony is usually numbered the Eighth, but the correct numbering of Schubert's symphonies presents an involved problem. The Symphony is interesting in many respects. It was written by a young man of twenty-five, when Beethoven was still living, and when the Romantic movement was not even a name. It was still the era of the classical conception of the symphony. Yet Schubert's Symphony in B minor departs from the classical tradition. Beethoven introduces the trombones for the finale of the Fifth Symphony, yet Schubert uses them as an integral part of the orchestra from the very first.

But the form is classical, and both movements are built on the model of the classical sonata.

M-MM-330, London Philharmonic Orchestra, Sir Thomas Beecham. Conducting.
M-MM-485, Leopold Stokowski Conducting the All-American Orchestra.

DIE WINTERREISE

Die Winterreise is the second of the two great cycles of songs written by Schubert to the words of the German lyrical poet, Wilhelm Müller. There is a curious parallelism between Müller's life and Schubert's. The poet was born two years before Schubert, and died a year before Schubert died. Schubert died some two months short of his thirty-second birthday; Müller died a week before this thirty-third birthday. Müller wrote strophic poetry, in which every stanza contained an allotted number of lines, and every line an allotted number of syllables. Schubert's music is also overwhelming strophic, with musical phrases composed of even periods, and a well-defined cadence at the end of each period.

Schubert wrote the twenty-four songs comprising the cycle *Die*

[408]

Winterreise in 1827, the year of Müller's death, and the last complete year of Schubert's life. Not all of these poems relate to winter travel, but all have the air of gloomy resignation. It must be remembered that the year of 1827 was the winter of Schubert's life. It was a year marked by illness, by disillusionment and frustration; it was the year in which Schubert's idol, Beethoven, died. The heavy atmosphere of pessimism which hung so heavily over Schubert pervades these songs. Newman Flower describes the last of these songs as "an epic in sadness, the blending of two moods of beauty—both in verse and in music—overshadowed by death."

The songs reflect the thoughts of a young poet, spurned by the woman he loves, who wanders aimlessly through the countryside, vainly seeking solace and rest.

Schubert turned over the last part of *Die Winterreise* to the publisher Haslinger in September 1828, only two months before he died. For these sublime creations he received the grand sum of about twenty cents a song.

M-MM-466, M-MM-587, Lotte Lehmann, Soprano, and Paul Ulanowsky, Piano.

Robert Schumann

1810–1856

IN LIFE as well as in art Schumann was the most Romantic composer of the nineteenth century. His early loves, his great
romance with Clara Wieck, even his final insanity, one of the
symptoms of which was that he constantly heard the note A, as if
his brain needed tuning—all this creates the image of a perpetual
youth who went through life as an actor in a play devised by himself, and acted with an impersonal interest in the actions and feelings
of Robert Schumann, as viewed by someone other than himself. His
letters were literary to the point of an attitude, and yet he felt deeply
about the matters of love, art, and humanity. His music was a medium for his intellectual and romantic messages, and it abounded in
private symbols, themes that spelled in musical notes the name of
the town where his sweetheart lived, or titles that reflected the
imaginary doings of an imaginary society to combat the Philistines.

Schumann had, from the beginning, immediate though casual contact with literature. His father was a bookseller and in a small way a
publisher; and Robert lived with literature, quite *en famille,* and with
the dependence upon it which he might have felt toward his older
brothers, were they more congenial. After his father's death, he was
spiritually a kind of orphan; for his mother had very straight-laced
notions about music as a profession, and Robert was quite unable to
fulfill her wish that he enter the profession of the law. Jean Paul
Richter, accordingly, and other imaginative persons like him, became
Robert's foster brothers. They taught him little, perhaps, that was
useful; nor had he, for long, the kind of instruction in music that a
composer must have. But he grew in his own way—which was far
better than his mother's—and being inordinately intelligent as well
as imaginative, he managed to extract from the music of Bach and

[410]

from that of his Romantic contemporaries enough for the formation of a highly individual style.

He fell in love with Clara Wieck, some ten years younger than himself, the daughter of his piano teacher. Father Wieck did not want to give his gifted child into the custody of a young man who was unable to provide for her. He taught Robert well, but saw too clearly his inferiority to Clara, as pianist, to be willing to consent to their marriage. He was obstinate by nature, and so continued to oppose the match, even after Robert had proved—by composition rather than by playing—that he could make a sufficient way in the world. But although his love affair ran thus roughly, it contributed a good deal to that extraversion which ultimately made a symphonist of him.

In 1840, Robert suddenly found that he was a song writer; and so stimulating was this excursion into an untried field, and so inspiring was his new life with his Clara (the marriage took place September 12, 1840), that in the following year he boldly essayed the problem of the symphony. In that one year he produced three symphonic works—the *Spring* Symphony, a *Symphonic Fantasie* (which ultimately became the Fourth Symphony), and the *Overture, Scherzo and Finale*. In 1842, he produced much chamber music, likewise written with incredible speed; in 1843 came choral composition— prepared for, as to vocal technique, only by the wealth of songs already written, but eventuating in the extraordinary *Paradise and the Peri;* and in 1844 he gave up composition for a time, making an extended tour of Russia with his wife. He had been reluctant to leave the pleasant routine of his domestic life, but was so agreeably impressed that he began to plan a tour of England. This, however, never occurred. His extraordinary concentration upon his work had begun to tell on his health. He became very nervous; he was compelled to cease composing, even to avoid hearing music, which seriously overstimulated him; and he had to give up his professorship of piano and composition at the Leipzig Conservatory. He removed to Dresden where, as he said, "one can get back the old lost longing for music, there is so little to hear!"

When at length he was again strong enough to compose, the style of his work showed a great increase in polyphonic intricacy. Among many other things there are ten fugues, of which six are on the musical notes in the letters of the name BACH. Even in youth, Schumann had been a Bach-lover, and from that example had contrived a process of weaving his rather improvisatory harmony out of independently moving strands of melody. This, perhaps, is the most notable acquisition during the interim.

After 1850, the mental and nervous disorders became more and more aggravated. Schumann felt that the great composers of the past were dictating melodies to him; and he was tortured by the maze of sounds that filled his mind. His mental condition deteriorated so badly that early in 1854 Schumann tried unsuccessfully to commit suicide. He was confined to an asylum near Bonn where he fluctuated between brief periods of sanity and prolonged periods of stifling morbidity. He died in the asylum in 1856.

THIS series of twenty-one fragmentary pieces—which Schumann sub-titled *Scènes mignonnes sur quatre notes* ("Little Scenes on Four Notes")—was intended by the composer to depict "manifold states of the soul." He peopled his imaginary masked ball with a number of characters, some real, others fanciful.

While still a student in Leipzig, Schumann fell in love with Ernestine von Fricken, who lived in the small town of Asch. Typical Romantic that he was, Schumann delighted (and saw metaphysical connotations) in anagrams. He was greatly impressed to learn that "Asch" comprised the only musical letters to be found in the name "Schumann." (Note: In German, "Es"—pronounced S—is E-flat; H is B-natural; As is A-flat.) Schumann decided to use the four letters of Asch as the basis for his thematic material, using them in three different combinations: EsCHA, AsCH, and AEsCH. These themes are cryptically stated in a three-bar section called *Sphinxes*, and perform a corybantic dance in *Lettres dansantes*.

This set of piano pieces is full of delightful caricatures, portraits, pictures. Masked characters appear under their time-tested names of *Pierrot, Arlequin, Pantalon et Colombine*. Chopin and Paganini are caricatured (Schumann pokes fun at Chopin's then unconventional method of fingering). *Estrella* is unfaithful Ernestine—her number is the poorest of the set, and the easiest to play. Clara Wieck, a pianist of extraordinary promise at the-then age of fifteen, received one of the most difficult pieces in the work, *Chiarina*. Schumann represents himself and his dual personality of *Eusebius* and *Florestan* (the latter piece contains a direct quotation from one of Schumann's earlier piano works, *Papillons*). In between such pieces there are valses, and numbers depicting likely happenings at a ball. The set which begins in a festival carnival mood (*Préambule*) concludes with a belligerent *March of the Davidsbündler against the Philistines* which symbolizes the march of Schumann himself, his co-editors on his *Zeitschrift*, Mendelssohn, Moscheles, Chopin, and Liszt against the conservatives headed by Czerny.

Carnaval was introduced by Franz Liszt in Leipzig, but the public reaction was cool—so cool that Liszt never again played Schumann's works in public.

In 1909 Rimsky-Korsakov orchestrated it for Diaghilev who presented it as a ballet at a ball in St. Petersburg with Nijinsky and Karsavina in the cast.

CONCERTO IN A MINOR, OP. 54, FOR PIANO AND ORCHESTRA

Allegro affetuoso · *Andante grazioso* · *Allegro vivace*

IT SEEMS strange that among Schumann's many compositions for the piano there is only one concerto, and stranger still when we find that from his earliest days he evidently wished to write one. His first attempt was in 1827 when he was but seventeen. At that time he knew hardly anything about the technicalities of music and absolutely nothing about the orchestra, so, as might be expected, the attempt was a failure. Three years later, while studying law at Heidelberg, he made another attempt, but this also came to nothing, probably from the same reason as the first.

It was in 1841 that Schumann turned his attention seriously to orchestral music, and in that year the germ of the Piano Concerto was born, though it was not conceived as a complete work. In 1841 he wrote a *Fantasia* for Piano and Orchestra. It was rehearsed and performed privately by Madame Schumann in August, 1841, and was apparently laid aside until 1845. Then the composer added the lovely little Intermezzo and a Finale, using the 1841 *Fantasia* as a first movement, and so made a complete Concerto.

Madame Schumann first performed the Concerto in public at the Gewandhaus in Leipzig in December 1845. It was in her repertoire during her tour in 1845–46, and achieved general success except in England where, on the first performance of the work in April 1856, it was severely condemned by critics, a verdict which has now been entirely reversed. Today the Concerto is regarded as one of the most personal and beautiful works that this great romantic composer has left us.

The older concertos always started with a long orchestral section in which all the main themes of the first movement were introduced before the solo instrument entered. But Schumann brings in the piano at once. Then he makes another change in form. In the older concertos a pause was inserted in the orchestral parts near the end of the first movement, and the soloist was expected to exercise his skill in improvising on some theme from the earlier part of the movement. Composers soon realized that this was a rather dangerous procedure and, to prevent their works from being ruined by unsuitable interpolations, they began to write their own cadenzas. The first of these appeared in Beethoven's *Emperor* Concerto and in the present work by Schumann.

M-MM-196, Yves Nat, Piano, with Symphony Orchestra Conducted by Eugène Bigot.

DICHTERLIEBE, OP. 48

COMPOSED in the year of Schumann's marriage, this exquisite selection from Heine's *Buch der Lieder* contains some of Schumann's vocal masterpieces. In them he covers a world of delicate emotion; and, in his effort to give musical expression to the subtlest nuances, he introduces numerous novel elements of song-writing. The first song, for example (*Im wunderschönen Monat Mai*), ends on the half-cadence to suggest the vagueness with which the poem dissolves; the ending of the second song (*Aus meinen Tränen spriessen*) is dramatized by means of suspense; the third (*Die Rose, die Lilie, die Taube, die Sonne*) is in breezy parlando style; the seventh (*Ich grolle nicht*) exploits some unique harmonic effects; in the ninth (*Das ist ein Flöten und Geigen*) the piano part is almost entirely independent of the voice; in the sixteenth (*Die alten, bösen Lieder*) the melody anticipates the conclusion of the poem, and the piano epilogue contributes new musical thoughts.

In all these songs the piano stresses the underlying thoughts of the poem. The melodic treatment is usually declamatory, attributing singular importance to the proper accentuation of the words.

M-MM-486, Lotte Lehmann, Soprano, and Bruno Walter, Piano.

THIS song cycle tells the simple story of a young woman's love: her first amazement at discovering she is falling in love; her happiness over her engagement; her wedding; her sorrow over her beloved's death. In typically Romantic fashion, there are here allusions to the remote past in exotic countries. The piano epilogue is musically related to the first song: the young widow, retiring within herself, relives the days of her young love.

Schumann borrowed eight of the nine lyrics from the cycle of the same name by Adalbert Chamisso. The poems, it must be confessed are rather mediocre, involved, oversensitive. On the other hand, Schumann's setting reveals the deepest insight into a woman's feelings. Much of his own happiness over his recent marriage to Clara is reflected in these songs: the second and third songs of the cycle (*Er, der Herrlichste von allen* and *Ich kann's nicht fassen, nicht glauben*) are among the most ebullient and the most ecstatic in all song literature.

M-MM-539, Lotte Lehmann, Soprano, with Bruno Walter at the Piano.

QUARTET NO. 1 IN A MINOR, OP. 41, NO. 1
Allegro · Adagio · Scherzo · Presto

SCHUMANN came late to chamber music. In the summer of 1839 he thought of writing a string quartet. He felt that the piano was becoming too narrow for him. He wrote to Clara Wieck that his ideas were contrapuntal, that in composing a theme he could instantly foresee its use in canonic imitation, and further, in inversion, rhythmic variation, and so on. At that time, as editor of the *Zeitschrift für Musik,* he published in his magazine a series of articles on Beethoven's quartets, written by a scholar and friend.

There were also regular morning musicales at Ferdinand David's house in Leipzig, at which quartets, new and old, were regularly performed. All this gave Schumann the necessary impetus to try his own hand at chamber music. In June 1842, at the age of thirty-two, and then happily married to Clara Wieck, he undertook the composition of three quartets. He wrote them one after another with great ease. The quartets were published much later, on Schumann's thirty-ninth birthday, and it took a great deal of persuasive letter writing by Schumann to his publishers before they consented to undertake such an unprofitable publication.

There is a story that Mendelssohn, to whom the First Quartet is dedicated, called on Schumann in the summer of 1842, and invited him to a walk in the sunshine. Schumann would not go; he was working on the quartets. Mendelssohn is supposed to have remarked that a walk would profit Schumann much more than a quartet. Schumann, who was sensitive about his first attempt in the new field, took offense. The dedication to Mendelssohn seems to contradict the implication of the story, but perhaps Schumann knew Mendelssohn well enough to appreciate a good-natured joke.

The A minor Quartet is unmistakably Schumannesque in its structure, in its free modulatory plan, and in its characteristic anacrustic rhythm. George Bernard Shaw, writing music criticism in London under the signature Corno di Bassetto (which is the clarinet in F), shrewdly observed that Schumann's Quartet in A minor was in reality in F major. Indeed, the F major tonality is the main key of the initial Allegro as well as that of Adagio. But the Scherzo is in A minor, and so is the concluding movement, Presto.

The Quartet ends in A major. The major ending for a work in a minor key is a development of a device known as the Third of Picardy —the use of the major third instead of a minor in the cadence. The best possible explanation of the term is that the major ending in minor modes was prevalent in the Gregorian melodies as sung in the cathedrals of Picardy, in France. The reason why composers of modern times employ this device in an enlarged form is simply that major tonality is acoustically more brilliant than minor.

M-MM-454, Roth String Quartet.

QUARTET IN A MAJOR, OP. 41, NO. 3

Andante espressivo; Allegro molto moderato · Assai agitato; Un poco adagio · Adagio molto · Finale: allegro molto vivace

THE QUARTET in A major was composed in 1842 when Schumann was thirty-two years old. From the technical point of view, and apart from

[417]

its musical merits, this Quartet is interesting, for Schumann exploits a separate musical device in each movement. In the first movement it is the "fifth," and its complementary interval, the "fourth." In the second movement the changes are rung on a rising "fourth" and this interval is also prominent in the slow movement, although the "seventh" is used dramatically there, while the salient feature of the main theme of the finale is the scale passages interrupted by the fall of a "sixth."

M-MM-319, Lener String Quartet.

QUINTET IN E-FLAT, OP. 44, FOR PIANO AND STRINGS

Allegro brillante · *Un poco largamente* · *Molto vivace* · *Allegro ma non troppo*

WITH this work, composed when he was thirty-two, Schumann invented the chamber-music combination of the piano quintet. Strange to say, the union of piano and string quartet was not realized with composers like Mozart and Beethoven, both of whom were pianists. Schumann, however, who had recently completed his three string quartets, thought it natural to add his beloved instrument, the piano, to his newly won resources in chamber-music composition.

Besides being historically important, this Quintet is also of surpassing beauty. The vigorous opening, with the piano dominant, establishes the tone for the entire work. The second movement, subtitled "In modo d'una marcia," begins with a theme suggestive of a funeral march; the gloomy atmosphere is further intensified by the second theme, melancholy in character, announced by the violin over a rich harmonic background. The Scherzo is based on the E-flat major scale—the prototype of simplicity, in spite of its colorful animation and rhythmic variety; it has two trios, the second of which was composed after the Quintet had been introduced in public. The finale is remarkable for the concluding double fugue built on the main themes of the first and last movements.

M-MM-533, Rudolf Serkin, Piano, and the Busch Quartet.

SONGS

"I can hardly tell you," Schumann wrote to Clara early in 1840, "how delightful it is to write for the voice. . . . I laughed and cried with delight. . . . I cannot tear myself away from vocal music."

Schumann seemed to have a one-track creative mind: He concentrated on one form at a time, nearly exhausted its artistic possibilities, then proceeded to the next. During the period of his stormy courtship he wrote most of the great piano works which reflect both his keen mind and progressive spirit as well as his emotional maladjustment of the time. Then, in 1840, when his marriage to Clara became a certainty, he burst out with song. In that year alone he wrote his major song cycles, and a number of other groups not especially entitled, bringing the number of songs composed in 1840 to almost 140. Approximately two years after that, his interest shifted to other forms (which, however, include his part-songs for male, female, or mixed voices). In 1850, he took up song writing again, continuing now to cultivate this form until shortly before his removal to the asylum.

Schumann excelled in the smaller forms—intimate expressions of sentiment, color, and detail. Like the piano pieces, his songs were often joined into cycles, sometimes completely integrated under specific titles, at other times only loosely connected.

It must be remembered that Schumann grew up in literary circles and almost became a poet himself. Well acquainted with the literary production of his own day, and a fervent proponent of all things Romantic, he was the first great composer to turn to song writing driven by literary impulses. He did not have Schubert's naïve sweetness and charm. But he did introduce into song composition a sophisticated, even intellectual, approach to poetry. The unity of words, melody and accompaniment was carried out by him far beyond that achieved even by Schubert. He did not merely set poems to music; he added to them a musical poetry, a work of art complete in itself.

Most of his piano accompaniments would make excellent little piano pieces. The instrumental epilogues which he attached to many of his songs are exquisite mood pictures, often built out of altogether new material. The piano seems to uncover the hidden significance of the poem.

Thus Schumann represents in some respects the acme of song composition. He stands midway between the pure music of Schubert and the word-tone picture of Hugo Wolf. He had a highly original feeling for color effects, for harmonic details, for melodic variety. Thus in *Die Nonne,* where the poem ends with a feeling of vagueness, the music concludes with an imperfect cadence.

Schumann's favorite poets were Heine and the other great Romanticists of his day (Eichendorff, Kerner, Rückert, Chamisso, Möricke, etc.). He had a decided preference for love poetry, but on occasion ventured into the field of the dramatic ballad. His best known songs include *Im Walde, Nussbaum* (with the melody treated rather sketchily over an illustrative accompaniment), *Widmung, Liebesbotschaft* (with its exuberant, soaring vocal line), *Lotosblume, Ich grolle nicht, Der Himmel hat eine Träne geweint,* and some of his exquisite morsels for children.

17297-D, Widmung, Risë Stevens, Mezzo-Soprano.

SYMPHONIC ETUDES, OP. 13, FOR PIANO

THE *Etudes en forme de variations,* as this work is officially known in the original, were written in 1834, and dedicated to an all-but-forgotten English musician, William Sterndale Bennett. It is among the most aggressive of the composer's works, and consists, as its title suggests, of a theme and twelve variations.

The theme is in characteristic Schumann style—graceful, quiet, and introspective. Several of the variations, notably the second, remind the listener of the influence Chopin had upon Schumann.

The twelfth, or Finale, is of quite heroic proportions, and from it one can understand how the group came to be known as the *Symphonic Etudes.*

The same year that Schumann gave the world the famous *Symphonic Etudes,* also saw the birth of the *New Musical Journal,* the composer's idealistic paper devoted to a more virile and genuine musical criticism. The *Journal,* as one might not suppose, had a long and useful career, and exerted considerable influence on the musical affairs of Germany. Fortunately, it appears not to have interfered seriously with Schumann's composing, for periods of his greatest musical fertility coincide with those when he was most active in literature. In compensation for his silence of tongue, he possessed a literary and critical talent equaled by few other composers. He has been said to demonstrate that criticism and composition are but two aspects of a common dedication to music.

In the *Symphonic Etudes*, Schumann represents Romanticism at its best. He is sincere, sympathetic, and intimate, but never presumptuous. "Everything that occurs in the world affects me, politics, literature, humanity," he wrote to his wife. "But for this very reason many of my compositions are so difficult to understand, because they are associated with remote interests. Often also they are significant because everything strange moves me, and I must then express it musically."

X-MX-162, Edward Kilenyi, Piano.

SYMPHONY NO. 1 IN B-FLAT MAJOR, OP. 38

Andante un poco maestoso; Allegro molto vivace · Larghetto · Molto vivace · Allegro animato e grazioso

THE SYMPHONY No. 1 in B-flat was sketched in the remarkably short space of four days. This was near the end of January, 1841, and the entire work was completed by February 20.

Schumann frequently referred to the work as the *Spring* Symphony. In a letter to his friend, E. F. Wenzel, he said: "Within the last few days I have completed, at least in outline, a labor which kept me in a state of bliss, but also exhausted me. Think of it! A whole Symphony—and moreover a *Spring* Symphony!" And in November 1842, the composer wrote to Spohr: "I composed the Symphony toward the end of the winter of 1841, under the impulse of that vernal ardor which carries away man even at the most advanced age, and seizes upon him anew every year. I did not aim to describe or portray; but I do believe that the season in which the Symphony originated has influenced its form and made it what it is."

He went into even greater detail in writing of the Symphony to Wilhelm Taubert, who was to conduct it in Berlin. His letter of January, 1843, read: "I should be pleased if you could imbue your orchestra with something of the mood of Springtime. This I had particularly in mind when I wrote the Symphony in February 1841. I should like to have the very opening trumpet call sound as if it came from on high like a summons to awakening. By what follows the introduction I might then suggest how on all sides the green leaves are sprouting, perhaps how a butterfly appears, and by the Allegro how gradually everything that belongs to Spring bursts forth. But these are fancies which occurred to me after I had completed the work. Regarding the last movement, however, I would say that I imagined it to represent the departure of Spring, and would like to have it played in a manner not too frivolous."

The true inspiration of the First Symphony, however, was revealed in October 1842, when Schumann sent a portrait of himself to the German poet Adolph Böttger. On it was inscribed the opening phrase for trumpets and horns from the B-flat Symphony, with the words: "Beginning of a symphony inspired by a poem of Adolph Böttger. To the poet, in remembrance of Robert Schumann."

The Symphony is dedicated to Friedrich August, King of Saxony. It was first heard at a concert by the Gewandhaus Orchestra in Leipzig on March 31, 1841. Felix Mendelssohn conducted, and Clara Schumann performed several piano solos on the same program.

Musicians have long decried Schumann's lack of skill in orchestration, and practically every conductor makes alterations in the scoring of certain passages when he performs the symphonies. Yet there is no one today who will deny that the Symphony in B-flat abounds in melodic freshness and inspiration. Like so many great creations, this work has outlived its detractors by many, many years.

M-MM-617, Cleveland Orchestra, Erich Leinsdorf Conducting.

SYMPHONY NO. 2 IN C MAJOR, OP. 61

Sostenuto assai; Allegro ma non troppo · *Scherzo: allegro vivace*
Adagio espressivo · *Allegro molto vivace*

SCHUMANN's Second Symphony was first performed under Mendelssohn's direction at the Leipzig Gewandhaus in November 1846. The

[422]

carefully prepared performance was highly gratifying to the composer, and the work was taken up by other conductors and equally well received. To one of these—Otten, at Hamburg—Schumann wrote:

"I composed the Symphony in December 1845, while I was still half sick. It seems to me that one must hear this in the music. In the Finale I first began to feel myself, and indeed I was much better after I had finished the work. Yet, as I have said, it recalls to me a dark period in my life. That such tones of pain, in spite of all, can awaken interest, shows me your sympathetic attitude. Everything you say about the work also shows me how thoroughly you understand music; and that my melancholy bassoon in the Adagio, which I introduced in that spot with especial fondness, has not escaped your notice, gives me especial pleasure."

Schumann was first of all a pianist, and his understanding and development of the possibilities of the piano amounted to genius. But in his devotion to this instrument he neglected other branches of music, and his symphonic scoring is often criticized. In the Second Symphony, for instance, he used violins in the gay Scherzo and carried them so far into the trio that his good friend Mendelssohn hinted that woodwinds at this point might be an effective relief.

This Symphony, though called the Second, was actually the third. The second symphony in order of composition was withdrawn after its performance and was not published until several years later, and is now known as the Fourth Symphony.

M-MM-503, Minneapolis Symphony Orchestra, Dimitri Mitropoulos Conducting.

SYMPHONY NO. 3 (RHENISH) IN E-FLAT MAJOR, OP. 97

Allegro · *Scherzo* · *Andante* · *Lento* · *Allegro finale*

THE *Rhenish* Symphony was one of Schumann's later works. It was written in little more than a month, toward the end of 1850, soon after Schumann had gone from Dresden to become Music Director at Düsseldorf. A little while before, Robert and Clara Schumann had gone on a pleasure trip to Cologne, and they were deeply impressed not only by the physical surroundings of the city on the Rhine, but also by its magnificent Gothic cathedral. The composer was especially moved by the ceremonial pomp attendant upon the installation of the Archbishop of Cologne as Cardinal, a ceremony duly immortalized in the fourth movement of the Symphony.

The Rhine had strong associations for Schumann. And although he was born at Zwickau, far to the east, he was as warm a worshiper of the German river as any of his compatriots. Two of his songs, *Sonntags am Rhein* ("Sunday on the Rhine") and *Im Rhein, im heiligen Strome* ("In the Rhine, Holy Stream"), bear witness to this reverence. It is perhaps not mere coincidence, but rather a symptom of the period, that the German patriotic song *Die Wacht am Rhein*, by Carl Wilhelm, was composed less than four years after the *Rhenish* Symphony.

Associations between scene and music, so characteristic among Romantic composers, are frequently to be observed as the *Rhenish* Symphony runs its course, even though the associations may be general rather than specific. Schumann himself used to say that, aside from the fourth movement, the music was intended to have a popular or national character.

The *Rhenish* Symphony was Schumann's last essay in that form. The D minor Symphony, usually called the Fourth because it was the last to be published, was originally projected and performed as the Second, almost ten years earlier. The *Rhenish* was, like its fellows, symphony principally in name. The ideas and their presentation have not the tautness and compression nor, at the other extreme, the expansiveness previously characteristic of most symphonic writing. But rules and textbooks do not produce the charm that is in the *Rhenish* Symphony, nor guarantee music which animates the spirit and conjures the essence of a distant time and scene.

M-MM-464, Philharmonic-Symphony Orchestra of New York, Bruno Walter Conducting.

SYMPHONY NO. 4 IN D MINOR, OP. 120

Introduction · Allegro · Romanze · Scherzo · Finale in einem Satze

SCHUMANN's symphonies were essentially suites of musical pictures, symphonically blended. It is a commonplace of musical criticism that Schumann's greatness lies in his songs and piano compositions, and not in his orchestral works. Schumann's orchestra is conventional; there are few contrasts between instrumental groups; the woodwind quartet is rarely if ever used independently; the brass merely underlines the rhythmical passages; instrumental solos are rare and doublings are prevalent—as if Schumann had deemed it imprudent to leave the flute unsupported by the violins, the oboe and clarinet by the violins or violas, the bassoon by the 'cellos. The pages of a Schumann orchestral score are uniformly filled with notes, suggesting secure sonority but little color.

The completeness of Schumann's orchestra and the ensuing monotony of instrumental color cannot be ascribed to Schumann's inexpertness. The example of the Symphony in D shows that this type of orchestration was Schumann's chosen technique. The Symphony was originally orchestrated in a much more transparent fashion, and was performed on December 6, 1841, as the Second Symphony. Then it was laid aside for ten years.

In the meantime, Schumann wrote two more symphonies, which went as Symphony No. 2 and No. 3. In 1851, he reorchestrated the Symphony in D, renamed it Fourth Symphony, and conducted the definitive version in Düsseldorf on March 3, 1853. Its full title emphasizes the continuity of movements without pause.

The continuity of development in Schumann's Symphony in D is indicated by the use of principal themes in different sections. Thus, the nostalgic theme of the Introduction reappears as the alternate subject in Romanze, and the lively subject of the first Allegro is used in the prelude to the Finale. In place of formal treatment of thematic material by the process of forming new melodic and rhythmic variants, the themes follow one another in free association, and do not change in shape when they reappear.

M-MM-475, Chicago Symphony Orchestra, Frederick Stock Conducting.

Dmitri Shostakovitch

1906–

No composer in modern times has created such a stir throughout the musical world as has the young Soviet artist Dmitri
Shostakovitch. Usually a creative musician must conduct a
never-ending search for someone to give his works a public hearing
But such has not been the case with Shostakovitch. Instead, conductors vie with one another for the privilege of giving his new compositions their initial performance. This eagerness has been carried to
such an extent that in 1942 the score for his Seventh Symphony was
photographed on microfilm and specially flown from Russia to America for its Western Hemisphere première, while two years later a
correspondent of the Columbia Broadcasting System was entrusted
with the task of bringing the score for the Eighth Symphony from
Moscow to New York for the same purpose.

Shostakovitch was born in Leningrad on September 25, 1906. Both
of his parents were musical, and it was from his mother that the boy
received his first music lessons at the age of nine. The Revolution
of 1917 brought financial difficulties to the family, and young Shostakovitch, then a student at the Leningrad Conservatory, was obliged
to aid his family by playing piano in the local motion picture theatres

World-wide recognition first came to the composer when his First
Symphony, written as his graduation piece at the Conservatory, was
performed by the Leningrad Philharmonic in 1926. From then on his
rise to fame was rapid. He was appointed as an instructor at the
Conservatory, and continued to compose prolifically. Most of his
compositions during the next ten years were either satirical, political
or both. His Second Symphony, dedicated to the October Revolution
appeared in 1927; the Third—or *May Day*—Symphony came three
years later.

Shostakovitch has twice invaded the field of opera, with *The Nose* and *Lady Macbeth of Mzensk,* the latter creating quite a controversial stir when it was performed in this country. There were also a Concerto for Piano and Orchestra and three ballets: *The Golden Age, The Bolt,* and *The Limpid Stream.* For the piano Shostakovitch composed a Sonata and a set of twenty-four Preludes.

In 1936, the composer went through a serious artistic crisis. The newspaper *Pravda* came out with two articles condemning his music —particularly *Lady Macbeth of Mzensk* and *The Limpid Stream*— as being expressive of "petty-bourgeois sensationalism" and full of "formalist confusion." These articles unloosed a wave of anti-Shostakovitch criticism throughout Russia. The composer immediately withdrew his Fourth Symphony after but one very unsatisfactory rehearsal. His days as a writer of satirical music were over, and he set out to find a more mature medium for expression.

His return to grace came with the triumphal appearance of his Fifth Symphony in 1937, followed two years later by the Sixth. Once again, he was a leading figure in Soviet music.

The coming of the war to his homeland did not interrupt the flow of compositions from Shostakovitch's pen. Instead, he merely added to his duties that of fire-fighter in Leningrad, and produced the war-inspired Seventh and Eighth Symphonies, musical reflections of the fateful days of 1941 and 1942.

But Shostakovitch has not limited himself to writing symphonies. Notable among the many exceptions are the String Quartet, Op. 49, the Quintet for Piano and Strings, Op. 57, an orchestration of Mussorgsky's opera *Boris Godounov,* and the now popular *Song of the United Nations.* In addition, he has composed a considerable amount of music for the films. Foremost among the aforementioned works is the Quintet, which created a sensation when it was first performed in Moscow in 1940.

CONCERTO, OP. 35, FOR PIANO
AND ORCHESTRA

Allegro moderato; Allegro vivace · Lento · Moderato · Allegro
brio: presto

THIS Concerto, composed in the early thirties, was first performed
in the United States at a Youth Concert conducted by Leopold Sto
kowski in Philadelphia on December 12, 1934. The soloist was the
young American pianist Eugene List. A year later New York heard
the Concerto at a concert of the Philharmonic-Symphony Orchestra
Its popularity has increased steadily since—a development which is
likely to continue, for it has all the qualities that contribute to the
growing esteem in which Shostakovitch's music is held by the public
Though Shostakovitch has had the benefit in this country of a
good deal of publicity unrelated to musical considerations, no important part of the success of his larger works—the symphonies, the
Piano Concerto, the opera *Lady Macbeth of Mzensk,* the Quintet
and Quartet—is to be attributed to this circumstance. However exaggerated one may feel some estimates of his talents and abilities to
be, it is impossible not to recognize in him a truly musical personality,
and this is particularly in evidence in this Concerto.

The Concerto for Piano, with an orchestra of strings and trumpet,
is in four movements, of which the first and second, and the third
and fourth, are connected. No key is designated, but C minor prevails
in the first movement and the finale.

M-MM-527, Eileen Joyce, Piano, Arthur Lockwood, Trumpet, and the Hallé Orchestra, Leslie Heward Conducting.

SYMPHONY NO. 1 IN F MAJOR, OP. 10

Allegretto; Allegro non troppo · Allegro · Lento; Largo
Allegro molto

IT IS a curious fortune of many composers that their first works remain the most popular in the general repertoire. Mendelssohn wrote
the Overture to *A Midsummer Night's Dream* at the age of seventeen. Rachmaninoff composed the celebrated C-sharp minor Prelude

[428]

hen he was nineteen, and Gretchaninoff wrote his well-known *ullaby* when he was a Conservatory student. Neither Rachmaninoff or Gretchaninoff had the foresight to copyright these early compositions, with the resultant loss of earnings.

Dmitri Shostakovitch composed his First Symphony as a graduaion piece at the Leningrad Conservatory. He was nineteen years of ge. The Symphony was performed by the Leningrad Philharmonic n May 12, 1926, but failed to produce an immediate sensation comarable to that made by the First Symphony of Glazunov forty-four ears before. This first symphonic work by the sixteen-year-old Glaunov was hailed as a token of continuity of the great Russian Iational School, and Glazunov was adopted by Rimsky-Korsakov, Balakirev, and Borodin as the sixth member of the Mighty Five. Now Glazunov was Director of the Conservatory at which Shostaovitch produced a Symphony, alien to the spirit of magnificent conervation symbolized by the St. Petersburg tradition.

The First Symphony remains more popular than any of Shostaovitch's later symphonies. Why? Perhaps because in these later vorks Shostakovitch was made self-conscious by the necessity of earching for a style. In the First Symphony Shostakovitch found that tyle instinctively. Here are all the characteristic vignettes of his hythmic and melodic inspirations, the typical dash-dot-dot rhythms, vhich Shostakovitch has so skillfully employed in so many of his quick movements in polka time, and the equally typical diatonic unes in slow waltz time. Here is the characteristic rhythmic abanlon, and the quasi-vulgarity of brilliant endings, shocking and irreistible at the same time.

In orchestration of his symphonies Shostakovitch adheres to the nethods of Tchaikovsky rather than those of the National Russian School. The composition of the orchestra is conservative, and no newangled instruments are included in his symphonic scores, the only exception being the introduction of the factory whistle in one place n his Second Symphony.

The First Symphony is in four movements. The first movement opens with a short phrase for the trumpet in a dialogue with the bassoon. The second important theme is given out by the clarinet. It is of a light dancing character. A contrasting lyric subject appears in the flute, against the waltz-time accompaniment of the pizzicato strings. These three themes are thoroughly developed, but in the recapitulation their order of appearance is reversed: the flute theme appears first, the clarinet theme second. The original trumpet theme is given again to the clarinet, and it serves as a coda. This change of order of appearance in the recapitulation remains a typical device of Shostakovitch's use of sonata form in his later works as well.

The main subject of the second movement features the character istic dash-dot-dot rhythm, in a quick movement. The clarinet introduces it in a distorted atonal form, before the violins take it up in clear A minor. It appears then in the piano part, and in the bassoon. The middle section of the movement is in a slow waltz movement with the wind instruments playing a theme whose modal character is not obstructed by slight chromaticism. As in the first movement of this Symphony, and as in many other waltz-time passages of many other works of Shostakovitch, the woodwinds are accompanied by tremolos and pizzicatos of the strings. The dash-dot-dot theme returns, but the brilliant conclusion of the movement is followed by curiously unnecessary chords in the piano part, after which there is a coda in pianissimo.

The third movement is a Lento. The opening theme of the oboe is, in its rhythmic construction and the direction of the intervals, a clearly recognizable version of the clarinet theme of the first movement, played four times as slowly. It is characteristically projected against the background of tremolo strings. There is a marching theme introduced for contrast. The movement fades out in pianissimo.

The last movement opens with a slow introduction, after which a fast propulsive rhythmic figure sets the pace. The pattern is chromatic, and even ultra-chromatic, for here Shostakovitch introduces the glissando effect in the strings. This device, too, has remained a favorite arrow in Shostakovitch's musical archery. A lyrical passage in the strings repeats the slow version of the original clarinet theme of the first movement. From then on, it is all a galloping dash. But before the end there is a short interlude with sinister beats in the kettledrums. The movement is resumed at an accelerated galloping pace, and ends explosively on the tonic of F, the key of the Symphony.

M-MM-472, Cleveland Orchestra, Artur Rodzinski Conducting.

SYMPHONY NO. 5, OP. 47

Moderato; Allegro non troppo · *Allegretto* · *Largo* · *Allegro non troppo*

IN 1936, the arbiters of Soviet opinion reached the conclusion that the music of Dmitri Shostakovitch was politically heterodox. This was a sudden and surprising reversal of their previous views and must have occasioned Shostakovitch much bewilderment. The leading Soviet composer of his generation, accustomed for ten years to the honors due a hero of the arts, he awoke one morning to find that his music had been condemned as "bourgeois," "counter-revolutionary," by molders of opinion—the editors of *Pravda* and *Izvestia* —who had repeatedly hailed him as the composer laureate of the Soviet State.

Performances of many of his works abruptly ceased and Shostakovitch, understandably alarmed by the turn of events, himself hastily withdrew still others from circulation. The manuscript of the Fourth Symphony was at the time in the hands of the Leningrad Philharmonic, which had announced its forthcoming première. But Shostakovitch reclaimed it and to this day it remains unplayed, unheard.

There followed a period of retirement and stock-taking for the composer. One can only guess what must have been his state of mind. He had already publicly espoused orthodoxy in his political and artistic views, saying in 1931, "I am a Soviet composer, and I see our epoch as something heroic, spirited and joyous. Music cannot help having a political basis—an idea that the bourgeoisie are slow to comprehend. There can be no music without ideology. The old composers were bolstering the rule of the upper classes. We, as revolutionists, have a different conception. . . .

"Good music lifts and heartens and lightens people for work and effort. It may be tragic, but it must be strong. It is no longer an end in itself, but a vital weapon in the struggle." Having paid his tribute to the chauvinism of class in these terms, Shostakovitch must have asked himself what more he could say—what, if anything, he could possibly do to rehabilitate himself in the eyes of the authorities.

What he did eventually was to write the Fifth Symphony. For reasons which we shall probably never know, this had the desired

[431]

effect. Performed in connection with the celebration of the twentieth anniversary of the Soviet State, it was received with enthusiasm by the press and public alike. There was nothing in the Fifth Symphony to indicate an artistic *volte face* on Shostakovitch's part; it marked a further stage in his development as a composer, but a further stage predictable on the basis of his earlier works. There was in it more emphasis on form, on the extended and serious-minded development of the basic musical ideas, and less emphasis on effects created by merely harmonic or instrumental means. But this was in line with tendencies already clearly marked in the succession of Shostakovitch's works, and to sympathetic bourgeois, or capitalist, ears, it was evidence merely of an expected advance toward artistic maturity.

In the Soviet press another view was expressed. A reviewer for the *Moscow Daily News* wrote: "The fetters of musical formalism which held Shostakovitch captive for so long, preventing him from creating works profound in conception, have been torn off. He must follow up this new trend in his work. He must turn more boldly toward Soviet reality. He must understand it more profoundly and find in it a new stimulus for his work."

In his Fifth Symphony, Shostakovitch has struck a note of courage, belief in life, has sung a noble song of man's faith in himself and the universe of which he is a part.

M-MM-520, Cleveland Orchestra, Artur Rodzinski Conducting.

SYMPHONY NO. 9, OP. 70

Allegro · Moderato · Presto · Largo · Allegretto

WITH his Ninth Symphony, Dmitri Shostakovitch brings to a close the most ambitious and certainly the most dramatically publicized artistic trilogy of the Second World War. The Seventh Symphony, the commencement of this huge musical saga, belongs to the last months of 1941 when Shostakovitch's native Leningrad was being brutally besieged by the Nazis and the composer was combining his duties as artist with those of a patriotic firefighter. It was inspired, he said, by the heroism and intrepidity of a people under siege. In the succeeding Eighth Symphony, completed by November, 1943,

[432]

while Russian armies were driving the invaders back, the young Russian musician sought to express musically "the new optimism found by a long-suffering people" and to record "the spirit of the new Red Army as it takes the offensive after discouraging retreat." A little later he hinted at a Ninth Symphony which would "create a musical interpretation of our triumph over barbarism and express the greatness of our people." He began it shortly after V-E Day and finished it six weeks later—just as the world was celebrating the end of the war in the East.

The first to hear the music was a group of four newspaper correspondents and critics for whom Shostakovitch played the score on his piano. "Looking pale and tired but nervously alive, Shostakovitch came into the house . . . hardly said hello, rushed to the piano, paused as if remembering that etiquette demanded that he be asked to play, and when he was asked, started without any preliminary explanations," wrote Robert Magidoff, the New York *Times* correspondent who was one of the guests. The performance finished, Shostakovitch arose, rubbed his hands together gleefully, and said, "It is a merry little piece. Musicians will love to play it and critics will delight in blasting it."

In view of the fabulous length of the Seventh and Eighth Symphonies (each takes more than one hour to play) and their many intensely tragic pages, the Ninth Symphony took listeners by surprise. "It is," said Mr. Magidoff, "the simplest piece the mature Shostakovitch has ever written, also the gayest, most youthful, and most melodious." Thoughts of Haydn and other Eighteenth Century classicists immediately came to mind, and it was learned that Shostakovitch and his fellow-composer, Kabalevsky, had spent many an evening playing four-hand arrangements of Haydn and Mozart and early Beethoven symphonies during the time the Ninth Symphony was being written. After its first orchestral performance on November 3, 1945, by the Leningrad Philharmonic Orchestra, the critic Gregori Schneerson found that the work "transported us at once to a bright and pleasant world" and he felt in its spirited rhythms "joyous abandon, the warm pulsation of life and the exuberance of youth."

M-MM-668, Philharmonic-Symphony Orchestra of New York, Efrem Kurtz Conducting.

Jean Sibelius

1865–

JEAN SIBELIUS is the last of the great symphonists. In an age that saw the upheaval of musical traditions, and the birth of many new styles, forms, and schools, Sibelius remained true to the symphonic form and to the idiom of his great symphonic predecessors. He has proved again that a creator of power and passion need not shatter existing rules to be original; that he can be original if he succeeds in transferring to his music his own identity and, by the same token, the identity of his people.

If Sibelius is a national hero in Finland it is not only because he is its greatest composer, but more especially because he has brought so much of his native land into his music. Sibelius's music is as much a part of the soul of Finland as is the *Kalevala*. The windswept melodies, the often bleak atmospheres, the cold harmonies, the restrained force give us a tonal picture of Finland's forest and lakes and people; and the melodies, though never borrowed from folklore sources, are so national in spirit and construction that some of them are frequently mistaken for authentic folk songs.

Sibelius was born in Tavastehus, Finland, in 1865. His early music study took place in Helsingfors with Martin Wegelius and Ferruccio Busoni. During travels in Germany and Austria he brought his studies to a close with Robert Fuchs and Karl Goldmark.

An intense national flame burned hot within him, and it at once ignited his inspiration. After returning to his land, he began composing works which were strongly national, imbued with patriotism, drenched with the backgrounds and lore of his country. These works included several which have since become highly successful, notably *Finlandia* and *En Saga*.

In 1897, an annual government grant made it possible for Sibelius to give up his teaching chores and to devote himself entirely to comosition. His time was now divided between composition and extensive travels: on one of his travels, in 1914, Sibelius visited the United States, and conducted several of his works at the Norfolk Festival of Music.

By the time World War I broke out, Sibelius was an international figure in music, having produced most of his famous shorter works, as well as five symphonies and a violin concerto. After World War I, there was a diminution in the rate of his production, though not in his powers, as his extraordinary Seventh Symphony proved. He suffered greatly in the period of storm and stress that followed World War I, and again in 1940 when his country was involved in war with the Soviet Union. During the period of World War II, he was frequently in great want.

His eightieth birthday, in 1945, was the occasion for worldwide celebrations in which his imperial position in the music of our times was once again emphasized.

FINLANDIA

T HAS frequently been said that Sibelius's *Finlandia* is more representative of Finland to the outside world than its national anthem. So genuinely is it a testament of Finland that its moving melody for reeds is often considered (and erroneously) to be a genuine Finnish folk song.

Sibelius composed it in 1899, during a period of storm and stress in his country's history, when it was suffering severe repressions at the hands of Imperial Russia. It is not difficult to read in this proud and majestic music the determination of a people to be free. Indeed, others too read this message in it: for a long time *Finlandia* suffered censorship by the Russian authorities. Not until 1905 was it allowed to be performed in Finland, and from that time on it became a musical symbol of the aspirations of the Finnish people, and their faith in the ultimate victory of their ideals.

11178-D, Cleveland Orchestra, Artur Rodzinski Conducting.

THE SWAN OF TUONELA

OF THE four sections of Sibelius's orchestral suite, *Lemminkainen* Op. 22 (inspired by the *Kalevala*), the most celebrated is the third— *The Swan of Tuonela*. The composer explains in his score: "Tuonela the Kingdom of Death . . . is surrounded by a broad river of blac water and rapid currents, in which the Swan of Tuonela glides in majestic fashion and sings."

This tone picture is one of the most exquisite pages of music com posed by Sibelius, in which the principal melody—a theme for Eng lish horn—beautifully describes the swan. The music rises to a clima after which the final strains of the swan's song are heard.

11388-D, Chicago Symphony Orchestra, Frederick Stock Conducting.

SYMPHONY NO. 1 IN E MINOR, OP. 39

Andante ma non troppo; Allegro energico · Andante ma non tropp lento · Allegro · Finale quasi una fantasia; Andante; Allegro molt

SIBELIUS composed his First Symphony in 1899. When he wrote i Sibelius was already a famous man. He had *En Saga,* the *Karelia Suite,* the orchestral *Legends* of Op. 22 (including the celebrate *Swan of Tuonela*), and *Finlandia* to his credit, and the Finnish Parlia ment had conferred on him an annual pension in recognition of hi talent and his contributions to Finnish national culture.

It is customary now to divide Sibelius's life into "periods" and t find in the works of each period certain distinguishing character istics. However, Sibelius's work from first to last is very much of piece, and its essential Sibelius features are always present. The chie difference between the early and the late Sibelius works is to b found in the increasing domination, in the latter, of certain manner isms of speech which intrude only occasionally in the former.

Sibelius has admired both Grieg and Tchaikovsky. The fact is de tectable in the First Symphony, where melodies of Tchaikovskia profile are to be found, and climaxes wrought with the aid of Tcha kovskian formulas. Nevertheless, the work is authentically an origina expression—and a masterpiece.

[436]

Those works of Sibelius which will longest endure may not be the mannered, tangential works which most impress some critics, but the tone poems *En Saga* and *The Swan of Tuonela,* the First and Second symphonies, and the Violin Concerto—works in which Sibelius is at once himself and a link in the chain of Western music.

M-MM-532, Philharmonic-Symphony Orchestra of New York, John Barbirolli Conducting.

SYMPHONY NO. 2 IN D MAJOR, OP. 43

Allegretto · Andante, ma rubato · Vivacissimo · Finale: allegro moderato

JEAN SIBELIUS was the first great name produced by Finnish music, and critics proceeded to apply such expressions as bleak, dark, solitary, Nordic, and even arctic to Sibelius's music, although the composer lived no nearer to the arctic circle than Rimsky-Korsakov, Glazunov, and other Russians of the St. Petersburg group. Music critics of the "geographic school" proceed on the assumption that every great musical personality necessarily reflects the characteristics of the country of origin. Then, by process of easy substitution, adjectives descriptive of the country's climate are applied to the music produced by its nationals. This method is particularly effective in the case of countries musically young, possessing a climate and a way of life different from those of middle Europe.

The symphonies of Sibelius, seven in number, were all composed between 1899 and 1925, with intervals of one to nine years between each two. The First Symphony is in the orthodox Romantic tradition. But beginning with the Second Symphony Sibelius evolves his own style, characterized by extraordinary freedom from symphonic tradition. It is known that the strongest influence Sibelius felt in his music was Beethoven—specifically the Beethoven of the last quartets. And Sibelius begins where Beethoven left off.

In the Second Symphony of Sibelius, and in his later symphonies, the element of form is as little binding as in the "third style" of Beethoven. But this freedom also means the freedom of being conventional, and both Sibelius and Beethoven are apt to include a

[437]

movement, or a section, based on a simple dancelike tune, treated in conventional manner. Then again, there are queer breaks, strange "general pauses," fragments of themes scattered among orchestral instruments, and musical chasms, when all movement stops. Perhaps the definition "bleakness and solitary grandeur" is permissible in application to such moods.

The Second Symphony was composed in 1901–02, and Sibelius conducted its first performance in Helsingfors on March 8, 1902. The first movement, Allegretto, derives its power from an iterated figure, slowly rising from the third to the fifth tone of the scale, harmonized by full chords. The whole movement is based on this powerful respiration, at times falling to a repeated drumbeat, at times rising to great intensity.

In the second movement, Andante ma rubato, a characteristically modal melody is projected on the rhythmic background, prepared by the movement in triplets. This melody suggests a folk song, but it is not allowed to develop. In place of development, there is accumulation of energy, repetition in various registers, and interplay of orchestral groups. The movement slackens; there is an Andante sostenuto, conceived as a chorale—solemn and sonorous.

The third movement, Vivacissimo, offers an interlude in lyric vein; then there is a characteristic interruption of motion, so that the music seems to stand still. A new mood is expressed in the section marked Lento e suave. The quick movement is resumed for a brief space, and the Lento reappears, leading to a slow but sonorous transition. There is no break between this movement and the Finale, marked Allegro moderato.

This Finale is in the stately sarabande time of 3-2, with majestic unisons, Beethovenlike. The themes are characteristically short, with a falling cadence separating the musical sentences. The movement grows heavier, but picks up quickly, leading to the final section of the Symphony. The conclusion is based on an obvious but effective formula of building up a theme of three ascending notes, first in slow time, then twice as fast, and finally four times as fast. The original tempo returns, and the lyric episode is repeated, as a final preparation for a slow but powerful and grandiloquent ending.

M-MM-423, Philharmonic-Symphony Orchestra of New York, John Barbirolli Conducting.

SYMPHONY NO. 4 IN A MINOR, OP. 63

Tempo molto moderato quasi adagio · Allegro molto · Il tempo largo
Allegro

SIBELIUS completed his Fourth Symphony in 1911, and it was first performed at Helsingfors on April 3 of that year. The score calls for an orchestra consisting of two flutes, two oboes, two clarinets, two bassoons, four horns, two trumpets, three trombones, kettledrums, bells, and the usual strings. This is a remarkably conservative and compact orchestra for a work by a composer of today, but the very nature of the music would not allow for an expansive instrumentation.

The first movement is almost depressing in its gloomy aspect. This mood is only partially dispelled by the brief scherzo, which never dares become really light-hearted. The ending of this movement is sudden and strange. Il tempo largo is the indication for the third movement, which is broad and sonorous, and is the most conventional of the four parts of the Symphony. The finale starts in an almost casual manner, but grows in dramatic intensity as it progresses. Included are several marchlike sections, the thematic content of which resembles a chant.

M-MM-665, Philharmonic-Symphony Orchestra of New York, Artur Rodzinski Conducting.

SYMPHONY NO. 5 IN E-FLAT, OP. 82

Tempo molto moderato; Allegro moderato, ma poco a poco stretto
Andante mosso quasi allegretto · Allegro molto

WHEN in August 1914, Austria declared war on Russia, Finland was reluctantly involved, for Finland then was part of Russia. As an artist and a humanist, Sibelius was profoundly shocked by this latest evidence of man's irremediable folly. As a Finn he felt keenly the tragic irony of his country's position. Horror and bitterness for a time made work impossible for him. But he had great powers of spiritual recuperation which presently he exerted.

An entry in Sibelius's diary, dated September 14, reads: "In a deep valley again. But dimly I begin to see the mountain which certainly I shall scale. For a moment God opens His door and His orchestra plays the Fifth Symphony." So, in an evil time, was born the noblest, most confident of his works.

The E-flat Symphony was performed for the first time in Helsingfors on December 8, 1915. The occasion was a special concert honoring the composer on his fiftieth birthday. Sibelius was not satisfied with the work and made certain changes in it. The new version was brought out under his direction the following year. Further revisions followed.

Sibelius's diary contains the following entry in May 1918: "The Fifth Symphony in a new form, practically composed anew. I work every day. Movement 1 is entirely new; Movement 2 reminiscent of the old one; movement 3 reminiscent of the end of the old first movement. Movement 4, the old subjects, but made stronger by revision. The whole, if I may say so, a vital climax to the end. Triumphal." The third version was played in Helsingfors on November 24, 1919. At last Sibelius was satisfied with his work and allowed it to be printed.

Much ingenuity has been shown in the invention of programs for Sibelius symphonies, including the Fifth, but none of these programs has received the approval of the composer. It may be assumed that when Sibelius composes to a program, he acknowledges the fact in the title of his piece—*Pohjola's Daughter, The Swan of Tuonela, Nightride and Sunrise;* that the symphonies are definitely not program pieces, but abstractions—communications of experience in purely musical terms.

In the dark hours of the first World War, Sibelius experienced despair; then a revival of faith in life. He thought and felt his way through a crisis, and the Fifth Symphony is the record of that thinking and feeling. Thus, the clue to the meaning of this music is to be sought not in a picture, a poem, a legend, but in the experience of the listener himself. Every man at some time has asked himself the questions this music answers.

The Symphony is in four movements, but the first and second are telescoped, and the work as a whole is set forth in three parts.

M-MM-514, Cleveland Orchestra, Artur Rodzinski Conducting.

SYMPHONY NO. 7, OP. 105

SIBELIUS published his Symphony No. 7 in 1925. In the same year, at the request of Walter Damrosch, he composed the symphonic poem *Tapiola* for the Symphony Society of New York. Very little has been heard from him since, his further output consisting almost entirely of some small choral works and a few short pieces for violin and piano and for piano solo.

There have been rumors of an eighth symphony from Sibelius and of other large-scale works, but they have remained rumors. It would be interesting to hear an explanation of these curious facts from Sibelius himself. Such an explanation might have a merely personal significance; as possibly, it might shed light on the mysterious and tragic decline of creative power that in the past quarter of a century has affected virtually all living composers, the younger generation of today excepted.

In the case of Sibelius there has been no decline of creative power. He has simply ceased to exert the power that was and very possibly still is his. The Symphony No. 7 and *Tapiola* are among his most original, most powerful, and most successful works; they represent him in the full possession and exercise of his very great gifts. Here, there is no reliance on formulas devised in earlier works. On the contrary, in both symphony and tone poem the artist poses new problems of construction and expression and finds for them magnificent solutions.

The one-movement form of the Symphony No. 7 is unique; so, too, is its sustained elevation and intensity of thought and feeling. It is the creation of a man to whom a vision of truth has been vouchsafed; the serenity in which all passionate experience is finally comprehended is nowhere in music more eloquently epitomized.

M-MM-524, Philharmonic-Symphony Orchestra of New York, Sir Thomas Beecham Conducting.

VALSE TRISTE

THE FANTASTIC but beautiful *Valse triste* is from the incidental music that Sibelius composed for Arvid Järnefelt's drama *Kuolema*—(Death). The music is explained in the following words:

It is night. A son, who has been watching beside the bed of his sick mother, has fallen asleep from sheer weariness. Gradually a light is diffused through the room; there is a sound of distant music; the glow and the music come nearer until the melody of a waltz is distantly heard. The sleeping mother wakes, rises from her bed and, in her long white garment, which takes the semblance of a ball gown, begins to move silently and slowly to and fro. She waves her hands and beckons in time to the music, as though summoning a crowd of invisible guests.

Now they appear, these strange visionary couples, turning and gliding to an unearthly waltz rhythm. The dying woman mingles with the dancers; she tries to make them look into her eyes, but the shadowy guests avoid her glance. She sinks exhausted on her bed and the music breaks off.

Presently she gathers all her strength and invokes the dance once more, with more energy than before. The shadowy dancers return, gyrating in a wild, mad rhythm. The weird gaiety reaches a climax; there is a knock at the door, which flies open; the mother utters a despairing cry; the spectral guests vanish; the music dies away. Death stands on the threshold.

X-MX-240, Columbia Broadcasting Symphony, Howard Barlow Conducting.

Elie Siegmeister

1909–

Few living American composers have done as much to publicize and popularize the folk music of this country as has Elie Siegmeister. Born in Brooklyn on January 15, 1909, he attended Columbia University, where he earned his Phi Beta Kappa key, then went on to study composition with Wallingford Riegger. Later, he won a three-year fellowship at the Juilliard Graduate School, where he studied conducting with the late Albert Stoessel. Further study with Nadia Boulanger in Paris followed, after which he journeyed through France, Italy, and Russia.

Returning to America, Siegmeister founded and conducted the American Ballad Singers, and has toured all over the country with this group, collecting and performing American folk ballads, old and new. Since 1933, he has composed and had published numerous major compositions ranging from a children's musical production to large symphonic works. In addition, he has found time to write several books on music, notable among which are *A Treasury of American Song* (edited in collaboration with Olin Downes), and *The Music Lover's Handbook*.

WHEN asked whether he spent much time in the Ozarks gathering material for the *Ozark Set,* the composer replied: "I wrote it very much like Debussy wrote *Iberia*—without journeying to the country which inspired the music. True, I have passed through the Ozarks on several occasions, but have never made any prolonged stops. Then, too, I have heard many singers and fiddlers from the territory and have presented a number of Ozark songs with the American Ballad Singers.

"As a matter of fact, the music was composed a long way from the Ozarks. It was written in Brooklyn, in July 1943. I received a call from the Theatre Guild who wanted some music for a play about the Ozarks which they planned to produce. They asked me if I had any examples of Ozark music to show them, but I had none. Consequently, I went home and in four days sketched out a piano version of what turned out later to be the *Ozark Set.* By this time, I was pretty enthusiastic about the whole thing. My enthusiasm was short-lived, however, for when I phoned the Guild I found that the entire project had been dropped.

"The story did have a happy ending, though. About a year later I received another call from the Guild, requesting that I play them some of my music, and it was on the strength of the *Ozark Set* that I was asked to compose and conduct the music for their hit production, *Sing Out, Sweet Land."*

The word "set" in the title of the present composition is the American equivalent of the more frequently used French word "suite." For example, a group of American square dances is usually referred to as a "square set."

The *Ozark Set* depicts musically the life of the Ozark Mountain people of Missouri and Arkansas. While the music employs certain characteristic Ozark rhythms and thematic phrases, all of the melodies are original. "I have tried to write music," says Siegmeister, "as clear and familiar to the average American as a story by Mark Twain."

The composition is divided into four sections, which are described in the printed score as follows:

"I. *Morning in the Hills:* A quiet back-country landscape; the stillness of dawn; the gradually awakening sounds of early morning; the full warmth of daylight as the people start their daily rounds.

"II. *Camp Meeting:* The lively sounds of a camp meeting in full progress: the enthusiasm, the wild exuberance of a great crowd roaring, stamping, singing, shouting. Snatches of joyful camp meeting tunes are mingled with the laughter, cries, hallelujahs.

"III. *Lazy Afternoon:* The feeling of lonely valleys, open fields and prairies and of men working slowly, taking time off to enjoy the warm sun, the sweet smells and quietness of a summer day.

"IV. *Saturday Night:* When Saturday Night rolls around there is the inevitable Square Dance. The fiddlers scrape out a lively breakdown, the caller shouts, and the boys swing their girls. This is the night to 'blow the lid off.'"

The *Ozark Set* was first performed by Dimitri Mitropoulos and the Minneapolis Symphony Orchestra in Minneapolis on November 11, 1944. The work was presented as part of an all-American program by the State Symphony Orchestra of the USSR, conducted by Nikolai Antonosov, in Moscow on July 3, 1945.

X-MX-262, Minneapolis Symphony Orchestra, Dimitri Mitropoulos Conducting.

Bedřich Smetana

1824–1884

THAT wars and revolutions sometimes have their good points as well as their evil is eloquently proven by the effect which the European revolutionary wave of 1848 had on the future of a then obscure young music teacher in Prague, Bohemia—by name, Bedřich Smetana.

Little did he realize at the time that this revolutionary movement in which he took an active part would later result in his creating a Bohemian nationalist music which would be the delight of countless thousands throughout the Western world. For after his name became suspect with the Austrian overlords of Bohemia, Smetana and his young wife went to Gothenburg, Sweden, where he was highly successful as a teacher of music and conductor of the local Philharmonic Society. He also composed a number of symphonic poems, none in any way reminiscent of his native land.

Just as Smetana was about to take up permanent residence in Gothenburg, his wife's health failed; and she died en route to Prague.

When the composer returned to the capital of his homeland, in 1861, he found the whole country seething with newly awakened national consciousness, and immediately he took up the cudgels in behalf of Bohemian music, at that time a non-existent entity. He organized what later became the great Czech Philharmonic Orchestra and accepted the post of director of the newly formed National Theater. Meanwhile, a whole mass of new compositions flowed unceasingly from his pen—all based on subjects of Bohemian history or folklore and flavored with the earthy, sparkling quality of the songs and dances of the Bohemian peasants.

Finally, in 1874, nervous strain and overwork took its toll. Resignation from conductorship of the Prague National Theater soon followed; then, after a period of ten years, insanity and death in an asylum.

THE BARTERED BRIDE

THIS gay and colorful folk opera is Smetana's masterpiece, and one of the classics in the literature of Bohemian national music. It has humor, sometimes even burlesque; it has pageantry; it has wonderful folk dances; and it is ever rich with local Bohemian flavors.

It was first heard at the National Theater in Prague on May 30, 1866. Soon after this, Smetana revised it, extending the original two acts into three and replacing the former spoken dialogue by recitatives. In this new version, *The Bartered Bride* became a world favorite, particularly after a spectacular production at the Vienna Opera in 1892. And it has maintained its great popularity on all the operatic stages since then. In recent performances at the Metropolitan Opera House it has been given in English.

The opera concerns Wenzel, the idiot son of a wealthy landowner, who is selected by Marie's parents to marry her. But Marie is in love with Hans, a stranger to the town, and of mysterious origin. Hans is prevailed upon by the local marriage broker to renounce Marie for a price, but he does so only on the specific agreement that Marie be allowed to marry only the son of the landowner. It turns out that Hans is a long lost son of the landowner and that, consequently, he can live up to his bargain even while marrying her.

The overture and dances (particularly the Polka and the Dance of the Comedians) are the most frequently heard parts of the opera; but it is also full of wonderful melodies. The entire opera has an irrepressible verve and vivacity that explain its great popular appeal.

12210-D, Dance of the Comedians, Philadelphia Orchestra "Pops," Eugene Ormandy Conducting.
19003-D, Overture, Philharmonic-Symphony Orchestra of New York, John Barbirolli Conducting.
71049-D, Polka and Furiant, Columbia Broadcasting Symphony, Howard Barlow Conducting.

QUARTET NO. 1 IN E MINOR
(FROM MY LIFE)

Allegro vivo appassionata · Allegro moderato à la polka · Largo sostenuto · Vivace

SMETANA had this to say of his Quartet in E minor: "As to the style of my quartet, I am not in the lest vexed if it does not please, since it

[447]

stands quite apart from the accepted quartet style. With me the form of each work is the outcome of the subject. And thus it is that this Quartet has made its own form. I wanted to paint, in sounds, the course of my life.

"The first movement depicts my early love of art and native folk music, my romantic tendency and unsatisfied yearnings. There is also a warning of future misfortune.

"The Polka recalls memories of my gay youth, when I used to write dance music and gave it away right and left.

"The slow movement recalls the bliss of my first love for a girl who afterward became my wife.

"The joy of the last movement is the result of the discovery of how to treat the Bohemian national elements in music. The coda brings an interruption of the catastrophe, the beginning of my deafness, a glimpse into the melancholy future. A persistent high note is heard which was the first symptom of my trouble. There is a ray of hope, an improvement, at the remembrance of all that was promised by my early career, at the same time a sense of madness."

This music consists of folk tunes and dances and is as gay and peasantlike. Lively rhythms and sharply articulated dance accents predominate. Here is found the Slavonic music that inspired Dvořák as well as Smetana. Two themes stand out—one Slavonic, the other Russian, in character. Both enjoy extensive treatment.

M-MM-405, Curtis String Quartet.

VLTAVA (THE MOLDAU)

Vltava, or *The Moldau* as it is commonly known in this country, is the second part of the magnificent cycle of tone poems glorifying Smetana's native land *Má Vlast* ("My Country"). The others are *Vysehrad* ("The High Castle"), *Sárka* (The Bohemian Amazon who takes a bloody revenge upon the race of men), *Z českých luhův a hayův* ("From Bohemia's Meadows and Forests"), *Tábor* ("The Hussite Fortress"), and *Blaník* (the mountain in which the Hussite warriors sleep awaiting the resurrection).

Vltava, because of its melodic charm and gorgeously colorful in-

[448]

strumentation, is probably the most successful piece of purely descriptive music ever written. In a note appended to the score, the composer asserts that the music is meant to picture in tone the scenes through which the great Moldau River passes on its way to the sea.

The source of the river lies in the center of the Bohemian forest where two streams meet. As the brook rushes through the woods the sound of hunting horns is heard, and as they die away the music becomes gay with the song and dance of a peasant wedding. Then, as night falls, the composer suggests the play of mysterious water sprites as the stream shimmers in the bright moonlight. Gradually the current gathers speed, and soon reaches the roaring, tumbling rapids of St. John. The stream widens into a river just above the city of Prague. As it flows majestically beneath the great legendary castle of Bysehrad, the entire orchestra, led by the brasses, bursts into an exultant hymn of national pride. The music ends with a last glimpse of the broad stream of the Moldau disappearing endlessly into the distance.

X-MX-211, Philharmonic-Symphony Orchestra of New York, Bruno Walter Conducting.

Johann Strauss II

1825–1899

J OHANN STRAUSS gives us in his waltzes the quintessence of the Vienna that was. Because of their seductive rhythm, variety of expression, and opulent harmony, these waltzes have held undisputed first place over all the other popular music of the Western World.

Johann Strauss, Jr. was born in Vienna, October 25, 1825, and was educated to become a clerk in a savings bank. With his mother's help he had secretly taken lessons on the violin and studied composition, and at the age of six wrote his first waltz, his mother writing down the notes. Just before he was 19, the young Johann could no longer resist the passion for a musical career and throwing off all parental restraint, made his debut as a conductor at the fashionable Café Dommayer, at Hietzing, near Vienna. This concert also was the debut of Johann Jr. as a composer for he conducted waltzes of his own as well as his father's. On the death of his father, Johann combined his parent's orchestra with his own and made a series of tours.

During the course of his long life, Johann Strauss, Jr. toured with his superb orchestra through all the great capitals of Europe. He came to America just once. On Independence Day of 1872 he conducted a gigantic chorus of more than 1,000 voices at the second of the celebrated Gilmore International Peace Jubilees in Boston.

The title of "Waltz King" is a most deserving one for this prolific composer wrote over 400 waltzes, probably the most famous as well as most popular being *On the Beautiful Blue Danube*. His music is full of melody, rhythm and charm, and is penetrated with Viennese gaiety and spirit.

Johannes Brahms wrote to a friend visiting Vienna, "You must go to the Volksgarten on Friday evening when Johann Strauss will conduct his waltzes. There is a master!" The great and serious composer

Brahms was completely captivated by Strauss's music. A widely quoted story that gives further evidence of Brahms's admiration for the Waltz King claims that when Madame Strauss asked Brahms to inscribe his name upon her autograph fan he jotted down the opening bars of the *Blue Danube* and commented, "Alas, not by Brahms."

"The Strauss waltzes," observed Dr. Riemann, "certainly belong to those works calculated to please the million . . . yet their rhythm and melody, and especially their refined instrumentation, deserve recognition on the part of musicians." There certainly can be no doubt to this statement for to this day every musician as well as music lover falls under the magic spell of this great composer's music, especially his waltzes.

Felix Weingartner found in the Strauss waltz "something tragic." The eminent German critic, Paul Bekker, observed that "a waltz of Strauss contains more melodies than a symphony of Beethoven, and the aggregate of Straussian melodies is surely greater than the aggregate of Beethoven's."

The great Waltz King died at the age of seventy-four, on June 3, 1899. His grave in the Central Cemetery in Vienna flanks that of his friend and admirer, Brahms, and lies opposite that of Schubert.

The best known and best loved Strauss waltzes include *Tales from the Vienna Woods, Artist's Life, Wine, Women and Song, The Blue Danube*, the *Emperor* Waltz, etc.

M-MM-481, André Kostelanetz and his Orchestra.
M-MM-389, Columbia Broadcasting Symphony, Howard Barlow Conducting.

DIE FLEDERMAUS (THE BAT)

Die Fledermaus is surely one of the greatest operettas of all time. By bringing the Waltz into the theatre, Strauss also brought a new kind of effervescence (as sparkling as the champagne that is apotheosized in one of the operetta's greatest waltzes), and a new kind of magic which the operetta stage had not known before this.

It is based on a French comedy, *Reveillon* (by Meilhac and Halévy) which was adapted for Strauss's use by Genée and Haffner. The first performance took place at the Theater-an-der-Wien on April 16, 1874. Vienna at this time was in the midst of a bleak depression. Notwithstanding this fact, the operetta was a sensation; the waltzes were encored; and the Waltz King was further deified. Since then it has, of course, become one of the most frequently performed and best loved operettas of the Viennese school.

The libretto is a frothy one, a brilliant foil for Strauss's engaging score. Baron von Eisenstein is to be arrested for a small offense. Instead of going to jail, he makes for the brilliant masquerade at the palace of Prince Orloff. Meanwhile, the Baron's wife entertains an old suitor who, mistaken for the Baron, is unceremoniously herded off to jail. The wife goes to the Orloff ball and there she carries on an amusing flirtation with her own husband.

Indicative of the fact that *Fledermaus* is much more than an engaging piece of musical entertainment—that it is actually a work of art—is that it is often produced by leading opera houses in Europe and with the foremost conductors directing.

9080-M, Overture, Berlin State Opera Orchestra, Bruno Walter Conducting.
71733-D, Fantasy, Lily Pons, Soprano, with Orchestra Conducted by Maurice Abravanel.

Richard Strauss

1864–

WHILE it is quite true that during the past three decades Richard Strauss has been artistically sterile, it cannot be denied that for all that he remains the *grand homme* of modern music. The works of his early manhood—those magnificent tone poems, the best operas, and his exquisite songs—are now so universally accepted as classics that it becomes amusing to recall that in its day this music shocked its contemporaries with its iconoclastic writing. The shock and the daring are gone. What remain are his brilliant orchestral palette of many colors, his sensual harmonies, his sweeping melodic lines, his Gargantuan climaxes, his extraordinary talent in transferring poetic and programmatic ideas into music, his passion and power and tenderness, all of which brought a new wealth of tonal expression to music.

Strauss, who was born in Munich in 1864, was the son of a famous horn player who played in Richard Wagner's orchestra. Father Strauss was, as a matter of fact, a violent opponent of Wagner's music; and it is one of the paradoxes of the music of our times that the son should, on the other hand, later become one of Wagner's most ardent protagonists.

Strauss went through an intensive musical training at the same time completing academic studies at the Munich University. In 1885, his great talent attracted the attention of Hans von Bülow, who made Strauss his assistant with the Meiningen Orchestra. Strauss soon succeeded Hans von Bülow as principal conductor. It was in Meiningen that he fell under the influence of Brahms, and the early works from young Strauss's pen—a symphony, concertos for violin and French horn, chamber music and some solo pieces—reflect that influence. Then he met Alexander Ritter, a musician thirty years his senior who was a great advocate of the program music of Liszt and

[453]

Wagner—music which was closely allied with works of literature. In Strauss's own words, "Ritter was exceptionally well read in all the philosophers, ancient and modern, and a man of the highest culture. His influence was in the nature of a storm wind. He urged me on to the development of the poetic, the expressive, in music, as exemplified in the works of Liszt, Wagner and Berlioz."

The result of the contact with Ritter was the creation by Strauss of his greatest contributions to music—his symphonic poems. The first of these, *Macbeth,* was written in 1886–87. *Don Juan* appeared in 1888, and that same year saw the beginning of *Death and Transfiguration,* which was completed in 1889.

Through their genius as well as novelty, the tone poems electrified the music world and made the composer famous and notorious at one and the same time. In 1905 came the first of Strauss's great operas, *Salome.*

Strauss outlived the scandals and riots of his early years to become an Olympian figure in the world of music, whose presence in the company of the great musical masters of all time was acknowledged. Together with his career as composer, Strauss pursued that of conductor, achieving particular note as an interpreter of the music of Mozart and Wagner in the leading capitals of Europe. In 1904 he visited the United States for the first time, conducting concerts of his own works, including the world première of his *Sinfonia Domestica.*

With the rise of the Nazis, Strauss allied himself openly with the new government by becoming president of the *Reichmusikkammer.* But he soon was at odds with his political superiors and withdrew from the limelight to the quiet and obscurity of his home in Garmisch-Partenkirchen, where he lived during the years of World War II.

ALSO SPRACH ZARATHUSTRA (THUS SPAKE ZARATHUSTRA), OP. 30

A PHILOSOPHICAL tone poem is an art form invented entirely by Richard Strauss. For this philosophical tone poem, Strauss selected the text from Friedrich Nietzsche's *Also Sprach Zarathustra*, written during the last years before insanity overtook the philosopher. The preachment of bodily health, strong leadership, and cold science was the wishful tribute of a philosopher on the brink of physical and mental disintegration, and it is an ironic commentary that this authoritarian outlook on life has found its eventual expression years later in the Nazi-sponsored movement of "strength through joy."

Richard Strauss stated that his tone poem is but a free paraphrase of Nietzsche. The score carries the following quotation from *Also Sprach Zarathustra:* "Having attained the age of thirty, Zarathustra left his home and went into the mountains. There he rejoiced in his spirit and his loneliness, and for ten years did not grow weary of it. But at last his heart turned. One morning he got up with the dawn, stepped into the presence of the Sun, and thus spake unto him:

"'Thou great star! What would be thy happiness, were it not for those on whom thou shinest? For ten years thou hast come up here to my cave. Thou wouldst have got sick of thy light and thy journey but for me, mine eagle, and my serpent. But we waited for thee every morning, and, receiving from thee thine abundance, blessed thee for it. Lo! I am weary of my wisdom, like the bee that hath collected too much honey. I need hands reaching out for it. I would fain grant and distribute, until the wise among men could once more enjoy their folly, and the poor once more their riches.

"'For that end I must descend to the depths, as thou dost at even, when, sinking behind the sea, thou givest light to the lower regions, thou resplendent star! I must, like thee, go down, as men say—men to whom I would descend. Then bless me, thou impassive eye, that canst look without envy upon overmuch happiness. Bless the cup which is about to overflow, so that the water, golden-flowing out of it, may carry everywhere the reflection of thy rapture. Lo! this cup is about to empty itself again, and Zarathustra will once again become a man.' Thus Zarathustra's descent began."

The tone poem is separated into several sections which are marked

by a change of movement or thematic content. After a solemn introduction, with a climax in C major, there is a section marked "Of the
Dwellers of the World in the Rear" (*Hinterweltler*). The horns introduce the religious theme *Credo in unum deum* as a quotation from
Gregorian Chant.

In the following section, "Of Profound Yearning," there is another Gregorian quotation from the Magnificat. This corresponds to
the program of the work, which reflects man's feeling for the power
of God. Strauss accepts this feeling as Christian and not as pagan sun-
worship.

The individual longings of man turn him to passion, illustrated in
the division marked "Of Joys and Sorrows." Then follows the mournful *Song of the Grave*. After religion and passion, the interest is turned
to science. Its theme, opening with the progression C — G — C, underlying the entire tone poem, is interesting in that it covers all
twelve tones of the scale, and forms four mutually exclusive triads (if
we start from the upper C and adjoin it to the last note of the theme)
to indicate the thorough exploration in scientific research. The theme
is treated fugally, illustrating man's attempt to solve the riddle of life.

The continuation of this section, marked "The Convalescent,"
treats the science theme with additional counterpoint in clipped,
rhythmically diversified figures. Then comes a waltz, in which man
finds his individual joy. The night descends; the *Song of the Night
Wanderer* is heard. The bell strikes twelve. There is a conflict of the
theme of the ideal expressed in the bitonality of B major in the high
register, and the unresolved chord in the trombones. The theme
C — G — C is repeated in the double basses, and its significance is
revealed: it is the world riddle.

Strauss himself gave little elucidation on the philosophical content of *Zarathustra*, and even denied that it was conceived as a philosophical tone poem. Strauss wrote the music in 1896 in Munich,
and conducted the first performance himself at Frankfort on November 27 of the same year.

M-MM-421, Chicago Symphony Orchestra, Frederick Stock Conducting.

[456]

DEATH AND TRANSFIGURATION
(TOD UND VERKLÄRUNG), OP. 24

Death and Transfiguration is the third of that extraordinary series of tone poems with which Richard Strauss astounded the musical world of his day. It was written in 1888–89, and in the flyleaf of the score is an unsigned poem by Strauss's friend Alexander Ritter. Unfortunately for the more romantic-minded program analysts, Ritter's poem was written *after* he had become acquainted with the music of *Death and Transfiguration*. Thus, it is not possible to claim for Strauss's music an unreservedly literary basis. However, since Ritter was intimately associated with the composer at the time *Death and Transfiguration* was set to paper, the poem may be accepted as an authentic guide to what Strauss was trying to say.

The following anonymous English prose translation of Ritter's verses appeared on the occasion of the first London performance of *Death and Transfiguration*, December 7, 1897:

"A sick man lies upon his mattress in a poor and squalid garret, lit by the flickering glare of a candle burnt almost to its stump. Exhausted by a desperate fight with death, he has sunk into sleep; no sound breaks the silence of approaching dissolution, save the low monotonous ticking of a clock on the wall. A plaintive smile from time to time lights up the man's wan features; at life's last limit, dreams are telling him of childhood's golden days.

"But death will not long grant its victim sleep and dreams. Dreadly it plucks at him, and once again begins the strife: desire of life against might of death! A gruesome combat! Neither yet gains the victory; the dying man sinks back upon his couch, and silence reigns once more.

"Weary with struggling, reft of sleep, in the delirium of fever he sees his life unrolled before him, stage by stage. First the dawn of childhood, radiant with pure innocence. Next the youth who tests and practices his forces for manhood's fight. And then the man in battle for life's greatest prize: to realize a high ideal, and make it all the higher by his act. All that his heart ever longed for, he seeks it still in death's last sweat—seeks, but never finds it! Though now he sees it more and more plainly; though now it shines before him, he yet can ne'er achieve it wholly, ne'er put the last touch to his endeavor. Then sounds the iron stroke of death's chill hammer; and breaks the earthly shell in twain. But now from on high comes sounds of triumph; what here on earth he sought in vain, from heaven it greets him: Deliverance, Transfiguration."

The music falls into four sections corresponding to those of Ritter's poem. The first opens Largo, in C minor, with darkly suggestive phrases for second violins and violas, punctuated by a sinister rhythm on the kettledrums. The key changes to D-flat major as woodwinds and harps suggest childhood memories; but soon the instruments sink back into the key of C minor, the quiet rhythm of the kettledrums ever more ominous.

M-MM-613, Philadelphia Orchestra, Eugene Ormandy Conducting.

DON JUAN, OP. 20

Don Juan is the first of Strauss's tone poems, if we disregard the earlier orchestral work, *Macbeth,* which has not been retained in the active repertoire. Strauss wrote *Don Juan* when he was twenty-four years old, and conducted its first performance at Weimar on November 11, 1889. The program carried a quotation from the poem *Don Juan,* written by the morbid Austrian poet Nicolaus Lenau. This poem, representing the hero as a tragic figure frustrated by his easy triumphs, it the only program that Strauss ever acknowledged.

The portion of Lenau's poem which is published in Strauss's score pictures a romantic Don Juan, insatiable in his conquests. He expresses the desire to die from a kiss on the lips of the last of his women. He elevates the plurality of his affections to a dogma, and poetizes the manifold charms of beautiful womanhood. He cries: "Out and away to ever new conquests." But he is reconciled to death, a lightning from above that finally strikes a deadly blow to his love power.

Don Juan is now a classic of the orchestral repertoire. The bombast of this music, as of all symphonic poems of Richard Strauss, is still offensive to many musicians, but we are inclined to regard it as a thing of the past, while fifty years ago, at the time when *Don Juan*

[458]

was young, it was a music of the future, the violent offspring of the Wagnerian school.

X-MX-190, Pittsburgh Symphony Orchestra, Fritz Reiner Conducting.

DON QUIXOTE, OP. 35

THE FULL title of this famous work is *Don Quixote: Introduction, Theme and Variations: Fantastic Variations on a Theme of Knightly Character.* It is the last but one of the great tone poems that Strauss composed in the decade 1888 to 1898.

Of all the composers who have attempted musical portraits of the Don, Strauss has treated him with the greatest understanding, compassion, and humor. The theme that represents him is a curious blend of the noble, the gallant, and the absurd—altogether one of Strauss's happiest inspirations. In a succession of variations, it is subjected to musical adventures which parallel those of Cervantes' hero. There are other themes for Sancho Panza, the Don's squire, and Dulcinea, his Ideal Woman, and they companion the Don's theme throughout.

The Introduction shows the Don in his study, deep in the lore of chivalry. "In the end, through his little sleep and much reading, he dried up his brains in such sort, as he lost wholly his judgment." Strange dissonances intrude into the development of his theme: the Don is mad. A fermata leads to the theme. Here the Don is characterized by the solo 'cello, Sancho Panza by clarinet and tenor tuba (later the viola). Ten Variations and a Finale follow:

Variation 1. Inspired by the beautiful Dulcinea, the Don sets out on a career of knight-errantry, with Sancho at his side. He encounters windmills, imagines them to be giants, and spurs to the attack. The revolving sails unseat him.

Variation 2. The Don encounters a flock of sheep. In his disordered imagination the harmless creatures are transformed into the armies of the Emperor Alifanfaron. He charges and routs them.

Variation 3. The Don and Sancho converse. Sancho questions the value of the life of chivalry, laments lost creature comforts. The Don instructs him. They dispute. The Don loses his temper and silences his squire.

Variation 4. The Don mistakes a band of pilgrims for robbers and attacks them. He is worsted and left senseless on the ground. Sancho laments.

Variation 5. While Sancho sleeps, the Don keeps knightly vigil, meditating on the Ideal. This variation is an extended solo for 'cello, Adagio, interrupted by a rhapsodic cadenza for strings and harp.

Variation 6. The Don and Dulcinea. A peasant wench meets the Don and Sancho on the road. Sancho decides to have some fun with his master and tells him that this is Dulcinea. At first incredulous, the Don concludes in the end that Dulcinea has been bewitched.

Variation 7. The Ride through the Air. Blindfolded, the Don and Sancho mount a wooden horse which they are told will carry them through the air. An orchestral storm, in which a wind-machine figures, describes their imaginary flight.

Variation 8. The Don and Sancho find an empty boat by a river's edge. The Don believes that it was sent by a supernatural power to bear him to some glorious adventure. He and Sancho embark. In midstream the boat capsizes, but knight and squire succeed in reaching shore, where they shake out their wet clothes and offer a prayer of thanksgiving.

Variation 9. The Don meets two monks and mistakes them for evil magicians. He charges them and they flee.

Variation 10. A townsman of the Don decides to bring him to his senses. Announcing himself as the Knight of the White Moon, he challenges the Don to combat, defeats him, and forces him to retire to his home. Divested of his illusions, the Don resolves to become a shepherd. A gradual simplification and clarification of the music's harmonic texture indicates the Don's returning sanity.

Finale. The Death of Don Quixote. The Don lies on his deathbed. A fever shakes him, but he has intervals of peace. He recalls his former life, realizing its folly. He speaks a few last words and dies.

M-MM-506, Gregor Piatigorsky, Solo 'Cellist, and the Pittsburgh Symphony Orchestra, Fritz Reiner Conducting.

EIN HELDENLEBEN (A HERO'S LIFE), OP. 40

Ein Heldenleben, the symphonic poem, depicts the life of a Hero grievously misunderstood by his fellow men and his fellow enemies. The Hero is essentially a peacemaker but, thanks to the intrigues of the petty objectors, he is driven to war. He confounds his enemies on the battlefield, and is then free to build a new order, in which peace is the only supreme law, after every conscious and unconscious foe has been crushed into the dust. The Hero then reminisces.

In Strauss's symphonic poem the reminiscences are from his own earlier works, twenty-three of them altogether, taken from six earlier symphonic works, one opera, and a song. But the world lying at the Hero's feet is still unresponsive. Fury rages in the Hero's soul, and he seeks solace in solitude. Even nature itself reminds him of his conquered foe. His soaring leitmotif rises. There is complete tranquillity in him and silence in the world. The poem ends in a solemn mood.

When Richard Strauss was completing *Ein Heldenleben* in Berlin on December 27, 1898, he was writing his own life story. He was at that time a ranking modernist, center of the greatest disturbance in the world of music after Wagner, and a grateful subject for musical cartoonists. He conducted *Ein Heldenleben* from the manuscript in Frankfort on March 3, 1899. The hall was packed to the doors, and the audience was shocked, intrigued, and delighted. The indignant correspondent of the *Musical Courier* of New York called the work "an alleged symphony." He was shocked by Strauss's self-assertion: "The plan of the work reveals conclusively that the composer indulges in a self-glorification of the most barefaced kind, for he passes muster in the chief themes of his work, and hence we cannot but assume that, with the hero under musical description, Strauss means nobody but himself. . . ."

The composer was extremely fortunate in having a host of commentators and exegetes who wrote expansive programs for every one of his symphonic poems. Strauss's music is not merely program music; it is a musical subject index. Every instrumental quirk, squib, or sinuosity signalizes an event, a mood, or an appearance. When these themes combine, the subjects and events are combined, too. Yet Strauss is reported to have said that the only program in *Ein Heldenleben* is a hero fighting his enemies.

M-441, Josef Fuchs, Violin Solo, and the Cleveland Orchestra, Artur Rodzinski Conducting.

"How BEAUTIFUL *was* Princess Salome"—thus did mocking critics paraphrase the first line of *Salome* in comparing the earlier work with *Elektra*. In their opinion, Strauss's newest operatic brainchild was the ultimate in ugliness and perversity.

Elektra is actually one of the few examples in music in which ugliness receives its true aesthetic value. The vocal declamation is masterful in its fullest exploitation of theatrical resources, and frequently achieves gruesome quality. The often ultra-modern orchestration is a coat of many colors, some of them dark and somber.

Drawing the very last consequences from the chromaticism of *Tristan*, Strauss here proved that effective and progressive music could be written within the diatonic framework. More than any other work by Strauss, *Elektra* is the answer to the intellectual, semi-scholarly experiments with harmonic revolutions undertaken by so many of Strauss's less gifted contemporaries. It is one of the greatest serious operas written after *Otello*. Womanly warmth and passion transcend even the hysteria of the heroine: the "Recognition Scene" between Elektra and Orestes is surely one of the most deeply moving passages in all opera.

Elektra was the first of six collaborative ventures between Strauss and the Austrian poet Hugo von Hofmannsthal. With Strauss possessing keen literary insight, and with Hugo von Hofmannsthal being a trained musician, they could work together harmoniously, each appreciative of the other's problems and achievements.

The book is a version of the old Greek legend describing the return of Orestes to avenge his father's murder, with his half-crazed sister, Elektra, in the foreground of events. Orestes kills the murderer before Elektra is able to consummate her own scheme of revenge. Ecstatically, Elektra dances until she falls dead.

Based on Sophocles, the libretto combines the grandeur of ancient tragedy with a twentieth-century approach to psychopathic problems.

Elektra was first heard at the Dresden Opera on January 25, 1909.

DER ROSENKAVALIER

"Now I am going to write a Mozart opera," announced Strauss as he settled down to set Hofmannsthal's nimble libretto to music. And many critics have, indeed, found a striking similarity between *Der Rosenkavalier* and *The Marriage of Figaro*. Others, however, have felt that there is much more of Johann Strauss in it than Mozart.

The setting is 18th century Vienna, a period of tragic undercurrents beneath a surface of calm. It was a day of romances in white, red and gold boudoirs, hunting parties, Prater parades, easy money— and unabashed corruption. Tinged with a bit of Viennese irony, Hofmannsthal and Strauss created a play in which the two principal characters are alive and vital: the middle-aged Marschallin, and her impoverished, pretentious, somewhat repulsive relative from the country, Baron Ochs. Ochs is a true descendent of the comic basso in the old *commedia dell' arte*. As Strauss wrote the part, he had a definite singer in mind—Richard Mayr of the Vienna Court Opera. When Mayr was informed by Strauss that this role was written for him, he responded in assumed dismay: "Now I don't know, Dr. Strauss, if this is meant to be a compliment to me, or an insult!"

Der Rosenkavalier is a comedy of love and intrigue set to the most sparkling and vivacious music Strauss ever wrote. Baron Ochs wishes a silver rose to be sent to his betrothed, Sophie; and the Marschallin suggests that her seventeen-year-old lover, Octavian, be the bearer. Octavian falls in love with Sophie, and when Baron Ochs accuses him of duplicity, a duel ensues in which the Baron is slightly wounded. However, the Baron is not wounded sufficiently to prevent him from making advances to—and arranging a rendezvous with— the Marschallin's maid. This maid turns out to be none other than Octavian in disguise, placing Baron Ochs in a highly ridiculous position. Octavian is now free to marry Sophie, with the Marschallin's magnanimous consent.

For his emotional outpourings and for dramatic denouements, Strauss went to the sweeping melodic line of the waltz; the waltzes of *Der Rosenkavalier* are among the most intoxicating and buoyant musical pages in the opera, and have achieved considerable fame, apart from the opera, in performances at symphony concerts. Writing these waltzes, Strauss proved himself indeed to have Strauss blood in his veins: they are Viennese to the very core.

Apart from these waltzes, which made the opera internationally famous, there are many passages of striking beauty, principal among which are the moving and emotional monologue of the Marschallin in the first act, the meeting of Sophie and Octavian in the second, and the Mozartian trio of the three female characters in the third.

The opera's première took place in Dresden on January 26, 1911.

11542-D, Waltzes, Cleveland Orchestra, Artur Rodzinski Conducting.

SALOME

Salome, first performed in Dresden on December 9, 1905, was based on the famous play of Oscar Wilde (translated into German by Hedwig Lachmann) which, in turn, was a variant of the scriptural account of the death of John the Baptist.

Strauss had completed this, his first important opera, in 1903. He was then in his fortieth year, a famed composer of orchestral music, the prophet of the orchestral tone poem. His operas have often been called tone poems with words. The human voice is used as merely one other instrument in the eloquent orchestration. Strauss, however, insisted on proper accentuation and pronunciation of the text, and he wanted the melody to be clearly distinguishable.

Salome is supremely effective on the stage. It shows that Strauss understands the theatre the way Mozart, Verdi, and Wagner did before him. It contains beautiful, intense, passionate melodies, sumptuous harmonies, glittering (sometimes often garish) colors.

When it was first produced it caused something of a shock. It was said that the subject was rendered only so much more objectionable because of the sensuous music. Strauss was called decadent, impertinent, criminal. Newspapers raged; the Kaiser protested; the opera was temporarily banned from the Berlin Court Opera. In America, too, it was a cause célèbre—its première taking place in 1907. The morality of the times was offended by the subject of Wilde's play and the equally shocking nature of Strauss's music, and after one performance it was banned.

[464]

Oscar Wilde's play is familiar. It tells about Salome who asks that the imprisoned Jochanaan be brought before her. In vain does she try to seduce him, and failing to do so asks for his head from Herod. Her request is granted after she dances the celebrated Dance of the Seven Veils. When the head of Jochanaan is brought to her on a tray, Salome kisses its lips sensuously, an act that so revolts Herod that he orders her death.

One of the most famous pages in this opera is the music—as erotic as any that can be found in operatic literature—for Salome's Dance of the Seven Veils.

11781-D, Dance of the Seven Veils, Cleveland Orchestra, Artur Rodzinski Conducting.

SONGS

THE SONGS which Strauss has written, more than 135 of them, are often overshadowed by the highly successful tone poems and operas associated with the period of his greatest productivity. Among these early songs are many masterpieces which are clearly the work of genius, a consummate ability still in full flower and giving promise of infinite riches to come. Although the promise was never fulfilled, the early songs themselves lose none of their beauty or appeal because of this; they remain miniature masterpieces of enduring value.

The songs generally accepted as Strauss's greatest were written before the composer's thirtieth year. They are now established classics in the Lieder repertoire and undoubtedly will remain so indefinitely. They include:

Ständchen (Serenade). Awake, awake, come softly to me in the garden. Let us enjoy this secret hour of our love.

Morgen (Tomorrow). And tomorrow the sun will shine again. We shall be united in its radiance and we shall slowly go down to the white beach; and standing there shall gaze into each other's eyes, feeling deep silence of happiness.

Allerseelen (All Souls' Day). Bring the last flowers of autumn— this is the day on which we may speak of our love as we used to in spring. I will hold your hand, not caring who may see it. This is the day of remembrance—come into my arms as once in spring!

Zueignung (Dedication). You know, beloved, that I suffer when I am far from you! But even this suffering is exultation. Thank you! Once I lived a full life, but you have understood and blessed me—thank you! You have freed me from evil and in your sacred love I have been reborn. Thank you!

Traum durch die Dämmerung (Dream through the Twilight). Spreading meadows in the dusk of eve! The sun has gone down, the stars appear—and I now go to the beautiful maid, far over the meads, in the dusk of eve. Through the shades of eve to lovers' land, I speed not too fast, nor haste to leave. I am led to a soft and velvet land at the close of day, to the lovers' land, in the twilight blue of eve.

X-MX-270, Lotte Lehmann, Soprano, Paul Ulanowsky, Piano.

TILL EULENSPIEGELS LUSTIGE STREICHE, OP. 28

IMAGINING all horn players to be as good as his father, Richard Strauss wrote a Concerto for Horn and Orchestra, under his father's inspiration. In *Till Eulenspiegel* he entrusted to the horn one of the most difficult solo passages ever written for the instrument. It is said that the idea for this solo came to him from listening to the first horn player of the Weimar Orchestra practice before each rehearsal. When at the first rehearsal of *Till Eulenspiegel* the horn player complained about the difficulty of the passage, Strauss replied: "Nonsense! I heard you practice it every morning."

Strauss's father was an excellent player on the French horn, and knew other orchestral instruments well. He taught Strauss never to force an instrument to play beyond its natural capacities. Once, looking over an orchestral score written by his son, he suddenly turned toward him, and gave him a slap on the face. *"Lausbub,"* he exclaimed, "so you are writing a high B-flat for the flute! Mozart and Beethoven never used it; neither should you." Strauss had great respect for his father as an educator and a musician and he remembered his lessons well.

Strauss completed the composition of *Till Eulenspiegel* on May 6, 1895, and the first performance took place in Cologne on November 5 of the same year. The complete title of the piece is *Till Eulenspiegels lustige Streiche,* which is usually translated *Till Eulenspiegel's Merry Pranks.*

The composition is defined by Strauss himself as a scherzo in rondo form. In it the career of Till Eulenspiegel, a cheat and a rogue, is described, from his early pranks to his termination at the gallows. Till Eulenspiegel is a universal character. In the Russian folklore he is Ivan the Fool; in Italy, he is Polichinello; in Spain, Portugal, and Latin America, he is Pedro Malazarte, the master of evil arts. Not all of these legendary figures end on the gallows; Till gets caught because he is not clever enough.

X-MX-210, Cleveland Orchestra, Artur Rodzinski Conducting.

Igor Stravinsky

1882–

Around the music of Igor Stravinsky has raged more controversy and conflict, critically speaking, than can be said of the creations of any of his contemporaries—excepting, as we must always in this connection, Richard Strauss and, on occasion, Claude Debussy. Stravinsky perhaps introduced more of the revolutionary tonalities that have been labeled "modernistic," to say nothing of "futuristic," than any of his predecessors, and while some have in latter days apparently sought to outstrip him in this respect it may be doubted whether any have combined such advanced ideas with forms that are genuinely and understandably musical. His *Le Sacre du printemps* (The Rite of Spring) a ballet in the most abstruse modern idiom, created what can only be termed a commotion when first heard, some thirty years ago. Insensibly, however, the musical world grows up to advanced ideas, provided, of course, that these have a sound—however revolutionary—foundation, and *Le Sacre du printemps* is already regarded with more or less complacency. Stravinsky's admirers—and they are many—claim for him that he attains an apotheosis of "absolute" music, that is to say, music that depends upon no extraneous devices of literary, pictorial or dramatic significance to convey its message. His earlier works, such as *Petrouchka* and *The Firebird*, adhere more or less to established traditions.

Stravinsky was born June 17, 1882, at Oranienbaum, near St. Petersburg, Russia. His father, a prominent singer and actor, was quick to recognize his son's musical talent. But he also was familiar with the precariousness of an artistic career, and was therefore determined that Igor should learn a profession. Consequently, young Stravinsky entered the St. Petersburg University as a law student, pursuing music only for recreation.

In 1902, however, while on a trip to Germany, Stravinsky met Rimsky-Korsakov, who, immediately aware of the young man's musical ability, persuaded him to give up the study of law and adopt music as his profession. Stravinsky became a pupil of Rimsky-Korsakov, and learned much from him in the way of composition and orchestration. In 1907, his first important composition, a symphony, appeared. The following year, while Stravinsky was at work on another orchestral piece, *Fireworks*, which he was writing to commemorate the marriage of Rimsky-Korsakov's daughter, the master died.

Stravinsky considers the first performance of *Fireworks*, on February 6, 1909, as one of the most important events in his life. For present at this concert in St. Petersburg was the great Russian impresario, Sergei Diaghilev. As a result, Diaghilev commissioned Stravinsky to orchestrate a group of Chopin pieces for the coming ballet season in Paris. Diaghilev then asked him to write an original ballet based on the Russian fairy tale, *The Firebird*. This great work had its première at Paris on June 25, 1910, and proved to be the first of a monumental trilogy of Stravinsky ballets. The other two, *Petrouchka* and *Le Sacre du printemps* appeared, respectively, in 1911 and 1913. The last of the ballets that Stravinsky composed for Diaghilev was *Le Chant du Rossignol*, which first saw the light in 1917.

During this whole period, Stravinsky had been spending all his time in France, Italy and Switzerland. Finally, he became a French citizen and settled in Paris. It was then that his musical path took a sudden turn. His compositions became neo-classic—that is, modern works based upon the forms and styles of the leading composers of the seventeenth and eighteenth centuries, particularly Bach and Handel. The principal works of this, his latest period, have been *Les Noces* for voices and orchestra, *Oedipus Rex*, *L'Histoire du soldat*, the comic opera *Mavra*, *Symphonie des Psaumes* for chorus and orchestra, Capriccio for Piano and Orchestra, *Ragtime* for eleven instruments, an octet, and the ballets *Apollon Musagète*, *Jeu de Cartes* and the recently composed *Danses Concertantes*.

After the outbreak of World War II, Stravinsky came to the United States, and now spends most of his time in California.

The compositions of his earlier—or so-called "Russian"—period have had a tremendous effect upon present-day composers. This is especially true of *Le Sacre du printemps*, which created such wild demonstrations of disapproval during the early days of its existence. Yet Stravinsky feels that this second—or neo-classic—period is far more important. Only time will tell us whether or not he is right.

THE FIREBIRD SUITE (L'OISEAU DE FEU)

FOR MANY years before 1910 the firebird soared on its imaginary wings through Russian legends and fairy tales. It remained for the youthful genius of Stravinsky to capture its scintillating brilliance and change fantasy into reality with a brilliant orchestral score. Since then the firebird has been the property of everyone; throughout the world wherever symphony orchestras play, the glittering plumage of this fanciful creature has become as familiar as it has been to past generations of wide-eyed Russian children listening to thrice-familiar fairy tales at bedtime.

The distinguished dancer and choreographer, Michel Fokine, had been developing a series of ideas for the Diaghilev ballet based on the firebird legend. After a conference between the two men, a commission to create the score was offered to and accepted by Anatol Liadov, best known today as the composer of the irrepressible *Musical Snuff Box*. Liadov's muse proved to be reluctant, however, and time passed rapidly without seeing the *Firebird* come any closer to orchestral reality. Finally, more or less in desperation, Fokine and Diaghilev, late in 1909, thought again of the twenty-seven-year-old Stravinsky. Another commission for the score was offered to the young composer with a strong implication that reasonable speed was of the essence. By May of 1910, the *Firebird* was ready, and to add that it more than fulfilled the hopes and wishes of its sponsors is almost superfluous. One month later the first performance was given in Paris, on June 25, 1910, with Fokine in the role of Ivan Tsarevitch. Gabriel Pierné was the conductor. Later, the Diaghilev troupe presented the first performance of the new work in this country at the Century Theater in New York, on January 17, 1916, with Ernest Ansermet in command of the orchestra.

The story of the ballet represents a compilation from several of the firebird fairy tales, in most of which Ivan Tsarevitch appears as the hero. The ballet opens in the enchanted wood which surrounds the castle of Kastchei, an evil magician. Ivan wanders into this wood while on a hunting expedition. Great is his wonder when he finds a magic tree richly hung with golden fruit. While he is still marveling at the sight, a dazzling creature flies into view and lights on the tree. It is the Firebird. Overcome with excitement, Ivan shoots an arrow

[470]

at the bird, and misses. The startled Firebird flies away but returns in a few minutes and is captured by Ivan. The enchanted bird pleads for its life so eloquently that the hunter releases it and is rewarded with a single golden feather.

Hardly has the bird disappeared than twelve lovely maidens appear and dance around the magic tree. When Ivan reveals himself, they warn him at once to leave, lest he fall under the power of Kastchei and be transformed into stone. Despite this warning, the hero determines to remain and test his strength against the powers of the magician.

He soon has his chance. Darkness descends, the maidens flee in fright, and a pack of demons swarms upon Ivan just as the terrible magician himself appears. As the dread conjuror begins his spell, Ivan fights back using the power of the magic feather. The Firebird comes to his aid, leading off the demons in a wild dance, after which they fall exhausted and sleep.

Now the Firebird reveals to Ivan the hiding place of an enchanted egg which contains the source of all of Kastchei's power. Ivan breaks the egg which, in one wondrous moment, shatters the evil powers of the wizard. Kastchei and his demons vanish, the castle disappears, and scores of liberated youths and maidens rush to hail Ivan as their champion. In this moment of supreme triumph Ivan is offered the dazzling prospect of selecting the loveliest of the maidens to be his wife. In this completely enviable position, Ivan makes his choice as the curtain falls.

Stravinsky has made three orchestral suites of his ballet masterpiece. Suite No. 1 made use of an exceptionally large orchestra, a situation which presented some performance problems. In Suite No. 2 Stravinsky reduced the size of the orchestra to bring it down to workable proportions and also eliminated sections two and three, the Adagio and Scherzo. The third suite utilizes the same orchestra called for in the second but restores the two previously deleted sections. In addition, Stravinsky has provided, to quote his own words, "short pantomimic episodes" between the various sections, so that the work now flows in a continuous, unbroken sequence.

PETROUCHKA

Petrouchka was Stravinsky's second ballet written for Diaghilev, and it did not assume the shape of a ballet at once. For a time Stravinsky toyed with the idea of composing a short piece for piano and orchestra, in the manner of Weber's *Concertstück*. It was to be a compressed piano concerto, and the piano part was largely ready when Stravinsky decided to put a new meaning into the piece.

Petrouchka is a diminutive for Peter, used by Russian peasants, but specifically it is the name of a puppet popular at Russian fairs after Lent. Thus, Petrouchka is the counterpart of the English Punch and Judy show. He is usually the pathetic lover, who gets beaten up by the villain, and is thwarted in all his enterprises. He is quarrelsome without cunning, and aggressive without caution. However, it was not Stravinsky's intention to write a musical biography of Petrouchka, in the manner of Strauss's *Till Eulenspiegel*. Stravinsky's score is a panorama of the Russian post-Lent Festival *Maslianitza*, which means, literally, Butter Time.

There are many sideshows in Stravinsky's ballet: the organ grinder, the magician with his flute, and a dancing bear. Among the crowds there are two categories of typical visitors: children's nurses and coachmen. Petrouchka's tragedy is a part of the show. He quarrels with the Moor over the love of a ballerina, and gets his skull cracked.

Stravinsky completed the composition of *Petrouchka* in Rome in May 1911. The ballet was produced by Diaghilev in Paris on June 13, 1911, and its success was instantaneous, but quite lacking in the riotous quality that accompanied the production of *Le Sacre du printemps*.

The three scores *The Firebird, Petrouchka,* and *Le Sacre* constitute the "Russian" period in Stravinsky's evolution. In all three, the subjects are intensely Russian, and in *Petrouchka* Stravinsky actually uses the themes of popular Russian songs in the score. It is the only work in which he does so openly.

The subtitle of *Petrouchka* reads: "Burlesque scenes in four tableaux," which establishes the character of the score as stage music. Yet the orchestral Suite from *Petrouchka* has proved extremely effective without the visual theatre, although early critics of the score in Europe and America wrote that ballet action was essential to illustrate the music. Historically, Stravinsky was right in acknowledging Diaghilev as the animator of his creative work, but the ballet was to Stravinsky merely a medium of expression, and his music, divorced from action, remains undiminished in its artistic power.

X-MX-177, Philharmonic-Symphony Orchestra of New York, Igor Stravinsky Conducting.

LE SACRE DU PRINTEMPS
(THE RITE OF SPRING)

ON THE night of May 29, 1913, the Russian Ballet of the famous impresario Sergei Diaghilev produced in Paris a new ballet, *Le Sacre du primtemps*, by a thirty-year-old Russian composer, Igor Stravinsky, whose name was familiar to Paris musicians by his earlier ballet music. The Parisians expected to hear a modern composition that would be very Russian, very brilliant, and perhaps a little too noisy.

But no sooner were the first bars of the music played than the audience became aware that this kind of music was entirely different from all schools of composition, classical or modern. The very opening, a bassoon solo in an absurdly high register, stirred the audience to nervous laughter. According to reports, Saint-Saëns, who was present, inquired sarcastically: "What instrument is that?" and walked out of the theatre. The following section, which was characterized by some critic as a barnyard come to life, unloosened the nervous energy of the public. Members of the audience, ordinarily respectable citizens, lost their natural restraint, and became vocal with protest.

Of many stories, there is a report that Roland-Manuel, a young progressive French composer, has for years preserved the torn collar of his shirt which was his share in the sacrifice for the new art and musical tolerance. Old Countess Pourtalès brandished her fan, and shouted in her extreme indignation: "It is the first time in sixty years that anyone has dared to make a fool of me." There was so much noise and altercation in the audience that at times the music could not be heard at all.

Stravinsky himself was with Nijinsky behind the stage throughout the performance, and became aware of the trouble only when the electrician, acting on Diaghilev's orders, began to blink the lights to pacify the passions. Nijinsky made an attempt to jump on the stage and start a counter-riot against the disturbers of the peace, but was held back by Stravinsky.

The complexities of *Le Sacre* are mostly visual. There are constant changes of meter, and in the final Sacred Dance the changing measures in sixteenth notes necessitate a great deal of geometrical time-beating on the part of the conductor. In one place, the C major scale is written in B-sharp, which has twelve sharps, counting two sharps for a double sharp. But the underlying melodic structure is diatonic, even though melodies may be treated in consecutive major sevenths rather than octaves. In other words, there are elements of polytonality, or writing in two or more keys simultaneously, but little atonality, inasmuch as the melodic line follows a tonal pattern. The rhythms, though formidable in appearance on paper, are products of two or more lines of perfectly regular beats, which results in polyrhythmy, or the use of several rhythms simultaneously. The harmonies are essentially tonal, and are treated in blocks, contrary to the classical conception of voice-leading and modulation.

Le Sacre du printemps, as a ballet, has a definite program. Each section represents a game, or a ritual of pagan Russia, and is clearly differentiated. There is no difficulty in identifying each dance by its specific rhythm, or its theme. The music is entirely pictorial.

M-MM-417, Philharmonic-Symphony Orchestra of New York, Igor Stravinsky Conducting.

Deems Taylor

1885–

THE magnificent versatility which is a distinguished feature of Deems Taylor has obscured the fact that he is primarily a composer. In his varied career, he has been a war correspondent, teacher of musical theory, translator, music critic, and music editor; radio orator, narrator, and commentator; the author of a best-selling book on music, genial master of ceremonies at many a socially musical occasion, and lastly the moderator in Walt Disney's luxurious *Fantasia*. He is an amateur artist, and has designed the cover of *Peter Ibbetson* (two silhouetted children looking at a dream castle beyond a poetic lake, under the crescent moon). He has also successfully composed a French folk song.

The price of this versatility has been that even the best friends and admirers of Deems Taylor allow themselves to treat his status as composer lightly, while praising half a dozen of his more conspicuous achievements. Yet, as an American-born composer, Deems Taylor has achieved a world record. His first opera *The King's Henchman*, produced at the Metropolitan Opera House in New York in 1926, had fourteen performances in three seasons, and his second opera *Peter Ibbetson*, produced at the Metropolitan in 1931, held on for sixteen performances in four seasons. The figures, numerically not impressive, constitute two consecutive world records for any American opera produced at the Metropolitan.

Deems Taylor was born in New York, December 22, 1885. Educated at the Ethical Culture School and the New York University, he obtained an A.B. degree in 1906 expecting to make his way in the world as an architect. During his days at the New York University he wrote a number of the college shows. Victor Herbert was induced, much against his will, to attend one of these shows. It was Herbert's encouragement that prompted young Taylor to study music. In 1908, he became a harmony pupil of Oscar Coon, an obscure musician who was later to win the posthumous tribute of a chapter in his former pupil's book, *Of Men and Music*. Aside from this study, Mr. Taylor is a self-taught composer.

Another veteran talent of Taylor's is journalism. When World War I broke out, the New York *Tribune* sent Taylor to France as a correspondent. In 1921, he became music critic for the New York *World*. In 1925, the composer ended his association with the *World* so as to write his first grand opera, *The King's Henchman*. Mr. Taylor has been editor of *Musical America*, associate editor of *Collier's Weekly* and the New York *Tribune*. He has been narrator for the Metropolitan Opera Company broadcasts and commentator for the Sunday afternoon broadcasts of the New York Philharmonic Orchestra. At present, he is the musical advisor for the Columbia Broadcasting Company.

PETER IBBETSON

For *Peter Ibbetson*, Deems Taylor conceived the idea of using a bilingual text, for the action of the famous play by Du Maurier unrolls alternately on both sides of the Channel. Before deciding on this libretto, Deems Taylor experimented with Heywood Broun's *Gandle Follows His Nose* and Elmer Rice's *Street Scene*, but neither supplied the necessary inspiration.

Peter Ibbetson is typical of the dreamy melodrama of Du Maurier's nineteenth-century mind. Briefly, the story is this: Peter Ibbetson is haunted by the memories of his happy childhood with Mimsey, who is now, in 1857, the Duchess of Towers. The children learned to "dream true," which allows them in their later life to divorce themselves from actual reality and plunge into poetic potentiality. Peter recognizes Mimsey when she appears as the Duchess of Towers in a French inn. The sound of the Fate motif from Beethoven's Fifth Symphony accompanies Mimsey's statement that she is not free. Peter's uncle slanders the memory of Peter's mother in a London drawing room, by implying that he is Peter's real father. Peter kills him with his cane, and is sentenced to prison. Mimsey sends him a message to "dream true," which transports him into the realm of his happy childhood. Many years later Mimsey is dead, and Peter dies, too, as the vision of Mimsey appears.

When his earlier opera *The King's Henchman* was produced, Deems Taylor stated openly that he believed in Wagner as an operatic ideal. In *Peter Ibbetson,* however, he changed his mind. "I am not sure just what the form of *Peter Ibbetson* is, but it is not Wagnerian," he stated in an interview. "I started writing it in the expectation that the score would contain the usual assortment of leit-motifs developed in the accepted way. But the music did not work out that way. There are almost no character themes, the music following the situation rather than one individual. Where there is a theme repeated, it recurs not so much as a motif, but rather in a new and further extended form."

The harmonic idiom of the opera has elements of Wagner, quite a modicum of the post-Puccini Italian opera, and just a trace of Debussy. In his war-correspondent days Deems Taylor learned French well, and the vocal line of the French text is remarkably accurate. In the passage where the old inn-keeper suggests to Peter various items on the menu, the characteristic inflection of the pitch placing the tonic accent on the first syllable in *POtage, SAUmone,* and so on, is conveyed with literal precision. In the childhood scenes Deems Taylor has made ample use of French folk songs. When he needed a song to fit contrapuntally with the Polonaise in the first act, he wrote a French folk song himself.

The composer completed the opera in 1930, and dedicated it to Walter Damrosch.

From *Peter Ibbetson* Deems Taylor drew an orchestral suite. Two scenes from the opera, the "Inn Music" from Act II, and the "Dream Music" and "Finale" from Act III were performed by the New York Philharmonic, John Barbirolli conducting, on March 26, 1938.

X-MX-204, Suite, Columbia Broadcasting Symphony, Howard Barlow Conducting.

Peter Ilitch Tchaikovsky

1840–1893

PETER ILITCH TCHAIKOVSKY, the second of five sons, was born in Kamsko-Votkinsk in the Viatka Government, Russia. Though he is regarded as a typical Russian, his ancestry was half French. Tchaikovsky's family seems to have been unaware of his early musical talent, for when he was five his French governess began encouraging his interest in literature, while curtailing his time at the piano.

At seven he did receive regular piano instruction, however, and when the Tchaikovsky family moved to St. Petersburg in 1850 he was placed under the tutelage of Philipov. In time he began the study of jurisprudence and later entered the Ministry of Justice. Perfunctory musical studies continued during this period, as Tchaikovsky had piano lessons under Kündinger and joined a choral class of the famous master Lomakin.

Gradually music came to be the greatest of Tchaikovsky's pleasures, but he had not yet demonstrated any particular originality or ability. An abrupt and dramatic change occurred when he reached the age of twenty. There came an awakening, a sense of disillusion and futility in the realization that he had missed his calling. He saw that his labors for the government were a subterfuge, and that the fulfillment of his destiny lay in another direction.

Tchaikovsky began remedying this by the serious study of theory with Zaremba in 1861, but he cautiously retained his government post until 1863. Then, despite his father's financial reverses, he decided to devote himself exclusively to music.

Students were forthcoming from Anton Rubinstein, founder and director of the St. Petersburg Conservatory, but the income from them was meager, seldom amounting to more than twenty-five dollars a month. In 1865, Tchaikovsky completed his own courses at the

[478]

Conservatory, offering as his thesis a work on Schiller's *Ode to Joy*.

When Nicholas Rubinstein, brother of the famous pianist, organized the Conservatory at Moscow, the young composer was given the post of professor of harmony, and provided with a fortunate opportunity for the public performance of his compositions. In two years he had composed three works of widely varying character—a Festival Overture on the Danish Hymn, a symphony, and an opera.

In 1868, Tchaikovsky came in contact with the nationalist composers' group at St. Petersburg, among whom were Balakirev and Rimsky-Korsakov. While they temporarily influenced his choice of subject matter, he soon returned to his extra-nationalistic attitude, and later spoke of the nationalists with derision.

The next years of his life were increasingly active. There were the emotional upheavals of a short-lived romance with Désirée Artôt, the renowned dramatic soprano; his unfortunate marriage to and separation from Antonina Ivanovna Milyukoff, with his resulting nervous and physical collapse; a continuance of financial worries; and his strange and memorable friendship with his benefactress Nadejda Filaretovna von Meck. Despite these harrowing circumstances, some of his most spontaneous and delightful music was composed during this period.

At Mme. von Meck's tactful insistence Tchaikovsky accepted an allowance which permitted him to compose at will, free from financial concern. From 1880 his fame grew, and he was in demand throughout Europe and in the United States as a conductor of his own works. Alternately he would journey abroad and then retire to the quiet of the Russian countryside to live the life of a recluse, alone save for one or two friends, his garden, and his work.

In 1893, Tchaikovsky became a victim of the cholera epidemic and died at Klin.

CAPRICCIO ITALIEN, OP. 45

DURING the winter of 1879–80 Tchaikovsky, an inveterate traveler, spent three months in Rome. He had been there scarcely a week when he wrote Mme. von Meck that he had heard a "charming popular song" which he expected to use some day. That this song inspired the *Capriccio italien* is a legitimate inference from subsequent correspondence. Thus, in February he informed Mme. von Meck that he was at work on the sketch of an Italian Fantasy for orchestra, based upon folk songs. "Thanks to the charming themes, some of which I have taken from collections and some of which I have heard in the streets, this work will be effective." The instrumentation was finished at Kamenka, after Tchaikovsky's return to Russia.

Tchaikovsky had a good opinion of the work and maintained it, despite the slighting comments of the Moscow and the St. Petersburg press. There was a vein of stubbornness in his character which opposition to his opinions would sometimes expose.

In Moscow, where the *Capriccio* was first heard, it was dubbed "cheap and coarse." A performance in St. Petersburg soon after gave César Cui the chance to express his scorn of Peter Ilitch. "The *Capriccio*," he wrote in his paper, "is certainly no work of art, but it is a valuable gift to the programs of open-air concerts." Cui's venom was unconcealed on this and other occasions when he was called upon to review a new work by Tchaikovsky. This was occasioned by the antipathy, both professional and personal, that the St. Petersburg nationalists, of whom Cui was the mouthpiece, felt for the Moscow cosmopolitan. Tchaikovsky's own attitude toward The Five (Balakirev, Borodin, Cui, Mussorgsky, Rimsky-Korsakov) was far more generous; it also revealed his good critical sense. "Cui," he once told Mme. von Meck, "is a gifted amateur. His music is not original, but it is graceful and elegant. We cannot deny that he is talented."

In one sense, Cui's comments on the *Capriccio italien* proved accurate enough. It was a valuable gift to the programs of open-air concerts. It is one of the pieces in which Tchaikovsky says nothing of any great importance, but says it very well indeed.

X-MX-229, Philharmonic-Symphony Orchestra of New York, Sir Thomas Beecham Conducting.

CONCERTO NO. 1 IN B-FLAT MINOR, OP. 23, FOR PIANO AND ORCHESTRA

Allegro non troppo e molto maestoso · *Allegro con spirito*
Andantino semplice · *Allegro con fuoco*

THIS extremely popular work was composed within the space of one month. Tchaikovsky had long wished to write a piano concerto for his friend and patron Nicholas Rubinstein, the celebrated pianist at the Moscow Conservatory. The composer accordingly invited Rubinstein and a friend to a private performance of the work on Christmas Eve. Tchaikovsky looked forward to the sympathy and encouragement which Rubinstein had extended toward other works. It was therefore a shock when Rubinstein, to whom the score had been dedicated, showed a very indifferent spirit. In the first place, he was annoyed that Tchaikovsky had written the work in secret, and had not consulted him concerning the pianistic passages.

Tchaikovsky described the scene as follows: "I left the room without a word and went upstairs. I could not have spoken for anger and agitation. Presently Rubinstein came to me and, seeing how upset I was, called me into another room. There he repeated that my concerto was impossible, pointed out many places where it needed to be completely revised, and said that if I would suit the concerto to his requirements, he would bring it out at his concert. 'I shall not alter a single note,' I replied. 'I shall publish the work precisely as it stands.' This intention I actually carried out."

Actually, Tchaikovsky did make alterations, a number of them allegedly proposed by Edward Dannreuther when he first played it in London.

This was not its première, for after the rebuke by Rubinstein, Tchaikovsky offered to dedicate the concerto to Hans von Bülow. In a warm letter of thanks, Bülow wrote: "The ideas are so original, so noble, so powerful; the details are so interesting, and though there are many of them, they do not impair the clearness and the unity of the work. The form is so mature, ripe, distinguished in style, for intention and labor are everywhere concealed. I should weary you if I were to enumerate all the characteristics of your work—characteristics which compel me to congratulate equally the composer, as

[481]

well as all those who shall enjoy actively or passively (respectively) the work."

The first performance of the Concerto took place in Boston on October 25, 1875, with Hans von Bülow at the piano. The composer commented upon its reception by New Englanders thus: "The Americans think that the first movement of my Concerto 'suffers in consequence of the absence of a central idea'—and in the finale this reviewer has found 'syncopation in trills, spasmodic pauses in the theme, and disturbing octave passages!' Think what healthy appetites these Americans must have: each time von Bülow was obliged to repeat *the entire Finale* of my Concerto! Nothing like this happens in our country!"

An interesting repercussion was the victory in store for Tchaikovsky. Rubinstein disavowed his earlier opinions, and performed the Concerto publicly thereafter with much success.

The main theme of the first movement is a Malo-Russian air sung by blind beggars at village fairs. The "Hit Parade" song *Tonight We Love* was taken from this first movement.

The lively section of the Andantino semplice is a French song *Il faut s'amuser, danser et rire*, which the composer's brothers used to hum "in remembrance of a certain charming singer" (Désirée Artôt).

The last movement, Allegro con fuoco, opens with a wild Cossack dance, a rondo of strongly national flavor.

M-MM-318, Egon Petri, Piano, and the London Philharmonic Orchestra, Walter Goehr Conducting.

CONCERTO IN D MAJOR, OP. 35, FOR VIOLIN AND ORCHESTRA

Allegro moderato · Canzonetta · Finale: allegro vivacissimo

TCHAIKOVSKY wrote the Violin Concerto in D major in the spring of 1878 at Clarens, a peaceful little town on the lake of Geneva.

The work was dedicated to the celebrated violinist Leopold Auer who, oddly enough, showed no interest in it. Auer explained his indifference by saying that the Concerto was too difficult and too radical to play. Therefore, it remained unplayed for three years—until Adolf Brodsky picked it up. He had been attracted to the beauty of the composition from the first, and he said that for two years he had been waiting only for the courage to learn the demanding work.

Brodsky performed the Concerto for the first time in Vienna in December 1881, with Hans Richter conducting. But his first rendition was not an unqualified success. The Viennese critic Hanslick (whom Wagner caricatured in the person of Beckmesser in his opera *Die Meistersinger*) was well known for his invective, and wrote that "the violin was not played, but beaten black and blue." He also objected to the last movement of the Concerto which he called "odorously Russian." Tchaikovsky said that he would never forget this.

Stimulated rather than discouraged by the unfavorable criticism of the work, Brodsky enthusiastically insisted that he would "continue playing the concerto forever." Richter and Brodsky again presented it, this time in London, with tremendous success. The audience's happy reaction to this performance cheered Tchaikovsky's sensitive soul.

The composition had its first Russian hearing in Moscow—and Brodsky, as soloist, seemed on the way to "playing the concerto forever." The response was great, and Tchaikovsky was called to the stage again and again.

M-MM-413, Nathan Milstein, Violin, and the Chicago Symphony Orchestra, Frederick Stock Conducting.

MARCHE SLAVE, OP. 31

THE MARCH is in three parts, the first of which is a funeral hymn, the middle a trio composed of two brilliant Russian folk dances, and the concluding part a conversion of the opening hymn into a song of victory. Tchaikovsky wrote this work in 1876 for a benefit concert held in honor of the wounded Slavic soldiers of the Turko-Serbian war, and it is not difficult to find in this music that Tchaikovsky's sympathies lay with the Slavs and that through it he was forecasting a Slavic victory.

C-11567-D, Cleveland Orchestra, Artur Rodzinski Conducting.

NUTCRACKER SUITE, OP. 71a

EARLY in 1891, the St. Petersburg Opera commissioned Tchaikovsky to write music for a ballet to the libretto *Casse-Noisette* by Dumas, based on E. T. A. Hoffman's fairy tale *The Nutcracker and the Mouse King*. The ballet was produced at the end of the following year, and the suite of dances in the second act won for the composer great acclaim.

The story of the ballet deals with little Marie, who gives a Christmas party for her friends. She becomes particularly attached to one of her gifts, a wooden nutcracker in the form of an old man with large jaws. During the party the nutcracker is broken by rough boys. That night Marie is unable to sleep, and steals out of bed to have another look at her favorite toy. She is amazed to find that her Christmas tree and all the toys have come to life. A group of mice wage war on the toys, and the nutcracker challenges the mouse king to single combat. The nutcracker is about to be defeated, when Marie saves his life by killing the mouse king with her shoe. At this point the nutcracker turns into a handsome young prince, and takes Marie with him to his enchanted kingdom.

The second scene depicts a mountain of jam, the realm of the Sugarplum Fairy. Marie and the Prince arrive, and the fairies of the court perform a series of dances for their amusement. It is these dances that comprise the so-called *Nutcracker Suite*.

OUVERTURE MINIATURE ("Miniature Overture"): The Overture is written only for higher strings and woodwinds, and is the only part of the Suite which has much relation to the story on which it is based. The triangle adds a piquant touch, and horns are the gravest voice to be heard.

DANSE RUSSE TREPAK ("Russian Dance"): The Russian Dance is a fiery tune played first by the strings, with the woodwinds coming in on the accented beats. Then other choirs take it up while the strings give a staccato accompaniment, and finally the whole orchestra joins in wild abandon.

MARCHE ("March"): In the March, Tchaikovsky takes a simple little tune and works it out with remarkable invention. While the tempo is not slow, there is a slightly mechanical feeling which sug-

[484]

gests a procession of dolls. The music was written for the assembling of the wedding guests in the ballet.

DANSE DE LA FÉE-DRAGÉE ("Dance of the Sugarplum Fairy"): The Dance of the Sugarplum Fairy employed the celesta for the first time. It is heard with the bass clarinet and the English horn.

DANSE ARABE ("Arabian Dance"): The Arabian Dance is a slow, sensuous piece of music which became a great favorite as an "atmospheric" during the days of silent moving pictures. No one could fail to recognize its Oriental flavor. Strings provide a drone bass against which woodwinds intone the lazy theme. English horn and oboe suggest the tone of a musette.

DANSE CHINOISE ("Chinese Dance"): An abrupt change of color and tempo takes us a few thousand miles farther into the Orient. Bassoons and flutes carry most of the motion, with strings and woodwinds thrown in for support. Violins, pizzicato, play a countermelody against the flutes.

DANSE DES MIRLITONS ("Reed-pipe Dance"): The Reed-pipe Dance is a piece of fragile charm, in every way expressive of its name. Three flutes first take the melody, then give way to a contrasting section for trumpets, and return to close the movement with the first theme.

VALSE DES FLEURS ("Waltz of the Flowers"): The Waltz of the Flowers is the thirteenth waltz of the second act of the ballet, and the most pretentious number in the group. There are fifteen measures of introduction in which the theme is presented hesitantly by the woodwinds. After a harp cadenza, the waltz begins. First it is played by the horns with a rippling melody following on the clarinets. Subsequent parts are heard in flutes and piccolo. As the waltz continues, the use of all the resources of the orchestra, in both small and large groups, marks the composer as a master of orchestral writing.

M-MM-627, Philharmonic-Symphony Orchestra of New York, Artur Rodzinski Conducting.

OVERTURE 1812

ALONG with the *Marche Slave* and the *Nutcracker Suite,* the *Overture 1812* seems destined to remain among Tchaikovsky's most popular works with the general public. All have the same qualities in common, stirring themes and brilliant orchestration.

Nicholas Rubinstein suggested to Tchaikovsky in the spring of 1880 that he write a *pièce d'occasion* for the consecration of the Temple of Christ in Moscow. This was to be part of a festival to commemorate the events of 1812, the year of Napoleon's ill-fated attempt to subdue the Russian Empire in the interests of his "new order for Europe." Tchaikovsky's Overture was to be performed in the public square before the cathedral by a colossal orchestra, the big drums to be replaced by salvos of artillery electrically controlled from the conductor's podium. The composition was finished in 1880, but apparently never received its scheduled performance (with artillery obbligato) at the festival. Its official première took place in Moscow on August 20, 1882.

The overture opens quietly with the subject of the old Russian hymn *God Preserve Thy People.* This is worked up to a brief climax followed by quiet, foreboding passages. There follows the main section of the overture, representing the Battle of Borodino. Here snatches of Russian folk music are brought into violent conflict with the *Marseillaise* amid deafening salvos from the orchestral battery. The uproar subsides as the orchestra recapitulates a quiet episode, reminiscent of a Russian peasant tune. The distant horns intone the *Marseillaise.* Then, choir by choir, the full orchestra rejoins the fray in a giant crescendo. The entire string section embarks on probably the longest orchestral cadenza ever written, and the overture ends with the Russian National Hymn triumphant amid the jubilant peal of the bells of Moscow.

X-MX-205, Cleveland Orchestra, Artur Rodzinski Conducting.

ROMEO AND JULIET, OVERTURE-FANTASIA

Romeo and Juliet is an "Overture-Fantasia after Shakespeare," with contents obviously programmatic. When Tchaikovsky wrote the work, Balakirev, dean of the neo-Russian school of composers, supplied Tchaikovsky with considerable gratuitous advice. Balakirev was then living in Moscow.

Tchaikovsky wrote thus to his brother Anatol: "I must confess that his [Balakirev's] presence makes me rather uncomfortable: he obliges me to be with him the whole day, and this is a great bore. It's true he is a very good man, and he is deeply interested in me; but—I don't know why—it is hard work for me to be intimate with him. The narrowness of his musical opinions and his brusque manner do not please me. . . . Nevertheless, his presence has helped me in many ways." And, upon Balakirev's departure: "If he was in my opinion irritating and a bore, justice compels me to say that I consider him to be an honorable and a good man, and an artist that stands immeasurably higher than the crowd. We parted with true emotion."

Tchaikovsky was not, however, desolated by Balakirev's departure. The latter continued to advise him by letter, and Tchaikovsky received from him the following words: "It seems to me that your inactivity comes from the fact that you do not concentrate yourself in spite of your 'friendly hovel' of a lodging. . . . You should know that in thus planning Balakirev's own overture, *King Lear*, I had not as yet any determined ideas. These came later, and began to adjust themselves to the traced outlines of the forms. I believe that all this would happen in your case, if you would only first be enthusiastic over the scheme." Balakirev then offered a thematic suggestion of five measures, and advised Tchaikovsky to meditate upon it while walking briskly along the boulevards.

Tchaikovsky later sent Balakirev the chief themes of *Romeo and Juliet*, perhaps as a courteous acknowledgment of the latter's interest. Balakirev replied with a fussy, wearisome critique of this outline, disparaging much, but enthusiastically applauding one theme.

Tchaikovsky did not take these criticisms as seriously as Balakirev himself did, but made some changes and submitted the result again for Balakirev's remarks. Further criticisms were forthcoming. The overture was completed and scored by November, 1869, but Balakirev was not yet satisfied. "It's a pity that you, or rather, N. Rubin-stein, were in such a hurry about the publication of the overture. Although the new introduction is far more beautiful, I had the ir-resistible wish to change certain passages . . . and not to dismiss it so quickly. . . . I hope that Jurgenson [the publisher] will not refuse to give the score of the newly revised and finally improved overture to the engraver a second time."

Romeo and Juliet received its première in Moscow, in March, 1870. By an unfortunate coincidence, Nicholas Rubinstein, the con-ductor, had been in difficulties at the Moscow Conservatory. Public sentiment was strongly in his favor, and, when he appeared for the concert he was greeted by an overwhelming ovation. In the excite-ment the music was all but forgotten. Tchaikovsky wrote thus of the occasion: "My overture had no success at all here, and was wholly ignored. . . . During the whole evening no one spoke to me a word about the overture. And yet I longed for sympathy and recognition."

In the summer of 1870, while traveling in Switzerland, the com-poser completely rewrote the Overture, with a new introduction, many changes in orchestration, and the removal of a death march which appeared toward the end in the first score. Still further re-visions were made before publication of the second edition in 1881.

M-MM-478, Cleveland Orchestra, Artur Rodzinski Conducting.

SYMPHONY NO. 4 IN F MINOR, OP. 36

Andante sostenuto; Moderato con anima · *Andantino in modo di canzona* · *Scherzo: pizzicato ostinato* · *Finale: allegro con fuoco*

TCHAIKOVSKY was the first and he remains the greatest of the Russian symphonists. The fact that both Rimsky-Korsakov and Borodin ex-perimented with the form before Tchaikovsky got around to it is immaterial. Rimsky's First Symphony (1865) and Borodin's (1867) were palpably the work of amateurs; Tchaikovsky's (1868) was, on the other hand, a thoroughly professional essay, for Tchaikovsky at twenty-eight was already a craftsman of knowledge and skill. He was the most professional musician in the group of his contemporaries.

[488]

Tchaikovsky's own words best tell the story of the F minor Symphony. His letter to Mme. von Meck is here reprinted:

"The Introduction is the kernel, the quintessence, the chief thought of the whole symphony" (opening theme, sounded by horns and bassoons, Andante, F minor, 3-4). "This is Fate, the fatal power which hinders one in the pursuit of happiness from gaining the goal, which jealously provides that peace and comfort do not prevail, that the sky is not free from clouds—a might that swings, like the sword of Damocles, constantly over the head, that poisons continually the soul. This might is overpowering and invincible. There is nothing to do but to submit and vainly complain" (theme for strings, Moderato con anima, F minor, 9-8). "The feeling of despondency and despair grows ever stronger and more passionate. It is better to turn from the realities and to lull one's self in dreams" (clarinet solo with accompaniment of strings). "O Joy! What a fine sweet dream! A radiant being, promising happiness, floats before me and beckons me. The importunate first theme of the allegro is now heard afar off, and now the soul is wholly enwrapped with dreams. There is no thought of gloom and cheerlessness. Happiness! Happiness! Happiness! No, they are only dreams, and Fate dispels them. The whole of life is only a constant alternation between dismal reality and flattering dreams of happiness. There is no port: you will be tossed hither and thither by the waves, until the sea swallows you. Such is the programme, in substance, of the first movement.

"The second movement shows another phase of sadness. Here is that melancholy feeling which enwraps one when he sits at night alone in the house, exhausted by work; the book which he had taken to read has slipped from his hand; a swarm of reminiscences has arisen. How sad it is that so much has already been and gone, and yet it is a pleasure to think of the early years. One mourns the past and has neither the courage nor the will to begin a new life. One is rather tired of life. One wishes to recruit his strength and to look back, to revive many things in the memory. One thinks on the gladsome hours, when the young blood boiled and bubbled and there was satisfaction in life. One thinks also on the sad moments, on irrevocable losses. And all this is now so far away, so far away. And it is all so sad and yet so sweet to muse over the past.

"There is no determined feeling, no exact expression in the third

[489]

movement. Here are capricious arabesques, vague figures which slip into the imagination when one has taken wine and is slightly intoxicated. The mood is now gay, now mournful. One thinks about nothing; one gives the fancy loose reins, and there is pleasure in drawings of marvellous lines. Suddenly rush into the imagination the picture of a drunken peasant and a gutter-song. Military music is heard passing by in the distance. These are disconnected pictures, which come and go in the brain of the sleeper. They have nothing to do with reality; they are unintelligible, bizarre, out-at-elbows.

"Fourth movement. If you find no pleasure in yourself, look about you. Go to the people. See how it understands to be jolly, how it surrenders itself to gaiety. The picture of a folk-holiday. Scarcely have you forgotten yourself, scarcely have you had time to be absorbed in the happiness of others, before untiring Fate again announces its approach. The other children of men are not concerned with you. They neither see nor feel that you are lonely and sad. How they enjoy themselves, how happy they are! And will you maintain that everything in the world is sad and gloomy? There is still happiness, simple, naïve happiness.

"This is all that I can tell you, my dear friend, about the symphony. Rejoice in the happiness of others—and you can still live. My words naturally are not sufficiently clear and exhaustive. It is the characteristic feature of instrumental music, that it does not allow analysis."

M-MM-468, Minneapolis Symphony Orchestra, Dimitri Mitropoulos Conducting.

SYMPHONY NO. 5 IN E MINOR, OP. 64

Andante; Allegro con anima · *Andante cantabile* · *Valse* · *Finale*

TCHAIKOVSKY was disturbed by doubts when, in the spring of 1888, he began to work on his new Symphony. He wrote to his brother Modeste, bemoaning his lack of impulse for creative work, and asking whether he had written himself out. A month later he wrote to his benefactress Nadejda von Meck in a slightly more hopeful vein, that he was anxious to prove both to himself and to others that he had not "sung himself out as a composer."

The Symphony No. 5 was completed in August of that year, and the first two performances within a week in November tended to renew Tchaikovsky's fears. "There is something repellent about it," he wrote, "a patchiness and insincerity and 'manufacturedness' which the public instinctively recognizes." It is strange to read these words about the popular Fifth Symphony which won the affections of a wide public—and holds them after half a century. Tchaikovsky is not *yet* played out, though according to ordinary standards, he ought to be.

Critics have maintained that although Tchaikovsky wrote six symphonies, as well as other large instrumental works, he was not a symphonic composer at all, but rather a writer of ballet suites. He employed symphonic forms because the rules demanded them, not because he had fashioned them, as had Beethoven, or believed in them, as did Brahms. Tchaikovsky himself said that in his instrumental works "the seams show"; there is "no organic union between the separate episodes."

Perhaps the seams show in the Fifth Symphony, which is in some respects a remarkable example of symphonic organization. But after the passage of years, the formal defects seem of relatively small consequence beside the enormous emotional impact of the work. The best explanation is the simplest, although it is but a restatement of the matter: Tchaikovsky was a great composer, whose faults not only do not obscure his virtues, but seem almost to enhance them. Such is the enigma of greatness.

M-MM-470, London Philharmonic Orchestra, Sir Thomas Beecham Conducting.

SYMPHONY NO. 6 (PATHÉTIQUE) IN B MINOR

Adagio; Allegro non troppo · Allegro con grazia · Allegro molto vivace · Finale

THE TITLE *Pathétique* for his Sixth Symphony was suggested to Tchaikovsky by his brother Modeste, a librettist and biographer. The word *pathétique*, in the Russian or French spoken by the Tchaikovsky brothers, has a more immediate reference to *pathos*, the Greek word for *suffering*, than has the corresponding English word. Thus,

[491]

Tchaikovsky's Sixth Symphony was named in effect a "Symphony of Suffering." The naming was done after the Symphony was completed, and some analysts' attempts to connect the Sixth Symphony with Beethoven's *Sonata pathétique* are entirely gratuitous.

Tchaikovsky dedicated the Sixth Symphony to his nephew Davidov, of whom he was passionately fond. He wrote to him on February 11, 1893: "During my journey [to America] I conceived a plan of a symphony with a program, but with a program that will remain a secret to everyone. . . . Let them guess, and I will name it simply a *symphony with a program*." In another letter he wrote that the program was full of personal meaning. Tchaikovsky's state of emotional stress was particularly acute during the last two years of his life, the period when the Sixth Symphony was conceived and written. "Often, during my travels, I was mentally composing my symphony, and wept, and wept," wrote Tchaikovsky.

Scattered sketches for a program of the symphony were found in Tchaikovsky's notebooks and papers. An early program written in Tchaikovsky's characteristic handwriting in large letters reads: "These sketches are for a symphony, LIFE. The first movement is all hope, conviction, thirst for action. It should be short. . . . *Finale*, DEATH, result of destruction." In parenthesis, there was given a program for the second movement, Love, and third movement, Disillusion. In another place, Tchaikovsky made notes for a program of the first version of the Symphony: "Motif: for what purpose? What for? The beginning and the main idea of the whole symphony."

This program of utter futility was nothing new in Tchaikovsky's mental outlook. The Fourth and the Fifth symphonies were similarly outlined, with Fate as the supreme arbiter of human strivings. In the Sixth Symphony, the apotheosis of human suffering goes farther than in Tchaikovsky's other music. The first movement of the Symphony gives away the hidden intent by the inclusion of the Russian hymn of mourning "Let him rest with the Saints," which appears in the brass after the nervous fugato. Further confirmation of the program is found in a letter Tchaikovsky wrote to Grand Duke Constantin, in reply to the latter's suggestion that Tchaikovsky should compose music to the poem *Requiem*, by the contemporary Russian poet Apukhtin, a classmate of Tchaikovsky.

"I am a little embarrassed," wrote Tchaikovsky, "by the circumstance that my symphony, which I have just finished, is in its mood very close to the *Requiem*. I believe my symphony is a successful work, and I fear I would repeat myself if I would undertake a composition so close in its spirit and character to its predecessor." Tchaikovsky considered the Sixth Symphony his greatest accomplishment. He wrote to Davidov on August 3, 1893: "I consider the Symphony positively my best and my sincerest work, and I love it as I have never loved any of my musical offspring."

However successful the Sixth Symphony was in the eyes of its creator and in the eyes of the world, it did not come to Tchaikovsky spontaneously. In fact, he labored over it more than over any of his large works. The numerous sketches of the early version of the Symphony were quite different from the ultimate product. In a letter to Ippolitov-Ivanov, dated March 24, 1893, Tchaikovsky says that he had a complete symphony all ready, and that he tore it up. "But I have written a new symphony," adds Tchaikovsky, "and most certainly, I will not tear it up."

The tragic significance of the Sixth Symphony is enhanced by the fact that Tchaikovsky died eight days after he conducted the world première at St. Petersburg, on October 28, 1893. In America, where the memories of Tchaikovsky's visit were fresh, Walter Damrosch announced the première of Tchaikovsky's last symphony. The score and parts of the Symphony, which Tchaikovsky had sent to Damrosch, arrived after Tchaikovsky's death.

M-MM-558, New York Philharmonic-Symphony Orchestra, Artur Rodzinski Conducting.
M-MM-432, Leopold Stokowski Conducting the All-American Youth Orchestra.

Virgil Thomson

1896–

VIRGIL THOMSON was born in Kansas City, Missouri, in 1896. After serving in the first World War, he pursued his musical studies at Harvard and in Paris. For a time he taught at Harvard, conducted the Harvard Glee Club, and played the organ at King's Chapel in Boston. He later returned to Paris, where he lived and composed until the arrival of the Germans; he came to New York. Now music critic for the New York *Herald Tribune,* he has also appeared as guest conductor of his own compositions with the Philadelphia Orchestra, the Philharmonic-Symphony Orchestra of New York, the Cincinnati Symphony, Indianapolis Symphony, and St. Louis Symphony.

Foremost among Thomson's works are the opera, *Four Saints in Three Acts,* with a libretto by Gertrude Stein, music for the Pare Lorentz films *The Plow That Broke the Plains* and *The River,* and *Symphony on a Hymn Tune.* He is the author of two books: *The State of Music* and *The Musical Scene.*

FIVE PORTRAITS

BUGLES AND BIRDS	TANGO LULLABY
PERCUSSION PIECE	FUGUE
CANTABILE FOR STRINGS	

THE COMPOSER himself has supplied the following description of his *Five Portraits:*

"The description of character through music is an ancient preoccupation of composers. Among those who have practiced it assiduously are Forqueray the Elder and the great François Couperin. Robert Schumann included personal sketches in his *Carnaval.* Anton Rubinstein made a set of twelve likenesses under the title of *Kam-*

menoi Ostrow, the well-known Prelude to these being a picture of his island home, where the persons depicted had on one occasion all been gathered together. Sir Edward Elgar's *Enigma Variations* are likewise portraits of friends.

"I first started making musical portraits in 1928. The gallery of them now includes over a hundred. These are scored for various instruments and combinations of instruments—for piano, for violin alone, for violin and piano, for organ, for string quartet, for a quartet of clarinets, for larger chamber groups, and for full orchestra. The subject sits for his likeness as he would for a painter, and the music is composed in front of him, usually at one sitting. Orchestral scoring is worked out in detail later.

"The musical style of the pieces varies with the personality of the subject. Sometimes it is harmonious, sometimes dissonant, sometimes straightforwardly tuneful, sometimes thematically or contrapuntally developed. An effort has been made to catch in all cases a likeness recognizable to persons acquainted with the sitter. The interest of these pieces for the musical public at large, however, must depend, of course, on whatever intrinsic merit they may be found to possess."

The five movements in the Suite are thus described by Mr. Thomson:

"*Bugles and Birds,* a portrait of the painter Pablo Picasso, is a representation of the man, not of his work, save in so far as certain traits of character are marked in both. . . .

"The *Percussion Piece* depicts Mrs. Chester Whitin Lasell of Whitinsville, Massachusetts, a California lady long resident in New England. . . .

"The *Cantabile for Strings* describes a young painter of Russian birth, Nicolas de Chatelain. . . .

"The *Tango Lullaby* depicts as a young girl Mademoiselle Flavie Alvarez de Tolédo (now Madame Jean-Pierre Cazelles), daughter of the Marquis and Marquise de Casa Fuerte. . . .

"The *Fugue* is a representation of the American conductor Alexander Smallens. . . ."

The *Five Portraits* received their first concert performance in orchestral form at a concert of the Philadelphia Orchestra, the composer conducting, on November 17, 1944.

X-MX-255, Philadelphia Orchestra, Virgil Thomson Conducting.

[495]

Giuseppe Verdi

1813–1901

G IUSEPPE VERDI was born in 1813 in the small village of Le Ron-
cole, in the province of Parma, Italy. His father was the
owner of a shabby inn. It is said that the boy's musical talent
was discovered by a strolling musician who played in front of the
father's inn.

In his early 'teens, Verdi was apprenticed to a cobbler in the town
of Busseto, three miles away. After two years, a wealthy merchant,
Barezzi, hired him as a grocery clerk and musical assistant (for
Barezzi was also the sponsor of the local orchestra which rehearsed
in his house). Copying out the orchestral parts, coaching, and composing his first pieces brought Verdi the musical experience he felt
would enable him to enter the Milan Conservatory. He was, however, turned down. He was not only over-age (nineteen), but poorly
dressed, awkward, not a particularly good performer on the piano,
and with a still limited compositorial technique. Verdi never forgot
this humiliation, and as an old and famous man often referred to it
with bitterness.

He studied privately with the La Scala coach and opera composer,
Lavigna, and acquired enough of a technique to be able to write his
first opera, *Oberto*. *Oberto* was produced at La Scala (November 17,
1839) and was such a remarkable success that offers came to the
composer from the publisher Ricordi, and Merelli, the La Scala director.

. The future began to look promising, when tragedy struck, and
struck hard. First Verdi fell ill. Then, within the space of a few weeks,
both his young wife and small daughter died. Finally, the first opera
he wrote for La Scala—written during these dark days—was an outright failure. Verdi, obsessed by gloom and futility, secluded himself
in an attic where he spent his time reading trashy novels. He might

have abandoned composing altogether if Merelli of La Scala did not finally prevail upon him to set the biblical theme of Nebuchadnezzar to music. Performed at La Scala in 1842 as *Nabucco,* the opera was an immediate success. The chorus, "Fly, my thoughts, on golden wings," took Italy by storm. Verdi was now acclaimed the opera-composer of the future; his days of want and struggle were at an end.

He was showered with commissions for operas. *Ernani* (1844) established his fame abroad; *I Masnadieri* (1847) was his first opera commissioned by a foreign opera house—London.

With the composition of *Luisa Miller* (1849), Verdi entered a new phase, generally identified today as his middle period. From now on, human beings—very much alive with their personal problems and passions—dominated the stage of his operas. Between 1851 and 1853 came a succession of masterpieces which made him the most famous opera composer of his day: *Rigoletto, II Trovatore,* and (though this work was originally a failure) *La Traviata.*

At about the time that *Rigoletto* went into rehearsal, the exiled Wagner issued another of his voluminous treatises about the principles of opera composition. Some critics soon found a direct association between these theories and the development of Verdi's style at the time. From *Rigoletto* through *Aïda,* Verdi was told (with increasing emphasis and annoying persistence) that he was a disciple of Wagner, and owed much of his success to the German's spiritual guidance. Verdi grew increasingly annoyed at these charges—particularly since he disliked the Germans, and had little use for Wagner's theories. His irritation grew particularly strong after the production of *Aïda* and played no small part in his decision to retire. He was firmly convinced that as a creative artist he was through; that his operas were no longer understood or wanted. For sixteen years he wrote nothing but the Requiem and his only string quartet. Finally, Ricordi virtually tricked him into his glorious come-back with *Otello* (1887) and *Falstaff* (1893), in which an even greater Verdi emerges.

On the morning of January 21, 1901, Verdi suffered a stroke while dressing. He never regained consciousness, and died six days later. His last will called for a simple funeral—no pomp, speeches, or even music. His wish was carried out.

AÏDA

THIS noble example of Verdi's genius at its maturest period of development was first performed at Cairo on the 24th of December, 1871. It was not, as is generally stated, commissioned by the Khedive Ismail-Pasha for the opening of his new opera-house, which had been inaugurated nearly two years previously. It was intended to be a work that should bring honor to the new theatre by conferring distinction upon its repertoire; and this purpose it not only fulfilled then, but has continued to do so ever since. Aïda was an opera written for an Egyptian ruler (who paid £4,000 sterling for the privilege), dealing with an Egyptian story, and submitted in the Egyptian capital to the judgment of the Egyptian people. After satisfying that severe test, it was produced six weeks later—February 7th, 1872—at La Scala, Milan; at the Théâtre Italien, Paris, on April 22nd, 1876; at Covent Garden on June 22nd, 1876; and thenceforward went the round of the world with triumphant and ever-increasing success.

The story of Aïda, Egyptian as it is in patriotic character and local color, is in no sense historical. The idea of the drama originated with a distinguished French Egyptologist named Mariette Bey, who having sketched out the plot, entrusted it to another clever Frenchman, Camille du Locle, an experienced playwright and librettist. M. du Locle was staying at the time with Verdi, at his villa near Busseto, and, under the master's own supervision, laid out the story as a four-act drama, writing it in French and in prose, with all the wealth of local archaeological detail that Mariette Bey had suggested. The task of converting this into operatic form and free Italian verse was undertaken by Antonio Ghislanzoni, who acquitted himself of it with a poetic skill and dramatic force altogether new to the Italian libretti of that epoch. Around the love of Rhadames (captain of the Egyptian guard) for the slave Aïda, daughter of the King of Ethiopia, a powerful story was constructed. Rhadames conquers the Ethiopians in battle, and captures their king, who prevails on his daughter to steal the battle plans from Rhadames. She does this, and when Rhadames is discovered he is punished by being sealed in a tomb. There he finds Aïda waiting for him. It should be noted that Verdi's own share in the construction of the various scenes had been an important and practical one, and, according to M. du Locle, "the idea f the finale of the last act, with its two stages one above the other, belongs especially to him."

To this fact must be attributed no small measure of the inspiration that wrought in the music of Aïda so remarkable a change of harmonic treatment and style on the part of the gifted composer (now in his 56th year)—a change only slightly foreshadowed in his preceding operas, La Forza del Destino and Don Carlos. When it was first heard, the majority of the critics were inclined to perceive in the score of Aïda all the traces of a powerful Wagnerian influence. On subsequent reflection—especially as they became better acquainted with the music and methods of the Bayreuth master—they gradually modified their opinion. Certain resemblances there might be; but it was hard to lay a finger on them, still harder to analyze them. This new and beautiful music, these strange and poignant harmonic progressions, might be "advanced" Verdi, but they were still pure Verdi, and not modeled upon any other school, "advanced" German or otherwise.

Today Aïda is recognized as one of the most original as well as one of the most impressive and satisfying works in the entire range of the lyric drama. Replete throughout with character and rich coloring, it attains its climax of tonal grandeur in the superb ensemble of the second act, only to leave a reserve of further climaxes, rare in their musical beauty, their dramatic intensity, and their wealth of phrases, alike grateful for the singer and full of haunting, enduring charm for the listener.

OP-MOP-3, Lombardi, Lindi, Borgioli, Passero, and Chorus and Orchestra of La Scala, Lorenzo Molajoli Conducting.

FALSTAFF

THREE years after the production of Otello, Verdi and Boïto happened to discuss the subject of comic opera. "What do you think Rossini meant when he said to me that I could never treat a comic subject?" Verdi asked his friend and librettist. The question inspired Boïto to write a libretto for the great composer, a comic libretto based on Shakespeare's The Merry Wives of Windsor.

[499]

Reluctantly, Verdi—then on the eve of his eightieth birthday—consented to write the music for it. He worked only two hours a day to avoid strain. To the very last he insisted that he would not allow the opera to be performed, that he considered it only as an idle pastime.

However, Verdi finally did permit *Falstaff* to be performed—at La Scala on February 9, 1893. It was his last opera; and there are many musicians (Richard Strauss among them) who consider it his greatest. The musical principle governing *Otello* was transferred into the world of comedy: there is the same continuous flow of music supporting and illustrating the action. *Falstaff* moves at a breath-taking pace. Breezy, gossipy, extremely alive, the recitatives seem to course in and out of the ensemble numbers with the utmost flexibility. The musical variety of the score is extraordinary. Melodies, or snatches of melodies, follow each other, intertwine, overlap. Characterizations are often compressed in a single bar. The orchestration is so subtle, brilliant, and ingenious that each measure is a miniature masterpiece of instrumental writing. The same consummate skill went into the vocal ensembles. Even the severest musical form, that of the fugue, was made to express merriment and mockery; and it is singularly ironical that this master of the Italian lyric line should have ended his career as an operatic composer not with a beautiful aria but with a magnificent eight-voice fugue, sung to the words *Tutto nel mond'è burla* ("It's all fun in this world").

Music and play blend magnificently; for Boïto's libretto is as gay and as sparkling as Verdi's music. Falstaff, the rotund rake, writes identical love notes to two women, who, learning this, decide to give him a lesson. One of these women, Mrs. Ford, invites him to her home. The arrival of the other woman, Mrs. Page, forces Falstaff to hide in a clothes basket, from which he is soon afterwards unceremoniously dumped out of the window. Later, Mrs. Ford invites Falstaff to a park where a love scene ensues. Her husband and his friends, disguised as nymphs and elves, burst in upon this idyllic scene and give Falstaff a thorough beating.

OP-MOP-16, Rimini, Tassinari, Buades, Tellini, Nessi, D'Alessio, Baccaloni, Venturini, and Chorus and Orchestra of La Scala, Lorenzo Molajoli Conducting.

OTELLO

THE STORY of the composition of *Otello* actually began as early as 1862 when Verdi met the young Arrigo Boïto in Paris, recognized his remarkable talent, and commissioned him to prepare the words for *The Hymn of the Nations*. Subsequently the two became estranged when Boïto embraced the cult of Wagnerism. When, in the early 1870's Boïto repudiated Wagner, he found Verdi unapproachable.

Meanwhile, Verdi produced *Aïda* and retired. Ricordi knew that only a first-rate libretto could tempt Verdi to return to composition. At a dinner party arranged by Ricordi in 1879, the publisher injected the name of Boïto into the conversation. The very next day he sent the younger man to visit Verdi. Reconciliation was now effected, and three days later, Boïto returned with an outline of an *Otello* libretto.

Verdi completed his opera in 1886. The first performance in February of the following year was anticipated feverishly. The première was a sensation. After the performance crowds followed Verdi to his hotel, shouting his name under his windows. They were not only paying personal tribute to the aged composer who could still write music so convincingly passionate, but they also celebrated this event as a victory of their own art over that of the Germans.

Otello was genuine music drama, but Verdi's own kind of music drama, in which emphasis was placed on the characterizations of human beings. Verdi's melodies are here less sweeping and dramatic than in his earlier operas. It is the orchestra which illustrates the action, situation, meditations; a continuous stream of music carries the action, only rarely interrupted by a static vocal number.

Melodic refinement, exquisite taste, an expressive harmonic pattern characterize *Otello*. The three major scenes of Otello and Desdemona proceed gradually toward the catastrophe: the love duet in the first act is lyrical and moving; the exciting duet in the third act contrasts her bewildered innocence with Otello's demoniac jealousy; the last scene is a gripping psychological drama, poignant with emotion. The dramatic highlight of the entire opera is probably the "Oath" duet in the second act, in which the sinister, agile, scheming baritone is brought into contrast with the ponderous, helplessly desperate tenor.

Verdi himself personally supervised the production of his opera and was able to achieve not only a unity between words and music, but also a unity of words and music and stage. Thus, in his own way, Verdi achieved a Wagnerian synthesis of the arts, and in doing so created one of his outstanding masterpieces.

The Shakespeare drama, on which Boïto based his libretto, is famous. Otello, a Moor, is passionately in love with his wife Desdemona. Insanely jealous of her, he suspects her, and without justification, of being unfaithful, and finally kills her.

7299-M, Credo, Riccardo Stracciari, Baritone, with Orchestra.

71389-D, Death of Otello, Lauritz Melchior, Tenor, and Columbia Opera Orchestra, Erich Leinsdorf Conducting.

71389-D, Monologue of Otello, Lauritz Melchior, Tenor, and Columbia Opera Orchestra, Erich Leinsdorf Conducting.

REQUIEM

WHEN Rossini died in 1868, Verdi arranged an ambitious project whereby twelve Italian composers were to collaborate with him in writing a Requiem Mass. He himself composed the last movement—the fugue, "Libera me." Inconsistencies of style and outlook jeopardized the execution of this project. Mazzucato of the Milan Conservatory saw Verdi's portion and suggested that he write the entire Requiem himself. Verdi sketched some of the movements, but his interest in the composition was pushed to a background by *Aïda*.

On May 22, 1873, the famous Italian poet and novelist, Alessandro Manzoni, died. Verdi, who worshiped the writer, was so deeply affected that he was incapable of going to the funeral, but instead made a secret visit to the grave a few days later. To honor Manzoni, he decided to write a Requiem Mass.

The first performance of this work took place on the anniversary of Manzoni's death, on May 22, 1874, at the Chiesa di San Marco in Milan. Verdi, who conducted himself, had carefully prepared the performance. Its success at its première, and in subsequent Italian performance, was overwhelming. Verdi and Ricordi had to take special precautions to prevent unauthorized performances: in Bologna, for example, it was performed not by an orchestra but by four pianos, while in Ferrara it was given by the local military band. During

1875, Verdi took the Requiem on tour, visiting Paris, London, and Vienna; in Vienna, it was given four times to full houses in spite of prohibitive prices and excessive summer heat.

The Requiem is filled with wonderful Verdi melodies, Verdi taste, and Verdi compositorial skill. The first movement (Requiem and Kyrie) is quiet and exalted, to which the dramatic Dies Ira provides an effective contrast. The Tuba mirum is introduced by trumpets. The Domine Jesu, Sanctus, and Agnus Dei are the three portions in which the operatic style is particularly evident. The Lux aeterna, a beautiful trio, leads to the concluding fugue, Libera me.

In May 1923, Arturo Toscanini conducted a memorable performance of the Requiem in Milan in honor of the fiftieth anniversary of Manzoni's death.

RIGOLETTO

VERDI's seventeenth opera, *Rigoletto*, was based on Victor Hugo's *Le Roi s'amuse*, a political play which was banned after the first-night performance because of its satiric overtones. The libretto by Francesco Maria Piave is one of the best that Verdi set to music. It has dramatic impact, and strong characterization. The central figure, the hunchback jester of the Duke of Mantua—"deformed and ridiculous, but full of love and passion," was the way Verdi described him —offers the basis for the development of the entire opera through the contrasts in his character. And the veiled father-daughter fixation (a favorite Verdi motive) is the driving force behind the plot.

Rigoletto collaborates with the courtiers of the Duke of Mantua to abduct a Countess with whom the latter is in love. But Rigoletto is duped. Blindfolded, he is led to his own home where his daughter, Gilda, is the victim. When Rigoletto learns that it is his daughter who has been seized for the Duke he vows vengeance, and hires an assassin to murder him. The assassin reneges on the bargain and decides to murder the first person he meets and pass him off as the dead Duke. Satisfied that justice has been done, Rigoletto carries a sack with the dead body to throw it in the river when, from the distance, he hears the voice of the Duke. Rigoletto looks into the sack, only to discover that it is his own daughter who has been murdered.

Rigoletto, among the most popular operas of all time, contains three lyrical numbers constantly heard apart from the opera: the coloratura aria, *"Caro nome,"* the famous tenor aria, *"La Donna è mobile,"* and the famous quartet in the last act, *"Bella figlia."*

The première of the opera at the Teatro Fenice in Venice on March 11, 1851 was an instantaneous success. Even Victor Hugo, who did not like operas, had to confess that *Rigoletto* had won him over. *Rigoletto* quickly became the rage in Italy and, within a few years, in Central and Western Europe as well.

OP-MOP-18, Caspir, Borgioli, Mannarini, Stracciari, with Chorus and Orchestra of La Scala, Lorenzo Molajoli Conducting.

LA TRAVIATA

Francesco Maria Piave based his libretto on Dumas's famous play *La Dame aux camelias,* which deals with a courtesan in whom true love awakens. It gives a vivid picture of the Paris of that time, and the heroine was modeled on the notorious demi-mondaine, Marie Duplessis. Piave intensified the emotions, omitted minor characters, but, on the whole, kept to Dumas's pattern. For the first time, a serious opera was removed from the world of kings, intrigues, and political plots into the drawing room in which the bourgeois world struggled with personal human problems.

The intimacy and warmth of feeling which the book demanded received their due from the composer. *La Traviata* has been called a chamber opera; the orchestra is somewhat smaller than in other Verdi operas and handled with greater lucidity and refinement. The lovely preludes to the first and third acts are sensitive and restrained. The two soprano arias (*"Ah! fors è lui"* and *"Addio del passato"*) brim over with feeling.

La Traviata was the forerunner of the realistic operas of Puccini, Leoncavallo, etc. In its own day, however, it was fiercely denounced. Objections were raised against it on moral and aesthetic grounds, for it was considered highly improper to show a courtesan dying of consumption.

At the world première, at the Teatro Fenice in Venice on March 6, 1853, *La Traviata* was one of the great fiascos in operatic history. A bad production was partly responsible; partly responsible, too, were some of the innovations, such as having the characters wear the street clothes of the day. The melancholy atmosphere of the entire work irritated the audience. "*La Traviata* yesterday was a fiasco," Verdi wrote to a friend. "Was the fault mine or the singers'? Time will tell."

Fourteen months later the opera was revived in a different theatre, with a different cast (wearing costumes from the Louis XIII period), and with slight revisions. This performance established the opera as a favorite. In 1856, *La Traviata* reached England, where it was fiercely attacked in the pulpit. Clerical resistance aroused the curiosity of the public, and the success of the opera actually saved Her Majesty's Theatre from financial ruin.

The story of the opera is well-known. The courtesan, Violetta, decides to turn over a new leaf because of her great love for Alfred Germont. Alfred's father intervenes and succeeds in convincing Violetta to give up her lover. She returns to her old life. One evening, she meets Alfred who, ignorant that she had renounced him for his own good, avoids her. When Alfred does learn the truth it is too late, for Violetta is on her death-bed with consumption. Before she dies, she hears from Alfred of his great love for her.

OP-MOP-25, Soloists, Chorus, and Orchestra of Rome Opera House, Vincenzo Bellezza Conducting.

IL TROVATORE

THE STARTLING success of *Rigoletto* in 1851 enabled Verdi to rest for a period of nearly two years. He emerged from this mental hibernation, refreshed and invigorated. At the end of 1852, he decided to set music to a text arranged by Cammarano, adapted from a tragedy by a young Spanish author. This opera, *Il Trovatore* eventually proved to be the most popular of all works of its kind. Based on a plot none too cheerful or credible, the composition might well have been doomed to failure but for the melodic fecundity of Verdi's genius. Two emotional conflicts—expressed in beautiful lyric episodes—though dramatically in violent contrast, became harmonious by Verdi's exquisite treatment. One of the vilest of operatic characters (the Count di Luna), is given a song of imperishable beauty. The melancholy atmosphere of the drama is counteracted by the transcendent charm of it luxuriant melodies. Even poets have been inspired to surround the opera with the glittering glamor of their Muse. One of the English poets, Alfred Noyes, became ecstatic about Verdi when he wrote:—

"Verdi, Verdi, when you wrote *Il Trovatore* did you dream
　　Of the City when the sun sinks low.
Of the organ and the monkey and the many coloured Stream
On the Piccadilly pavement, of the myriad eyes that seem
To be litten for a moment with a wild Italian gleam
As *A che la morte* parodies the world's eternal theme
　　And pulses with the sunset-glow?"

The story of *Il Trovatore* came from the pen of a Spanish youth, who at 17 years of age wrote and completed the drama in verse. This young dramatist, Antonio Garcia Gutierrez, was about to be conscripted into the army, when he was notified of the decision to produce his play. Its immediate success gained for him the right to pay for a substitute to perform his military service, so enabling him to pursue a successful literary career.

The excitement prevailing before the production in Rome was astonishing. The day before the first presentation (which took place at the Teatro Apollo in Rome, on January 19, 1853), the Tiber had overflowed its banks. All the approaches to the Apollo Theatre were flooded. Hundreds of Verdi's enthusiastic admirers formed a lengthy queue, ankle to knee-deep in water, waiting from early morning until evening to obtain places for the first performance. Needless to say, the opera was a brilliant success.

It might be said with justification that the parts of *Il Trovatore* are greater than the whole. The opera is complicated and diffuse, but portions of it are among the most famous in all opera, notably the Anvil and Soldier choruses, the *"Miserere,"* the *"Stride la vampa,"* the *"Il balen,"* and the *"Ai nostri monti."*

OP-MOP-9, Scacciati, Zinetti, Merli, Molinari, Zambelli, Mannarini, Venturini, Arnaldi, with Chorus and Orchestra of La Scala, Lorenzo Molajoli Conducting.

[506]

Heitor Villa-Lobos

1881–

HEITOR VILLA-LOBOS probably the greatest and most prolific of all contemporary South American composers, is almost entirely self-taught. He combines in his music the elements of typical South American rhythms, the primitive, exotic qualities of the native music of the Indian tribes in the Brazilian hinterland, and the many original ideas that he has evolved from his own fertile imagination. So interested was he in the indigenous music of Brazil that he made an expedition into some of the unexplored territories of the country in order to collect specimens of Indian songs and dances. This native folk music had a permanent influence on Villa-Lobos's own style of composition, for he fused into his own idiom qualities of the Brazilian folk song.

He was born in Rio de Janeiro in 1881. His father taught him the 'cello and piano. This, with the exception of a brief but unsatisfactory period at the National Institute of Music, was Villa-Lobos's only formal instruction. After his father died, Villa-Lobos—then eleven—earned his living playing in commercial orchestras. In 1912, he made the first of his scientific expeditions into the interior of Brazil for the purpose of uncovering native folk songs and dances. Three years after this, the first concert devoted to his works took place in Rio de Janeiro. From then on his reputation increased. In 1922, he was enabled to live and study in Paris by virtue of a government subsidy. When he returned to his native land, Villa-Lobos not only assumed a position of pre-eminent importance among the composers of Brazil, but he also took an active part in the educational life of the country, revolutionizing its school system in his office as Supervisor and Director of Music Education. In November 1944, he visited the United States for the first time.

BACHIANAS BRASILEIRAS

The strange fusion of the style of Johann Sebastian Bach with elements of Brazilian folk music has resulted in seven suites, which are among Villa-Lobos's most popular works. Each suite is divided into several movements, all of which have duplicate titles, one set being of a classical nature in true Bach tradition (Prelude, Chorale, Aria, Toccata), the other with intimate Brazilian allusions. The second of these suites, for example, has the following alternate titles: I. Prelude (Song of the Hoodlum); II. Aria (Song of Our Country); III. Danza (Woodland Memory); IV. Toccata (The Little Train to Caipira). Written for various combinations of instruments, these suites have been uniquely successful in incorporating the rich native colors, the sensuous moods, the dynamic rhythms of Brazil's folk idioms with the mobile and lucid counterpoint of Bach.

71760, No. 5, Bidu Sayao, Soprano, with Orchestra Conducted by the Composer.

SERÉSTAS

The *Seréstas*—or Serenades—contain a combination of the qualities most often found in Villa-Lobos's music. Though they were written in 1925–26, during the composer's eight-year sojourn in Paris, they are distinctly Brazilian in flavor and are punctuated throughout with infectious South American rhythms. The original set contained twelve *Seréstas*, and Villa-Lobos added two more in 1943. Of especial interest is the *Modinha*, the Brazilian form of a melancholy love song, supposed to have been inspired by the old Italian operatic arias.

X-MX-249, Jennie Tourel, Mezzo Soprano, with Orchestra Conducted by Heitor Villa-Lobos.

Antonio Vivaldi

1675–1741

VIVALDI belongs with Corelli to that early school of Italian composers who were responsible for the development of instrumental music in general, and the concert form in particular. It is quite true that Vivaldi wrote numerous operas and choral works as well; but it is his music in the concerto form which has kept his name significant in musical history.

Vivaldi was born in Venice in or about 1675. In his fifteenth year he decided to enter the Church, and in 1703 he was ordained a priest. Meanwhile he began music study and acquired a considerable reputation as a virtuoso of the violin. Music began to assume such a prominent role in his life that he finally decided to leave the Church and to devote himself entirely to the practice of his art. In 1714, he became music master of the Ospedale della Pieta—a foundling hospital in Venice—where he remained to the end of his life.

CONCERTI GROSSI

VIVALDI wrote two sets of concerti grossi. The first of these (Op. 3) he called *L'Estro harmonico* (Harmonic Inspiration), which was published in Amsterdam between 1714 and 1716. Containing twelve works, this set is most notable for the eleventh concerto in D minor, which is probably the best known of Vivaldi's works to present-day concertgoers. This work is in three movements, the first of which is a robust Allegro, the second a highly poetic and beautiful Intermezzo, and the third a sweeping and dramatic Allegro.

In the second set, Op. 8—published in Amsterdam at an unknown date under the title *Il Cimento dell' Armonia e dell' Invenzioni* (The Trial of Harmony and Invention)—the first four works are most notable. These are in turn subtitled *Le quattro staggioni* (The Four Seasons), and beginning with Spring give fascinating tonal pictures, often literally programmatic, of the four seasons of the year.

[509]

Richard Wagner

1813–1883

THE conception of the music drama, as distinguished from that
of opera (the pioneers of which were Gluck and Weber),
reached its completest and fullest realization with Richard
Wagner. By regarding the music drama as the synthesis of several
different arts (each one significant in its own right), Wagner virtually evolved a new art form, uniquely his, which opened a new world
for the opera. Wagner's wonderful sense for good theater—a sense
which never seemed to desert him; his revolutionary concept of what
opera should be—away from the concept of set numbers and arias
and toward the realization of perpetually flowing melody; his incomparable technical skill in handling music of Gargantuan design;
his infinite harmonic, contrapuntal and melodic resources; his ability
to achieve through music an expressiveness, an articulateness not
known before; his adroit use of the *leitmotif*—a leading theme descriptive of a character, situation or emotion—to integrate and unify
his operas; his incomparable gift at characterization; his literary powers which made it possible for him to write his own poetic dramas—
all these were some of the talents which, miraculously combined in
one man, helped to create a Wagner.

Richard Wagner was born in Leipzig in 1813. For a long time the
question of his parentage has been in great doubt. But in recent
years, as a result of a lifelong research, Ernest Newman has come to
the conclusion that Wagner's father was not (as was generally believed) Karl Friedrich Wagner, a police court clerk, but the Jewish
actor-playwright, Ludwig Geyer, a dear friend of the Wagner family.
After Karl Friedrich's death, Richard's mother married Ludwig
Geyer.

Wagner attended the Kreuzschule in Dresden where he showed at
first a far greater talent for literature than for music. In his fourteenth

year, he heard a Beethoven symphony for the first time. That event sealed his fate, for he knew that henceforth music not literature was to be his chosen profession. He plunged into study of harmony and counterpoint, and produced several youthful efforts, including an orchestral overture which was performed in Leipzig.

In 1830, Wagner entered the University of Leipzig, during which period his preoccupation with music was no less intense. He studied compositions passionately, and wrote many works, two of which—an overture and a symphony—were performed by the Gewandhaus Orchestra. A position as chorus master at the Würzburg Theater turned his interests from symphonic to operatic music. In 1834 he wrote his first opera, *Die Feen,* following this was the writing of *Das Liebesverbot* (based on Shakespeare's *Measure for Measure*). Neither opera was produced.

His next position was as director of a small opera company in Magdeburg, one of whose members was Minna Planer. After the collapse of this company, Wagner and Minna Planer were married—on November 24, 1836.

Wagner's next stop was Riga, where he came to accept a post as music director. There he plunged so deeply into debt that, to escape prison, he had to smuggle himself and his wife across the Russian border. The Wagners went on to London, and from there to Paris. The three years he spent in Paris were in some respects the most difficult in his life. He failed in his efforts to interest the Paris Opéra in his latest work, *Rienzi.* He failed even to gain a satisfactory post. To keep himself and his wife from starvation, he was compelled to accept the most degrading kind of hack work. But his powerful creative urge could not be stifled by his personal misfortunes: during these difficult years he worked assiduously on a new opera, *The Flying Dutchman.*

But eventually there was to be a change of fortune. In 1842, *Rienzi* was performed in Dresden with such success that the opera house then and there scheduled *The Flying Dutchman* for the following season. This, too, was successful. Wagner, inspired by these victories, now produced new and greater operas: *Tannhäuser,* produced in Dresden (and not too successfully) in 1845, and *Lohengrin,* completed in 1848 and first performed by Franz Liszt in Weimar two years later.

During the revolutionary period of 1848, Wagner allied himself with the revolution which, when overcome, made it necessary for him to flee for his life. He found refuge for a while in the home of Franz Liszt—thus beginning a historic friendship; then he fled on to Paris; and finally he settled for a twelve-year period in Zürich.

These years in Zurich were spent in the production of several literary volumes, and in the formulating of his theories on the opera which were to send him into altogether new artistic directions. This was the period when he first conceived of the Gargantuan project to set the *Nibelungen Lied* into a trilogy of operas; and this was the period when he not only completed all of the *Rheingold, Die Walküre,* and a part of *Siegfried,* but also wrote another opera, not part of the *Ring* cycle—*Tristan und Isolde.*

In 1860, Wagner was given an official pardon for his radical activities of 1848, and was now free to return to his native land. At this time, he met and became a friend of Ludwig II, the young king of Bavaria, who became so profoundly impressed by Wagner's ideals and achievements that he decided to become the composer's patron.

Meanwhile, a love affair was developing between Wagner and Cosima, the wife of his dear friend, Hans von Bülow. After the death of his own wife, and after Cosima had borne him two children, Wagner fled with her to Triebschen, near the Lake of Lucerne, to establish their home together there. In June of 1869 a son was born to them, Siegfried.

During this emotionally tempestuous period in Wagner's life he was deep at work on his opera—his only comic opera—*Die Meistersinger.* Completing it, he returned to the monumental *Ring,* which he had left unfinished twelve years earlier. The extravagant proportions of this great trilogy, and the prodigious demands it made on singers, orchestra and stage hands, gave Wagner the idea for the erection of a festival theatre in which this trilogy might be produced. Funds were solicited in all parts of the world, and in 1872—on Wagner's birthday—the cornerstone was laid for a festival theatre in Bayreuth. Four years after this, the theatre was officially opened, with the first complete production of the *Ring.*

On June 28, 1882, the world première of Wagner's last music drama took place in Bayreuth—*Parsifal.* Shortly after these performances, Wagner went on vacation to Venice. There he suffered a heart attack, and died on February 13, 1883.

GÖTTERDÄMMERUNG (THE DUSK OF THE GODS)

See THE RING OF THE NIBELUNGS

LOHENGRIN

Lohengrin, the first of two operas dealing with the Knights of the Holy Grail, was planned at Marienbad in the summer of 1845. Wagner spent the following winter on the libretto. Liszt conducted the initial performance of the opera at Weimar in August, 1850, at a time when Wagner himself was a political exile from Germany and, owing to the failure of *The Flying Dutchman* and *Tannhäuser,* in poor repute as a composer. It was a great act of courage for the idolized Liszt to risk his position to produce the work. His chance was well taken; *Lohengrin* attained such popularity that Wagner, still in exile, was later able to make his famous remark to the effect that he was the only German who had not heard *Lohengrin.*

The action of the opera takes place in the tenth century. Duke Godfrey of Brabant, who is still a boy, has disappeared and his sister Elsa is accused of his murder. Armed combat is to determine her innocence or guilt. A summons is sounded, but Elsa's position appears hopeless when no one can be found who will defend her name. Suddenly, a boat is seen coming down the river drawn by a single swan and bearing a knight who has come to be Elsa's champion. He quickly defeats her accuser, establishing her innocence, and wins her promise to marry him on the morrow. The condition is imposed that she must never ask him his name or whence he came.

The following day, in a magnificent ceremony, Elsa and her knight are married, but not before their wedding is almost ruined by Frederick of Telramund and his sorceress wife, Ortrud, who accuse the unknown knight of having won his victory through witchcraft. Happily alone with her husband in their bridal chamber, Elsa cannot drive Ortrud's accusations from her mind. At last, able to contain herself no longer, she asks the forbidden question. As she does so, Frederick rushes into the chamber intent on murdering Elsa's champion. She quickly hands her husband his sword with which he strikes Frederick dead.

The fatal question asked, it must now be answered. On the bank of the river the people are gathered together. In a magnificent narration the unknown knight reveals himself to be a champion of the Holy Grail, Lohengrin, the son of Parsifal. The swan reappears to take him away. Ortrud, seeking to prove her power, declares that the swan is actually the missing Godfrey, cast in this form by her magic, and destined so to remain. Lohengrin kneels in prayer, a dove of the Grail appears, and the liberated youth springs up in place of the swan. As the dove draws the boat, bearing Lohengrin away, Elsa finds her emotions too much to bear and sinks lifeless to the ground.

The famous Prelude is a development of the theme of the Holy Grail. Wagner himself wrote a long program note for this ethereal music, describing the angelic host descending earthward bearing the Grail. As it nears the earth it is revealed in a blaze of glory, and the beholder is purified by its presence.

The Prelude to Act III is also well-known. This joyous music introduces the festivities attending the wedding of Lohengrin and Elsa, and leads directly into the famous Bridal Chorus.

M-MM-549, Preludes to Act I and Act III, Pittsburgh Symphony Orchestra, Fritz Reiner Conducting.

X-MX-261, Bridal Chamber Scene, Helen Traubel, Soprano, Kurt Baum, Tenor, and the Philharmonic-Symphony Orchestra of New York, Artur Rodzinski Conducting.

12321-D, Elsa's Dream, Helen Traubel, Soprano, and the Philharmonic-Symphony Orchestra of New York, Artur Rodzinski Conducting.

17354-D, Elsa's Song to the Air, Astrid Varnay, Soprano, with Orchestra conducted by Erich Leinsdorf.

9146-M, In Fernem Land, Charles Kullman, Tenor, with Orchestra.

DIE MEISTERSINGER VON NÜRNBERG

OF ALL Wagner's operatic masterpieces, *Die Meistersinger* is the most perfect, the most completely convincing in every detail. While its music does not rise to the grandiose heights of certain portions of the *Ring* or achieve the searing intensity of *Tristan,* it is infinitely more consistent in its inspiration from beginning to end. The same is even more true of the libretto, incomparably Wagner's finest, and completely free of the narrative padding which hampers so much of the dramatic action in the *Ring*.

Wagner composed his only comic opera as a humorous sequel to the contest of song in *Tannhäuser*. It is based on the story of the sixteenth-century guild of Mastersingers, headed by the beloved cobbler-poet Hans Sachs.

Although the young knight, Walther von Stolzing, intended as a portrayal of Wagner himself, is the ostensible hero of the plot, the central figure of the opera is Hans Sachs. Walther represents the new and youthful in art, while Sachs symbolizes an enlightened and tolerant conservatism. Against these are pitted the forces of blind prejudice, represented by the Mastersingers and the ludicrous figure of Beckmesser. It is significant that Wagner had originally intended this character to bear the name of Hans Lick, after his bitter Viennese critic Eduard Hanslick.

Lovely Eva is the character around which the plot revolves. Her father has announced that only he who can win a song contest will get her hand in marriage, and both Walther and Beckmesser are rivals. In a first trial, Walther is eliminated because the judge—who is Beckmesser himself—decrees that his song is full of errors. At the contest, however, Beckmesser is eliminated because his song is grotesque; and Walther, who demands that he be heard, is acknowledged the victor as a result of his moving "Prize Song."

Die Meistersinger was first heard at the Munich Opera on June 21, 1868. The often-heard Prelude, however, was completed six years earlier and received its first performance in November 1862 at a Gewandhaus concert in Leipzig, the composer conducting.

The Prelude opens with a stirring Procession of the Mastersingers. A tender melody follows. A second marchlike Mastersinger theme then makes its appearance—the Guild (or Banner) theme. A lyrical suggestion of the famous Prize Song is followed by a scherzo in which the first Mastersinger theme is parodied to represent the playful Apprentices.

The climax is reached as the two Mastersinger themes and the Prize Song are combined in a magnificent display of counterpoint. This was Wagner's way of silencing forever the critics who said that he was unable to compose in the polyphonic forms of the classical period.

Perhaps the crowning glory of *Die Meistersinger* is the final act, which gives us not only the most magnificent choral writing in all Wagner, but also brings to its fullest flowering the composer's character portrait of Hans Sachs. Here Sachs is revealed as more than just a kindly adviser to the aspiring Walther. In the great *"Wahn"* monologue he is seen as the sensitive poet brooding over the power of human passions to turn men into selfish, spiteful brutes. But he is convinced in his heart that these same passions can be made to create great and noble works.

The Prelude to Act III of *Die Meistersinger* is a tone portrait of Hans Sachs, and is one of Wagner's most exalted and poetic creations. The composer has given us his own comments on the music:

"The opening theme for the 'cellos has already been heard in the third strophe of Sachs' cobbler song in Act II. There it expressed the bitter cry of the man who has determined to renounce his personal happiness, yet who shows the world a cheerful, resolute exterior. That smothered cry was understood by Eva, and so deeply did it pierce her heart that she fain would fly away, if only to hear this cheerful-seeming song no longer.

"Now, in the Introduction to Act III, this motive is played alone by the 'cellos, and developed in the other strings till it dies away in resignation; but forthwith, and as from out the distance, the horns intone the solemn song wherewith Hans Sachs greeted Luther and the Reformation, which had won the poet such incomparable popularity. After the first strophe the strings again take single phrases of the cobbler song, very softly and much slower, as though the man were turning his gaze from his handiwork heavenwards, and lost in tender musings. Then, with increased sonority, the horns pursue the master's hymn, with which Hans Sachs, at the end of the act, is greeted by the populace of Nuremberg. Next reappears the strings' first motive, with grandiose expression of the anguish of a deeply stirred soul; calmed and allayed, it attains the utmost serenity of a blest and peaceful resignation."

The "Dance of the Apprentices" and "Procession of the Mastersingers" occur early in the second and final scene of Act III. The curtain rises on a festive crowd on the banks of the River Pegnitz, just outside the city of Nuremberg. Final preparations are being made for the song contest. Members of the Shoemakers Guild have just arrived singing a lusty tune in praise of their patron St. Crispin. Then come the Tailors, followed by the Bakers, and these in turn by the Apprentices. A decorated boat arrives full of young girls in colorful peasant dress. The Apprentices rush to the bank and lift the girls out of the boat. In the dance that follows, the Journeymen seek to "cut in" and lure the girls elsewhere. At the height of the merriment is heard a fanfare of trumpets. The dance comes to a sudden end and all make way for the procession of the Meistersingers, who now arrive at the center of the stage amid the jubilant acclamation of the Nuremberg populace.

M-MM-549, Overture, Pittsburgh Symphony Orchestra, Fritz Reiner Conducting.
X-MX-218, Excerpts from Act III, Pittsburgh Symphony Orchestra, Fritz Reiner Conducting.
9146-M, Prize Song, Charles Kullman, Tenor, with Orchestra.

PARSIFAL

LIKE *Tannhäuser*, the last of the Wagnerian music dramas, *Parsifal*, is built around the Knights of the Holy Grail. These Knights guard two holy relics on Montsalvat: the spear that pierced Christ, and the cup He used at the Last Supper which now contains his blood. Amfortas, leader of this holy group, is mortally ill, and can be cured only if one, pure of heart, touches the wound with the edge of the spear. Parsifal, who resists the lure of the flower maiden Kundry, proves to be that pure man, and he effects Amfortas's cure.

Wagner described this music drama as a "consecrational festival play," and he imbued it with a spirituality, mysticism, and a profound religious feeling not found in his other works. Just as *Tristan* is probably the last word in the expression of love and passion in music, so *Parsifal* is the ultimate in the tonal delineation of the emotions of suffering, exaltation, and devout reverence.

Parsifal may not be Wagner's greatest work: it is too full of long and repetitious monologues and wordy and dull religious and philosophic expositions. It nevertheless contains some of the greatest music he ever wrote: the spiritual Prelude, the sensuous Flower Maiden Music of Act II, and one of the most awe-inspiring religious pieces of music ever penned, the "Good Friday Spell" in Act III.

[517]

Parsifal was written by Wagner expressly for Bayreuth, specifying that for a period of fifty years it was not to be permitted a performance elsewhere. And in Bayreuth the première took place on July 26, 1882, one year before Wagner's death.

For twenty years, *Parsifal* was performed only at Bayreuth. Then the Metropolitan Opera House, in violation of Wagner's wishes, launched a performance of its own which resulted in one of the historic musical battles of the early 20th century. David Ewen, in his book *Music Comes to America*, tells about it:

"Arguments for and against the production split New York into two battle camps. There were those who sided with Cosima Wagner: on legal grounds, because she held the exclusive rights to Parsifal and had the privilege of prohibiting its performance out of Bayreuth if she so desired; on religious grounds, because they felt it sacrilegious to present a devout subject on a public stage; on sentimental grounds, because the master had written the work for Bayreuth and there it belonged. Others, however, were with Conried when he argued that Parsifal had, after all, been given a New York performance in 1890 without interference (in a concert version, it was true; but a performance nevertheless); also, that it was the artistic duty of Cosima to permit a masterpiece of such dimensions to be witnessed by the world at large.

"The battle was bitter. It grew more vitriolic as it was prolonged. Letters poured into the newspapers in which the general public expressed its opinion, pro and con. Sermons were preached in the pulpit throughout the country. Bayreuth had issued a warning that anyone participating in the performance would be boycotted in all future Wagnerian performances at the shrine; Felix Mottl, as a matter of fact (imported expressly to conduct the music drama in New York), announced flatly that he would have nothing whatsoever to do with the venture. Some, looking upon Conried's attempted performance as an outright theft, bitterly renamed the drama *The Rape of Parsifal*.

"All this succeeded in stirring the curiosity of all in the provocative opera. When, therefore, Conried won his legal fight and announced that the performance would definitely take place, the sale of tickets reached prodigious proportions, even though the prices of admission had been practically doubled. Out-of-town orders were so numerous

[518]

that most of them had to be turned down. Special Parsifal excursion trains were run to bring out-of-town music lovers to the performance. A few minutes before five o'clock, on the afternoon of December 24, 1903, a group of trumpeters advanced to the main entrance of the Metropolitan and blew several motives from Parsifal to announce the arrival of curtain time. Such was the eagerness of the public to witness this publicized spectacle that—wonderful to say!—it came on time. Until midnight, an excited audience witnessed the first American production of *Parsifal* conducted by Alfred Hertz. The cast included Ternina, Louise Homer, Journet, and Van Rooy.

"For the rest of that season, *Parsifal* remained the most exciting opera in the Metropolitan repertoire. It played to sold-out houses. In place of the originally scheduled five performances there were eleven, bringing almost $200,000 in receipts. Meanwhile performances were so eagerly attended in major cities throughout the country, brought there by wandering companies, such as the Savage production (in English) and one by the Walter Damrosch company. Drama lectures on Parsifal were conducted with stereopticon slides; a variety of shows with the legend of Parsifal as their subject were hurriedly contrived."

But America eventually had too much of *Parsifal*. After all, the audiences had thronged the opera house to hear the work mainly because of curiosity over a highly publicized novelty. These audiences were too immature to recognize in it a masterpiece of profound and searching beauty. When the novelty wore off, there remained only the long monologues, the static action, the lack of singable melodies to provoke boredom. In New York, interest in *Parsifal* died down to such an extent that by 1905 it was exhibited at the normal scale of admission prices, while in 1906 tickets could be procured virtually free for the asking. There are many who now derisively spoke of the *Parsifal* performances as "Metropolitan prayer meetings."

M-MM-337, Excerpts, Ernst Wolff, Tenor, Alexander Kipnis, Bass, and the Bayreuth Festival Orchestra, Karl Muck and Siegfried Wagner Conducting.

DAS RHEINGOLD

See THE RING OF THE NIBELUNGS

THE RING OF THE NIBELUNGS

DAS RHEINGOLD
DIE WALKÜRE (THE VALKYRIE)
SIEGFRIED

GÖTTERDÄMMERUNG (THE DUSK OF
THE GODS)

In 1848 Wagner, looking around for a subject for a new opera, decided to write his next work on a text derived from the Nibelungen myths. The political upheaval of 1849, however, forced him to leave Germany. After spending a short time in Paris, he moved to Zurich, where he resumed work on what he thought was going to be only one new opera, *The Death of Siegfried*.

But as Wagner himself put it: "When I tried to dramatize the most important moment of the mythos of the Nibelungen in *Siegfried's Tod*, I found it necessary to indicate a vast number of antecedent facts, so as to put the main incidents in the proper light. But I could only *narrate* these subordinate matters, whereas I felt it imperative that they should be embodied in the action. Thus I came to write *Siegfried*. But here again the same difficulty troubled me. Finally I wrote *Die Walküre* and *Das Rheingold*, and thus contrived to incorporate all that was needful to make the action tell its own story."

Thus it was that the libretti for the four operas of *The Ring of the Nibelungs*—as the group came to be called—were written in reverse order. They were completed in 1853, whereupon Wagner set to work composing the music. Here he worked in the proper sequence, completing *Das Rheingold* in 1854 and *Die Walküre* two years later. At this stage, however, he was forced to turn to something more remunerative, an opera of lesser scope that could be produced shortly after it was written. He therefore stopped work on *The Ring* and wrote *Tristan und Isolde*.

It was about this time that Wagner received an offer from King Ludwig II, the young, erratic ruler of Bavaria, to come to Munich where a stipend from the King would enable him to finish composing *The Ring*. Consequently, in 1864, he went to Munich and worked on the music for *Siegfried*. Wagner's political opponents, however, forced him to leave Munich the following year, and he retired to a villa on Lake Lucerne. Once again, the composition of *The Ring* was interrupted for the creation of another music drama—this time *Die Meistersinger*.

Not until 1869 did Wagner have a chance to resume his labor of love, and he required another two years to finish *Siegfried*. Then he received an invitation from the municipality of Bayreuth to build his proposed festival theatre there. Besides working on the final opera of *The Ring*, *Götterdämmerung* (a change in title from *Siegfried's Death* to *The Dusk of the Gods*), he spent much time and effort raising funds for the erection of the new opera house. In 1874, *Götterdämmerung* was completed, and finally, between August 13 and 17, 1876, the entire *Ring* cycle was presented for the first time, before a distinguished gathering of the world's musical and political elite. This was not the first time that either *Das Rheingold* or *Die Walküre* had been performed, however; the former was first heard at Munich on September 22, 1869, and the latter received its première on the following June 26th, in the same city. Wagner objected to both performances, since he wanted *The Ring* to be presented as an entity. But the earlier performances were given at the request of King Ludwig, who, after all, had been footing the bills for the creation of *The Ring*.

With the complete presentation of *The Ring* at Bayreuth, Wagner saw the fulfillment of his great dream. He now had at his disposal the most perfectly constructed opera house in the world, the finest singers of the day and the best orchestral players obtainable. Needless to say, the performances were a great artistic success; *The Ring* had to be repeated twice more before the summer was over. Financially, however, the venture was a fiasco, and the composer-impresario found himself with a large deficit on his hands. It was some time, therefore, before the festivals were resumed.

The Ring of the Nibelungs, though it is composed of four operas, is usually referred to as a trilogy, as *Das Rheingold* is considered a sort of prelude to the gigantic drama.

The story of *The Ring* is long and complicated. Essentially, it deals with the theft of the hoard of Rhinegold from the Rhinemaidens by the Nibelung dwarf, Alberich, and the consequent trouble this theft brings. Alberich forces his brother, Mime, to fashion a magic ring and helmet from the gold, so that he may assume great power and amass huge wealth. But Alberich is tricked by Wotan, ruler of the gods, who steals the gold from him and gives it to the giants, Fafner and Fasolt, in payment for the great castle of Valhalla which they have built for the gods. This much of the story is related in *Das Rheingold*. Wotan has been warned of the impending doom of the gods, and since he fears that Alberich may be the eventual cause of their downfall, he moves heaven and earth to reclaim the accursed treasure. It is these efforts with which the action of the ensuing three operas is concerned. Having once given a gift, Wotan is powerless to take it back. But he so plans events that the hero, Siegfried, kills Fafner and takes the Rhinegold. The curse which Alberich placed on the gold, however, eventually does its work; Siegfried is killed, Valhalla is destroyed, and the gold is returned to the Rhinemaidens.

Since the music of *The Ring* is almost as familiar in the symphony hall as in the opera house, a few words about the more significant excerpts from each opera are in order.

The most famous single orchestral excerpt from *Das Rheingold* is the majestic "Entrance of the Gods into Valhalla" with which the opera closes and which is largely constructed from the motifs of the Rhine and Valhalla.

Die Walküre includes the magnificent love music between Siegmund and Sieglinde (Act I), the "Ride of the Valkyries" (Act III), and "Wotan's Farewell and Magic Fire Scene" (Act III). The "Ride of the Valkyries" is Wagner's concert version of the fiery Prelude to Act III in the opera. "Wotan's Farewell and Magic Fire Scene" brings the opera to a close as the music gives a tonal description of the flames which rise and leap around the rock on which Brünnhilde is left sleeping.

In *Siegfried* we have the dynamic "Forging Scene" (Act I), in which Siegfried forges his famous sword; the exquisite "Forest Murmurs," (Act II) accompanying the scene before the dragon Fafner's cave and describing the daydreaming of the hero Siegfried amid the rustle of the forest, and the ecstatic love music from Act III with which the opera comes to an end.

Götterdämmerung contains some of the most famous orchestral excerpts from the entire *Ring*—notably, "Siegfried's Rhine Journey" (which forms the transition from the Prologue to Act I), and "Siegfried's Death Music" and "Brünnhilde's Apostrophe" both from Act III. Through a skillful use of all the *leitmotifs* connected with Siegfried's life, the "Death Music" becomes a sort of a tonal biography of

[522]

the hero. "Brünnhilde's Apostrophe," with which she brings herself to death just before the collapse of Valhalla, is the close of the opera.

67373-D, Entrance of the Gods into Valhalla, Bayreuth Festival Orchestra, Von Hösslin Conducting.

M-MM-618, Love Music, Die Walküre, Helen Traubel, Soprano, Emery Darcy, Tenor, and the Philharmonic-Symphony Orchestra, Artur Rodzinski Conducting.

M-MM-581, Act III, Die Walküre, Helen Traubel, Soprano, Herbert Janssen, Baritone, Vocal Ensemble of the Metropolitan Opera Association, and the Philharmonic-Symphony Orchestra, Artur Rodzinski Conducting.

67372-D, Forging Scene, Siegfried, Bayreuth Festival Orchestra, Von Hösslin Conducting .

M-MM-549, Forest Murmurs, Siegfried, Pittsburgh Symphony Orchestra, Fritz Reiner Conducting.

67372-D, Prelude Act III, Siegfried, Bayreuth Festival Orchestra, Von Hösslin Conducting.

68044-D, Siegfried's Funeral Music, Götterdämmerung, Bruno Walter and Symphony Orchestra.

X-MX-224, Siegfried's Rhine Journey, Götterdämmerung, Orchestre de la Société des Concerts du Conservatoire, Felix Weingartner Conducting.

SIEGFRIED

See above, THE RING OF THE NIBELUNGS

SIEGFRIED IDYLL

On July 6, 1869, a son was born to Richard Wagner and Cosima von Bülow at Triebschen, their quiet retreat on Lake Lucerne. Quite appropriately, the boy was named Siegfried, after the great hero of Wagner's operatic trilogy, The Ring of the Nibelungs. It was more than a year later that Cosima was finally able to obtain her divorce from Hans von Bülow and marry Wagner.

Cosima's thirty-third birthday fell on Christmas Day, 1870, and Wagner, wishing to present her with a particularly fine gift, composed during the previous month the Siegfried Idyll. All of the preparations for the first performance were made in the utmost secrecy. On December 4th, Wagner gave the score to the conductor, Hans Richter, who copied out the parts. Richter was also responsible for engaging and rehearsing the musicians, whom he secured from Zürich. The first rehearsal took place December 21st, in the foyer of the old Zürich Theatre, and the composer himself directed the final reheaisal, which was held on Christmas Eve in the Hotel du Lac in Lucerne.

Early on Christmas morning, the members of the little orchestra stole into the Wagner house, tuned their instruments quietly in the kitchen, and took their places on the stairs leading to Cosima's bedroom. Wagner, who conducted, stood at the top of the stairs. Below him stretched the wind instruments, then the violins and violas, while the 'cellist and double-bass player were entirely out of sight. Altogether, there were sixteen instruments in this first performance of the *Siegfried Idyll*. Actually there were only fifteen players, for Richter doubled at the viola and trumpet.

Promptly at 7:30 the performance began. Cosima must have experienced a wonderful sensation, waking to the lovely strains of her husband's most charming and unaffected composition. For several years she cherished the work as her own personal possession. When, in 1878, Wagner was obliged by financial difficulties to release the *Siegfried Idyll* for publication, Cosima wrote in her diary: "My secret treasure is becoming common property; may the joy it will bring mankind be commensurate with the sacrifice that I am making."

The *Idyll* is constructed principally from themes used by Wagner in the third act of his music-drama, *Siegfried*. Much of this material, it is said, was originally planned for use in some trios and string quartets, but was later expanded to fit into the operatic mold. It is not surprising, then, that the *Siegfried* music lends itself so admirably to the intimate requirements of the *Idyll*. A homey touch is added with the inclusion of the folk lullaby, *Schlaf', mein Kind, schlaf' ein*.

When it was first composed, the work was known as the *Triebschener Idyll,* and because of the circumstances of the first performance, Cosima's children referred to it as the "Steps-Music."

X-MX-265, Philharmonic-Symphony Orchestra of New York, Artur Rodzinski Conducting.

TANNHÄUSER

TANNHÄUSER was no mythical personage. There lived in the thirteenth century a Minnesinger named Tanhuser, who wrote poems. He also went to the Holy Land as a Crusader. In folk tales he has been made into a legendary knight who comes to Venusberg, or, in terms of actual geography, Hörselberg in Thuringia, and meets the German counterpart of Venus in a mountain cavern.

He remains with Venus, but later recalls his higher ideals, and goes to Rome to beg forgiveness from the Pope. He is told that forgiveness for the sin of consorting with a pagan goddess is as impossible as the flowering of a bare rod. But Tannhäuser's rod does blossom forth, and he now knows that he can die in peace.

Such is the folk legend, which was used by several German poets before Wagner. In his brochure *Drei Operndichtungen*, published in Leipzig in 1852, Wagner relates the story of his writing of *Tannhäuser*. He thought of connecting *Tannhäuser* with another story, that of a "singers' war" at Wartburg. Hence, the double title of the opera, *Tannhäuser oder der Sängerkrieg auf Wartburg*.

Tannhäuser was Wagner's first "Wagnerian" opera. In it Wagner opened the cycle of operas based on Germanic folklore, and in it he clearly outlined the importance of stage setting. He describes the events that led him to the composition of *Tannhäuser* in the following words:

"My third trip to Dresden took me through the valleys of Thuringia, from where one can see Wartburg towering above. How near was that sight to my heart! Yet, strangely enough, it was not until seven years later that I visited Wartburg for the first time, and it was from Wartburg that I cast the last glance at the German soil, which I had trod with heartfelt joy, and which I had to abandon as an outlaw, a refugee. . . ."

The reference to his status as an outlaw is explained by the fact that Wagner went into exile as a participant in the Dresden Revolution of 1848. As late as 1852, he was talked about in Germany as "that red revolutionary." When the question of a production of *Tannhäuser* at the Munich Opera House came up, an article in the press suggested that "the proper place for the Orpheus who, during the May revolt in Dresden, raised barricades with his lyre, is not the Munich Opera House, but prison."

Wagner's idea of *Tannhäuser* was far from pietistic. He describes his state of mind during the composition of the opera: "How silly are the critics who, amidst their wanton living, have suddenly become spiritual, and who impute to my *Tannhäuser* a specifically Christian, impotently celestialized tendency. . . . I was in a state of highly sensuous agitation which brought my blood and my nervous system to the point of feverish excitement when I conceived and carried out the composition of the music. . . . From this high state my eager vision became aware of a Woman; the Woman for whom the Flying Dutchman hankered from the sea-depths of his misery; the Woman who showed Tannhäuser the way to Heaven, and the one who brought Lohengrin from the sunlit heights down to the warm breast of the earth."

Wagner began the music of *Tannhäuser* at Dresden in the summer of 1843, in his thirty-first year, and finished the score in the spring of 1845. So excited was he while writing *Tannhäuser*, he tells us, that he was haunted by an idea that sudden death would prevent him from finishing it. Here again he was embodying in artistic form another fragment of his own experiences.

He suffered at this time from "a longing for the highest form of Love," springing out of his "loathing of the modern world." Himself no stranger to sensuous passion, there was bound to come—sooner or later—the longing for more spiritual delights. This found expression directly in *Tannhäuser*, where sensuality and chastity are opposed in sharp antithesis. As in *The Flying Dutchman*, there is predominant the theme of redemption; for Tannhäuser is redeemed by the saintly Elizabeth.

The first performance of *Tannhäuser* took place at the Dresden Opera on October 19, 1845. Wagner himself conducted. The enlarged version of the orchestral Bacchanale was added to the score for the Paris performance of March 13, 1861, a performance that made history because of the hostile manifestations in the audience, which forced the withdrawal of the opera after the third performance.

The Paris humorous periodical *Charivari* printed a cartoon representing a young woman playing the piano, and her mother sitting in a chair in the same room. "You are playing wrong notes," says the mother. "But, *Maman*, I am playing *Tannhäuser*," the young lady replies. "Oh, that's different," remarks *Maman*.

In the same spirit of innocent mockery, some bright Conservatoire student transcribed the *Tannhäuser* Overture for piano and a whisk broom, the latter to play the rapid violin passages in the high treble.

It is well to remind ourselves of what Wagner really intended to depict in the music of the Overture to *Tannhäuser*. Fortunately, he has left us his own explanation of its meaning. The composer wrote it at the request of the players in the orchestra who were rehearsing the Overture for a performance in Zürich, Switzerland. It was published in the *Neue Zeitschrift für Musik* of January 14, 1853.

"To begin with, the orchestra leads before us the Pilgrims' Chant alone; it draws near, then swells into a mighty outpour, and passes finally away.—Evenfall; last echo of the chant. As night breaks, magic sights and sounds appear, a rosy mist floats up, exultant shouts assail our ear; the whirlings of a fearsomely voluptuous dance are seen. These are the 'Venusberg's' seductive spells, that show themselves at dead of night to those whose breast is fired by daring of the senses.

"Attracted by the tempting show, a shapely human form draws nigh: 'tis Tannhäuser, Love's minstrel. He sounds his jubilant Song of Love in joyous challenge, as though to force the wanton witchery to do his bidding. Wild cries of riot answer him: the rosy cloud grows denser 'round him, entrancing perfumes hem him in and steal away his senses.

"In the most seductive of half-lights, his wonder-seeing eye beholds a female form; he hears a voice that sweetly murmurs out the siren-call, which promises contentment of the darer's wildest wishes. Venus herself it is, this woman who appears to him. Then heart and senses burn within him; a fierce devouring passion fires the blood in all his veins; with irresistible constraint it thrusts him nearer; before the Goddess' self he steps with that canticle of love triumphant, and now he sings it in ecstatic praise of her.

"As though a wizard's spell were upon him, the wonders of the Venusberg unroll. Tumultuous shouts and savage cries of joy mount up on every hand; in drunken glee Bacchantes drive their raging dance and drag Tannhäuser to the warm caresses of Love's Goddess, who throws her glowing arms around the mortal drowned with bliss, and bears him where no step dare tread, to the realm of Being-no-more.

"A scurry, like the sound of the Wild Hunt, and speedily the storm is laid. Merely a wanton whir still pulses in the breeze, a wave of weird voluptuousness, like the sensuous breath of unblest love, still soughs above the spot where impious charms had shed their raptures, and over which the night now broods once more.

"But dawn begins to break already; from afar is heard again the

[527]

Pilgrims' Chant. As this chant draws closer yet and closer, as the day drives farther back the night, that whir and soughing of the air—which had erewhile sounded like the eerie cries of souls condemned—now rises, too, to ever gladder waves; so that when the sun ascends at last in splendor, and the Pilgrims' Chant proclaims in ecstasy to all the world, to all that lives and moves thereon, Salvation won, this wave itself swells out the tidings of sublimest joy.

" 'Tis the carol of the Venusberg itself, redeemed from curse of impiousness, this cry we hear amid the hymn of God. So wells and leaps each pulse of Life in chorus of Redemption; and both dissevered elements, both soul and senses, God and Nature, unite in the atoning kiss of hallowed Love."

OP-MOP-24, Müller, Andresen, Janssen, Bayreuth Festival Orchestra and Chorus, Karl Elmendorff Conducting.

TRISTAN UND ISOLDE

ALL OF the arts have painted the passion and ecstasy and despair of love. Poetry, painting, dance, drama, sculpture have all given us wonderful examples of their eloquence to portray love. Even architecture, which at first would seem to be remote from this form of expression, has given us abiding creations such as the Taj Mahal and the Marble Pavilion at Fatehpur Sikri. But the perfect expression of love among the arts is music. And probably the most intense and deeply felt of all is *Tristan und Isolde* of Wagner.

All through the three acts of the music drama of *Tristan* the despair and ecstasy of love are sounded, but its supreme expression is in the garden scene of the second act, and in the last scene of the third act.

Wagner composed *Tristan* during the period in which he was planning and working on the Gargantuan outlines of his *Ring*, and finished it in 1859. A great part of the opera was written while Wagner was a guest at the home of Otto Wesendonck, and it is generally assumed that the passionate music was created under the stimulus of an illicit love-affair between Wagner and Otto Wesendonck's wife, Mathilde. On June 10, 1865, the opera was introduced at the Munich Opera.

The love of Tristan and Isolde is famous in legend and literature.

Tristan, nephew of King Mark of Cornwall, is despatched to Ireland to bring back to his uncle Isolde, daughter of the Irish king. Isolde, in love with Tristan, has her nurse Brangäne prepare a death potion for Tristan, but Brangäne gives him a love potion instead. Both Tristan and Isolde drink it, and then are drawn to each other by an irresistible force. They carry on their ardent love affair in King Mark's castle. They are discovered in the garden by King Mark, who denounces Tristan for treachery; at the same time, Melot, one of Mark's men, stabs Tristan. Tristan goes off to Brittany, nursed by Kurwenal, and Isolde follows him. Eventually King Mark has a change of heart, and comes to Brittany to forgive the lovers. But he comes too late, for Tristan and Isolde die in each other's arms.

The Prelude and Finale are among the most famous of all Wagnerian excerpts. For many years there has existed a general misunderstanding and misnaming of these two pieces: Practically every concert program listed the Prelude and Finale of this opera as "Prelude and *Liebestod*."

When Wagner conducted these two excerpts at a concert in Vienna in 1863—the same year that he completed the opera—he programmed them as *Vorspiel* (*Liebestod*) and *Schluss* (*Verklärung*)— "Prelude (Love Death)" and "Finale (Transfiguration)." William Ashton Ellis has translated the program note that Wagner himself wrote on this occasion:

Prelude (Love Death): "Tristan as bridal envoy conducts Isolde to his uncle, the King. They love each other. From the first stifled moan of quenchless longing, from the faintest tremor to unpent avowal of a hopeless love, the heart goes through each phase of unvictorious battling with its inner fever, till, swooning back upon itself, it seems extinguished as in death.

Finale (Transfiguration): "Yet, what Fate divided from this life, in death revives transfigured; the gate of union opens. Above the body of Tristan, dying Isolde sees transcendent consummation of their passionate desire, eternal union in unmeasured realms, nor bond nor barrier, indivisible!"

It was Franz Liszt who was responsible for transferring the name *Liebestod* from the Prelude to the Finale. In preparing his piano transcription of the Finale, he used as an introduction a brief passage from the Love Duet in the second act, in which the word *Liebestod* appears. Consequently, he called his transcription of the Finale *Liebestod*, and the misnomer has stuck to this day.

The music of the Prelude, compounded from themes in the opera, soars to great heights of ecstasy. Ending on a somber note, it presages the tragic but beautiful story that is to unfold on the stage. The voices of the instruments in the orchestra glide over each other voluptuously, or spring upwards with abandon, and the whole tonal design of the orchestra is seething unendingly as the creative energy of love pours itself into life expression.

The love music of the second act is one of the most passionate and sensual pages in music. Wagner created for himself a new style, a new technique, new harmonic sequences, new combinations of timbres, and a new orchestral palette for *Tristan*. He conceived of sound with a new tonal perspective, so that we hear the hunting horns so far away that they are merely a suggestion of harmony and rhythm. Nearer we hear the sounds of the trees swaying in the forest during the *Liebesnacht*. From above, high up in the tower of the castle, we hear the song of *Brangäne* warning the lovers below of the treachery that may overcome them in the night.

This is music of the utmost beauty, and unforgettable for its fatalistic and melancholy loveliness. At other times, the music leaps toward us like a flame with burning impulsiveness. It mounts up into great climaxes of luminous sound.

This love music maintains its overpowering eloquence when words cannot continue, when even life cannot further express itself. It is the supreme and ultimate of the poetry of love.

The Prelude to Act III is a passage of a slow and somber character, full of haunting beauty, sets the stage for the desolate scene that is the third act.

OP-MOP-23, Larsen-Todsen, Graarud, Helm, Bockelmann, Andresen, Bayreuth Chorus and Orchestra, Karl Elmendorff Conducting.
M-MM-573, Excerpts, Helen Traubel, Soprano, and the Philharmonic-Symphony Orchestra of New York, Artur Rodzinski Conducting.
M-MM-550, Excerpts Act III, Lauritz Melchior, Tenor, Herbert Janssen, Baritone, the Colon Opera Orchestra, Roberto Kinsky Conducting, and the Columbia Opera Orchestra, Erich Leinsdorf Conducting.

DIE WALKÜRE (THE VALKYRIE)
See THE RING OF THE NIBELUNGS

Karl Maria von Weber

1786–1826

KARL MARIA VON WEBER was born in 1786 in Eutin (Oldenburg) where his father, an army officer, conducted the town band. Father Weber subsequently became the impresario of a traveling opera company, and little Karl (born with a hip disease which made him somewhat lame) was compelled to lead a nomadic life as a child. In Salzburg, he studied with Michael Haydn, joined the cathedral choir, and published his first compositions (six fughettas). In Munich, he wrote his first opera (later destroyed by fire), gave his first piano recital, and, becoming interested in lithography, himself printed his second opus, a set of piano variations.

In the autumn of 1803, Weber went to Vienna where he became a pupil of Abbé Vogler. Vogler recommended him to Breslau as an opera conductor, a post he occupied from 1804 to 1806. After a brief interlude at a Silesian court, he became secretary to Duke Louis at Stuttgart (brother of the King of Württemberg). Twice arrested for financial irregularities, Weber was finally banished from the kingdom just before the performance of his new opera *Silvana*. He went on a long concert tour, and during this period started writing a novel, composed his first symphony, supervised a performance of *Silvana* at Frankfurt and produced his one-act comic opera *Abu Hassan*. His reputation grew to such an extent that in 1813 he was appointed director of the National Theatre in Prague, where he proved himself to be a remarkable organizer and conductor. He also fervently embraced the cause of German nationalism during this time. His patriotic songs and choruses endeared him to German soldiers and students.

In 1817 he went to Dresden as director of the German opera, and it was then that he began to work on his first masterpiece, *Der Freischütz*. Performed in 1821, this opera made him famous throughout all of Germany. His next important opera was *Euryanthe,* the first "grand" opera in German written throughout in declamatory style. *Euryanthe* did not please Rossini-mad Vienna, but had more success in Berlin.

Weber's last opera *Oberon* was commissioned by Covent Garden in England. The composition of this last opera was frequently delayed through ill health. Though sick, Weber rehearsed and conducted the opera, but succumbed to consumption a few weeks after the première in 1826. His remains were reburied in Dresden in 1844, during the ceremony of which Richard Wagner spoke the eulogy and conducted a funeral march made up of themes from *Euryanthe* as well as a funeral ode of his own creation.

Though physically handicapped, Weber was considered an attractive man. He was extremely versatile—the first musical representative of German romanticism. Except for a few arias from his operas, a handful of great overtures, the *Concertstück* for piano and orchestra, and the celebrated *Invitation to the Dance,* Weber's music is barely known today, so much so that it is sometimes difficult to remember that he left over 100 songs, masses, symphonies, concerti, a volume of piano pieces and incidental music.

DER FREISCHÜTZ

WEBER discovered the source for his opera in a ghost story by Apel and Laun in 1810, and seven years later asked Friedrich Kind to prepare a libretto for him. The composition proceeded by fits and starts, and was not completed until 1820. On June 18, 1821, it was introduced at the Schauspielhaus in Berlin.

Weber's success was enormous. It established him as a sort of national hero overnight. His audience (composed largely of German *Landswehr* who had marched to his patriotic songs) realized that he had created German opera as an answer to the alluring stage works of the Italian Spontini. Mendelssohn, Heine, and E. T. A. Hoffmann were present, and the last-named crowned the composer with a laurel wreath. The overture and one aria were repeated; other numbers were enthusiastically applauded. Weber, according to a report in his diary, was showered with verses; but he did not explain that some of these were full of mockery, that a few of these critics called the work a caricature, devoid of music.

Weber's music was inspired by his ardent German nationalism. He appealed to the German enthusiasm for their own legends and folk music, for the German horn and German woods. He stirred their fearful superstitions. He took the German Singspiel with its sentimental characters, borrowed time-tested devices from the Viennese fairy burlesque and applied these to characters from the German fairy tale. From his idol Mozart he borrowed the device of "through-composition" in the dramatic scene, Wolf's Glen. In this scene lies the historical importance of the opera, for it paved the way for *Euryanthe* which in turn became the model for *Lohengrin*. In this scene Weber also employed tone painting to a degree that definitely heralded music-drama.

Weber's sometimes over-effective orchestration provided color; the story brought drama; the folk songs (such as *"Leise, leise, fromme Weise"*) and choruses (Huntsmen's Chorus in Act III) contributed simplicity. These qualities helped to endear *Der Freischütz* to German audiences, who considered it the paragon of German opera.

As usual with Weber's operas, the overture has survived. It contains some of the most effective melodies from the opera, and creates an interesting contrast of sinister grandeur and simplicity. Berlioz

[533]

called it the "crowned queen," and quoted the clarinet passage as the most perfect example of clarinet-writing.

OBERON

SINCE it was commissioned by Covent Garden, the libretto of *Oberon* was written in English. Its author was James Robinson Planché who drew his story from Villeneuve's *Huon de Bordeaux* and Wieland's *Oberon*. Weber himself took 153 lessons in English in order that he might understand the text, which, truth to tell, he did not like. For the librettist, cautioned by the initial near-failure of *Der Freischütz* in London, had decided to prepare a melodrama rather than an operatic text. Weber complained about the presence of so many non-singing actors on the stage, and the inclusion of important scenes requiring no music. He believed that these factors would prevent performances of the opera in Continental opera houses, and make for bad publicity for the composer. In spite of this inadequate book, and his displeasure with it, Weber did succeed in pouring a good deal of chivalric spirit and beautiful music into his score.

Yet *Oberon* has hardly survived its composer, for all the sincere efforts by musicians, conductors, and scholars to keep it alive, and make it suitable for modern opera houses. The discrepancies between the action on the stage and the music are not easily bridged. Besides, the work in its entirety is frankly dull.

It has, however, a few highlights which are of unforgettable inspiration: the arias of Huon and Rezia, and the remarkable overture, probably Weber's greatest. The fairy music set the example for Mendelssohn who was to produce some of his greatest music in this vein.

Weber began composing the opera in January 1825 and completed it on April 9, 1826. When he came to London, he was a very sick man, almost unable to stand without assistance. He rehearsed, and conduced the première performance on April 12, 1826, from the piano. On June 5, he died of consumption. Thus he never heard his opera performed in Germany.

Henri Wieniawski

1835–1880

W IENIAWSKI was born in Lublin in 1835. Like many another artist he made his debut while still a child, giving his first concert when only thirteen. After a tour of Poland and Russia, he wisely returned to the study of music perfecting himself both as a virtuoso and also as a musical technician. When at last he felt his preparation to be complete, he made a European tour with his brother Joseph, a pianist. Together the brothers met with sufficient success to win for Henri a position as solo violinist to the Czar of Russia and a teaching position at the St. Petersburg (Leningrad) Conservatory. In 1872 he toured the United States with Anton Rubinstein, the distinguished Russian pianist.

Upon his return to Europe Wieniawski taught at the Conservatory of Brussels, but after a few years resigned his position due to failing health and a naturally restless temperament which demanded change. After a brief interval, he returned once more to the concert stage and to the life of travel which he loved so well. His health continued to cause him difficulty; he was, in fact, suffering from a mortal disease, although there is no indication that he was then aware of the fact.

Wieniawski; his health badly shattered, turned toward Russia. Upon reaching Odessa, he broke down completely and had to be conveyed to Moscow where he died on April 2, 1880, only forty-four years of age. Today his reputation rests most securely on the second of the two concerti which he wrote for his own instrument.

CONCERTO NO. 2 IN D MINOR, OP. 22

Allegro moderato · *Andante non troppo* · *A la Zingara*

THE CONCERTO NO. 2 in D minor is scored in the full Romantic tradition, which is to say that it is richly endowed with melody, feeling and beauty of line rather than relying upon form and counterpoint. The work won the praise of Tchaikovsky when he wrote to Madame von Meck on March 22, 1880: "Your benevolence to poor dying Wieniawski touches me deeply. . . . I pity him greatly. In him we shall lose an incomparable violinist and a gifted composer. In this respect, I think Wieniawski very talented . . . parts of the D minor Concerto show a true creative gift."

The first movement of the Concerto displays almost at once the Romantic aspects which permeate the whole work. The development, as such, does not follow the customary pattern. Instead, the composer has turned to pure virtuosity. Without the fact being too clearly evident, the solo violinist faces highly challenging technical problems on almost every page.

Properly executed, the music flows smoothly with the collaboration between solo instrument and the orchestra well integrated and presenting few problems to the listener. The second movement, a Romance, is written in 12-8 time. Once again the feeling for sentiment is uppermost as the music unfolds; at the conclusion of the movement a cadenza for the solo violin leads into the third and final movement, *A la Zingara* (Gypsy style). The music sparkles with gaiety and verve with the soloist once more called upon to perform minor miracles of technique. The principal themes of the first two movements reappear in varied form and then with a final tutti highly suggestive of the main theme of the work, the Concerto concludes.

M-MM-656, Isaac Stern, Violin, and the Philharmonic-Symphony Orchestra of New York, Efrem Kurtz Conducting.

Ralph Vaughan Williams

1872–

RALPH VAUGHAN WILLIAMS, the septuagenarian dean of the English school of music, was born at Down Ampney, Gloucestershire, England, on October 12, 1872. The son of a clergyman, he received his general education at Trinity College, Cambridge (1892–95), and at the Royal College of Music in London, where he took his degree of Bachelor of Music. Incidentally, he is now a professor at that institution. Although primarily interested in composition, he directed the London Bach Choir in 1920 for a period of eight years. His interest in the piano, in the organ, and in conducting were purely supplementary, though he was the organist of the South Lambeth Church in London in 1896, and has given extremely intelligent readings of both his own works and those of other composers.

It was in 1901 that Vaughan Williams was awarded his Doctor's degree in Music at Cambridge. Shortly thereafter, he became passionately interested in collecting English folk songs—particularly those of Norfolk. In 1904 he joined the Folk-Song Society. This affiliation led indirectly to his engagement at the famous Leeds Festival of 1907, where he conducted two of his settings of Walt Whitman's poems: *Toward the Unknown Region* and *A Sea Symphony.*

America welcomed this composer in the Summer of 1922, when he attended the festival at Norfolk, Connecticut, conducting his *Pastoral* Symphony. It is interesting to note that Vaughan Williams studied under two quite different composers without in any way being influenced by them as to form or method. These were Max Bruch, who was associated with the Akademie der Kunste in Berlin in 1909, and the popular French modernist, Maurice Ravel.

During World War I, Vaughan Williams served in the ranks,

[537]

though he later was commissioned an officer. When hostilities ceased, he joined the staff of the Royal College of Music. In 1935 he had the rare distinction of having conferred on him the Order of Merit.

Without doubt the most distinguished of the older living British composers, Vaughan Williams is a man of great and protean talent. As one critic has observed: "Only something super-English, insular, and parochial in his personality has kept him from being of great world-wide popularity. Almost alone among English composers of his generation, he has known how to make large musical statements without becoming windy or orotund. His treatment of folk music might be a model for all other composers."

This composer's work includes many songs of great worth, hymns, his operas *The Poisoned Kiss* and *Hugh the Drover* (based on folk songs), and five symphonies. The Fifth Symphony received its first performance in America at New York's Carnegie Hall on November 30, 1944, with Artur Rodzinski conducting the Philharmonic-Symphony Orchestra of New York. It was accorded a very favorable reception.

Olin Downes says that "Vaughan Williams seeks in the recesses of his own soul for the truth that endures."

ENGLISH FOLK SONGS, SUITE

MARCH: SEVENTEEN COME SUNDAY   FOLK SONGS FROM SOMERSET
MY BONNY BOY

THESE three folk songs make a well-balanced Suite, with first and third movements in quick tempo, and with a slow middle section.

Seventeen Come Sunday, the first, is presented in a robust, colorful, contrapuntal orchestration, which does not disguise its Elizabethan character. It is fast but not sprightly. Even the melody taken by the basses, near the end, conveys an impression more of severity than of joy.

My Bonny Boy is of a pastorale character. The theme is first given to the oboe, which is accompanied by a somber string background. The violin takes the melody, and then the 'cello, with counter-melody in the violin. In the second part the woodwinds are made to sound like shepherds' pipes.

Folk Songs from Somerset is in a more popular idiom, with the infectious rhythms, strong melodic lines, and bold thematic material of pronounced contemporary appeal. The composer has welded together a number of tunes in a thrilling medley exploiting all the orchestral choirs. A catchy tune which recurs in the clarinet serves as an identifying mark, and will long remain in the listener's mind.

X-MX-159, Columbia Broadcasting Symphony, Howard Barlow Conducting.

FANTASIA ON A THEME BY THOMAS TALLIS

THOMAS TALLIS was a 16th century English composer, Gentleman of the Chapel Royal, whose music Vaughan Williams discovered in his numerous explorations into the forgotten music of England's past. Tallis composed the theme, on which Vaughan Williams embroiders his Fantasia, in 1567, and is the third of eight tunes found in the Metrical Psalter of Matthew Parker, Archbishop of Canterbury.

The Fantasia was composed for doubled string orchestra, the strings being divided into two orchestras and a quartet of soloists thereby retaining the antiphonal character of the original music. The theme appears after a brief introduction against a background of tremolo violins, and then is allowed to expand and develop in design until it reaches an effective climax; then the theme is heard again, this time on solo violin, after which the music comes to a quiet and contemplative ending.

A LONDON SYMPHONY

Lento; Allegro risoluto · Lento · Scherzo · Andante con moto; Maestose alla marcia; Andante sostenuto

VAUGHAN WILLIAMS twice revised this Symphony before he pronounced it satisfactory. Its final revision was introduced by Albert Coates conducting the London Symphony Orchestra on May 4, 1920, seven years after the writing of the first version.

The composer had this to say about his Symphony: "The title . . . may suggest to some hearers a descriptive piece, but this is not the intention of the composer. A better title would perhaps be, *Symphony by a Londoner*, that is to say the life of London (including possibly its various sights and sounds) has suggested to the composer an attempt at musical expression; but it would be no help to the hearer to describe these in words. The music is intended to be self-impressive, and must stand or fall as 'absolute' music. Therefore, if listeners recognize suggestions of such things as the Westminster Chimes or the *Lavender Cry* they are asked to consider these as accidents, not essentials of the music."

Notwithstanding the composer's intentions to avoid a program for this Symphony, the following has been provided as a key to the music: In the first movement, "London sleeps. The Thames flows serenely through the city. The city awakens. We get glimpses of different parts of the city, its varied character. We get a glimpse of its good humor, of its activity.

"Second movement: Portrait of a region known as Bloomsbury. Dusk. Damp and foggy twilight. Poverty. Tragedy. An old musician outside a 'pub' plays *Sweet Lavender*. Gloom deepens and the movement ends with the musician still playing his sad tune.

"Third movement: Sitting late one Saturday evening at the Temple Embankment. One side of the river is slums. Other side, the quiet and stately majesty of Houses of Parliament. The Thames flows serenely.

"Fourth movement: A picture of the crueler aspects of the city. Unemployed. The unfortunate. Music ends with chimes of Big Ben on Westminster Tower. Epilogue—a picture of London as a whole. The symphony ends as it began—the Thames flowing silently, serenely. . . ."

SERENADE TO MUSIC

THE CIRCUMSTANCES surrounding the composition of the *Serenade to Music* are noteworthy. In 1901, Vaughan Williams wished to pay tribute to Sir Henry J. Wood, the noted British conductor whose avowed aim was "democratizing the message of music."

Looking about for an appropriate subject to honor his friend, Vaughan Williams wrote this lovely piece of music, based on part of Shakespeare's tragi-comedy, *The Merchant of Venice*. It was used presumably as background music for Act V, where the two pairs of lovers, Portia and Bassanio, and Jessica and Lorenzo, meet in the moonlit garden. *Serenade to Music* is a minor work, consuming about twenty minutes. It was originally written for chorus and orchestra, with solo parts for eight or more voices. It can be sung with four soloists, and has also been arranged for orchestra only. Malcolm Sargent says that "at the celebration, each soloist sang a short section to honor the conductor."

The piece begins quietly. One hears the harp and strings, suggestive of Debussy. Then follows the passage in which the chorus sings: "Now streams the moonlight." This is followed by an air for the soprano soloist. Afterwards, we hear the baritone sing: "Lo! how the flower of Heaven!" This passage is reminiscent of Delius's setting to Walt Whitman's *Sea Drift*. This serenade ends on a high note of the chorus, who proclaim: "Come home!" Of particular interest is the use of the harp throughout this composition.

X-MX-121, Soloists and the B.B.C. Symphony Orchestra, Sir Henry J. Wood Conducting.

Hugo Wolf

1860–1903

H<small>UGO</small> W<small>OLF</small> was born in Windischgrätz, Austria, in 1860. From his father (a leather dealer) and a local musician he received his first lessons on the violin and piano. In the fall of 1875, he entered the Vienna Conservatory. Hardly arrived in the Austrian capital, Wolf went to see Richard Wagner who was in that city in conjunction with a *Tannhäuser* performance. A few encouraging words from the master swelled Wolf's admiration for Wagner into outright fanaticism.

Unwilling to submit to routine, Wolf was an unresponsive student at the Conservatory. In 1877, he fell in disfavor with the director and was asked to leave the school. He never again had any formal instruction.

For a while he earned his living by giving piano lessons. At the same time he wrote his first songs and his one string quartet. In the fall of 1881 he became second conductor at the Salzburg Opera (then directed by Karl Muck), but was so unhappy in this position that he left it a few months later. He was better fitted temperamentally for his next assignment—music critic of the *Salonblatt*, holding this post from 1884 to 1887. During this period he continued to write songs, a few choruses, and one big work for orchestra, the symphonic poem *Penthesilea*. By 1887, he had won the support of several sponsors who made it possible for him to give up his regular job, and who paid for the publication of his first two volumes of song.

Hugo Wolf now proved to be uniquely productive, writing numerous songs, the *Italian Serenade,* and an opera *Der Corregidor.* The opera was introduced in Mannheim in 1896, but was not successful and had only two performances during Wolf's lifetime. Nevertheless, he began writing a second opera, *Manuel Venegas*, which he was never destined to finish.

Meanwhile, mental disintegration was taking place. On September 20, 1897 he had to be taken to a private institution. He recovered sufficiently to be able to be discharged early in 1898. For a short period he traveled in Italy and Upper Austria. Suddenly, insanity returned. After an unsuccessful attempt at suicide, Wolf was confined to an asylum in Vienna. There he lingered on for a few more years. The Vienna Hugo Wolf Verein, founded in 1897 to spread propaganda for that composer's works, took care of his expenses. Wolf died in 1903, and was buried near Schubert, Beethoven and Brahms.

Wolf's name is pre-eminently identified with his songs which number well over 300. Most of them were written while he was comparatively young, yet they represent the third (and last) important phase in the development of the form which Schubert had originated.

Wolf created the word tone-poem, the miniature counterpart of the music drama. Its relationship to the melodic song (Schubert, Brahms) is the same of that of music drama to opera. The accompaniment in a Wolf song has the same function as the orchestra in a work by Wagner. Wolf extended the elaborate preludes and postludes (introduced by Schumann). Sometimes the piano part is an independent musical piece (as in *Auf dem grünen Balkon*), while on other occasions a small figure or phrase contains the germ motive for the entire song (*Komm' O Tod!*).

Wolf applied the Wagnerian idiom to song composition in the same way that Bruckner did to the symphony. Yet it would be a mistake to call him an imitator of Wagner. The new musical language, for which Wagner found the most convincing and alluring expression, had developed gradually, and was either adopted or rejected (but hardly ever ignored) by Wagner's contemporaries and successors. Wolf—hyper-sensitive, slightly degenerate, highly intellectual, and violently opposed to any restraint—passionately waved the flag of the new movement which recommended expressive chromaticism, freedom of form, poetic elaboration of detail.

Wolf was extremely well read and had a strong predilection for poets who wrote musical (rather than dramatic) verse. His working habits were strange and indicate his mental maladjustment. Over

200 of his songs were written in a mere four years, or rather in about 170 working days during this period. Once a poet caught his fancy, he would compose an entire volume of his verse, almost forgetting to eat and sleep. When the spell was over, he suffered dismal periods of depression.

It has been said of him that he did not compose music for poems, but for "entire poets." He became intensely interested in the man's personality, in the manner in which he expressed himself on various subjects. Each song is a faithful image of the poem—with meter, declamation, modulations even the key deriving from language phrases and turns. Each volume gives a faithful portrait of the poet in the manner of musical monographs. Those collections are no song cycles, since there is no underlying story or continuous development; but the arrangement of the songs is well planned and cannot be changed.

Wolf wrote six such volumes, three devoted to his favorite authors (Mörike, Eichendorff, Goethe), one to Spanish, and two to Italian folk poetry. Smaller groups are included in a few volumes, summarily entitled *Lieder nach verschiedenen Dichtern*. They include the six *Alte Weisen* to words by Gottfried Keller; some by Heine, Scheffel and other German poets; one by Shakespeare; two by Lord Byron; three by Michelangelo. Twelve of Wolf's earliest songs were published separately in a volume called *Lieder aus der Jugendzeit*.

EICHENDORFF LIEDERBUCH

BARON JOSEPH VON EICHENDORFF was a well-known Roman Catholic writer and poet, prominently identified with the Romantic movement. Wolf set twenty of Eichendorff's poems to music in the summer of 1888. These songs have a curious blend of mirth and melancholy. Schumann, who had also composed songs to Eichendorff poems, had written dreamy, nocturnal music. Wolf brought a note of realism, virility, vivid color. *Erwartung* and *Verschwiegene Liebe* (with interesting modulations) are the most famous from the collection. The volume originally contained twenty-three songs, but three were omitted by Wolf himself and published separately.

GOETHE LIEDERBUCH

IN HIS fifty-one songs after poems of Goethe, Wolf's genius found its subtlest forms of expression. They are highly sensitive, depicting every psychological nuance. They were composed between October 1888 and February 1889, and include three songs from *Mignon*, three *Harfenspieler* songs, *Anakreon's Grab*, *Rattenfänger*, *Grenzen der Menschheit*, etc. The gamut of emotion found in these songs is a wide one, ranging from tender lyricism to passionate outbursts, from melancholy ballads to humorous expressions.

ITALIENISCHES LIEDERBUCH

THESE forty-six songs were written in two installments, the first in 1890–91, the second in the summer of 1896. They are simpler than some of Wolf's earlier songs. The fusion of words and music make constant progress, as does Wolf's ability to obtain a maximum of effect with a minimum of means. Brevity, and intensity of speech, are the distinguishing traits of many of these songs, particularly in the second volume where the last songs are virtual miniatures and are particularly effective when sung in groups ("as if gathered into bouquets," as Josef Schalk once put it). *Auch kleine Dinge, Wenn doch gemalt all deine Reize wären, Du denkst mit einem Fädchen mich zu binden, Sterb' ich, so hüllt in Blumen* are a few of the gems in this collection.

MÖRIKE LIEDERBUCH

WOLF had occupied himself with song-writing for ten years when he became acquainted with the poetry of the Swabian pastor, Eduard Mörike. As Wolf himself stated, this experience set him off in a new direction. Until then he had frequently used old-fashioned strophic forms and a conventional accompaniment. Now he made the greatest effort to avoid unnecessary repetition of words, and developed his compositorial technique in free forms. The volume consists of 53 songs, all but ten of which were composed between February and May of 1888. *Agnes, Er ist's* and *Der Feuerreiter* are among the most famous of these songs.

SPANISCHES LIEDERBUCH

THESE 44 songs, composed between the fall of 1889 and April 1890, constituted perhaps Wolf's most remarkable collection. Although he had never been to Spain, Wolf loved its spirit and its art so intensely that he succeeded in rendering an authentic and convincing description of the millieu. The volume contains a few poems set to music by other composers as well. It is interesting to compare the composition of *In dem Schatten meiner Locken* by the two rivals—Wolf and Brahms. Brahms modulated less strongly than Wolf, but his vocal part is more melodic and cannot boast Wolf's flawless declamation. *Herz, verzage nicht geschwind, Geh' Geliebter, geh' jetzt, sagt ihm, dass er zu mir komme,* are some of the most famous in the collection.

17297-D, In dem Schatten meiner Locken, Risë Stevens, Mezzo-Soprano.